# Built on Diana Hacker's vision

diananacker.com/bedhandbook

The
Bedford
Handbook
SEVENTH EDITION

Diana Hacker

2006, 876 pages
Paperbound ISBN 0–312–41933–3
Clothbound ISBN 0–312–41932–5
Instructor's Annotated Edition
ISBN 0–312–44337–4
diananacker.com/bedhandbook

Diana Hacker's handbooks, assigned at more than half of the two- and four-year colleges in the United States, are the most successful college handbooks of all time. Students and instructors alike praise them for being the easiest handbooks to use, giving students the advice they need in a way they can understand. *The Bedford Handbook* is unique in that it combines a quick, easy reference with a comprehensive, full-sized handbook.

Diana's ideas for this edition grew out of her work in the writing center at Prince George's Community College, where she taught for 35 years. She mapped out her goals: bring in insights from writing center tutors, offer help for writers who struggle to maintain their own voice while integrating sources, help students distinguish among types of research sources on the Web, offer practical approaches for students who write in courses other than composition, and update the book's design.

With the help of expert composition teachers and writing center directors — and with the advice of many thoughtful and candid reviewers — this book achieves Diana Hacker's vision. *The Bedford Handbook* has always worked both as a classroom tool and as a reference tool. Now you'll find that it works even better.

> "I've tried to look squarely at the problems students face and come up with practical solutions."
>
> — Diana Hacker

# Help with the seventh edition

**Contributors.** Diana Hacker mapped out her goals for the seventh edition with her editorial team. Throughout the development of the new edition, we called on several contributing writers to help us develop Diana's goals. These individuals truly understood and put themselves at the service of the book and of Diana's vision.

- Nancy Sommers, Tom Jehn, and Jane Rosenzweig
  *Harvard University*
- Terry Myers Zawacki and Scott Berg
  *George Mason University*
- Lue Cobene
  *Solano Community College*
- Dànielle DeVoss
  *Michigan State University*
- Barbara Fister
  *Gustavus Adolphus College*

"Diana Hacker was a dedicated and talented teacher of writing, and *The Bedford Handbook* reflects her 35 years of experience. None of the imitators offers students the straightforward, respectful, and specific guidance of a Hacker handbook. When my colleagues and I joined the project, we sought to understand and honor the changes, large and small, that Diana had already set in motion for the seventh edition. We wanted to fulfill Diana's vision by making the handbook an even stronger resource for academic writing."

— Nancy Sommers,
*Harvard University*

**Editorial Advisory Board.** More than 100 dedicated and experienced composition instructors reviewed the seventh edition. A group served as an editorial advisory board, carefully reviewing all of the new material for the seventh edition, making sure it would work as well for their students as it always had.

- Linda L. Black
  *St. Johns River Community College*
- Karen Castellucci Cox
  *City College of San Francisco*
- Rosemary Day
  *Albuquerque TVI Community College*
- Michel A. de Benedictis
  *Miami Dade College*
- Allison Green
  *Highline Community College*
- Katherine L. Hall
  *Roger Williams University*
- Iris Hart
  *Santa Fe Community College*
- Lauren Sewell Ingraham
  *University of Tennessee at Chattanooga*

- John F. Jebb
  *University of Delaware*
- Paul Kleinpoppen
  *Florida Community College*
- Laurie F. Leach
  *Hawaii Pacific University*
- Jennifer Swartout
  *Heartland Community College*
- Tom Treffinger
  *Greenville Technical College*
- Heidi Van Dixhorn-Nesser
  *Minneapolis Community and Technical College*
- William Vaughn
  *Central Missouri State University*
- Lisa A. Wilde
  *Howard Community College*

# The one full-sized handbook that also works as a quick reference

▶ **Comprehensive coverage of writing, research, grammar, argument, and design** gives students all the help they need for the composition course. Nine sample papers, ample charts and illustrations, and clear, thorough discussions provide useful models and guidelines.

▶ **At its core, a grammar handbook that works.** Diana Hacker's commonsense language and class-tested exercises provide a solid foundation that helps students find and fix errors in their writing.

▶ **Clear, concise writing style and friendly, unpretentious tone.** Students know they can rely on the accessible explanations and straightforward advice that come directly from the author's classroom experience.

▶ **Trademark Diana Hacker reference features** — menus, tabs, hand-edited sentences, user-friendly index, tutorials, and charts — help students find the information they need and then use what they find.

▶ **An uncluttered page design.** As always, the book's pages lay out complex material and visual elements simply — allowing students to find answers to their questions quickly.

---

Pronoun reference | **ref 23a** | 279

## 23

### Make pronoun references clear.

Pronouns substitute for nouns; they are a kind of shorthand. In a sentence like *After Andrew intercepted the ball, he kicked it as hard as he could,* the pronouns *he* and *it* substitute for the nouns *Andrew* and *ball.* The word a pronoun refers to is called its *antecedent.*

> ✓ GRAMMAR CHECKERS do not flag problems with faulty pronoun reference. Although a computer program can identify pronouns, it has no way of knowing which words, if any, they refer to. For example, grammar checkers miss the fact that the pronoun *it* has an ambiguous reference in the following sentence: *The thief stole the woman's purse and her car and then destroyed it.* Did the thief destroy the purse or the car? It takes human judgment to realize that readers might be confused.

**23a** Avoid ambiguous or remote pronoun reference.

Ambiguous pronoun reference occurs when a pronoun could refer to two possible antecedents.

> The pitcher broke when Gloria set it
> ▶ ~~When Gloria set the pitcher~~ on the glass-topped table~~, it broke.~~
>
> "You have
> ▶ Tom told James, ~~that he had~~ won the lottery."
>
> What broke — the table or the pitcher? Who won the lottery — Tom or James? The revisions eliminate the ambiguity.

# Meeting challenges with smart innovations

## New help from the writing center

**Insights from the writing center.** Throughout the seventh edition, writing tutors share their experiences as writers and offer peer-to-peer advice about the real challenges of college writing. Twenty new boxes offer tips on topics like understanding assignments, thinking critically about a first draft, evaluating and integrating sources, avoiding plagiarism, and understanding academic conventions.

▼

**TIPS FROM WRITING TUTORS**

"In writing a conclusion, above all a writer has to try to answer the question 'So what?' Put yourself in your readers' position: Why should readers care about this subject? Has your argument convinced them? What makes your topic and argument so important?"
— *Nanda Srikantaiah, University of Maryland*

"I love this new feature. These tutor quotes will catch students' attention and help them focus on writing as a process. The quotes are clearly directed to all college writers, helping dispel the notion that tutoring centers are only for basic skills."

— Karen Castellucci Cox, *City College of San Francisco*

*editorial adviser*

The Bedford Handbook
Diana Hacker
SEVENTH EDITION

◀ **Resources for writers and tutors.** This area of the companion site includes practical materials for writers and writing tutors: tip sheets on visiting the writing center, guidelines for using feedback, sample papers, revision checklists, and links to additional tutoring resources. Helpsheets for common writing problems — the same kinds of handouts students see in the writing center — are available in printable format.

# More practical guidance for research writers

▶ **Advice that helps students maintain their voice while writing from sources.** Revised coverage of integrating sources teaches students how to go beyond patchwork research writing and put source material in the context of their own argument.

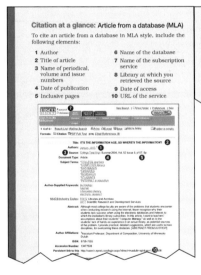

**Citation at a glance:** Article from a database (MLA)

To cite an article from a database in MLA style, include the following elements:

1 Author
2 Title of article
3 Name of periodical, volume and issue numbers
4 Date of publication
5 Inclusive pages
6 Name of the database
7 Name of the subscription service
8 Library at which you retrieved the source
9 Date of access
10 URL of the service

**WORKS CITED ENTRY FOR AN ARTICLE FROM A DATABASE**

Jenson, Jill D. "It's the Information Age, so Where's the Information?" *College Teaching* 52.3 (2004): 107–12. Academic Search Premier. EBSCOhost. St. Johns River Community Coll. Lib., Palatka, FL. 2 Feb. 2005 <http://search.epnet.com>.

For more on citing articles from a database in MLA style, see pages 000... citing arti... m a databa... PA

◀ **New visuals teach citation at a glance.** New full-color, annotated pages from original sources show students where to look for publication information and help students cite print and online materials responsibly.

▶ **More help with recognizing types of sources.** A new section helps students puzzle out common questions as they conduct research: *Is this from a Web site or a database? Is this a scholarly source? Is this an abstract or a full-text article?* Sound advice and clear visuals offer practical guidance.

# More help with academic writing

**New chapter on writing in the disciplines** helps students with writing for all their courses by helping them understand the common features of good college writing and providing practical advice for approaching writing assignments in the disciplines.

> "You've improved the book by adding material on disciplinary writing. It's important to prepare students for writing in multiple disciplines. Many at our community college don't realize they'll be writing in science."
>
> — Heidi Van Dixhorn-Nesser,
> *Minneapolis Community
> and Technical College*

## 49

### Writing in the disciplines

Writing is a fact of college life. No matter what you study, you will be expected to write for a variety of audiences in a variety of formats. College courses expose you to the thinking of scholars in many disciplines, such as the humanities (literature, music, art), the social sciences (psychology, anthropology, sociology), and the sciences (biology, physics, chemistry). Writing in any discipline provides the opportunity to practice the methods used by scholars in these fields and to enter into their debates.

Each field has its own questions, evidence, language, and methods. But all disciplines share certain expectations for good writing. As you write in college courses, be aware of both the commonalities and the variations in different fields.

### 49a Find commonalities across disciplines.

A good paper in any field needs to communicate a writer's purpose to an audience (see 1a) and to explore an engaging question about a subject (see 1b). All effective writers make an argument and support their claims with evidence (see 47). Writers in any field need to show readers the thesis they're developing (or, in the sciences, the hypothesis they're testing) and how they counter opposing explanations or objections of other writers. All disciplines require writers to document where they found their evidence and from whom they borrowed ideas (see 49e). If you understand the features that are common to writing in all disciplines, you will have an easier time sorting out the unique aspects of writing in a particular field.

▶ **A new emphasis on inquiry.** Throughout the writing process, students are prompted to stop, think, and pose questions — a practice that prepares them for all academic work.

> "Far and away, the single greatest improvement [to the critical thinking sections] may be the new stress on the importance of counterargument."
>
> — Paul Kleinpoppen,
> *Florida Community
> College*

▶ **More help with writing arguments.** A new section teaches students how to strengthen their writing by responding to objections. A new annotated sample paper demonstrates effective counterargument.

▶ **Expanded guidelines for writing about both verbal and visual texts.** The new edition includes more advice for analyzing traditional verbal texts, such as essays, and new guidance for writing about visual texts, such as advertisements and photographs.

# Better tools for student writers

**Guidelines for active reading**

The following questions will help you understand your responses to a text's meaning. It may not be necessary to address all of these questions for every assignment. Also, you
don't need to address them one at a time—or in just this
order. (See also 1a.)

*Familiarize yourself with the basic features and struc-
ture of a text.*

- What kind of text are you reading? An essay? An editorial?
  A scholarly article? An advertisement?
- What is the author's purpose? To inform? To persuade?
  To call to action?
- Who is the author's audience? How does the author
  attempt to appeal to the audience?
- What is the author's thesis? What question does the text
  attempt to answer?
- What evidence does the author provide to support the thesis?

*Note details that surprise, puzzle, or intrigue you.*

- Has the author revealed a fact or made a point that runs
  counter to what you had assumed was true? What exactly
  is surprising?
- Has the author made a generalization you disagree with?
  Can you think of evidence that would challenge the generalization?
- Are there any contradictions or inconsistencies in the text
  that don't make sense to you?
- Are there any words, statements, or phrases in the text
  that you don't understand? If so, what reference materials
  do you need to consult?

*Read and reread to discover meaning.*

- What do you notice on a second, third, or fourth reading
  that you didn't notice earlier?

(continued)

◀ **New quick-access charts**
help writers navigate
common writing challenges:
understanding a writing
assignment, using advice
from peer reviewers, writing
conclusions, reading actively,
and analyzing visuals.

editorial adviser

"In 32 years of
teaching, I have
used various
texts. But the best
handbook that I
have ever used is
what we, a faculty
of 60, call 'The
Hacker.' That text is
*The Bedford
Handbook.*"

— Iris Hart, *Santa Fe
Community College*

**New ESL tips** help nonnative speakers
by addressing some of their most
common rhetorical concerns: writing
thesis statements, writing arguments,
and understanding plagiarism.

▼

 If you come from a culture that prefers an indirect
approach in writing, you may feel that asserting a thesis
early in an essay sounds unrefined and even rude. In
the United States, however, readers appreciate a direct
approach; when you state your point as directly as possible, you show that you value your readers' time.

▶ **Expanded document design guidelines** include more examples of layout
options and better guidance on writing with visuals, including citing visuals.

▶ **New exercise items** reflect a diversity of experience and offer practice
through high-interest topics.

▶ **Updated grammar checker boxes.** A Diana Hacker innovation, these fifty
boxes have been totally updated — and continue to give students helpful
advice about the capabilities and limitations of these electronic tools.

# Ancillaries

## Print resources

**Instructor's Annotated Edition,** Diana Hacker, with updates
by Terry Myers Zawacki, George Mason University.
ISBN 0–312–44337–4

Easy to use in the classroom, this instructor's edition extends
lengthwise so that it can be held in your hand. Annotations at the
bottom of the page include answers to all of the exercises, annotated
bibliographic references, quotations from well-known writers and
scholars, and cross-references to the handbook's print and electronic
ancillaries. Answer Key ISBN 0–312–44338–2

**Developmental Exercises,**
Wanda Van Goor, Prince George's Community
College, and Diana Hacker.
ISBN 0–312–44341–2
Answer Key ISBN 0–312–44342–0

**Quizzes and Diagnostic Tests,**
Wanda Van Goor, Prince George's Community
College, and Diana Hacker.
ISBN 0–312–44340–4; also available online.

**Transparency Masters,** Diana Hacker. ISBN 0–312–44728–0; also available online.

**Language Debates,** Second Edition,
Diana Hacker, with updates by *Atlantic Monthly* columnist
Barbara Wallraff.
ISBN 0–312–44727–2; also available online.

**The Bedford Guide for Writing Tutors,**
Fourth Edition, Leigh Ryan, University of Maryland, and
Lisa Zimmerelli, Montgomery College.
ISBN 0–312–44068–5

**Research and Documentation in the Electronic Age,**
Fourth Edition, Diana Hacker and Barbara Fister, Gustavus
Adolphus College. ISBN 0–312–44339–0; also available online.

**Working with Sources:
Exercises to Accompany**
*The Bedford Handbook,* Diana Hacker.
ISBN 0–312–44003–0

Fifty exercises — with thorough feedback — allow
students to practice key research skills: avoiding
plagiarism, integrating sources, identifying citation
information, and documenting sources.

# Electronic resources

## The Electronic Bedford Handbook 7.0

Available on CD-ROM and online, the electronic
edition offers the complete contents of the print book
for quick help whenever students need it. ISBN when
packaged with paperbound book 0–312–43792–7, with
clothbound book 0–312–43776–5.

## Electronic Exercises for *The Bedford Handbook*

This CD-ROM version of the online exercises is available for free when packaged with
the text. ISBN when packaged with paperbound book 0–312–45400–7, with
clothbound book 0–312–45398–1.

## Comment with *The Bedford Handbook*

A powerful Web-based response tool, *Comment* makes it
easy for students and instructors to give writers feedback on
their writing. *Comment* also includes the complete handbook
online, letting reviewers include direct links in their comments to the pages of the handbook. ISBN when packaged
with paperbound book 0–312–43789–7, with clothbound
book 0–312–43753–6.

## Book Companion Site
dianahacker.com/bedhandbook

Throughout the text, On the Web boxes
direct students to this rich collection of
resources: interactive grammar, writing, and
research exercises; model papers; *Research
and Documentation Online*, a guide to finding
and documenting sources in 30 disciplines;
*Language Debates*, brief essays on
controversial matters of style; instructor
resources; and writing center resources.

## Support for Course Management Software

A variety of student and
instructor resources developed
for the handbook are ready for
use in WebCT, Blackboard,
Desire2Learn, and Angel.

editorial adviser

"The book retains a singular voice
and approach. I do believe it will
work for student writers no matter
what type of school they attend.
That's the beauty of a well-written,
well-rounded handbook. It's a sem-
inal reference work for everyone."

— Michel A. de Benedictis,
*Miami Dade College*

# Other Hacker handbooks

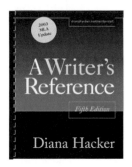

## A Writer's Reference, Fifth Edition
Diana Hacker
2003 Comb-bound with MLA Update 499 pages
ISBN 0-312-41262-2
dianahacker.com/writersref

Class-tested by nearly 3,000,000 students at over 1,500 schools, *A Writer's Reference* is the most widely adopted composition handbook. This is a book that students can — and will — use on their own. The fifth edition expands coverage of research and argument and is now thoroughly integrated with an enhanced companion Web site developed by Diana Hacker. On the Web and in print, *A Writer's Reference* remains the source students and instructors can trust. ● ● ● ● ● ● ● ● ● ● ● ● ● ● ● ● ● ● ● ●

## Rules for Writers, Fifth Edition
Diana Hacker
2004 Spiral-bound 624 pages ISBN 0-312-40685-1
Instructor's Edition ISBN 0-312-41050-6
dianahacker.com/rules

From the best-selling family of handbooks, *Rules for Writers* features comprehensive coverage, with exercises — now thoroughly integrated with a companion Web site and updated with crucial advice on researching in the digital age, working with sources, and avoiding plagiarism. *Rules* offers Hacker handbook coverage at a low price and Hacker Web content for free. ● ● ● ● ● ● ● ● ● ● ● ● ● ● ● ● ● ●

## A Pocket Syle Manual, Fourth Edition
Diana Hacker
2004 Spiral-bound 288 pages ISBN 0-312-40684-3
dianahacker.com/pocket

Adopted at more than 1,600 schools across the country in more than 20 different academic disciplines, *A Pocket Style Manual* is a straightforward, inexpensive quick reference to the essentials of writing and research. This best-selling pocket resource is now accompanied by a robust companion Web site — developed by Diana Hacker. ● ● ● ● ● ● ● ● ● ●

# Practical student resources at Re:Writing

Bedford/St. Martin's is pleased to present **Re:Writing**, the best FREE collection of online resources for the writing class. Our resources are all free, all open, all easy to access, and all of the high quality you expect from Bedford/St. Martin's.

From brainstorming to citing and everything in between, **Re:Writing**'s content and tutorials are written by our most widely adopted authors — such as Mike Palmquist, Mike Markel, and Diana Hacker — so you know your students are getting helpful advice from experts in their fields.

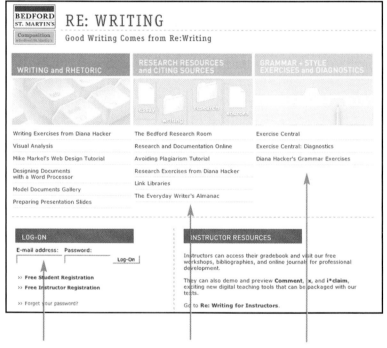

Because **Re:Writing** is free, there are no access codes to lose or books to purchase. Students simply register and immediately begin practicing grammar or accessing tutorials. Any scored work can then be viewed by their instructors.

With the largest collection of writing exercises, exciting visual analysis activities, useful research guides, plagiarism tutorials, and more, **Re:Writing** is the most comprehensive resource available.

# Extensive instructor resources at Re:Writing

**Re:Writing** is a useful resource for instructors as well as students. Instructors can assign any of the activities or tutorials and view records for any of the scored activities either online or in an e-mail. **Re:Writing** is also a portal for all of Bedford/St. Martin's excellent online and print professional resources written by some of the top names in the field.

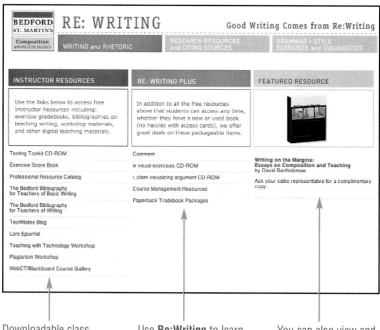

**BEDFORD ST. MARTIN'S**
Composition
*Bedford/St.Martin's*

## RE: WRITING

Good Writing Comes from Re:Writing

WRITING and RHETORIC    RESEARCH RESOURCES and CITING SOURCES    GRAMMAR + STYLE EXERCISES and DIAGNOSTICS

### INSTRUCTOR RESOURCES

Use the links below to access free Instructor Resources including: exercise gradebooks, bibliographies on teaching writing, workshop materials, and other digital teaching materials.

Testing Toolkit CD-ROM

Exercise Score Book

Professional Resource Catalog

The Bedford Bibliography for Teachers of Basic Writing

The Bedford Bibliography for Teachers of Writing

TechNotes Blog

Lore Ejournal

Teaching with Technology Workshop

Plagiarism Workshop

WebCT/Blackboard Course Gallery

### RE: WRITING PLUS

In addition to all the free resources above that students can access any time, whether they have a new or used book (no hassles with access cards), we offer great deals on these packageable items.

Comment

ix visual exercises CD-ROM

i_claim visualizing argument CD-ROM

Course Management Resources

Paperback Tradebook Packages

### FEATURED RESOURCE

**Writing on the Margins: Essays on Composition and Teaching**
by David Bartholomae

Ask your sales representative for a complimentary copy.

Downloadable class materials such as handouts on plagiarism, author-written workshops, and e-journals to help you keep up with the changing field of composition are all available for free at **Re:Writing.**

Use **Re:Writing** to learn about our great packageables, free resources, and exciting promotions — such as 50% off best-selling and award-winning trade books — that are available to users of Bedford/St. Martin's textbooks.

You can also view and order complimentary copies of our professional development books, including *The Bedford Bibliography for Teachers of Writing, The St. Martin's Guide for Teaching Writing,* and *Visual Rhetoric in a Digital Age.*

# Professional resources for instructors

## The Bedford Bibliography for Teachers of Writing

Nedra Reynolds, *University of Rhode Island*
Patricia Bizzell, *College of the Holy Cross*
Bruce Herzberg, *Bentley College*
2003 Paper 267 pages ISBN 0-312-40501-4
bedfordstmartins.com/bb

An essential, highly praised resource for writing teachers for over
15 years, *The Bedford Bibliography* provides an annotated list of
books, articles, and periodicals devoted to composition and rhetoric —
updated to include the most recent research — together with a historical
overview of these fields.

## Second-Language Writing in the Composition Classroom
A Critical Sourcebook

Paul Kei Matsuda, *University of New Hampshire*
Michelle Cox, *University of New Hampshire*
Jay Jordan, *Penn State*
Christina Ortmeier-Hooper, *University of New Hampshire*
2006 Paper 400 pages (approx.) ISBN 0-312-44473-7

*Second-Language Writing* addresses key issues for instructors working with
multilingual writers in first-year composition. Framed with insightful introductory material, this sourcebook provides both theoretical context and practical
resources for designing courses, negotiating differences among students, and
responding to and assessing second-language writing.

## The Elements of Teaching Writing

Katherine Gottschalk, Keith Hjortshoj, *Cornell University*
2004 Paper 180 pages ISBN 0-312-40683-5

Drawing on their extensive experience training instructors in all disciplines,
Gottschalk and Hjortshoj provide strategies and guidance in this brief, well-
written reference. Accommodating a wide range of teaching styles and class
sizes, *Elements* offers advice about how to design effective writing assignments and how to respond to and evaluate student writing in any course.

## A TA's Guide to Teaching Writing in All Disciplines

Beth Hedengren, *Brigham Young University*
2004 Paper 160 pages ISBN 0-312-40714-9
bedfordstmartins.com/ta_guide

Written specifically for teaching assistants responsible for WAC or WID
courses, *A TA's Guide to Teaching Writing in All Disciplines* provides
the practical advice that teaching assistants need in order to teach
and evaluate writing effectively. This informative text is perfectly suited
to a teaching assistant training course, or it can serve as a reference for
teaching assistants to use on their own.

## Portfolio Teaching, Second Edition

Nedra Reynolds, *University of Rhode Island*
Rich Rice, *Texas Tech University*
2006 Paper 74 pages ISBN 0-312-41911-2

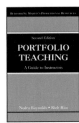

Providing the practical information instructors and writing program
administrators need to use the portfolio method successfully in a writing
course, *Portfolio Teaching* is an ideal companion to *Portfolio Keeping*.

## Teaching Composition

**T. R. Johnson,** *Tulane University*
2005 608 pages  ISBN 0–312–41529–X

Professional readings on composition and rhetoric written by leaders in the field such as Peter Elbow, Nancy Sommers, and David Bartholomae are accompanied by chapter introductions, headnotes, and activities for classroom use.

## Teaching Argument in the Composition Course

**Timothy Barnett,** *Northeastern Illinois University*
2001 Paper 470 pages  ISBN 0–312–39161–7

Offering a range of perspectives, from Aristotle to the present day, on argument and on teaching argument, the 28 readings — many of them classic works in the field — present essential insights and practical information for instructors using any of Bedford/St. Martin's argument texts and readers.

## Writing on the Margins: Essays on Composition and Teaching

**David Bartholomae,** *University of Pittsburgh*
2004 Paper 386 pages  ISBN 0–312–25869–0

This collection of essays by David Bartholomae includes 21 selections that have helped shape the discipline of composition studies. It brings together Bartholomae's most important and influential work and serves as a valuable reference and as a powerful introduction to crucial  issues in the field of composition.

## An Open Language
Selected Writing on Literacy, Learning, and Opportunity

**Mike Rose,** *University of California, Los Angeles*
2006 Paper 400 pages (approx.)  ISBN 0–312–44474–5

*An Open Language* by Mike Rose chronicles the development of one of the most widely read and influential writers in the fields of composition and education. Rose contextualizes each of the 30 selections with commentary that illuminates the historical, cultural, and personal issues at stake in his research and writing. An invaluable resource for graduate students and new scholars, this collection offers unique insight into the process of building a meaningful career — one that makes a difference both in the academy and beyond.

## Visual Rhetoric in a Digital World

**Carolyn Handa,** *University of Alabama*
2004 Paper 504 pages  ISBN 0–312–40975–3

This sourcebook helps composition instructors consider what it means to teach visual rhetoric in the multimedia classroom. Readings address visual argument, rhetoric of the image and design, and the role of culture in shaping visual understanding.

For a complete list, visit bedfordstmartins.com/professionalresources.

**Bedford / St. Martin's and the Two-Year College Association of NCTE proudly cosponsor**

# The Diana Hacker TYCA Outstanding Programs in English Awards

The Diana Hacker TYCA Outstanding Programs in English Awards honor the achievements of two-year college English teachers who, together with administrators, community leaders, and/or colleagues in other disciplines or programs, create exemplary programs and initiatives to enhance language learning and to enable students of diverse interests and backgrounds to achieve their college, career, and personal goals.

To learn about award categories, criteria, and submission instructions, visit ncte.org/groups/tyca/awards.

The
Bedford
Handbook

Seventh Edition

# The Bedford Handbook

## Diana Hacker

**Bedford/St. Martin's**
Boston ◆ New York

**Instructor's Annotated Edition**

*For Bedford/St. Martin's*

*Executive Editor:* Michelle M. Clark
*Senior Production Editor:* Anne Noonan
*Senior Production Supervisor:* Dennis Conroy
*Marketing Manager:* Kevin Feyen
*Development Editor:* Caroline Thompson
*Editorial Assistants:* Jennifer Ambrose, Kaitlin Hannon, and Amy Hurd Gershman
*Production Assistant:* Amy Derjue
*Copyeditor:* Barbara G. Flanagan
*Text Design:* Claire Seng-Niemoeller
*Cover Design:* Hannus Design Associates
*Composition:* Monotype, LLC
*Printing and Binding:* RR Donnelley and Sons Company

*President:* Joan E. Feinberg
*Editorial Director:* Denise B. Wydra
*Editor in Chief:* Karen S. Henry
*Director of Marketing:* Karen Melton Soeltz
*Director of Editing, Design, and Production:* Marcia Cohen
*Managing Editor:* Elizabeth M. Schaaf

Library of Congress Control Number: 2004118170

Manufactured in the United States of America.

0   9   8   7   6   5
f   e   d   c   b   a

*For information, write:* Bedford/St. Martin's, 75 Arlington Street, Boston, MA 02116 (617-399-4000)

ISBN:  0-312-44337-4 (Instructor's Annotated Edition)   EAN: 978-0-312-44337-5
       0-312-41932-5 (hardcover Student Edition)              978-0-312-41932-5
       0-312-41933-3 (softcover Student Edition)              978-0-312-41933-2

*Acknowledgments*
Table from Africa Recovery (June 2004), United Nations Department of Public Information, www.un.org/ecosocdev/geninfo/afrec/vol15no1/drugpr1.htm. Reprinted with permission.

*Acknowledgments and copyrights are continued at the back of the book on pages 875–76, which constitute an extension of the copyright page. It is a violation of the law to reproduce these selections by any means whatsoever without the written permission of the copyright holders.*

# Preface for Instructors

*Publisher's Note*

> This book is grounded in my many years of teaching first- and second-year composition to a wide range of students: young and mature, mainstream and multiethnic, talented and underprepared. As I've drafted and revised *The Bedford Handbook*, my goal has never been to sell students on my personal views about language and politics—or to endorse popular trends in the teaching of English. Instead, I've tried to look squarely at the problems students face and come up with practical solutions.
>
> —Diana Hacker, from the preface to
> *The Bedford Handbook*, Sixth Edition

First and foremost a teacher, Diana Hacker (1942–2004) was clear about why her handbooks have been so success- ful: They give students practical solutions to real writing problems. Her many innovations—both large and small— were always at the service of giving students the advice they need in a way they can understand. She was able to take everything she knew from her thirty-five years of teaching and put it to work on every page of her books. As a result, she was one of the most successful college textbook authors of all time, with her handbooks assigned at more than half of the two- and four-year colleges in the United States.

Diana wanted handbooks to be helpful, and she wanted them to work. The list of innovations that first appeared in a Hacker handbook is impressive: hand-edited sentences, grammar checker boxes, an index with student-friendly entries, a special section on ESL issues, coverage of document design, and discipline-specific research advice. With every edition of every book, Diana identified the new challenges students faced and came up with solutions. Her hand-edited sentences changed the way examples were presented in a handbook, but she had developed them initially for her own students because they didn't know what editing looked like. She developed her grammar checker boxes because she had started seeing what she called "strange errors" in her students' papers from their use of grammar and spell checkers, and she wanted to show students how to use these tools critically.

In this seventh edition, you will see Diana's solutions to some of the new challenges students face at the beginning of the twenty-first century. Many of her ideas for this edition came from her work over the past ten years at the Prince George's Community College writing center, which serves writers in all disciplines. She believed deeply in the value of the writing center and in the ability of student tutors to help their peers. She was determined to bring the insights of these tutors into the book because they speak directly to students' experiences. From her work in the classroom and in the writing center, she knew how students struggle to integrate sources into their writing while still maintaining their own voice. She saw that students often can't distinguish different kinds of Web sources. From her work in the writing center she saw the problems students face in their writing for other courses. She also felt that her coverage of the writing process needed to be updated to better reflect how much reading students now do in a writing course. She was determined to provide help for all of these situations in the new edition of *The Bedford Handbook*.

With her team of Bedford editors, Diana mapped out a detailed plan for the seventh edition and began the careful process of revising each section. A talented group of composition instructors helped us finish the revision with Diana's plan as a guide. All of these people knew Diana and her work well; in turn, they are all people whose work Diana admired, and they are committed to carrying out her vision. To help with the new writing center feature, Terry Myers Zawacki and Scott Berg, director and associate director of the Writing Center at George Mason University, were the perfect contributors. Scott had gotten to know Diana well when he wrote an article about her for the *Washington Post.* Terry is a longtime user of Hacker handbooks and brought her expertise from her professional work on writing centers and writing across the curriculum. Terry's early scholarly work focused on teaching writing in the two-year college. Nancy Sommers and two of her colleagues in the Harvard Expository Writing Program, Tom Jehn and Jane Rosenzweig, helped revise the coverage of the writing process and research. Diana was a huge fan of Nancy's work because it focused on student writing, drawing on Nancy's teaching at the University of Oklahoma and Rutgers as well as at Harvard. Diana acknowledged that Nancy's article on revision greatly informed both her own teaching and her approach to the writing process in *The Bedford Handbook.* Nancy's recent longitudinal study of student writing gave Diana ideas for ways to help students as they work with sources, and she wanted to get these insights into her books.

Diana was particularly proud of her exercises. The exercise items all came from her own students' papers, so they were realistic models of errors students actually make. For this edition, she wanted the topics to reflect the wide range of students in composition classrooms. Lue Cobene from Solano Community College (CA), a school with a diverse student body similar to that of Prince George's Community College, provided a broader range of topics in two hundred new exercise items. Lue and Diana shared a passion for teaching grammar and style. Dànielle DeVoss of Michigan State University, who specializes in visual rhetoric, skillfully updated and expanded the coverage of analyzing and using visuals effectively. Barbara Fister, reference librarian at Gustavus Adolphus College (MN), continued to do the work she has done on every edition of Diana's books to make the research coverage the most up-to-date and useful of any handbook.

To ensure that the new material met the high standards of a Hacker handbook, we formed an editorial board of users of *The Bedford Handbook* who read and commented on every word. They made sure that the new edition would work as well for them in the classroom as the previous editions had done. We are extraordinarily grateful for their advice and for their commitment to the book. With the help of our contributors, our editorial board, and our other reviewers (see pp. xviii–xxiv), the classroom experiences of committed teachers has continued to inform *The Bedford Handbook*.

*The Bedford Handbook* has always been a team effort between Diana and her editors at Bedford/St. Martin's. The Hacker team is still in place. I worked with Diana on the first edition of her first book and on every book since, and so have other members of the team, including Boston editor in chief Karen Henry and Boston managing editor Elizabeth Schaaf. Karen and Elizabeth have worked on these books from the beginning and remain committed to Diana's vision and to maintaining the high level of quality of Hacker handbooks. A number of wonderful developmental editors have worked on Hacker handbooks over the years, but none have had the editorial skill, managerial ability, cheerful temperament, and deep understanding of the books that Michelle Clark has. She developed several editions with Diana, talking with her every day. Michelle walked through every page of *The Bedford Handbook* with Diana to make sure she understood Diana's ideas for the new edition. Also an integral part of the team is Anne Noonan, longtime Hacker production editor, who kept us all on track with her persistence, sharp eye, and concern for every detail. Claire Seng-Niemoeller has designed every Hacker handbook since the first and has again retained the clean, uncluttered look of the book while making more use of color. Having copy-edited every Hacker handbook, Barbara Flanagan has been hearing Diana's voice for more than twenty years. Diana credited her with the clarity and consistency that is a Hacker hallmark. With help from former Hacker editor Ellen Kuhl, Barbara made sure that every word in this book sounds like Diana's voice. Editorial director Denise Wydra consulted at every stage of development and reminded us of the high standards we need to maintain. New media editor Katie Schooling brought her expert skills to the development of the Hacker Web site and the electronic handbook. Associate editor Caroline Thompson immersed herself in the community of writing center directors to integrate their point of view into the book. She also coordinated a number of ancillaries and worked with Barbara Flanagan to expand and update the electronic exercises. Our stellar editorial assistants Amy Hurd Gershman, Kaitlin Hannon, and Jennifer Ambrose managed numerous small projects. Production assistant Amy Derjue provided detailed assistance throughout the page proof review.

Special thanks go to Chuck Christensen for understanding what makes a great handbook author and for knowing he had found one in Diana Hacker. We are also grateful to Bob Hacker, Diana's husband of many years, for his continued interest in her handbooks and for his support of the work we have done.

Diana taught us well. We have tried to honor her memory by working hard to maintain the same high standards that have informed every Hacker handbook, and we feel that this new edition achieves the goals Diana set out for herself and for us. We always kept in mind, as Diana herself said, "that errors, a natural by-product of the writing process, are simply problems waiting to be solved."

Joan Feinberg
President, Bedford/St. Martin's

## Features of the Seventh Edition

### What's new

**INSIGHTS FROM THE WRITING CENTER.** New boxes called "Tips from Writing Tutors" feature quotations from and photos of writing center tutors who share their experiences as writers and offer peer-to-peer advice about the real challenges of college writing.

**ADVICE THAT HELPS STUDENTS MAINTAIN THEIR VOICE WHILE WRITING FROM SOURCES.** Thoroughly revised coverage of integrating sources teaches students how to go beyond patchwork research writing. Section 56 shows students how to lead into—and get out of—sources while keeping the source material in context and maintaining their own line of argument.

**MORE HELP WITH RECOGNIZING TYPES OF SOURCES.** Technology has granted wide access to information, but some students still struggle when almost every type of source—from books and articles to Web sites—appears on a computer screen. A new section (51b) helps students puzzle out typical questions as they conduct research: *Is this a scholarly source? Is this an abstract or a full-text article? Is this from a Web site or a database?* Clear explanations and helpful visuals offer practical guidance.

**NEW VISUALS TEACH CITATION AT A GLANCE.** New full-color, annotated facsimiles of original sources show students where to look for publication information in a book, a periodical, a Web site, and a source accessed in a database. These visuals help students find the information they need to cite print and online materials accurately and responsibly.

**MORE HELP WITH WRITING ARGUMENTS.** Revised coverage of counterargument teaches students how to strengthen their writing by anticipating and responding to objections. A new annotated sample paper demonstrates the effective use of counterargument.

**A NEW SECTION ON WRITING IN THE DISCIPLINES.** A new section 49, "Writing in the Disciplines," helps students with writing in all their courses. It explains the common features of all good college writing and provides practical advice for approaching writing assignments in all disciplines.

**NEW QUICK-ACCESS CHARTS.** The seventh edition features new charts to help writers navigate common writing challenges: understanding a writing assignment, making use of advice from peer reviewers, writing a conclusion, reading actively, and analyzing visuals.

**EXPANDED GUIDELINES FOR WRITING ABOUT BOTH WRITTEN AND VISUAL TEXTS.** The section on writing about texts (46) now includes additional helpful guidelines for analyzing written texts, such as essays. New guidance for writing about visual texts helps students apply critical thinking skills to advertisements, photographs, cartoons, and other visual material.

**AN UNCLUTTERED PAGE DESIGN.** The book's new, more colorful design presents complex material and new visual elements as simply as possible. Because grammar rules and hand-edited examples are highlighted in color, students can easily skim the book's central sections for quick answers to questions. Charts and boxes are easy to find and, just as important, easy to skip.

**NEW SAMPLE PAPERS.** A new APA-style paper, a review of the literature on treatments for childhood obesity, uses current print and electronic sources and is annotated to show both good writing and proper formatting. New essays in section 46, "Writing about Texts," demonstrate effective analysis of both an article and an advertisement.

**NEW EXERCISE ITEMS.** Revisions of two hundred exercise items reflect a diversity of experience and offer practice through high-interest topics. These new items, along with the existing ones, provide students abundant opportunities for practice on every topic in the handbook.

**NEW ESL TIPS.**  Additional ESL boxes help students who are unfamiliar with American academic writing deal with some of the most common and challenging rhetorical concerns: writing thesis statements, writing arguments, and understanding plagiarism.

**UPDATED GRAMMAR CHECKER BOXES.**  A Diana Hacker innovation, the fifty grammar checker boxes have been updated to reflect the way current grammar and spell checker programs work. We repeated the research Diana Hacker did nearly ten years ago, running all of the exercise items through current grammar checkers to give students helpful advice about the programs' capabilities and limitations. The results, summarized in boxes throughout the book, explain that grammar checkers help with some but by no means all of the typical problems in a draft.

### What's the same

The seventh edition is built on Diana Hacker's vision and was developed according to a plan she mapped out with her editorial team. We have kept the features that have made *The Bedford Handbook* work so well for so many students and instructors. These features, detailed here, will be familiar to users of the previous edition. The section starts with Diana's description of the beginnings of *The Bedford Handbook*.

When I began writing this book, I had been teaching long enough to know just what I wanted in a handbook. At Prince George's Community College, our teaching load is fifteen hours per semester, so there is all too little time for individualized grammar lessons. I wanted a handbook so clear and accessible that our students could learn from it on their own. I had in mind a book that would give students what they seem to prefer — straightforward rules — but without suggesting that rules are absolutes or that writing well is simply a matter of following the rules.

Further, because our students have such a range of abilities, I hoped for a book that would be useful for all of them, offering a little help or a lot of help depending on their needs. Finally, I envisioned a handbook that would support the philosophy of composition that we work so hard to convey in the classroom. Writing is a process, we tell our students, and revision is central to that process. Revision is not a punishment for failing to get things right the first time. Nor is it a perfunctory clean-up exercise. It occurs right on the pages of a rough draft, often messily, with cross-outs and insertions, and it requires an active mind, a mind willing to look at a draft from the point of view of the reader, to spot problems, and to choose solutions.

With these aims in mind, then, I began writing this book. And it was with them in mind that I rewrote it again and again, with each draft edging closer to my vision. Central to my vision — then and now — is the belief that a handbook, whether brief or full, should work primarily as a reference that students can use on their own.

**A BRIEF MENU AND A USER-FRIENDLY INDEX.** Designed for student use, a brief menu inside the front cover displays the book's eleven parts and lists only the numbered sections. The traditional, more detailed handbook menu, which is useful for instructors but too daunting for many students, appears inside the back cover.

The handbook's index (which Diana wrote herself and which was carefully updated for this edition) helps students find what they are looking for even if they don't know grammatical terminology. When facing a choice between *I* and *me*, for example, students may not know to look up "Case" or even "Pronoun, case of." They are more likely to look up "*I*" or "*me*," so the index includes entries for "*I* vs. *me*" and "*me* vs. *I*." Similar user-friendly entries appear throughout the index.

**QUICK-REFERENCE CHARTS.** Many of the handbook's charts help students review for common problems in their own writing, such as fragments and subject-verb agreement.

Other charts summarize important material: a checklist for global revision, strategies for avoiding sexist language, guidelines for evaluating Web sites, and so on.

**HELP FOR CULTURALLY DIVERSE STUDENTS.**   More than ten years ago, Diana Hacker was the first handbook author to write a special section for nonnative speakers of English. Over the years, she expanded the section and added a number of ESL boxes throughout the book. ESL students are the primary audience, but many instructors and tutors who work with culturally diverse students have also found this material helpful.

**EXTENSIVE EXERCISES, SOME WITH ANSWERS.**   At least one exercise set accompanies nearly every section of the book. Most sets begin with five lettered sentences with answers in the back of the book so students can test their understanding independently. The sets then continue with numbered sentences whose answers appear only in the Instructor's Annotated Edition. Students who need more practice can go to the book's companion Web site (see p. xv for details).

**DISCIPLINE-SPECIFIC RHETORICAL ADVICE FOR MLA, APA, AND *CHICAGO* STYLES.**   Advice on drafting a thesis, avoiding plagiarism, and integrating sources is illustrated for all three major documentation styles—MLA, APA, and *Chicago*—in three color-coded sections. Examples are tied to topics appropriate to the disciplines that typically use each style: English and other humanities (MLA), social sciences (APA), and history (*Chicago*).

### What's on the companion Web site

The companion Web site for the seventh edition includes a rich collection of resources that supplements rather than repeats the material in the text. Developed by Diana Hacker, the Web resources provide practical help for students as they write online. On the Web boxes throughout the text direct students to appropriate online help.

The features described here are intended for students. Instructor resources, both print and electronic, are listed on pages xvii–xviii.

**RESOURCES FOR WRITERS AND TUTORS.**   New writing center resources on the companion Web site offer help for both tutors and writers: checklists for responding to a wide array of assignments, tips for preparing for a visit to the writing center, hints for making the best use of advice from tutors, and helpsheets for common writing problems—the same kinds of handouts students see in the writing center—all available in printable format.

**ELECTRONIC GRAMMAR EXERCISES.**   For online practice, students can access more than one thousand exercise items—on every topic in the handbook—with feedback written by Diana Hacker. Most of the exercises are scorable. Exercises that call for editing are labeled "edit and compare." They ask students to edit sentences and compare their versions with possible revisions.

**ELECTRONIC RESEARCH AND WRITING EXERCISES.**   Scorable electronic exercises on matters such as avoiding plagiarism, integrating sources, using MLA documentation, and identifying citation elements give students ample practice with these critical topics. Scorable exercises on thesis statements, peer review, point of view, transitions, and other writing topics accompany Part I, "The Writing Process."

**LANGUAGE DEBATES.**   To encourage students to think about the rationales for a rule and then make their own rhetorical decisions, Diana Hacker wrote twenty brief essays that explore controversial issues of grammar and usage, such as split infinitives and *who* versus *whom.* The Web site for the seventh edition features two additional debates written by style expert Barbara Wallraff.

**LINKS LIBRARY.**    From the companion Web site students can access resources such as online writing centers, tutorials on creating Web sites, and online libraries.

**MODEL PAPERS.**    Model papers for MLA, APA, *Chicago,* and CBE/CSE styles illustrate both the design and the content of researched writing. Annotations highlight key points about each paper's style, content, and documentation.

**RESEARCH AND DOCUMENTATION ONLINE.**    This online resource helps students conduct research and document their sources. Reference librarian Barbara Fister has updated her advice on finding sources and has provided new links to resources in a variety of disciplines; she continues to maintain the research portion of the site. Guidelines for documenting print and online sources in MLA, APA, *Chicago,* and CBE/CSE styles are also kept up-to-date.

### Ancillaries for students

Both print and electronic ancillaries are available for students.

**PRINT RESOURCES**

*Developmental Exercises to Accompany* THE BEDFORD HANDBOOK

*Answers to Exercises in* THE BEDFORD HANDBOOK

*Research and Documentation in the Electronic Age,* Fourth Edition

**ELECTRONIC RESOURCES**

*The Electronic Bedford Handbook*

*The Bedford Handbook* companion Web site (see the On the Web box on p. xxx)

*Comment* with *The Bedford Handbook*

### Ancillaries for instructors

Classroom and professional resources for instructors are available in print form. Other resources appear on the instructor portion of the book's companion Web site.

#### CLASSROOM RESOURCES FOR INSTRUCTORS

Instructor's Annotated Edition

*Quizzes and Diagnostic Tests to Accompany* THE BEDFORD HANDBOOK

*Transparency Masters to Accompany* THE BEDFORD HANDBOOK

*Working with Sources: Exercises to Accompany* THE BEDFORD HANDBOOK

*Language Debates,* Second Edition

#### PROFESSIONAL RESOURCES FOR INSTRUCTORS

*Teaching Composition: Background Readings*

*The Bedford Guide for Writing Tutors,* Fourth Edition

*The Bedford Bibliography for Teachers of Writing,* Sixth Edition

#### WEB RESOURCES FOR INSTRUCTORS

*The Bedford Handbook* instructor site <http://dianahacker.com/bedhandbook/instructor>

- Exercise Masters, print-format versions of all the exercises in the book
- Quiz Masters, print-format quizzes on key topics in the book

- Electronic Diagnostic Tests, a test bank for instructors' use
- Transparency Masters, useful charts, examples, and visuals from the book
- *Preparing for the CLAST*
- *Preparing for the THEA*

In addition, all of the resources within *Re:Writing* (http://bedfordstmartins.com/rewriting) are available to users of *The Bedford Handbook.* Resources include tutorials, exercises, diagnostics, technology help, and model documents—all written by our most widely adopted authors.

## Acknowledgments

Diana Hacker worked with us to map out her goals for the seventh edition. We called on a number of individuals to help us develop the seventh edition according to Diana's plan.

### Contributors

The following contributing writers understood the goals of the revision and put themselves at the service of the book and of Diana's vision. For their commitment to the project, we are grateful.

**Nancy Sommers, Tom Jehn, and Jane Rosenzweig** (Harvard University) strengthened the material on the writing process, on critical thinking, and on researched writing; they also co-authored a new section on writing in the disciplines.

**Terry Myers Zawacki and Scott Berg** (George Mason University, VA) developed the new writing center tips based on surveys of writing tutors from across the country. Terry Zawacki also took on the major responsibility of revising the Instructor's Annotated Edition.

**Lue Cobene** (Solano Community College, CA) met the challenge of writing two hundred new grammar, style, punctuation, and mechanics exercises—no small task, considering how meticulous Diana Hacker was about the exercises in her handbooks.

**Dànielle DeVoss** (Michigan State University) updated and expanded the coverage of document design.

**Barbara Fister** (Gustavus Adolphus College, MN) helped refine the sections on research strategy.

### *Editorial Advisory Board*

We asked a number of longtime users of the book and several nonusers to serve as editorial advisers. They looked carefully at all new and substantially revised sections of the seventh edition to make certain that the book is still as effective as it has always been in their classrooms. We thank them for their thoughtful and candid reviews.

Linda L. Black, St. Johns River Community College (FL)

Karen Castellucci Cox, City College of San Francisco (CA)

Rosemary Day, Albuquerque TVI Community College (NM)

Michel A. de Benedictis, Miami Dade College (FL)

Allison Green, Highline Community College (WA)

Katherine L. Hall, Roger Williams University (RI)

Iris Hart, Santa Fe Community College (FL)

Lauren Sewell Ingraham, University of Tennessee at Chattanooga

John F. Jebb, University of Delaware

Paul Kleinpoppen, Florida Community College

Laurie F. Leach, Hawaii Pacific University

Jennifer Swartout, Heartland Community College (IL)

Tom Treffinger, Greenville Technical College (SC)

Heidi Van Dixhorn-Nesser, Minneapolis Community and Technical College (MN)

William Vaughn, Central Missouri State University

Lisa A. Wilde, Howard Community College (MD)

## Reviewers

For their many helpful suggestions, we would like to thank a perceptive group of reviewers. Some answered a detailed questionnaire about the sixth edition; others reviewed manuscript for the seventh edition.

Kathryn Adams, Allan Hancock College (CA); Teresa Aggen, Pikes Peak Community College (CO); Ted Allder, University of Arkansas Community College, Batesville; Marta Amezquita, St. Mary's University (TX); Valerie K. Anderson, York College, City University of New York; Paul Andrews, St. Johns River Community College (FL); Dee Baer, University of Delaware; Mark Balhorn, University of Wisconsin, Stevens Point; Susan Beebe, Texas State University, San Marcos; Joseph Bizup, Columbia University (NY); Shane Borrowman, Gonzaga University (WA); Jennifer Boswell, University of Western Ontario; Arnold Jay Bradford, Northern Virginia Community College; Amy Braziller, Red Rocks Community College (CO); Melanie Rosen Brown, St. Johns River Community College (FL); Laurie E. Buchanan, Clark State Community College (OH); Joy H. Calico, Vanderbilt University (TN); Norton Bradley Christie, Erskine College (SC); Frank Cioffi, Princeton University (NJ); Patrick Clauss, Butler University (IN); Andrea Bewick Collins, Napa Valley College (CA); Dawn Comer, Albion College (MI); Gill Creel, Minneapolis Community and Technical College (MN); Michael J. Cripps, York College, City University of New York; Marylynne Diggs, Clark College (WA); Keith Dorwick, Vanderbilt University (TN); Caroline Eisner, University of Michigan; Brennan Enos, Palm Beach Community College (FL); Gwyn Enright, San Diego City College (CA); Kim Fobes, University of Mobile (AL); Lynne Gaillet, Georgia State University; Ruth Ann Gambino, Palo Alto College (TX); Gay Goss, California State University, Dominguez Hills; Natalie Grinnell, Wofford College (SC); Mickey Hall, Volunteer State Community College (TN); John L. Hare, Montgomery College, Germantown (MD); Susanna Harrington, Indiana University–Purdue University, Indianapolis; Mary L. Hays, University of Illinois; Ana Hernandez, Miami Dade College (FL); Bryan Hiatt, Frederick Community College (MD); Karyn Hollis, Villanova University

(PA); Jeffrey Hotz, Montgomery College, Takoma Park (MD); Carol Howard, Warren Wilson College (NC); Doug Hunt, University of Missouri, Columbia; Melissa Joarder, Cabrini College (PA); T. R. Johnson, University of New Orleans (LA); Jennie Joiner, University of Kansas; Edmund Jones, Seton Hall University (NJ); Sarah Jordan, Albion College (MI); William Kazarian, Hawaii Pacific University; Valerie Kinloch, Teachers College, Columbia University (NY); Deborah Kirkman, University of Kentucky; Ray Korpi, Clark College (WA); Michael Kulycky, South Suburban College (IL); Maureen Lauder, Michigan State University; Nancy Lecourt, Pacific Union College (CA); Jerri Lindblad, Frederick Community College (MD); Frank Littler, Palm Beach Community College (CA); Judith Lockyer, Albion College (MI); Thomas E. Logan, American River College (CA); Ian MacInnes, Albion College (MI); Paul Matsuda, University of New Hampshire; Miles McCrimmon, J. Sargeant Reynolds Community College (VA); Nora Michaels, St. Johns River Community College (FL); Margie Monforton, Michigan State University; Roger E. Moore, Vanderbilt University (TN); Rhonda Morris, Santa Fe Community College (FL); Roger Munger, Boise State University (ID); Harriet Napierkowski, University of Colorado; Luis Nazario, Pueblo Community College (CO); Betty Palmer Nelson, Volunteer State College (TN); Diana Nystedt, Palo Alto College (TX); Ildiko Olasz, Michigan State University; Kim A. Parker, Palm Beach Community College (FL); David Porter, Clark College (WA); Margaret Price, University of Massachusetts, Amherst; Lynne Paris Purtle, Western Connecticut State University; Ellen Raphaeli, Northern Virginia Community College; Kathy Reynolds, Western Nevada Community College; Michael Ritterbrown, Glendale College (CA); Julie Rivera, California State University, Long Beach; David Russell, Iowa State University; David Sabrio, Texas A&M University, Kingsville; Ed Sams, San Jose State University (CA); Rick Saucier, St. John's University (NY); Shannin Schroeder, Southern Arkansas University; Ann Selby, Portland Community College (OR); Michelle Sidler, Auburn University (AL); Kathleen Ann Simonitsch, Western Connecticut State University; Gary Sligh, Lake-Sumter Community College (FL); Mary Stahoviak-Hall, Victoria College (TX); Erin Mary Sullivan, Humboldt State University (CA); Margaret

Judith Sullivan, Western Connecticut State University; Judy Swan, Princeton University (NJ); R. Swigger, Albuquerque TVI Community College (NM); James D. Thayer, Gonzaga University (WA); Tom Thompson, The Citadel (SC); Matthew T. Usner, Harold Washington College (IL); Barbara Voigt, Hawaii Pacific University; Wendy Wagner, Johnson and Wales University (RI); Cordell M. Waldron, University of Northern Iowa; Albert Keith Whitaker, Boston University (MA); Ian W. Wilson, Centre College (KY); and Joel Wingard, Moravian College (PA)

### Writing center directors

We would like to thank the following writing center directors who helped us think about the new writing center boxes and who involved their own tutors in the revision process.

Deborah Bacharach, Highline Community College (WA); Jennifer Beech, University of Tennessee at Chattanooga; Shane Borrowman, Gonzaga University (WA); Elizabeth Caulfield, Palm Beach Community College (FL); Laurie J. C. Cella, University of Connecticut; Paula Dean, Lord Fairfax Community College (VA); Harry Denny, State University of New York, Stony Brook; Anita Duneer, University of Connecticut; Paul Ellis, Northern Kentucky University; Jane Fife, University of Western Kentucky; Marsha Fisher, Northern Virginia Community College; Diane Flores-Kagan, Antelope Valley College (CA); Mary Jo Garcia, Palo Alto College (TX); Margaret Garroway, Howard Community College (MD); Deanne Gute, University of Northern Iowa; Scott Hendrix, Albion College (MI); Troy Hicks, Michigan State University; Joyce Hinnefeld, Moravian College (PA); Beth Kupper-Herr, Leeward Community College (HI); Leslie Leach, College of the Redwoods (CA); William L. Magrino, Rutgers University (NJ); Felicia Monticelli, Frederick Community College (MD); Ann Osborn, Everett Community College (WA); Grace Rhodes, Shoreline Community College (WA); Herbert Shapiro, Empire State College (NY); Ruth Ulvin, North Hennepin Community College (MN); Jackie Walsh, Boston University (MA); and Stephen Whitney, Pasadena City College (CA)

### Writing center tutors

Many writing center tutors responded to a questionnaire, sharing with us both their own best practices as writers and their best advice for successful college writing.

From Cardozo College (NY): Shuling J. Wu; from Central Missouri State University: Matt Groner; from College of the Redwoods (CA): Sarah Short; from Columbus State University (GA): Suzanne Alford, Shannon Hofer; from Empire State College (NY): Harry W. Aurand, Leslie Edwards; from Everett Community College (WA): Elizabeth Massengale, Leah Phillips; from Frederick Community College (MD): Kenneth Pitts; from Gonzaga University (WA): Lauren M. Carlson, Kelly Lynch, Kristen Marshall, Megan McKee, Kimberly E. Morgan, Thomas Perry, Jarrett Sacks, John Stewart; from Highline Community College (WA): Errol Chua; from Leeward Community College (HI): Rebecca McGee; from Michigan State University: Geoffrey A. Johns; from Moravian College (PA): Amy Ambler, Brandi Fogel, Courtney L. Werner; from Northern Kentucky University: Becky Anderson, Heather L. Burns, Susanne Firestone, Beth Kamradt, Laura M. Klein, Amber Weiss; from Northern Virginia Community College: Rebecca T. Elliott; from North Hennepin Community College (MN): Joan Baldwin, Jessica Estrada, Julia Hill; from Palm Beach Community College (FL): Jessica L. Asam, Katerine Rodriguez; from Palo Alto College (TX): Guadalupe Flores; from Rutgers University (NJ): Karen Gosselink, Melanie Holm, Bliss L. Kern, Alexander Obercian, Heather Robinson, Yana Zeltser; from Shoreline Community College (WA): Margarete Gail Cayford, Jana Norton; from State University of New York, Stony Brook: Kei Terauchi; from Western Kentucky University: Lindsey Bale, Thomas S. Johnson, Aubrey Videtto; from University of Connecticut: Kellan Chatelain, Mackenzie Dunn, Simona Herdan, Melanie Kelly, Dana Loch, Carrie Thibodeau; from University of Houston (TX): Alpha Holland, Kissanet Taffere, Cari-Sue Wilmot; from University of Maryland: Abigail Anne DuFour, David Dumas, Shanti Gonzales, Jennifer D. Sciubba, Michelle Solomon, Nanda Srikantaiah; from University of Northern Iowa: Amy Bly, Gabriel Smith, Eric Warren, Beth Wendland; and from

University of Tennessee at Chattanooga: Melanie Griffin, Diva Rutledge, Robert A. Trail, Amanda Womac, Lorenzo Woods

### Student contributors

We are indebted to the students whose essays appear in this edition—Ned Bishop, Angela Daly, Dan Larson, Albert Lee, Paul Levi, Carmen Lopez, Aaron Lund, Luisa Mirano, Margaret Peel, Matt Watson, and Tom Weitzel—not only for permission to use their work but also for allowing us to adapt it for pedagogical purposes. Our thanks also go to the students who granted permission to use their paragraphs: Celeste Barrus, Rosa Broderick, Diana Crawford, Jim Drew, Connie Hailey, Craig Lee Hetherington, William G. Hill, Linda Lavelle, Kathleen Lewis, Laurie McDonough, Chris Mileski, Leon Nage, Julie Reardon, Kevin Smith, Margaret Smith, Margaret Stack, John Clyde Thatcher, and David Warren.

### Authors of the ancillaries

Thanks are due to the authors of the book's ancillaries: to Leigh Ryan and Lisa Zimmerelli for their ambitious revision of *The Bedford Guide for Writing Tutors;* to Wanda Van Goor and Mitch Evich for their work on *Quizzes and Diagnostic Tests;* to Wanda Van Goor for her creative *Developmental Exercises;* to Barbara Fister for her expert contribution to *Research and Documentation in the Electronic Age,* Fourth Edition; to Barbara Wallraff for her clever new Language Debates; and to Barbara Sloan and Carolyn Christensen West and to Ellen Shull and Paula Tran for their useful guides *Preparing for the CLAST* and *Preparing for the THEA,* respectively.

# How to Use This Book and Its Web Site

Though it is small enough to hold in your hand, *The Bedford Handbook* will answer most of the questions you are likely to ask as you plan, draft, and revise a piece of writing: How do I choose and narrow a topic? What can I do if I get stuck? How do I know when to begin a new paragraph? Should I write *each was* or *each were*? When does a comma belong before *and*? What is the difference between *accept* and *except*? How do I cite a source from the Web?

The book's companion Web site extends the book beyond its covers. See page xxx for details.

## How to find information with an instructor's help

When you are revising an essay that has been marked by your instructor, tracking down information is simple. If your instructor marks problems with a number such as *16* or a number and letter such as *12e,* you can turn directly to the appropriate section of the handbook. Just flip through the olive-colored tabs at the top of the pages until you find the number in question. The number *16,* for example, leads you to the rule "Tighten wordy sentences," and *12e* takes you to the subrule "Repair dangling modifiers." If your instructor uses an abbreviation such as *w* or *dm* instead of a number, consult the list of abbreviations and revision symbols on the next to the last page of the book. There you will find the name of the problem (*wordy; dangling modifier*) and the number of the section to consult.

## How to find information on your own

With a little practice, you will be able to find information in this book without an instructor's help — usually by consulting the brief menu inside the front cover. At times, you may consult the detailed menu inside the back cover, the index, the Glossary of Usage, the list of revision symbols (as below), or one of the directories to documentation models. The tutorials on pages xxxi–xxxiv give you opportunities to practice finding information in different ways.

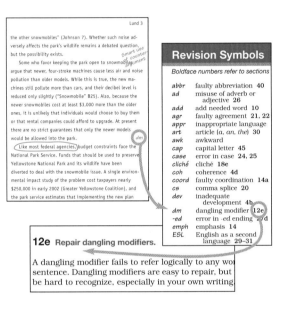

**THE BRIEF MENU.** The brief menu inside the front cover displays the book's contents as briefly and simply as possible.

Let's say that you are having problems writing parallel sentences. Your first step is to scan the menu for the appropriate numbered topic—in this case "9 Parallelism." Then you can use the olive-colored tabs at the top of the pages to find section 9. The information in the tabs—the section number and the symbol for parallelism—will tell you that you are in the section you need.

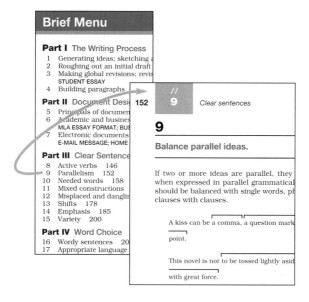

**Brief Menu**

**Part I** The Writing Process
1   Generating ideas; sketching a
2   Roughing out an initial draft
3   Making global revisions; revis
    STUDENT ESSAY
4   Building paragraphs

**Part II** Document Desi   152
5   Principals of documen
6   Academic and busines
    MLA ESSAY FORMAT; BUS
7   Electronic documents
    E-MAIL MESSAGE; HOME

**Part III** Clear Sentence
8   Active verbs   146
9   Parallelism   152
10  Needed words   158
11  Mixed constructions
12  Misplaced and danglir
13  Shifts   178
14  Emphasis   185
15  Variety   200

**Part IV** Word Choice
16  Wordy sentences   20
17  Appropriate language

// 9   *Clear sentences*

# 9

**Balance parallel ideas.**

If two or more ideas are parallel, they
when expressed in parallel grammatical
should be balanced with single words, ph
clauses with clauses.

A kiss can be a comma, a question mark
point.

This novel is not to be tossed lightly asid
with great force.

**THE DETAILED MENU.**   The detailed menu appears inside the back cover. When the numbered section you're looking for is broken up into quite a few lettered subsections, try consulting this menu. For instance, if you have a question about the proper use of commas after introductory elements, this menu will lead you quickly to section 32b.

Once you find the right lettered subsection, you will see three kinds of advice to help you edit your writing—a rule, an explanation, and one or more hand-edited examples.

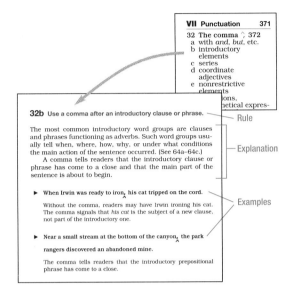

**THE INDEX.**   If you aren't sure which topic to choose from one of the menus, consult the index at the back of the book. For example, you may not realize that the issue of whether to use *have* or *has* is a matter of subject-verb agreement (section 21). In that case, simply look up "*has* vs. *have*" in the index and you will be directed to specific pages in two sections covering the topic of subject-verb agreement.

**THE GLOSSARY OF USAGE.**   When in doubt about the correct use of a particular word (such as *affect* and *effect*, *among* and *between,* or *hopefully*), consult the Glossary of Usage at the back of the book. This glossary explains the difference between commonly confused words; it also lists words that are inappropriate in formal written English.

**DIRECTORIES TO DOCUMENTATION MODELS.**   When you are documenting a research paper with MLA, APA, or *Chicago* style, you can find documentation models by consulting the appropriate directories. For MLA in-text citation and works cited directories, see the pages marked with a vertical band of blue; for APA in-text citation and reference list directories, see the pages marked with a vertical band of olive; and for the *Chicago* directory, see the pages marked with a vertical band of brown.

## How to use this book and its Web site for self-study

In a composition class, most of your time should be spent writing. So it is unlikely that you will study all of the chapters in this book in detail. Instead you should focus on the problems that tend to crop up in your own writing. Your instructor (or a tutor in your college's writing center) can help you design a program of self-study.

The Bedford Handbook has been designed so that you can learn from it on your own. By providing answers to some exercise sentences, it allows you to test your understanding of the material. Most exercise sets begin with five sentences lettered a–e and conclude with five or ten numbered sentences. Answers to the lettered sentences appear in an appendix at the end of the book.

The chart on page xxx describes the features on the book's companion Web site <dianahacker.com/bedhandbook>. Each feature—whether an electronic exercise or a Language Debate or a writing center helpsheet—has been developed for you to use on your own whenever you need it.

**ON THE WEB**

Throughout *The Bedford Handbook,* Seventh Edition, On the Web boxes direct you to relevant resources on the book's companion Web site.

Simply go to **dianahacker.com/bedhandbook** and click on

▶ **Electronic writing exercises**
Interactive exercises on topics such as choosing a thesis statement and conducting a peer review

▶ **Electronic grammar exercises**
Interactive exercises on grammar, style, and punctuation

▶ **Electronic research exercises**
Interactive exercises on topics such as integrating quotations and documenting sources in MLA, APA, and *Chicago* styles

▶ **Language Debates**
Mini-essays exploring controversial issues of grammar and usage, such as split infinitives

▶ **Resources for writers and tutors**
Revision checklists and helpsheets for common writing problems

▶ **Model papers**
Annotated sample papers in MLA, APA, *Chicago,* and CBE/CSE styles; a paper in progress; and two argument papers

▶ **Research and Documentation Online**
Advice on finding sources in a variety of disciplines and up-to-date guidelines for documenting print and online sources in MLA, APA, *Chicago,* and CBE/CSE styles

▶ **Additional resources**
Print-format versions of the exercises in the book and links to additional online resources for every part of the book

## TUTORIALS

The following tutorials will give you practice using the book's menus, index, Glossary of Usage, and MLA directory. Answers to the tutorials begin on page 859.

### TUTORIAL 1 Using the menus

Each of the following "rules" violates the principle it expresses. Using the brief menu inside the front cover or the detailed menu inside the back cover, find the section in *The Bedford Handbook* that explains the principle. Then fix the problem. Examples:

> *Tutors in*
> ~~In~~ the writing center/ ~~they~~ say that vague pronoun reference
> ^
> is unacceptable.   *23*
>
>                                   *come*
> Be alert for irregular verbs that have ~~came~~ to you in the
>                                   ^
> wrong form.   *27a*

1. A verb have to agree with its subject.
2. Each pronoun should agree with their antecedent.
3. About sentence fragments. You should avoid them.
4. Its important to use apostrophe's correctly.
5. Check for *-ed* verb endings that have been drop.
6. Discriminate careful between adjectives and adverbs.
7. If your sentence begins with a long introductory word group use a comma to separate the word group from the rest of the sentence.
8. Don't write a run-on sentence, you must connect independent clauses with a comma and a coordinating conjunction or with a semicolon.
9. A writer must be careful not to shift your point of view.
10. When dangling, watch your modifiers.

For answers to Tutorial 1, see page 859.

## TUTORIAL 2  Using the index

Assume that you have written the following sentences and want to know the answers to the questions in brackets. Use the index at the back of the book to locate the information you need, and edit the sentences if necessary.

1. Each of the candidates have decided to participate in tonight's debate. [Should the verb be *has* or *have* to agree with *Each*?]
2. We had intended to go surfing but spent most of our vacation lying on the beach. [Should I use *lying* or *laying*?]
3. We only looked at two houses before buying the house of our dreams. [Is *only* in the right place?]
4. In Saudi Arabia it is considered ill mannered for you to accept a gift. [Is it okay to use *you* to mean "anyone in general"?]
5. In Canada, Joanne picked up several bottles of maple syrup for her sister and me. [Should I write *for her sister and I*?]

## TUTORIAL 3  Using the menus or the index

Imagine that you are in the following situations. Using either the menus or the index, find the information you need.

1. You are Ray Farley, a community college student who has been out of high school for ten years. You recall learning to put a comma between all items in a series except the last two. But you have noticed that most writers use a comma between all items. You're curious about the current rule. Which section of *The Bedford Handbook* will you consult?
2. You are Maria Sanchez, a peer tutor in your university's writing center. Mike Lee, a nonnative speaker of English, has come to you for help. He is working on a rough draft that contains a number of problems with articles (*a, an,* and *the*). You know how to use articles, but you aren't able to explain the complicated rules on their correct use. Which section of *The Bedford Handbook* will you and Mike Lee consult?
3. You are John Pell, engaged to marry Jane Dalton. In a note to Jane's parents, you have written, "Thank you for giving Jane

For answers to Tutorial 2, see page 859.
For answers to Tutorial 3, see page 860.

and myself such a generous contribution toward our honey-moon." You wonder if you should write "Jane and I" or "Jane and me." What does *The Bedford Handbook* say?

4. You are Selena Young, an intern supervisor at a housing agency. Two of your interns, Jake Gilliam and Susan Green, have writing problems involving -s endings on verbs. Jake tends to drop -s endings; Susan tends to add them where they don't belong. You suspect that both problems stem from non-standard dialects spoken at home.

   Susan and Jake are in danger of losing their jobs because your boss thinks that anyone who writes "the tenant refuse" or "the landlords agrees" is beyond hope. You disagree. Susan and Jake have asked for your help. Where in *The Bedford Handbook* can they find the rules they need?

5. You are Joe Thompson, a first-year college student. Your friend Samantha, who has completed two years of college, seems to enjoy correcting your English. Just yesterday she corrected your sentence "I felt badly about her death" to "I felt bad about her death." You're sure you've heard many educated people, including professors, say "I felt badly." Upon consulting *The Bedford Handbook*, what do you discover?

---

## TUTORIAL 4  Using the Glossary of Usage

Consult the Glossary of Usage to see if the italicized words are used correctly. Then edit any sentences containing incorrect usage. If a sentence is correct, write "correct" after it. Example:

*an*
The pediatrician gave my daughter a̶ injection for her allergy.

1. Changing attitudes *toward* alcohol have *effected* the beer industry.
2. It is *mankind's* nature to think wisely and act foolishly.
3. This afternoon I plan to *lie* out in the sun and work on my tan.
4. Our goal this year is to *grow* our profits by 9 percent.
5. Most sleds are pulled by no *less* than two dogs and no more than ten.

For answers to Tutorial 4, see page 860.

## TUTORIAL 5 Using the directory to MLA works cited models

Assume that you have written a short research essay on the origins of hip-hop music. You have cited the following sources in your essay, using MLA documentation, and you are ready to type your list of works cited. Turn to page 622 and use the MLA directory to locate the appropriate models. Then write a correct entry for each source and arrange the entries in a properly formatted list of works cited.

A book by Jeff Chang titled *Can't Stop, Won't Stop: A History of the Hip-Hop Generation.* The book was published in New York by St. Martin's Press in 2005.

An online article by Kay Randall called "Studying a Hip-Hop Nation." The article appeared on the University of Texas at Austin Web site, which you accessed on April 13, 2005. The last update was April 11, 2005, and the URL is <http://www.utexas.edu/features/archive/2003/hiphop.html>.

A journal article by H. Samy Alim titled "360 Degreez of Black Art Comin at You: Sista Sonia Sanchez and the Dimensions of a Black Arts Continuum." The article appears in the journal *BMa: The Sonia Sanchez Literary Review,* which is paginated by issue. The article appears on pages 15–33. The volume number is 6, the issue number is 1, and the year is 2000.

A sound recording entitled "Rapper's Delight" performed by the Sugarhill Gang on the LP *The Sugarhill Gang.* The album was released in 1979 by Sugarhill Records.

A magazine article accessed through the *InfoTrac* database *Expanded Academic ASAP.* The article, "The Roots Redefine Hip-Hop's Past," was written by Kimberly Davis and published in *Ebony* magazine in June 2003. The article appears on pages 162–64. You found this article at the Ray Cosgrove Library at Truman College in Chicago on April 13, 2005, using the URL <http://infotrac.galegroup.com>.

For answers to Tutorial 5, see page 860.

# Contents

---

✳ **NEW TO THIS EDITION**

Part I includes new tips from writing tutors, new charts, an emphasis on asking questions, updated grammar checker advice, and new ESL boxes.

| | |
|---|---|
| 1 | New tips from writing tutors: the writing process |
| 1a | New ESL box; new chart on understanding assignments |
| 1c | New chart on testing a tentative thesis |
| 2 | New tips from writing tutors: drafting and writing conclusions |
| 2a | Revised advice on thesis statements; new ESL box |
| 2c | New chart on writing conclusions |
| 3 | New tips from writing tutors: revising and proofreading |
| 3a | New guidelines for using reviewers' comments |

---

**✳ NEW TO THIS EDITION**

**Part II** includes more examples of documents and updated advice on document design principles.

5     New visuals to show elements of design: brochure, newsletter, flyer, charts, graphs, table, clip art, photograph, diagram, and figures

5d    Revised advice on using visuals effectively and responsibly

**Part III** features new exercise items and updated grammar checker boxes.

# ✳ PART IV
## Word Choice     205

✳ **NEW TO THIS EDITION**
**Part IV** features new exercise items and updated grammar checker boxes.

## ✳ **PART V**
## **Grammatical Sentences**     **237**

---

✳ **NEW TO THIS EDITION**

**Part V** features new exercise items and updated grammar checker boxes.

✳ **NEW TO THIS EDITION**

## ✳ PART VI
### ESL Trouble Spots     **335**

---

✳ **NEW TO THIS EDITION**

**Part VI** features new exercise items and updated grammar checker boxes.

✳ **NEW TO THIS EDITION**

**Part VII** features new exercise items and updated grammar checker boxes.

✳ **NEW TO THIS EDITION**

36a New language debate on the companion Web site: -'s for singular nouns ending in -s

## ✳ PART VIII
## Mechanics                                                 **433**

✳ **NEW TO THIS EDITION**

**Part VIII** features new exercise items and updated grammar
checker boxes.

✳ **NEW TO THIS EDITION**

**Part IX** includes new coverage of writing about visual texts, new sample papers, revised treatment of counterargument, and a new chapter on writing in the disciplines.

46 New sample summary, outline, and analysis based on an annotated reading (by Jane Goodall) included in the book

New tips from writing tutors: annotating texts, reading

46a New guidelines for active reading

✳ **NEW TO THIS EDITION**

| 46c | New guidelines for writing a summary |
| 46d | New guidelines for writing an analysis |
|  | New student paper: analysis of a written text |
| 46e | New coverage of writing about visual texts; new student analysis paper |
| 47 | New ESL box on writing arguments |
|  | New tips from writing tutors: writing argument as an ESL student |
| 47f | Revised coverage on the importance of counterargument |
|  | New guidelines for anticipating and countering objections |
|  | New argument paper on snowmobiles in national parks |

---

✳ **NEW TO THIS EDITION**

  56  New tips from writing tutors: integrating sources

       Revised advice on integrating sources and using signal phrases in MLA papers

  56c  New section on putting source material in context

  57  Revised advice on documenting print and online sources in MLA style

  57b  New annotated visuals (Citation at a glance) that help students identify publication information needed to cite books, articles in periodicals, Web documents, and sources from databases

✳ **NEW TO THIS EDITION**

  60c   Revised advice on integrating sources and using signal phrases
         New section on putting source material in context
  60d   Revised advice on documenting print and online sources
         New annotated visuals (Citation at a glance) that help students identify publication information needed to cite articles in periodicals, books, sources from databases, and Web documents
  60f   New sample paper on treatments for childhood obesity, in APA style
  61c   Revised advice on integrating sources and using signal phrases
         New section on putting source material in context
  61d   Revised advice on documenting print and online sources

# Part I

# The Writing Process

1 Generate ideas and sketch a plan.

2 Rough out an initial draft.

3 Make global revisions; then revise sentences.
   • Student essay

4 Build effective paragraphs.

ON THE WEB

**dianahacker.com/bedhandbook/instructor**
▶ Exercise masters
▶ Quiz masters
▶ Transparency masters

1

Since it's not possible to think about everything all at once, most experienced writers approach a piece of writing in stages. You will generally move from planning to drafting to revising. Writing, however, is not a matter of recording already developed thoughts but a process of figuring out what you think. Be prepared to return to earlier stages as your ideas develop.

# 1

## Generate ideas and sketch a plan.

Before attempting a first draft, spend some time generating ideas. Mull over your subject while listening to music or driving to work, jot down inspirations on scratch paper, and explore your insights with anyone willing to listen. Ask yourself questions: What do you find puzzling, striking, or interesting about your subject? What would you like to know more about? What will interest your readers? At this stage, you should be collecting information and experimenting with ways of focusing and organizing it to reach your readers.

### 1a  Assess the writing situation.

Begin by taking a look at the writing situation in which you find yourself. The key elements of the writing situation include your subject, the sources of information available to you, your purpose, your audience, and constraints such as length, document design, review sessions, and deadlines.

It is likely that you will make final decisions about all of these matters later in the writing process—after a first draft, for example. Nevertheless, you can save yourself time

**SCHOLARS ON THE TEACHING SITUATION**

Logan, Shirley Wilson. "Changing Missions, Shifting Positions, and Breaking Silences." *College Composition and Communication* 55 (2003): 330–42. In this version of her address as chair of the 2003 CCCC convention, Logan reviews eleven important position statements that the CCCC has made on professional standards and students' linguistic rights, beginning with the 1974 statement "Students' Right to Their Own Language" and ending with the 2001 "Statement on Second Language Writing and Writers." After her 2003 address, Logan appointed a committee to create the position statement "Teaching, Learning, and Assessing Writing in Digital Environments," which was adopted in February 2004. All the position statements can be accessed at <http://www.ncte.org/groups/cccc/positions>.

by thinking about as many of them as possible in advance. For a quick checklist, see the chart on this page.

 **ESL** What counts as good writing varies from culture to culture and even among groups within cultures. In some situations, you will need to become familiar with the writing styles — such as direct or indirect, personal or impersonal, plain or embellished — that are valued by the culture or discourse community for which you are writing.

## Checklist for assessing the writing situation

At the beginning of the writing process, you may not be able to answer all of the questions on this checklist. That's fine. Just be prepared to think about them later. It is not necessary to think about the elements of a writing situation in the exact order listed in this chart.

### Subject

- Has the subject (or a range of possible subjects) been given to you, or are you free to choose your own?
- What interests you about your subject? What questions would you like to explore?
- Why is your subject worth writing about? How might readers benefit from reading about it?
- How broadly can you cover the subject? Do you need to narrow it to a more specific topic (because of length restrictions, for instance)?

### Sources of information

- Where will your information come from: Personal experience? Reading? Direct observation? Interviews? Questionnaires?
- What sort of documentation is required?

*(continued)*

**SCHOLARS ON THE TEACHING SITUATION**

Roberts-Miller, Trish. "Discursive Conflict in Communities and Classrooms." *College Composition and Communication* 54 (2003): 536–57. Roberts-Miller discusses the emphasis in critical pedagogy on using productive conflict in the classroom to understand and negotiate differences and maintain civility. She critiques another teacher's published narrative of her students' attempts to negotiate civilly with a homophobic student and argues that we cannot assume it is inherently valuable for different viewpoints to be expressed or that students can negotiate as equals. We also cannot downplay the pressures on students to reach consensus and conform to prevailing views. We need to provide space for students to listen and to argue so that they can "begin to form their own voices as writers and intellectuals."

## Checklist for assessing the writing situation (*continued*)

### Purpose

- Why are you writing: To inform readers? To persuade them? To entertain them? To call them to action? Some combination of these?
- Will your readers care about your purpose? Why do they need to be informed, persuaded, entertained, or called to action?

### Audience

- Who are your readers? How well informed are they about the subject? What do you want them to learn about the subject?
- How interested and attentive are they likely to be? Will they resist any of your ideas?
- What is your relationship to them: Citizen to citizen? Expert to novice? Scholar to scholar? Student to instructor? Employee to supervisor?
- How much time are they willing to spend reading?

### Length and document design

- Do you have any length specifications? If not, what length seems appropriate, given your subject, purpose, and audience?
- Must you use a particular format for your document? If so, do you have guidelines to follow or examples that you can consult?

### Reviewers and deadlines

- Who will be reviewing your draft in progress: Your instructor? A writing center tutor? Your classmates? A friend? Someone in your family?
- What are your deadlines? How much time will you need to allow for the various stages of writing, including proofreading the final draft and printing?

---

**ADDITIONAL RESOURCE ON THE TEACHING SITUATION**

*Lore* <http://bedfordstmartins.com/lore>. This e-journal, published by Bedford/St. Martin's, provides a forum for graduate students and adjunct composition teachers to discuss everyday teaching issues, to reflect on their teaching, and to become informed about professional matters.

## *Subject*

Frequently your subject will be given to you. In a psychology class, for example, you might be asked to explain Bruno Bettelheim's Freudian analysis of fairy tales. Or in a course on the history of filmmaking, you might be assigned an essay on the impact of D. W. Griffith's silent film *The Birth of a Nation.* In the business world, your assignment might be to draft a quarterly sales report or to craft a diplomatic e-mail to a customer who has complained about your firm's software.

At other times you will be free to choose your own subject. Then you will be wise to select a subject that you are curious to learn more about. If you studied television, print advertising, radio, and the Internet in a communications course, for example, you might ask yourself which of these subjects interests you most. Perhaps you are intrigued by children's television. In that case, look back through your readings and class notes and see if you can identify any questions you'd like to explore further. If you are puzzled by the relation between some children's violent behavior and violence in television programming, you can explore that question in your essay.

Make sure that you can reasonably investigate your subject in the space you have. If you are limited to a few pages, for example, you could not possibly do justice to a subject as broad as "television violence." You would be wise to restrict your focus to one aspect of the subject that will intrigue both you and your readers — perhaps experts' contradictory claims about the psychological effects of television violence on children. The chart on the next page suggests specific ways to narrow a subject to a manageable paper topic.

Whether or not you choose your own subject, it's important to be aware of the expectations of each writing situation. The chart on pages 10–11 suggests ways to interpret assignments.

### SCHOLARS ON THE TEACHING SITUATION

Corbett, Edward, Nancy Myers, and Gary Tate. *The Writing Teacher's Sourcebook.* 4th ed. New York: Oxford UP, 2000. The most recent edition of this well-regarded collection on the pedagogical concerns of classroom teachers includes thirty-six previously published articles on theories and approaches to teaching composition, constructing assignments, and responding to writing, among other topics.

## Ways to narrow a subject to a topic

### Subdividing your subject

Many subjects can be divided into smaller pieces. One way to subdivide a subject is to ask questions sparked by reading or talking to your classmates. If you are writing about teen pregnancy, for example, you might wonder why some cities have different rates of teen pregnancy. Or you might ask whether high schools should provide child care for teen mothers. Either question would give you a manageable topic for a short paper.

### Restricting your purpose

Often you can restrict your purpose. For example, if your subject is preventing teen pregnancy, you might at first hope to call readers to action. Upon further reflection, you might realize that this goal is more than you could hope to accomplish, given your word limit. By adopting a more limited purpose — to show that an experimental health class targeted at sixth graders results in lower rates of teen pregnancy or to argue for more funding for educational programs — you would have a manageable topic and a better chance of success.

### Restricting your audience

Consider writing for a particular audience. For example, instead of writing for a general audience on a broad subject such as teenage pregnancy, you might address groups with a special interest in the subject: young people, parents, educators, or politicians.

### Considering the information available to you

Look at the information you have collected. If you have gathered a great deal of information on one aspect of your subject (for example, counseling programs for pregnant teenagers) and less information on other aspects (such as birth control education or the rights of teen fathers), you may have found your topic.

**SCHOLARS ON THE TEACHING SITUATION**

Hacker, Diana. "Following the Tao." *Teaching English in the Two-Year College* 27 (2000): 297–300. Hacker suggests that the Chinese classic *Tao Te Ching*, which offers advice to rulers, can benefit teachers as well. In fact, she says, many of the *Tao*'s insights have become accepted wisdom in the teaching of composition over the past twenty-five years. Hacker's article is organized around five of her favorite lines from the *Tao:* Practice nonaction. Yield and overcome; bend and be straight. In action, watch the timing. Give up learning and put an end to your troubles. Achieve greatness in little things.

**ON THE WEB**

**dianahacker.com/bedhandbook**
▶ Additional resources
   ▶ Subjects for writing

*Sources of information*

Where will your facts, details, and examples come from? Can you develop your topic from personal experience, or will you need to search for relevant information through direct observation, interviews, questionnaires, or reading? Your sources of information will affect how you approach your topic and what kinds of questions you ask.

**PERSONAL EXPERIENCE**   If your interest in a subject stems from your personal experience, you will want to ask yourself what it is about your experience that would interest your audience and why. For example, if you volunteered at a homeless shelter, you might have spent some time talking to homeless children and learned about their fears. Perhaps you can use your experience to broaden your readers' understanding of the issues involved, to persuade an organization to fund an after-school program for homeless children, or to propose changes in legislation.

**READING**   Reading is an important way to deepen your understanding of a topic and enlarge your perspective. Reading will be your primary source of information for many college assignments, which will generally be of two kinds: (1) analytical essays that call for a close reading of one book, essay, or literary work and (2) research assignments that ask you to find and consult a variety of sources on a topic. (See the chart "Guidelines for active reading" on p. 470.)

For an analytical essay, you will select details from the work not to inform readers but to support an interpretation.

**ADDITIONAL RESOURCE ON THE TEACHING SITUATION**

Johnson, T. R., ed. *Teaching Composition: Background Readings.* 2nd ed. Boston: Bedford, 2005. This collection of thirty readings, both classic and contemporary, by leading scholars in the field provides an introduction to composition theory and practice. Suggested classroom applications and questions for reflection accompany each reading.

You can often assume that your readers are familiar with the work and have a copy of it on hand, but provide enough context so that someone who doesn't know the work well can still follow your interpretation. When you quote from the work, page references are usually sufficient. When in doubt about the need for documentation, consult your instructor.

For a research paper, you cannot assume that your readers are familiar with your sources. Therefore, you must formally document all quoted, summarized, or paraphrased material (see 53).

**DIRECT OBSERVATION**    Direct observation is an excellent means of collecting information about a wide range of subjects, such as male-female relationships on a popular television program, the clichéd language of a sports announcer, or the appeal of a local art museum. For such subjects, do not rely on your memory alone; your information will be fresher and more detailed if you actively collect it, with a notebook or tape recorder in hand. As writer Stuart Chase advised young journalists assigned to report on their city's water system, "You will write a better article if you heave yourself out of a comfortable chair and go down in tunnel 3 and get soaked."

**INTERVIEWS AND QUESTIONNAIRES**    Interviews and questionnaires can supply you with detailed and interesting information on a variety of subjects. A nursing student

---

**TIPS FROM WRITING TUTORS**

"I read a lot more now than I did when I started college, so it's easier for me to spot when my own argument is weak or when my writing is disorganized. Reading a lot also helps me to combat grammar and punctuation problems in my own writing."
— *Shanthi Gonzales, University of Maryland, College Park*

---

**SCHOLARS ON THE WRITING SITUATION**

Sommers, Nancy, and Laura Saltz. "The Novice as Expert: Writing the Freshman Year." *College Composition and Communication* 56 (2004): 124–49. Using their findings from a longitudinal study of four hundred Harvard undergraduates, the authors describe the students' writing experiences in their first-year courses other than English. They discuss the teaching methods that helped successful students realize that they "get something" more than just a grade if the writing matters to them and that they have some knowledge to "give" to their teachers. At two extremes on the spectrum of writing experience were students for whom the only value in writing was a grade or a means of personal expression and students who understood that writing is "the heart of what they know and learn."

interested in the care of terminally ill patients might inter-view nurses at a hospice; a political science major might speak with a local judge to learn about alternative sentenc-ing for first offenders; a future teacher might conduct a sur-vey on the classroom use of computers in local elementary schools.

It is a good idea to tape-record interviews to preserve any lively quotations that you might want to weave into your essay. Circulating questionnaires by e-mail will facilitate re-sponses. Keep questions simple and specify a deadline to ensure that you get a reasonable number of replies. (See also 50g.)

### Purpose

Your purpose will often be dictated by your specific writing situation. Perhaps you have been asked to draft a proposal requesting funding for a student organization, to report the results of a biology experiment, or to write about the stem cell research controversy for the school newspaper. Even though your overall purpose is fairly obvious in such situa-tions, a closer look at the assignment can help you make a variety of necessary decisions. How detailed should the pro-posal be? What will persuade the student government to grant your organization the funds it needs: a summary of past projects or a list of plans for the future? How technical does your biology professor want your report to be? Are you supposed to share your laboratory results or evaluate the data you collected? Do you want to inform students about the stem cell research controversy or change their attitudes toward it?

In many writing situations, part of your challenge will be discovering a purpose. Asking yourself why readers should care about what you are saying can help you decide what your purpose might be. Perhaps you have chosen the subject magnet schools—schools that draw students from

**SCHOLARS ON THE WRITING SITUATION**

Curtis, Marcia, and Anne Herrington. "Writing Development in the College Years: By Whose Definition?" *College Composition and Communication* 55 (2003): 69–90. As a follow-up to the authors' longitudinal study of the development of four undergraduate writ-ers, *Persons in Process* (Urbana: NCTE, 2000), this article looks at how writing tasks from courses across the disciplines contribute to students' academic and personal growth. Students use writing, including assigned writing, to reflect on and fashion public and private identities. Rather than taking a narrow view of writing com-petence, the authors urge, we should attend to students' cognitive, emotional, and ethical development, all important aspects of the writerly selves they are creating and equally important aspects of the writing assignments we create.

## Understanding an assignment

For many college papers, you will be given a written assignment that outlines your instructor's expectations. When you receive an assignment, read through it carefully. Don't assume that all writing assignments are alike—spend some time making sure you understand what is required of you. When in doubt, ask your instructor.

### Determining the purpose of the assignment

Instructors assign writing projects for a variety of reasons. You might be expected to summarize information from textbooks, lectures, or research (see 46c); to analyze ideas and concepts (see 46d); to take a position on a topic and defend it with evidence (see 47); or to create an original argument by combining ideas from different sources (see 47). Usually the wording of the assignment will suggest which of these purposes your instructor has in mind.

### Understanding how to answer an assignment's question

Many assignments will ask you to answer a *how* or *why* question. Such a question cannot be answered using only facts;

different neighborhoods because of features such as advanced science classes or a concentration on the arts. If you have already discussed magnet schools in class, a basic description of how these schools work probably will not interest you or your readers. But maybe you have discovered that your county's magnet schools are not promoting racial integration as had been planned and you want to call your readers to action. Or maybe you are interested in comparing student performance at magnet schools and traditional schools.

Although no precise guidelines will lead you to a purpose, you can begin by asking yourself which one or more of the following aims you hope to accomplish.

**WRITING CENTER DIRECTORS ON THE WRITING SITUATION**

"Many students think only of the teacher when they write papers, but the teacher as audience is problematic because often he or she knows more about the subject than the student author. The student may also think the teacher has no real interest in what he or she is writing. Both of these scenarios make it difficult for student writers to focus sharply on the purpose for writing. The writing center offers a space for the student writer to have a fully attentive and careful reader for the paper, one who can engage with the topic and who doesn't have to evaluate the paper for a grade."

—Paul Ellis, director, Learning Assistance Program,
Northern Kentucky University

you will need to take a position. For example, the question "*What* are the survival rates for leukemia patients?" can be answered by reporting facts. The question "*Why* are the survival rates for leukemia patients in one state lower than in a neighboring state?" must be answered with both facts and interpretation. If a list of prompts appears in the assignment, be careful—instructors rarely expect you to answer all of the questions in order. Look instead for topics, themes, or ideas that will help you ask your own questions.

### Recognizing implied questions

When you are asked to *discuss, analyze, agree or disagree,* or *consider* a topic, your instructor will often expect you to answer a *how* or *why* question. For example, "*Discuss* the effects of the No Child Left Behind Act on special education programs" is really another way of saying "*How* has the No Child Left Behind Act affected special education programs?" Similarly, the assignment "*Consider* the recent rise of attention deficit hyperactivity disorder diagnoses" is asking you to answer the question "*Why* are diagnoses of attention deficit hyperactivity disorder rising?"

**PURPOSES FOR WRITING**

| | |
|---|---|
| to inform | to evaluate |
| to persuade | to recommend |
| to entertain | to request |
| to call readers to action | to propose |
| to change attitudes | to provoke thought |
| to analyze | to express feelings |
| to argue | to summarize |

Writers often misjudge their own purposes, summarizing when they should be analyzing or expressing feelings about problems instead of proposing solutions. Before beginning any writing task, pause to ask, "Why am I communicating with my readers?" This question will lead you to another important question: "Just who are my readers?"

**SCHOLARS ON THE WRITING SITUATION**

Hillocks, George, Jr. "The Composing Process: A Model." *Teaching Writing as Reflective Practice.* New York: Teachers Coll. P, 1995. 76–95. Hillocks asks us to think of a piece of writing as having three sorts of purpose: one related to "the substance of the writing," another connected to audience, and a third tied to the writer.

*Audience*

Audience analysis can often lead you to an effective strategy for reaching your readers. One writer, whose purpose was to persuade teenagers not to smoke, jotted down the following observations about her audience:

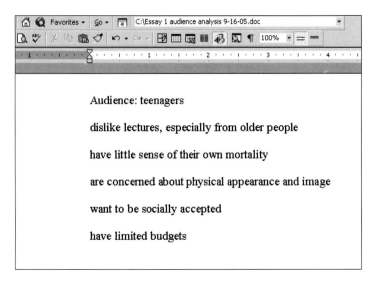

Audience: teenagers

dislike lectures, especially from older people

have little sense of their own mortality

are concerned about physical appearance and image

want to be socially accepted

have limited budgets

This analysis led the writer to focus more on the social aspects of smoking than on the health risks. Her audience analysis also warned her against adopting a preachy tone that her readers might find offensive. Instead of lecturing, she decided to draw examples from her own experience as a smoker: burning holes in her best sweater, driving in zero-degree weather late at night in search of an open convenience store to buy cigarettes, and so on. The result was an essay that reached its readers instead of alienating them.

Of course, in some writing situations the audience will not be neatly defined for you. Nevertheless, many of the

**SCHOLARS ON THE WRITING SITUATION**

Bartholomae, David. "Inventing the University." *When a Writer Can't Write: Studies in Writer's Block and Other Composing Problems.* Ed. Mike Rose. New York: Guilford, 1985. 134–65. Bartholomae argues that students writing in the university are attempting "to learn to speak our language, to speak as we do, to try on the peculiar ways of knowing, selecting, evaluating, reporting, concluding, and arguing that define the . . . various discourses of our community." Assessing the writing situation, then, is complex.

choices you make as you write will tell readers who you think they are (novices or experts, for example), so it is best to be consistent—even if this means creating an audience that is in some sense a fiction.

For help with audience analysis, see the chart on pages 3–4.

**ACADEMIC AUDIENCES** In the academic world, considerations of audience can be more complex than they seem at first. Your instructor will read your essay, of course, but most instructors play multiple roles while reading. Their first and most obvious roles are as coach and judge; less obvious is their role as an intelligent and objective reader, the kind of person who might reasonably be informed, convinced, entertained, or called to action by what you have to say.

Some instructors create writing assignments that specify an audience, such as a hypothetical supervisor, readers of a local newspaper, or fellow academics in a particular field of study. Other instructors expect you to imagine an audience appropriate to your purpose and your subject. Still others prefer that you write for a general audience of educated readers—nonspecialists who can be expected to read with an intelligent, critical eye. When in doubt about an appropriate audience for a particular assignment, check with your instructor.

**BUSINESS AUDIENCES** Writers in the business world often find themselves writing for multiple audiences. A letter to a client, for instance, might be distributed to sales representatives as well. Readers of a report might include persons with and without technical expertise or readers who want details and those who prefer a quick overview.

To satisfy the demands of multiple audiences, business writers have developed a variety of strategies: attaching cover letters to detailed reports, adding boldface headings, placing summaries in the left margin, and so on.

### SCHOLARS ON THE WRITING SITUATION

Kinneavy, James L. *A Theory of Discourse.* New York: Norton, 1980. 17–40, 48–68. In this classic work, Kinneavy makes explicit the "communication triangle" and the several "aims" of discourse, providing the foundation for much of the later thought on what it means to assess the writing situation.

### SCHOLARS ON AUDIENCE

Adler-Kassner, Linda, and Susanmarie Harrington. *Questioning Authority: Stories Told in School.* Ann Arbor: U of Michigan P, 2001. The twelve "stories" that make up this collection explore the ways experienced teachers define and teach the expository essay, including the role of personal narrative in helping students talk with and back to the authoritative voices of the academy.

## Length and document design

Writers seldom have complete control over length. Journalists usually write within strict word limits set by their editors, businesspeople routinely aim for conciseness, and most college assignments specify an approximate length.

Certain document designs may be required by your writing situation. Specific formats are used in the business world for letters, memos, reports, budget analyses, and personnel records. In the academic world, you may need to learn precise conventions for lab reports, critiques, research papers, and so on. For most undergraduate essays, a standard format is acceptable (see 6a).

In some writing situations, you will be free to create your own design, complete with headings, displayed lists, and perhaps even visuals, such as charts and graphs. As software becomes more sophisticated, both writers and readers are becoming increasingly interested in designs that improve readability. For a discussion of the principles of document design, see 5.

## Reviewers and deadlines

Professional and business writers rarely work alone. They work with reviewers, often called editors, who offer advice throughout the writing process. In college classes, too, the use of reviewers is common. Some instructors will play the role of reviewer for you; others may ask you to visit your college's writing center. Still others schedule peer review sessions to be conducted in class or online. Such sessions give you a chance to hear what other students think about your draft in progress—and to play the role of reviewer yourself. For peer review guidelines, see the chart on page 46.

Deadlines are a key element of any writing situation. They help you plan your time and map out what you can accomplish in that time. For complex writing projects, such as research papers, you'll need to plan your time quite care-

**SCHOLARS ON AUDIENCE**

Rafoth, Bennett A. "Discourse Community: Where Writers, Readers, and Texts Come Together." *The Social Construction of Written Communication.* Ed. Bennett A. Rafoth and Donald L. Rubin. Norwood: Ablex, 1988. 131–46. Drawing on theoretical work in rhetoric, literary criticism, and linguistics, Rafoth argues that a "focus on discourse community differs from approaches to audience in composition, where perspectives that emphasize either writers, texts, or readers emerge not from a single, underlying framework but stand more or less independent of, and sometimes in opposition to, each other."

fully. By working backward from the final deadline, you can create a schedule of target dates for completing various parts of the process. (See p. 529 for an example.)

**EXERCISE 1-1**   Narrow five of the following subjects into topics that would be manageable for an essay of two to five pages.

 1.  Domestic violence and the courts
 2.  Performing as a musician
 3.  Treatments for mental illness
 4.  An experience with racism or sexism
 5.  Computers in the classroom
 6.  Images of women in video games
 7.  Mandatory drug testing
 8.  Olympic gymnasts
 9.  Presidential campaign funding
10.  The films of Quentin Tarantino

**EXERCISE 1-2**   Suggest a purpose and an audience for five of the following subjects.

 1.  Science fiction as a serious form of literature
 2.  Cloning human beings
 3.  Government subsidies to farmers
 4.  The future of online advertising
 5.  Working with special needs children
 6.  The challenges facing single parents
 7.  Smoking and lung disease
 8.  Growing up in a large family
 9.  The influence of African art on Picasso
10.  Hybrid cars

**ON THE WEB**   **dianahacker.com/bedhandbook**
  ▶ Electronic writing exercises
    ▶ E-ex 1-1

**SCHOLARS ON AUDIENCE**

Elbow, Peter. "Closing My Eyes as I Speak: An Argument for Ignoring Audience." *College English* 49 (1987): 50–69. Elbow argues that premature attention to audience can inhibit writers, stifling their natural voices. In some situations, writers should ignore audience until the revision stage.

**1b** Experiment with ways to explore your subject.

Instead of just plunging into a first draft, experiment with one or more techniques for exploring your subject, perhaps one of these:

> talking and listening
>
> annotating texts and taking notes
>
> listing
>
> clustering
>
> freewriting
>
> asking the journalist's questions
>
> keeping a journal

You can use most of these techniques whether you are working on paper or on a computer.

Whatever technique you turn to, the goal is the same: to generate a wealth of ideas that will lead you to a question, a problem, or an issue that you want to explore further. At this early stage of the writing process, don't censor yourself. Sometimes an idea that initially seems trivial or far-fetched will actually turn out to be worthwhile.

### Talking and listening

Since writing is a process of figuring out what you think about a subject, it can be useful to try out your ideas on other people — early and often. Conversation can deepen and refine your ideas before you even begin to set them down on paper. By talking and listening to others, you can also discover what they find interesting, what they are curious about, and where they disagree with you. If you are planning to advance an argument, you can try it out on listeners with other points of view.

---

**SCHOLARS ON THE WRITING PROCESS**

Dunn, Patricia A. *Talking, Sketching, Moving: Multiple Literacies in the Teaching of Writing.* Portsmouth: Boynton, 2001. Dunn argues that too many students are excluded by our "print-loving pedagogies" and that we can all benefit if we make space for the multiple literacies students bring to our writing classrooms. In a lengthy and very useful third chapter, she describes a variety of strategies — visual, aural, and kinesthetic — that teachers can use to help even the most proficient writers generate ideas and organize their texts in more insightful ways. Strategies include "rhetorical proof cards," which can be moved around to form arguments and counterarguments; sketching-to-learn and moving-to-learn activities; sketching to generate metaphors; and connecting ideas through oral outlines and oral journals.

Many writers begin a writing project by brainstorming ideas in a group, debating a point with friends, or chatting with an instructor. Others turn to themselves for company — by talking into a tape recorder. Some writers "virtually converse" by exchanging ideas through e-mail or instant messaging, by joining an Internet chat group, or by following a mailing list discussion. If you are part of a networked classroom, you may be encouraged to exchange ideas with your classmates and instructor in an electronic workshop. One advantage of engaging in such discussions is that while you are "talking" you are actually writing. For example, a student who participated in the following chat was able to refine her argument before she started drafting her essay on presidential campaign funding.

**CONVERSATION ABOUT A SUBJECT**

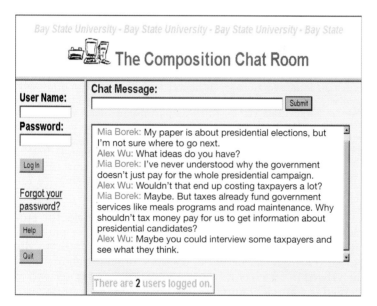

*Bay State University - Bay State University - Bay State University - Bay State*

## The Composition Chat Room

**User Name:**

**Password:**

Log In

Forgot your password?

Help

Quit

**Chat Message:**

Submit

> Mia Borek: My paper is about presidential elections, but I'm not sure where to go next.
> Alex Wu: What ideas do you have?
> Mia Borek: I've never understood why the government doesn't just pay for the whole presidential campaign.
> Alex Wu: Wouldn't that end up costing taxpayers a lot?
> Mia Borek: Maybe. But taxes already fund government services like meals programs and road maintenance. Why shouldn't tax money pay for us to get information about presidential candidates?
> Alex Wu: Maybe you could interview some taxpayers and see what they think.

There are **2** users logged on.

**SCHOLARS ON THE WRITING PROCESS**

Gallehr, Donald R. "What Is the Sound of No Hand Writing? The Use of Secularized Zen Koans in the Teaching of Writing." *The Spiritual Side of Writing.* Ed. Regina Foehr and Susan Schiller. Portsmouth: Boynton, 1997. Gallehr describes how he uses Zen koans (questions intended to bring about enlightenment) in his composition classroom to help students clear their minds and begin to think intuitively and holistically. He begins with the question "What does society want my writing to become?" followed by "What do I want my writing to become?" Finally, after several weeks, he poses the question "What does my writing want to become?" It is this last question, Gallehr says, that allows students to relax and let their writing flow. He also teaches students to focus on the last question when they begin to revise their work.

### Annotating texts and taking notes

When you write about reading, one of the best ways to explore ideas is to mark up the work — on the pages themselves if you own a copy, on photocopies if you don't. Annotating a text encourages you to look at it more carefully — to underline key concepts, to note possible contradictions in an argument, to raise questions for further investigation. (See also 46a.) Here, for example, is a paragraph from an essay on medical ethics as one student annotated it.

*What break-throughs?*
*Do all break-throughs have the same consequences?*

*Is everyone really uneasy?*
*Is something a breakthrough if it creates a predicament?*

Breakthroughs in genetics present us with a promise and a predicament. The promise is that we may soon be able to treat and prevent a host of debilitating diseases. The predicament is that our newfound genetic knowledge may also enable us to manipulate our own nature — to enhance our muscles, memories, and moods; to choose the sex, height, and other genetic traits of our children; to make ourselves "better than well." When science moves faster than (moral understanding), as it does today, men and women struggle to articulate their unease. In liberal societies they reach first for the language of autonomy, fairness, and individual rights. But this part of our moral vocabulary is ill equipped to address the hardest questions posed by genetic engineering. The genomic revolution has induced a kind of moral vertigo.
  — Michael Sandel, "The Case against Perfection"

*Stem cell research?*

*What does he mean by "moral understanding"?*

*Which questions? He doesn't seem to be taking sides.*

After reading and annotating the entire article, the student read through his annotations and looked for patterns. He noticed that several of his annotations pointed to the larger question of whether a scientific breakthrough should be viewed in terms of its moral consequences. He decided to reread the article, taking detailed notes on his reading, with this question in mind. (See also 52c.)

---

**WRITING CENTER DIRECTORS ON THE WRITING PROCESS**

"Many regular users of the writing center recognize that they can integrate the way the tutors work with their own writing process, so that one step includes working with a draft or a series of ideas or an outline, another getting feedback. When feedback thus also becomes part of their writing process, they learn to build time into their long-range writing plans for tutor/peer interaction instead of trying to cram their paper into the keyboard at the last minute. This global state of mind — seeing one's writing as part of larger processes involving the writing center, the professor's expectations, the world of research and ideas, other audiences (real or imagined) — is a key factor in the development of effective writers."
  — Scott Hendrix, director of writing, Albion College

## Listing

Listing ideas is a good way to figure out what you know and what questions you have. You might begin by simply putting ideas down in the order in which they occur to you — a technique sometimes known as *brainstorming*. Here is a list one student writer jotted down for an essay about funding for college athletics:

- Football receives the most funding of any sport.
- Funding comes from ticket sales, fundraisers, alumni contributions.
- Biggest women's sport is soccer.
- Women's soccer team is only ten years old; football team is fifty years old.
- Football graduates have had time to earn more money than soccer graduates.
- Soccer games don't draw as many fans.
- Should funding be equal for all teams?
- Do alumni have the right to fund whatever they want?

The ideas and questions appear here in the order in which they first occurred to the writer. Later she felt free to rearrange them, to group them under general categories, to delete some, and to add others. These initial thoughts led the writer to questions that helped her narrow her topic. In other words, she treated her early list as a source of ideas and a springboard to new ideas, not as an outline.

## Clustering

Unlike listing, the technique of clustering highlights relationships among ideas. To cluster ideas, write your topic in the center of a sheet of paper, draw a circle around it, and surround the circle with related ideas connected to it with lines. If some of the satellite ideas lead to more specific clusters, write them down as well. The writer of the following diagram was exploring ideas for an essay on obesity in children.

**SCHOLARS ON THE WRITING PROCESS**

Lindemann, Erika. *A Rhetoric for Writing Teachers.* 3rd ed. New York: Oxford UP, 1995. 21–34. Lindemann traces how views of the writing process have developed since the 1970s. She recommends that we treat writing as social interaction and asks us to reexamine "what goes on in writing classes, what textbooks recommend, even what our own experiences as writers suggest."

**CLUSTER DIAGRAM**

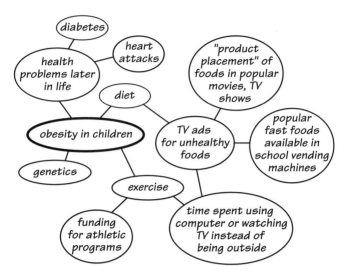

The writer drew several lines between television advertising and related thoughts. This small cluster of ideas indicates that the relationship between advertising and childhood obesity might be a promising paper topic.

*Freewriting*

In its purest form, freewriting is simply nonstop writing. You set aside ten minutes or so and write whatever comes to mind, without pausing to think about word choice, spelling, or even meaning. If you get stuck, you can write about being stuck, but you should keep your fingers moving. The point is to loosen up and see what happens. Even if nothing much happens, you have lost only ten minutes. It's more likely, though, that something interesting will emerge—perhaps a surprising observation, an honest expression of feeling, or a thought worth exploring. Freewriting also lets you ask ques-

**SCHOLARS ON FREEWRITING**

Marsella, Joy, and Thomas L. Hilgers. "Exploring the Potential of Freewriting." *Nothing Begins with N: New Investigations of Freewriting.* Ed. Pat Belanoff, Peter Elbow, and Sheryl I. Fontaine. Carbondale: Southern Illinois UP, 1991. 93–110. The authors argue for "the use of freewriting as a broad heuristic . . . that prompts not only ideas but also analysis of those ideas." They describe a three-step sequence derived from Elbow's *Writing without Teachers* (New York: Oxford UP, 1973) and explain their expanded use and understanding of freewriting.

tions without feeling that you have to answer them. Sometimes a question that emerges at this stage will point you in an unexpected direction.

To explore ideas on a particular topic, consider using a technique known as *focused freewriting.* Again, you write quickly and freely—without regard for punctuation, word choice, spelling, or paragraphing—but this time you focus on a subject and pay some attention to the connections among your ideas. For example, the student who made the cluster diagram about childhood obesity on page 20 used freewriting to explore the link between advertising and the rise in children's average weight. Here is what she came up with.

**FOCUSED FREEWRITING**

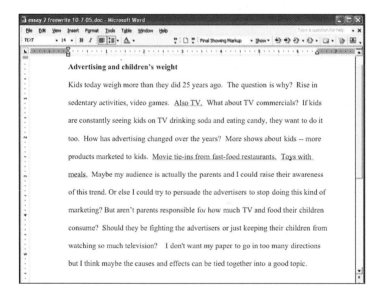

**TIP:** If you get stuck while freewriting, try imagining that you are writing an e-mail to a friend about your subject.

**SCHOLARS ON FREEWRITING**

Reynolds, Mark. "Make Free Writing More Productive." *College Composition and Communication* 39 (1988): 81–82. Reynolds provides some questions, activities, and guidelines to help students make freewriting "more productive and generative."

Elbow, Peter. *Writing with Power: Techniques for Mastering the Writing Process.* New York: Oxford UP, 1981. In his first two chapters, Elbow describes prewriting strategies, including freewriting.

## TIPS FROM WRITING TUTORS

"The first word is the hardest. It's the perfectionist in me that doesn't allow me to just write away, right away. I have that nagging feeling that it needs to be right the first time. Often, I get beyond this by writing my thoughts on the sources that I plan to use. I may not use this first bit of writing, but it gets the ideas flowing without so much pressure."
                                        —*Aubrey Videtto, Western Kentucky University*

### Asking the journalist's questions

By asking questions, you can generate many ideas—and you can make sure that you have adequately explored your subject. When gathering material for a story, journalists routinely ask themselves Who? What? When? Where? Why? and How? In addition to helping journalists get started, these questions ensure that they will not overlook an important fact: the date of a prospective summit meeting, for example, or the exact location of a neighborhood burglary.

Whenever you are writing about events, whether current or historical, asking the journalist's questions is one way to get started. One student, whose topic was the negative reaction in 1915 to D. W. Griffith's silent film *The Birth of a Nation,* began exploring her topic with this set of questions:

*Who* objected to the film?

*What* were the objections?

*When* were protests first voiced?

*Where* were protests most strongly expressed?

*Why* did protesters object to the film?

*How* did protesters make their views known?

As often happens, the answers to these questions led to another question the writer wanted to explore further. After she discovered that protesters objected to the film's racist

### SCHOLARS ON JOURNAL WRITING

Autrey, Ken. "Entries into Teaching with Journals." *Genre by Example: Writing What We Teach.* Ed. David Starkey. Portsmouth: Boynton, 2001. 41–52. Using a journal format, Autrey shows the changes in his thinking about the value of journal writing assignments in his composition classes. He questions the common assumption that the audience for a journal is the self. When journals are assigned in class, he argues, the teacher is the primary audience and the "self" is secondary. Instead he wants the journal to be an academic space for students to think critically and creatively and to blend the personal and the public. In his own journal, he reflects on ways he might make this happen.

portrayal of African Americans, she wondered whether their protests had changed attitudes. This question prompted an interesting topic for a paper: Did the film's stereotypes lead to positive, if unintended, consequences?

In the academic world, scholars often generate ideas with questions related to a specific discipline: one set of questions for analyzing short stories, another for evaluating experiments in social psychology, still another for reporting field experiences in anthropology. If you are writing in a particular discipline, try to discover the questions that its scholars typically explore. (See 49.)

### Keeping a journal

A journal is a collection of personal, exploratory writing. An entry in a journal can be any length—from a single sentence to several pages—and it is likely to be informal and experimental.

In a journal, often meant for your eyes only, you can take risks. In one entry, for example, you might do some freewriting. In another, you might pose a series of questions, whether or not you have the answers. You might comment on an interesting idea from one of your classes or keep a list of questions that occur to you while reading. A journal is also an excellent place to play around with language for the sheer fun of it: experimenting with prose style, for instance, or parodying a favorite author or songwriter.

Keeping a journal can be an enriching experience in its own right, since it allows you to explore issues of concern to you without worrying about what someone else thinks. A journal can also serve as a sourcebook of ideas to draw on in future essays; on rare occasions, in fact, a journal entry may emerge as a polished essay of interest to readers other than yourself. Some writers find that they do their best work when writing for themselves, deliberately ignoring the constraints of a formal writing situation.

**SCHOLARS ON JOURNAL WRITING**

Fulwiler, Toby, ed. *The Journal Book.* Portsmouth: Boynton, 1987. The forty-two essays in this collection are especially useful for teachers interested in promoting journal writing across the curriculum. The essays provide examples of journal prompts and suggest ways of responding to student journals. The introduction reprints NCTE's "Guidelines for Using Journals in School Settings."

**EXERCISE 1–3**  Using one of the methods discussed in this section—listing, clustering, freewriting—explore one of the subjects in either Exercise 1–1 or Exercise 1–2. Then write down at least one question you could explore further if you were writing an essay on the subject.

## 1c Formulate a tentative thesis.

As you explore your topic and begin to identify questions you would like to investigate, you will begin to see possible ways to focus your material. At this point, try to settle on a tentative central idea. The more complex your topic, the more your initial central idea will change as your drafts evolve.

For many types of writing, you will be able to assert your central idea in a sentence or two. Such a statement, which will ordinarily appear in the opening paragraph of your finished essay, is called a *thesis*. A thesis is often the answer to a question you have posed, the resolution of a problem you have identified, or a statement that takes a position on a debatable topic. A successful thesis—like the following, which are all taken from articles in *Smithsonian*—points both the writer and the reader in a definite direction.

> Much maligned and the subject of unwarranted fears, most bats are harmless and highly beneficial.

> Geometric forms known as fractals may have a profound effect on how we view the world, not only in art and film but in many branches of science and technology, from astronomy to economics to predicting the weather.

> Aside from his more famous identities as colonel of the Rough Riders and president of the United States, Theodore Roosevelt was a lifelong professional man of letters.

**SCHOLARS ON PREWRITING AND INVENTION**

Ballenger, Bruce. "The Importance of Writing Badly." *Genre by Example: Writing What We Teach.* Ed. David Starkey. Portsmouth: Boynton, 2001. 86–102. It is important to give students the space to write badly "without feeling bad about it," Ballenger argues, and so he doesn't collect students' journals or freewriting. To show what he means, Ballenger re-creates the journal writing process he used to prepare a conference paper on students' use of the Internet for research. He shows readers the contradictory conclusions he comes to as he works out ideas in his journal.

The thesis sentence usually contains a key word or controlling idea that limits its focus. The preceding sentences, for example, prepare for essays that focus on the *beneficial* aspects of bats, the *effect* of fractals on how we view the world, and Roosevelt's identity as a writer, or *man of letters.*

It's a good idea to formulate a tentative thesis early in the writing process, perhaps by jotting it on scratch paper, by putting it at the head of a rough outline, or by writing an introductory paragraph that includes it. This tentative thesis will help you organize your draft. It will probably be less graceful than the thesis you include in the final version of your essay. Don't worry too soon about the exact wording of your thesis because your main point may change — often drastically — as you refine your ideas. Here, for example, is one student's early effort:

> In *Rebel without a Cause,* the protagonist, Jim Stark, is often seen literally on the edge of physical danger — walking too close to the swimming pool, leaning over an observation deck, and driving his car toward a cliff.

This tentative thesis offers a useful place to start writing, but it doesn't give readers a reason to continue reading. The thesis that appeared in the student's final draft not only was more polished but also reflected the evolution of the student's ideas.

> The scenes in which Jim Stark is seen on the edge of physical danger — walking too close to the swimming pool, leaning over an observation deck, driving his car toward a cliff — provide viewers with a visual metaphor for his mental state; as Jim teeters on the edge of physical danger, he also becomes more and more agitated by the constraints of family and society.

For a more detailed discussion of the thesis, see 2a.

**SCHOLARS ON PREWRITING AND INVENTION**

Shafer, Gregory. "Using Letters for Process and Change in the Basic Writing Class." *Teaching English in the Two-Year College* 28 (2000): 285–92. Shafer asked his developmental writing students to write letters to one another and to him in an effort to help them overcome their fears, anxieties, and frustrations. Shafer explains his rationale for the assignments and shares his experience using one of his own letters as a model in class discussion.

Gorrell, Donna. "Central Question for Prewriting and Revising." *Teaching English in the Two-Year College* 23 (1996): 34–38. Gorrell suggests that students begin their writing process not with a thesis statement but with a question. She offers concise examples and two helpful lists: questions to develop a focus and questions to guide revisions.

## Testing a tentative thesis

Once you have come up with a tentative thesis, you can use the following questions to refine it.

- Does the thesis require an essay's worth of development? Will you be able to include all of your support? Or will you run out of points too quickly?
- Is the thesis too obvious? If you cannot come up with interpretations that oppose your own, consider revising your thesis.
- Can you support your thesis with the evidence available?
- Can you explain why readers will want to read an essay with this thesis?

## 1d Sketch a plan.

Once you have generated some ideas and formulated a tentative thesis, you might want to sketch an informal outline to see how you will support your thesis and to figure out a tentative structure for your ideas. Informal outlines can take many forms. Perhaps the most common is simply the thesis followed by a list of major ideas.

> Thesis: Television advertising should be regulated to help prevent childhood obesity.
>
> - Children watch more television than ever.
> - Snacks marketed to children are often unhealthy and fattening.
> - Childhood obesity can cause diabetes and other health problems.
> - Solving these health problems costs taxpayers billions of dollars.
> - Therefore, these ads are actually costing the public money.
> - But if advertising is free speech, do we have the right to regulate it?
> - We regulate liquor and cigarette ads on television, so why not advertising aimed at children?

**SCHOLARS ON PREWRITING AND INVENTION**

Lindemann, Erika. "Prewriting Techniques." *A Rhetoric for Writing Teachers.* 3rd ed. New York: Oxford UP, 1995. 105–25. Lindemann offers several strategies for teaching prewriting and invention. She cautions that "most students . . . begin drafting too soon, before they have sufficiently probed the subject, developing their own point of view and making a commitment to the message."

Young, Richard, and Yameng Liu, eds. *Landmark Essays on Rhetorical Invention in Writing.* Davis: Hermagoras, 1994. Nineteen essays trace scholarly views on invention beginning with a 1943 essay by Kenneth Burke.

If you began by jotting down a list of ideas (see p. 19), you may be able to turn the list into a rough outline by crossing out some ideas, adding others, and putting the ideas in a logical order.

### Planning with headings

When writing a long college paper or a business document, consider using headings to guide readers. In addition to helping readers follow the organization of your final draft, headings can be a powerful planning tool, especially if you are working on a computer. You can type in your tentative thesis and then experiment with possible headings; once you have settled on the headings that work best, you can begin typing in chunks of text beneath each heading. Here, for example, is what Ned Bishop, a history student, typed into his computer when planning a history research paper. The headings, written in the form of questions, are centered.

> Although we will never know whether Nathan Bedford Forrest directly ordered the massacre of Union troops at Fort Pillow, evidence strongly suggests that he was responsible for it.
>
> 
>
> What happened at Fort Pillow?
>
> Did Forrest have reasons to order the massacre?
>
> Did the men have reason to think Forrest wanted a massacre?
>
> Can Forrest be held responsible for the massacre?
>
> 

For more detailed advice about using headings, see 5b. For examples of papers that use headings, see pages 743–55 and 785–90.

**SCHOLARS ON PLANNING**

Starkey, David, ed. *Genre by Example: Writing What We Teach.* Portsmouth: Boynton, 2001. In this collection of essays, scholars experiment with a variety of forms and genres to show, not just tell, readers how their theories might work in practice. Each essay, through its form, argues that the academic essay is not the only way to convey scholarly ideas. The book comprises four sections: "Reclaiming a Space for the Personal in Academic Essays," "Planning, Invention, and Revision: New Strategies for Teaching and Writing Essays," "It Takes Two: Dialogues, Arguments, and Letters," and "Poetry, Fiction, and 'Other' Writing."

---

**TIPS FROM WRITING TUTORS**

"A lot of bad writing habits come from the mythology we've built up around the college experience: that it's supposed to be a time of struggle and all-nighters and caffeine and procrastination. This attitude holds back a lot of potentially fabulous writers. I wish someone had told me sooner the value of breaking a paper into parts with enough time to think and revise."

—*Ann Marie Pietrantonio, George Mason University*

---

### When to use a formal outline

Early in the writing process, rough outlines have certain advantages over their more formal counterparts: They can be produced more quickly, they are more obviously tentative, and they can be revised more easily should the need arise. However, a formal outline may be useful later in the writing process, after you have written a rough draft, especially if your topic is complex.

A formal outline helps you see whether the parts of your essay work together and whether your essay's structure is logical. A formal outline does not set your paper in stone. In fact, it will often make clear which parts of your draft should be rearranged and which parts don't fit at all.

The following formal outline brought order to a complex topic, methods for limiting and disposing of nuclear waste. Notice that the student's thesis is an important part of the outline. Everything else in the outline supports it, either directly or indirectly.

> Thesis: Although various methods for limiting or disposing of nuclear wastes have been proposed, each has serious drawbacks.
>
> I. The process of limiting nuclear waste through partitioning and transmutation has serious drawbacks.
>    A. The process is complex and costly.
>    B. Nuclear workers' exposure to radiation would increase.

---

**WRITING CENTER DIRECTORS ON PLANNING**

"One thing that seems to help less experienced writers a great deal is when they realize that most successful student writers don't just write their final draft the night before a paper is due and receive an A. Students who write A papers understand their own writing process and the elements of a good essay. And they spend quite a lot of time writing, thinking, revising, thinking some more, and revising again. I sometimes quote Michelangelo to discouraged students: 'If people knew how hard I worked, they wouldn't think I'm a genius.' The myth of the writer producing focused, clear, coherent, interesting prose all alone late at night is still alive and well. Students need to understand the reality of the good writer."   —Leslie R. Leach, writing center coordinator, College of the Redwoods

II. Antarctic ice sheet disposal is a problem for scientific and legal reasons.
   A. Our understanding of ice sheet behavior is too limited.
   B. An international treaty prohibits disposal in Antarctica.
III. Space disposal is unthinkable.
   A. The risk of an accident and resulting worldwide disaster is great.
   B. The cost is prohibitive.
   C. The method would be unpopular at home and abroad.
IV. Seabed disposal is unwise because we do not know enough about the procedure or its impact.
   A. Scientists have not yet solved technical difficulties.
   B. We do not fully understand the impact of such disposal on the ocean's ecology.
V. Deep underground disposal threatens public safety and creates political problems.
   A. Geologists disagree about the safest disposal sites, and no sites are completely safe.
   B. There is much political pressure against the plan from citizens who do not want their states to become nuclear dumps.

## Guidelines for constructing an outline

1. Put the thesis at the top.
2. Make items at the same level of generality as parallel as possible (see 9).
3. Use sentences unless phrases are clear.
4. Use the conventional system of numbers and letters for the levels of generality.

   I.
       A.
       B.
               1.
               2.
                       a.
                       b.

*(continued)*

II.
  A.
  B.
    1.
    2.
      a.
      b.

5. Always use at least two subdivisions for a category, since nothing can be divided into fewer than two parts.
6. Limit the number of major sections in the outline; if the list of roman numerals begins to look like a laundry list, find some way of clustering the items into a few major categories with more subcategories.
7. Be flexible; be prepared to change your outline as your drafts evolve.

# 2

## Rough out an initial draft.

As you rough out an initial draft, focus your attention on ideas and organization. You can deal with sentence structure and word choice later.

Before you begin to write, gather your prewriting materials — lists, diagrams, outlines, freewriting, and so on. In addition to helping you get started, such notes and blueprints will encourage you to keep moving. With your earlier thoughts close by, you won't need to stare at a blank page or screen in search of ideas. Writing tends to flow better when it is drafted relatively quickly, without many stops and starts. The trick, of course, is to relax — to overcome the fear that grips many of us when we face that blank page.

If writer's block becomes a problem for you, consider whether you're being too hard on yourself. Do you demand that your sentences all be stylish and perfectly grammatical right from the start? Do you expect your ideas to emerge full-blown, like Athena from the head of Zeus? Do you get stuck trying to perfect your introduction—the hardest part—before you can move forward?

Professional writers look at drafting as a process of discovery, so they expect their first attempts to be messy. Jacques Barzun, for example, lets his rough-draft sentences be "as stupid" as they wish. Most writers discover ideas as they write. As Joan Didion puts it, "I write entirely to find out what I'm thinking, what I'm looking at, what I see, and what it means."

**TIP:** Take another look at your assignment and make sure you understand what you are being asked to do. If you have questions, set aside time to e-mail or visit your instructor before you sit down to write. Tutors at your writing center might also help; they have been trained to analyze assignments and give you suggestions on getting started. They can also help later in the writing process—after you have written a rough draft.

---

**ON THE WEB**

**dianahacker.com/bedhandbook**
▶ Additional resources
  ▶ Links Library
    ▶ The writing process

---

**2a** For most types of writing, draft an introduction that includes a thesis.

The introduction announces the main point; the body develops it, usually in several paragraphs; the conclusion drives it home. You can begin drafting, however, at any point. If you

---

**SCHOLARS ON WRITER'S BLOCK**

Rose, Mike. "Rigid Rules, Inflexible Plans, and the Stifling of Language: A Cognitivist Analysis of Writer's Block." *College Composition and Communication* 31 (1980): 389–401. In a study of blocked and nonblocked writers, Rose discovered that the blocked writers were all working within a set of rigid rules and inflexible plans. One writer, for example, believed that an introduction must always dazzle readers, and another invariably planned her writing with a complex outline. The nonblocked writers worked with rules as well, but they viewed them quite differently—as guidelines or "rules of thumb" to be followed in most instances, but to be rejected when they conflicted with common sense.

find it difficult to introduce a paper that you have not yet written, try drafting the body first and saving the introduction for later.

Your introduction will usually be a paragraph of 50 to 150 words (in a longer paper, it may be more than one paragraph). Perhaps the most common strategy is to open with a few sentences that engage the reader and establish your purpose for writing, your main point. The sentence stating the main point is called a *thesis*. (See also 1c.) In the following examples, the thesis has been italicized.

> In "When I Heard the Learn'd Astronomer," Walt Whitman expresses a feeling we all know: a desire to look at things simply. According to the poet, only the most analytical minds would prefer attending a dry lecture to taking in "the mystical moist night-air." Beyond stating his preference for innocent wonder, though, Whitman implies that astronomers are missing something when they reduce nature to equations. Scientists are able to describe the motions of objects overhead, but the mystery of the night sky, the way that we are awed and inspired by a vast blackness seemingly perforated with images of monsters and heroes, cannot be described so logically. All that matters, according to Whitman, is the beauty in the stars; astronomical data do nothing but distract the viewer from the true nighttime splendor. But in searching for immediate and spiritual satisfaction, Whitman fails to realize that he cannot see all the splendor of the night sky because it is not all visible to the naked eye. *Scientific knowledge does not detract from, but rather deepens, one's emotional reaction to beauty.*
> —Craig Lee Hetherington, student

> As the United States industrialized in the nineteenth century, using desperate immigrant labor, social concerns took a backseat to the task of building a prosperous nation. The government did not regulate industries and did not provide an effective safety net for the poor or for those who became sick or injured on the job. Luckily, immigrants and the poor did have a few advocates. Settlement houses such as Hull-House in Chicago provided information, services, and

---

**WRITERS ON WRITING**

Convince yourself that you are working in clay, not marble, on paper not eternal bronze: Let that first sentence be as stupid as it wishes.  —Jacques Barzun

Prose is architecture, not interior decoration.
  —Ernest Hemingway

Get it down. Take chances. It may be bad, but it's the only way you can do anything really good.  —William Faulkner

a place for reform-minded individuals to gather and work to improve the conditions of the urban poor. Alice Hamilton was one of these reformers. Her work at Hull-House spanned twenty-two years and later expanded throughout the nation. *Hamilton's efforts helped to improve the lives of immigrants and drew attention and respect to the problems and people that until then had been virtually ignored.*

—Laurie McDonough, student

Ideally, the sentences leading to the thesis should hook the reader, perhaps with one of the following:

a startling statistic or an unusual fact

a vivid example

a description

a paradoxical statement

a quotation or a bit of dialogue

a question

an analogy

an anecdote

Whether you are writing for a scholarly audience, a professional audience, or a general audience, you cannot assume your readers' interest in the topic. The hook should spark curiosity and offer readers a reason to continue reading.

Although the thesis frequently appears at the end of the introduction, it can just as easily appear at the beginning. Much work-related writing, in which a straightforward approach is most effective, commonly begins with the thesis.

*Flextime scheduling, which has proved its effectiveness at the Library of Congress, should be introduced on a trial basis at the main branch of the Montgomery County Public Library.* By offering flexible work hours, the library can boost employee morale, cut down on absenteeism, and expand its hours of operation.

—David Warren, student

### SCHOLARS ON INTRODUCTIONS

Hilbert, Betsy S. "It Was a Dark and Nasty Night It Was a Dark and You Would Not Believe How Dark It Was a Hard Beginning." *College Composition and Communication* 43 (1992): 75–80. In her insightful meditation on students' problems with openings, Hilbert discusses several reasons for their difficulties. Students fear being unable to live up to the expectations that an effective opening should establish, and they fear "that the words on the page will never be as wonderful" as the words in their heads. Hilbert offers this advice: "At the beginning, a writer must trust the sense of the work. He or she must believe that it can be written. He or she must be secure, above all, that no one will laugh or sneer. . . . The writer must understand, also, that not everything devolves on this one piece now under construction."

For some types of writing, it may be difficult or impossible to express the central idea in a thesis sentence; or it may be unwise or unnecessary to put a thesis sentence in the essay itself. A personal narrative, for example, may have a focus too subtle to be distilled in a single sentence, and such a sentence might ruin the story. Strictly informative writing, like that found in many business memos, may be difficult to summarize in a thesis. In such instances, do not try to force the central idea into a thesis sentence. Instead, think in terms of an overriding purpose, which may or may not be stated directly.

### Characteristics of an effective thesis

An effective thesis sentence should be a central idea that requires supporting evidence; it should be of adequate scope for an essay of the assigned length; and it should be sharply focused. (See also 1c.)

When constructing a thesis sentence, you should ask yourself whether you can successfully develop it with the sources available to you and for the purpose you've identified. Also ask yourself if you can explain why readers should be interested in reading an essay that explores this thesis. If your thesis addresses a question or problem that intrigues you, then it will probably interest your readers as well. If

**WRITERS ON WRITING**

The idea is to get the pencil moving quickly.
— Bernard Malamud

It is the lead that gives the writer control over his [or her] subject.
— Donald M. Murray

Once your mind is caught on the right snag, there's nothing so hard about the mechanics of writing.
— Anne Tyler

Thomas Huxley taught me the importance of giving to every argument a simple sentence.
— H. L. Mencken

your thesis would be obvious to everyone, then your readers will be less compelled to read on.

A thesis must require proof or further development through facts and details; it cannot itself be a fact or a description.

| | |
|---|---|
| **TOO FACTUAL** | The first polygraph was developed by Dr. John A. Larson in 1921. |
| **REVISED** | Because the polygraph has not been proved reliable, even under the most controlled conditions, its use by private employers should be banned. |
| **TOO FACTUAL** | John F. Kennedy's assassination on November 22, 1963, left many of his administration's projects unfinished. |
| **REVISED** | Although John F. Kennedy sent the first American troops to Vietnam before he died, an analysis of his foreign policy suggests that he would not have escalated the war had he lived. |

A thesis should be of sufficient scope for your assignment, not too broad and not too narrow. Unless you are writing a book or a very long research paper, the following thesis is too broad.

| | |
|---|---|
| **TOO BROAD** | Mapping the human genome has many implications for health and science. |
| **TOO NARROW** | A person who carries a genetic mutation linked to a particular disease might or might not develop that disease. |
| **REVISED** | Although scientists can now detect genetic predisposition to specific diseases, not everyone should be tested for these diseases. |

A thesis should be sharply focused, not too vague. Avoid fuzzy, hard-to-define words such as *interesting, good,* or *disgusting.*

> **TOO VAGUE**  The way the TV show *ER* portrays doctors and nurses is interesting.

The word *interesting* is needlessly vague. To sharpen the focus of this thesis, the writer should be more specific.

> **REVISED**  In dramatizing the experiences of doctors and nurses as they treat patients, navigate medical bureaucracy, and negotiate bioethical dilemmas, the TV show *ER* portrays health care professionals as unfailingly caring and noble.

In the process of making a too-vague thesis more precise, you may find yourself outlining the major sections of your paper, as in the preceding example. This technique, known as *blueprinting,* helps readers know exactly what to expect as they read on. It also helps you, the writer, control the shape of your essay.

## Tips for drafting a thesis sentence

- View your initial thesis as tentative. As you draft an essay, you may discover a main idea that is more interesting than the one you began with. As writer E. M. Forster put it, "How do I know what I think until I see what I say?"
- Instead of writing the thesis sentence by itself, try drafting the whole introduction, placing the thesis sentence in context (usually at the end of the introduction). This will help you see whether your thesis is clear.
- Don't take on too much. If you try to begin with a grand, sweeping statement, you may not have the evidence to support it.

The thesis sentence is central to so many types of writing that it is discussed in several other sections of this book:

- in 46, writing about texts
- in 47, writing arguments
- in 54, MLA research papers
- in 59, MLA literature papers
- in 60 and 61, APA and *Chicago* research papers

 If you come from a culture that prefers an indirect approach in writing, you may feel that asserting a thesis early in an essay sounds unrefined and even rude. In the United States, however, readers appreciate a direct approach; when you state your point as directly as possible, you show that you value your readers' time.

**EXERCISE 2–1**  In each of the following pairs, which sentence might work well as a thesis for a short paper? What is the problem with the other one? Is it too factual? Too broad? Too vague?

1a. By networking with friends, a single parent can manage to strike a balance among work, school, a social life, and family.
  b. Single parents face many challenges as they try to juggle all of their responsibilities.
2a. At the Special Olympics, disabled athletes are taught that with hard work and support from others they can accomplish anything: that they can indeed be winners.
  b. Working with the Special Olympics program is rewarding.
3a. History 201, taught by Professor Brown, is offered at 10:00 a.m. on Tuesdays and Thursdays.
  b. Whoever said that history is nothing but polishing tombstones must have missed History 201, because in Professor Brown's class history is very much alive.
4a. So far, research suggests that zero-emissions vehicles are not a sensible solution to the problem of steadily increasing air pollution.

**EXERCISE 2–1  Answers:**

1. a; b is too broad
2. a; b is too vague
3. b; a is too factual
4. a; b is too broad
5. b; a is too factual

b. Because air pollution is of serious concern to many people today, several US government agencies have implemented plans to begin solving the problem.

5a. Anorexia nervosa is a dangerous and sometimes deadly eating disorder occurring mainly in young, upper-middle-class teenagers.

b. The eating disorder anorexia nervosa is rarely cured by one treatment alone; only by combining drug therapy with psychotherapy and family therapy can the patient begin the long, torturous journey to wellness.

---

**ON THE WEB**

**dianahacker.com/bedhandbook**
▶ Electronic writing exercises
  ▶ E-ex 2–1 and 2–2

---

## 2b Fill out the body.

The body of the essay develops support for your thesis, so it's important to have at least a tentative thesis before you start writing. What does your thesis promise readers? Try to keep your response to that question in mind as you draft the body.

**NOTE:** You may already have written an introduction that includes your thesis. If not, as long as you have a thesis you can begin developing the body and return later to the introduction.

If your thesis sentence suggests a plan (see 2a) or if you have sketched a preliminary outline, try to block out your paragraphs accordingly. Draft the body of your essay by writing a paragraph about each supporting point you listed in the planning stage. If you do not have a plan, you would be wise to pause for a moment and sketch one (see 1d).

---

### SCHOLARS ON THE WRITING PROCESS

Tobin, Lad, and Thomas Newkirk, eds. *Taking Stock: The Writing Process Movement in the '90s.* Portsmouth: Boynton, 1994. This collection of sixteen essays explores the past, present, and future of writing instruction, challenging and extending the process pedagogy.

Faigley, Lester. "Competing Theories of Process: A Critique and a Proposal." *College English* 48 (1986): 527–42. Recognizing that "conceptions of writing as a process vary from theorist to theorist," Faigley surveys the three prevailing perspectives—the expressive view, the cognitive view, and the social view. He contrasts the assumptions of the views and proposes a synthesis of all three.

Keep in mind that often you might not know what you want to say until you have written a draft. Don't be discouraged if your ideas are rough or incomplete. It is possible to begin without a plan—assuming you are prepared to treat your first attempt as a "discovery draft" that will almost certainly be tossed (or radically rewritten) once you discover what you really want to say. Whether or not you have a plan when you begin drafting, you can often figure out a workable order for your ideas by stopping each time you start a new paragraph to think about what your readers will need to know to follow your train of thought.

If you are drafting on a computer, you will be able to move blocks of text around to see how your ideas fit together. Keep in mind, though, that it can also be helpful to print out your draft and look at different paragraphs in relation to one another rather than just one screen at a time.

For more detailed advice about paragraphs in the body of an essay, see 4.

## 2c Attempt a conclusion.

A conclusion should remind readers of the essay's main idea without dully repeating it. Often the concluding paragraph can be relatively short. By the end of the essay, readers should already understand your main point; your conclusion simply drives it home and, perhaps, leaves readers with something larger to consider.

---

**TIPS FROM WRITING TUTORS**

"In writing a conclusion, above all a writer has to try to answer the question 'So what?' Put yourself in your readers' position: Why should readers care about this subject? Has your argument convinced them? What makes your topic and argument so important?"

—*Nanda Srikantaiah, University of Maryland*

---

**SCHOLARS ON THE WRITING PROCESS**

Flower, Linda, and John R. Hayes. "A Cognitive Process Theory of Writing." *College Composition and Communication* 32 (1981): 365–87. Flower and Hayes propose a theory of the cognitive processes involved in composing: Writing is a set of thinking processes, those processes are hierarchical and interrelated, composing is goal-directed, and writers create their own goals.

Emig, Janet. *The Composing Processes of Twelfth Graders.* NCTE Research Rept. No. 13. Urbana: NCTE, 1971. Emig investigated the writing process by asking eight students to compose aloud. Her study has been influential both for its methodology and for its emphasis on process.

In addition to echoing your main idea, a conclusion might briefly summarize the essay's key points, propose a course of action, discuss the topic's wider significance, offer advice, or pose a question for future study. To conclude an essay analyzing the shifting roles of women in the military services, one student discusses her topic's implications for society as a whole:

> As the military continues to train women in jobs formerly reserved for men, our understanding of women's roles in society will no doubt continue to change. When news reports of women training for and taking part in combat operations become commonplace, reports of women becoming CEOs, police chiefs, and even president of the United States will cease to surprise us. Or perhaps we have already reached this point.
>
> —Rosa Broderick, student

To make the conclusion memorable, you might include a detail, an example, or an image from the introduction to bring readers full circle; a quotation or a bit of dialogue; an anecdote; or a humorous, witty, or ironic comment. To end a narrative describing a cash register holdup, one student uses an anecdote that includes some dialogue:

> It took me a long time to get over that incident. Countless times I found myself gasping as someone "pointed" a dollar bill at me. On one such occasion, a jovial little man buying a toy gun for his son came up to me and said in a Humphrey Bogart impression, "Give me all your money, Sweetheart." I didn't laugh. Instead, my heart skipped a beat, for I had heard those words before.
>
> —Diana Crawford, student

Whatever concluding strategy you choose, avoid introducing wholly new or unrelated ideas at the end of an essay. Also avoid apologies and other limp, indeterminate endings. Do not become discouraged if the perfect conclusion eludes you at the rough-draft stage. Because the conclusion is so closely tied to the rest of the essay in both content and tone,

**WRITERS ON WRITING**

Grab a pen and put down some words—your name even—and a title: something to see, to revise, to carve, to do over in the opposite way. —Jacques Barzun

I keep six honest serving-men
(They taught me all I knew);
Their names are What and Why and When
And How and Where and Who. —Rudyard Kipling

By writing an outline you really are writing in a way, because you're creating the structure of what you're going to do. Once I really know what I'm going to write, I don't find the actual writing takes all that long. —Tom Wolfe

you may well decide to rework it (or even replace it) at a later stage.

**TIP:** Because your ideas will evolve as you draft your essay, you may find that your draft conclusion contains a statement of your thesis that is more developed than the thesis in your original introduction. If this is the case, make sure that your introduction reflects the revised thesis.

## Strategies for concluding an essay

Good conclusions generally use at least one of these strategies; the strategies can also be combined.

### Summarize your essay's key points.

While it's not necessary to revisit every point in an essay, it can be useful to summarize your main points, especially if you have made a complex argument. A brief summary also allows you to create continuity between your introduction and your conclusion by bringing your ideas full circle.

### Propose a course of action or offer a recommendation.

Where appropriate, consider proposing a course of action for your readers. For example, if you have argued that advertising snack foods on television contributes to obesity in children, you might conclude by suggesting that parents restrict the hours of television their children watch.

### Discuss the wider significance or implications of your essay.

The conclusion is an appropriate place to put your ideas into a larger context. At the end of an essay about online voting technology, you might suggest that simplifying the voting process could strengthen American democracy by empowering a new generation of voters.

*(continued)*

### WRITERS ON WRITING

When you're ready to stop, stop. If you have presented all the facts and made the point that you want to make, look for the nearest exit. —William Zinsser

There's still a strange moment with every book when I move from the position of writer to the position of reader and I suddenly see my words with the eyes of the cold public. It gives me a terrible sense of exposure, as if I'd gotten sunburned. —Eudora Welty

## Strategies for concluding an essay (*continued*)

### Offer advice to your readers.

Where appropriate, conclude by offering advice to your readers. If you have written a personal essay about working with children with special needs, for example, you might conclude by giving some general tips on how to interact with such children.

### Pose a question for future study.

Sometimes in the process of exploring a question, other, more complex questions that are beyond the scope of your essay will occur to you. If your essay explores the benefits of organic produce, for example, you might conclude by suggesting that a study of organic farming and its economic impact on conventional farmers would add to our understanding of this issue. Make sure that any question you pose in your conclusion is a natural extension of the ideas you've discussed in your essay rather than a completely new idea.

# 3

## Make global revisions; then revise sentences.

For most experienced writers, revising is rarely a one-step process. Global matters — focus, purpose, organization, content, and overall strategy — generally receive attention first. Improvements in sentence structure, word choice, grammar, punctuation, and mechanics come later.

By the time you've written a draft, your ideas will probably have gone in directions you couldn't have predicted ahead of time. As a result, global revisions can be quite dra-

### SCHOLARS ON REVISION

Horning, Alice S. "Reflection and Revision: Intimacy in College Writing." *Composition Chronicle* 9 (1997): 4–7. Horning suggests that as portfolios become more popular, we will need to involve students in assessing their own writing processes and products. In Horning's classes, for each paper they write, students submit a "writing process statement" in which they reflect on some aspect of their drafting and revising process. Horning offers a number of prompts for reflective writing along with student examples of such writing.

matic. It's possible, for example, that your thesis will evolve as you figure out how your ideas fit together. You might end up dropping whole paragraphs of text and adding others. Material once stretched over two or three paragraphs might need to be condensed into one. You could decide to rearrange entire sections. You will save yourself time if you handle global revisions before turning to sentence-level issues, because there is little sense in revising sentences that may not appear in your final draft.

Many of us resist global revisions because we find it difficult to view our work from our audience's perspective. To distance yourself from a draft, put it aside for a while, preferably overnight or even longer. When you return to it, try to play the role of your audience as you read. Ask questions such as "What is the main point of this paragraph?" "Why have I put these paragraphs in this order?" "How will readers respond to this point?" If possible, enlist the help of reviewers to play the role of audience for you.

Professors often set aside class time for peer review sessions in which students respond to one another's drafts in written comments, discussions, or both. In some courses, students use e-mail or other forms of electronic communication to send and receive comments on one another's rough drafts. Before you revise, it's a good idea to visit your school's writing center. Ask your reviewers to focus on the larger issues of writing, not on the fine points. The checklist for global revision on page 49 as well as the guidelines for reviewers on pages 46–47 may help them get started. Tips for how to use the feedback you receive appear on pages 50–51.

| ON | **dianahacker.com/bedhandbook** |
| THE | ▶ Resources for writers and tutors |
| WEB | ▶ Preparing to visit the writing center |

**SCHOLARS ON REVISION**

Moran, Mary Hurley. "Connections between Reading and Successful Revision." *Journal of Basic Writing* 16.2 (1997): 76–89. Moran's study found that when basic writers who were proficient readers read their drafts aloud, their revisions led to better papers. Although this activity did not help writers who were struggling readers, Moran suggests that basic writers can benefit in courses that integrate reading and revision activities.

| ON | dianahacker.com/bedhandbook |
| THE | ▶ Electronic writing exercises |
| WEB | ▶ E-ex 3–1 |

**EXAMPLE OF GLOBAL REVISIONS**

Sports on TV--A Win or a Loss?

Team sports are as much a part of Americain life as Mom and
apple pie, and they have a good tendency to bring people together.
They encourage team members to cooperate with one another, they
also create shared enthusiasm among fans. Thanks to television, this
togetherness now seems available to nearly all of us at the flick of a
switch. We do not have to buy tickets, and travel to a stadium, to see
the World Series or the Super Bowl, these games are on television. We
can enjoy the game in the comfort of our own living room. ~~After
Thanksgiving or Christmas dinner, the whole family may gather around
the TV set to watch football together.~~ It would appear that television
has done us a great service. But is this really the case?

*Although television does make sports more accessible, it also
creates a distance between the sport and the fans and between
athletes and the teams they play for.*

*The advantage of television is that it provides sports fans
with greater convenience.*

[insert] ◀

*We can see more games than if we had to attend each one in per-
son, and we can follow greater varieties of sports.*

**EXAMPLE OF SENTENCE-LEVEL REVISIONS**

*Televised*
Sports ~~on TV~~--A Win or a Loss?

Team sports**,** ~~are~~ as much a part of American life as Mom and
*tend*                                           *us*
apple pie, ~~and they have a good tendency~~ to bring ~~people~~ together.
*and*
They encourage team members to cooperate with one another**,** they
*Because of*
~~also~~ create shared enthusiasm among fans. ~~Thanks to~~ television, this

togetherness now seems available ~~to nearly all of us~~ at the flick of a

switch. ~~It would appear that television has done us a great service.~~
*makes*
But is this really the case? Although television ~~does make~~ sports more

accessible, it also creates a distance between the sport and the fans
*their*
and between athletes and ~~the~~ teams**.** ~~they play for.~~

The advantage of television is that it provides sports fans with

greater convenience. We do not have to buy tickets**/** and travel to a
*but*
stadium**/** to see the World Series or the Super Bowl**/** ~~these games are~~
*any*
~~on television. We~~ can enjoy ~~the~~ game in the comfort of our own living
*rooms.*
~~room.~~ We can see more games than if we had to attend each one in
*a       variety*
person, and we can follow greater ~~varieties~~ of sports.

## Guidelines for peer reviewers

### View yourself as a coach, not a judge.

Think of yourself as a proposer of possibilities, not a dictator of revisions. It is the writer, after all, who will have to grapple with the task of improving the essay.

### Restate the writer's main ideas.

It's helpful for the writer to see if you understand the main point of the essay. For example, if the writer's subject is televised sports, you might comment, "I think your thesis is that although television makes sports more accessible, it also creates a distance between the sport and the fans. Your purpose seems to be to question whether televising sports really allows more fans to share the experience." Paraphrasing each paragraph of the draft will also help the writer see if the essay's points are clearly expressed.

### Where possible, give specific compliments.

Vague compliments (such as "I liked your essay") sound insincere—and they aren't helpful. Point out specific successes. For example, you might mention that you particularly

## 3a Approach global revision in cycles.

Major revising can be difficult, sometimes even painful. You might discover, for example, that an essay's first three paragraphs are nothing but padding, that its central argument tilts the wrong way, and that you sound like a stuffed shirt throughout. But the sheer fact that you can see such problems in your own writing is a sign of hope. Those opening paragraphs can be dropped, the argument's slant realigned, the voice made more approachable.

Because the process of global revision can be overwhelming, approach it in cycles, with each cycle encompass-

**SCHOLARS ON PEER REVIEW**

Butts, Elizabeth A. "Overcoming Student Resistance to Group Work." *Teaching English in the Two-Year College* 28 (2000): 81–83. Students resist group assignments, in part because assignments are not structured effectively and in part because teachers often don't help students get the most out of group work. Butts shares a specific assignment sequence she uses to help students succeed in a group environment.

admire how the writer examines the opposing viewpoint in the second paragraph before challenging it in the third.

***Link suggestions for improvement to the writer's goals.***

Criticism is constructive when it is offered in the right spirit. For example, you might advise the writer to put the most dramatic example last, where it will have the maximum impact on readers. Or you might suggest that a passage would gain power if the writer replaced abstractions with concrete details.

***Ask questions and tell the writer where you would like to hear more.***

Note passages that you found either confusing or especially interesting. By asking for clarification, you will help the writer see what needs to be revised. Indicating an interest in hearing more about a topic will often inspire the writer to come up with useful and vivid details.

***Express interest in reading the next draft.***

When your interest is sincere, expressing it can be a powerful motivation for a writer.

---

ing a particular purpose for revising. Five common cycles of global revision are discussed in this section:

- Engaging the audience
- Sharpening the focus
- Improving the organization
- Strengthening the content
- Clarifying the point of view

You can handle these cycles in nearly any order, and you may even skip or combine some of them. A chart summarizing these cycles appears on page 48.

**SCHOLARS ON PEER REVIEW**

Lawrence, Sandra M., and Elizabeth Sommers. "From the Park Bench to the (Writing) Workshop Table: Encouraging Collaboration among Inexperienced Writers." *Teaching English in the Two-Year College* 23 (1996): 101–11. Acknowledging both the value of peer collaboration and the resistance to it in writing classes, the authors provide a detailed explanation for establishing, developing, and maintaining effective peer feedback groups. In addition to sample handouts, they share results of a small study they conducted that support their suggestions.

## Checklist for global revision (for writers)

### Engaging the audience

Look for opportunities

- to let readers know why they are reading
- to motivate readers to read on
- to use a more appropriate tone

### Sharpening the focus

Look for opportunities

- to clarify the introduction (especially the thesis)
- to delete text that is off the point

### Improving the organization

Look for opportunities

- to add or sharpen topic sentences
- to move blocks of text
- to add headings

### Strengthening the content

Look for opportunities

- to rethink your thesis
- to emphasize major ideas
- to add specific facts, details, and examples

### Clarifying the point of view

Look for opportunities

- to make the point of view more consistent
- to use a more appropriate point of view

### SCHOLARS ON PEER REVIEW

Brooke, Robert, Ruth Mirtz, and Rick Evans. *Small Groups in Writing Workshops: Invitations to a Writer's Life.* Urbana: NCTE, 1994. The authors explain the theoretical principles and suggest practical methods for using small groups in writing classrooms.

Bruffee, Kenneth A. "Writing and Collaboration." *Collaborative Learning: Higher Education, Interdependence, and the Authority of Knowledge.* Baltimore: Johns Hopkins UP, 1993. 52–62. Bruffee proposes that we view writing as a "social, collaborative, constructive conversational act," and he explains several ways in which conversation can help writers.

## Checklist for global revision (for reviewers)

### Purpose and audience

- Does the draft accomplish its purpose—to inform readers, persuade them, entertain them, call them to action?
- Is the draft appropriate for its audience? Does it account for the audience's knowledge of the subject, level of interest in the subject, and possible attitudes toward the subject?

### Focus

- Do the introduction and conclusion focus clearly on the central idea?
- Is the thesis clear? Is it prominently placed? (See "Testing a tentative thesis," p. 26.)
- If there is no thesis, is there a good reason for omitting one?
- Are any ideas obviously off the point?

### Organization and paragraphing

- Are there enough organizational cues for readers (such as topic sentences and headings)?
- Are ideas presented in a logical order?
- Are any paragraphs too long or too short for easy reading?

### Content

- Is the supporting material relevant and persuasive?
- Which ideas need further development?
- Are the parts proportioned sensibly? Do major ideas receive enough attention?
- Where might material be deleted?

### Point of view

- Is the draft free of distracting shifts in point of view (from *I* to *you*, for example, or from *it* to *they*)?
- Is the dominant point of view—*I, we, you, he, she, it, one,* or *they*—appropriate for your purpose and audience?

## Guidelines for using reviewers' comments

### Don't take criticism personally.

Your reader is responding to your essay, not to you. It may be frustrating to hear that you still have work ahead of you, but taking feedback seriously will make your essay stronger.

### Pay attention to ideas that contradict your own.

If comments show that a reviewer doesn't understand what you're trying to do, don't be defensive. Instead, consider why your reader is confused and figure out how to clarify your point. Responding to readers' objections—instead of dismissing them—will strengthen your ideas and make your essay more persuasive.

### Look for global concerns.

Your reviewers will probably make more suggestions than you can use. To keep things manageable, focus on the comments that relate to your thesis, organization, and evidence. Do your readers understand your main idea? Can they follow your

If someone has reviewed your draft, you have already begun to see which of these cycles most need your attention (see the chart on p. 48). Giving some thought to your overall purpose and audience should let you see even more clearly where your essay does—and does not—need revision.

**TIP:** When working on a computer, print out a hard copy and read the draft as a whole rather than screen by screen. Once you have decided what global revisions may be needed, the computer is an excellent tool for experimenting. Should you combine two paragraphs? Would your conclusion make a good introduction? Might several paragraphs be rearranged

**WRITING CENTER DIRECTORS ON PEER REVIEW**

"Strong writers trust feedback and also understand that not all feedback is created equal. Weaker writers tend to see feedback as an indicator of what needs to be fixed, and they fix only the things that are most clearly marked."

—Shane Borrowman, director of the Writing Lab,
Gonzaga University

train of thought? Are they looking for more supporting ideas or facts?

### Weigh feedback carefully.

As you begin revising, you may find yourself sorting through comments and suggestions from many people, including instructors, writing tutors, and peer reviewers. Sometimes these different readers will be in agreement, but often their advice will differ greatly. It's important to carefully sort through all of the comments you receive with your original goals in mind — otherwise you'll find yourself with the nearly impossible task of trying to incorporate everyone's advice.

### Keep a revision and editing log.

Make a clear and simple list of the global and sentence-level concerns that keep coming up from most of your reviewers. Such a list can serve as a starting point each time you revise a paper. When you take charge of your own writing in this way, comments will become a valuable resource rather than something to dread.

for greater impact? With little risk, you can explore the possibilities. When a revision misfires, it is easy to return to your original draft.

### Engaging the audience

Considerations of audience can contribute to global revision. Often a rough draft needs a major overhaul because it is directed at no audience at all for no apparent purpose — written in a vacuum, so to speak. Readers are put off by such writing because when they don't know *why* they are reading, they suspect that a writer may be wasting their

**SCHOLARS ON THE WRITING PROCESS**

Qualley, Donna. *Turns of Thought: Teaching Composition as Reflexive Inquiry.* Portsmouth: Boynton, 1997. Qualley describes a method for teaching students to think about their reading and writing practices. She demonstrates by reflecting on her own practices and noting the ways she had to "unlearn" and revise some of her basic assumptions about teaching writing and responding to student writers.

time. A good question to ask yourself, therefore, is the toughest question that a reader might ask: "So what?" If your draft can't pass the "So what?" test, you will need to rethink your entire approach; in fact, you may even decide to scrap the draft and start over.

Once you have made sure that your draft is directed at an audience — readers who stand to benefit in some way by reading it — you may still need to refine your tone. The tone of a piece of writing expresses the writer's feelings toward the audience, so it is important to get it right. If the tone seems too self-centered — or too flippant, stuffy, bossy, patronizing, opinionated, or hostile — modify it.

For example, the following paragraph was drafted by a student who hoped to persuade his audience to buy organic produce.

> If you choose to buy organic produce, you are supporting local farmers as well as demonstrating your opposition to chemical pesticides. As more and more supermarkets carry organic fruits and vegetables, consumers have fewer reasons not to buy organic. Some consumers do not buy organic produce because they are not willing to spend the extra money. But if you care at all about the environment or the small farmer, you should be willing to support organic farms in your area.

When he reviewed this draft, the writer saw the need to be more diplomatic. He didn't want to alienate his readers by accusing them of being unwilling to spend money or uninterested in helping the environment. He revised the paragraph to offer readers positive reasons to support his cause.

> By choosing to buy organic produce, you have the opportunity to support local farmers, to oppose the use of chemical pesticides, and to taste some of the freshest produce available. Because more supermarkets carry organic produce than ever, you won't even have to miss out on any of your favorite fruits

### SCHOLARS ON REVISION

Murray, Donald M. *The Craft of Revision.* 2nd ed. Orlando: Harbrace, 1995. Murray argues that "we build effective writing more from increasing the strengths of a text than from eliminating error." He shows how writers can increase strengths by paying attention to global matters such as focus, organization, development, and voice.

Harris, Muriel. "Composing Behaviors of One- and Multi-Draft Writers." *College English* 51 (1989): 174–90. Harris contrasts the revision behaviors of writers who produce one draft and those who produce many drafts and argues that we should "use this diversity [of behaviors] as a source for helping students with different types of problems and concerns."

or vegetables. Although organic produce can be more expensive than conventional produce, the costs are not prohibitive. For example, a pound of organic bananas at my local grocery store is eighty-nine cents, while the conventional bananas are sixty-nine cents a pound. If you can afford this small price difference, you will have the opportunity to make a difference for the environment and for the small farmer.

—Leon Nage, student

### Sharpening the focus

A clearly focused draft fixes readers' attention on one central idea and does not stray from that idea. You can sharpen the focus of a draft by clarifying the introduction (especially the thesis) and by deleting any text that is off the point.

**CLARIFYING THE INTRODUCTION**    Make sure that your introduction looks and reads like an introduction. Can readers tell where the introduction stops and the body of the essay begins? Have you perhaps included material in the introduction that really belongs in the body of the essay? Is your introduction long-winded?

Next check to see whether the introduction focuses on the essay's main point. Does it let readers know what to expect as they read on? Does it make the significance of the subject clear so that readers will want to read on?

The most important sentence in the introduction is the thesis. (See 2a.) If your essay lacks a thesis, add one now or have a good reason for not including one. If your thesis is poorly focused or if it doesn't accurately state the real point of the essay, revise it.

**DELETING TEXT THAT IS OFF THE POINT**    Compare the introduction, particularly the thesis sentence, with the body of the essay. Does the body fulfill the promise of the introduction? If not, you will need to adjust one or the other. Either

### SCHOLARS ON REVISION

Flower, Linda, et al. "Detection, Diagnosis, and the Strategies of Revision." *College Composition and Communication* 37 (1986): 16–55. Flower and her coauthors view revision as a "distributed process of detection, diagnosis, and strategic action." They suggest that future research on revision should focus on the "distinctive features of the expert's revision process that we might be able to teach."

Faigley, Lester, and Stephen Witte. "Analyzing Revision." *College Composition and Communication* 32 (1981): 400–14. Faigley and Witte classify the kinds of revisions that student writers typically make, distinguishing between changes in surface features of the text and changes in meaning.

rebuild the introduction to fit the body or keep the introduction and delete any sentences or paragraphs that stray from its point.

### Improving the organization

A draft is well organized when its major divisions are logical and easy to follow. To improve the organization of your draft, consider taking one or more of the following actions: adding or sharpening topic sentences, moving blocks of text, and inserting headings.

**ADDING OR SHARPENING TOPIC SENTENCES**   Topic sentences state the main ideas of the paragraphs in the body of an essay. (See 4a.) Topic sentences act as signposts for readers, announcing ideas to come.

You can review the organization of a draft by reading only the topic sentences. Do they clearly support the essay's main idea? Do they make a reasonable sentence outline of the paper? If your draft lacks topic sentences, either add them or have a good reason for omitting these important signposts.

**MOVING BLOCKS OF TEXT**   Improving the organization of a draft can be as simple as moving a few sentences from one paragraph to another or reordering paragraphs. You may

**SCHOLARS ON PEER REVIEW**

Harris, Muriel. "Collaboration Is Not Collaboration Is Not Collaboration: Writing Center Tutorials vs. Peer-Response Groups." *College Composition and Communication* 43 (1992): 369–83. Harris cautions teachers not to confuse different meanings of the term *collaboration.* Separating collaborative writing from collaborative learning about writing, Harris explains the differences between tutoring and group work and argues that teachers should help students take advantage of both forms of collaboration.

also find that you can clarify the organization of a draft by combining choppy paragraphs or by dividing those that are too long for easy reading. (See 4e.) Often, however, the process is more complex. As you move blocks of text, you may need to supply transitions to make them fit smoothly in the new positions; you may also need to rework topic sentences to make your new organization clear.

Before moving text, consider sketching a revised outline. Divisions in the outline might become topic sentences in the restructured essay. (See 1d.)

**INSERTING HEADINGS** In long documents, such as research papers or business reports, headings can help readers follow your organization. Typically, headings are presented as phrases, declarative or imperative sentences, or questions. To draw attention to headings, you can center them, put them in boldface, underline them, use all capital letters, or some combination of these. (See also 5b.)

**TIP:** Construct an outline of your draft after you have written it (see 1d). By going through your draft paragraph by paragraph and listing the most important ideas, you can see how the parts work together and whether each paragraph has a clear focus.

### Strengthening the content

In reviewing the content of a draft, consider whether any text (sentences, paragraphs, or longer passages) should be added or deleted, keeping in mind your readers' needs. Then, if your purpose is to argue a point, consider how persuasively you have proved your point to an intelligent, discerning audience. When necessary, rethink your argument.

**RETHINKING YOUR ARGUMENT** A first draft presents you with an opportunity for rethinking your argument. You can

**SCHOLARS ON PEER REVIEW**

Bishop, Wendy. "Helping Peer Writing Groups Succeed." *Teaching English in the Two-Year College* 15 (1988): 120–25. Bishop reviews research on writing groups and lists reasons for their success and failure. She also outlines what teachers should know before using groups and suggests strategies for training, monitoring, and evaluating them.

often deepen your ideas about a subject by asking yourself some hard questions: Is your claim more sweeping than the evidence allows? Have you left out an important step in the argument? Have you dealt with the arguments of the opposition? Is your draft free of faulty reasoning? The more challenging your subject, the more likely you will find yourself adjusting your early thoughts. (For more about writing arguments, see 47.)

**ADDING TEXT**    If any paragraphs or sections of the essay are developed too skimpily to be clear and convincing (a common flaw in rough drafts), add specific facts, details, and examples. Go back to the beginning of the writing process: listing specifics, brainstorming ideas with friends or classmates, perhaps doing more research.

**DELETING TEXT**    Look for sentences and paragraphs that can be cut without serious loss of meaning. Perhaps you have repeated yourself or strayed from your point. Maybe you have given undue emphasis to minor ideas. Cuts may also be necessitated by word limits, such as those imposed by a college assignment or by the realities of the business world, where readers are often pressed for time.

### Clarifying the point of view

If the point of view of a draft shifts confusingly or if it seems not quite appropriate for your purpose, audience, and subject, consider adjusting it.

There are three basic points of view: the first person (*I* or *we*), the second person (*you*), and the third person (*he, she, it, one,* or *they*). Each point of view is appropriate in at least some contexts, and you may need to experiment before discovering which one best suits your needs.

**THE THIRD-PERSON POINT OF VIEW**    Much academic and professional writing is best presented from the third-person

---

**SCHOLARS ON PEER REVIEW**

Spear, Karen. *Sharing Writing: Peer Response Groups in English Classes.* Portsmouth: Boynton, 1988. In this now classic text, Spear discusses the challenges of using peer response groups and the ways in which they help students grow as writers. She offers advice on organizing, managing, and guiding peer groups and on teaching students to read their peers' writing in progress, to be careful listeners, and to give effective feedback.

point of view (*he, she, it, one,* or *they*), which puts the subject in the foreground. The *I* point of view is usually inappropriate in such contexts because, by focusing attention on the writer, it pushes the subject into the background. Consider, for example, one student's first-draft description of the behavior of a species of frog he had observed in the field.

> Each frog that *I* was able to locate in trees remained in its given tree during the entirety of *my* observation period. However, *I* noticed that there was considerable movement within the home tree.

Here the *I* point of view is distracting, as the student himself noticed when he began to revise his report. His revision focuses more on the frogs, less on himself.

> Each frog located in a tree remained in that tree throughout the observation period. The frogs moved about considerably, however, within their home trees.

Just as the first-person pronoun *I* can draw too much attention to the writer, the second-person pronoun *you* can focus unnecessarily on the reader. In the following sentence from a memo, for example, a supervisor writing to a sales manager needlessly draws attention to the reader.

> When *you* look at the numbers, *you* can clearly see that travel expenses must be cut back.

This sentence would be clearer and more direct if presented without the distraction of the *you* point of view.

> The numbers clearly show that travel expenses must be cut back.

Although the third-person point of view is often a better choice than the *I* or *you* point of view, it is by no means trouble-free. Writers can run into problems when they want to use singular pronouns in an indefinite sense. For example, the following sentence sounds stuffy and ambiguous: "Jogging improves *one's* emotional health and makes *one* feel better about *oneself*." Some years ago Americans would have said "improves a person's emotional health and makes *him* feel better about *himself*," with the understanding that *him* really meant *him or her*. Today, however, this use of *him* is offensive to many readers and is best avoided. But "makes *him or her* feel better about *himself or herself*" is awkward.

One solution is to try switching to the plural: *Joggers run to improve their emotional health and to make them feel better about themselves.* A writer could also restructure the sentence altogether: *Jogging improves a person's emotional health and self-image.* (See 17f and 22a.)

**THE SECOND-PERSON POINT OF VIEW**    The *you* point of view, which puts the reader in the foreground, is appropriate for advising readers directly, as in giving tips on raising children or instructions on flower arranging. All imperative sentences, such as the advice for writers in this book, are written from the *you* point of view, although the word itself is frequently omitted. "Sketch a plan" means "*You* should sketch a plan."

In the course of giving advice or instructions, the actual word *you* may be appropriate and even desired. In advising gardeners about walkways, for example, newspaper columnist Henry Mitchell feels free to use the words *you* and *your* as the need arises:

> If *your* main walk is less than four feet wide, and if it is white concrete, then widen it, no matter what has to be sacrificed . . . and resurface it with brick, stone, or something less glaring and dull. Three flowers against a good-looking pavement will do more for *you* than thirty flowers against white concrete. [Italics added.]

Mitchell might have written this passage from the third-person point of view instead ("If *the gardener's* walk is less than four feet wide . . ."), but the effect would have seemed oddly indirect. Even at the risk of sounding a bit bossy, Mitchell has wisely selected the imperative (*you*) approach instead.

Notice that Mitchell's *you* means "you, the reader." It does not mean "you, anyone in general." Indefinite uses of *you,* such as in the following example, are inappropriate in formal writing. (See 23d.)

> Young Japanese women wired together electronic products on a piece-rate system: The more *you* wired, the more *you* were paid.

Here the writer should have stayed with the third-person point of view.

> The more *they* wired, the more *they* were paid.

**THE FIRST-PERSON POINT OF VIEW**   If much of a writer's material comes from personal experience, the *I* point of view will prove most natural. It is difficult to imagine, for example, how James Thurber could have avoided the word *I* in describing his early university days:

> *I* passed all the other courses that *I* took at my university, but *I* could never pass botany. This was because all botany students had to spend several hours a week in a laboratory looking through a microscope at plant cells, and *I* could never see through a microscope. *I* never once saw a cell through a microscope. This used to enrage my instructor. [Italics added.]
> —James Thurber, "University Days"

Thurber's *I* point of view puts the writer in the foreground, since the writer is in fact the subject.

Writers who are aware that the first-person point of view is sometimes seen as inappropriate in academic writing often overgeneralize the rule. Concluding that the word *I* is never appropriate, they go to extreme lengths to avoid it.

> Mama read with such color and detail that *one* could fancy *oneself* as the hero of the story.

Since the paper in which this sentence appeared was a personal reminiscence, the entire paper sounded more natural once the writer allowed himself to use the word *I*.

> Mama read with such color and detail that *I* could fancy *myself* as the hero of the story.

**ON THE WEB**

**dianahacker.com/bedhandbook**
▶ Electronic writing exercises
　▶ E-ex 3–2

## 3b　Revise and edit sentences; proofread the final draft.

When you revise sentences, you focus on effectiveness; when you edit, you check for correctness. Proofreading is a slow and careful reading in search of typos and other obvious mistakes.

### Revising and editing sentences

As with global revision, sentence-level revision may be approached in cycles, with each cycle focusing on a different purpose for making changes. The main purposes for revising sentences—to strengthen, clarify, vary, and refine them—

**SCHOLARS ON CONFERENCING**

Boynton, Linda. "See Me: Conference Strategies for Developmental Writers." *Teaching English in the Two-Year College* 30 (2003): 391–402. Boynton describes twenty-five strategies teachers can use with basic writers to help them feel at home in a college environment. She categorizes these according to what can be done before, during, and after a conference.

"I used to rely on the teacher to tell me exactly what to fix, and then I would fix it without thinking about the paper as a whole. I'd just add in the changes and hand the paper back without a second look. Now I've learned to think about how the changes the teacher recommends might affect the whole paper and what other parts I might need to revise."
— *Amy Amoroso, George Mason University*

are detailed in the chart on page 64. A checklist on editing for grammar, punctuation, and mechanics appears on page 65.

Some writers handle most sentence-level revisions directly at the computer, experimenting on-screen with a variety of possible improvements. Other writers prefer to print out a hard copy of the draft, mark it up, and then return to the computer to enter their revisions. Here, for example, is a rough-draft paragraph as one student edited it for a variety of sentence-level problems:

> Although some cities have found creative ways to improve access to public transportation for physically handicapped passengers, ~~and to fund other programs, there have been problems in~~ our city has struggled with ~~due to the need to address~~ budget constraints and competing ~~needs~~ priorities. ~~This~~ The budget crunch has led citizens to question how funds are distributed.~~?~~ For example, last year ~~when~~ city officials voted to use available funds to support ~~had to choose between allocating funds for accessible transportation or allocating funds to~~ after-school programs rather than transportation upgrades. ~~, they voted for the after-school programs.~~ It is not clear to some citizens why ~~these~~ after-school programs are more important.

The original paragraph was flawed by wordiness, a problem that can be addressed through any number of revisions. The following revision would also be acceptable.

### SCHOLARS ON CONFERENCING

Good, Tina Lavonne. "Individual Student Conferences and Community Workshops: Is There a Conflict?" *In Our Own Voice: Graduate Students Teach Writing.* Ed. Tina Lavonne Good and Leanne B. Warshauer. Boston: Allyn, 2000. 231–30. Good suggests that in our enthusiasm for peer workshops we should not abandon student-teacher conferences. The student-teacher conference, in Good's view, should "encourage reflection," not direct the student's revision. Good asks students to engage in peer review first; then, in a conference, she uses the results of the peer review to promote individual reflection. To encourage true reflection Good feels, we must engage in a dialogue with our students.

Some cities have funded improved access to public transportation for physically handicapped passengers. Because of budget constraints, our city chose to fund after-school programs rather than transportation programs. As a result, citizens have begun to question how funds are distributed and why certain programs are more important than others.

Some of the paragraph's improvements do not involve choice and must be fixed in any revision. The hyphen in *after-school programs* is necessary; a noun must be substituted for the pronoun *these* in the last sentence; and the question mark in the second sentence must be changed to a period.

**GRAMMAR CHECKERS** on your computer can help with some but by no means all of the sentence-level problems in a typical draft. Many problems—such as faulty parallelism and misplaced modifiers—require an understanding of grammatical structure that computer programs lack. Such problems often slip right past the grammar checker. Grammar checkers also can go overboard, flagging sentence elements that are not faulty or offering suggestions that cause more problems than they solve.

When the grammar checker makes a suggestion for revising a sentence it considers faulty, it is your responsibility as the writer to determine whether the suggestion makes grammatical sense and is more effective than your original. You should be wary of automatically accepting a grammar checker's recommendations.

Throughout this book, you will find grammar checker boxes that look like the one you are now reading. The boxes explain how well grammar checkers can flag specific problems such as dangling modifiers, run-on sentences, and so on. The information in these boxes is based on a large sample of correct and faulty sentences that were run through the most widely used grammar checker program.

**SCHOLARS ON CONFERENCING**

Gay, Pamela. "Dialogizing Response in the Writing Classroom: Students Answer Back." *Journal of Basic Writing* 17.1 (1998): 3–17. Gay points out that while composition teachers use interaction and dialogue among student writers to promote invention, revision, and evaluation of work in progress, these same teachers may not regularly invite students to discuss teachers' responses. She shares strategies that she uses in her classes to initiate a dialogue between teacher and writer.

## *Proofreading*

After revising and editing, you are ready to prepare the final manuscript. (See 6a for guidelines.) Make sure to allow yourself enough time for proofreading—the final and most important step in manuscript preparation.

Proofreading is a special kind of reading: a slow and methodical search for misspellings, typographical mistakes, and omitted words or word endings. Such errors can be difficult to spot in your own work because you may read what you intended to write, not what is actually on the page. To fight this tendency, try proofreading out loud, articulating each word as it is actually written. You might also try proofreading your sentences in reverse order, a strategy that takes your attention away from the meanings you intended and forces you to think about small surface features instead.

Although proofreading may be dull, it is crucial. Errors strewn throughout an essay are distracting and annoying. If the writer doesn't care about this piece of writing, thinks the reader, why should I? A carefully proofread essay, however, sends a positive message: It shows that you value your writing and respect your readers.

 **SPELL CHECKERS** are much more reliable than grammar checkers, but they too must be used with caution. Many typographical errors (such as *quiet* for *quite*) and misused words (such as *effect* for *affect*) slip past the spell checker because it flags only words not found in its dictionary. The following example shows (in italics) the errors that remained after the sentence was run through a spell checker.

> To *by* a new house, Mark and Julia submitted *thee* letters of reference and a five-*age* application *from*.

The spell checker approved *by* for *buy, thee* for *three, age* for *page*, and *from* for *form*. (Also see Exercise 43–1 on p. 455.)

### SCHOLARS ON CONFERENCING

Harris, Muriel. *Teaching One-to-One.* Urbana: NCTE, 1986. Harris provides a rationale for conference teaching and gives practical tips for working "elbow-to-elbow" with students.

Murray, Donald M. "Teaching the Other Self: The Writer's First Reader." *College Composition and Communication* 33 (1982): 140–47. Murray describes a conference technique in which the teacher does "as little as possible to interfere with [the students'] learning." Students need to develop "the other self," an internal critic who guides the student through the writing process: reading, evaluating, rethinking, and revising.

## Checklist for sentence-level revision

The numbers in the chart refer to sections in this handbook.

### Strengthening sentences

Look for opportunities

- to use more active verbs (8a)
- to prune excess words (16)

### Clarifying sentences

Look for opportunities

- to balance parallel ideas (9)
- to supply missing words (10)
- to untangle mixed constructions (11)
- to repair misplaced or dangling modifiers (12)
- to eliminate distracting shifts (13)
- to emphasize key ideas using coordination and subordination (14a)
- to combine choppy sentences (14b)
- to break up long sentences (14e)

### Introducing variety

Look for opportunities

- to vary sentence openings (15a)
- to vary sentence structures (15b)
- to vary the order of sentence elements (15c)

### Refining the style

Look for opportunities

- to choose language more appropriate for the subject and audience (17)
- to choose more exact words (18)

---

**WRITING CENTER DIRECTORS ON THE TUTOR'S ROLE**

"Sometimes students make unspoken comparisons between writing center visits and visits to other services. Meeting with a tutor is not like a doctor's visit, with a tutor writing out a prescription to make the paper better. It's not like taking dirty clothes to the laundry, with the student dropping off the paper and picking it up later all cleaned up. Instead a writing tutor is a student's partner in improving either the written product or the processes involved in creating it or, most often, both. Students can be expected to *do* things in a session: practice a strategy, record ideas, mark their own papers for revision, rewrite sentences, ask and answer questions. And they should expect to apply the practices and information they've gained from the session on their own."

—Deanne Gute, writing specialist, University of Northern Iowa

## An editing checklist

At first this checklist may seem overwhelming, but as your instructor responds to your writing and as you become familiar with the rules in this handbook, you'll begin to see which problems, if any, tend to cause you trouble. You can then devise a personal checklist of errors to look for as you edit. (The numbers in the chart refer to sections in this handbook.)

### Grammar

Sentence fragments (19)
Run-on sentences (20)
Subject-verb agreement (21)
Pronoun-antecedent agreement (22)
Pronoun reference (23)
Case of nouns and pronouns (24)
Case of *who* and *whom* (25)
Adjectives and adverbs (26)
Standard English verb forms (27)
Verb tense, mood, and voice (28, 8)
ESL problems (29, 30, 31)

### Punctuation

The comma and unnecessary commas (32, 33)
The semicolon (34)
The colon (35)
The apostrophe (36)

Quotation marks (37)
End punctuation (38)
Other punctuation marks (39)

### Mechanics

Abbreviations and numbers (40, 41)
Italics (underlining) (42)
Spelling and the hyphen (43, 44)
Capital letters (45)

---

**ADDITIONAL RESOURCE ON THE TUTOR'S ROLE**

Ryan, Leigh, and Lisa Zimmerelli. *The Bedford Guide for Writing Tutors.* 4th ed. Boston: Bedford, 2006. The authors offer practical guidelines for conferencing with students at all stages of the writing process, helping students with varied backgrounds and learning styles, tutoring students who are writing in various disciplines, coping with difficult tutoring situations, and tutoring online or with computers.

## STUDENT ESSAY

Matt Watson, who wrote "Hooked on Credit Cards" (pp. 72–75), was responding to the following assignment.

> In an essay of 500–1,000 words, discuss a significant problem facing today's college students. Assume that your audience consists of general readers, not simply college students.
>
> If you use any sources, document them with in-text citations and a list of works cited in MLA style (see section 57 in *The Bedford Handbook*).

When he received the assignment, Watson considered several possibilities before settling on the topic of credit cards. He already knew something about the topic because his older sister had run up large credit card bills while in college and was working hard to pay them off. Because the assignment required him to *discuss* a problem, he decided that a good strategy would be to identify a *how* or *why* question to answer.

To get started on his paper, Watson interviewed his sister over the phone and then typed the following ideas into his computer.

> easy to get hooked on credit cards and run up huge debts
>
> Why do credit card companies try to sign up students? Aren't we a bad risk? But they must be profiting, or they'd stop. High interest rates.
>
> advertisements for credit cards appear all over campus and on the Web
>
> using plastic doesn't seem like spending money
>
> tactics used by the companies--offering low interest rates at first, setting high credit limits, allowing a revolving balance
>
> What happens to students who get in debt but don't have parents who can bail them out?

### SCHOLARS ON WRITING CENTERS

Briggs, Lynn C., and Meg Woolbright, eds. *Stories from the Center: Connecting Narrative and Theory in the Writing Center.* Urbana: NCTE, 2000. The essays in this collection focus on the stories writing center directors and tutors tell about their work with student writers, including the conflicts that occur when the writer and the tutor have different goals for the sessions or when a tutor encounters instructor comments or methods that seem misguided.

After he listed these ideas, Watson realized that what puzzled him most was why credit card companies would put so many resources into soliciting students in spite of their poor credit profiles. He decided that his purpose would be to answer this question for himself and his audience. He wrote his first draft quickly, focusing more on ideas than on grammar, style, and mechanics. Then he made some additions and deletions and fixed a few typos before submitting the draft for peer review in a networked classroom. Here is the draft he submitted, together with the most helpful comments he received from classmates. The peer reviewers were asked to comment on global issues—audience appeal, focus, organization, content, and point of view—and to ignore any problems with grammar and punctuation.

**ROUGH DRAFT**

Good question. Seems like there might be more to the answer than you've written here. That is, why are these companies trying to hook us? (Mark)

Some students do have jobs. (Sara)

The assignment asks for a general audience; your thesis shouldn't be about "us." (Sara)

Shouldn't your thesis also explain *how* the companies hook students? (Tim)

Good point. I never thought of it that way. (Sara)

Maybe you could also mention the solicitors who show up during orientation. (Mark)

Hooked on Credit Cards

Credit card companies love to extend credit to college students. You see ads for these cards on campus bulletin boards and also on the Web. Why do companies market their product to a population that has no job and lacks a substantial credit history? They seem to be trying to hook us on their cards; unfortunately many of us do get hooked on a cycle of spending that leads to financial ruin.

Banks require applicants for a loan to demonstrate a good credit history and some evidence of a source of income, but credit card companies don't. On campus, students are bombarded with

**SCHOLARS ON WRITING CENTERS**

Hawthorne, Joan. "'We Don't Proofread Here': Re-visioning the Writing Center to Better Meet Student Needs." *Writing Lab Newsletter* 23.8 (1999): 1–7. Hawthorne questions the standard writing center goal: to improve the writer, not the writing. Instead of dismissing "directive tutoring," Hawthorne explores how it can be part of a larger sequence of activities that engage the writer in the process of improving his or her writing.

This sentence sounds less formal than the rest of your essay. (Tim)

offers of preapproved credit cards. Then there are the Web sites. Sites with lots of student traffic are plastered with banner ads like this one: "To get a credit card, you need to establish credit. To establish credit, you need a credit card. Stop the vicious cycle! Apply for our student MasterCard."

I like this example. (Mark)

Why not give us some numbers here? Just how low and how high? (Sara)

Credit card companies often entice students with low interest rates, then they jack up the rates later. A student may not think about the cost of interest. That new stereo or back-to-school wardrobe can get pretty expensive at 17.9% interest if it's compounded over several months. Would you have bought that $600 item if you knew it would end up costing you $900?

The shift to "you" seems odd. (Sara)

Most cards allow the holder to keep a revolving balance, which means that they don't have to pay the whole bill, they just pay a minimum amount. The minimum is usually not too much, but a young person may be tempted to keep running up debt. The companies also give students an unrealistically high credit limit. I've heard of undergraduates who had a limit as high as $4,000.

Maybe you could search Lexis-Nexis for some statistical information. (Mark)

This paragraph seems sort of skimpy. (Tim)

This would be more convincing if you provided some evidence to back up your claim. (Mark)

Card companies make money not just from high interest rates. Often they charge fees for late payments. I've heard of penalties for going over the credit limit too.

## SCHOLARS ON WRITING CENTERS

Sherwood, Steve. "Censoring Students, Censoring Ourselves: Constraining Conversations in the Writing Center." *Writing Center Journal* 20.1 (1999): 51–60. Writing center tutors struggle with ways to help students whose work may be offensive or controversial, to the tutor or to the intended audience. Sherwood explores options for and consequences of dealing with these kinds of pieces and cautions tutors to avoid their "own political and ideological agendas."

Often students discover too late that they are thoroughly trapped. Some drop out of school, others graduate and then can't find a good job because they have a poor credit rating. There are psychological problems too. Your parents may bail you out of debt, but you'll probably feel guilty. On a Web site, I read that two students felt so bad they committed suicide.

Credit cards are a part of life these days, and everyone is probably wise to have a charge account for emergencies. But every college student must take a hard look at their financial picture. The very things that make those cards so convenient and easy to use can lead to a mountain of debt that will take years to pay off.

*Professor Mills won't like your shifts to "you" and "I" here. (Sara)*

*Also, he wants us to cite our sources. (Sara)*

*Your paper focuses on the tactics that the companies use, but your conclusion doesn't mention them. (Tim)*

Some instructors will ask you to write letters to your classmates about their drafts. Here is what one student, Sara Colecchi, wrote to Watson after she had read his essay and written comments in the margins.

Dear Matt:

I enjoyed reading your essay. My roommate has $2,000 in credit card debt and she's always complaining about it, so I found this topic particularly interesting. I never thought about how banks require all sorts of proof before they let you have an account, but credit card companies just give you the card.

As I understand it, your purpose is to explain why credit card companies give credit to college students, and your thesis is that they are trying to hook us on their cards. Your introduction seems pretty clear, but I wonder if you could explain

**SCHOLARS ON WRITING CENTERS**

Thompson, Jan C. "Beyond Fixing Today's Paper: Promoting Metacognition and Writing Development in the Tutorial through Self-Questioning." *Writing Lab Newsletter* 23.6 (1999): 1–6. Thompson discusses several ways to use questions to shape the tutorial dialogue and explains how tutors can help writers learn to use the same strategies independently. Thompson's strategies and suggestions are meant for all levels of students, including those who have learning disabilities.

a bit more. Why would credit card companies want to hook people who have no money? What do the companies gain?

Overall, your essay seems organized, but it's not clear how the last few paragraphs fit together. Maybe you could work on your topic sentences. I also wonder whether you could bring in some more evidence for your point about how card companies make money.

You shift sometimes between points of view, which made me wonder whether you are writing for an audience of other students or for a different audience. Since the assignment said we should write for a general audience, you should take another look at your point of view.

A couple of other questions: Is there anything good about being able to get a credit card? For example, letting people build a credit history? Or are you saying that everyone should avoid credit cards?

Overall, this is a really interesting draft. I would be happy to read it again after you revise it.

                                             Sara Colecchi

After rereading his draft and considering the feedback from his classmates, Watson realized that he needed to develop his thesis further. He thought that Colecchi's question about what credit card companies gain by hooking students was a good one, and he decided that his paper would be stronger if he could answer it. He decided to work on expanding his explanation of both why and how credit card companies market cards to students.

Watson also decided that he needed more evidence to back up his claims about how credit card companies hook students. He located several Web sites with relevant information and rejected those that were obviously promotional. He relied on sites sponsored by two reputable organizations, the student loan provider Nellie Mae and the Consumer Federation of America.

In his next draft, Watson reworked his introduction to explain why credit card companies profit from students who have no steady source of income. Then he strengthened his content by supplying more facts. While adding facts, he discovered ways to improve the organization. He also adjusted his point of view so that his essay would be appropriate for a general audience, not just for other students. When he was more or less satisfied with the paper as a whole, he worked to polish his sentences. Watson's final draft begins on the next page.

Watson 1

Matt Watson
Professor Mills
English 101
12 March 2001

Hooked on Credit Cards

Introduction orients readers and ends with a thesis.

Introduction poses a question to engage readers and lead them to the thesis.

Thesis announces the writer's main point.

Clear topic sentences guide readers through the body of the paper.

Credit card companies love to extend credit to college students, especially those just out of high school. Ads for credit cards line campus bulletin boards, flash across commercial Web sites for students, and get stuffed into shopping bags at college bookstores. Why do the companies market their product so vigorously to a population that lacks a substantial credit history and often has no steady source of income? The answer is that significant profits can be earned through high interest rates and assorted penalties and fees. By granting college students liberal lending arrangements, credit card companies often hook them on a cycle of spending that can ultimately lead to financial ruin.

Whereas banks require applicants for a loan to demonstrate a good credit history and some evidence of an income flow, credit card companies make no such demands on students. On campus, students find themselves bombarded with offers of preapproved cards --and not just on flyers pinned to bulletin boards. Many campuses allow credit card vendors to solicit applications during orientation week. In addition to offering preapproved cards, these vendors often give away T-shirts or CDs to entice students to apply. Students are bombarded on the Web as well. Sites with heavy student traffic are emblazoned with banner ads like this one: "To get a credit card, you

Marginal annotations indicate MLA-style formatting and effective writing.

need to establish credit. To establish credit, you need a credit
card. Stop the vicious cycle! Apply for our student MasterCard."

Credit card companies often entice students with low
"teaser" interest rates of 13% and later raise those rates to
18% or even higher. Others charge high rates up front, trusting
that students won't read the fine print. Some young people
don't think about the cost of interest, let alone the cost of
interest compounding month after month. That back-to-school
wardrobe can get pretty expensive at 17.9% interest compounded over several months. A $600 trip to Fort Lauderdale is
not such a bargain when in the long run it costs $900 or more.

In addition to charging high interest rates, credit card
companies try to maximize the amount of interest generated.
One tactic is to extend an unreasonably high credit limit to
students. According to Nellie Mae statistics, in 1998 undergraduates were granted an average credit limit of $3,683; for
graduate students, the figure jumped to $15,721. Nearly 10%
of the students in the Nellie Mae study carried balances near or
exceeding these credit limits (Blair).

Another tactic is to allow students to maintain a revolving
balance. A revolving balance permits the debtor to pay only
part of a current bill, often an amount just a little larger than
the accumulated interest. The indebted student is tempted to
keep on charging, paying a minimum amount every month, because there aren't any immediate consequences to doing so.

Once a student is hooked on a cycle of debt, the companies profit even further by assessing a variety of fees and
penalties. According to a press release issued by Consumer

Body paragraphs
are developed
with details and
examples.

Transition serves as
a bridge between
paragraphs.

Summary of the
source is in the stu-
dent's own words.

Source is docu-
mented with an
MLA in-text citation.

Writer cites a Web
article from a rep-
utable source.

Watson 3

Action and the Consumer Federation of America, many credit card companies charge late fees and "over the limit" penalties as high as $29 per month. In addition, grace periods are often shortened to ensure that late fees kick in earlier. Many companies also raise interest rates for those who fail to pay on time or who exceed the credit limit. Those "penalty" rates can climb as high as 25% (1-2).

Often students discover too late that they are thoroughly hooked. The results can be catastrophic. Some students are forced to drop out of school and take low-paying full-time jobs. Others, once they graduate, have difficulty landing good jobs because of their poor credit rating. Many students suffer psychologically as well. Even those who have parents willing to bail them out of debt often experience a great deal of anxiety and guilt. Two students recently grew so stressed by their accumulating debt that they committed suicide (Consumer Federation of Amer. 3).

Credit cards are a part of life these days, and there is nothing wrong with having one or two of them. Before signing up for a particular card, however, college students should take the time to read the fine print and do some comparison shopping. Students also need to learn to resist the many seductive offers that credit card companies extend to them once they have signed up. Students who can't "just say no" to temptations such as high credit limits and revolving balances could well become hooked on a cycle of debt from which there is no easy escape.

Conclusion echoes the writer's main idea.

Works Cited

Blair, Alan D. "A High Wire Act: Balancing Student Loan and
    Credit Card Debt." <u>Nellie Mae</u>. 1999. 6 Mar. 2001
    <http://www.nelliemae.com/shared/bal.htm>.

Consumer Action and Consumer Federation of America. "Card
    Issuers Hike Fees and Rates to Bolster Profits." <u>Consumer
    Federation of America</u>. 5 Nov. 1998. 5 pp. 6 Mar. 2001
    <http://www.consumerfed.org/cardissuerspr.pdf>.

Consumer Federation of America. "Credit Card Debt Imposes
    Huge Costs on Many College Students." <u>Consumer
    Federation of America</u>. 8 June 1999. 7 pp. 6 Mar. 2001
    <http://www.consumerfed.org/ccstudent.pdf>.

Works cited page
follows MLA format.

# 4

## Build effective paragraphs.

Except for special-purpose paragraphs, such as introductions and conclusions (see 2a and 2c), paragraphs are clusters of information supporting an essay's main point (or advancing a story's action). Aim for paragraphs that are clearly focused, well developed, organized, coherent, and neither too long nor too short for easy reading.

### 4a Focus on a main point.

A paragraph should be unified around a main point. The point should be clear to readers, and all sentences in the paragraph should relate to it.

#### Stating the main point in a topic sentence

As readers move into a paragraph, they need to know where they are—in relation to the whole essay—and what to expect in the sentences to come. A good topic sentence, a one-sentence summary of the paragraph's main point, acts as a signpost pointing in two directions: backward toward the thesis of the essay and forward toward the body of the paragraph.

Like a thesis sentence (see 1c and 2a), a topic sentence is more general than the material supporting it. Usually the topic sentence (italicized in the following examples) comes first in the paragraph.

> *Nearly all living creatures manage some form of communication.* The dance patterns of bees in their hive help to point

---

**SCHOLARS ON COHERENCE**

Lan, Haixia. "Contrastive Rhetoric: A Must in Cross-Cultural Inquiries." *ALT DIS: Alternative Discourses and the Academy.* Ed. Christopher Schroeder, Helen Fox, and Patricia Bizzell. Portsmouth: Boynton, 2002. 68–79. Lan traces the cultural and discursive differences in Western and Chinese orientations toward constructing analytical arguments. She shows how philosophically different views affect every aspect of written communication, from invention to the shape of a thesis to ways of reasoning and constructing coherent texts. Cultures shape texts, she argues, but discursive practices also shape cultural perspectives.

the way to distant flower fields or announce successful forag-
ing. Male stickleback fish regularly swim upside-down to indicate outrage in a courtship contest. Male deer and lemurs
mark territorial ownership by rubbing their own body secre-
tions on boundary stones or trees. Everyone has seen a frightened dog put his tail between his legs and run in panic. We,
too, use gestures, expressions, postures, and movement to
give our words point. [Italics added.]

— Olivia Vlahos, *Human Beginnings*

Sometimes the topic sentence is introduced by a transitional sentence linking it to earlier material. In the following
paragraph, the topic sentence has been delayed to allow for
a transition.

But flowers are not the only source of spectacle in the
wilderness. *An opportunity for late color is provided by the
berries of wildflowers, shrubs, and trees.* Baneberry presents
its tiny white flowers in spring but in late summer bursts forth
with clusters of red berries. Bunchberry, a ground-cover plant,
puts out red berries in the fall, and the red berries of winter-
green last from autumn well into winter. In California, the
bright red, fist-sized clusters of Christmas berries can be seen
growing beside highways for up to six months of the year.
[Italics added.]

— James Crockett et al., *Wildflower Gardening*

Occasionally the topic sentence may be withheld until
the end of the paragraph — but only if the earlier sentences
hang together so well that readers perceive their direction, if
not their exact point. The opening sentences of the following
paragraph state facts, so they are supporting material rather
than topic sentences, but they strongly suggest a central
idea. The topic sentence at the end is hardly a surprise.

Tobacco chewing starts as soon as people begin stirring.
Those who have fresh supplies soak the new leaves in water
and add ashes from the hearth to the wad. Men, women, and

**SCHOLARS ON COHERENCE**

Powell, Malea. "Listening to Ghosts: An Alternative (Non)Argu-
ment." *ALT DIS: Alternative Discourses and the Academy.* Ed.
Christopher Schroeder, Helen Fox, and Patricia Bizzell. Portsmouth: Boynton, 2002. 11–22. In this evocative essay, which mixes
stories and analysis, Powell, a Native American scholar, invites
readers to rethink the logic of the traditional argument essay. She
questions the assumptions that underlie notions of coherence
and invites teachers, by her example, to imagine discourse practices that challenge inherited standards and to "reinvent our writ-
ings in another voice, another language."

children chew tobacco and all are addicted to it. Once there was a shortage of tobacco in Kaobawa's village and I was plagued for a week by early morning visitors who requested permission to collect my cigarette butts in order to make a wad of chewing tobacco. Normally, if anyone is short of tobacco, he can request a share of someone else's already chewed wad, or simply borrow the entire wad when its owner puts it down somewhere. *Tobacco is so important to them that their word for "poverty" translates as "being without tobacco."* [Italics added.]

— Napoleon A. Chagnon, *Yanomamo: The Fierce People*

You will find that some professional writers, especially journalists and informal essayists, do not always use clear topic sentences. In college writing, however, topic sentences are often necessary for clarifying the lines of an argument or reporting the research in a field. In business writing, topic sentences (along with headings) are essential, since readers often scan for information.

Try to develop a flexible approach to writing. Although it is generally wise to use topic sentences, at times they are unnecessary, even in college papers. A topic sentence may not be needed if a paragraph continues developing an idea clearly introduced in a previous paragraph, if the details of the paragraph unmistakably suggest its main point, or if the paragraph appears in a narrative of events where generalizations might interrupt the flow of the story.

**TIP:** If you're not sure what key idea to express in the topic sentence for each paragraph, try jotting down an informal outline before you begin writing your paper; then write a topic sentence for each major point in the outline. Or after you have written a draft, go back and make an outline, checking that each paragraph has a topic sentence reflecting one main point. If you discover that you are making more than one point in a paragraph, consider breaking the paragraph into several shorter paragraphs.

### SCHOLARS ON PARAGRAPHS

Lindemann, Erika. *A Rhetoric for Writing Teachers.* 3rd ed. New York: Oxford UP, 1995. 141–57. Lindemann distinguishes among views of "paragraphs-as-products" and "paragraphing-as-process," arguing that the former view is less effective in helping students become better writers. Building on the work of Christensen and Winterowd, she offers a sequence of lessons for teaching paragraphing and advises teachers to focus on student writing whenever possible.

*Sticking to the point*

Sentences that do not support the topic sentence destroy the unity of a paragraph. If the paragraph is otherwise well focused, such offending sentences can simply be deleted or perhaps moved elsewhere. In the following paragraph describing the inadequate facilities in a high school, the information about the word processing instructor (in italics) is clearly off the point.

> As the result of tax cuts, the educational facilities of Lincoln High School have reached an all-time low. Some of the books date back to 1985 and have long since shed their covers. The lack of lab equipment makes it necessary for four or five students to work at one table, with most watching rather than performing experiments. The few computers in working order must share one dot matrix printer. *Also, the word processing instructor left to have a baby at the beginning of the semester, and most of the students don't like the substitute.* As for the furniture, many of the upright chairs have become recliners, and the desk legs are so unbalanced that they play seesaw on the floor. [Italics added.]

Sometimes the solution for a disunified paragraph is not as simple as deleting or moving material. Writers often wander into uncharted territory because they cannot think of enough evidence to support a topic sentence. Feeling that it is too soon to break into a new paragraph, they move on to new ideas for which they have not prepared the reader. When this happens, the writer is faced with a choice: Either find more evidence to support the topic sentence or adjust the topic sentence to mesh with the evidence that is available.

**EXERCISE 4–1**   Underline the topic sentence in the following paragraph and cross out any material that does not clarify or develop the central idea.

**EXERCISE 4–1   Answers:**

Topic sentence: Quilt making has served as an important means of social, political, and artistic expression for women. Eliminate the following sentence: They used dyed cotton fabrics much like the fabrics quilters use today; surprisingly, quilters' basic materials haven't changed that much over the years.

Quilt making has served as an important means of social, political, and artistic expression for women. In the nineteenth century, quilting circles provided one of the few opportunities for women to forge social bonds outside of their families. Once a week or more, they came together to sew as well as trade small talk, advice, and news. They used dyed cotton fabrics much like the fabrics quilters use today; surprisingly, quilters' basic materials haven't changed that much over the years. Sometimes the women joined their efforts in the support of a political cause, making quilts that would be raffled to raise money for temperance societies, hospitals for sick and wounded soldiers, and the fight against slavery. Quilt making also afforded women a means of artistic expression at a time when they had few other creative outlets. Within their socially acceptable roles as homemakers, many quilters subtly pushed back at the restrictions placed on them by experimenting with color, design, and technique.

| ON THE WEB | **dianahacker.com/bedhandbook** |
|---|---|
| | ▶ Electronic writing exercises |
| | ▶ E-ex 4–1 |

## 4b Develop the main point.

Though an occasional short paragraph is fine, particularly if it functions as a transition or emphasizes a point, a series of brief paragraphs suggests inadequate development. How much development is enough? That varies, depending on the writer's purpose and audience. For example, when she wrote a paragraph attempting to convince readers that it is impossible to lose fat quickly, health columnist Jane Brody knew that she would have to present a great deal of evidence because many dieters want to believe the opposite. She did *not* write:

---

**WRITING CENTER DIRECTORS ON COHERENCE**

"Writing is meant to be read, and that understanding—that movement from writing for the self to writing for readers—is essential if students are to improve their writing. One key role tutors play is that of the experienced reader, one who can point out what's clear, what needs support, what coheres, and so on. Once student writers get the concept of writing for a reader, they are likely to improve in all of those areas—clarity, unity, coherence—on their own."                                     —Leslie R. Leach, writing center coordinator, College of the Redwoods

> When you think about it, it's impossible to lose—as many diets suggest—10 pounds of *fat* in ten days, even on a total fast. Even a moderately active person cannot lose so much weight so fast. A less active person hasn't a prayer.

This three-sentence paragraph is too skimpy to be convincing. But the paragraph that Brody wrote contains enough evidence to convince even skeptical readers.

> When you think about it, it's impossible to lose—as many diets suggest—10 pounds of *fat* in ten days, even on a total fast. A pound of body fat represents 3,500 calories. To lose 1 pound of fat, you must expend 3,500 more calories than you consume. Let's say you weigh 170 pounds and, as a moderately active person, you burn 2,500 calories a day. If your diet contains only 1,500 calories, you'd have an energy deficit of 1,000 calories a day. In a week's time that would add up to a 7,000-calorie deficit, or 2 pounds of real fat. In ten days, the accumulated deficit would represent nearly 3 pounds of lost body fat. Even if you ate nothing at all for ten days and maintained your usual level of activity, your caloric deficit would add up to 25,000 calories. . . . At 3,500 calories per pound of fat, that's still only 7 pounds of lost fat.
> —Jane Brody, *Jane Brody's Nutrition Book*

## 4c Choose a suitable pattern of organization.

Although paragraphs (and indeed whole essays) may be patterned in any number of ways, certain patterns of organization occur frequently, either alone or in combination: examples and illustrations, narration, description, process, comparison and contrast, analogy, cause and effect, classification and division, and definition. There is nothing particularly magical about these patterns (sometimes called *methods of development*). They simply reflect some of the ways in which we think.

**SCHOLARS ON WRITING CENTERS**

Blau, Susan R., John Hall, and Tracy Strauss. "Exploring the Tutor/Client Conversation: A Linguistic Analysis." *Writing Center Journal* 19.1 (1998): 19–48. The authors report on an ongoing study of tutor-client relationships, focusing on the ways that the language used during the tutorial shapes and determines these relationships. Their analysis of questions, echoing, and qualifiers as prominent features in tutorials helps tutors recognize not only how they create relationships but also what *kinds* of relationships they create with their student clients.

*Examples and illustrations*

Examples, perhaps the most common pattern of development, are appropriate whenever the reader might be tempted to ask, "For example?" Though examples are just selected instances, not a complete catalog, they are enough to suggest the truth of many topic sentences, as in the following paragraph.

> Normally my parents abided scrupulously by "The Budget," but several times a year Dad would dip into his battered black strongbox and splurge on some irrational, totally satisfying luxury. Once he bought over a hundred comic books at a flea market, doled out to us thereafter at the tantalizing rate of two a week. He always got a whole flat of pansies, Mom's favorite flower, for us to give her on Mother's Day. One day a boy stopped at our house selling fifty-cent raffle tickets on a sailboat and Dad bought every ticket the boy had left—three books' worth.          — Connie Hailey, student

Illustrations are extended examples, frequently presented in story form. Because they require several sentences apiece, they are used more sparingly than examples. When well selected, however, they can be a vivid and effective means of developing a point. The writer of the following paragraph uses illustrations to demonstrate that Harriet

Tubman, famous conductor on the underground railroad for escaping slaves, was a genius at knowing how and when to retreat.

> Part of Harriet Tubman's strategy of conducting was, as in all battle-field operations, the knowledge of how and when to retreat. Numerous allusions have been made to her moves when she suspected that she was in danger. When she feared the party was closely pursued, she would take it for a time on a train southward bound. No one seeing Negroes going in this direction would for an instant suppose them to be fugitives. Once on her return she was at a railway station. She saw some men reading a poster and she heard one of them reading it aloud. It was a description of her, offering a reward for her capture. She took a southbound train to avert suspicion. At another time when Harriet heard men talking about her, she pretended to read a book which she carried. One man remarked, "This cannot be the woman. The one we want can't read or write." Harriet devoutly hoped the book was right side up.                          —Earl Conrad, *Harriet Tubman*

### Narration

A paragraph of narration tells a story or part of a story. Narrative paragraphs are usually arranged in chronological order, but they may also contain flashbacks, interruptions that take the story back to an earlier time. The following paragraph, from Jane Goodall's *In the Shadow of Man,* recounts one of the author's experiences in the African wild.

> One evening when I was wading in the shallows of the lake to pass a rocky outcrop, I suddenly stopped dead as I saw the sinuous black body of a snake in the water. It was all of six feet long, and from the slight hood and the dark stripes at the back of the neck I knew it to be a Storm's water cobra—a deadly reptile for the bite of which there was, at that time, no serum. As I stared at it an incoming wave gently deposited

**SCHOLARS ON WRITING CENTERS**

Harris, Muriel. "Talking in the Middle: Why Writers Need Writing Tutors." *College English* 57 (1995): 27–42. Harris says tutors play four critical roles in tutoring sessions: They encourage independence through collaborative talk about writing; they assist with the acquisition of strategic knowledge; they allow students to discuss their feelings about writing; and they help students interpret the meaning of academic language, including the comments teachers write on papers.

North, Stephen. "The Idea of the Writing Center." *College English* 46 (1984): 433–46. North proposes that writing center instructors focus not on producing better individual student texts but on producing better student writers.

part of its body on one of my feet. I remained motionless, not even breathing, until the wave rolled back into the lake, drawing the snake with it. Then I leaped out of the water as fast as I could, my heart hammering.

—Jane Goodall, *In the Shadow of Man*

### Description

A descriptive paragraph sketches a portrait of a person, place, or thing by using concrete and specific details that appeal to one or more of our senses—sight, sound, smell, taste, and touch. Consider, for example, the following description of the grasshopper invasions that devastated the midwestern landscape in the late 1860s.

> They came like dive bombers out of the west. They came by the millions with the rustle of their wings roaring overhead. They came in waves, like the rolls of the sea, descending with a terrifying speed, breaking now and again like a mighty surf. They came with the force of a williwaw and they formed a huge, ominous, dark brown cloud that eclipsed the sun. They dipped and touched earth, hitting objects and people like hailstones. But they were not hail. These were live demons. They popped, snapped, crackled, and roared. They were dark brown, an inch or longer in length, plump in the middle and tapered at the ends. They had transparent wings, slender legs, and two black eyes that flashed with a fierce intelligence.
>
> —Eugene Boe, "Pioneers to Eternity"

### Process

A process paragraph is patterned in time order, usually chronologically. A writer may choose this pattern either to describe a process or to show readers how to perform a process. The following paragraph describes what happens when water freezes.

---

**SCHOLARS ON THE HISTORY OF WRITING INSTRUCTION**

Russell, David R. *Writing in the Academic Disciplines: A Curricular History.* 2nd ed. Carbondale: Southern Illinois UP, 2002. Russell's book provides a useful parallel to histories of writing instruction in English departments. He examines "the broader, though largely tacit traditions students encounter in the whole curriculum" to understand the ways students learn to write in their fields. Writing, he argues, is not a single skill that can be taught once and for all in a general composition course; rather it is deeply embedded in the diverse practices of disciplinary discourse communities. His chapters trace the effects of increasingly specialized disciplines on writing instruction, the role of writing in general education reforms, the evolution of the writing-across-the-curriculum (WAC) movement, and the distinction between and curricular models for WAC and writing in the disciplines (WID).

In school we learned that with few exceptions the solid phase of matter is more dense than the liquid phase. Water, alone among common substances, violates this rule. As water begins to cool, it contracts and becomes more dense, in a perfectly typical way. But about four degrees above the freezing point, something remarkable happens. It ceases to contract and begins expanding, becoming less dense. At the freezing point the expansion is abrupt and drastic. As water turns to ice, it adds about one-eleventh to its liquid volume.

— Chet Raymo, "Curious Stuff, Water and Ice"

Here is a paragraph explaining how to perform a "roll cast," a popular fly-fishing technique.

Begin by taking up a suitable stance, with one foot slightly in front of the other and the rod pointing down the line. Then begin a smooth, steady draw, raising your rod hand to just above shoulder height and lifting the rod to the 10:30 or 11:00 position. This steady draw allows a loop of line to form between the rod top and the water. While the line is still moving, raise the rod slightly, then punch it rapidly forward and down. The rod is now flexed and under maximum compression, and the line follows its path, bellying out slightly behind you and coming off the water close to your feet. As you power the rod down through the 3:00 position, the belly of the line will roll forward. Follow through smoothly so that the line unfolds and straightens above the water.

— *The Dorling Kindersley Encyclopedia of Fishing*

## Comparison and contrast

To compare two subjects is to draw attention to their similarities, although the word *compare* also has a broader meaning that includes a consideration of differences. To contrast is to focus only on differences.

Whether a comparison-and-contrast paragraph stresses similarities or differences, it may be patterned in one of two

**SCHOLARS ON THE HISTORY OF WRITING INSTRUCTION**

Murphy, James J., ed. *A Short History of Writing Instruction: From Ancient Greece to Modern America.* Mahwah: Erlbaum, 2001. This collection of articles traces the development of writing instruction from its roots in ancient Greece, where it supplemented oral instruction and trained the mind in abstract thinking and self-reflection. The book then covers the instructional materials and methods of the Middle Ages and the Renaissance and the teaching practices that evolved in Britain and America. The discussion of the evolution of writing instruction in the United States begins in the seventeenth century and covers the emergence of rhetoric and composition as a discipline, its major theories, and the literacy "crises" to which it has responded over the last century.

ways. The two subjects may be presented one at a time, block style, as in the following paragraph of contrast.

> So Grant and Lee were in complete contrast, representing two diametrically opposed elements in American life. Grant was the modern man emerging; beyond him, ready to come on the stage, was the great age of steel and machinery, of crowded cities and a restless burgeoning vitality. Lee might have ridden down from the old age of chivalry, lance in hand, silken banner fluttering over his head. Each man was the perfect champion of his cause, drawing both his strengths and weaknesses from the people he led.
> —Bruce Catton, "Grant and Lee: A Study in Contrasts"

Or a paragraph may proceed point by point, treating the two subjects together, one aspect at a time. The following paragraph uses the point-by-point method to contrast the writer's academic experiences in an American high school with those in an Irish convent.

> Strangely enough, instead of being academically inferior to my my American high school, the Irish convent was superior. In my class at home, *Love Story* was considered pretty heavy reading, so imagine my surprise at finding Irish students who could recite passages from *War and Peace*. In high school we complained about having to study *Romeo and Juliet* in one semester, whereas in Ireland we simultaneously studied *Macbeth* and Dickens's *Hard Times*, in addition to writing a composition a day in English class. In high school, I didn't even begin algebra until the ninth grade, while at the convent seventh graders (or their Irish equivalent) were doing calculus and trigonometry.                        —Margaret Stack, student

### Analogy

Analogies draw comparisons between items that appear to have little in common. Writers turn to analogies for a variety of reasons: to make the unfamiliar seem familiar, to provide

**SCHOLARS ON THE HISTORY OF WRITING INSTRUCTION**

Connors, Robert J. "Personal Writing Assignments." *College Composition and Communication* 38 (1987): 166–83. Connors tracks the shift in writing instruction from assignments on "impersonal," abstract topics, which asked students to draw from their own store of knowledge and reading, to assignments based on personal experience that became dominant in the late 1800s when it was believed that students would write better essays if they wrote about themselves.

a concrete understanding of an abstract topic, to argue a point, or to provoke fresh thoughts or changed feelings about a subject. In the following paragraph, physician Lewis Thomas draws an analogy between the behavior of ants and that of humans. Thomas's analogy helps us understand the social behavior of ants and forces us to question the superiority of our own human societies.

> Ants are so much like human beings as to be an embarrassment. They farm fungi, raise aphids as livestock, launch armies into wars, use chemical sprays to alarm and confuse enemies, capture slaves. The families of weaver ants engage in child labor, holding their larvae like shuttles to spin out the thread that sews the leaves together for their fungus gardens. They exchange information ceaselessly. They do everything but watch television.
> —Lewis Thomas, "On Societies as Organisms"

Although analogies can be a powerful tool for illuminating a subject, they should be used with caution in arguments. Just because two things may be alike in one respect, we cannot conclude that they are alike in all respects. (See "false analogy," p. 507.)

### Cause and effect

When causes and effects are a matter of argument, they are too complex to be reduced to a simple pattern (see p. 509). However, if a writer wishes merely to describe a cause-and-effect relationship that is generally accepted, then the effect may be stated in the topic sentence, with the causes listed in the body of the paragraph.

> The fantastic water clarity of the Mount Gambier sink-holes results from several factors. The holes are fed from aquifers holding rainwater that fell decades—even centuries—ago, and that has been filtered through miles of limestone. The

**SCHOLARS ON RESPONDING TO STUDENT WRITING**

Tobin, Lad. *Reading Student Writing: Confessions, Meditations, and Rants.* Portsmouth: Boynton, 2004. Writing in an engagingly personal voice, Tobin discusses the way our identities, values, and assumptions shape the way we read and respond to our students' writing. He combines memoir, stories of the classroom, and self-reflection to argue that we can read even the most problematic student texts more generously if we reflect on our own experiences as adolescents and student writers and if we recognize that teacher burnout and institutional attitudes toward student writing may be the cause, not the effect, of "bad" student writing.

high level of calcium that limestone adds causes the silty detritus from dead plants and animals to cling together and settle quickly to the bottom. Abundant bottom vegetation in the shallow sinkholes also helps bind the silt. And the rapid turnover of water prohibits stagnation.

—Hillary Hauser, "Exploring a Sunken Realm in Australia"

Or the paragraph may move from cause to effects, as in this paragraph from a student paper on the effects of the industrial revolution on American farms.

The rise of rail transport in the nineteenth century forever changed American farming—for better and for worse. Farmers who once raised crops and livestock to sustain just their own families could now make a profit by selling their goods in towns and cities miles away. These new markets improved the living standard of struggling farm families and encouraged them to seek out innovations that would increase their profits. On the downside, the competition fostered by the new markets sometimes created hostility among neighboring farm families where there had once been a spirit of cooperation. Those farmers who couldn't compete with their neighbors left farming forever, facing poverty worse than they had ever known.

—Chris Mileski, student

### Classification and division

Classification is the grouping of items into categories according to some consistent principle. Philosopher Francis Bacon was using classification when he wrote that "some books are to be tasted, others to be swallowed, and some few to be chewed and digested." Bacon's principle for classifying books is the degree to which they are worthy of our attention, but books of course can be classified according to other principles. For example, an elementary school teacher might classify children's books according to their level of difficulty, or a librarian might group them by subject matter. The principle of classification that a writer chooses ultimately depends on the purpose of the classification.

**SCHOLARS ON RESPONDING TO STUDENT WRITING**

Ransdell, D. R. "Directive versus Facilitative Commentary." *Teaching English in the Two-Year College* 26 (1999): 269–76. Responding to work by Richard Straub, who recommends facilitative rather than directive comments on student writing, Ransdell argues that both styles of commentary can be useful. Ransdell showed her students each type of comment on side-by-side versions of the same draft and asked them which style they preferred. The students were divided in their preferences, offering good rationales for both styles.

The following paragraph classifies species of electric fish.

> Scientists sort electric fishes into three categories. The first comprises the strongly electric species like the marine electric rays or the freshwater African electric catfish and South American electric eel. Known since the dawn of history, these deliver a punch strong enough to stun a human. In recent years, biologists have focused on a second category: weakly electric fish in the South American and African rivers that use tiny voltages for communication and navigation. The third group contains sharks, nonelectric rays, and catfish, which do not emit a field but possess sensors that enable them to detect the minute amounts of electricity that leak out of other organisms.
> —Anne Rudloe and Jack Rudloe, "Electric Warfare: The Fish That Kill with Thunderbolts"

Division takes one item and divides it into parts. As with classification, division should be made according to some consistent principle. Dividing a tree into roots, trunk, branches, and leaves makes sense; listing its components as branches, wood, water, and sap does not, for the categories overlap.

The following passage describes the components that make up a baseball.

> Like the game itself, a baseball is composed of many layers. One of the delicious joys of childhood is to take apart a baseball and examine the wonders within. You begin by removing the red cotton thread and peeling off the leather cover—which comes from the hide of a Holstein cow and has been tanned, cut, printed, and punched with holes. Beneath the cover is a thin layer of cotton string, followed by several hundred yards of woolen yarn, which make up the bulk of the ball. Finally, in the middle is a rubber ball, or "pill," which is a little smaller than a golf ball. Slice into the rubber and you'll find the ball's heart—a cork core. The cork is from Portugal, the rubber from southeast Asia, the covers are American, and the balls are assembled in Costa Rica.
> —Dan Gutman, *The Way Baseball Works*

**SCHOLARS ON RESPONDING TO STUDENT WRITING**

Sweeney, Marilyn Ruth. "Relating Revision Skills to Teacher Commentary." *Teaching English in the Two-Year College* 27 (1999): 213–18. Sweeney reports on a semester-long study that examined the connections between her response style—both deductive and inductive—and revisions made by students receiving her comments. Students who received direct response about a problem, with a suggested solution, revised more than students who received nondirective, inductive responses, even in a subsequent writing assignment for which they received no comments. However, over the course of the semester, students receiving inductive comments doubled (then redoubled) the revisions they did; this result suggests that students can learn to think inductively about their writing and revision.

*Definition*

A definition puts a word or concept into a general class and then provides enough details to distinguish it from others in the same class. For example, in one of its senses the term *grit* names the class of things that birds eat, but it is restricted to those items — such as small pebbles, eggshell, and ashes — that help the bird grind food.

Many definitions may be presented in a sentence or two, but abstract or difficult concepts may require a paragraph or even a full essay of definition. In the following paragraph, the writer defines *envy* as a special kind of desire.

> Envy is so integral and so painful a part of what animates human behavior in market societies that many people have forgotten the full meaning of the word, simplifying it into one of the synonyms of desire. It is that, which may be why it flourishes in market societies: democracies of desire, they might be called, with money for ballots, stuffing permitted. But envy is more or less than desire. It begins with the almost frantic sense of emptiness inside oneself, as if the pump of one's heart were sucking on air. One has to be blind to perceive the emptiness, of course, but that's just what envy is, a selective blindness. *Invidia*, Latin for envy, translates as "nonsight," and Dante had the envious plodding along under cloaks of lead, their eyes sewn shut with leaden wire. What they are blind to is what they have, God-given and humanly nurtured, in themselves.
>
> —Nelson W. Aldrich Jr., *Old Money*

**EXERCISE 4–2** After you have drafted an essay, go through it paragraph by paragraph and identify the patterns of organization that you have used.

**EXERCISE 4–3** As you write a draft of your essay, experiment with organizing your paragraphs according to the different patterns of organization. Try at least two different patterns.

**SCHOLARS ON RESPONDING TO STUDENT WRITING**

O'Neill, Peggy. "From the Writing Process to the Responding Sequence: Incorporating Self-Assessment and Reflection in the Classroom." *Teaching English in the Two-Year College* 26 (1998): 61–70. Because research suggests that successful writers have internalized the process of self-assessment, O'Neill calls on us to teach students to assess their own work. O'Neill asks her students to comment on their drafts, and then she responds in writing to the students' comments and questions. She offers several practical suggestions for making this sort of dialogue between teacher and student work.

## 4d Make paragraphs coherent.

When sentences and paragraphs flow from one to another without discernible bumps, gaps, or shifts, they are said to be coherent. Coherence can be improved by strengthening the various ties between old information and new. A number of techniques for strengthening those ties are detailed in this section.

### Linking ideas clearly

Readers expect to learn a paragraph's main point in a topic sentence early in the paragraph. Then, as they move into the body of the paragraph, they expect to encounter specific details, facts, or examples that support the topic sentence — either directly or indirectly. In the following paragraph, all of the sentences following the topic sentence directly support it.

> A passenger list of the early years of the Orient Express would read like a *Who's Who of the World,* from art to politics. Sarah Bernhardt and her Italian counterpart Eleonora Duse used the train to thrill the stages of Europe. For musicians there were Toscanini and Mahler. Dancers Nijinsky and Pavlova were there, while lesser performers like Harry Houdini and the girls of the Ziegfeld Follies also rode the rails. Violinists were allowed to practice on the train, and occasionally one might see trapeze artists hanging like bats from the baggage racks.
>
> — Barnaby Conrad III, "Train of Kings"

If a sentence does not support the topic sentence directly, readers expect it to support another sentence in the paragraph and therefore to support the topic sentence indirectly. The following paragraph begins with a topic sentence. The italicized sentences are direct supports, and the rest of the sentences are indirect supports.

**SCHOLARS ON RESPONDING TO STUDENT WRITING**

Zak, Frances, and Christopher C. Weaver, eds. *The Theory and Practice of Grading Writing.* Albany: State U of New York P, 1998. Particularly useful among the fifteen essays in this collection are Bruce Speck and Tammy Jones's "Direction in the Grading of Writing: What the Literature on the Grading of Writing Does and Doesn't Tell Us" and Peter Elbow's "Changing Grading While Working with Grades."

Though the open-space classroom works for many children, it is not practical for my son, David. *First, David is hyperactive.* When he was placed in an open-space classroom, he became distracted and confused. He was tempted to watch the movement going on around him instead of concentrating on his own work. *Second, David has a tendency to transpose letters and numbers, a tendency that can be overcome only by individual attention from the instructor.* In the open classroom he was moved from teacher to teacher, with each one responsible for a different subject. No single teacher worked with David long enough to diagnose the problem, let alone help him with it. *Finally, David is not a highly motivated learner.* In the open classroom, he was graded "at his own level," not by criteria for a certain grade. He could receive a B in reading and still be a grade level behind, because he was doing satisfactory work "at his own level." [Italics added.]

—Margaret Smith, student

### Repeating key words

Repetition of key words is an important technique for gaining coherence. To prevent repetitions from becoming dull, you can use variations of a key word (*hike, hiker, hiking*), pronouns referring to the word (*gamblers . . . they*), and synonyms (*run, spring, race, dash*). In the following paragraph describing plots among indentured servants in the seventeenth century, historian Richard Hofstadter binds sentences together by repeating the key word *plots* and echoing it with a variety of synonyms (which are italicized).

*Plots* hatched by several servants to run away together occurred mostly in the plantation colonies, and the few recorded servant *uprisings* were entirely limited to those colonies. Virginia had been forced from its very earliest years to take stringent steps against *mutinous plots,* and severe punishments for *such behavior* were recorded. Most servant *plots* occurred in the seventeenth century: A contemplated *uprising*

**SCHOLARS ON RESPONDING TO STUDENT WRITING**

Smith, Summer. "The Genre of the End Comment: Conventions in Teacher Responses to Student Writing." *College Composition and Communication* 48 (1997): 249–68. Examining more than three hundred end comments written on student writing, Smith identifies sixteen "primary genres" divided further into three categories: "judging genres," "reader response genres," and "coaching genres." Smith also examines the ways that teachers choose from among these genres—such as evaluation of style, of effort, of correctness—to construct a particular end comment. Smith suggests that generic end comments are less helpful to students, while comments that focus on a particular writer's performance are more helpful.

was nipped in the bud in York County in 1661; apparently led by some left-wing offshoots of the *Great Rebellion*, servants *plotted* an *insurrection* in Gloucester County in 1663, and four leaders were condemned and executed; some discontented servants apparently joined *Bacon's Rebellion* in the 1670s. In the 1680s the planters became newly apprehensive of discontent among the servants "owing to their great necessities and want of clothes," and it was feared that they would *rise up* and *plunder* the storehouses and ships; in 1682 there were plant-cutting *riots* in which servants and laborers, as well as some planters, took part. [Italics added.]

—Richard Hofstadter, *America at 1750*

### Using parallel structures

Parallel structures are frequently used within sentences to underscore the similarity of ideas (see 9). They may also be used to bind together a series of sentences expressing similar information. In the following passage describing folk beliefs, anthropologist Margaret Mead presents similar information in parallel grammatical form.

Actually, almost every day, even in the most sophisticated home, something is likely to happen that evokes the memory of some old folk belief. The salt spills. A knife falls to the floor. Your nose tickles. Then perhaps, with a slightly embarrassed smile, the person who spilled the salt tosses a pinch over his left shoulder. Or someone recites the old rhyme, "Knife falls, gentleman calls." Or as you rub your nose you think, That means a letter. I wonder who's writing?

—Margaret Mead, "New Superstitions for Old"

A less skilled writer might have varied the structure, perhaps like this: *The salt gets spilled. Mother drops a knife on the floor. Your nose begins to tickle.* But these sentences are less effective; Mead's parallel structures help tie the passage together.

**SCHOLARS ON RESPONDING TO STUDENT WRITING**

Straub, Richard. "The Concept of Control in Teacher Response: Defining the Varieties of 'Directive' and 'Facilitative' Commentary." *College Composition and Communication* 47 (1996): 223–51. Straub challenges the prevailing ways of labeling teacher responses—as either directive or facilitative—pointing out that each category includes a rich variety of useful responses.

White, Edward M. *Assigning, Responding, Evaluating: A Writing Teacher's Guide.* 3rd ed. New York: St. Martin's, 1995. White offers advice on developing assignments; on different methods of assessing, evaluating, and responding to student writing; and on conducting large-scale exit or proficiency exams.

*Maintaining consistency*

Coherence suffers whenever a draft shifts confusingly from one point of view to another or from one verb tense to another. (See 13.) In addition, coherence can suffer when new information is introduced with the subject of each sentence. As a rule, a sentence's subject should echo a subject or object in the previous sentence.

The following rough-draft paragraph is needlessly hard to read because so few of the sentences' subjects are tied to earlier subjects or objects. The subjects appear in italics.

> *One* goes about trapping in this manner. At the very outset *one* acquires a "trapping" state of mind. A *library* of books must be read, and preferably *someone* with experience should educate the novice. *Preparing* for the first expedition takes several steps. The *purchase* of traps is first. A *pair* of rubber gloves, waterproof *boots,* and the grubbiest *clothes* capable of withstanding human use come next to outfit the trapper for his adventure. Finally, the *decision* has to be made on just what kind of animals to seek, what sort of bait to use, and where to place the traps. [Italics added.]

Although the writer repeats a number of key words, such as *trapping,* the paragraph seems disconnected because new information is introduced with the subject of each sentence.

To improve the paragraph, the writer used the first-person pronoun as the subject of every sentence. The revision is much easier to read.

> *I* went about trapping in this manner. To acquire a "trapping" state of mind, *I* read a library of books and talked at length with an experienced trapper, my father. Then *I* purchased the traps and outfitted myself by collecting a pair of rubber gloves, waterproof boots, and the grubbiest clothes capable of withstanding human use. Finally, *I* decided just what kinds of animals to seek, what sort of bait to use, and where to place my traps. [Italics added.]
>
> —John Clyde Thatcher, student

**WRITERS ON WRITING**

The purpose of paragraphing is to give the reader a rest. The writer is saying . . . : Have you got that? If so, I'll go to the next point.
— H. W. Fowler

Short paragraphs put air around what you write and make it look inviting, whereas one long chunk of type can discourage the reader from even starting to read.   — William Zinsser

No one can write decently who is distrustful of the reader's intelligence, or whose attitude is patronizing.   — E. B. White

We often refuse to accept an idea merely because the tone of voice in which it has been expressed is unsympathetic to us.
— Friedrich Nietzsche

Notice that Thatcher combined some of his original sentences. By doing so, he was able to avoid excessive repetitions of the pronoun *I.* Notice, too, that he varied his sentence openings (most sentences do not begin with *I*) so that readers are not likely to find the repetitions tiresome.

### Providing transitions

Transitions are bridges between what has been read and what is about to be read. Transitions help readers move from sentence to sentence; they also alert readers to more global connections of ideas — those between paragraphs or even larger blocks of text.

**SENTENCE-LEVEL TRANSITIONS**  Certain words and phrases signal connections between (or within) sentences. Frequently used transitions are included in the following list.

**TO SHOW ADDITION**
and, also, besides, further, furthermore, in addition, moreover, next, too, first, second

**TO GIVE EXAMPLES**
for example, for instance, to illustrate, in fact, specifically

**TO COMPARE**
also, in the same manner, similarly, likewise

**TO CONTRAST**
but, however, on the other hand, in contrast, nevertheless, still, even though, on the contrary, yet, although

**TO SUMMARIZE OR CONCLUDE**
in other words, in short, in summary, in conclusion, to sum up, that is, therefore

**TO SHOW TIME**
after, as, before, next, during, later, finally, meanwhile, then, when, while, immediately

---

**WRITERS ON WRITING**

Write freely and as rapidly as possible and throw the whole thing on paper. Never correct or rewrite until the whole thing is down. Rewrite in process is usually found to be an excuse for not going on.  —John Steinbeck

The act of composition is a series of discoveries.
—E. L. Doctorow

**TO SHOW PLACE OR DIRECTION**
above, below, beyond, farther on, nearby, opposite, close, to the left

**TO INDICATE LOGICAL RELATIONSHIP**
if, so, therefore, consequently, thus, as a result, for this reason, since

Skilled writers use transitional expressions with care, making sure, for example, not to use *consequently* when an *also* would be more precise. They are also careful to select transitions with an appropriate tone, perhaps preferring *so* to *thus* in an informal piece, *in summary* to *in short* for a scholarly essay.

In the following paragraph, taken from an argument that dinosaurs had the "'right-sized' brains for reptiles of their body size," biologist Stephen Jay Gould uses transitions (italicized) with skill.

> I don't wish to deny that the flattened, minuscule head of the large bodied "Stegosaurus" houses little brain from our subjective, top-heavy perspective, *but* I do wish to assert that we should not expect more of the beast. *First of all,* large animals have relatively smaller brains than related, small animals. The correlation of brain size with body size among kindred animals (all reptiles, all mammals, *for example*) is remarkably regular. *As* we move from small to large animals, from mice to elephants or small lizards to Komodo dragons, brain size increases, *but* not so fast as body size. *In other words,* bodies grow faster than brains, *and* large animals have low ratios of brain weight to body weight. *In fact,* brains grow only about two-thirds as fast as bodies. *Since* we have no reason to believe that large animals are consistently stupider than their smaller relatives, we must conclude that large animals require relatively less brain to do as well as smaller animals. *If* we do not recognize this relationship, we are likely to underestimate the mental power of very large animals, dinosaurs *in particular.* [Italics added.]
> —Stephen Jay Gould, "Were Dinosaurs Dumb?"

**TIP:** Do not self-consciously plug in transition words while you are drafting sentences; overuse of these signals can seem heavy-handed. Usually, you will use transitions quite naturally, just where readers need them. If you (or your reviewers) discover places where readers cannot easily move from sentence to sentence in your rough draft, you can always add transition words as you revise.

| ON THE WEB | **dianahacker.com/bedhandbook**<br>▶ Electronic writing exercises<br>  ▶ E-ex 4–2 |
| --- | --- |

**PARAGRAPH-LEVEL TRANSITIONS**  Paragraph-level transitions usually link the *first* sentence of a new paragraph with the *first* sentence of the previous paragraph. In other words, the topic sentences signal global connections.

Look for opportunities to allude to the subject of a previous paragraph (as summed up in its topic sentence) in the topic sentence of the next one. In his essay "Little Green Lies," Jonathan H. Alder uses this strategy in the following topic sentences, which appear in a passage describing the benefits of plastic packaging.

> Consider aseptic packaging, the synthetic packaging for the "juice boxes" so many children bring to school with their lunch. [*Rest of paragraph omitted.*]

> What is true for juice boxes is also true for other forms of synthetic packaging. [*Rest of paragraph omitted.*]

**TRANSITIONS BETWEEN BLOCKS OF TEXT**  In long essays, you will need to alert readers to connections between blocks of text more than one paragraph long. You can do this by inserting transitional sentences or short paragraphs at key points in the essay. Here, for example, is a transitional paragraph from a student research paper. It announces that the first part of the paper has come to a close and the second part is about to begin.

> Although the great apes have demonstrated significant language skills, one central question remains: Can they be taught to use that uniquely human language tool we call grammar, to learn the difference, for instance, between "ape bite human" and "human bite ape"? In other words, can an ape create a sentence?

Another strategy to help readers move from one block of text to another is to insert headings in your essay. Headings, which usually sit above blocks of text, allow you to announce a new topic boldly, without the need for subtle transitions. (See 5b.)

## 4e If necessary, adjust paragraph length.

Most readers feel comfortable reading paragraphs that range between one hundred and two hundred words. Shorter paragraphs force too much starting and stopping, and longer ones strain readers' attention span. There are exceptions to this guideline, however. Paragraphs longer than two hundred words frequently appear in scholarly writing, where they suggest seriousness and depth. Paragraphs shorter than one hundred words occur in newspapers because of narrow columns; in informal essays to quicken the pace; and in business writing and Web sites, where readers routinely skim for main ideas.

In an essay, the first and last paragraphs will ordinarily be the introduction and the conclusion. These special-purpose paragraphs are likely to be shorter than the paragraphs in the body of the essay. Typically, the body paragraphs will follow the essay's outline: one paragraph per point in short essays, a group of paragraphs per point in longer ones. Some ideas require more development than others, however, so it is best to be flexible. If an idea stretches to a length unreasonable for a paragraph, you should divide the paragraph, even if you have presented comparable points in the essay in single paragraphs.

Paragraph breaks are not always made for strictly logical reasons. Writers use them for the following reasons as well.

**REASONS FOR BEGINNING A NEW PARAGRAPH**

- to mark off the introduction and conclusion
- to signal a shift to a new idea
- to indicate an important shift in time or place
- to emphasize a point (by placing it at the beginning or the end, not in the middle, of a paragraph)
- to highlight a contrast
- to signal a change of speakers (in dialogue)
- to provide readers with a needed pause
- to break up text that looks too dense

Beware of using too many short, choppy paragraphs, however. Readers want to see how your ideas connect, and they become irritated when you break their momentum by forcing them to pause every few sentences. Here are some reasons you might have for combining some of the paragraphs in a rough draft.

**REASONS FOR COMBINING PARAGRAPHS**

- to clarify the essay's organization
- to connect closely related ideas
- to bind together text that looks too choppy

# Part II

## Document Design

**ON THE WEB**

**dianahacker.com/bedhandbook/instructor**
▶ Exercise masters
▶ Quiz masters
▶ Transparency masters

101

The term *document* is broad enough to describe anything you might write in a college class, in the business world, and in everyday life. How you design a document (format it for the printed page or for a computer screen) will affect how readers respond to it.

Word processing software presents you with abundant design and formatting options. As you prepare a document, make sure that your design choices are based on careful consideration of your purpose and audience.

# 5

## Become familiar with the principles of document design.

Good document design promotes readability, but what *readability* means depends on your purpose and audience and perhaps on other elements of your writing situation, such as your subject, length restrictions, or any other specific requirements (see the checklist on pp. 3–4). All of your design choices — layout, word processing options such as margins and fonts, headings, and lists — should be made in light of your writing situation. Likewise, different types of visuals — tables, charts, and images — can support your writing if they are used appropriately.

### 5a Select appropriate format options.

Similar types of documents share similar design features. Taken together, these features — layout, margins and line spacing, alignment, fonts, and font styles — form an appearance that helps to guide readers.

**SCHOLARS ON DOCUMENT DESIGN**

Bridgeford, Tracy, Karla Saari Kitalong, and Dickie Selfe, eds. *Innovative Approaches to Teaching Technical Communication.* Logan: Utah State UP, 2004. This collection emphasizes the creativity that is present, though often not explicit, in the theories of teaching technical communication. The essays, which are organized into sections on pedagogical perspectives, practices, and partnerships, all focus on teaching approaches, activities, and projects that have the potential to reenergize the field. Part 2, "Pedagogical Practices," includes a number of essays with detailed descriptions of assignments and activities, such as how to use "stories," "role plays," and "technology autobiographies" to help students understand the literacies they possess and those they must learn to be successful communicators.

## Layout

Most readers have set ideas about how different kinds of documents should look. Advertisements, for example, have a distinctive appearance, as do newsletters, flyers, brochures, and menus. Instructors have expectations about how a college paper should look (see 6a). Employers too expect documents such as letters, résumés, and memos to be presented in standard ways (see 6b). And anyone who reads your writing online will appreciate a recognizable layout (see 7).

Unless you have a compelling reason to stray from convention, it's best to choose a document layout that conforms to your readers' expectations. If you're not sure what readers expect, look at examples of the kind of document you are producing.

**BROCHURE**

**SCHOLARS ON DOCUMENT DESIGN**

Brumberger, Eva R. "The Rhetoric of Typography: Effects on Reading Time, Reading Comprehension, and Perceptions of Ethos." *Technical Communication* 51 (2004): 13–24. Brumberger begins with a review of the literature on the rhetoric of typography. Then, building on two of her previous studies on the personalities readers attribute to particular typefaces, Brumberger offers empirical evidence that typefaces and texts interact in different ways during the reading process depending on the rhetorical context. She concludes that in visual rhetoric, as in verbal rhetoric, "context is crucial, and each communication situation requires a carefully considered and appropriately tailored solution" rather than a formulaic approach to design.

**NEWSLETTER**

**FLYER**

## Margins and line spacing

Margins help control the look of a page. For most academic and business documents, leave a margin of one to one and a half inches on all sides. These margins create a visual frame for the text and provide room for annotations, such as an instructor's comments or an editor's suggestions. Tight margins generally make a page crowded and difficult to read.

Most manuscripts in progress are double-spaced to allow room for editing. Final copy is often double-spaced as well, since single-spacing is less inviting to read. If you are unsure about margin and spacing requirements for your document, check with your instructor or consult documents similar to the one you are writing.

At times, the advantages of wide margins and double-spaced lines are offset by other considerations. For example, most business and technical documents are single-spaced, with double-spacing between paragraphs, to save paper and promote quick scanning. Similarly, newsletters and trifold

**SCHOLARS ON DOCUMENT DESIGN**

Williams, Robin. *The Non-Designer's Design Book: Design and Typographic Principles for the Visual Novice.* 2nd ed. Berkeley: Peachpit, 2004. In Part 1 of this basic introduction to design, Williams discusses the principles of proximity, alignment, repetition, and contrast. Part 2 explores typeface categories, characteristics, and contrasts.

**SINGLE-SPACED, UNFORMATTED**

**DOUBLE-SPACED, FORMATTED**

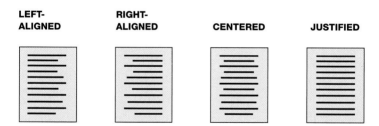

brochures tend to use narrow margins and single-spaced lines to conserve space (see the examples on pp. 104 and 103). Your document's purpose and context should determine appropriate margins and line spacing.

## *Alignment*

Word processing programs allow you to align text and visuals on a page in four ways:

**LEFT-ALIGNED**  **RIGHT-ALIGNED**  **CENTERED**  **JUSTIFIED**

## SCHOLARS ON DOCUMENT DESIGN

Markel, Mike. "What Students See: Word Processing and the Perception of Visual Design." *Computers and Composition* 15 (1998): 373–86. Markel's study of first-year students found that students who had more experience with word processing software were more aware of basic page design elements. Because visual rhetoric is becoming more important in all forms of written communication, Markel suggests that teachers use word processing packages specifically to help students explore and understand the use and importance of basic design elements.

*Left-aligned* text lines up at the left margin but has a ragged right margin. Because it is what most Americans are accustomed to reading, use left alignment for most of your documents, including essays, reports, letters, and e-mails.

*Right-aligned* text lines up at the right margin, with a ragged left margin. Avoid right-aligned text because it is generally difficult to read.

*Centered* text aligns words at the center of the page, with ragged left and right margins. Centered text can make titles and headings stand out from the rest of the text in a document (see 5b). Use it sparingly.

*Justified* text is aligned against both the left and the right margins, as on a typeset page like the one you are reading. Unfortunately, using the justify setting on a computer can add distracting gaps between words, making passages hard to read. Avoid using the justify setting.

### Fonts

If you have a choice, select a font that fits your writing situation in an easy-to-read size (usually 10 to 12 points). Although offbeat fonts may seem attractive, they slow readers down and can distract them from your ideas. For example, using comic sans, a font with a handwritten, childish feel, can make an essay seem too informal or unpolished, regardless of how well it's written. Similarly, an aggressive font like XBAND ROUGH might lead readers to perceive your message as hostile.

Fonts that are easy to read and appropriate for college and workplace documents include the following.

| | |
|---|---|
| Arial | Tahoma |
| Courier | Times New Roman |
| Garamond | Verdana |
| Georgia | |

**SCHOLARS ON DOCUMENT DESIGN**

Parker, Roger C. *Looking Good in Print.* 4th ed. Scottsdale: Corialis, 1998. Parker explains the basics of graphic design for desktop publishing and suggests many revision strategies for improving the design of a document. Examples of documents include newsletters, newspapers, advertisements, sales materials, and various business communications.

Fonts that are funky, decorative, or stylish, such as the following, should be used sparingly and only when they seem appropriate for your subject and audience.

*Amazone*

Bradley Hand

Curlz

elementric

Harting

TacoSalad

Zombie-Noize

## Font styles

Font styles—such as boldface, italics, underlining, and so on—can be useful for calling attention to parts of a document.

| | |
|---|---|
| **boldface** | color |
| *italics* | larger |
| <u>underlining</u> | smaller |
| CAPITAL LETTERS | SMALL CAPS |

On the whole, it is best to use restraint when selecting styles. Applying too many different styles within a document can result in busy-looking pages. The technique defeats its own purpose, since readers have trouble sorting out which elements are most important. The sample business card on page 108 shows an effective use of font styles to highlight important information.

**SCHOLARS ON DOCUMENT DESIGN**

Andrews, Deborah C., and Marilyn Dyrud, eds. *Document Design: Part I.* Special issue of *Business Communication Quarterly* 59.3 (1996): 65–76. The following brief articles provide practical suggestions for teaching document design: "Teaching the Rhetoric of Document Design" by Michael J. Hassett; "Teaching by Example: Suggestions for Assignment Design" by Marilyn A. Dyrud; "Teaching the Page as a Visual Unit" by Bill Hart-Davidson.

**EFFECTIVE USE OF FONT STYLES**

**JENNIFER HAYNES**
Graphic Designer & Art Consultant

197 Broad Street, Suite 412
New York, NY 10001
202/555-1212

www.jenniferhaynes.com
jen@jenniferhaynes.com

**TIP:** Never write a document in all capital or all lowercase letters. Readers experience frustration when they read more than a few consecutive words printed in all capital letters, and typing in all capitals is often perceived as shouting. Although some readers have become accustomed to instant messages and e-mails that omit capital letters entirely, their absence makes a message difficult to read and can reflect poorly on the writer.

## 5b Consider using headings.

You will have little need for headings in short essays, especially if you use paragraphing and clear topic sentences to guide readers. In more complex documents, however, such as research papers, grant proposals, business reports, and Web sites, headings can be a useful visual cue for readers.

Headings help readers see at a glance the organization of a document. If more than one level of heading is used, the headings also indicate the hierarchy of ideas—as they do throughout this book.

Headings serve a number of functions, depending on the needs of different readers. When readers are simply looking

**SCHOLARS ON DOCUMENT DESIGN**

Kramer, Robert, and Stephen A. Bernhardt. "Teaching Text Design." *Technical Communication Quarterly* 5 (1996): 35–60. Rpt. in *Teaching Technical Communication: Critical Issues for the Classroom.* Ed. James M. Dubinsky. Boston: Bedford, 2004. 240–64. Arguing that writers must learn to become text designers, the authors attempt to "not only *tell* but *show*" their guidelines for designing documents. Beginning with two pages typeset in a traditional academic format, the article progresses through a sequence of design changes involving the page grid; active white space; text structures such as margins, headings, and lists; and typographic design. The authors show how design decisions not only demonstrate the writer's skill with word processing tools but also help the writer bring organization and coherence to the text.

up information, headings will help them find it quickly. When readers are scanning, hoping to pick up the gist of things, headings will guide them. Even when readers are committed enough to read every word, headings can help. Efficient readers preview a document before they begin reading; when previewing and while reading, they are guided by any visual cues the writer provides.

**TIP:** Avoid using more headings or more levels of headings than you really need. Excessive use of headings can make a text choppy.

### Phrasing headings

Headings should be as brief and as informative as possible. Certain styles of headings—the most common being *-ing* phrases, noun phrases, questions, and imperative sentences—work better for some purposes, audiences, and subjects than others.

Whatever style you choose, use it consistently for headings on the same level. In other words, headings on the same level of organization should be written in parallel structure (see 9), as in the following examples. The first set of headings appeared in a report written for an environmental think tank, the second in a history textbook, and the third in a mutual fund brochure. The excerpt from a garden designer's newsletter on page 110 uses imperative sentences as headings.

**-ING HEADINGS**

Safeguarding the earth's atmosphere

Charting the path to sustainable energy

Conserving global forests

Triggering the technological revolution

**NOUN PHRASE HEADINGS**

The economics of slavery

The sociology of slavery

The psychological effects of slavery

**QUESTIONS AS HEADINGS**

How do I buy shares?

How do I redeem shares?

What is the history of the fund's performance?

What are the tax consequences of investing in the fund?

**IMPERATIVE SENTENCES AS HEADINGS**

*caring for Roses*

**Fertilize roses in the fall.**
In late fall, when the air becomes crisp and cool, and after the first nighttime frost or two, fertilize the soil in which your roses grow. If you fertilize before first frost, you run some risk of having the roses absorb the fertilizer and new growth appear in the fall. If you wait until after the frost begins, however, the fertilizer will remain dormant until the weather warms again in spring.

**Feed them again in the spring.**
The initial fertilizer applied in fall will help fuel the growth of your roses in the spring, but you will need to reapply fertilizer in the spring. You can purchase, at a local greenhouse, a soil analysis kit that will allow you to evaluate the residual fertilizer in the soil and to apply the appropriate amount of new fertilizer.

**Prune roses when dormant and after flowering.**
Clipping your roses when they are in bud can be traumatic to the entire plant. It is best to wait to prune your roses until after the rose plant or bush has gone dormant (after the first freeze) or after the plant has fully flowered.

*Placing and highlighting headings*

Headings on the same level of organization should be positioned and styled in a consistent way. For example, in the garden designer's newsletter on page 110, the headings are left-aligned and in boldface. If you have more than one level of heading, you might center your first-level headings and make them boldface; then you might make the second-level headings left-aligned and italicized, like this:

**First-level heading**

*Second-level heading*

A college paper with headings typically has only one level, and the headings are usually centered, as in the sample paper on pages 743–55. See the memo on page 134 for a business memo that includes headings.

You can use some of the font styles listed on page 107 to make your headings stand out. Important headings can be highlighted by using white space around them. Less important headings can be downplayed by using less white space or by running them into the text (as with the small all-capital headings on p. 127).

## 5c Consider using lists.

Lists are easy to read or scan when they are displayed rather than run into your text. You might choose to display the following kinds of lists:

- steps in a process
- materials needed for a project
- parts of an object
- advice or recommendations
- items to be discussed
- criteria for evaluation (as in checklists)

**ADDITIONAL RESOURCE ON DOCUMENT DESIGN**
Muth, Marcia F., and Karla Saari Kitalong. *Getting the Picture: A Brief Guide to Understanding and Creating Visual Texts.* Boston: Bedford, 2004. This slender booklet instructs students on the critical tools they need to manage communication in visual environments. The first part of the booklet focuses on strategies for document design, the second part on strategies for understanding visual representations. Both authors are well known for their work in visual and technical communication.

Lists should usually be introduced with an independent clause followed by a colon (see 35a and the preceding list). Periods are not used after items in a list unless the items are complete sentences.

Lists are most readable when they are presented in parallel grammatical form (see 9). In the list on page 111, for instance, the items are all noun phrases. As with headings, some kinds of lists might be more appropriate presented as *-ing* phrases, as imperative sentences, or as questions.

If the order of items is not important, use bullets (circles or squares) or dashes to draw readers' eyes to a list. The bulleted list at the bottom of this page, from the government Web site <http://www.ready.gov>, provides tips for stocking an emergency food supply.

If you are describing a sequence or a set of steps, number your list with arabic numerals (1, 2, 3) followed by periods. The numbered list on page 113 outlines the process of entering a science competition.

Although lists can be useful visual cues, don't overdo them. Too many of them will give a document a choppy, cluttered look. Avoid lists that are very long as well. Readers can hold only so many ideas in their short-term memory, so if a list grows too long, you should find some way of making it more concise or clustering similar items.

**BULLETED LIST**

**Food**

- Store *at least* a three-day supply of non-perishable food.
- Select foods that require no refrigeration, preparation, or cooking, and little or no water.
- Pack a manual can opener and eating utensils.
- Choose foods your family will eat.

**SCHOLARS ON VISUAL RHETORIC**

Hill, Charles A. "Reading the Visual in College Writing Classes." *Intertexts: Reading Pedagogy in College Writing Classrooms.* Ed. Marguerite Helmers. Mahwah: Erlbaum, 2003. 123–50. Hill analyzes some of the underlying assumptions about visual expression that have caused it to be neglected in the teaching of composition. He then discusses some of the challenges of developing a useful way to teach visual rhetoric. Hill argues that even without an established pedagogy, instructors should encourage students to analyze and experiment with page design and visual texts. He concludes that for such a pedagogy to be established, universities need to create multidepartmental rhetoric programs.

**NUMBERED LIST**

5th Annual

**SCIENCE RESEARCH COMPETITION**

Entry Instructions

Entries are due by **Friday, October 28**. All entries must be complete; each entry must include the student's signature and the signature of the student's research adviser. For more details, see the SRC Web site (www.usscienceresearchcompetition.org).

Steps for entering your project in the SRC:
1. Print out and complete an SRC entry form.
2. Print out and sign the SRC "Terms and Conditions" statement.
3. Have your adviser sign both forms.
4. Submit your completed entry form and your signed "Terms and Conditions" statement to the address on the Web site.
5. Register on the SRC Web site.

## 5d Consider adding visuals.

Visuals can convey information concisely and powerfully. Charts, graphs, and tables, for example, can simplify complex numerical information. Images — including clip art, photographs, and diagrams — often express an idea more vividly than words can. Images can amplify a message in both print and electronic media. With access to the Internet, digital photography, and word processing or desktop publishing software, you can download or create your own visuals to enhance an essay, a report, or a Web site.

Use visuals to supplement your writing, not to supplant it. Always consider how a visual supports your purpose and how your audience might respond to it. As you draft and revise a document, choose carefully the visuals that best support your main point, and avoid overloading your text with too many.

**SCHOLARS ON VISUAL RHETORIC**

Hocks, Mary E. "Understanding Visual Rhetoric in Digital Writing Environments." *College Composition and Communication* 54 (2003): 629–56. Hocks defines some of the features of digital rhetoric and explores the ways in which they function in examples of scholarly hypertexts. She builds on this analysis to explore the value of assignments that ask students to design multimodal projects.

## Using charts, graphs, and tables

Flowcharts can help readers follow the steps or parts of a process (for an example, see p. 239). Organizational charts are useful for explaining relationships, as in the following example.

**ORGANIZATIONAL CHART**

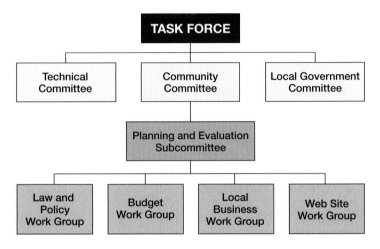

Pie charts are a visual way of organizing data to compare the parts of a whole. The parts are displayed as segments of the pie, represented as percentages of the whole (which is always 100 percent). The pie chart on the next page organizes visitors to the George Mason University writing center into seven groups, each group displayed as a percentage of the total visitors.

Line graphs, which display numerical data, show trends, a rising or falling of the data over a period of time. You might, for instance, illustrate trends in sales, in population growth, or, as in the graph on the next page, in number of hits on a Web site in the same months one year apart.

**SCHOLARS ON VISUAL RHETORIC**

George, Diana. "From Analysis to Design: Visual Communication in the Teaching of Writing." *College Composition and Communication* 54 (2002): 11–39. George offers a brief history of the role of the visual in English composition, drawing on examples from several popular composition textbooks. She argues that by casting the visual as subordinate to the written word, composition teachers limit the kinds of assignments that are possible in the classroom. She suggests through examples of her own students' visual arguments that students "have a much richer imagination for what we might accomplish with the visual than our journals have yet to address."

**PIE CHART**

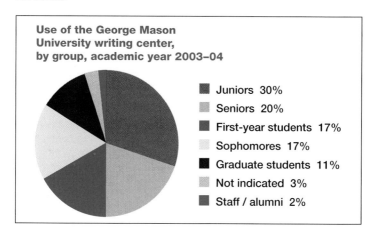

**LINE GRAPH**

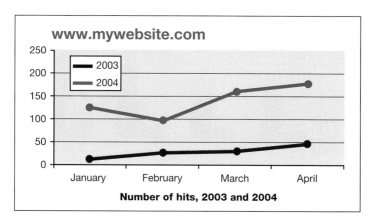

Bar graphs can be used for the same purpose as line graphs. (The bar graph on page 116 displays the same data as in the line graph on this page.)

Though sometimes less visually interesting than charts and graphs, tables can organize complicated numerical data into a digestible format. The table at the right compares information on the cost of AIDS medications in different countries. Its creator added visual interest by printing the numerical data over a relevant photograph.

**TABLE**

### Prices of daily doses of AIDS drugs
(US$)

| Drug | Brazil | Uganda | Côte d'Ivoire | US |
|------|--------|--------|---------------|-----|
| 3TC (Lamuvidine) | 1.66 | 3.28 | 2.95 | 8.70 |
| ddC (Zalcitabine) | 0.24 | 4.17 | 3.75 | 8.80 |
| Didanosine | 2.04 | 5.26 | 3.48 | 7.25 |
| Efavirenz | 6.96 | n/a | 6.41 | 13.13 |
| Indinavir | 10.32 | 12.79 | 9.07 | 14.93 |
| Nelfinavir | 4.14 | 4.45 | 4.39 | 6.47 |
| Nevirapine | 5.04 | n/a | n/a | 8.48 |
| Saquinavir | 6.24 | 7.37 | 5.52 | 6.50 |
| Stavudine | 0.56 | 6.19 | 4.10 | 9.07 |
| ZDV/3TC | 1.44 | 7.34 | n/a | 18.78 |
| Zidovudine | 1.08 | 4.34 | 2.43 | 10.12 |

Source: UNAIDS, 2000

**BAR GRAPH**

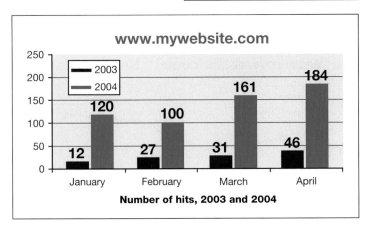

*Using clip art, photographs, and diagrams*

A picture may be worth a thousand words, but if you choose to use one in a document, be sure that you have carefully considered your reasons for including it. When used judiciously, clip art and photographs can enhance your message; but inserted randomly or for decoration, they can distract or annoy your readers.

Clip art—uncopyrighted symbols, icons, and drawings—can be useful when a visual representation is important but specific details are irrelevant; for instance, clip art can effectively illustrate abstract ideas on a flyer (see the example on p. 104) or in a business presentation. Although it is easy to obtain, clip art is almost never appropriate for academic writing.

Photographs are best used to represent details discussed in a text. In a paper about antidrug campaigns, for example, including an image from the 1987 "This is your brain on drugs" public service announcement below might help you explain how the Partnership for a Drug-Free America used a vivid image to demonstrate the physiological effects of narcotics.

**CLIP ART**

**PHOTOGRAPH**

**DIAGRAM**

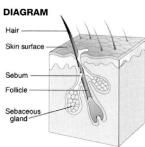

Diagrams are useful in scientific and technical writing. The diagram at the right, for example, explains the structure of human skin more vividly than words could do.

*Placing and labeling visuals*

A visual may be placed in the text of a document near a discussion to which it relates, or it can be put in an appendix, labeled, and referred to in the text.

    Placing visuals in the text of a document can be tricky. Usually you will want the visual to appear close to the sentences that relate to it, but page breaks won't always allow this placement. At times you may need to insert the visual at a later point and tell readers where it can be found; sometimes, with the help of software, you can make the text flow around the visual. No matter where you place a visual, refer to it in your text. Don't expect visuals to speak for themselves.

**VISUAL WITH A FIGURE NUMBER**

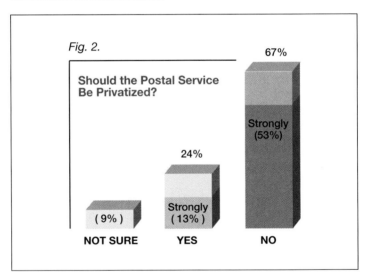

**VISUAL WITH A TITLE**

Fig. 4. Location of Postal Service Mail Processing Facilities

Most of the visuals you include in a document will require some sort of label. Labels are typically placed above or under the visual. Labels are brief but descriptive. Most commonly, a visual is labeled with the word "Figure" or the abbreviation "Fig.," followed by a number. Sometimes a title might be included to explain how the visual relates to the text.

*Using visuals responsibly*

Most word processing and spreadsheet software will allow you to produce your own visuals. If you created a chart, a table, or a graph using information from your research, you must cite the source of the information even though the visual is your own. The table on page 120 credits the source of its data.

**VISUAL WITH A SOURCE CREDITED**

*Fig. 6.*

## Postal Service Size, by Number of Employees

| | Among the Global 500 | | | Among US Companies | |
|---|---|---|---|---|---|
| Rank | Company | Employees as of 2002 | Rank | Company | Employees as of 2002 |
| 1 | Wal-Mart Stores | 1,300,000 | 1 | Wal-Mart Stores | 1,300,000 |
| 2 | China National Petroleum | 1,146,194 | **2** | **US Postal Service** | **854,376** |
| 3 | Sinopec | 917,000 | 3 | McDonald's | 413,000 |
| **4** | **US Postal Service** | **854,376** | 4 | United Parcel Service | 360,000 |
| 5 | Agricultural Bank of China | 490,999 | 5 | Ford Motor | 350,321 |
| 6 | Siemens | 426,000 | 6 | General Motors | 350,000 |
| 7 | McDonald's | 413,000 | 7 | Intl. Business Machines | 315,889 |
| 8 | Ind. & Comm. Bank of China | 405,000 | 8 | General Electric | 315,000 |
| 9 | Carrefour | 396,662 | 9 | Target | 306,000 |
| 10 | Compass Group | 392,352 | 10 | Home Depot | 300,000 |
| 11 | China Telecomm | 365,778 | 11 | Kroger | 289,000 |
| 12 | DaimlerChrysler | 365,571 | 12 | Sears Roebuck | 289,000 |
| 13 | United Parcel Service | 360,000 | 13 | Tyco International | 267,000 |
| 14 | Ford Motor | 350,321 | 14 | Citigroup | 252,500 |
| 15 | General Motors | 350,000 | 15 | Verizon Communications | 229,497 |

Source: Number of employees rankings by *Fortune Magazine,* April 14, 2003.

If you download a photograph from the Web or scan an image from a magazine or book, you must credit the person or organization that created it, just as you would cite any other source you use in a college paper (see 52). If your document is written for a public audience (outside the classroom), you may also need to request written permission to use any visual you borrow.

**ON THE WEB**   **dianahacker.com/bedhandbook**
▶ Additional resources
  ▶ Links Library
    ▶ Document design

# 6

## Use standard academic and business formats.

**6a** Use the manuscript format required by your academic discipline.

If your instructor provides guidelines for formatting an essay, report, or research paper, you should of course follow them. Otherwise, use the manuscript format that is recommended for your academic discipline.

In most English and humanities classes, you will be asked to use the MLA (Modern Language Association) format. The essay on pages 122–23 illustrates this format. For more detailed advice about MLA manuscript guidelines, along with a sample MLA research paper, see 58. If you have been asked to use APA (American Psychological Association) guidelines, see 60. *Chicago Manual of Style* guidelines appear in 61.

**6b** Use standard business formats.

This section provides guidelines for preparing business letters, résumés, and memos. For a more detailed discussion of these and other business documents—proposals, reports, executive summaries, and so on—consult a business writing textbook or look at current examples at the organization for which you are writing.

### Business letters

In writing a business letter, be direct, clear, and courteous, but do not hesitate to be firm if necessary. State your purpose or request at the beginning of the letter and include

---

**SCHOLARS ON BUSINESS WRITING**

Cyphert, Dale. "The Problem of PowerPoint: Visual Aid or Visual Rhetoric?" *Business Communication Quarterly* 67.1 (2004): 80–84. Cyphert suggests that rather than teaching students about presentation software as a means to create visual aids, instructors should adopt a more rhetorical approach that encourages students to see presentations as a form of communication requiring the same eloquence as other workplace communications.

**MLA ESSAY FORMAT**

↕ 1″
Weitzel 1

Double-spacing used throughout.

Tom Weitzel

Dr. Fry

English 101

18 April 2005

Title is centered.

Who Goes to the Races?

½″ indent

A favorite pastime of mine is observing people, and my favorite place to observe is at the horse races. After many encounters with the racing crowd, I have discovered that there are four distinct groups at the track: the once-a-year bunch, the professionals, the clubhouse set, and the unemployed.

The largest group at the track consists of those who show up once a year. They know little about horses or betting and rely strictly on racetrack gimmick sheets and newspaper predictions for selecting possible winners. If that strategy doesn't work, they use intuition, lucky numbers, favorite colors, or appealing names. They bet larger amounts as the day goes along, gambling on every race, including long-shot bets on exactas and daily doubles. The vast majority go home broke and frustrated.

1″

1″

More subtle and quiet are the professionals. They follow the horses from track to track and live in campers and motor homes. Many are married couples, some are retired, and all are easily spotted with their lunch sacks, water jugs, and binoculars. Since most know one another, they section themselves off in a particular area of the stadium. All rely on the racing form and on personal knowledge of each horse, jockey, and track in

1″

Marginal annotations indicate MLA-style formatting.

**MLA ESSAY FORMAT (*continued*)**

1"

½"
Weitzel 2

making the proper bet. They bet only on the smart races, rarely on the favorites. Never do they bet on exactas or daily doubles. More often than not they either break even or go home winners.

Isolated from the others is the clubhouse set. Found either at the cocktail lounge or in the restaurant, usually involved in business transactions, these racing fans rarely see a race in person; instead they do their betting via the waiter. It's difficult to tell whether they go home sad, happy, or in between. They keep their emotions to themselves.

1"

The most interesting members of the racetrack population are the unemployed. They will be found not in the clubhouse, but right down at the rail next to the finish line. Here one can discover the real emotion of the racetrack--the screaming, the cursing, and the pushing. The unemployed are not in it for the sport. Betting is not a game for them, but a battle for survival. If they lose, they must borrow enough money to carry them until the next check comes in, and then, of course, they head right back to the track. This particular group arrives at the track beaten and leaves beaten.

I have probably lost more money than I have won at the track, but observing these four interesting groups of people makes it all worthwhile.

only relevant information in the body. By being as direct and concise as possible, you show that you value your reader's time.

For the format of the letter, stick to established business conventions. A sample business letter appears below. This

**BUSINESS LETTER IN FULL BLOCK STYLE**

## SCHOLARS ON BUSINESS WRITING

Campbell, Nittaya. "Getting Rid of the Yawn Factor: Using a Portfolio Assignment to Motivate Students in a Professional Writing Class." *Business Communication Quarterly* 65.3 (2002): 42–54. Campbell describes using a portfolio assignment to teach writing and to motivate students by contributing to their job searches. The assignment asks students to take on the role of writing consultant or communication officer for a real or fictitious company and then produce a set of related business documents based on that company's needs. Campbell argues that a portfolio approach motivates students more than separate writing assignments because it brings personal relevance, continuity, and coherence to their writing tasks. Students finish the class with a professional product to show to prospective employers.

letter is typed in what is known as *full block* style. Paragraphs are not indented and are typed single-spaced, with double-spacing between them. This style is usually preferred when the letter is typed on letterhead stationery, as in the example.

Slightly less formal is the *modified block* style (see the example on p. 126). The return address and date at the top and the close and signature at the bottom are indented to the middle of the page. As with full block style, the inside address, the salutation, and the body paragraphs are all left-justified, and the paragraphs are not indented. If you choose to indent your paragraphs, you are using *semiblock* style, which is considered the least formal.

When writing to a woman, use the abbreviation *Ms.* in the salutation unless you know that the woman prefers another form of address. If you are not writing to a particular person, you can use a generic salutation (*Dear Sir or Madam:*), the position title (*Dear Personnel Manager:*), or the name of the company itself (*Dear Solar Technology:*).

Below the signature, aligned at the left, you may include the abbreviation *Enc.* to indicate that something is enclosed with the letter or the abbreviation *cc* followed by a colon and the name of someone who is receiving a copy of the letter.

### Résumés and cover letters

An effective résumé gives relevant information in a clear and concise form. The cover letter gives a prospective employer a reason to look at your résumé. The trick is to present yourself in a favorable light without including unnecessary details and wasting your reader's time.

You may be asked to produce a traditional résumé, a scannable résumé, or a Web résumé. Brief guidelines for each type of résumé appear in this section, along with examples.

**SCHOLARS ON BUSINESS WRITING**

Ellis, Shelley M. "Up Close and Personal: A Real-World Audience Awareness Assignment." *Teaching English in the Two-Year College* 26 (1999): 286–90. Ellis describes an assignment meant to help writers recognize that different audiences have different needs. Using a modified "real-world" case study, Ellis provides students with complaint letters and asks them to consider options for responding as employees who received the letters. The article explains the process of introducing the assignment and includes samples of student responses and analyses of the assignment.

**BUSINESS LETTER IN MODIFIED BLOCK STYLE (COVER LETTER)**

Return address ——————— 121 Knox Road, #6
College Park, MD 20740
March 4, 2004

Linda Hennessee, Managing Editor
*World Discovery* ——————— Inside address
1650 K Street, NW
Washington, DC 20036

Dear Ms. Hennessee: ——————— Salutation

Body

Please accept my application for the summer editorial internship listed with the Career Development Center at the University of Maryland. Currently I am a junior at the University of Maryland, with a double major in English and Latin American studies.

Over the past three years I have gained considerable experience in newspaper and magazine journalism, as you will see on my enclosed résumé. I am familiar with the basic procedures of editing and photographic development, but my primary interests lie in feature writing and landscape photography. My professional goal is to work as a photojournalist with an international focus, preferably for a major magazine. I cannot imagine a better introduction to that career than a summer at *World Discovery.*

I am available for an interview almost any time and can be reached at 301-555-2651. My e-mail address is jrichardson@jrichardson.localhost. My portfolio is online at http://jrichardson.localhost/jrportfolio.htm.

I look forward to hearing from you.

Close ——————— Sincerely,

Signature ——————— *Jeffrey Richardson*
Jeffrey Richardson

Enc.

**COVER LETTERS**   When you send out your résumé, always include a cover letter that introduces yourself, states the position you seek, and tells where you learned about it (see p. 126). The letter should also highlight past experiences that qualify you for the position and emphasize what you can do for the employer (not what the job will do for you). End the letter with a suggestion for a meeting, and tell your prospective employer when you will be available.

**TRADITIONAL RÉSUMÉS**   Traditional résumés are produced on paper, and they are screened by people, not by computers. Because screeners may face stacks of applications, they often spend very little time looking at each résumé. Therefore, you will need to make your résumé as reader-friendly as possible. Here are a few guidelines:

- Limit your résumé to one page if possible, two pages at the most. (If your résumé is longer than a page, repeat your name at the top of the second page.)
- Organize your information into clear categories — Education, Experience, and so on.
- Present the information in each category in reverse chronological order to highlight your most recent accomplishments.
- Use bulleted lists or some other simple, clear visual device to organize information.
- Use strong, active verbs to emphasize your accomplishments. (Use present-tense verbs, such as *manage*, for current activities and past-tense verbs, such as *managed*, for past activities.)

A sample traditional résumé appears on page 128.

**SCANNABLE RÉSUMÉS**   Scannable résumés might be submitted on paper, by e-mail, or through an online employment service. The prospective employer scans and searches

**SCHOLARS ON RÉSUMÉ WRITING**

Davis, Barbara, and Clive Muir. "Résumé Writing and the Minority Student." *Business Communication Quarterly* 66.3 (2003): 39–51. Davis and Muir explore the temptation of minority students to de-emphasize or conceal their ethnic background on their résumés, and they show how doing so can be counterproductive when students end up de-emphasizing their achievements or qualifications. The authors suggest ways for instructors to guide students through the challenges of creating an accurate résumé while acknowledging the reality of hiring discrimination.

**TRADITIONAL RÉSUMÉ**

---

### Jeffrey Richardson

121 Knox Road, #6
College Park, MD 20740
301–555–2651
jrichardson@jrichardson.localhost

---

**OBJECTIVE**        To obtain an editorial internship with a magazine

**EDUCATION**
Fall 2001–        University of Maryland
present          • BA expected in June 2005
                 • Double major: English and Latin American studies
                 • GPA: 3.7 (on a 4-point scale)

**EXPERIENCE**
Fall 2003–        Associate editor, *Latino Voice*, newsletter of Latino Club
present          • Assign and edit feature articles
                 • Coordinate community outreach

Fall 2002–        Photo editor, *The Diamondback*, college paper
present          • Shoot and print photographs
                 • Select and lay out photographs and other visuals

Summer 2003       Intern, *The Globe,* Fairfax, Virginia
                 • Wrote stories about local issues and personalities
                 • Interviewed political candidates
                 • Edited and proofread copy
                 • Coedited "The Landscapes of Northern Virginia:
                   A Photoessay"

Summers          Tutor, Fairfax County ESL Program
2002, 2003       • Tutored Latino students in English as a Second Language
                 • Trained new tutors

**ACTIVITIES**      Photographers' Workshop, Latino Club

**PORTFOLIO**      Available at http://jrichardson.localhost/jrportfolio.htm

**REFERENCES**     Available upon request

**SCANNABLE RÉSUMÉ**

Jeffrey Richardson
121 Knox Road, #6
College Park, MD 20740
301-555-2651
jrichardson@jrichardson.localhost

OBJECTIVE
To obtain an editorial internship with a magazine

EDUCATION
Fall 2001-present
University of Maryland
BA expected in June 2005
Double major: English and Latin American studies
GPA: 3.7 (on a 4-point scale)

EXPERIENCE
Fall 2003-present
Associate editor, _Latino Voice_, newsletter of Latino Club
Assign and edit feature articles
Coordinate community outreach

Fall 2002-present
Photo editor, _The Diamondback_, college paper
Shoot and print photographs
Select and lay out photographs and other visuals

Summer 2003
Intern, _The Globe_, Fairfax, Virginia
Wrote stories about local issues and personalities
Interviewed political candidates
Edited and proofread copy
Coedited "The Landscapes of Northern Virginia: A Photoessay"

Summers 2002, 2003
Tutor, Fairfax County ESL Program
Tutored Latino students in English as a Second Language
Trained new tutors

ACTIVITIES
Photographers  Workshop, Latino Club

PORTFOLIO
http://jrichardson.localhost/jrportfolio.htm

REFERENCES
Available upon request

KEYWORDS
editorial internship, magazine, photo editor, layout, photographs,
writer, interviewer, editor, proofreader, tutor, trainer, Spanish, Latino

the résumé electronically; a database matches keywords in the employer's job description with keywords in the résumé. A human screener then looks through the résumés filtered out by the database matching.

A scannable résumé must be very simply formatted so that the scanner can accurately pick up its content. In general, follow these guidelines when preparing a scannable résumé:

- Include a Keywords section that lists words likely to be searched by a scanner. (You will often find these words embedded in the employer's job description.) Use nouns such as *manager,* not verbs such as *manage* or *managed.*
- Use standard résumé headings (for example, Education, Experience, References).
- Avoid special characters, graphics, or font styles such as boldface or italics.
- Avoid formatting features such as tabs, indents, columns, or tables.
- Use plain, white, 8½″ × 11″ paper and a high-quality printer. Watermarks or ridges on the paper may interrupt scanning; poorly printed or smudged type may also confuse the scanner. Avoid folding or stapling the document.

A sample scannable résumé appears on page 129.

**WEB RÉSUMÉS**   A Web résumé is an easy way to provide prospective employers with recent information about your employment goals and accomplishments. It also allows you to present details about yourself without overwhelming your readers.

Web résumés can vary considerably in scope and depth. Most guidelines for traditional résumés apply to Web résumés, but if you choose to post your résumé to your personal Web site, consider the following guidelines.

- Keep the opening screen of your Web site (home page) simple and concise. Provide links to take readers farther down the page or to other sections of your site.
- Include identifying information—at least your name and a link to your e-mail address—on every page of your Web site. Also include a link to your home page on every internal page.
- Consider including links on your home page and on your résumé to your portfolio, which presents electronic examples of your work.

**HOME PAGE**

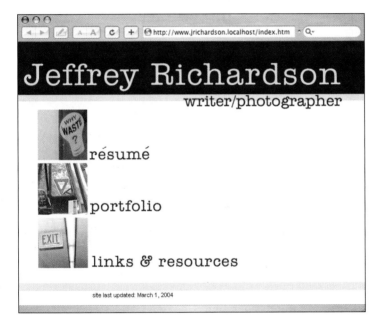

**WEB RÉSUMÉ**

# Jeffrey Richardson
### résumé

| | |
|---|---|
| PRINT VERSION | http://jrichardson.localhost/resume.pdf |
| CONTACT | 121 Knox Road, #6<br>College Park, MD 20740<br>301-555-2651<br>jrichardson@jrichardson.localhost |
| OBJECTIVE | To obtain an editorial internship with a magazine |
| EDUCATION | Fall 2001-present, University of Maryland<br>• BA expected in June 2005<br>• Double major: English and Latin American studies<br>• GPA: 3.7 (on a 4-point scale) |
| EXPERIENCE | Fall 2003-present, associate editor, *Latino Voice*,<br>newsletter of Latino Club<br>• Assign and edit feature articles<br>• Coordinate community outreach<br><br>Fall 2002-present, photo editor, *The Diamondback*, a college paper<br>• Shoot and print photographs<br>• Select and lay out photographs and other visuals<br><br>Summer 2003, intern, *The Globe*, Fairfax, Virginia<br>• Wrote stories about local issues and personalities<br>• Interviewed political candidates<br>• Edited and proofread copy<br>• Coedited "The Landscapes of Northern Virginia: A Photoessay"<br><br>Summers 2002, 2003, tutor, Fairfax County ESL Program<br>• Tutored Latino students in English as a Second Language<br>• Trained new tutors |
| ACTIVITIES | Photographers' Workshop, Latino Club |
| PORTFOLIO | http://jrichardson.localhost/jrportfolio.htm |
| REFERENCES | Available upon request |

*last updated: March 1, 2004*

- Consider including both an HTML version and a downloadable/printable version (a PDF file, for instance) of your résumé.
- Include identifying information—your name, address, and phone number and a link to your e-mail address—at the top of your résumé page.
- Keep your online résumé current; note the date that you last updated it.

For a sample home page, see page 131. A sample Web résumé is at the top of this page. (See also 7b.)

**ON THE WEB**

**dianahacker.com/bedhandbook**
▶ Additional resources
  ▶ Links Library
    ▶ Document design

### Memos

Business memos are typically used within a company or organization. Usually brief and to the point, a memo reports information, makes a request, or recommends an action. The format of a memo, which varies from company to company, is designed for easy distribution, quick reading, and efficient filing.

Most memos display the date, the name of the recipient, the name of the sender, and the subject on separate lines at the top. Many companies have preprinted forms for memos, and some word processing programs have memo templates. Memos also may be distributed via e-mail to be read on-screen.

The subject line of a memo, on paper or in e-mail, should describe the topic as clearly and concisely as possible, and the introductory paragraph should get right to the point. In addition, the body of the memo should be well organized and easy to skim. To promote skimming, use headings where possible and display any items that deserve special attention by setting them off from the text — in a list, for example, or in boldface. (In e-mail, it is best to avoid special features such as boldface or nonstandard characters.) A sample memo with headings and a displayed list appears on page 134; a sample e-mail memo appears on page 135.

**TIP:** For e-mail memos, use plain-text formatting — asterisks instead of bullets, for example, and capital letters instead of underlining — to ensure that your message is readable by all recipients. (See also 7a.)

**BUSINESS MEMO**

## Commonwealth Press

MEMORANDUM

February 28, 2005

To:        Production, promotion, and editorial assistants

cc:        Stephen Chapman

From:      Helen Brown

Subject:   New computers for staff

We will receive the new personal computers next week for the assistants in production, promotion, and editorial. In preparation, I would like you to take part in a training program and to rearrange your work areas to accommodate the new equipment.

Training Program

A computer consultant will teach in-house workshops on how to use our spreadsheet program. If you have already tried the program, be prepared to discuss any problems you have encountered.

Workshops for our three departments will be held in the training room at the following times:

- Production: Monday, March 7, 10:00 a.m. to 2:00 p.m.
- Promotion: Wednesday, March 9, 10:00 a.m. to 2:00 p.m.
- Editorial: Friday, March 11, 10:00 a.m. to 2:00 p.m.

Lunch will be provided in the cafeteria. If you cannot attend, please let me know by March 4.

Allocation and Setup

To give everyone access to a computer, we will set up the new computers as follows: two in the assistants' workspace in production; two in the area outside the conference room for the promotion assistants; and two in the library for the editorial assistants.

Assistants in all three departments should see me before the end of the week to discuss preparation of the spaces for the new equipment.

**SCHOLARS ON E-MAIL**

Borsheim, Carlin. "Email Partnerships: Conversations That Changed the Way My Students Read." *English Journal* 93.5 (2004): 60–65. Borsheim describes a classroom project that paired ninth-grade students with undergraduate students for e-mail discussions of a work of literature. The high school students became more engaged, critical readers of the work—more successful at forming, articulating, and defending their interpretations.

**E-MAIL MEMO**

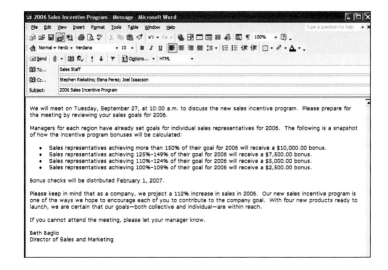

# 7

---

## Create effective electronic documents.

---

**7a** Follow the conventions of electronic communication.

E-mail is fast replacing regular mail in the business world and in most people's personal lives. E-mail is also being used in the academic world for communication between professors and their students and among students in a class.

As with all writing, you should keep your purpose and audience in mind as you draft e-mail. But you should also be aware of the special conventions of this fast-paced form of communication.

**SCHOLARS ON E-MAIL**

Munter, Mary, Priscilla S. Rogers, and Jone Rymer. "Business E-mail: Guidelines for Users." *Business Communication Quarterly* 66.1 (2003): 26–40. The authors offer practical guidelines for composing e-mail with readers' needs in mind and for processing and managing e-mail. They discuss e-mail as a hybrid form of oral and written communication and examine its advantages and disadvantages.

*Keeping messages reader-friendly*

Especially in business and academic settings, you will want to show readers that you value their time. Your message may be just one of many that your readers have to wade through. Although you may need to spend more of your own time to create reader-friendly e-mail, readers will appreciate your extra care. For a sample e-mail message, see page 137.

Here are some strategies you can use to make your messages reader-friendly:

- Fill in the subject line with a meaningful, concise subject to help readers sort through messages and set priorities.
- Put the most important part of your message at the beginning so it will be seen on the first screen.
- For long, detailed messages, consider providing a summary at the beginning.
- Write concisely and keep paragraphs fairly short, especially if your audience is likely to read your message on-screen. (In e-mails meant to be printed out, paragraphs can be somewhat longer.)
- Avoid writing in all capital letters or all lowercase letters, a practice that is easy on the writer but hard on the reader.
- Keep in mind that a recipient's e-mail system may not accept attachments. When possible, include the text of an attachment in the body of the e-mail.
- Proofread for typos and obvious errors that are likely to slow down or annoy readers.

*Using an appropriate tone*

The language and level of formality you might use for one audience and medium may not be appropriate for another. Because e-mail is fast-paced and often informal, it is easy to strike an unprofessional tone if you are not careful. For example, if you omit the greeting line in an e-mail (such as *Hello,*

---

**WRITING CENTER DIRECTORS ON TECHNOLOGY**

"Because of the ease of word processing, students generally have a greater facility with writing—a tendency to write more and to prepare neater, more orderly written assignments. However, these benefits can become problems if students resist necessary revision. Frequent use of e-mail and instant messaging has also brought greater informality to student writing. When it represents simple carelessness, informality is a problem; but, if it means students get closer to finding their own voices as writers, it can be a very good thing."

—Joyce Hinnefeld, assistant professor of English, Moravian College

**E-MAIL MESSAGE**

Date:     Fri, 18 Nov 2005 22:31:45-0500
To:       rdayson@newhoriz.org
cc:       Helen Tran <htran@umb.edu>
From:     Danielle Portes <dportes@umb.edu>
Subject:  Telephone interview on Dec. 5

Dear Ms. Dayson:

Thank you for taking the time to speak with me last week about my research project. As we agreed, I am sending some questions for you to consider before our phone interview on December 5 at 2:00 p.m.

QUESTIONS ABOUT GUESTS

What symptoms of stress do guests--both women and their children--show when they first arrive at the shelter?

What problems, in addition to the abuse itself, must guests deal with (for example, lack of support from family or friends, financial concerns, problems in dealing with police and courts)?

Can you think of any past or current guests who might agree to an interview?

QUESTIONS ABOUT STAFFERS

What are the main stresses that staffers face? How do they cope with these stresses?

What do staffers see as the rewards as well as the drawbacks of the job?

On average, how many guests does each staffer work with every day? Every week?

Can you think of any past or current staffers who might agree to an interview?

I appreciate your considering these questions and look forward to our interview.

Sincerely,
Danielle Portes
Phone: 617-555-7777

**SCHOLARS ON TEACHING WITH TECHNOLOGY**

Selber, Stuart A. *Multiliteracies for a Digital Age.* Carbondale: Southern Illinois UP, 2004. This book offers comprehensive instructional guidelines for those who are teaching with technology or want to understand online literacies. While his larger goal is to lay out a framework for conceptualizing computer literacy, Selber includes in each chapter heuristics, assignments, and suggestions for syllabi so that teachers can put the concepts and his three approaches to literacy—functional, critical, and rhetorical—into practice.

*Gloria* or *Dear Professor Hart*), some readers may feel they are being treated unprofessionally. The same is true if you omit a brief closing (such as *Bye for now* or *Sincerely,* followed by your name). In the business and academic worlds, many readers are put off by flippant language or inappropriate jokes. Even when a joke may be appropriate, you can't be sure that all readers will understand it in the spirit you intend.

Because part of your tone will be set by the way you identify yourself, select your screen name carefully. Although clever names like *PrettyPrincess809* and *KingofSin* are fine for informal communications, they are not appropriate for an academic or workplace environment. Choose a simple name that readers will readily recognize as yours, such as your first initial and last name.

Some e-mailers and instant messagers use emoticons (combinations of symbols that look like faces turned sideways) and abbreviations (such as *TIA* for "thanks in advance" and *LOL* for "laughing out loud"). Though these shortcuts are appropriate among friends, they may confuse or even annoy readers in business and academic settings.

Obviously you should resist the temptation to "flame" — to spout off angry or insulting messages. One problem with e-mail and instant messages is that it's so easy to press the send button — and then regret what you've done. When you have written a heated message, print it out and take a cool look at it. Chances are you will decide to tone it down before sending it, or you may choose not to send it at all.

### Respecting privacy rights

E-mail programs make it easy to forward a message you received to another person or even to a large group of people. You should do this only when you are absolutely certain that the original sender would approve. It is always best to check first. If you decide to forward the message, send a copy to the sender as well so the sender can see exactly who has received it.

**SCHOLARS ON TEACHING WITH TECHNOLOGY**

Selber, Stuart A. "Reimagining the Functional Side of Computer Literacy." *College Composition and Communication* 55 (2004): 470–503. Selber describes what a computer-literate student should be able to do and what a teacher needs to know to educate that student. Rather than make a list of requirements for functional literacy, Selber focuses on performance parameters and related strategies that teachers and programs can use as a guide: educational goals, social conventions, specialized discourses, management activities, and technological impasses.

## 7b Create effective Web sites.

Web sites in the academic and business worlds are usually aimed at audiences looking for ideas and information, not entertainment. You may have noticed that the most effective informational Web sites give you quick and easy access to what you're looking for.

A Web site generally consists of a home page and any number of internal pages linked to the home page. Deciding what to put on the home page and how to organize internal pages can present a challenge. When making such crucial decisions, consider your readers' needs and expectations.

Why are they visiting your site?

What are they expecting to find?

What is their level of interest?

Do they plan to read on-screen or to print out a hard copy?

The design of your site—from its home page to its structure to its page layout and even to its writing style—will depend on the answers to such questions.

### The home page

A home page consists of text and visuals on an opening screen and any other material that can be reached by scrolling. The home page should introduce visitors to the site, give them an overview of its contents, and show them that you have their needs in mind. It should also include navigational links, words or images that, at the click of the mouse, will send them to other locations or pages within the site. Usually these links are clustered—often along the top of the screen or on one side—leaving room in the center for your name or the sponsor, the title, a relevant visual or two, and an indication of the purpose of the site. The example on page 140 illustrates a well-designed opening screen; the site is for

**SCHOLARS ON TEACHING WITH TECHNOLOGY**

Cambridge, Barbara L., ed. *Electronic Portfolios: Emerging Practices in Student, Faculty, and Institutional Learning.* Washington: Amer. Assn. of Higher Educ., 2001. This book describes the potential of electronic portfolios for continuous reflection and updating as well as the inclusion of interactive hyperlinks to engage readers in revision. The first section of the book consists of articles on helping students develop, construct, and manage e-portfolios in the humanities, nursing, and management. Kathleen Yancey opens the section with an introduction to digitized portfolios and concludes it with observations on general patterns in e-portfolio pedagogy and recommendations for the future.

**HOME PAGE**

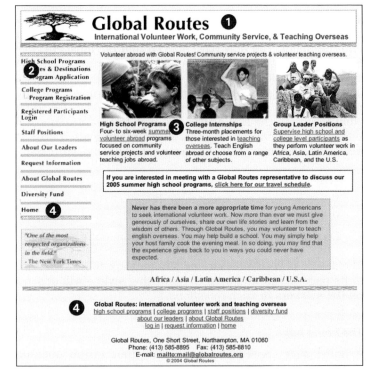

❶ The sponsoring organization and purpose of the site are clearly defined at the top of the page.

❷ By highlighting the main audiences for the site, this home page allows readers to skip information that is not relevant to them.

❸ Appealing visual images emphasize the site's three main audiences.

❹ Links to internal pages are consistently placed on the left side of the screen and in the footer to help readers navigate the site.

### SCHOLARS ON TEACHING WITH TECHNOLOGY

Moran, Charles. "Technology and the Teaching of Writing." *A Guide to Composition Pedagogies.* Ed. Gary Tate, Amy Rupiper, and Kurt Schick. New York: Oxford UP, 2001. 203–23. Moran provides a thorough overview of technology and writing instruction and focuses on how instructors can use technology to enhance their teaching.

Anson, Chris. "Distant Voices: Teaching and Writing in a Culture of Technology." *College English* 61 (1999): 261–80. Anson explores the ways that technology is changing writing instruction, the nature of the classroom itself, and face-to-face interactions between students and instructors.

an organization that sponsors community service and teaching internships for students.

Keep the copy on your home page relatively short—an easily digested chunk of information—with links to equally brief internal pages. You can assume that visitors will skip some links but follow others.

### Structure and navigation

Web sites consisting of more than one page usually have hierarchical structures: General pages link to more specific pages, which in turn may link to even more specific pages. At the bottom of this page is an example of a Web site structure for a doctors' practice.

How shallow or how deep should your hierarchy be? In other words, how many levels make sense? The answer depends on the complexity of your material and your audience's needs, but two cautions are in order. A structure is too shallow if your readers must deal with long "laundry

**SAMPLE WEB SITE STRUCTURE**

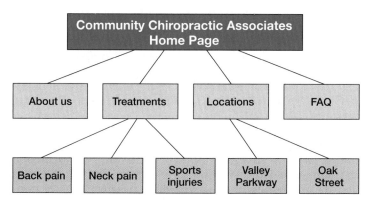

**SCHOLARS ON TEACHING WITH TECHNOLOGY**

Hawisher, Gail E., and Cynthia L. Selfe, eds. *Passions, Pedagogies and Twenty-first Century Technologies.* Logan: Utah State UP; Urbana: NCTE, 1999. A winner of the 2000 Computers and Composition Award, this collection is divided into four parts, of which Parts 1 and 2 speak most directly to teaching practices, technological change, and conceptions of literacy in an electronic world.

lists" of choices (unless the choices can be arranged alphabetically or chronologically). A structure is too deep if readers are needlessly forced to drill down through several layers to reach what they need.

Visitors to your site will navigate it in different ways, depending on their interests. They will choose some links and ignore others, landing on internal pages in an order that you can't predict. Indeed, some visitors may arrive at one of your internal pages without having gone through your home page. Because of this unpredictability, provide as much context as possible for each internal page.

- Put key information on each internal page: a title, a link to the home page, and perhaps a list of links to other pages. Such lists are really an outline of the site, a useful aid for readers.
- Provide a brief overview that puts the internal page in context; make sure the content of the page can be understood on its own.
- Repeat design elements so that visitors will feel at home. Place navigational aids consistently and use consistent background colors, fonts, visual motifs, and formatting.

In addition to providing links within your site, you may want to link to other sites. When you decide that an external link enhances the message of your site, provide enough information about it so that visitors will understand why it is worthwhile and what to expect if they follow it. Avoid external links that are distracting or unnecessary. Remember that an external link sends visitors into unfamiliar territory, where they may get lost or, worse, decide not to return.

Because a link to another site is an implicit endorsement of that site, you should evaluate potential sites before linking to them. As a courtesy to readers, periodically visit the sites you have linked to; remove any links to sites that are nonfunctioning, and update links to sites that have moved.

### SCHOLARS ON ELECTRONIC DOCUMENTS

Gregory, Judy. "Writing for the Web versus Writing for Print: Are They Really So Different?" *Technical Communication* 51 (2004): 276–85. Writing for technical communicators, Gregory compares writing guidelines for the Web with those for print. She argues that a genre-based approach to developing guidelines would allow writers to focus on audience and purpose rather than on medium.

Wysocki, Anne. "The Multiple Media of Texts: How Onscreen and Paper Texts Incorporate Words, Images, and Other Media." *What Writing Does and How It Does It: An Introduction to Analyzing Texts and Textual Practices.* Ed. Charles Bazerman and Paul Pryor. Mahwah: Erlbaum, 2004. 123–64. Wysocki explores the vi-

## Page layout and writing style

Don't expect Web site visitors to read in the traditional way: word by word. Most will scan your site, looking for information of interest and ignoring the rest. To keep the attention of a Web audience, make your page layout and writing style as user-friendly as possible.

**EXCEPTION:** If content on your site is scholarly work meant to be printed out, you can assume that your audience is motivated to read, not just to scan. Even so, visitors will appreciate a reader-friendly page layout and writing style.

**PAGE LAYOUT** To promote easy scanning, break up your text with headings and displayed lists and, when appropriate, display information with graphics such as clip art, photos, and charts. (See 5b–5d.)

Some common design practices make a site needlessly hard to read. If you are an experienced Web user, you no doubt could have written the following advice:

- Don't stretch lines of text across the full width of the screen. The reader's eye gets lost as it swoops from line to line.
- Limit the page width so that readers don't need to scroll sideways.
- Avoid ALL CAPS or *all italic* text. It slows readers down.
- Avoid busy backgrounds that make the print illegible.
- Steer clear of animations. They are distracting.

Graphics and other media, such as films and sound clips, can add interest to a Web site, but use them thoughtfully—to support your message. For example, one student enhanced his Web site about Ralph Ellison's *The Invisible Man* by using a dissolving graphic, a visual representation of the novel's theme of invisibility. Too often, however, Web graphics and sound clips are used just for show. Most visitors to a site are annoyed by art that takes a long time to download and then turns out to be a distraction.

**SCHOLARS ON ELECTRONIC DOCUMENTS (continued)**

sual elements—such as typography, photographs, and charts—that can appear in paper texts as well as additional elements such as animation and sound that can appear in on-screen texts. She suggests an approach for analyzing multimedia texts and demonstrates it through analysis of three types of text.

Lawrence, Sally F. "Analysis Report Project: Audience, E-writing, and Information Design." *Business Communication Quarterly* 66.1 (2003): 47–60. Lawrence describes a five-week assignment designed to teach business students to analyze Web site effectiveness and develop their own writing skills for electronic media. Appendices include practical handouts.

In addition, consider how your text and visuals will look when printed out. To prevent some printers from chopping off words and images at the right margin, limit the width of your pages. If you've used a lot of graphics, provide a printable version of your text without the graphics; graphics can be slow to print and may be irrelevant for your readers' purposes.

**WRITING STYLE**   Visitors to your Web site value their time. As a rule, they want concise, factual information that is easy to understand. For example, they expect to learn the key idea of a paragraph in its first sentence; if it's not there, they might move on. They also prefer sentences that waste no words; a verbose style will send them elsewhere.

Web users are also sensitive to tone. There is so much promotional hype on the Web that many users have a keen ear for it. The tone of your site will depend on your purpose and audience, of course, but in general aim for an objective—not a promotional—tone.

**PROMOTIONAL**
Our site tells you everything you want to know about hang gliding! Check out our awesome video clips and click on links to the coolest sites on the Web.

**OBJECTIVE**
Whether you're a beginning hang glider or a seasoned flier, this site will show you how and where to glide. Visit our <u>Video Window</u> for an animated bird's-eye view.

An objective tone enhances your credibility and makes it likely that readers will trust you enough to stay with you.

| ON THE WEB | **dianahacker.com/bedhandbook** |
|---|---|
| | ▶ Additional resources |
| | ▶ Links Library |
| | ▶ Document design |

---

**SCHOLARS ON ELECTRONIC DOCUMENTS**

Wysocki, Anne, et al. *Writing New Media: Theory and Applications for Expanding the Teaching of Composition.* Logan: Utah State UP, 2004. Each chapter provides a rationale for teaching new media, a theoretical framework, and a series of useful activities and assignments, all of which are described in step-by-step detail. Some chapters also include suggestions for assessing students' work. The chapter "Students Who Teach Us," for example, includes four pages of prompts to help students write their "technological literacy autobiographies" as well as detailed instructions for three activities that ask students to analyze and create new media texts.

# Part III

# Clear
# Sentences

**ON THE WEB**

**dianahacker.com/bedhandbook/instructor**
▶ Exercise masters
▶ Quiz masters
▶ Transparency masters

# 8

## Prefer active verbs.

As a rule, choose an active verb and pair it with a subject that names the person or thing doing the action. Active verbs express meaning more emphatically and vigorously than their weaker counterparts—forms of the verb *be* or verbs in the passive voice.

| | |
|---|---|
| **PASSIVE** | The pumps *were destroyed* by a surge of power. |
| ***BE* VERB** | A surge of power *was* responsible for the destruction of the pumps. |
| **ACTIVE** | A surge of power *destroyed* the pumps. |

Verbs in the passive voice lack strength because their subjects receive the action instead of doing it. Forms of the verb *be* (*be, am, is, are, was, were, being, been*) lack vigor because they convey no action.

Although passive verbs and the forms of *be* have legitimate uses, if an active verb can carry your meaning, use it. Even among active verbs, some are more active—and therefore more vigorous and colorful—than others. Carefully selected verbs can energize a piece of writing.

▶ The goalie crouched low, ~~reached~~ *swept* out his stick, and ~~sent~~ *hooked* the

rebound away from the mouth of the net.

 Some speakers of English as a second language avoid the passive voice even when it is appropriate. For advice on transforming an active sentence to the passive, see 63c.

---

**SCHOLARS ON ACTIVE AND PASSIVE VOICE**

Robinson, William S. "Sentence Focus, Cohesion, and the Active and Passive Voices." *Teaching English in the Two-Year College* 27 (2000): 440–45. Robinson argues that even skilled writers don't consciously choose the active or the passive voice. Instead, they select subjects that name what they are talking about, a technique that produces a cohesive text. Both the active and passive voices can play a role in cohesion, as topic-comment theorists have pointed out. Robinson suggests that when students produce texts lacking cohesion, they may be mimicking academic style. The cure, says Robinson, is to advise students to focus on what they're talking about and make their subjects personal rather than abstract.

GRAMMAR CHECKERS are fairly good at flagging passive verbs, such as *is used.* However, because passive verbs are sometimes appropriate, you—not the computer program—must decide whether to change a verb from passive to active. Grammar checkers tend to suggest revisions only when the passive sentence contains a *by* phrase (*Carbon dating is used by scientists to determine an object's approximate age*). Occasionally they make inappropriate suggestions for revision (*Scientists to determine an object's approximate age use carbon dating*). Only you can determine the most sensible word order for your sentence.

**8a** Use the active voice unless you have a good reason for choosing the passive.

In the active voice, the subject does the action; in the passive voice, the subject receives the action (see also 63c). Although both voices are grammatically correct, the active voice is usually more effective because it is simpler and more direct.

**ACTIVE**     Hernando *caught* the fly ball.

**PASSIVE**     The fly ball *was caught* by Hernando.

In passive sentences, the actor (in this case Hernando) frequently disappears from the sentence: *The fly ball was caught.*

In most cases, you will want to emphasize the actor, so you should use the active voice. To replace a passive verb with an active alternative, make the actor the subject of the sentence.

> A bolt of lightning struck the transformer.
> ▶ ~~The transformer was struck by a bolt of lightning.~~
>   ^

The active verb (*struck*) makes the point more forcefully than the passive verb (*was struck*).

**SCHOLARS ON ACTIVE AND PASSIVE VOICE**

Frischkorn, Craig. "Style in Advanced Composition: Active Students and Passive Voice." *Teaching English in the Two-Year College* 26 (1999): 415–18. Partly because most grammar checkers blindly condemn the passive voice, Frischkorn thinks we need to teach students to make their own decisions. By using newspaper articles from financial, sports, and even self-help columns, Frischkorn engages his students in rich and lively discussions of the rhetoric of the passive voice.

▶ The settlers stripped the land of timber before realizing  
~~The land was stripped of timber before the settlers realized~~  
the consequences of their actions.

The revision emphasizes the actors (*settlers*) by naming them in the subject.

▶ We did not take down the  
~~The~~ holiday decorations ~~were not taken down~~ until  
Valentine's Day.

Often the actor does not appear in a passive-voice sentence. To turn such a sentence into the active voice, the writer must decide on an appropriate subject, in this case *We*.

### Appropriate uses of the passive

The passive voice is appropriate if you wish to emphasize the receiver of the action or to minimize the importance of the actor.

**APPROPRIATE PASSIVE**  Many native Hawaiians *are forced* to leave their beautiful beaches to make room for hotels and condominiums.

**APPROPRIATE PASSIVE**  As the time for harvest approaches, the tobacco plants *are sprayed* with a chemical to retard the growth of suckers.

The writer of the first sentence wished to emphasize the receiver of the action, *Hawaiians*. The writer of the second sentence wished to focus on the tobacco plants, not on the people spraying them.

In much scientific writing, the passive voice properly emphasizes the experiment or process being described, not the researcher.

**SCHOLARS ON ACTIVE AND PASSIVE VOICE**

Scriven, Karen. "Actively Teaching the Passive Voice." *Teaching English in the Two-Year College* 16 (1989): 89–93. Scriven argues that passives "are not the mark of flawed writing . . . but are instead frequent and effective stylistic variants." She suggests that instead of condemning the passive voice, we should show students when it might be effective. For example, at times the passive voice allows the writer to put old information in the subject position, thus preserving what has been called the "given-new contract." Readers usually expect to hear old information in the subject and new information later.

| APPROPRIATE PASSIVE | The solution *was heated* to the boiling point, and then it *was reduced* in volume by 50 percent. |

---

| ON THE WEB | **dianahacker.com/bedhandbook**<br>▶ Language Debates<br>  ▶ Passive voice |

---

**8b** Replace *be* verbs that result in dull or wordy sentences.

Not every *be* verb needs replacing. The forms of *be* (*be, am, is, are, was, were, being, been*) work well when you want to link a subject to a noun that clearly renames it or to an adjective that describes it: *History is a bucket of ashes. Scoundrels are always sociable.* And when used as helping verbs before present participles (*is flying, are disappearing*) to express ongoing action, *be* verbs are fine: *Derrick was plowing the field when his wife went into labor.* (See 29a.)

If using a *be* verb makes a sentence needlessly dull and wordy, however, consider replacing it. Often a phrase following the verb will contain a word (such as *violation*) that suggests a more vigorous, active alternative (*violate*).

▶ Burying nuclear waste in Antarctica would ~~be in violation of~~ *violate* an international treaty.

    *Violate* is less wordy and more vigorous than *be in violation of.*

▶ When Rosa Parks ~~was resistant to~~ *resisted* giving up her seat on the bus, she became a civil rights hero.

    *Resisted* is stronger than *was resistant to.*

---

**WRITERS ON WRITING**

God is a verb, not a noun.     —Buckminster Fuller

Nouns and verbs are almost pure metal; adjectives are cheaper ore.     —Marie Gilchrist

Use strong, active verbs. . . . Don't let the agents wiggle out of your sentences; expose the villains lurking behind foul deeds and commend the folks who have made the world a better place.     —Sally James

Avoid the passive voice whenever possible. University term papers bleed with the passive voice. It seems to be the accepted style of academia. Dump it.     —Rita Mae Brown

> **GRAMMAR CHECKERS** usually do not flag wordiness caused
> by *be* verbs: *is in violation of.* Only you can find ways to
> strengthen your sentences by using vigorous, active verbs
> in place of *be.*

**8c** As a rule, choose a subject that names the person or
thing doing the action.

In weak, unemphatic prose, both the actor and the action
may be buried in sentence elements other than the subject
and the verb. In the following sentence, for example, the actor
and the action both appear in prepositional phrases, word
groups that do not receive much attention from readers.

> **WEAK**     Exposure to Dr. Martinez's excellent teaching had
>              the effect of inspiring me to major in education.
>
> **EMPHATIC**  Dr. Martinez's excellent teaching inspired me to
>              major in education.

Consider the subjects and verbs of the two versions — *Exposure had* versus *teaching inspired.* Clearly the latter expresses the writer's point more emphatically.

> ~~The use of cocaine~~ by pregnant women can ~~be a major~~
>      *Cocaine used*                                   *cause*
> ~~contributor to~~ severe brain damage in infants.

In the original version, the subject and verb — *use can be* — express the point blandly. *Cocaine can cause* alerts readers to the
dangers of cocaine more emphatically than *use can be.*

**EXERCISE 8–1**     Revise any weak, unemphatic sentences by replacing *be* verbs or passive verbs with active alternatives and, if

---

**EXERCISE 8–1     Possible revisions:**
a. The Prussians defeated the Saxons in 1745.
b. Ahmed, the producer, manages the entire operation.
c. The video game programmers awkwardly paddled the sea kayaks.
d. Emphatic and active; no change
e. Protesters were shouting on the courthouse steps.

necessary, by naming in the subject the person or thing doing the action. Some sentences are emphatic; do not change them. Revisions of lettered sentences appear in the back of the book. Example:

> *The ranger doused the campfire before giving us*
> ~~The campfire was doused by the ranger before we were given~~
> ^
> a ticket for unauthorized use of a campsite.

a. The Prussians were victorious over the Saxons in 1745.
b. The entire operation is managed by Ahmed, the producer.
c. The sea kayaks were awkwardly paddled by the video game programmers.
d. At the crack of rocket and mortar blasts, I jumped from the top bunk and landed on my buddy below, who was crawling on the floor looking for his boots.
e. There were shouting protesters on the courthouse steps.

1. A strange sound was made in the willow tree by the monkey that had escaped from the zoo.
2. Her letter was in acknowledgment of the student's participation in the literacy program.
3. The bomb bay doors rumbled open, and freezing air whipped through the plane.
4. The work of Paul Oakenfold and Sandra Collins was influential in my choice of music for my audition.
5. The only responsibility I was given by my parents was putting gas in the brand-new Mitsubishi they bought me my senior year.

---

**ON THE WEB**

**dianahacker.com/bedhandbook**
▶ Electronic grammar exercises
   ▶ E-ex 8–1 to 8–3

---

**EXERCISE 8–1 (continued)**

1. The monkey that had escaped from the zoo made a strange sound in the willow tree.
2. Her letter acknowledged the student's participation in the literacy program.
3. Emphatic and active; no change
4. The work of Paul Oakenfold and Sandra Collins influenced my choice of music for my audition.
5. The only responsibility my parents gave me was putting gas in the brand-new Mitsubishi they bought me my senior year.

# 9

## Balance parallel ideas.

If two or more ideas are parallel, they are easier to grasp when expressed in parallel grammatical form. Single words should be balanced with single words, phrases with phrases, clauses with clauses.

> A kiss can be a comma, a question mark, or an exclamation point.
> — Mistinguett

> This novel is not to be tossed lightly aside, but to be hurled with great force.
> — Dorothy Parker

> In matters of principle, stand like a rock; in matters of taste, swim with the current.
> — Thomas Jefferson

Writers often use parallelism to create emphasis. (See p. 198.)

 **GRAMMAR CHECKERS** only occasionally flag faulty parallelism. Because the programs cannot assess whether ideas are parallel in grammatical form, they fail to catch the faulty parallelism in sentences such as this: *In my high school, boys were either jocks, preppies, or studied constantly.*

**WRITERS ON WRITING**

All the fun's in how you say a thing. — Robert Frost

Nothing is more satisfying than to write a good sentence.
— Barbara Tuchman

There is the first satisfaction of arranging it on a bit of paper; after many, many false tries, false moves, finally you have the sentence you recognize as the one you are looking for.
— Vladimir Nabokov

## 9a Balance parallel ideas in a series.

Readers expect items in a series to appear in parallel grammatical form. When one or more of the items violate readers' expectations, a sentence will be needlessly awkward.

▶ Abused children commonly exhibit one or more of the

   following symptoms: withdrawal, rebelliousness, restlessness,
   *depression.*
   and ~~they are depressed.~~
       ^

   The revision presents all of the items as nouns.

▶ Hooked on romance novels, I learned that there is nothing
                                                  *having*
   more important than being rich, looking good, and ~~to have~~ a
                                                      ^
   good time.

   The revision uses *-ing* forms for all items in the series.

▶ After assuring us that he was sober, Sam drove down the
                                         *went through*
   middle of the road, ran one red light, and ~~two stop signs.~~
                                             ^
   The revision adds a verb to make the three items parallel:
   *drove..., ran..., went through....*

**NOTE:** In headings and lists, aim for as much parallelism as the content allows. (See 5b and 5c.)

## 9b Balance parallel ideas presented as pairs.

When pairing ideas, underscore their connection by expressing them in similar grammatical form. Paired ideas are usually connected in one of these ways:

**SCHOLARS ON PARALLELISM**

Corbett, Edward P. J. *Classical Rhetoric for the Modern Student.*
4th ed. New York: Oxford UP, 1998. 354–58. In his discussion of
the "composition of the sentence," Corbett identifies parallelism
as a significant feature of effective style.

- with a coordinating conjunction such as *and, but,* or *or*
- with a pair of correlative conjunctions such as *either...or* or *not only...but also*
- with a word introducing a comparison, usually *than* or *as*

### Parallel ideas linked with coordinating conjunctions

Coordinating conjunctions (*and, but, or, nor, for, so,* and *yet*) link ideas of equal importance. When those ideas are closely parallel in content, they should be expressed in parallel grammatical form.

▶ At Lincoln High School, vandalism can result in suspension
  *expulsion*
  or even ~~being expelled~~ from school.
            ^

The revision balances the nouns *suspension* and *expulsion.*

▶ Many states are reducing property taxes for home owners
  *extending*
  and ~~extend~~ financial aid in the form of tax credits to renters.
      ^

The revision balances the verb *reducing* with the verb *extending.*

### Parallel ideas linked with correlative conjunctions

Correlative conjunctions come in pairs: *either...or, neither ...nor, not only...but also, both...and, whether...or.* Make sure that the grammatical structure following the second half of the pair is the same as that following the first half.

▶ Thomas Edison was not only a prolific inventor but also ~~was~~

  a successful entrepreneur.

The words *a prolific inventor* follow *not only,* so *a successful entrepreneur* should follow *but also.* Repeating *was* creates an unbalanced effect.

---

**SCHOLARS ON PARALLELISM**

Graves, Richard L. "Symmetrical Form and the Rhetoric of the Sentence." *Rhetoric and Composition: A Sourcebook for Teachers and Writers.* Ed. Richard L. Graves. Upper Montclair: Boynton, 1984. 119–27. Graves asserts that symmetrical form is essential for effective writing and offers convincing empirical evidence. He argues that we should teach parallelism as more than a mechanical skill and should also recognize it as a "major means through which we perceive and structure reality."

▶ The harried clerk advised me either to change my flight or *to* take the train.

> *To change my flight,* which follows *either,* should be balanced with *to take the train,* which follows *or.*

### Comparisons linked with than or as

In comparisons linked with *than* or *as,* the elements being compared should be expressed in parallel grammatical structure.

▶ It is easier to speak in abstractions than ~~grounding~~ *to ground* one's thoughts in reality.

▶ Mother could not persuade me that giving is as much a joy as *receiving.* ~~to receive.~~

> *To speak in abstractions* is balanced with *to ground one's thoughts in reality. Giving* is balanced with *receiving.*

**NOTE:** Comparisons should also be logical and complete. (See 10c.)

## 9c Repeat function words to clarify parallels.

Function words such as prepositions (*by, to*) and subordinating conjunctions (*that, because*) signal the grammatical nature of the word groups to follow. Although they can sometimes be omitted, include them whenever they signal parallel structures that might otherwise be missed by readers.

**SCHOLARS ON PARALLELISM**

Walker, Robert L. "The Common Writer: A Case for Parallel Structure." *College Composition and Communication* 21 (1970): 373–79. Written when Francis Christensen's "cumulative sentence" instruction was in vogue, this essay argues that parallelism is essential to good prose. Walker calls for explicit instruction in parallelism, and he offers evidence that professional writers rely more on parallel structures than on the "free modifiers" that Christensen values so highly.

▶ Many smokers try switching to a brand they find distasteful
  *to*
or a low tar and nicotine cigarette.
  ^

In the original sentence, the prepositional phrase was too complex for easy reading. The repetition of the preposition *to* prevents readers from losing their way.

▶ The ophthalmologist told me that Julie was extremely far-
         *that*
sighted but corrective lenses would help considerably.
          ^

A second subordinating conjunction helps readers sort out the two parallel ideas: *that* Julie was extremely farsighted and *that* corrective lenses would help.

**NOTE:** If it is possible to streamline the sentence, repetition of the function word may not be necessary.

▶ The board reported that its investments had done well

in the first quarter but ~~that they~~ had since dropped in

value.

Instead of linking two subordinate clauses beginning with *that,* the revision streamlines the sentence by balancing the two parts of a compound predicate — *had done well in the first quarter* and *had since dropped in value.*

**EXERCISE 9–1**  Edit the following sentences to correct faulty parallelism. Revisions of lettered sentences appear in the back of the book. Example:

Rowena began her work day by pouring a cup of coffee and
*checking*
~~checked~~ her e-mail.
  ^

a. Police dogs are used for finding lost children, tracking criminals, and the detection of bombs and illegal drugs.

b. Hannah told her rock climbing partner that she bought a new harness and of her desire to climb Otter Cliffs.

c. It is more difficult to sustain an exercise program than starting one.

d. During basic training, I was not only told what to do but also what to think.

e. Jan wanted to drive to the wine country or at least Sausalito.

1. Activities on Wednesday afternoons include fishing trips, dance lessons, and computers.

2. Arriving at Lake Powell in a thunderstorm, the campers found it safer to remain in their cars than setting up their tents.

3. The streets were not only too steep but also were too narrow for anything other than pedestrian traffic.

4. More digital artists in the show are from the South Shore than the North Shore.

5. To load her toolbox, Anika the Clown gathered hats of different sizes, put in two tubes of face paint, arranged a bundle of extra-long straws, added a bag of colored balloons, and a battery-powered hair dryer.

| ON THE WEB | **dianahacker.com/bedhandbook** |
|---|---|
| | ▶ Electronic grammar exercises |
| | ▶ E-ex 9–1 to 9–3 |

**EXERCISE 9–2**  Describe the parallel structure in the following passages and discuss how the use of parallelism contributes to the effectiveness of each. (Also see 14f, which discusses parallel structure.)

1. All respect we may have had for politicians, preachers, lawyers, governors, presidents, senators, congressmen was utterly destroyed as we watched them temporizing and compromising over right and wrong, over legality and illegality, over constitutionality and unconstitutionality.  — Eldridge Cleaver

**EXERCISE 9–1 (continued)**

1. Activities on Wednesday afternoons include fishing trips, dance lessons, and computer classes.

2. Arriving at Lake Powell in a thunderstorm, the campers found it safer to remain in their cars than to set up their tents.

3. The streets were not only too steep but also too narrow for anything other than pedestrian traffic.

4. More digital artists in the show are from the South Shore than from the North Shore.

5. To load her toolbox, Anika the Clown gathered hats of different sizes, put in two tubes of face paint, arranged a bundle of extra-long straws, added a bag of colored balloons, and tossed in a battery-powered hair dryer.

2.  I learned three important things in college—to use a library, to memorize quickly and visually, to drop asleep at any time given a horizontal surface and fifteen minutes. What I could not learn was to think creatively on schedule.     —Agnes de Mille

3.  Knowing others is wisdom; knowing the self is enlightenment. Mastering others requires force; mastering the self needs strength.     —Lao-tzu

4.  How can I love the man who raped my mother, killed my father, enslaved my ancestors, dropped atomic bombs on Japan, killed off the Indians, and keeps me cooped up in the slums?
    —Malcolm X

5.  It is better to write a bad first draft than to write no first draft at all.     —Will Shetterly

# 10

## Add needed words.

Do not omit words necessary for grammatical or logical completeness. Readers need to see at a glance how the parts of a sentence are connected.

**ESL** Languages sometimes differ in the need for certain words. In particular, be alert for missing verbs, articles, subjects, or expletives. See 29e, 30, and 31a.

**GRAMMAR CHECKERS** do not flag the vast majority of missing words. They can, however, catch some missing verbs (see 27e). Although they can flag some missing articles (*a*, *an*, and *the*), they often suggest that an article is missing when in fact it is not. (See also 30.)

**WRITERS ON WRITING**

Easy writing makes hard reading.     —Ernest Hemingway

Most people won't realize that writing is a craft. You have to take your apprenticeship in it like anything else.
    —Katherine Anne Porter

I have rewritten—often several times—every word I have ever published. My pencils outlast their erasers.     —Vladimir Nabokov

**10a** Add words needed to complete compound structures.

In compound structures, words are often omitted for economy: *Tom is a man who means what he says and [who] says what he means.* Such omissions are perfectly acceptable as long as the omitted words are common to both parts of the compound structure.

If the shorter version defies grammar or idiom because an omitted word is not common to both parts of the compound structure, the word must be put back in.

▶ Some of the regulars are acquaintances whom we see at work
  *who*
  or live in our community.
  ^

  The word *who* must be included because *whom . . . live in our community* is not grammatically correct.

  *accepted*
▶ Mayor Davis never has and never will accept a bribe.
  ^

  *Has . . . accept* is not grammatically correct.

  *in*
▶ Many South Pacific islanders still believe and live by ancient
  ^
  laws.

  *Believe . . . by* is not idiomatic in English. (For a list of common idioms, see 18d.)

**NOTE:** Even when the omitted word is common to both parts of the compound structure, occasionally it must be inserted to avoid ambiguity. The sentence *My favorite English professor and mentor influenced my choice of a career* suggests that the professor and the mentor are the same person. If they are not, *my* must be repeated: *My favorite English professor and my mentor influenced my choice of a career.*

**WRITERS ON WRITING**

What is written without effort in general is read without pleasure.
— Samuel Johnson

I don't write easily or rapidly. My first draft usually has only a few elements worth keeping. I have to find what those are and build from them and throw out what doesn't work, or what simply is not alive.
— Susan Sontag

**10b** Add the word *that* if there is any danger of misreading without it.

If there is no danger of misreading, the word *that* may be omitted when it introduces a subordinate clause. *The value of a principle is the number of things [that] it will explain.* Occasionally, however, a sentence might be misread without *that*.

▶ Looking out the family room window, Sarah saw her favorite *that* tree, which she had climbed so often as a child, was gone.

Sarah didn't see the tree; she saw that the tree was gone. The word *that* tells readers to expect a clause, not just *tree*, as the direct object of *saw*.

**10c** Add words needed to make comparisons logical and complete.

Comparisons should be made between items that are alike. To compare unlike items is illogical and distracting.

▶ The forests of North America are much more extensive than *those of* Europe.

Forests must be compared with forests.

▶ ~~The graduation rate of our~~ *Our* student athletes ~~is higher~~ *graduate at a higher rate* than the rest of the student population.

A rate cannot be logically compared to a population. The writer could revise the sentence by inserting *that of* after *than*, but the preceding revision is more concise.

▶ Some say that Ella Fitzgerald's renditions of Cole Porter's
   *singer's.*
songs are better than any other ~~singer.~~
                               ^

Ella Fitzgerald's renditions cannot be logically compared with a
singer. The revision uses the possessive form *singer's*, with the
word *renditions* being implied.

Sometimes the word *other* must be inserted to make a
comparison logical.

                     *other*
▶ Jupiter is larger than any planet in our solar system.
                         ^

Jupiter cannot be larger than itself.

Sometimes the word *as* must be inserted to make a
comparison grammatically complete.

                        *as*
▶ The city of Lowell is as old, if not older than, the neighboring
                             ^

city of Lawrence.

The construction *as old* is not complete without a second *as: as
old as . . . the neighboring city of Lawrence.*

Finally, comparisons should be complete enough to ensure clarity. The reader should understand what is being
compared.

**INCOMPLETE**   Brand X is less salty.

**COMPLETE**   Brand X is less salty than Brand Y.

Also, comparisons should leave no ambiguity for readers. If
more than one interpretation is possible, revise the sentence
to state clearly which interpretation you intend. In the following sentence, two interpretations are possible.

| **AMBIGUOUS** | Ken helped me more than my roommate. |
| **CLEAR** | Ken helped me more than *he helped* my roommate. |
| **CLEAR** | Ken helped me more than my roommate *did*. |

**10d** Add the articles *a, an,* and *the* where necessary for grammatical completeness.

Articles are sometimes omitted in recipes and other instructions that are meant to be followed while they are being read. Such omissions are inappropriate, however, in nearly all other forms of writing, whether formal or informal.

▶ Blood can be drawn only by ^*a* doctor or by ^*an* authorized person who has been trained in ^*the* procedure.

It is not always necessary to repeat articles with paired items: *We bought a computer and printer.* However, if one of the items requires *a* and the other requires *an*, both articles must be included.

▶ We bought a computer and ^*an* antivirus program.

 **ESL** Articles can cause special problems for speakers of English as a second language. See 30.

**EXERCISE 10–1** Add any words needed for grammatical or logical completeness in the following sentences. Revisions of lettered sentences appear in the back of the book. Example:

**EXERCISE 10–1    Possible revisions:**
a. A good source of vitamin C is a grapefruit or an orange.
b. The women entering VMI can expect haircuts as short as those of the male cadets.
c. The driver went to investigate, only to find that one of the new tires had blown.
d. The graphic designers are interested in and knowledgeable about producing posters for the balloon race.
e. Reefs are home to more species than any other ecosystem in the sea.

                          *that*
The officer feared ⌃ the prisoner would escape.
                    ⌃

a. A good source of vitamin C is a grapefruit or orange.
b. The women entering VMI can expect haircuts as short as the male cadets.
c. The driver went to investigate, only to find one of the new tires had blown.
d. The graphic designers are interested and knowledgeable about producing posters for the balloon race.
e. Reefs are home to more species than any ecosystem in the sea.

1. Very few black doctors were allowed to serve in the Civil War, and their qualifications had to be higher than white doctors.
2. Producers of violent video games are not capable or interested in regulating themselves.
3. Vassily likes mathematics more than his teacher.
4. The inspection team saw many historic buildings had been damaged by the earthquake.
5. American English has borrowed more words from Spanish than from any language.

| ON THE WEB | **dianahacker.com/bedhandbook** ▶ Electronic grammar exercises ▶ E-ex 10–1 and 10–2 |

# 11

## Untangle mixed constructions.

A mixed construction contains parts that do not sensibly fit together. The mismatch may be a matter of grammar or of logic.

**EXERCISE 10–1 (continued)**

1. Very few black doctors were allowed to serve in the Civil War, and their qualifications had to be higher than those of white doctors.
2. Producers of violent video games are not capable of or interested in regulating themselves.
3. Vassily likes mathematics more than he likes his teacher. [or . . . more than his teacher does.]
4. The inspection team saw that many historic buildings had been damaged by the earthquake.
5. American English has borrowed more words from Spanish than from any other language.

> **GRAMMAR CHECKERS** can flag *is when, is where,* and
> *reason . . . is because* constructions (11c), but they fail
> to identify nearly all other mixed constructions, including
> sentences as tangled as this one: *Depending on our method
> of travel and our destination determines how many suit-
> cases we are allowed to pack.*

## 11a Untangle the grammatical structure.

Once you head into a sentence, your choices are limited by
the range of grammatical patterns in English. (See 63 and
64.) You cannot begin with one grammatical plan and switch
without warning to another.

**MIXED**    For most drivers who have a blood alcohol content
of .05 percent double their risk of causing an
accident.

**REVISED**    For most drivers who have a blood alcohol content
of .05 percent, the risk of causing an accident is
doubled.

**REVISED**    Most drivers who have a blood alcohol content of .05
percent double their risk of causing an accident.

The writer began with a long prepositional phrase that was
destined to be a modifier but then tried to press it into service
as the subject of the sentence. A prepositional phrase cannot
serve as the subject of a sentence. If the sentence is to begin
with the prepositional phrase, the writer must finish the sentence with a subject and verb (*risk . . . is doubled*). The writer
who wishes to stay with the original verb (*double*) must head
into the sentence another way: *Most drivers. . . .*

▶  *Being*
~~When an employee is~~ promoted without warning can be
   ^
alarming.

### SCHOLARS ON MIXED CONSTRUCTIONS

Freeman, Donald C. "Linguistics and Error Analysis: On Agency."
*The Territory of Language.* Ed. Donald A. McQuade. Carbondale:
Southern Illinois UP, 1986. 165–73. In discussing the use of linguistics to help students write grammatical sentences, Freeman
offers several examples of tangled syntax. He argues that instead
of attempting to apply rules to the problem, instructors should
draw the students' attention to the question of "agency" (who is
doing what) in the sentence. Thinking about agency often can help
students sense what is wrong and see how to fix the problem.

The adverb clause *When an employee is promoted without warning* cannot serve as the subject of the sentence. The revision replaces the adverb clause with a gerund phrase, a word group that can function as the subject. (See 64b and 64c.)

▶ **Although the United States is one of the wealthiest nations in the world, ~~but~~ more than twelve million of our children live in poverty.**

The *Although* clause is subordinate, so it cannot be linked to an independent clause with the coordinating conjunction *but.*

Occasionally a mixed construction is so tangled that it defies grammatical analysis. When this happens, back away from the sentence, rethink what you want to say, and then say it again as clearly as you can.

**MIXED**   In the whole-word method children learn to recognize entire words rather than by the phonics method in which they learn to sound out letters and groups of letters.

**REVISED**   The whole-word method teaches children to recognize entire words; the phonics method teaches them to sound out letters and groups of letters.

---

**ESL** English does not allow double subjects; nor does it allow an object or an adverb to be repeated in an adjective clause. See 31b and 31c.

▶ **The squirrel that came down our chimney ~~it~~ did much damage.**

▶ **Hearing screams, Serena ran over to the pool that her daughter was swimming in. ~~it.~~**

---

**SCHOLARS ON MIXED CONSTRUCTIONS**
Shaughnessy, Mina P. *Errors and Expectations: A Guide for the Teacher of Basic Writing.* New York: Oxford UP, 1979. 44–89. Shaughnessy suggests several causes of tangled syntax, which she calls "blurred constructions."

## 11b Straighten out the logical connections.

The subject and the predicate should make sense together; when they don't, the error is known as *faulty predication.*

> ► We decided that ~~Tiffany's welfare~~ would not be safe living
>      *Tiffany*
>
> with her mother.

Tiffany, not her welfare, may not be safe.

> ► Under the revised plan, the elderly/ ~~who now receive a double~~
>      *double personal exemption for the*
>
> ~~personal exemption,~~ will be abolished.

The exemption, not the elderly, will be abolished.

An appositive and the noun to which it refers should be logically equivalent. When they are not, the error is known as *faulty apposition.*

> ► ~~The tax accountant,~~ a very lucrative field, requires
>   *Tax accounting,*
>
> intelligence, patience, and attention to mathematical
>
> detail.

The tax accountant is a person, not a field.

## 11c Avoid *is when, is where,* and *reason . . . is because* constructions.

In formal English, many readers object to *is when, is where,* and *reason . . . is because* constructions on either grammatical or logical grounds. Grammatically, the verb *is* (as well as *are, was,* and *were*) should be followed by a noun that re-

---

**WRITERS ON WRITING**

It is the little uncertainty that matters—the small confusion, the modifier that isn't badly lost but only slightly misplaced. At such pauses along the trail, the reader's eye flickers and wanders— back up to the subject, down again to the verb.
                                                                    —James J. Kilpatrick

I see but one rule: to be clear.                                    —Stendhal

The demands I make on a sentence are the same demands I would make on a line of poetry.                                    —Cynthia Ozick

It helps to read the sentence aloud.                                —Harry Kemelman

names the subject or by an adjective that describes it, not by an adverb clause beginning with *when, where,* or *because.* (See 63b and 64b.) Logically, the words *when, where,* and *because* suggest relations of time, place, and cause — relations that do not always make sense with *is, was,* or *were.*

▶ Anorexia nervosa is ~~where people,~~ *a disorder suffered by people who,* believing they are too fat,

diet to the point of starvation.

Anorexia nervosa is a disorder, not a place.

▶ ~~The reason~~ I missed the exam ~~is~~ because my motorcycle

broke down.

The writer might have changed *because* to *that* (*The reason I missed the exam is that my motorcycle broke down*), but the preceding revision is more concise.

**EXERCISE 11–1**   Edit the following sentences to untangle mixed constructions. Revisions of lettered sentences appear in the back of the book. Example:

*Keeping*
~~By keeping~~ your wrists relaxed while rowing will help you

avoid injury.

a. Using surgical gloves is a precaution now worn by dentists to prevent contact with patients' blood and saliva.
b. A physician, the career my brother is pursuing, requires at least ten years of challenging work.
c. The reason the pharaohs had bad teeth was because tiny particles of sand found their way into Egyptian bread.
d. Recurring bouts of flu among team members set a record for number of games forfeited.
e. In this box contains the key to your future.

---

**EXERCISE 11–1   Possible revisions:**

a. Using surgical gloves is a precaution now taken by dentists to prevent contact with patients' blood and saliva.
b. A career in medicine, which my brother is pursuing, requires at least ten years of challenging work.
c. The pharaohs had bad teeth because tiny particles of sand found their way into Egyptian bread.
d. Recurring bouts of flu caused the team to forfeit a record number of games.
e. This box contains the key to your future.

1. Early diagnosis of prostate cancer is often curable.
2. Depending on our method of travel and our destination determines how many suitcases we are allowed to pack.
3. Dyslexia is where people have a learning disorder that impairs reading ability.
4. Even though Ellen had heard French spoken all her life, yet she could not speak it.
5. In understanding artificial intelligence code is a critical skill for computer game designers.

---

**ON THE WEB**

**dianahacker.com/bedhandbook**
- ▶ Electronic grammar exercises
  - ▶ E-ex 11–1 and 11–2

---

# 12

## Repair misplaced and dangling modifiers.

---

Modifiers, whether they are single words, phrases, or clauses, should point clearly to the words they modify. As a rule, related words should be kept together.

**GRAMMAR CHECKERS** can flag split infinitives, such as *to carefully and thoroughly sift* (12d). However, they don't alert you to other misplaced modifiers (*I only ate three radishes*) or dangling modifiers, including danglers like this one: *When a young man, my mother enrolled me in tap dance classes, hoping I would become the next Savion Glover.*

---

**EXERCISE 11–1 (continued)**

1. When prostate cancer is diagnosed early, it is often curable.
2. Our method of travel and our destination determine how many suitcases we are allowed to pack.
3. Dyslexia is a learning disorder that impairs reading ability.
4. Even though Ellen had heard French spoken all her life, she could not speak it.
5. Understanding artificial intelligence code is a critical skill for computer game designers.

**12a** Put limiting modifiers in front of the words they modify.

Limiting modifiers such as *only, even, almost, nearly,* and *just* should appear in front of a verb only if they modify the verb: *At first, I couldn't even touch my toes, much less grasp them.* If they limit the meaning of some other word in the sentence, they should be placed in front of that word.

▶ Lasers ~~only~~ destroy <sup>only</sup> the target, leaving the surrounding healthy tissue intact.

*Only* limits the meaning of *the target,* not *destroy.*

▶ The turtle ~~only~~ makes progress <sup>only</sup> when it sticks its neck out.

*Only* limits the meaning of the *when* clause.

When the limiting modifier *not* is misplaced, the sentence usually suggests a meaning the writer did not intend.

▶ In the United States in 1860, all black southerners were <sup>not</sup> ~~not~~ slaves.

The original sentence says that no black southerners were slaves. The revision makes the writer's real meaning clear: Some (but not all) black southerners were slaves.

**12b** Place phrases and clauses so that readers can see at a glance what they modify.

Although phrases and clauses can appear at some distance from the words they modify, make sure your meaning is clear. When phrases or clauses are oddly placed, absurd misreadings can result.

**WRITERS ON WRITING**

A sentence should read as if its author, had he held a plough instead of a pen, could have drawn a furrow deep and straight to the end.                                         —Henry David Thoreau

All those clauses, appositions, amplifications, qualifications, asides, God knows what else, hanging inside the poor old skeleton of one sentence like some kind of Spanish moss.          —Tom Wolfe

| MISPLACED | The soccer player returned to the clinic where he had undergone emergency surgery in 2004 in a limousine sent by Adidas. |
|---|---|
| REVISED | Traveling in a limousine sent by Adidas, the soccer player returned to the clinic where he had undergone emergency surgery in 2004. |

The revision corrects the false impression that the soccer player underwent emergency surgery in a limousine.

► *On the walls*
~~There~~ are many pictures of comedians who have performed at Gavin's. ~~on the walls.~~

The comedians weren't performing on the walls; the pictures were on the walls.

► The robber was described as a *150-pound,* six-foot-tall man with a heavy mustache. ~~weighing 150 pounds.~~

The robber, not the mustache, weighed 150 pounds. The revision makes this clear.

Occasionally the placement of a modifier leads to an ambiguity, in which case two revisions will be possible, depending on the writer's intended meaning.

| AMBIGUOUS | The exchange students we met for coffee occasionally questioned us about our latest slang. |
|---|---|
| CLEAR | The exchange students we occasionally met for coffee questioned us about our latest slang. |
| CLEAR | The exchange students we met for coffee questioned us occasionally about our latest slang. |

In the original version, it was not clear whether the meeting or the questioning happened occasionally. The revisions eliminate the ambiguity.

## 12c Move awkwardly placed modifiers.

As a rule, a sentence should flow from subject to verb to object, without lengthy detours along the way. When a long adverbial element separates a subject from its verb, a verb from its object, or a helping verb from its main verb, the result is often awkward.

▶ ~~Hong Kong,~~ *A* after more than 150 years of British rule, *Hong Kong* was

transferred back to Chinese control in 1997.

> There is no reason to separate the subject, *Hong Kong*, from the verb, *was transferred*, with a long phrase.

**EXCEPTION:** Occasionally a writer may choose to delay a verb or an object to create suspense. In the following passage, for example, Robert Mueller inserts the *after* phrase between the subject *women* and the verb *walk* to heighten the dramatic effect.

> I asked a Burmese why women, after centuries of following their men, now walk ahead. He said there were many unexploded land mines since the war.                      — Robert Mueller

---

**ESL**  English does not allow an adverb to appear between a verb and its object. See 31d.

*easily*
▶ Yolanda lifted ~~easily~~ the fifty-pound weight.

---

**WRITERS ON WRITING**

When I goes to work on an infinitive I don't just split it; I break it in little pieces.                      — Jimmy Durante

## 12d Avoid split infinitives when they are awkward.

An infinitive consists of *to* plus a verb: *to think, to breathe, to dance.* When a modifier appears between *to* and the verb, an infinitive is said to be "split": *to carefully balance, to completely understand.*

When a long word or a phrase appears between the parts of the infinitive, the result is usually awkward.

> ~~The~~ *If possible, the* patient should try to ~~if possible~~ avoid going up and down stairs.

Attempts to avoid split infinitives can result in equally awkward sentences. When alternative phrasing sounds unnatural, most experts allow — and even encourage — splitting the infinitive.

**AWKWARD**   We decided actually to enforce the law.

**BETTER**   We decided to actually enforce the law.

At times, neither the split infinitive nor its alternative sounds particularly awkward. In such situations, you may want to unsplit the infinitive, especially in formal writing.

> After consulting her family, the candidate decided to ~~formally~~ launch her campaign/ *formally.*

**ON THE WEB**

dianahacker.com/bedhandbook
> Language Debates
>> Split infinitives

---

**EXERCISE 12–1  Possible revisions:**

a. Our English professor asked us to reread the sonnet very carefully, looking for subtleties we had missed on a first reading.

b. The monarch arrived at the gate in a gold carriage pulled by four white horses.

c. Rhonda and Sam talked almost all night about her surgery.

d. A coolhunter is a person who can find the next wave of fashion in the unnoticed corners of modern society.

e. Not all geese fly beyond Narragansett for the winter.

**EXERCISE 12–1**   Edit the following sentences to correct misplaced or awkwardly placed modifiers. Revisions of lettered sentences appear in the back of the book. Example:

> *in a telephone survey*
> Answering questions can be annoying. ~~in a telephone survey.~~

a. Our English professor asked us to very carefully reread the sonnet, looking for subtleties we had missed on a first reading.

b. The monarch arrived in a gold carriage at the gate pulled by four white horses.

c. Rhonda and Sam almost talked all night about her surgery.

d. A coolhunter is a person who can find in the unnoticed corners of modern society the next wave of fashion.

e. All geese do not fly beyond Narragansett for the winter.

1. Carlos sat solemnly and didn't even smile once during the comedy.

2. Angelie wrote about collecting peacock feathers with her uncle David in her class notebook.

3. Several recent studies have encouraged heart patients to more carefully watch their cholesterol levels.

4. The garden's centerpiece is a huge sculpture that was carved by three women called *Walking in Place*.

5. The old Marlboro ads depicted a man on a horse smoking a cigarette.

**ON THE WEB**   **dianahacker.com/bedhandbook**
▶ Electronic grammar exercises
  ▶ E-ex 12–1 and 12–2

## 12e  Repair dangling modifiers.

A dangling modifier fails to refer logically to any word in the sentence. Dangling modifiers are easy to repair, but they can be hard to recognize, especially in your own writing.

**EXERCISE 12–1 (continued)**

1. Carlos sat solemnly and didn't smile even once during the comedy.

2. Angelie wrote in her class notebook about collecting peacock feathers with her uncle David.

3. Several recent studies have encouraged heart patients to watch their cholesterol levels more carefully.

4. The garden's centerpiece is a huge sculpture called *Walking in Place* that was carved by three women.

5. The old Marlboro ads depicted a man on horseback smoking a cigarette.

*Recognizing dangling modifiers*

Dangling modifiers are usually word groups (such as verbal phrases) that suggest but do not name an actor. When a sentence opens with such a modifier, readers expect the subject of the next clause to name the actor. If it doesn't, the modifier dangles.

▶ ~~Opening~~ *When the driver opened* the window to let out a huge bumblebee, the car accidentally swerved into an oncoming car.

The car didn't open the window; the driver did.

▶ After completing seminary training, ~~women's~~ *women have often been denied* access to the pulpit. ~~has often been denied.~~

The women (not their access to the pulpit) complete the training.

The following sentences illustrate four common kinds of dangling modifiers.

**DANGLING** *Deciding to join the navy,* the recruiter enthusiastically pumped Joe's hand. [Participial phrase]

**DANGLING** *Upon entering the doctor's office,* a skeleton caught my attention. [Preposition followed by a gerund phrase]

**DANGLING** *To please the children,* some fireworks were set off a day early. [Infinitive phrase]

**DANGLING** *Though only sixteen,* UCLA accepted Martha's application. [Elliptical clause with an understood subject and verb]

---

**SCHOLARS ON DANGLING MODIFIERS**

Williams, Joseph. *Style: Ten Lessons in Clarity and Grace.* 8th ed. New York: Longman, 2005. In his chapter on "managing long sentences," Williams discusses the dangers of dangling modifiers.

Jordan, Michael P. "Unattached Clauses in Technical Writing." *Journal of Technical Communication* 29.1 (1999): 65–93. Jordan argues that not all dangling (or "unattached") clauses affect meaning in negative ways. In technical writing, unattached clauses are sometimes acceptable, since the name of the agent (actor) may be irrelevant. Jordan suggests that on the issue of unattached clauses there may be cultural differences "between humanistic teachers and task-oriented engineers."

These dangling modifiers falsely suggest that the recruiter decided to join the navy, that the skeleton entered the doctor's office, that the fireworks intended to please the children, and that UCLA is only sixteen years old.

Although most readers will understand the writer's intended meaning in such sentences, the inadvertent humor can be distracting, and it can make the writer appear somewhat foolish.

| ON THE WEB | **dianahacker.com/bedhandbook** ▶ Language Debates  ▶ Dangling modifiers |
| --- | --- |

### Repairing dangling modifiers

To repair a dangling modifier, you can revise the sentence in one of two ways:

1. Name the actor in the subject of the sentence, or
2. name the actor in the modifier.

Depending on your sentence, one of these revision strategies may be more appropriate than the other.

**ACTOR NAMED IN SUBJECT**

▶ Upon entering the doctor's office, a skeleton. ~~caught my~~ ~~attention.~~ *I noticed*

▶ To please the children, some fireworks ~~were set off~~ a day early. *we set off*

---

**SCHOLARS ON DANGLING MODIFIERS**

Noguchi, Rei R. *Grammar and the Teaching of Writing: Limits and Possibilities.* Urbana: NCTE, 1991. 38–58. In his chapter on teaching a "writer's grammar," Noguchi recommends having students form "tag questions" and "yes and no questions" from original declarative sentences. He shows how this method is useful in identifying and clarifying "presentence modifiers."

**WRITERS ON WRITING**

Always suspect an *ing* word of dangling if it's near the front of a sentence; consider it guilty until proved innocent.

—Patricia O'Conner

## Checking for dangling modifiers

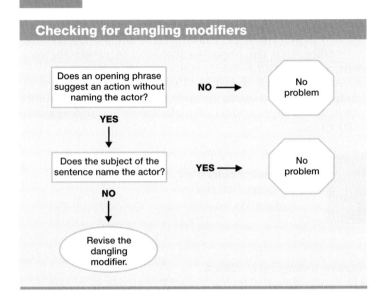

**ACTOR NAMED IN MODIFIER**

> *When Joe decided*
> ~~Deciding~~ to join the navy, the recruiter enthusiastically
>           *his*
> pumped ~~Joe's~~ hand.

>   *Martha was*                          *her*
> Though only sixteen, UCLA accepted ~~Martha's~~ application.

**NOTE:** You cannot repair a dangling modifier just by moving it. Consider, for example, the sentence about the skeleton. If you put the modifier at the end of the sentence (*A skeleton caught my attention upon entering the doctor's office*), you are still suggesting—absurdly, of course—that the skeleton entered the office. The only way to avoid the problem is to put the word *I* in the sentence, either as the subject or in the modifier.

---

**WRITERS ON WRITING**

I have never thought of myself as a good writer. . . . But I'm one of the world's great rewriters. —James Michener

Writing isn't hard—no harder than ditch digging.
—Patrick Dennis

Nothing you write, if you hope to be any good, will ever come out as you first hoped. —Lillian Hellman

Writing being what it is, print being what it is, and structures being what they are—you can't put everything into it. You have to choose, and trying to figure out what to choose is the hardest part.
—Paula Gunn Allen

> *I noticed*
▶ Upon entering the doctor's office, a skeleton. ~~caught my~~
> ^                                              ^
> ~~attention.~~

> *As I entered*
▶ ~~Upon entering~~ the doctor's office, a skeleton caught my
> ^
> attention.

**EXERCISE 12–2** Edit the following sentences to correct dangling modifiers. Most sentences can be revised in more than one way. Revisions of lettered sentences appear in the back of the book. Example:

> *a student must complete*
> To acquire a degree in almost any field, two science courses.
> ^                                          ^
> ~~must be completed.~~

a. At the age of ten, my parents took me on my first balloon ride.
b. To replace the gear mechanism, attached is a form to order the part by mail.
c. Nestled in the cockpit, the pounding of the engine was muffled only slightly by my helmet.
d. After studying polymer chemistry, computer games seemed less complex to Phuong.
e. When a young man, my mother enrolled me in tap dance classes, hoping I would become the next Savion Glover.

1. While working as a ranger in Everglades National Park, a Florida panther crossed the road in front of my truck one night.
2. By following this new procedure, our mailing costs will be reduced significantly.
3. Serving as president of the missionary circle, one of Grandmother's duties is to raise money for the church.
4. After buying an album by Ali Farka Toure, the rich and rolling rhythms of Malian music made more sense to Silas.
5. Understanding the high-tech needs of drivers, the Volkswagen Phaeton has an innovative dashboard design.

**EXERCISE 12–2  Possible revisions:**
a. When I was ten, my parents took me on my first balloon ride.
b. To replace the gear mechanism, you can use the attached form to order the part by mail.
c. As I nestled in the cockpit, the pounding of the engine was muffled only slightly by my helmet.
d. After studying polymer chemistry, Phuong found computer games less complex.
e. When I was a young man, my mother enrolled me in tap dance classes, hoping I would become the next Savion Glover.

| ON | dianahacker.com/bedhandbook |
| THE | ▶ Electronic grammar exercises |
| WEB | ▶ E-ex 12–3 and 12–4 |

# 13

## Eliminate distracting shifts.

 **GRAMMAR CHECKERS** usually do not flag shifts in point of view or in verb tense, mood, or voice. Even obvious errors, like the following shift in tense, slip right past the grammar checker: *My three-year-old fell into the pool and to my surprise she swims to the shallow end.*

Sometimes grammar checkers mark a shift from direct to indirect question or quotation but do not make any suggestions for revision. You must decide where the structure is faulty and determine how to fix it.

**13a** Make the point of view consistent in person and number.

The point of view of a piece of writing is the perspective from which it is written: first person (*I* or *we*), second person (*you*), or third person (*he, she, it, one,* or *they*).

The *I* (or *we*) point of view, which emphasizes the writer, is a good choice for informal letters and writing based primarily on personal experience. The *you* point of view, which emphasizes the reader, works well for giving advice or explaining how to do something. The third-person point of

**EXERCISE 12–2 (continued)**

1. While I was working as a ranger in Everglades National Park, a Florida panther crossed the road in front of my truck one night.
2. By following this new procedure, we will reduce our mailing costs significantly.
3. Serving as president of the missionary circle, Grandmother is responsible for raising money for the church.
4. After buying an album by Ali Farka Toure, Silas understood the rich and rolling rhythms of Malian music.
5. Understanding the high-tech needs of drivers, designers of the Volkswagen Phaeton have created an innovative dashboard.

view, which emphasizes the subject, is appropriate in formal academic and professional writing.

Writers who are having difficulty settling on an appropriate point of view sometimes shift confusingly from one to another. The solution is to choose a suitable perspective and then stay with it.

▶ One week our class met in a junkyard to practice rescuing a

victim trapped in a wrecked car. We learned to dismantle the

car with the essential tools. ~~You~~ *We* were graded on ~~your~~ *our* speed

and ~~your~~ *our* skill in extricating the victim.

The writer should have stayed with the *we* point of view. *You* is inappropriate because the writer is not addressing readers directly. *You* should not be used in a vague sense meaning "anyone." (See 23d.)

▶ ~~One needs~~ *You need* a password and a credit card number to access

this database. You will be billed at an hourly rate.

*You* is an appropriate choice because the writer is giving advice directly to readers.

▶ ~~A police officer is~~ *Police officers are* often criticized for always being there when

they aren't needed and never being there when they are.

Although the writer might have changed *they* to *he or she* (to match the singular *officer*), the revision in the plural is more concise. (See also 17f and 22a.)

**EXERCISE 13–1** Edit the following paragraph to eliminate distracting shifts in point of view (person and number).

**EXERCISE 13–1 Possible revisions:**

When online dating first became available, many people thought that it would simplify romance. Hopeful singles believed that they could type in a list of criteria—sense of humor, college education, green eyes, good job—and a database would select the perfect mate. Thousands of people signed up for services and filled out their profiles, confident that true love was only a few mouse clicks away. As it turns out, however, virtual dating is no easier than traditional dating. Online daters still have to contact the people they find, exchange e-mails and phone calls, and meet in the real world. Although a database might produce a list of possibilities and screen out obviously undesirable people, it can't

When online dating first became available, many people thought that it would simplify romance. We believed that you could type in a list of criteria—sense of humor, college education, green eyes, good job—and a database would select the perfect mate. Thousands of people signed up for services and filled out their profiles, confident that true love was only a few mouse clicks away. As it turns out, however, virtual dating is no easier than traditional dating. I still have to contact the people I find, exchange e-mails and phone calls, and meet him in the real world. Although a database might produce a list of possibilities and screen out obviously undesirable people, you can't predict chemistry. More often than not, people who seem perfect online just don't click in person. Electronic services do help a single person expand their pool of potential dates, but it's no substitute for the hard work of romance.

## 13b Maintain consistent verb tenses.

Consistent verb tenses clearly establish the time of the actions being described. When a passage begins in one tense and then shifts without warning and for no reason to another, readers are distracted and confused.

▶ There was no way I could fight the current and win. Just as I
was losing hope, a stranger ~~jumps~~ *jumped* off a passing boat and ~~swims~~ *swam*
toward me.

Writers often encounter difficulty with verb tenses when writing about literature. Because fictional events occur outside the time frames of real life, the past and the present tenses may seem equally appropriate. The literary conven-

---

**EXERCISE 13–1 (continued)**

predict chemistry. More often than not, people who seem perfect online just don't click in person. Electronic services do help single people expand their pool of potential dates, but they're no substitute for the hard work of romance.

tion, however, is to describe fictional events consistently in the present tense.

▶ The scarlet letter is a punishment sternly placed upon Hester's
breast by the community, and yet it ~~was~~ *is* an extremely fanciful
and imaginative product of Hester's own needlework.

**EXERCISE 13–2**  Edit the following paragraphs to eliminate distracting shifts in tense.

The English colonists who settled in Massachusetts received assistance at first from the local Indian tribes, but by 1675 there had been friction between the English and the Indians for many years. On June 20 of that year, Metacomet, whom the colonists called Philip, leads the Wampanoag tribe in the first of a series of attacks on the colonial settlements. The war, known today as King Philip's War, rages on for over a year and leaves three thousand Indians and six hundred colonists dead. Metacomet's attempt to retain power in his native land failed. Finally he too is killed, and the victorious colonists sell his wife and children into slavery.

The Indians did not leave records of their unfortunate encounters with the English settlers, but the settlers recorded some of their experiences at the hands of the Indians. One of the few accounts to survive was written by a captured colonist, Mrs. Mary Rowlandson. She is a minister's wife who is kidnapped by an Indian war party and held captive for eleven weeks in 1676. Her history, *A Narrative of the Captivity and Restoration of Mrs. Mary Rowlandson,* tells the story of her experiences with the Wampanoags. Although it did not paint a completely balanced picture of the Indians, Rowlandson's narrative, which is considered a classic early American text, showed its author to be a keen observer of life in an Indian camp.

**EXERCISE 13–2  Possible revisions:**

The English colonists who settled in Massachusetts received assistance at first from the local Indian tribes, but by 1675 there had been friction between the English and the Indians for many years. On June 20 of that year, Metacomet, whom the colonists called Philip, led the Wampanoag tribe in the first of a series of attacks on the colonial settlements. The war, known today as King Philip's War, raged on for over a year and left three thousand Indians and six hundred colonists dead. Metacomet's attempt to retain power in his native land failed. Finally he too was killed, and the victorious colonists sold his wife and children into slavery.

## 13c Make verbs consistent in mood and voice.

Unnecessary shifts in the mood of a verb can be as distracting as needless shifts in tense. There are three moods in English: the *indicative*, used for facts, opinions, and questions; the *imperative*, used for orders or advice; and the *subjunctive*, used in certain contexts to express wishes or conditions contrary to fact (see 28b).

The following passage shifts confusingly from the indicative to the imperative mood.

▶ The officers advised us against allowing anyone into our
homes without proper identification. ~~Also,~~ alert neighbors to
our vacation schedules.

*They also suggested that we*

Since the writer's purpose was to report the officers' advice, the revision puts both sentences in the indicative.

A verb may be in either the active voice (with the subject doing the action) or the passive voice (with the subject receiving the action). (See 8a.) If a writer shifts without warning from one to the other, readers may be left wondering why.

▶ When the tickets are ready, the travel agent notifies the
client/, ~~Each ticket is then listed~~ on a daily register form, and
a copy of the itinerary. ~~is filed.~~

*lists each ticket*

*files*

The passage began in the active voice (*agent notifies*) and then switched to the passive (*ticket is listed, copy is filed*). Because the active voice is clearer and more direct, the writer changed all the verbs to the active voice.

---

**EXERCISE 13–2 (continued)**

The Indians did not leave records of their unfortunate encounters with the English settlers, but the settlers recorded some of their experiences at the hands of the Indians. One of the few accounts to survive was written by a captured colonist, Mrs. Mary Rowlandson. She was a minister's wife who was kidnapped by an Indian war party and held captive for eleven weeks in 1676. Her history, *A Narrative of the Captivity and Restoration of Mrs. Mary Rowlandson*, tells the story of her experiences with the Wampanoags. Although it does not paint a completely balanced picture of the Indians, Rowlandson's narrative, which is considered a classic early American text, shows its author to be a keen observer of life in an Indian camp.

**13d** Avoid sudden shifts from indirect to direct questions or quotations.

An indirect question reports a question without asking it: *We asked whether we could visit Mimo.* A direct question asks directly: *Can we visit Mimo?* Sudden shifts from indirect to direct questions are awkward. In addition, sentences containing such shifts are impossible to punctuate because indirect questions must end with a period and direct questions must end with a question mark. (See 38b.)

▶ I wonder whether Karla knew of the theft and, if so, ~~did~~
   *whether she reported*
   ~~she report~~ it to the police~~?~~.

The revision poses both questions indirectly. The writer could also ask both questions directly: *Did Karla know of the theft and, if so, did she report it to the police?*

An indirect quotation reports someone's words without quoting word for word: *Annabelle said that she is a Virgo.* A direct quotation presents the exact words of a speaker or writer, set off with quotation marks: *Annabelle said, "I am a Virgo."* Unannounced shifts from indirect to direct quotations are distracting and confusing, especially when the writer fails to insert the necessary quotation marks, as in the following example.

                                           *asked me not to*
▶ Mother said that she would be late for dinner and ~~please do~~
                                    *came*
   ~~not~~ leave for choir practice until Dad ~~comes~~ home.

The revision reports all of the mother's words. The writer could also quote directly: *Mother said, "I will be late for dinner. Please do not leave for choir practice until Dad comes home."*

---

**WRITERS ON WRITING**

The art of writing is the art of applying the seat of the pants to the seat of the chair.                    —Mary Heaton Vosse

All good writing is swimming under water and holding your breath.
                                           —F. Scott Fitzgerald

The best reason for putting anything down on paper is that one may then change it.                    —Bernard De Voto

If someone tells you, "That's a terrible idea," there's a real danger that you'll believe [that person] when maybe it's not a terrible idea; maybe you just haven't articulated it right yet.
                                           —Ethan Hawke

**EXERCISE 13–3**  Edit the following sentences to eliminate distracting shifts. Revisions of lettered sentences appear in the back of the book. Example:

> For many first-year engineering students, adjusting to
> rigorous courses can be so challenging that ~~you~~ *they* sometimes
> feel overwhelmed.

a.  A courtroom lawyer has more than a touch of theater in their blood.

b.  The interviewer asked if we had brought our proof of birth and citizenship and did we bring our passports.

c.  The reconnaissance scout often has to make fast decisions and use sophisticated equipment to keep their team from detection.

d.  After the animators finish their scenes, the production designer arranges the clips according to the storyboard. Synchronization notes must also be made for the sound editor and the composer.

e.  Madame Defarge is a sinister figure in Dickens's *A Tale of Two Cities*. On a symbolic level, she represents fate; like the Greek Fates, she knitted the fabric of individual destiny.

1.  Everyone should protect yourself from the sun, especially on the first day of extensive exposure.

2.  Our neighbors told us that the island was being evacuated because of the coming storm. Also, take the northern route to the mainland.

3.  Rescue workers put water on her face and lifted her head gently onto a pillow. Finally, she opens her eyes.

4.  In my first tai chi class, the sensei asked if I had ever done yoga stretches and did I have good balance.

5.  The artist has often been seen as a threat to society, especially when they refuse to conform to conventional standards of taste.

**ON THE WEB**  **dianahacker.com/bedhandbook**
▶ Electronic grammar exercises
▶ E-ex 13–1 to 13–4

**EXERCISE 13–3  Possible revisions:**

a.  Courtroom lawyers have more than a touch of theater in their blood.

b.  The interviewer asked if we had brought our proof of birth and citizenship and our passports.

c.  Reconnaissance scouts often have to make fast decisions and use sophisticated equipment to keep their teams from detection.

d.  After the animators finish their scenes, the production designer arranges the clips according to the storyboard and makes synchronization notes for the sound editor and the composer.

e.  Madame Defarge is a sinister figure in Dickens's *A Tale of Two Cities*. On a symbolic level, she represents fate; like the Greek Fates, she knits the fabric of individual destiny.

# 14

## Emphasize key ideas.

Within each sentence, emphasize your point by expressing it in the subject and verb of an independent clause, the words that receive the most attention from readers (see 14a–14e).

Within longer stretches of prose, you can draw attention to ideas deserving special emphasis by using a variety of techniques, often involving an unusual twist or some element of surprise (see 14f).

**14a** Coordinate equal ideas; subordinate minor ideas.

When combining two or more ideas in one sentence, you have two choices: coordination or subordination. Choose coordination to indicate that the ideas are equal or nearly equal in importance. Choose subordination to indicate that one idea is less important than another.

GRAMMAR CHECKERS do not catch the problems with coordination and subordination discussed in this section. Not surprisingly, computer programs have no way of sensing the relative importance of ideas.

### Coordination

Coordination draws attention equally to two or more ideas. To coordinate single words or phrases, join them with a coordinating conjunction or with a pair of correlative conjunctions (see 62g). To coordinate independent clauses — word groups that could each stand alone as a sentence — join

**EXERCISE 13–3 (continued)**

1. You should protect yourself from the sun, especially on the first day of extensive exposure.
2. Our neighbors told us that the island was being evacuated because of the coming storm. They also suggested that we take the northern route to the mainland.
3. Rescue workers put water on her face and lifted her head gently onto a pillow. Finally, she opened her eyes.
4. In my first tai chi class, the sensei asked if I had ever done yoga stretches and if I had good balance.
5. Artists have often been seen as a threat to society, especially when they refuse to conform to conventional standards of taste.

them with a comma and a coordinating conjunction or with a semicolon:

| , and | , but | , or | , nor |
|-------|-------|-------|-------|
| , for | , so | , yet | ; |

The semicolon is often accompanied by a conjunctive adverb such as *moreover, furthermore, therefore,* or *however* or by a transitional phrase such as *for example, in other words,* or *as a matter of fact.* (For a longer list, see p. 187.)

Assume, for example, that your intention is to draw equal attention to the following two ideas.

> Grandmother lost her sight. Her hearing sharpened.

To coordinate these ideas, you can join them with a comma and the coordinating conjunction *but* or with a semicolon and the conjunctive adverb *however.*

> Grandmother lost her sight, but her hearing sharpened.

> Grandmother lost her sight; however, her hearing sharpened.

It is important to choose a coordinating conjunction or conjunctive adverb appropriate to your meaning. In the preceding example, the two ideas contrast with one another, calling for *but* or *however.*

### Subordination

To give unequal emphasis to two or more ideas, express the major idea in an independent clause and place any minor ideas in subordinate clauses or phrases. (For specific subordination strategies, see the chart on p. 188.)

**SCHOLARS ON SENTENCE RHETORIC**

Myers, Sharon A. "ReMembering the Sentence." *College Composition and Communication* 54 (2003): 610–28. Drawing on linguistics research and her background with ESL writers, Myers argues that composition teachers should place more emphasis on sentence-combining and imitation exercises to help students acquire a "feel" for written language. With systematic practice in manipulating words and phrasing at the sentence level, students will become more aware of the grammar and syntax options available to them. Over time, Myers claims, they will also begin to internalize ways of processing language. The article describes several strategies teachers can use to help students vary their sentences.

## Using coordination to combine sentences of equal importance

1. Consider using a comma and a coordinating conjunction. (See 32a.)

, and , but , or , nor
, for , so , yet

▶ In Orthodox Jewish funeral ceremonies, the shroud is
a simple linen vestment/. ~~The~~ *and the* coffin is plain wood with
no adornment.

2. Consider using a semicolon and a conjunctive adverb or transitional phrase. (See 34b.)

| | | |
|---|---|---|
| also | in addition | now |
| as a result | in fact | of course |
| besides | in other words | on the other hand |
| consequently | in the first place | otherwise |
| finally | meanwhile | still |
| for example | moreover | then |
| for instance | nevertheless | therefore |
| furthermore | next | thus |
| however | | |

▶ Alicia scored well on the SAT/; *moreover, she* ~~She also~~ had excellent
high school grades and a record of community
service.

3. Consider using a semicolon alone. (See 34a.)

▶ In youth we learn/; *in* ~~In~~ age we understand.

---

**SCHOLARS ON SENTENCE RHETORIC**

Lindemann, Erika. *A Rhetoric for Writing Teachers.* 4th ed. New York: Oxford UP, 2001. 163–74. In the chapter "Teaching about Sentences," Lindemann suggests that our teaching goal "should be to enlarge the student's repertoire of sentence options and rhetorical choices." She offers three approaches to helping students. First, we can help students consider the various expectations that readers bring to sentences. Second, we can encourage students to experiment with combining and decombining sentences, primarily in their own drafts. Third, we can use Christensen's "generative rhetoric" to help students explore alternative sentence constructions and understand how those constructions express relationships among ideas.

## Using subordination to combine sentences of unequal importance

1. Consider putting the less important idea in a subordinate clause beginning with one of the following words. (See 64b.)

| | | | |
|---|---|---|---|
| after | before | that | which |
| although | even though | unless | while |
| as | if | until | who |
| as if | since | when | whom |
| because | so that | where | whose |

▶ ~~My~~ *When my* son asked his grandmother to chaperone the class trip/, ~~She~~ *she* was thrilled.

▶ My sister owes much of her recovery to a yoga program/ *that she* ~~She~~ began ~~the program~~ three years ago.

2. Consider putting the less important idea in an appositive phrase. (See 64d.)

▶ Karate, ~~is~~ a discipline based on the philosophy of non-violence/, ~~It~~ teaches the art of self-defense.

3. Consider putting the less important idea in a participial phrase. (See 64c.)

▶ *Noticing* ~~I noticed~~ that smoke had filled the backyard/, I ran out to see where it was coming from.

▶ ~~Alvin was~~ *E*ncouraged by his professor to apply for the job/, ~~He~~ *Alvin* filed an application on Monday morning.

---

**SCHOLARS ON SENTENCE RHETORIC**

Connors, Robert J. "The Erasure of the Sentence." *College Composition and Communication* 52 (2000): 96–128. Connors describes sentence-based instruction that was scientifically tested in the 1960s and 1970s—generative rhetoric, imitation exercises, and sentence combining—and suggests why such instruction fell out of favor in the 1980s. "The usefulness of these sentence-based rhetorics was never disproved," writes Connors, "but a growing wave of anti-formalism, anti-behaviorism, and anti-empiricism . . . doomed them to a marginality under which they still exist today." In Connors's view, current trends in English studies marginalize not just the rhetoric of the sentence but also the whole notion that instructional effectiveness can be measured at all.

Deciding which idea to emphasize is not a matter of right and wrong but is determined by the meaning you intend. Consider the two ideas about Grandmother's sight and hearing.

Grandmother lost her sight. Her hearing sharpened.

If your purpose is to stress your grandmother's acute hearing rather than her blindness, subordinate the idea about her blindness.

*As Grandmother lost her sight,* her hearing sharpened.

To focus on your grandmother's growing blindness, subordinate the idea about her hearing.

*Though her hearing sharpened,* Grandmother gradually lost her sight.

## 14b Combine choppy sentences.

Short sentences demand attention, so you should use them primarily for emphasis. Too many short sentences, one after the other, make for a choppy style.

If an idea is not important enough to deserve its own sentence, try combining it with a sentence close by. Put any minor ideas in subordinate structures such as phrases or subordinate clauses. (See 64.)

▶ We keep our use of insecticides, herbicides, and fungicides to a minimum/ ~~We~~ *because we* are concerned about their effect on the environment.

A minor idea is now expressed in a subordinate clause beginning with *because.*

**SCHOLARS ON SENTENCE RHETORIC**

Weaver, Constance. *Teaching Grammar in Context.* Portsmouth: Boynton, 1996. 102–47. Weaver argues that sentence-combining and sentence-generating activities, presented in "mini-lessons," can promote syntactic complexity and diversity of style, two characteristics of effective writing. Her extensive appendix offers mini-lessons illustrating what she means by "teaching grammar in context."

▶ The Chesapeake and Ohio Canal, ~~is~~ a 184-mile waterway
   ∧
constructed in the 1800s/. ~~It~~ was a major source of
                         ∧
transportation for goods during the Civil War.

A minor idea is now expressed in an appositive phrase (*a
184-mile waterway constructed in the 1800s*).

                                       E
▶ ~~Sister Consilio was~~ ȩnveloped in a black robe with only her
                             *Sister Consilio*
face and hands visible/. ~~She~~ was an imposing figure.
                        ∧
A minor idea is now expressed in a participial phrase beginning
with *Enveloped.*

---

**ESL** When combining sentences, do not repeat the subject of
the sentence; also do not repeat an object or an adverb in
an adjective clause. See 31b and 31c.

▶ The apartment that we rented ~~it~~ needed repairs.

▶ Tanya climbed into the tree house that the boys were

playing in. ~~it.~~
            ∧

---

Although subordination is ordinarily the most effective
technique for combining short, choppy sentences, coordination is appropriate when the ideas are equal in importance.

▶ The hospital decides when patients sleep/. ~~It~~ dictates when
          *and*                              ∧
they eat/. ~~It~~ tells them when they may be with family.
          ∧
Equivalent ideas are expressed as parallel elements of a compound predicate: *decides . . . dictates . . . tells.*

---

**SCHOLARS ON SENTENCE COMBINING**

Killgallon, Don. "Sentence Composing: Notes on a New Rhetoric."
*Lessons to Share: On Teaching Grammar in Context.* Ed. Con-
                                      ∧
stance Weaver. Portsmouth: Boynton, 1998. Killgallon offers detailed descriptions of four kinds of sentence-composing activities
—unscrambling, imitating, combining, and expanding—all of
which are designed to help students learn to write sentences that
approximate the mature and stylistically varied sentences of professional writers.

**EXERCISE 14–1**   Combine the following sentences by subordinating minor ideas or by coordinating ideas of equal importance. You must decide which ideas are minor because the sentences are given out of context. Revisions of lettered sentences appear in the back of the book. Example:

> Agnes, ~~was~~ another girl I worked with/, ~~She~~ was a hyperactive child.

a. The X-Men comic books and Japanese woodcuts of kabuki dancers were part of Marlena's research project on popular culture. They covered the tabletop and the chairs.
b. Our waitress was costumed in a kimono. She had painted her face white. She had arranged her hair in an upswept lacquered beehive.
c. Students can apply for a spot in the foundation's leadership program. The program teaches thinking and communication skills.
d. Shore houses were flooded up to the first floor. Beaches were washed away. Brant's Lighthouse was swallowed by the sea.
e. Laura Thackray is an engineer at Volvo Car Corporation. She designed a pregnant crash-test dummy. She addressed women's safety needs.

1. I noticed that the sky was glowing orange and red. I bent down to crawl into the bunker.
2. The Market Inn is located on North Wharf. It doesn't look very impressive from the outside. The food, however, is excellent.
3. He walked up to the pitcher's mound. He dug his toe into the ground. He swung his arm around backward and forward. Then he threw the ball and struck the batter out.
4. Eryn and Maeve have decided to start a business. They have known each other since kindergarten. They will renovate homes for disabled people.
5. The first football card set was released by the Goudey Gum Company in 1933. The set featured only three football players. They were Red Grange, Bronko Nagurski, and Knute Rockne.

**EXERCISE 14–1   Possible revisions:**

a. **The X-Men comic books and Japanese woodcuts of kabuki dancers, all part of Marlena's research project on popular culture, covered the tabletop and the chairs.**
b. **Our waitress, costumed in a kimono, had painted her face white and arranged her hair in an upswept lacquered beehive.**
c. **Students can apply for a spot in the foundation's leadership program, which teaches thinking and communication skills.**
d. **Shore houses were flooded up to the first floor, beaches were washed away, and Brant's Lighthouse was swallowed by the sea.**
e. **Laura Thackray, an engineer at Volvo Car Corporation, designed a pregnant crash-test dummy to address women's safety needs.**

**ON THE WEB**  **dianahacker.com/bedhandbook**
▶ Electronic grammar exercises
▶ E-ex 14–1 and 14–2

**14c** Avoid ineffective or excessive coordination.

Coordinate structures are appropriate only when you intend to draw the reader's attention equally to two or more ideas: *Professor Sakellarios praises loudly, and she criticizes softly.* If one idea is more important than another — or if a coordinating conjunction does not clearly signal the relation between the ideas — you should subordinate the less important idea.

> **INEFFECTIVE** Closets were taxed as rooms, and most colonists stored their clothes in chests or clothes presses.

> **IMPROVED** Because closets were taxed as rooms, most colonists stored their clothes in chests or clothes presses.

The revision subordinates the less important idea (*closets were taxed as rooms*) by putting it in a subordinate clause. Notice that the subordinating conjunction *Because* signals the relation between the ideas more clearly than the coordinating conjunction *and.*

Because it is so easy to string ideas together with *and,* writers often rely too heavily on coordination in their rough drafts. The cure for excessive coordination is simple: Look for opportunities to tuck minor ideas into subordinate clauses or phrases.

**EXERCISE 14–1 (continued)**

1. Noticing that the sky was glowing orange and red, I bent down to crawl into the bunker.
2. The Market Inn, located on North Wharf, doesn't look very impressive from the outside. The food, however, is excellent.
3. He walked up to the pitcher's mound, dug his toe into the ground, and swung his arm around backward and forward. Then he threw the ball and struck the batter out.
4. Eryn and Maeve, who have known each other since kindergarten, have decided to start a business renovating homes for disabled people.
5. The first football card set, released by the Goudey Gum Company in 1933, featured only three football players: Red Grange, Bronko Nagurski, and Knute Rockne.

*When*
► Jason walked over to his new Mini Cooper, ~~and~~ he saw that
  ^
its windshield had been smashed.

The minor idea has become a subordinate clause beginning with *When.*

          *noticing*
► My uncle, ~~noticed~~ my frightened look, ~~and~~ told me that
      ^                       ^
Grandma had to feel my face because she was blind.

The less important idea has become a participial phrase modifying the noun *uncle.*

  *After four hours,*
► ~~Four hours went by, and~~ a rescue truck finally arrived, but by
  ^
that time we had been evacuated in a helicopter.

Three independent clauses were excessive. The least important idea has become a prepositional phrase.


**EXERCISE 14–2**   In the following sentences, ideas have been coordinated (joined with a coordinating conjunction or a semicolon). Restructure the sentences by subordinating minor ideas. You must decide which ideas are minor because the sentences are given out of context. Revisions of lettered sentences appear in the back of the book. Example:

                    *where they*
  The crew team finally returned to shore, ~~and~~ had a party on
    *to celebrate*            ^
  the beach ~~and celebrated~~ the start of the season.
     ^

a. These particles are known as "stealth liposomes," and they can hide in the body for a long time without detection.
b. Irena is a competitive gymnast and majors in biochemistry; her goal is to apply her athletic experience and her science degree to a career in sports medicine.


**EXERCISE 14–2   Possible revisions:**

a. These particles, known as "stealth liposomes," can hide in the body for a long time without detection.
b. Irena, a competitive gymnast majoring in biochemistry, intends to apply her athletic experience and her science degree to a career in sports medicine.
c. Because students, textile workers, and labor unions have loudly protested sweatshop abuses, apparel makers have been forced to examine their labor practices.
d. Developed in a European university, IRC (Internet Relay Chat) was created as a way for a group of graduate students to talk about projects from their dorm rooms.
e. The cafeteria's new menu, which has an international flavor, includes everything from enchiladas and pizza to pad thai and sauerbraten.

c. Students, textile workers, and labor unions have loudly protested sweatshop abuses, so apparel makers have been forced to examine their labor practices.
d. IRC (Internet Relay Chat) was developed in a European university; it was created as a way for a group of graduate students to talk about projects from their dorm rooms.
e. The cafeteria's new menu has an international flavor, and it includes everything from enchiladas and pizza to pad thai and sauerbraten.

1. Victor switched on his remote-control lawn mower, and it began to shudder and emit clouds of smoke.
2. Iguanas are dependent on ultraviolet rays from the sun, so in the winter months they must be put under ultraviolet-coated lights that can be purchased at most pet stores.
3. The Civil War Trust was founded in 1991; it spearheads a nationwide campaign to protect America's Civil War battlefields.
4. We did not expect to receive so many large orders so quickly, and we are short on inventory.
5. I am certain that Mother spread her love equally among us all, but she had a way of making each of us feel very special in our own way.

## 14d Do not subordinate major ideas.

If a sentence buries its major idea in a subordinate construction, readers may not give the idea enough attention. Express the major idea in an independent clause and subordinate any minor ideas.

▶ Lanie, who now walks with the help of braces/. ~~had polio as a~~ ~~child.~~
       *had polio as a child,*

The writer wanted to focus on Lanie's ability to walk, but the original sentence buried this information in an adjective clause. The revision puts the major idea in an independent

**EXERCISE 14–2 (continued)**
1. When Victor switched on his remote-control lawn mower, it began to shudder and emit clouds of smoke.
2. Because iguanas are dependent on ultraviolet rays from the sun, in the winter months they must be put under ultraviolet-coated lights that can be purchased at most pet stores.
3. Founded in 1991, the Civil War Trust spearheads a nationwide campaign to protect America's Civil War battlefields.
4. We are short on inventory because we did not expect to receive so many large orders so quickly.
5. Although I am certain that Mother spread her love equally among us all, she had a way of making each of us feel very special in our own way.

clause and tucks the less important idea into an adjective clause (*who had polio as a child*).

►   *As*
I was driving home from my new job, heading down Ranchitos
Road, ~~when~~ my car suddenly overheated.

The writer wanted to emphasize that the car overheated, not the fact of driving home. The revision expresses the major idea in an independent clause, the less important idea in an adverb clause (*As I was driving home from my new job*).

## 14e Do not subordinate excessively.

In attempting to avoid short, choppy sentences, writers sometimes go to the opposite extreme, putting more subordinate ideas into a sentence than its structure can bear. If a sentence collapses of its own weight, occasionally it can be restructured. More often, however, such sentences must be divided.

►   Our job is to stay between the stacker and the tie machine
                                        *If they do,*
  watching to see if the newspapers jam/. ~~in which case~~ we pull
the bundles off and stack them on a skid, because otherwise
they would back up in the stacker.

**EXERCISE 14–3**   In each of the following sentences, the idea that the writer wished to emphasize is buried in a subordinate construction. Restructure each sentence so that the independent clause expresses the major idea and lesser ideas are subordinated. Revisions of lettered sentences appear in the back of the book. Example:

**SCHOLARS ON SENTENCE COMBINING**

Elbow, Peter. "The Challenge for Sentence Combining." *Sentence Combining: A Rhetorical Perspective.* Ed. Don Daiker, Andrew Kerek, and Max Morenberg. Carbondale: Southern Illinois UP, 1985. 232–45. Elbow recognizes the value of sentence combining as a composing and revision strategy, but he also asks teachers to recognize the value of "decombining" and of leaving syntax alone.

Although
Catherine has weathered many hardships, ~~although~~ she has
^
rarely become discouraged. [*Emphasize that Catherine has*

*rarely become discouraged.*]

a. Gina worked as an aide for the relief agency, distributing food and medical supplies. [*Emphasize distributing food and medical supplies.*]

b. Janbir spent every Saturday learning tabla drumming, noticing with each hour of practice that his memory for complex patterns was growing stronger. [*Emphasize Janbir's memory.*]

c. The rotor hit, gouging a hole about an eighth of an inch deep in my helmet. [*Emphasize that the rotor gouged a hole in the helmet.*]

d. My grandfather, who raised his daughters the old-fashioned way, was born eighty years ago in Puerto Rico. [*Emphasize how the grandfather raised his daughters.*]

e. The Narcan reversed the depressive effect of the drug, saving the patient's life. [*Emphasize that the patient's life was saved.*]

1. Fatima, who studied Persian miniature painting after college, majored in early childhood education. [*Emphasize Fatima's studies after college.*]

2. I was losing consciousness when my will to live kicked in. [*Emphasize the will to live.*]

3. Using a sliding compound miter saw, the carpenter made intricate edges on the cabinets. [*Emphasize the carpenter's use of the saw.*]

4. Ernie was using origami to solve some tricky manufacturing problems when he decided to leave engineering and become an artist. [*Emphasize Ernie's decision.*]

5. As the undulating waves glinted in the sun, the paddlers synchronized their strokes. [*Emphasize the brightness of the waves.*]

**ON THE WEB**

**dianahacker.com/bedhandbook**
▶ Electronic grammar exercises
   ▶ E-ex 14–3

---

**EXERCISE 14–3   Possible revisions:**

a. **Working as an aide for the relief agency,** Gina distributed food and medical supplies.

b. Janbir, **who spent every Saturday learning tabla drumming,** noticed with each hour of practice that his memory for complex patterns was growing stronger.

c. **When the rotor hit, it** gouged a hole about an eighth of an inch deep in my helmet.

d. My grandfather, **who was born eighty years ago in Puerto Rico,** raised his daughters the old-fashioned way.

e. **By reversing the depressive effect of the drug,** the Narcan saved the patient's life.

**14f** Experiment with techniques for gaining special emphasis.

By experimenting with certain techniques, usually involving some element of surprise, you can draw attention to ideas that deserve special emphasis. Use such techniques sparingly, however, or they will lose their punch. The writer who tries to emphasize everything ends up emphasizing nothing.

*Using sentence endings for emphasis*

You can highlight an idea simply by withholding it until the end of a sentence. The technique works something like a punch line. In the following example, the sentence's meaning is not revealed until its very last word.

> The only completely consistent people are the dead.
> —Aldous Huxley

Two types of sentences that withhold information until the end are the inversion and the periodic sentence. The *inversion* reverses the normal subject-verb order, placing the subject at the end, where it receives unusual emphasis. (Also see 15c.)

> In golden pots are hidden the most deadly poisons.
> —Thomas Draxe

The *periodic* sentence opens with a pile-up of modifiers and withholds the subject and verb until the end. It draws attention to itself because it contrasts with the cumulative sentence, which is used more frequently. A *cumulative* sentence begins with the subject and verb and adds modifying elements at the end.

**EXERCISE 14–3 (continued)**

1. Fatima, who majored in early childhood education, studied Persian miniature painting after college.
2. As I was losing consciousness, my will to live kicked in.
3. The carpenter used a sliding compound miter saw to make intricate edges on the cabinets.
4. While using origami to solve some tricky manufacturing problems, Ernie decided to leave engineering and become an artist.
5. The undulating waves glinted in the sun as the paddlers synchronized their strokes.

**PERIODIC**

Twenty-five years ago, at the age of thirteen, while hiking in the mountains near my hometown of Vancouver, Washington, I came face to face with the legendary Goat Woman of Livingston Mountain. —Tom Weitzel, student

**CUMULATIVE**

A metaphysician is one who goes into a dark cellar at midnight without a light, looking for a black cat that is not there. —Baron Bowan of Colwood

### Using parallel structure for emphasis

Parallel grammatical structure draws special attention to paired ideas or to items in a series. (See 9.) When parallel ideas are paired, the emphasis falls on words that underscore comparisons or contrasts, especially when they occur at the end of a phrase or clause.

> We must *stop talking* about the *American dream* and *start listening* to the *dreams of Americans.* —Reubin Askew

In a parallel series, the emphasis falls at the end, so it is generally best to end with the most dramatic or climactic item in the series.

> Sister Charity enjoyed passing out writing punishments: translate the Ten Commandments into Latin, type a thousand-word essay on good manners, copy the New Testament with a quill pen. —Marie Visosky, student

### Using punctuation for emphasis

Obviously the exclamation point can add emphasis, but you should not overuse it. As a rule, the exclamation point is more appropriate in dialogue than in ordinary prose.

**SCHOLARS ON SENTENCE STYLE**

Shuster, Edgar H. *Breaking the Rules: Liberating Writers through Innovative Grammar Instruction.* Portsmouth: Heinemann, 2003. Shuster offers a nontraditional approach to teaching grammar, usage, and punctuation. He begins with a short history of traditional grammar instruction and the "counter traditions" offered in the research on language acquisition. The remaining chapters describe the "myth rules," those that have not offered meaningful help to students, and the "bedrock" rules, those that have been helpful. He lays out lesson plans for teaching the bedrock rules effectively so that they will "stay taught." Central to his approach is the belief that teachers should reflect on how their practices connect to the practices of the writers they most admire, professionals and students, in order to understand "which rules really rule."

I oozed a glob of white paint onto my palette, whipped some medium into it, loaded my brush, and announced to the class, "Move over, Michelangelo. Here I come!"
—Carolyn Goff, student

A dash or a colon may be used to draw attention to word groups worthy of special attention. (See 35a, 35b, and 39a.)

The middle of the road is where the white line is—and that's the worst place to drive.
—Robert Frost

I turned to see what the anemometer read: The needle had pegged out at 106 knots.
—Jonathan Shilk, student

Occasionally, a pair of dashes may be used to highlight a word or an idea.

[My friend] was a gay and impudent and satirical and delightful young black man—a slave—who daily preached sermons from the top of his master's woodpile, with me for sole audience.
—Mark Twain

### Using an occasional short sentence for emphasis

Too many short sentences in a row will fast become monotonous (see 14b), but an occasional short sentence, when played off against longer sentences in the same passage, will draw attention to an idea.

The great secret, known to internists and learned early in marriage by internists' wives [or husbands], but still hidden from the general public, is that most things get better by themselves. Most things, in fact, are better by morning.
—Lewis Thomas

**SCHOLARS ON SENTENCE STYLE**

Corbett, Edward P. J. *Classical Rhetoric for the Modern Student.* 4th ed. New York: Oxford UP, 1998. 359–76. In his chapter "Study of Style," Corbett lists features that determine prose style, including lengths of sentences, kinds of sentences, variety of sentence patterns, and coherence. He provides an example of student analysis, demonstrating the possible results.

Walpole, Jane R. "The Vigorous Pursuit of Grace and Style." *Writing Instructor* 1 (1982): 163–69. Walpole provides six short lessons to improve sentence style.

# 15

## Provide some variety.

When a rough draft is filled with too many same-sounding sentences, try injecting some variety — as long as you can do so without sacrificing clarity or ease of reading.

 **GRAMMAR CHECKERS** are of little help with sentence variety. It takes a human ear to know when and why sentence variety is needed.

Some programs tell you when you have used the same word to open several sentences, but sometimes it is a good idea to do so — if you are trying to highlight parallel ideas, for example (see p. 93).

### 15a Vary your sentence openings.

Most sentences in English begin with the subject, move to the verb, and continue to the object, with modifiers tucked in along the way or put at the end. For the most part, such sentences are fine. Put too many of them in a row, however, and they become monotonous.

Adverbial modifiers, being easily movable, can often be inserted ahead of the subject. Such modifiers might be single words, phrases, or clauses.

▶ *Eventually a*
 $\Lambda$ few drops of sap ~~eventually~~ began to trickle into the
   ^
   bucket.

Like most adverbs, *eventually* does not need to appear close to the verb it modifies (*began*).

**SCHOLARS ON SENTENCE STYLE**

Lanham, Richard. *Style: An Anti-Textbook.* New Haven: Yale UP, 1978. Resisting the call for clarity found in many textbooks, Lanham argues that we should teach students how to use a number of styles effectively.

Christensen, Francis. "A Generative Rhetoric of the Sentence." *College Composition and Communication* 14 (1963): 155–61. Rpt. in *Notes toward a New Rhetoric.* New York: Harper, 1967. 1–22. In this classic essay, Christensen introduces his concept of the cumulative sentence as one that generates ideas.

> *Just as the sun was coming up, a*
> ᴧ pair of black ducks flew over the pond. ~~just as the sun was~~
> ᴧ                                        ᴧ
> ~~coming up.~~

The adverb clause, which modifies the verb *flew,* is as clear at the beginning of the sentence as it is at the end.

Adjectives and participial phrases can frequently be moved to the beginning of a sentence without loss of clarity.

> *Dejected and withdrawn,*
> Edward/ ~~dejected and withdrawn,~~ nearly gave up his search
> ᴧ
> for a job.

>                  ᴧ                          *John and I*
> ~~John and I,~~ anticipating a peaceful evening, sat down at the
>              ᴧ                           ᴧ
> campfire to brew a cup of coffee.

**CAUTION:** When beginning a sentence with an adjective or a participial phrase, make sure that the subject of the sentence names the person or thing described in the introductory phrase. If it doesn't, the phrase will dangle. (See 12e.)

## 15b Use a variety of sentence structures.

A writer should not rely too heavily on simple sentences and compound sentences, for the effect tends to be both monotonous and choppy. (See 14b and 14c.) Too many complex or compound-complex sentences, however, can be equally monotonous. If your style tends to one or the other extreme, try to achieve a better mix of sentence types.

The major sentence types are illustrated in the following sentences, all taken from Flannery O'Connor's "The King of the Birds," an essay describing the author's pet peafowl.

**WRITERS ON WRITING**

I hate a style, as I do a garden, that is wholly flat and regular; that slides along like an eel, and never rises to what one can call an inequality.                                                    —William Shenstone

To shift the structure of a sentence alters the meaning of that sentence, as definitely and inflexibly as the position of a camera alters the meaning of the object photographed.                     —Joan Didion

A fluent writer always seems more talented than he [or she] is. To write well, one needs a natural facility and an acquired difficulty.
                                                                 —Joubert

| SIMPLE | Frequently the cock combines the lifting of his tail with the raising of his voice. |
|---|---|
| COMPOUND | Any chicken's dusting hole is out of place in a flower bed, but the peafowl's hole, being the size of a small crater, is more so. |
| COMPLEX | The peacock does most of his serious strutting in the spring and summer when he has a full tail to do it with. |
| COMPOUND-COMPLEX | The cock's plumage requires two years to attain its pattern, and for the rest of his life, this chicken will act as though he designed it himself. |

For a fuller discussion of sentence types, see 65a.

## 15c Try inverting sentences occasionally.

A sentence is inverted if it does not follow the normal subject-verb-object pattern (see 63c). Many inversions sound artificial and should be avoided except in the most formal contexts. But if an inversion sounds natural, it can provide a welcome touch of variety.

▶ *Opposite the produce section is a* A refrigerated case of mouth-watering cheeses; ~~is opposite the produce section;~~ a friendly attendant will cut off just the amount you want.

The revision inverts the normal subject-verb order by moving the verb, *is*, ahead of its subject, *case*.

▶ *Set at the top two corners of the stage were huge* ~~Huge~~ lavender hearts outlined in bright white lights. ~~were set at the top two corners of the stage.~~

**SCHOLARS ON SENTENCE VARIETY**

Williams, James D. *Preparing to Teach Writing.* 3rd ed. Mahwah: Erlbaum, 2003. Williams discusses common myths about sentence openings, closings, and length.

Laib, Nevin. "Conciseness and Amplification." *College Composition and Communication* 41 (1990): 443–59. Asserting that "conciseness is not an unqualified good," Laib argues that we should teach amplification as well as conciseness. Though much of his essay focuses on paragraph-level concerns, his suggestions for teaching amplification illustrate fifteen sentence types.

In the revision the subject, *hearts*, appears after the verb, *were set*. Notice that the two parts of the verb are also inverted—and separated from one another—without any awkwardness or loss of meaning.

Inverted sentences are used for emphasis as well as for variety (see 14f).

**15d** Consider adding an occasional question or quotation.

An occasional question can provide a welcome change of pace, especially at the beginning of a paragraph, where it engages the reader's interest.

> Virginia Woolf, in her book *A Room of One's Own,* wrote that in order for a woman to write fiction she must have two things, certainly: a room of her own (with key and lock) and enough money to support herself.
>    *What then are we to make of Phillis Wheatley, a slave, who owned not even herself?* This sickly, frail black girl who required a servant of her own at times—her health was so precarious—and who, had she been white, would have been easily considered the intellectual superior of all the women and most of the men in the society of her day. [Italics added.]
>                                                            —Alice Walker

Quotations can also provide variety, for they add other people's voices to your own. These other voices might be bits of dialogue.

> When we got back upstairs, Dr. Haney and Captain Shiller, the head nurse, were waiting for us by the elevator. As the nurse hurried off, pushing Todd, the doctor explained to us what would happen next.
>    "Mrs. Barrus," he began, "this last test is one we do only when absolutely necessary. It is very painful and hard on the

**WRITERS ON WRITING**
When I sit at my table to write, I never know what it's going to be till I'm under way. I trust in inspiration, which sometimes comes and sometimes doesn't. But I don't sit back waiting for it. I work *every* day.                                            —Alberto Moravia

patient but we have no other choice." Apologetically, he went on. "I cannot give him an anesthetic." He waited for the statement to sink in. —Celeste L. Barrus, student

Or they might be quotations from written sources.

> Even when she enters the hospital on the brink of death, the anorexic will refuse help from anyone and will continue to deny needing help, especially from a doctor. At this point, reports Dr. Steven Levenkron, the anorexic is most likely "a frightened, cold, lonely, starved, and physically tortured, exhausted person—not unlike an actual concentration camp inmate" (29). In this condition she is ultimately force-fed through a tube inserted in the chest. —Jim Drew, student

Notice that the quotation from a written source is documented with a citation in parentheses. (See Part X.)

**EXERCISE 15–1**   Edit the following paragraph to increase sentence variety.

> Making architectural models is a skill that requires patience and precision. It is an art that illuminates a design. Architects come up with a grand and intricate vision. Draftspersons convert that vision into blueprints. The model maker follows the blueprints. The model maker builds a miniature version of the structure. Modelers can work in traditional materials like wood and clay and paint. Modelers can work in newer materials like Styrofoam and liquid polymers. Some modelers still use cardboard, paper, and glue. Other modelers prefer glue guns, deformable plastic, and thin aluminum and brass wire. The modeler may seem to be making a small mess in the early stages of model building. In the end the modeler has completed a ¹⁄₁₀₀-scale structure. Architect Rem Koolhaas has insisted that plans reveal the logic of a design. He has argued that models expose the architect's vision. The model maker's art makes vision real.

**EXERCISE 15–1   Possible revisions:**

Making architectural models is a skill that requires patience and precision and also an art that illuminates a design. Architects come up with a grand and intricate vision and then draftspersons convert that vision into blueprints. The model maker follows the blueprints to build a miniature version of the structure. Modelers can work in traditional materials like wood and clay and paint or in newer materials like Styrofoam and liquid polymers. Some modelers still use cardboard, paper, and glue; other modelers prefer glue guns, deformable plastic, and thin aluminum and brass wire. Although the modeler may seem to be making a small mess in the early stages of model building, in the end the modeler has completed a ¹⁄₁₀₀-scale structure. Architect Rem Koolhaas has insisted that plans reveal the logic of a design and that models expose the architect's vision. The model maker's art makes vision real.

# Part IV

# Word Choice

ON THE WEB

**dianahacker.com/bedhandbook/instructor**
- ▶ Exercise masters
- ▶ Quiz masters
- ▶ Transparency masters

# 16

---

## Tighten wordy sentences.

---

In a rough draft we are rarely economical: We repeat ourselves, we belabor the obvious, we cushion our thoughts in verbiage. As a general rule, advises writer Sidney Smith, "run a pen through every other word you have written; you have no idea what vigor it will give your style."

Long sentences are not necessarily wordy, nor are short sentences always concise. A sentence is wordy if it can be tightened without loss of meaning.

>  **GRAMMAR CHECKERS** flag wordy constructions only occasionally. They sometimes alert you to common redundancies, such as *true fact,* but they overlook more redundancies than they catch. They may miss empty or inflated phrases, such as *in my opinion* and *in order that,* and they rarely identify sentences with needlessly complex structures. Grammar checkers are very good, however, at flagging and suggesting revisions for wordy constructions beginning with *there is* and *there are.*

### 16a Eliminate redundancies.

Writers often repeat themselves unnecessarily. Afraid, perhaps, that they won't be heard the first time, they insist that a teacup is small *in size* or yellow *in color,* that married people should cooperate *together,* that a fact is not just a fact but a *true* fact. Such redundancies may seem at first to add emphasis. In reality they do just the opposite, for they divide the reader's attention.

---

**WRITERS ON WRITING**

I apologize for this long letter; I didn't have time to shorten it.
—Pliny

To write simply is as difficult as to be good.
—W. Somerset Maugham

Clutter is the disease of American writing. We are a society strangling in unnecessary words, circular constructions, pompous frills, and meaningless jargon. —William Zinsser

I once said his prose is dipped in chicken fat.
—Oscar Levant, referring to David Susskind

▶ Twenty-somethings are often ~~thought of or~~ stereotyped as apathetic even though many are active in political and service groups.

▶ Daniel ~~is now employed~~ <sup>works</sup> at a private rehabilitation center ~~working~~ as a registered physical therapist.

Though modifiers ordinarily add meaning to the words they modify, occasionally they are redundant.

▶ Sylvia ~~very hurriedly~~ scribbled her name, address, and phone number on a greasy napkin.

▶ Joel was determined ~~in his mind~~ to lose weight.

The words *scribbled* and *determined* already contain the notions suggested by the modifiers *very hurriedly* and *in his mind.*

## 16b Avoid unnecessary repetition of words.

Though words may be repeated deliberately, for effect, repetitions will seem awkward if they are clearly unnecessary. When a more concise version is possible, choose it.

▶ Our fifth patient, in room six, is a mentally ill. ~~patient.~~

▶ The best teachers help each student to ~~become a better~~ <sup>grow</sup> ~~student~~ both academically and emotionally.

---

**WRITERS ON WRITING**

Remember the waterfront shack with the sign FRESH FISH SOLD HERE. Of course it's fresh, we're on the ocean. Of course it's for sale, we're not giving it away. Of course it's here, otherwise the sign would be someplace else. The final sign: FISH.

—Peggy Noonan

A sentence should contain no unnecessary words, a paragraph no unnecessary sentences, for the same reason that a drawing should have no unnecessary lines and a machine no unnecessary parts.

—William Strunk Jr. and E. B. White

**16c** Cut empty or inflated phrases.

An empty phrase can be cut with little or no loss of meaning. Common examples are introductory word groups that apologize or hedge: *in my opinion, I think that, it seems that, one must admit that,* and so on.

▶ ~~In my opinion,~~ *O*ur current immigration policy is misguided.

▶ ~~It seems that~~ *Harry Potter and the Half-Blood Prince* is
J. K. Rowling's darkest novel.

Readers understand without being told that they are hearing the writer's opinion or educated guess.

Inflated phrases can be reduced to a word or two without loss of meaning.

| INFLATED | CONCISE |
|---|---|
| along the lines of | like |
| as a matter of fact | in fact |
| at all times | always |
| at the present time | now, currently |
| at this point in time | now, currently |
| because of the fact that | because |
| by means of | by |
| by virtue of the fact that | because |
| due to the fact that | because |
| for the purpose of | for |
| for the reason that | because |
| have the ability to | be able to, can |
| in light of the fact that | because |
| in order to | to |
| in spite of the fact that | although, though |
| in the event that | if |
| in the final analysis | finally |

**WRITERS ON WRITING**

He can compress the most words into the smallest ideas of any man I ever met.
                    —Abraham Lincoln, referring to a political opponent

I might not know how to use thirty-four words where three would do, but that does not mean that I don't know what I'm talking about.                    —Ruth Shays

A writer wastes nothing.                    —F. Scott Fitzgerald

Concision is honesty, honesty concision—that's one thing you need to know.                    —John Simon

Epigrams succeed where epics fail.                    —Persian proverb

| INFLATED | CONCISE |
|---|---|
| in the nature of | like |
| in the neighborhood of | about |
| until such time as | until |

                                                      *if*
► We will file the appropriate papers ~~in the event that~~ we are
                                              ^
unable to meet the deadline.

## 16d Simplify the structure.

If the structure of a sentence is needlessly indirect, try simplifying it. Look for opportunities to strengthen the verb.

► The financial analyst claimed that because of volatile market

conditions she could not ~~make an~~ estimate ~~of~~ the company's

future profits.

The verb *estimate* is more vigorous and concise than *make an
estimate of.*

The colorless verbs *is, are, was,* and *were* frequently
generate excess words.

              *monitors and balances*
► Eduartina ~~is responsible for monitoring and balancing~~ the
           ^
budgets for travel, contract services, and personnel.

The revision is more direct and concise. Actions originally
appearing in subordinate structures have become verbs replacing *is.*

The expletive constructions *there is* and *there are* (or
*there was* and *there were*) can also generate excess words.

The same is true of expletive constructions beginning with
*it.* (See 63c.)

▶ ~~There is~~ A another module ~~that~~ tells the story of Charles

Darwin and introduces the theory of evolution.

▶ ~~It is imperative that~~ A ll police officers *must* follow strict

procedures when apprehending a suspect.

Expletive constructions do have legitimate uses, however.
For example, they are appropriate when a writer has a good
reason for delaying the subject. (See 63c.)

Finally, verbs in the passive voice may be needlessly indirect. When the active voice expresses your meaning as
well, use it. (See 8a.)

▶ All too often, *our coaches have recruited* athletes with marginal academic skills. ~~have~~

~~been recruited by our coaches.~~

**16e** Reduce clauses to phrases, phrases to single words.

Word groups functioning as modifiers can often be made
more compact. Look for any opportunities to reduce clauses
to phrases or phrases to single words.

▶ We took a side trip to Monticello, ~~which was~~ the home of

Thomas Jefferson.

▶ For her birthday we gave Jess a stylish vest. *silk* ~~made of silk.~~

**EXERCISE 16–1   Possible revisions:**
a. Martin Luther King Jr. set a high standard for future leaders.
b. Aanika has loved cooking since she could first peek over a kitchen tabletop.
c. Bloom's race for the governorship is futile.
d. A successful graphic designer must have technical knowledge and an eye for color and balance.
e. You will deliver mail to all employees.

**EXERCISE 16–1** Edit the following sentences for wordiness. Revisions of lettered sentences appear in the back of the book. Example:

> The Wilsons moved into the house ~~in spite of the fact that~~ *even though* ^ the back door was only ten yards from the train tracks.

a. Martin Luther King Jr. was a man who set a high standard for future leaders to meet.
b. Aanika has been deeply in love with cooking since she was little and could first peek over the edge of a big kitchen tabletop.
c. In my opinion, Bloom's race for the governorship is a futile exercise.
d. It is pretty important in being a successful graphic designer to have technical knowledge and at one and the same moment an eye for color and balance.
e. Your task will be the deliverance of correspondence to all employees in the company.

1. Seeing the barrels, the driver immediately slammed on his brakes.
2. A really well-stocked bookshelf should have classical literature on it as well as important modern works of the current day.
3. China's enormously huge work population has an effect on the global world of high-tech manufacturing of things.
4. A typical autocross course consists of at least two straightaways, and the rest of the course is made up of numerous slaloms and several sharp turns.
5. At breakfast time, Mehrdad always started his day with cantaloupe, lemon yogurt, and black coffee.

---

**ON THE WEB**

**dianahacker.com/bedhandbook**
▶ Electronic grammar exercises
　▶ E-ex 16–1 to 16–3

---

**EXERCISE 16–1 (continued)**

1. Seeing the barrels, the driver slammed on his brakes.
2. A well-stocked bookshelf should have classical literature and important modern works.
3. China's huge work population affects high-tech manufacturing globally.
4. A typical autocross course consists of at least two straightaways, numerous slaloms, and several sharp turns.
5. Mehrdad always had cantaloupe, lemon yogurt, and black coffee for breakfast.

**EXERCISE 16–2**    Edit the following business memo for wordiness.

| | |
|---|---|
| To: | District managers |
| From: | Margaret Davenport, Vice President |
| Subject: | Customer files |

It has recently been brought to my attention that a percentage of our sales representatives have been failing to log reports of their client calls in our electronic customer file each and every day. I have also learned that some representatives are not checking the customer file on a routine basis.

Our clients sometimes receive a multiple number of sales calls from us when a sales representative is not cognizant of the fact that the client has been contacted at a previous time. Repeated telephone calls from our representatives annoy our customers. These repeated telephone calls also portray our company as one that is lacking in organization.

Effective as of immediately, direct your representatives to do the following:

- Record each and every customer contact in the electronic file at the end of each day, without fail.
- Check the electronic file at the very beginning of each day to ensure that telephone communications will not be initiated with clients who have already been called.

Let me extend my appreciation to you for cooperating in this important matter.

# 17

## Choose appropriate language.

Language is appropriate when it suits your subject, engages your audience, and blends naturally with your own voice.

To some extent, your choice of language will be governed by the conventions of the genre in which you are writing.

**EXERCISE 16–2    Possible revisions:**

| | |
|---|---|
| To: | District managers |
| From: | Margaret Davenport, Vice President |
| Subject: | Customer files |

Some of our sales representatives have been failing to log daily reports of their client calls in our electronic customer file. Also, some representatives are not routinely checking the customer file.

Our clients sometimes receive repeated calls from us when a sales representative does not realize that the client has already been contacted. Repeated calls annoy our customers and make us appear disorganized.

Effective immediately, direct your representatives to do the following:

When in doubt about the conventions of a particular genre—lab reports, informal essays, business memos, and so on—look at models written by experts in the field.

## 17a Stay away from jargon.

Jargon is specialized language used among members of a trade, profession, or group. Use jargon only when readers will be familiar with it; even then, use it only when plain English will not do as well.

Sentences filled with jargon are likely to be long and lumpy. To revise such sentences, you must rewrite them, usually in fewer words.

> **JARGON** For years the indigenous body politic of South Africa attempted to negotiate legal enfranchisement without result.
>
> **REVISED** For years the indigenous people of South Africa negotiated in vain for the right to vote.

Though a political scientist might feel comfortable with the original version, jargon such as *body politic* and *legal enfranchisement* is needlessly complicated for ordinary readers.

Broadly defined, jargon includes puffed-up language designed more to impress readers than to inform them. The following are common examples from business, government, higher education, and the military, with plain English translations in parentheses.

| | |
|---|---|
| ameliorate (improve) | indicator (sign) |
| commence (begin) | optimal (best, most favorable) |
| components (parts) | parameters (boundaries, limits) |
| endeavor (try) | peruse (read, look over) |
| exit (leave) | prior to (before) |
| facilitate (help) | utilize (use) |
| factor (consideration, cause) | viable (workable) |
| impact (v.) (affect) | |

---

**EXERCISE 16–2 (continued)**

- Record each customer contact in the electronic file at the end of each day.
- Check the electronic file at the beginning of each day to guard against repeated calls.

Thank you for cooperating in this important matter.

**SCHOLARS ON JARGON AND DOUBLESPEAK**

Lutz, William. *The New Doublespeak: Why No One Knows What Anyone's Saying Anymore.* New York: Harper, 1996. The longtime editor of the *Quarterly Review of Doublespeak* continues his campaign to expose misleading language. He offers myriad examples from a wide range of public texts.

Sentences filled with jargon are hard to read, and they are often wordy as well.

▶ All ~~employees functioning in the capacity of~~ work-study students ~~are required to give evidence of current enrollment.~~ *must prove that they are currently enrolled.*

▶ Mayor Summers will ~~commence~~ *begin* his term of office by ~~ameliorating~~ *improving* living conditions in ~~economically deprived zones.~~ *poor neighborhoods.*

### 17b Avoid pretentious language, most euphemisms, and "doublespeak."

Hoping to sound profound or poetic, some writers embroider their thoughts with large words and flowery phrases, language that in fact sounds pretentious. Pretentious language is so ornate and often so wordy that it obscures the thought that lies beneath.

▶ When our ~~progenitors reach their silver-haired and golden years,~~ *parents become old,* we frequently ~~ensepulcher~~ *entomb* them in ~~homes for senescent beings~~ *old-age homes* as if they were already ~~among the deceased.~~ *dead.*

The writer of the original sentence had turned to a thesaurus (a dictionary of synonyms and antonyms) in an attempt to sound educated. When such a writer gains enough confidence to speak in his or her own voice, pretentious language disappears.

Related to pretentious language are euphemisms, nice-sounding words or phrases substituted for words thought to sound harsh or ugly. Like pretentious language, euphemisms are wordy and indirect. Unlike pretentious language, they are sometimes appropriate. It is our social

**WRITERS ON WRITING**

Stick close to the original form of a word. With every suffix you add to a word, you compromise its clarity and immediacy. As *institute* becomes *institution,* then *institutional,* then *institutionalize,* and finally *institutionalization,* readers cease to match precise meanings with the increasingly abstract terms. —Sally James

Many intelligent people, when about to write . . . , force on their minds a certain notion about style, just as they screw up their faces when they sit for their portraits. —G. C. Lichtenberg

custom, for example, to use euphemisms when speaking or writing about excretion (*I have to go to the bathroom*), sexual intercourse (*They did not sleep together until they were married*), and the like. We may also use euphemisms out of concern for someone's feelings. Telling parents, for example, that their daughter is "unmotivated" is more sensitive than saying she's lazy. Tact or politeness, then, can justify an occasional euphemism.

Most euphemisms, however, are needlessly evasive or even deceitful. Like pretentious language, they obscure the intended meaning.

| EUPHEMISM | PLAIN ENGLISH |
|---|---|
| adult entertainment | pornography |
| preowned automobile | used car |
| economically deprived | poor |
| selected out | fired |
| negative savings | debts |
| strategic withdrawal | retreat or defeat |
| revenue enhancers | taxes |
| chemical dependency | drug addiction |
| downsize | lay off |
| correctional facility | prison |

The term *doublespeak,* coined by George Orwell in his novel *1984,* applies to any deliberately evasive or deceptive language, including euphemisms. Doublespeak is especially common in politics, where missiles are named "Peacekeepers," airplane crashes are termed "uncontrolled contact with the ground," and a military retreat is described as "tactical redeployment." Business also gives us its share of doublespeak. When the manufacturer of a pacemaker writes that its product "may result in adverse health consequences in pacemaker-dependent patients as a result of sudden 'no output' failure," it takes an alert reader to grasp the message: The pacemakers might suddenly stop functioning and cause a heart attack or even death.

**WRITERS ON WRITING**

That must be fine, for I don't understand a word. —Molière

Read over your compositions, and wherever you meet with a passage which you think is particularly fine, strike it out.
—Samuel Johnson, quoting a college tutor

If I take refuge in ambiguity, I assure you it's quite conscious.
—Kingman Brewster Jr.

She calls a spade a delving instrument. —Rita Mae Brown

**GRAMMAR CHECKERS** rarely identify jargon and only occasionally flag pretentious language. Sometimes they flag language that is acceptable in academic writing. You should be alert to your own use of jargon and pretentious language and simplify it whenever possible. If your grammar checker continually questions language that is appropriate in an academic setting, check to see whether you can set it to a formal style level.

**EXERCISE 17–1**  Edit the following sentences to eliminate jargon, pretentious or flowery language, euphemisms, and doublespeak. You may need to make substantial changes in some sentences. Revisions of lettered sentences appear in the back of the book. Example:

> *mastered*
> After two weeks in the legal department, Sue has ~~worked~~
> *office                                   performance has*
> ~~into~~ the routine, ~~of the office,~~ and her ~~functional and self-~~
>
> ~~management skills have~~ exceeded all expectations.

a. In my youth, my family was under the constraints of difficult material circumstances.
b. In order that I may increase my expertise in the area of delivery of services to clients, I feel that participation in this conference will be beneficial.
c. Have you ever been accused of flagellating a deceased equine?
d. Governmentally sanctioned investigations into the continued value of after-school programs have begun to indicate a perceived need in the public realm at large.
e. Passengers should endeavor to finalize the customs declaration form prior to exiting the aircraft.

1. We learned that the mayor had been engaging in a creative transfer of city employees' pension funds.
2. After a cursory examination of brand-new research materials on textiles, Patricia and the members of her team made the de-

---

**EXERCISE 17–1  Possible revisions:**

a. In my youth, my family was poor.
b. This conference will help me serve my clients better.
c. Have you ever been accused of beating a dead horse?
d. Government studies show a need for after-school programs.
e. Passengers should try to complete the customs declaration form before leaving the plane.

1. We learned that the mayor had been embezzling money from city employees' pension funds.
2. After a quick look at new research on textiles, Patricia's team decided to visit local clothing manufacturers.
3. The nurse said that the patient had died because the surgeon had made a mistake.

cision to engage in a series of visits to fashion manufacturers in the local vicinity.

3. The nurse announced that there had been a negative patient-care outcome due to a therapeutic misadventure on the part of the surgeon.

4. A generally leisurely pace at the onset of tai chi exercises can yield a variety of beneficial points within a short period of time.

5. The bottom line is that the company is experiencing a negative cash flow.

**EXERCISE 17–2**   Edit the following e-mail message to eliminate jargon.

Dear Ms. Jackson:

We members of the Nakamura Reyes team value our external partnering arrangements with Creative Software, and I look forward to seeing you next week at the trade show in Fresno. Per Mr. Reyes, please let me know when you'll have some downtime there so that he and I can conduct a strategizing session with you concerning our production schedule. It's crucial that we all be on the same page re our 2004–2005 product release dates.

Before we have a face-to-face, however, I have some findings to share. Our customer-centric approach to the new products will necessitate that user testing periods trend upward. The enclosed data should help you effectuate any adjustments to your timeline; let me know ASAP if you require any additional information to facilitate the above.

Before we convene in Fresno, Mr. Reyes and I will agendize any further talking points. Thanks for your help.

Sincerely,

Sylvia Nakamura

**EXERCISE 17–1 (continued)**
4. Beginning tai chi slowly brings benefits quickly.
5. The important fact is that the company is losing money.

**EXERCISE 17–2   Possible revisions:**

Dear Ms. Jackson:

We at Nakamura Reyes value our relationship with Creative Software, and I look forward to seeing you next week at the trade show in Fresno. Please let me know when you will have time to meet with Mr. Reyes and me to discuss our production schedule. It's crucial that we all agree on our 2004–2005 product release dates.

Before we meet, however, I have some new information. Our user-friendly approach to the new products will make longer user test-

| ON THE WEB | **dianahacker.com/bedhandbook**
▶ Electronic grammar exercises
▶ E-ex 17–1 |

## 17c Avoid obsolete and invented words.

Although dictionaries list obsolete words such as *recomfort* and *reechy,* these words are not appropriate for current use. Invented words (also called *neologisms*) are too recently created to be part of standard English. Many invented words fade out of use without becoming standard. *Bling* and *technobabble* are neologisms that may not last. *Printout* and *flextime* are no longer neologisms; they have become standard English. Avoid using invented words in formal writing unless they are given in the dictionary as standard or unless no other word expresses your meaning.

## 17d In most contexts, avoid slang, regional expressions, and nonstandard English.

Slang is an informal and sometimes private vocabulary that expresses the solidarity of a group such as teenagers, rock musicians, or football fans; it is subject to more rapid change than standard English. For example, the slang teenagers use to express approval changes every few years; *cool, groovy, neat, awesome, phat,* and *sweet* have replaced one another within the last three decades. Sometimes slang becomes so widespread that it is accepted as standard vocabulary. *Jazz,* for example, started out as slang but is now generally accepted to describe a style of music.

Although slang has a certain vitality, it is a code that not everyone understands, and it is very informal. Therefore, it is inappropriate in most written work.

---

**EXERCISE 17–2 (continued)**

ing periods necessary. The enclosed data should help you adjust your timeline; let me know right away if you require any additional information before making these adjustments.

Before we meet in Fresno, Mr. Reyes and I will outline any other topics for discussion. Thanks for your help.

Sincerely,

Sylvia Nakamura

▶ If we don't begin studying for the final, a whole semester's
      *will be wasted.*
   work ~~is going down the tubes.~~
     ^

                                               *disgust you.*
▶ The government's "filth" guidelines for food will ~~gross you out.~~
                                                      ^

Regional expressions are common to a group in a geographical area. *Let's talk with the bark off* (for *Let's speak frankly*) is an expression in the southern United States, for example. Regional expressions have the same limitations as slang and are therefore inappropriate in most writing.

▶ John was four blocks from the house before he remembered
     *turn on*
   to ~~cut~~ the headlights. ~~on.~~
    ^                  ^

▶ I'm not ~~for~~ sure, but I think the dance has been postponed

   until tomorrow.

Standard English is the language used in all academic, business, and professional fields. Nonstandard English is spoken by people with a common regional or social heritage. Although nonstandard English may be appropriate when spoken within a close group, it is out of place in most formal and informal writing.

         *has*
▶ The counselor ~~have~~ so many problems in her own life that
   *doesn't*  ^
   she ~~don't~~ know how to advise anyone else.
    ^

If you speak a nonstandard dialect, try to identify the ways in which your dialect differs from standard English. Look especially for the following features of nonstandard English, which commonly cause problems in writing.

**WRITERS ON WRITING**

The best advice I ever had about writing was to do it as if you were writing for a friend.       — Helen Fielding

There is still no substitute for radical sincerity.      — Gish Jen

"Are you excavating a subterranean channel?" asked the scholar. "No sir," replied the farmer. "I am only digging a ditch."
            — An old joke

I know there are professors in this country who "ligate" arteries. Other surgeons only tie them, and it stops bleeding just as well.
            — Oliver Wendell Holmes Sr.

When an idea is wanting, a word can always be found to take its place.         — J. W. Goethe

Misuse of verb forms such as *began* and *begun* (See 27a.)

Omission of *-s* endings on verbs (See 27c.)

Omission of *-ed* endings on verbs (See 27d.)

Omission of necessary verbs (See 27e.)

Double negatives (See 26d.)

**17e** Choose an appropriate level of formality.

In deciding on a level of formality, consider both your subject and your audience. Does the subject demand a dignified treatment, or is a relaxed tone more suitable? Will readers be put off if you assume too close a relationship with them, or might you alienate them by seeming too distant?

For most college and professional writing, some degree of formality is appropriate. In a letter applying for a job, for example, it is a mistake to sound too breezy and informal.

> **TOO INFORMAL**   I'd like to get that technician job you've got in the paper.

> **MORE FORMAL**   I would like to apply for the technician position listed in the *Peoria Journal Star.*

Informal writing is appropriate for private letters, personal e-mail and instant messages, and business correspondence between close associates. Like spoken conversation, it allows contractions (*don't, I'll*) and colloquial words (*kids, buddy*). Vocabulary and sentence structure are rarely complex.

In choosing a level of formality, above all be consistent. When a writer's voice shifts from one level of formality to another, readers receive mixed messages.

**SCHOLARS ON NONSTANDARD ENGLISH**

Monseau, Virginia R., ed. *And Language for All.* Issue of *English Journal* 90.4 (2001). This issue of the journal for the secondary section of NCTE includes several articles on nonstandard English including "Standard English and the Migrant Community" by Gregory Shafer, "What's a (White) Teacher to Do about Black English?" by Sara Dalmas Jonsberg, and "Acknowledging the Language of African American Students: Instructional Strategies" by Sharroky Hollie.

▶ Once a pitcher for the Cincinnati Reds, Bob shared with me
the secrets of his trade. His lesson ~~commenced~~ *began* with his
famous curveball, ~~implemented~~ *thrown* by tucking the little finger
behind the ball instead of holding it straight out. Next he
~~elucidated~~ *revealed* the mysteries of the sucker pitch, a slow ball
coming behind a fast windup.

Words such as *commenced* and *elucidated* are inappropriate for
the subject matter, and they clash with informal terms such as
*sucker pitch* and *fast windup*.

---

**GRAMMAR CHECKERS** rarely flag slang and informal language. They do, however, flag contractions. If your ear tells you that a contraction such as *isn't* or *doesn't* strikes the right tone, stay with it.

---

## 17f Avoid sexist language.

Sexist language is language that stereotypes or demeans men or women, usually women. Using nonsexist language is a matter of courtesy—of respect for and sensitivity to the feelings of others.

### Recognizing sexist language

Some sexist language is easy to recognize because it reflects genuine contempt for women: referring to a woman as a "chick," for example, or calling a lawyer a "lady lawyer," or saying in an advertisement, "If our new sports car were a lady, it would get its bottom pinched."

---

**SCHOLARS ON NONSTANDARD ENGLISH**

Williams, James D. "Nonstandard English." *Preparing to Teach Writing*. 3rd ed. Mahwah: Erlbaum, 2003. Williams draws on several decades of sociolinguistic research to define "dialect," to discuss the characteristics of black English and Chicano English, and to explore how these forms of English affect writing performance. His bibliography is extensive.

Balester, Valerie M. *Cultural Divide: A Study of African-American College-Level Writers*. Portsmouth: Boynton, 1993. 77–151. In her study of eight African American college students, Balester explores how these writers draw on language strategies embedded in an African American rhetorical tradition, strategies that are often at odds with expectations for academic prose.

Other forms of sexist language are less blatant. The following practices, while they may not result from conscious sexism, reflect stereotypical thinking: referring to nurses as women and doctors as men, using different conventions when naming or identifying women and men, or assuming that all of one's readers are men.

**STEREOTYPICAL LANGUAGE**

After the nursing student graduates, *she* must face a difficult state board examination. [Not all nursing students are women.]

Running for city council are Jake Stein, an attorney, and *Mrs.* Cynthia Jones, a professor of English and *mother of three.* [The title *Mrs.* and the phrase *mother of three* are irrelevant.]

*Wives* of senior government officials are required to report any gifts they receive that are valued at more than $100. [Not all senior government officials are men.]

Still other forms of sexist language result from outmoded traditions. The pronouns *he, him,* and *his,* for instance, were traditionally used to refer generically to persons of either sex.

**GENERIC *HE* OR *HIS***

When a physician is harassed by managed care professionals, *he* may be tempted to leave the profession.

A journalist is stimulated by *his* deadline.

Today, however, such usage is widely viewed as sexist because it excludes women and encourages sex-role stereotyping—the view that men are somehow more suited than women to be doctors, journalists, and so on.

Like the pronouns *he, him,* and *his,* the nouns *man* and *men* were once used indefinitely to refer to persons of either

**SCHOLARS ON NONSTANDARD ENGLISH**

Giannasi, Jenefer M. "Language Varieties and Composition." *Teaching Composition.* Ed. Gary Tate. Rev. ed. Fort Worth: Texas Christian UP, 1987. Giannasi reviews sociolinguistic studies of variations in language and addresses issues that arise in the composition classroom because of differences among dialects.

Labov, William. *Language in the Inner City: Studies in the Black English Vernacular.* Philadelphia: U of Pennsylvania P, 1972. Labov describes the linguistic features of black English as spoken in inner cities. He also analyzes the cultural, social, and political dimensions of black English.

See also SCHOLARS ON STANDARD ENGLISH VERB FORMS (27).

sex. Current usage demands gender-neutral terms for references to both men and women.

| INAPPROPRIATE | APPROPRIATE |
|---|---|
| chairman | chairperson, moderator, chair, head |
| clergyman | member of the clergy, minister, pastor |
| congressman | member of Congress, representative, legislator |
| fireman | firefighter |
| foreman | supervisor |
| mailman | mail carrier, postal worker, letter carrier |
| (to) man | to operate, to staff |
| mankind | people, humans |
| manpower | personnel |
| policeman | police officer |
| salesman | salesperson, sales associate, salesclerk, sales representative |
| weatherman | weather forecaster, meteorologist |
| workman | worker, laborer |

**GRAMMAR CHECKERS** are good at flagging obviously sexist terms, such as *mankind* and *fireman,* but they do not flag language that might be demeaning to women (*woman doctor*) or stereotypical (referring to assistants as women and lawyers as men, for instance). They also have no way of identifying the generic use of *he* or *his* (*An obstetrician needs to be available to his patients at all hours*). All in all, you must use your common sense to tell when a word or a construction is offensive.

**ON THE WEB**

**dianahacker.com/bedhandbook**
▶ Language Debates
  ▶ Sexist language

---

**WRITERS ON WRITING**

Slang is a language that rolls up its sleeves, spits on its hands, and goes to work. —Carl Sandburg

You can be a little ungrammatical if you come from the right part of the country. —Robert Frost

## Revising sexist language

When revising sexist language, be sparing in your use of the wordy constructions *he or she* and *his or her.* Although these constructions are fine in small doses, they become awkward when repeated throughout an essay. A better revision strategy, many writers have discovered, is to write in the plural; yet another strategy is to recast the sentence so that the problem does not arise.

**SEXIST**

When a physician is harassed by managed care professionals, *he* may be tempted to leave the profession.

A journalist is stimulated by *his* deadline.

A good designer chooses *her* projects carefully.

**ACCEPTABLE BUT WORDY**

When a physician is harassed by managed care professionals, *he or she* may be tempted to leave the profession.

A journalist is stimulated by *his or her* deadline.

A good designer chooses *his or her* projects carefully.

**BETTER: USING THE PLURAL**

When *physicians* are harassed by managed care professionals, *they* may be tempted to leave the profession.

*Journalists* are stimulated by *their* deadlines.

Good designers choose *their* projects carefully.

**BETTER: RECASTING THE SENTENCE**

When harassed by managed care professionals, a *physician* may be tempted to leave the profession.

A journalist is stimulated by *a* deadline.

A good designer chooses projects carefully.

For more examples of these revision strategies, see 22.

**EXERCISE 17–3   Possible revisions:**

a. Dr. Geralyn Farmer is the chief surgeon at University Hospital. Dr. Paul Green is her assistant.
b. All applicants want to know how much they will make.
c. Elementary school teachers should understand the concept of nurturing if they intend to be successful.
d. Students of high-tech architecture pick a favorite when they study such inspirational architects as Renzo Piano and Zaha Hadid.
e. If we do not stop polluting our environment, we will perish.

**EXERCISE 17–3**   Edit the following sentences to eliminate sexist language or sexist assumptions. Revisions of lettered sentences appear in the back of the book. Example:

> *Scholarship athletes*                                        *their*
> ~~A scholarship athlete~~ must be as concerned about ~~his~~
>   ^                                            *they are*   *their*    ^
> academic performance as ~~he is~~ about ~~his~~ athletic
>                           ^              ^
>
> performance.

a. Mrs. Geralyn Farmer, who is the mayor's wife, is the chief surgeon at University Hospital. Dr. Paul Green is her assistant.
b. Every applicant wants to know how much he will make.
c. An elementary school teacher should understand the concept of nurturing if she intends to be a success.
d. Every student of high-tech architecture picks his favorite when he studies such inspirational architects as Renzo Piano and Zaha Hadid.
e. If man does not stop polluting his environment, mankind will perish.

1. A fireman must always be on call even when he is off duty.
2. The chairman for the new program in digital art is Ariana Tamlin, an accomplished portrait painter, computer programmer, and cookie baker.
3. In the gubernatorial race, Lena Weiss, a defense lawyer and mother of two, easily defeated Harvey Tower, an architect.
4. Recent military history has shown that lady combat helicopter pilots are as skilled, reliable, and resourceful as men.
5. An emergency room head nurse must know how to use sophisticated digital equipment if she is to keep track of all her patients' data and guide her medical team.

| ON THE WEB | **dianahacker.com/bedhandbook**<br>▶ Electronic grammar exercises<br>  ▶ E-ex 17–2 |
|---|---|

**EXERCISE 17–3 (continued)**

1. A firefighter must always be on call even when off duty.
2. The chairperson for the new program in digital art is Ariana Tamlin, an accomplished portrait painter and computer programmer.
3. In the gubernatorial race, Lena Weiss, a defense lawyer, easily defeated Harvey Tower, an architect.
4. Recent military history has shown that women and men are equally skilled, reliable, and resourceful as combat helicopter pilots.
5. An emergency room head nurse must know how to use sophisticated digital equipment to keep track of all patient data and guide the medical team.

**17g** Revise language that may offend groups of people.

Obviously it is impolite to use offensive terms such as *Polack* and *redneck*. But biased language can take more subtle forms. Because language evolves over time, names once thought acceptable may become offensive. When describing groups of people, choose names that the groups currently use to describe themselves.

▶ North Dakota takes its name from the ~~Indian~~ *Lakota* word meaning

"friend" or "ally."

▶ Many ~~Oriental~~ *Asian* immigrants have recently settled in our small

town in Tennessee.

Negative stereotypes (such as "drives like a teenager" or "haggard as an old crone") are of course offensive. But you should avoid stereotyping a person or a group even if you believe your generalization to be positive.

▶ It was no surprise that Greer, ~~a Chinese American,~~ *an excellent math and science student,* was

selected for the honors chemistry program.

# 18

## Find the exact words.

Two reference works (or their online equivalents) will help you find words to express your meaning exactly: a good dictionary, such as *The American Heritage Dictionary*, *Merriam-Webster's Collegiate Dictionary*, or *Webster's New World*

**WRITERS ON WRITING**

As societies grow decadent, the language grows decadent too. Words are used to disguise, not illuminate, action: you liberate a city by destroying it. —Gore Vidal

A van loaded with copies of *Roget's Thesaurus* collided with a taxi. Witnesses were astounded, shocked, taken aback, surprised, startled, dumbfounded, thunder-struck, and caught unawares.
—*Imprint*

Words fascinate me. They always have. For me, browsing in a dictionary is like being turned loose in a bank. —Eddie Cantor

*College Dictionary,* and a book of synonyms and antonyms, such as *Roget's International Thesaurus.*

**TIP:** Do not turn to a thesaurus in search of exotic, fancy words—such as *halcyon*—with which to embellish your essays. Look instead for words that exactly express your meaning. Most of the time these words—such as *tranquil*—will be familiar to both you and your readers.

**GRAMMAR CHECKERS** flag some nonstandard idioms, such as *comply to,* but few clichés. They do not identify commonly confused words, such as *principal* and *principle* or misused word forms, such as *significance* and *significant.* You must be alert for such words and use your dictionary if you are unsure of the correct form. Grammar checkers are of little help with the other problems discussed in 18: choosing words with appropriate connotations, using concrete language, and using figures of speech appropriately.

**18a** Select words with appropriate connotations.

In addition to their strict dictionary meanings (or *denotations*), words have *connotations,* emotional colorings that affect how readers respond to them. The word *steel* denotes "made of or resembling commercial iron that contains carbon," but it also calls up a cluster of images associated with steel, such as the sensation of touching it. These associations give the word its connotations—cold, smooth, unbending.

If the connotation of a word does not seem appropriate for your purpose, your audience, or your subject matter, you should change the word. When a more appropriate synonym does not come quickly to mind, consult a dictionary or a thesaurus.

**WRITERS ON WRITING**

A writer who does not speak out of a full experience uses torpid words, wooden or lifeless words, such words as "humanitary," which have a paralysis in their tails.    —Henry David Thoreau

Cut these words and they would bleed.    —Ralph Waldo Emerson

All my life I've looked at words as though I were seeing them for the first time.    —Ernest Hemingway

All meanings, we know, depend on the key of interpretation.
    —George Eliot

▶ The model was ~~skinny~~ and fashionable.
           *slender*

The connotation of the word *skinny* is too negative.

▶ As I covered the boats with marsh grass, the ~~perspiration~~ I
           *sweat*

had worked up evaporated in the wind, and the cold morning

air seemed even colder.

The term *perspiration* is too dainty for the context, which suggests vigorous exercise.

**EXERCISE 18–1**    Use a dictionary and a thesaurus to find at least four synonyms for each of the following words. Be prepared to explain any slight differences in meaning.

1. decay (verb)
2. difficult (adjective)
3. hurry (verb)
4. pleasure (noun)
5. secret (adjective)
6. talent (noun)

**EXERCISE 18–2**    For each of the words italicized in the following passages, consider alternatives that the writer might have chosen instead. (A dictionary and a thesaurus will lead to other possibilities.) Then discuss why the author probably selected the word he or she did.

1. The forest, *choked* by growth and *shadow*, was like a jungle; the air hung thick with heat, *muting* the sound of their progress. Breathing in a *pungent steam* of sweet grasses and tangy needles, rotting wood and sunbaked fungi, she followed as best she could, *plunging* through the thicket to keep up with the young man ahead.
   —Diana West

2. A change of just a few degrees in atmospheric temperature over the next century would be *catastrophic*. A *parade* of scientists appearing before a Senate committee in June *painted a graphic*

---

**EXERCISE 18–1    Possible answers:**

1. decay (verb): decompose, disintegrate, break up, corrode, rot, putrify, fester, molder; 2. difficult (adjective): hard, tough, rigorous, formidable, arduous, tricky, demanding, complex; 3. hurry (verb): rush, accelerate, bustle, speed up, scamper, scramble, quicken, hasten, dash, dart; 4. pleasure (noun): enjoyment, contentment, euphoria, gratification, satisfaction, relish, gusto, fun, entertainment, amusement; 5. secret (adjective): concealed, covert, cryptic, hidden, arcane, clandestine, undercover, furtive, stealthy, mysterious, unknown; 6. talent (noun): ability, genius, skill, faculty, flair, gift, power, forte

picture of what that could mean: melting icecaps and rising sea levels that would *inundate* seaboard cities and drown thousands in *fierce* storms; rainfall shifts that would make the deserts *bloom* and turn *breadbaskets* into *dustbowls;* and, of course, heat everywhere. —Matthew L. Wald

## 18b Prefer specific, concrete nouns.

Unlike general nouns, which refer to broad classes of things, specific nouns point to definite and particular items. *Film,* for example, names a general class, *fantasy film* names a narrower class, and *Lord of the Rings: Return of the King* is more specific still. Other examples: *team, football team, Denver Broncos; music, symphony, Beethoven's Ninth.*

Unlike abstract nouns, which refer to qualities and ideas (*justice, beauty, realism, dignity*), concrete nouns point to immediate, often sensory experience and to physical objects (*steeple, asphalt, lilac, stone, garlic*).

Specific, concrete nouns express meaning more vividly than general or abstract ones. Although general and abstract language is sometimes necessary to convey your meaning, ordinarily prefer specific, concrete alternatives.

▶ The senator spoke about the challenges of the future: *famine, pollution, dwindling resources, and terrorism.* ~~the environment and world peace.~~
   ^

Nouns such as *thing, area, aspect, factor,* and *individual* are especially dull and imprecise.

                                        *rewards.*
▶ A career in city planning offers many ~~things.~~
                                        ^

                          *experienced technician.*
▶ Try pairing a trainee with an ~~individual with technical~~
                          ^
   ~~experience.~~

---

### WRITERS ON WRITING

Do not be grand. Try to get the ordinary into your writing—breakfast tables rather than the solar system; Middletown today, not Mankind through the ages. —Darcy O'Brien

It is a good deal easier for most people to state an abstract idea than to describe and thus re-create some object they actually see. —Flannery O'Connor

An abstract style is always bad. Your sentences should be full of stones, metals, chairs, tables, animals, men, and women. —Alain de Lille

Words are loaded pistols. —Jean-Paul Sartre

**18c** Do not misuse words.

If a word is not in your active vocabulary, you may find yourself misusing it, sometimes with embarrassing consequences. Imagine the chagrin of the young woman who wrote that the "aroma of pumpkin pie and sage stuffing acted as an *aphrodisiac*" when she learned that aphrodisiacs are drugs or foods stimulating sexual desire. Such blunders are easily prevented: When in doubt, check the dictionary.

▶ The fans were ~~migrating~~ *climbing* up the bleachers in search of seats.

▶ Mrs. Johnson tried to fight but to no ~~prevail.~~ *avail.*

▶ The Internet has so ~~diffused~~ *permeated* our culture that it touches all segments of society.

Be especially alert for misused word forms — using a noun such as *absence, significance,* or *persistence,* for example, when your meaning requires the adjective *absent, significant,* or *persistent.*

▶ Most dieters are not ~~persistence~~ *persistent* enough to make a permanent change in their eating habits.

**EXERCISE 18–3** Edit the following sentences to correct misused words. Revisions of lettered sentences appear in the back of the book. Example:

The training required for a ballet dancer is ~~all-absorbent.~~ *all-absorbing.*

**EXERCISE 18–3  Possible revisions:**

a. We regret this delay; thank you for your patience.
b. Ada's plan is to acquire education and experience to prepare herself for a position as property manager.
c. Tiger Woods, the ultimate competitor, has earned millions of dollars just in endorsements.
d. Many people take for granted that public libraries have up-to-date networked computer systems.
e. The effect of Gao Xinjian's novels on Chinese exiles is hard to gauge.

a. We regret this delay; thank you for your patients.
b. Ada's plan is to require education and experience to prepare herself for a position as property manager.
c. Tiger Woods, the penultimate competitor, has earned millions of dollars just in endorsements.
d. Many people take for granite that public libraries have up-to-date networked computer systems.
e. The affect of Gao Xinjian's novels on Chinese exiles is hard to gauge.

1. Waste, misuse of government money, security and health violations, and even pilfering have become major dilemmas in some government agencies.
2. Designers of handheld devices have to understand that changes in ambience temperatures can damage the tiny circuit boards.
3. Grand Isle State Park is surrounded on three sides by water.
4. The Old World nuance of the restaurant intrigued us.
5. The person who complained to the human resources manager wishes to remain unanimous.

| ON THE WEB | **dianahacker.com/bedhandbook**<br>▶ Electronic grammar exercises<br>  ▶ E-ex 18–1 |
| --- | --- |

## 18d Use standard idioms.

Idioms are speech forms that follow no easily specified rules. The English say "Maria went *to hospital*," an idiom strange to American ears, which are accustomed to hearing *the* in front of *hospital*. Native speakers of a language seldom have problems with idioms, but prepositions sometimes cause trouble, especially when they follow certain verbs and adjectives. When in doubt, consult a dictionary.

**EXERCISE 18–3 (continued)**
1. Waste, misuse of government money, security and health violations, and even pilfering have become major problems in some government agencies.
2. Designers of handheld devices have to understand that changes in ambient temperatures can damage the tiny circuit boards.
3. Grand Isle State Park is bordered on three sides by water.
4. The Old World ambience of the restaurant intrigued us.
5. The person who complained to the human resources manager wishes to remain anonymous.

| UNIDIOMATIC | IDIOMATIC |
|---|---|
| abide with (a decision) | abide by (a decision) |
| according with | according to |
| agree to (an idea) | agree with (an idea) |
| angry at (a person) | angry with (a person) |
| capable to | capable of |
| comply to | comply with |
| desirous to | desirous of |
| different than (a person or thing) | different from (a person or thing) |
| intend on doing | intend to do |
| off of | off |
| plan on doing | plan to do |
| preferable than | preferable to |
| prior than | prior to |
| superior than | superior to |
| sure and | sure to |
| try and | try to |
| type of a | type of |

 Because idioms follow no particular rules, you must learn them individually. You may find it helpful to keep a list of idioms that you frequently encounter in conversation and in reading.

**EXERCISE 18–4**    Edit the following sentences to eliminate errors in the use of idiomatic expressions. If a sentence is correct, write "correct" after it. Answers to lettered sentences appear in the back of the book. Example:

We agreed to abide ~~with~~ by the decision of the judge.

a.   Queen Anne was so angry at Sarah Churchill that she refused to see her again.

**EXERCISE 18–4    Possible revisions:**

a.   Queen Anne was so angry with Sarah Churchill that she refused to see her again.
b.   Correct
c.   The parade moved off the street and onto the beach.
d.   The frightened refugees intend to make the dangerous trek across the mountains.
e.   What type of wedding are you planning?

1.   Be sure to report on the danger of releasing genetically engineered bacteria into the atmosphere.
2.   Why do you assume that embezzling bank assets is so different from robbing the bank?
3.   The wilderness guide seemed capable of showing us where the trail of petroglyphs was located.

b. Jean-Pierre's ambitious travel plans made it impossible for him to comply with the graduate program's residency requirement.
c. The parade moved off of the street and onto the beach.
d. The frightened refugees intend on making the dangerous trek across the mountains.
e. What type of a wedding are you planning?

1. Be sure and report on the danger of releasing genetically engineered bacteria into the atmosphere.
2. Why do you assume that embezzling bank assets is so different than robbing the bank?
3. The wilderness guide seemed capable to show us where the trail of petroglyphs was located.
4. In Evan's cautious mind, packing his own parachute seemed preferable to letting an indifferent teenager fold all that silk and cord into a small pack.
5. Andrea plans on joining the Peace Corps after graduation.

| **ON THE WEB** | **dianahacker.com/bedhandbook** |
| --- | --- |
| | ▶ Electronic grammar exercises |
| | ▶ E-ex 18–2 |

## 18e Do not rely heavily on clichés.

The pioneer who first announced that he had "slept like a log" no doubt amused his companions with a fresh and unlikely comparison. Today, however, that comparison is a cliché, a saying that has lost its dazzle from overuse. No longer can it surprise.

To see just how dully predictable clichés are, put your hand over the right-hand column on the following page and then finish the phrases on the left.

**EXERCISE 18–4 (continued)**
4. Correct
5. Andrea plans to join the Peace Corps after graduation.

**SCHOLARS ON CLICHÉS**

Kari, Daven M. "A Cliché a Day Keeps the Gray Away." *Teaching English in the Two-Year College* 19 (1992): 128–33. After pointing out that it is impossible to avoid clichés entirely, Kari argues that we should stop admonishing students to avoid them in all situations. Instead, we should show students how to revitalize clichés through a variety of techniques. For example, instead of saying that "a penny saved is a penny earned," we can invert the cliché: "In today's inflation-ridden economy, a penny saved is a penny lost."

| | |
|---|---|
| cool as a | cucumber |
| beat around | the bush |
| blind as a | bat |
| busy as a | bee, beaver |
| crystal | clear |
| dead as a | doornail |
| out of the frying pan and | into the fire |
| light as a | feather |
| like a bull | in a china shop |
| playing with | fire |
| nutty as a | fruitcake |
| selling like | hotcakes |
| starting out at the bottom | of the ladder |
| water under the | bridge |
| white as a | sheet, ghost |
| avoid clichés like the | plague |

The cure for clichés is frequently simple: Just delete them. When this won't work, try adding some element of surprise. One student, for example, who had written that she had butterflies in her stomach, revised her cliché like this:

> If all of the action in my stomach is caused by butterflies, there must be a horde of them, with horseshoes on.

The image of butterflies wearing horseshoes is fresh and unlikely, not dully predictable like the original cliché.

---

**ON THE WEB**

dianahacker.com/bedhandbook
▶ Language Debates
  ▶ Clichés

---

**SCHOLARS ON FIGURATIVE LANGUAGE**

Corbett, Edward P. J. *Classical Rhetoric for the Modern Student.* 4th ed. New York: Oxford UP, 1998. 377–410. Corbett provides succinct explanations of figures of speech, illustrated with examples. Exposure to figures of speech does not ensure that students will be able to use them, says Corbett, but at least they will be aware of the possibilities.

Devet, Bonnie. "Bringing Back More Figures of Speech into Composition." *Journal of Teaching Writing* 6 (1987): 293–304. Devet suggests that Kenneth Burke's theories of language, along with new composition theories, provide a current rationale for teaching figures of speech in composition classes.

## 18f Use figures of speech with care.

A figure of speech is an expression that uses words imaginatively (rather than literally) to make abstract ideas concrete. Most often, figures of speech compare two seemingly unlike things to reveal surprising similarities.

In a *simile,* the writer makes the comparison explicitly, usually by introducing it with *like* or *as*: "By the time cotton had to be picked, Grandfather's neck was as red as the clay he plowed." In a *metaphor,* the *like* or *as* is omitted, and the comparison is implied. For example, in the Old Testament Song of Solomon, a young woman compares the man she loves to a fruit tree: "With great delight I sat in his shadow, and his fruit was sweet to my taste."

Although figures of speech are useful devices, writers sometimes use them without thinking through the images they evoke. The result is sometimes a *mixed metaphor,* the combination of two or more images that don't make sense together.

► Crossing Utah's salt flats in his new convertible, my father flew *at jet speed.* ~~under a full head of steam.~~

*Flew* suggests an airplane, while *under a full head of steam* suggests a steamboat or a train. To clarify the image, the writer should stick with one comparison or the other.

► Our office decided to put all controversial issues on a

back burner ~~in a holding pattern~~ until the annual meeting

was over.

Here the writer is mixing stoves and airplanes. Simply deleting one of the images corrects the problem.

**EXERCISE 18–5 Possible revisions:**
a. John stormed into the room like a hurricane.
b. Some people insist that they'll always be available to help, even when they haven't been before.
c. The Cubs easily beat the Mets, who were in trouble early in the game today at Wrigley Field.
d. We ironed out the wrinkles in our relationship.
e. My mother accused me of evading her questions when in fact I was just saying the first thing that came to mind.

**EXERCISE 18–5** Edit the following sentences to replace worn-out expressions and clarify mixed figures of speech. Revisions of lettered sentences appear in the back of the book. Example:

> *the color drained from his face.*
> When he heard about the accident, ~~he turned white as a~~
> ^
> ~~sheet.~~

a. John stormed into the room like a bull in a china shop.
b. Some people insist that they'll always be there for you, even when they haven't been before.
c. The Cubs easily beat the Mets, who were in the soup early in the game today at Wrigley Field.
d. We ironed out the sticky spots in our relationship.
e. My mother accused me of beating around the bush when in fact I was just talking off the top of my head.

1. Patricia was used to burning the candle at both ends to get her assignments done.
2. No matter how many books he reads, André can never seem to quench his hunger for knowledge.
3. In an era of cutbacks and outsourcing, the best high-tech workers discover that being a jack of all trades is a solid gold key to continued success.
4. There are too many cooks in the broth at corporate headquarters.
5. Juanita told Kyle that keeping skeletons in the closet would be playing with fire.

| | |
|---|---|
| **ON THE WEB** | **dianahacker.com/bedhandbook**<br>▶ Electronic grammar exercises<br>　▶ E-ex 18–3 |

**EXERCISE 18–5 (continued)**

1. Patricia was used to working long hours to get her assignments done.
2. No matter how many books he reads, André can never seem to satisfy his hunger for knowledge.
3. In an era of cutbacks and outsourcing, the best high-tech workers discover that having diverse skills is essential to continued success.
4. There are too many managers at corporate headquarters.
5. Juanita told Kyle that keeping secrets would be dangerous.

# Part V

# Grammatical Sentences

# 19

## Repair sentence fragments.

A sentence fragment is a word group that pretends to be a sentence. Sentence fragments are easy to recognize when they appear out of context, like these:

> On the old wooden stool in the corner of my grandmother's kitchen.

> And immediately popped their flares and life vests.

When fragments appear next to related sentences, however, they are harder to spot.

> On that morning I sat in my usual spot. On the old wooden stool in the corner of my grandmother's kitchen.

> The pilots ejected from the burning plane, landing in the water not far from the ship. And immediately popped their flares and life vests.

### Recognizing sentence fragments

To be a sentence, a word group must consist of at least one full independent clause. An independent clause has a subject and a verb, and it either stands alone or could stand alone.

To test a word group for sentence completeness, use the flowchart on page 239. For example, by using the flowchart, you can see exactly why *On the old wooden stool in the corner of my grandmother's kitchen* is a fragment: It lacks both a subject and a verb. *And immediately popped their flares and life vests* is a fragment because it lacks a subject.

**ADDITIONAL RESOURCE ON TEACHING BASIC WRITING**

Adler-Kassner, Linda, and Gregory R. Glau. *The Bedford Bibliography for Teachers of Basic Writing.* Boston: Bedford, 2002. Compiled by members of the Conference on Basic Writing, this text provides an annotated list of hundreds of books, articles, and periodicals selected specifically for their value to teachers of basic writing. Topics include history and theory, pedagogical issues, curriculum development, and administration of basic writing programs. The complete text is available online at <http://bedfordstmartins.com/basicbib>.

## Test for sentence completeness

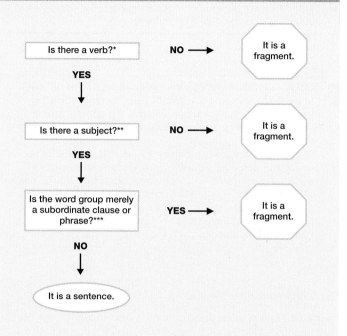

* Do not mistake verbals for verbs. (See 64c.)
** The subject of a sentence may be *you,* understood. (See 63a.)
*** A sentence may open with a subordinate clause, but the sentence must also include an independent clause. (See 65a.)

*If you find any fragments, try one of these methods of revision:*

1. Attach the fragment to a nearby sentence.
2. Turn the fragment into a sentence.

### SCHOLARS ON ERROR

Beason, Larry. "Ethos and Error: How Business People React to Errors." *College Composition and Communication* 53 (2001): 33–64. To understand the impact of error on nonacademic readers, Beason examined the responses of fourteen business professionals to a variety of error types. He concludes that readers in business judge the seriousness of errors in part by how much they think readers inside and outside the organization will be bothered by the errors. Teachers cannot assume, he argues, that some types of errors are more serious than others; nor can students assume that teachers are just being picky when they mark seemingly nonserious errors. Rather, teachers and students need to appreciate the larger ways that errors affect and "endanger" a writer's ethos and can reflect on the writer's overall capabilities.

ESL Unlike some languages, English does not allow omission of subjects (except in imperative sentences); nor does it allow omission of verbs. See 31a and 29e.

GRAMMAR CHECKERS can flag as many as half of the sentence fragments in a sample; but that means, of course, that they miss half or more of them. If fragments are a serious problem for you, you will still need to proofread for them.

Sometimes the grammar checker will identify "false positives," sentences that it flags but that are not fragments. For example, a grammar checker flagged this complete sentence as a possible fragment: *I bent down to crawl into the bunker.* When a program spots a possible fragment, you should check to see if it is really a fragment by using the flowchart on page 239.

### Repairing sentence fragments

You can repair most fragments in one of two ways: Either pull the fragment into a nearby sentence or turn the fragment into a sentence.

▶ On that morning I sat in my usual spot~~.~~, ~~On~~ the old wooden stool in the corner of my grandmother's kitchen.

▶ The pilots ejected from the burning plane, landing in the water not far from the ship. ~~And~~ They immediately popped their flares and life vests.

---

### SCHOLARS ON ERROR

Cogie, Jane, Kim Strain, and Sharon Lorinskas. "Avoiding the Proofreading Trap: The Value of the Error Correction Process." *Writing Center Journal* 19.2 (1999): 7–31. The authors describe a number of strategies that can be used to guide students through the process of self-editing so they can gain greater control over their revisions. While the strategies focus on ESL students, any student writer will find the strategies useful, particularly the advice about creating an error log to record and analyze errors made on a regular basis.

## 19a Attach fragmented subordinate clauses or turn them into sentences.

A subordinate clause is patterned like a sentence, with both a subject and a verb, but it begins with a word that marks it as subordinate. The following words commonly introduce subordinate clauses.

| | | | | |
|---|---|---|---|---|
| after | even though | so that | when | whom |
| although | how | than | where | whose |
| as | if | that | whether | why |
| as if | in order that | though | which | |
| because | rather than | unless | while | |
| before | since | until | who | |

Subordinate clauses function within sentences as adjectives, as adverbs, or as nouns. They cannot stand alone. (See 64b.)

Most fragmented clauses beg to be pulled into a sentence nearby.

► Americans have come to fear the West Nile virus/ ~~Because~~  *because*

it is transmitted by the common mosquito.

> *Because* introduces a subordinate clause. (For punctuation of a subordinate clause appearing at the end of a sentence, see 33f.)

► Although we seldom get to see wildlife in the city/, ~~At~~ the zoo  *at*

we can still find some of our favorites.

> *Although* introduces a subordinate clause. (For punctuation of subordinate clauses appearing at the beginning of a sentence, see 32b.)

### SCHOLARS ON ERROR

Connors, Robert J. *Composition-Rhetoric: Backgrounds, Theory, and Pedagogy.* Ithaca: Cornell UP, 1997. 112–70. Connors traces American attitudes toward grammar over the past two centuries. At times, class structures have contributed to an obsessive concern for correctness, with elites condemning "vulgarities" and the lower classes looking to improve themselves through language. In colleges, instructors over the years have tried to focus on rhetoric, but underprepared students and heavy workloads have often led them to focus on correctness (it's easier to mark errors than to comment on rhetoric). Connors writes that we will no doubt continue to investigate "how the balance between rhetoric and mechanics can best be struck."

If a fragmented clause cannot be attached to a nearby sentence or if you feel that attaching it would be awkward, try turning the clause into a sentence. The simplest way to do this is to delete the opening word or words that mark it as subordinate.

▶ Population increases and uncontrolled development are

taking a deadly toll on the environment. ~~So that in~~ *In* many

parts of the world, fragile ecosystems are collapsing.

## 19b Attach fragmented phrases or turn them into sentences.

Like subordinate clauses, phrases function within sentences as adjectives, as adverbs, or as nouns. They cannot stand alone. Fragmented phrases are often prepositional or verbal phrases; sometimes they are appositives, words or word groups that rename nouns or pronouns. (See 64a, 64c, and 64d.)

Often a fragmented phrase may simply be pulled into a nearby sentence.

▶ The archaeologists worked slowly/, ~~Examining~~ *examining* and labeling

every pottery shard they uncovered.

The word group beginning with *Examining* is a verbal phrase.

▶ Mary is suffering from agoraphobia/, ~~A~~ *a* fear of the outside

world.

*A fear of the outside world* is an appositive renaming the noun *agoraphobia*. (For punctuation of appositives, see 32e.)

### SCHOLARS ON ERROR

Harris, Joseph. *A Teaching Subject: Composition since 1966.* Upper Saddle River: Prentice, 1997. 76–90. Harris traces the role of error in teaching and research, beginning with Mina Shaughnessy's work. He explores the various ways our profession has dealt with error in the teaching of writing, comparing our attitudes and understandings with public perceptions.

The November 1996 issue of *English Journal* includes twenty articles that address the debate on teaching grammar and usage. Ranging across the political spectrum—from liberal to traditional approaches—the authors show that the issue still enlivens our professional conversations.

If a fragmented phrase cannot be pulled into a nearby sentence effectively, turn the phrase into a sentence. You may need to add a subject, a verb, or both.

> ► In the training session, Jamie explained how to access our
> *She also taught us*
> new database. ~~Also~~ how to submit expense reports and
>        ^
> request vendor payments.

The revision turns the fragmented phrase into a sentence by adding a subject and a verb.

## 19c Attach other fragmented word groups or turn them into sentences.

Other word groups that are commonly fragmented include parts of compound predicates, lists, and examples introduced by *such as, for example,* or similar expressions.

### Parts of compound predicates

A predicate consists of a verb and its objects, complements, and modifiers (see 63b). A compound predicate includes two or more predicates joined by a coordinating conjunction such as *and, but,* or *or.* Because the parts of a compound predicate have the same subject, they should appear in the same sentence.

> ► The woodpecker finch of the Galápagos Islands carefully
> *and*
> selects a twig of a certain size and shape/ ~~And~~ then uses this
>                                          ^
> tool to pry out grubs from trees.

Notice that no comma appears between the parts of a compound predicate. (See 33a.)

---

**SCHOLARS ON ERROR**

Devet, Bonnie. "Errors as Discoveries: An Assignment for Prospective English Teachers." *Journal of Teaching Writing* 15.1 (1996): 129–39. Devet urges us to see error "not as a dichotomous right-versus-wrong, but as a continuum that reflects the rhetorical context of writing." She describes an assignment that asks students to find errors in published materials, to identify the rule that has been broken, and to fix the error. The most important aspect of this exercise is that it encourages students to consider why writers — in particular rhetorical contexts — might intentionally break rules.

## Lists

When a list is mistakenly fragmented, it can often be attached to a nearby sentence with a colon or a dash. (See 35a and 39a.)

▶ It has been said that there are only three indigenous
American art forms*/:* ~~Musical~~ *musical* comedy, jazz, and soap
opera.

### Examples introduced by *such as, for example, or similar expressions*

Expressions that introduce examples (or explanations) can lead to unintentional fragments. Although you may begin a sentence with some of the following words or phrases, make sure that what you have written is a sentence, not a fragment.

| | | |
|---|---|---|
| also | for instance | or |
| and | in addition | such as |
| but | like | that is |
| especially | mainly | |
| for example | namely | |

Sometimes fragmented examples can be attached to the preceding sentence.

▶ In the twentieth century, the South produced some
great American writers*/,* ~~Such~~ *such* as Flannery O'Connor,
William Faulkner, Alice Walker, Tennessee Williams, and
Thomas Wolfe.

---

### SCHOLARS ON ERROR

Hull, Glynda. "Constructing Taxonomies for Error." *A Sourcebook for Basic Writing Teachers.* Ed. Theresa Enos. New York: McGraw, 1987. 231–44. Hull asks us to think of locating and editing errors in terms of three kinds of operations: "Sometimes editing begins with an act of comprehension as a writer attends to the meaning of a text. Sometimes it begins with a verbal representation of a rule. And sometimes it begins with a writer's sense that something is amiss, although he [or she] cannot specifically name what it is."

At times, however, it may be necessary to turn the fragment into a sentence.

▶ If Eric doesn't get his way, he goes into a fit of rage. For example, ~~lying~~ *he lies* on the floor screaming or ~~opening~~ *opens* the cabinet doors and then ~~slamming~~ *slams* them shut.

The writer corrected this fragment by adding a subject — *he* — and substituting verbs for the verbals *lying, opening,* and *slamming.*

## 19d Exception: Occasionally a fragment may be used deliberately, for effect.

Skilled writers occasionally use sentence fragments for the following special purposes.

| | |
|---|---|
| **FOR EMPHASIS** | Following the dramatic Americanization of their children, even my parents grew more publicly confident. *Especially my mother.*<br>— Richard Rodriguez |
| **TO ANSWER A QUESTION** | Are these new drug tests 100 percent reliable? *Not in the opinion of most experts.* |
| **AS TRANSITION** | *And now the opposing arguments.* |
| **EXCLAMATIONS** | *Not again!* |
| **IN ADVERTISING** | *Fewer carbs. Improved taste.* |

Although fragments are sometimes appropriate, writers and readers do not always agree on when they are appropriate. That's why you will find it safer to write in complete sentences.

### SCHOLARS ON ERROR

Williams, Joseph M. "The Phenomenology of Error." *College Composition and Communication* 32 (1981): 152–68. Williams humorously points out the contradictions involved in English teachers' varied reactions to errors of grammar and usage. When textbooks violate their own rules, even in the rules themselves (for example, "The passive voice should be avoided"), or when professional writers make mistakes, teachers often overlook the errors. Williams provides an intriguing case study to demonstrate the truth of his statements.

**EXERCISE 19–1**   Repair any fragment by attaching it to a nearby sentence or by rewriting it as a complete sentence. If a word group is correct, write "correct" after it. Revisions of lettered sentences appear in the back of the book. Example:

> One Greek island that should not be missed is Mykonos/, ̶A̶ ^*a*^
>
> vacation spot for Europeans and a playground for the rich
>
> and famous.

a.  Listening to the CD her sister had sent, Mia was overcome with a mix of emotions. Happiness, homesickness, nostalgia.

b.  Cortés and his soldiers were astonished when they looked down from the mountains and saw Tenochtitlán. The magnificent capital of the Aztecs.

c.  Although my spoken Spanish is not very good. I can read the language with ease.

d.  There are several reasons for not eating meat. One reason being that dangerous chemicals are used throughout the various stages of meat production.

e.  To learn how to sculpt beauty from everyday life. This is my intention in studying art and archaeology.

1.  The panther lay motionless behind the rock. Waiting silently for its prey.

2.  Mother loved to play all our favorite games. Canasta, Monopoly, hide-and-seek, and even kick-the-can.

3.  With machetes, the explorers cut their way through the tall grasses to the edge of the canyon. Then they began to lay out the tapes for the survey.

4.  The owners of the online grocery store rented a warehouse in the Market district. An area catering to small businesses.

5.  If a woman from the desert tribe showed anger toward her husband, she was whipped in front of the whole village. And shunned by the rest of the women.

---

**EXERCISE 19–1   Possible revisions:**

a.  Listening to the CD her sister had sent, Mia was overcome with a mix of emotions: happiness, homesickness, nostalgia.

b.  Cortés and his soldiers were astonished when they looked down from the mountains and saw Tenochtitlán, the magnificent capital of the Aztecs.

c.  Although my spoken Spanish is not very good, I can read the language with ease.

d.  There are several reasons for not eating meat. One reason is that dangerous chemicals are used throughout the various stages of meat production.

e.  To learn how to sculpt beauty from everyday life is my intention in studying art and archaeology.

**EXERCISE 19–2**   Repair each fragment in the following passage by attaching it to a sentence nearby or by rewriting it as a complete sentence.

Browsing the Web has become a way of life, but some people think it is destroying a way of life. That we will never recover. Our grandparents and parents feared that the age of television — starting with *Howdy Doody* and progressing through MTV and *The Apprentice* — would create generations of viewers who were content to sit for hours and hours. Passively watching images flit before their eyes. Cable television now offers far more passive entertainment than previous generations could ever have imagined. Hundreds of channels and an endless supply of round-the-clock programming. The World Wide Web has the potential to top even cable television's reach. Making access to information easy and available to people anywhere in the world at any time.

One major risk that our grandparents and parents feared is still an issue today. In a culture based on images, the written word may become an endangered species. As our brains eventually adapt to greater and greater levels of stimulation. Will we continue to be able to focus on a page of print? Before we send out too many alarms, however, we should remember that the World Wide Web is based more on words than television ever was. There is some evidence that those who spend time browsing the Web are doing more, not less, reading. Unlike TV viewers. Some Web surfers prefer to run their eyes over the words on the screen. An activity that is, after all, reading. Others download information and read the printouts. While it is true that television has reduced our nation's level of literacy, the World Wide Web could well advance it. Only the future will tell.

| ON THE WEB | **dianahacker.com/bedhandbook** ▶ Electronic grammar exercises ▶ E-ex 19–1 to 19–3 |

**EXERCISE 19–1 (continued)**

1. The panther lay motionless behind the rock, waiting silently for its prey.
2. Mother loved to play all our favorite games: canasta, Monopoly, hide-and-seek, and even kick-the-can.
3. Correct
4. The owners of the online grocery store rented a warehouse in the Market district, an area catering to small businesses.
5. If a woman from the desert tribe showed anger toward her husband, she was whipped in front of the whole village and shunned by the rest of the women.

# 20

---

## Revise run-on sentences.

---

Run-on sentences are independent clauses that have not been joined correctly. An independent clause is a word group that can stand alone as a sentence. (See 65a.) When two independent clauses appear in one sentence, they must be joined in one of these ways:

- with a comma and a coordinating conjunction (*and, but, or, nor, for, so, yet*)
- with a semicolon (or occasionally with a colon or a dash)

### *Recognizing run-on sentences*

There are two types of run-on sentences. When a writer puts no mark of punctuation and no coordinating conjunction between independent clauses, the result is called a *fused sentence.*

┌──────────────── INDEPENDENT CLAUSE ────────────────┐

**FUSED**   Gestures are a means of communication for everyone

┌──────────── INDEPENDENT CLAUSE ────────────┐

they are essential for the hearing-impaired.

A far more common type of run-on sentence is the *comma splice*—two or more independent clauses joined by a comma without a coordinating conjunction. In some comma splices, the comma appears alone.

**COMMA**   Gestures are a means of communication for everyone,
**SPLICE**   they are essential for the hearing-impaired.

---

**EXERCISE 19–2   Possible revisions:**

Browsing the Web has become a way of life, but some people think it is destroying a way of life that we will never recover. Our grandparents and parents feared that the age of television — starting with *Howdy Doody* and progressing through MTV and *The Apprentice* — would create generations of viewers who were content to sit for hours and hours, passively watching images flit before their eyes. Cable television now offers far more passive entertainment than previous generations could ever have imagined: hundreds of channels and an endless supply of round-the-clock programming. The World Wide Web has the potential to top even cable television's reach, making access to information easy and available to people anywhere in the world at any time.

## Recognizing run-on sentences

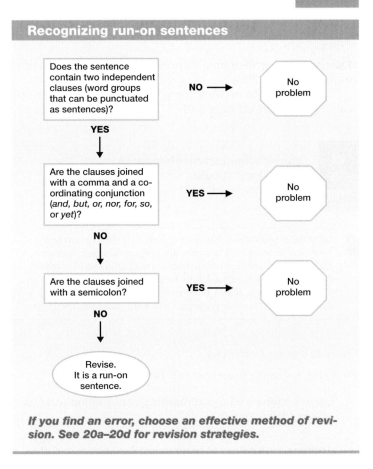

Does the sentence contain two independent clauses (word groups that can be punctuated as sentences)? **NO** → No problem

**YES** ↓

Are the clauses joined with a comma and a co-ordinating conjunction (*and, but, or, nor, for, so,* or *yet*)? **YES** → No problem

**NO** ↓

Are the clauses joined with a semicolon? **YES** → No problem

**NO** ↓

Revise. It is a run-on sentence.

*If you find an error, choose an effective method of revision. See 20a–20d for revision strategies.*

In other comma splices, the comma is accompanied by a joining word that is *not* a coordinating conjunction. There are only seven coordinating conjunctions in English: *and, but, or, nor, for, so,* and *yet.* Notice that all of these words are short—only two or three letters long.

**EXERCISE 19–2 (continued)**

One major risk that our grandparents and parents feared is still an issue today. In a culture based on images, the written word may become an endangered species. As our brains eventually adapt to greater and greater levels of stimulation, will we continue to be able to focus on a page of print? Before we send out too many alarms, however, we should remember that the World Wide Web is based more on words than television ever was. There is some evidence that those who spend time browsing the Web are doing more, not less, reading—unlike TV viewers. Some Web surfers prefer to run their eyes over the words on the screen, an activity that is, after all, reading. Others download information and read the printouts. While it is true that television has reduced our nation's level of literacy, the World Wide Web could well advance it. Only the future will tell.

| COMMA | Gestures are a means of communication for everyone, |
|-------|-----------------------------------------------------|
| SPLICE | however, they are essential for the hearing-impaired. |

*However* is a transitional expression, not a coordinating conjunction (see 20b).

To review your writing for possible run-on sentences, use the flowchart on page 249.

---

**ON THE WEB**   **dianahacker.com/bedhandbook**
  ► Language Debates
  ► Comma splices

---

 **GRAMMAR CHECKERS** flag fewer than half the run-on sentences in a sample. They usually suggest a semicolon as a method of revision, but you can consult 20a–20d for other revision strategies that might be more suitable in a particular situation. If you have repeated problems with run-ons, the flowchart on page 249 will help you identify them.

---

*Revising run-on sentences*

To revise a run-on sentence, you have four choices.

1. Use a comma and a coordinating conjunction (*and, but, or, nor, for, so, yet*).

      *but*
   ► Gestures are a means of communication for everyone, they
      ^
   are essential for the hearing-impaired.

2. Use a semicolon (or, if appropriate, a colon or a dash). A semicolon may be used alone; it can also be accompanied by a transitional expression.

---

**SCHOLARS ON RUN-ON SENTENCES**

Caroll, Joyce Armstrong, and Edward E. Wilson. *Acts of Teaching: How to Teach Writing.* Englewood: Teacher Ideas, 1993. 223–39. Caroll and Wilson point to run-on sentences and fragments as problems that disturb sentence sense. They suggest ways to explain the problems to students and recommend revision strategies. In addition, they advocate sentence combining to give students practice improving their decision-making skills and syntactic fluency.

▶ Gestures are a means of communication for everyone↓**; they**
  are essential for the hearing-impaired.

**; however,**
▶ Gestures are a means of communication for everyone↓ they
  are essential for the hearing-impaired.

3. Make the clauses into separate sentences.

**They**
▶ Gestures are a means of communication for everyone↓**. ~~they~~**
  are essential for the hearing-impaired.

4. Restructure the sentence, perhaps by subordinating one
   of the clauses.

**Although gestures**
▶ ~~Gestures~~ are a means of communication for everyone, they
  are essential for the hearing-impaired.

One of these revision techniques usually works better than
the others for a particular sentence. The fourth technique,
the one requiring the most extensive revision, is often the
most effective.

**20a** Consider separating the clauses with a comma and a
coordinating conjunction.

There are seven coordinating conjunctions in English: *and,*
*but, or, nor, for, so,* and *yet.* When a coordinating conjunction
joins independent clauses, it is usually preceded by a
comma. (See 32a.)

**SCHOLARS ON RUN-ON SENTENCES**
Kagan, Dona M. "Run-on and Fragment Sentences: An Error Analysis." *Research in the Teaching of English* 14 (1980): 127–38.
Kagan studied the features students consider when determining
whether a sentence is complete. She found that students tend to
focus on two features: a subject-verb construction of a certain
length and a construction including a prepositional phrase. Kagan
discusses possible explanations for the results of the study.

> *and*
▶ The paramedic asked where I was hurt, ~~as~~ soon as I told him,
   ∧

   he cut up the leg of my favorite pair of jeans.


▶ Many government officials privately admit that the polygraph
      *yet*
   is unreliable, ~~however,~~ they continue to use it as a security
      ∧

   measure.

   *However* is a transitional expression, not a coordinating conjunction, so it cannot be used with only a comma to join independent clauses. (See also 20b.)


**20b** Consider separating the clauses with a semicolon (or, if appropriate, with a colon or a dash).

When the independent clauses are closely related and their relation is clear without a coordinating conjunction, a semi-colon is an acceptable method of revision. (See 34a.)

▶ Tragedy depicts the individual confronted with the fact

   of death/; comedy depicts the adaptability of human
           ∧

   society.


A semicolon is required between independent clauses that have been linked with a transitional expression (such as *however, therefore, moreover, in fact,* or *for example*). For a longer list, see 34b.

▶ Handheld PDAs are gaining in popularity/; however, they are
                                         ∧

   not nearly as popular as cell phones.

**SCHOLARS ON RUN-ON SENTENCES**

Shaughnessy, Mina P. *Errors and Expectations: A Guide for the Teacher of Basic Writing.* New York: Oxford UP, 1979. 16–43. Diag-nosing comma splices as symptoms of more general difficulties with written English, Shaughnessy argues that students need to practice a variety of linking devices. She suggests a sequence of lessons focusing on both punctuation and sentence structure.

Bamberg, Betty. "Periods Are Basic: A Strategy for Eliminating Comma Faults and Run-on Sentences." *Teaching the Basics — Really!* Ed. Ouida Clapp. Urbana: NCTE, 1977. 97–99. Believing that students can avoid problems if they understand how "punctu-ation marks are related to the basic structure of the language," Bamberg outlines a five-stage procedure for instruction.

▶ Everyone in my outfit had a specific job/; as a matter of fact,

most of the officers had three or four duties.

If the first independent clause introduces the second or if the second clause summarizes or explains the first, a colon or a dash may be an appropriate method of revision. (See 35b and 39a.) In formal writing, the colon is usually preferred to the dash.

▶ Nuclear waste is hazardous ~~this~~ : This is an indisputable fact.

▶ The female black widow spider is often a widow of her own

making/ — she has been known to eat her partner after mating.

If the first independent clause introduces a quoted sentence, a colon is an appropriate method of revision.

▶ Feminist writer and scholar Carolyn Heilbrun has this to

say about the future/: "Today's shocks are tomorrow's

conventions."

## 20c Consider making the clauses into separate sentences.

▶ Why should we spend money on expensive space

exploration/? ~~we~~ We have enough underfunded programs here

on Earth.

Since one independent clause is a question and the other is a statement, they should be separate sentences.

▶ I gave the necessary papers to the police officer. ~~then~~ he said
_Then_ ^

I would have to accompany him to the police station, where

a counselor would talk with me and call my parents.

Because the second independent clause is quite long, a sensible revision is to use separate sentences.

**NOTE:** When two quoted independent clauses are divided by explanatory words, make each clause its own sentence.

▶ "It's always smart to learn from your mistakes," quipped my

supervisor. ~~"it's~~ even smarter to learn from the mistakes of
_"It's_ ^

others."

## 20d Consider restructuring the sentence, perhaps by subordinating one of the clauses.

If one of the independent clauses is less important than the other, turn it into a subordinate clause or phrase. (For more about subordination, see 14, especially the chart on p. 188.)

▶ One of the most famous advertising slogans is Wheaties

cereal's "Breakfast of Champions," ~~it~~ was penned
_which_ ^

in 1933.

▶ ~~Many~~ scholars dismiss the abominable snowman
_Although many_ ^

of the Himalayas as a myth, others claim it may be a

kind of ape.

**EXERCISE 20–1    Possible revisions:**

a. The city had one public swimming pool that stayed packed with children all summer long.

b. The building is being renovated, so at times we have no heat, water, or electricity.

c. The view was not what the travel agent had described. Where were the rolling hills and the shimmering rivers?

d. All those gnarled equations looked like toxic insects; maybe I was going to have to rethink my major.

e. The city government had good reason to fear a major earthquake: Most [or most] of the business district was built on landfill.

▶ Mary McLeod Bethune, ~~was~~ the seventeenth child of former
⌄
slaves, ~~she~~ founded the National Council of Negro Women in

1935.

Minor ideas in these sentences are now expressed in subordinate clauses or phrases.

**EXERCISE 20–1** Revise any run-on sentences using the method of revision suggested in brackets. Revisions of lettered sentences appear in the back of the book. Example:

*Because*
Orville had been obsessed with his weight as a teenager, he
⌄
rarely ate anything sweet. [*Restructure the sentence.*]

a. The city had one public swimming pool, it stayed packed with children all summer long. [*Restructure the sentence.*]
b. The building is being renovated, therefore at times we have no heat, water, or electricity. [*Use a comma and a coordinating conjunction.*]
c. The view was not what the travel agent had described, where were the rolling hills and the shimmering rivers? [*Make two sentences.*]
d. All those gnarled equations looked like toxic insects, maybe I was going to have to rethink my major. [*Use a semicolon.*]
e. The city government had good reason to fear a major earthquake, most of the business district was built on landfill. [*Use a colon.*]

1. The car was hardly worth trading, the frame was twisted and the block was warped. [*Restructure the sentence.*]
2. The next time an event is canceled because of bad weather, don't blame the meteorologist, blame nature. [*Make two sentences.*]
3. Ray was fluent in American Sign Language he could sign as easily as he could speak. [*Restructure the sentence.*]

1. The car was hardly worth trading because the frame was twisted and the block was warped.
2. The next time an event is canceled because of bad weather, don't blame the meteorologist. Blame nature.
3. Ray, who was fluent in American Sign Language, could sign as easily as he could speak.
4. Susanna arrived with a stack of her latest hats, hoping the gift shop would place a big winter order.
5. There was one major reason for John's wealth: His [*or* his] grandfather had been a multimillionaire.

4. Susanna arrived with a stack of her latest hats she hoped the gift shop would place a big winter order. [*Restructure the sentence.*]
5. There was one major reason for John's wealth, his grandfather had been a multimillionaire. [*Use a colon.*]

**EXERCISE 20–2**   Revise any run-on sentences using a technique that you find effective. If a sentence is correct, write "correct" after it. Revisions of lettered sentences appear in the back of the book. Example:

> Crossing so many time zones on an eight-hour flight, I knew
> I would be tired when I arrived, ~~however,~~ *but* I was too excited
> to sleep on the plane.

a. Wind power for the home is a supplementary source of energy, it can be combined with electricity, gas, or solar energy.
b. Aidan viewed Sofia Coppola's *Lost in Translation* three times and then wrote a paper describing the film as the work of a mysterious modern painter.
c. In the Middle Ages, the streets of London were dangerous places, it was safer to travel by boat along the Thames.
d. "He's not drunk," I said, "he's in a state of diabetic shock."
e. Are you able to endure boredom, isolation, and potential violence, then the army may well be the adventure for you.

1. Death Valley National Monument, located in southern California and Nevada, is one of the hottest places on earth, temperatures there have soared as high as 134 degrees Fahrenheit.
2. Anamaria opened the boxes crammed with toys, out sprang griffins, dragons, and phoenixes.
3. Subatomic physics is filled with strange and marvelous particles, tiny bodies of matter that shiver, wobble, pulse, and flatten to no thickness at all.
4. As his first major project, landscape architect Frederick Law Olmsted designed New York City's Central Park, one of the most beautiful urban parks in the United States.

**EXERCISE 20–2   Possible revisions:**

a. Wind power for the home is a supplementary source of energy that can be combined with electricity, gas, or solar energy.
b. Correct
c. In the Middle Ages, when the streets of London were dangerous places, it was safer to travel by boat along the Thames.
d. "He's not drunk," I said. "He's in a state of diabetic shock."
e. Are you able to endure boredom, isolation, and potential violence? Then the army may well be the adventure for you.

1. Death Valley National Monument, located in southern California and Nevada, is one of the hottest places on earth. Temperatures there have soared as high as 134 degrees Fahrenheit.
2. When Anamaria opened the boxes crammed with toys, out sprang griffins, dragons, and phoenixes.

5. The neurosurgeon explained that the medication could have one side effect, it might cause me to experience temporary memory loss.

**EXERCISE 20–3** In the following rough draft, revise any run-on sentences.

Some parents and educators argue that requiring uniforms in public schools would improve student behavior and performance. They think that uniforms give students a more professional attitude toward school, moreover, they believe that uniforms help create a sense of community among students from diverse backgrounds. But parents and educators should consider the drawbacks to requiring uniforms in public schools.

Uniforms do create a sense of community, they do this, however, by stamping out individuality. Youth is a time to express originality, it is a time to develop a sense of self. One important way young people express their identities is through the clothes they wear. Of course, it could be argued that the self-patrolled dress code of high school students is stricter than any school-imposed code, nevertheless, trying to control dress habits from above will only lead to resentment or to mindless conformity.

If children are going to act like adults, they need to be treated like adults, they need to be allowed to make their own choices. Telling young people what to wear to school merely prolongs their childhood. Requiring uniforms undermines the educational purpose of public schools, which is not just to teach facts and figures but to help young people grow into adults who are responsible for making their own choices.

**ON THE WEB**

**dianahacker.com/bedhandbook**
▶ Electronic grammar exercises
  ▶ E-ex 20–1 to 20–3

**EXERCISE 20–2 (continued)**

3. Correct
4. Correct
5. The neurosurgeon explained that the medication could have one side effect: It [or it] might cause me to experience temporary memory loss.

**EXERCISE 20–3** Possible revisions:

Some parents and educators argue that requiring uniforms in public schools would improve student behavior and performance. They think that uniforms give students a more professional attitude toward school; moreover, they believe that uniforms help create a sense of community among students from diverse backgrounds. But parents and educators should consider the drawbacks to requiring uniforms in public schools.

# 21

## Make subjects and verbs agree.

Native speakers of standard English know by ear that *he talks, she has,* and *it doesn't* (not *he talk, she have,* and *it don't*) are standard subject-verb combinations. For such speakers, problems with subject-verb agreement arise only in certain tricky situations, which are detailed in 21b–21k.

If you don't trust your ear—perhaps because you speak English as a second language or because you speak or hear nonstandard English in your community—you will need to learn the standard forms explained in 21a. Even if you do trust your ear, take a quick look at 21a to see what "subject-verb agreement" means.

### 21a Consult this section for standard subject-verb combinations.

In the present tense, verbs agree with their subjects in number (singular or plural) and in person (first, second, or third). The present-tense ending *-s* (or *-es*) is used on a verb if its subject is third-person singular; otherwise the verb takes no ending. Consider, for example, the present-tense forms of the verbs *love* and *try,* given at the beginning of the chart on the following page.

The verb *be* varies from this pattern; unlike any other verb, it has special forms in *both* the present and the past tense. These forms appear at the end of the chart.

If you aren't confident that you know the standard forms, use the charts on pages 259 and 260 as you proof-read for subject-verb agreement. You may also want to look at 27c on *-s* endings.

---

**EXERCISE 20–3 (continued)**

Although uniforms do create a sense of community, they do this by stamping out individuality. Youth is a time to express originality, a time to develop a sense of self. One important way young people express their identities is through the clothes they wear. Of course, it could be argued that the self-patrolled dress code of high school students is stricter than any school-imposed code. Nevertheless, trying to control dress habits from above will only lead to resentment or to mindless conformity.

If children are going to act like adults, they need to be treated like adults who are allowed to make their own choices. Telling young people what to wear to school merely prolongs their childhood. Requiring uniforms undermines the educational purpose of public schools, which is not just to teach facts and figures but

## Subject-verb agreement at a glance

### *Present-tense forms of love and try (typical verbs)*

| | SINGULAR | | PLURAL | |
|---|---|---|---|---|
| **FIRST PERSON** | I | love | we | love |
| **SECOND PERSON** | you | love | you | love |
| **THIRD PERSON** | he/she/it | loves | they | love |

| | SINGULAR | | PLURAL | |
|---|---|---|---|---|
| **FIRST PERSON** | I | try | we | try |
| **SECOND PERSON** | you | try | you | try |
| **THIRD PERSON** | he/she/it | tries | they | try |

### *Present-tense forms of have*

| | SINGULAR | | PLURAL | |
|---|---|---|---|---|
| **FIRST PERSON** | I | have | we | have |
| **SECOND PERSON** | you | have | you | have |
| **THIRD PERSON** | he/she/it | has | they | have |

### *Present-tense forms of do*

| | SINGULAR | | PLURAL | |
|---|---|---|---|---|
| **FIRST PERSON** | I | do/don't | we | do/don't |
| **SECOND PERSON** | you | do/don't | you | do/don't |
| **THIRD PERSON** | he/she/it | does/doesn't | they | do/don't |

### *Present-tense and past-tense forms of be*

| | SINGULAR | | PLURAL | |
|---|---|---|---|---|
| **FIRST PERSON** | I | am/was | we | are/were |
| **SECOND PERSON** | you | are/were | you | are/were |
| **THIRD PERSON** | he/she/it | is/was | they | are/were |

**EXERCISE 20–3 (continued)**

also to help young people grow into adults who are responsible for making their own choices.

### SCHOLARS ON SUBJECT-VERB AGREEMENT

Shaughnessy, Mina P. *Errors and Expectations: A Guide for the Teacher of Basic Writing.* New York: Oxford UP, 1979. 16–43. Shaughnessy points out that students who are confused about the inflectional system in standard English will make far more errors in subject-verb agreement than other students. She argues that such students need direct instruction in the use of the -s verb form.

See also SCHOLARS ON STANDARD ENGLISH VERB FORMS (27).

## When to use the -s (or -es) form of a present-tense verb

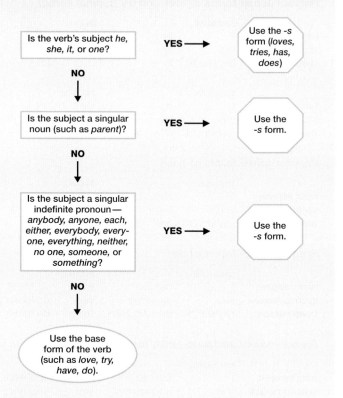

Is the verb's subject *he, she, it,* or *one*?

**YES** ⟶ Use the *-s* form (*loves, tries, has, does*)

**NO** ↓

Is the subject a singular noun (such as *parent*)?

**YES** ⟶ Use the *-s* form.

**NO** ↓

Is the subject a singular indefinite pronoun— *anybody, anyone, each, either, everybody, every- one, everything, neither, no one, someone,* or *something*?

**YES** ⟶ Use the *-s* form.

**NO** ↓

Use the base form of the verb (such as *love, try, have, do*).

**EXCEPTION:** Choosing the correct present-tense form of *be* (*am, is,* or *are*) is not quite so simple. See the chart on the previous page for both present- and past-tense forms of *be*.

**ESL TIP:** Do not use the *-s* form of a verb that follows a helping verb such as *can, must,* or *should*. (See 29a.)

---

**WRITERS ON WRITING**

Like everything metaphysical, the harmony between thought and reality is to be found in the grammar of the language.

—Ludwig Wittgenstein

GRAMMAR CHECKERS are fairly good at flagging subject-verb agreement problems. They occasionally flag a correct sentence, usually because they misidentify the subject, the verb, or both. Sometimes they miss an agreement problem because they don't recognize a pronoun's antecedent. In the following sentence, for example, the grammar checker did not detect that *eggs* is the antecedent of *which: Some animal rights groups oppose eating eggs, which comes from animals.* Because *eggs* is plural, the correct verb is *come.*

## 21b Make the verb agree with its subject, not with a word that comes between.

Word groups often come between the subject and the verb. Such word groups, usually modifying the subject, may contain a noun that at first appears to be the subject. By mentally stripping away such modifiers, you can isolate the noun that is in fact the subject.

The *samples* on the tray in the lab *need* testing.

▶ High levels of air pollution cause~~s~~ damage to the respiratory tract.

The subject is *levels*, not *pollution.* Strip away the phrase *of air pollution* to hear the correct verb: *levels cause.*

has
▶ The slaughter of pandas for their pelts ~~have~~ caused the
 ^
panda population to decline drastically.

The subject is *slaughter*, not *pandas* or *pelts.*

**WRITERS ON WRITING**
Grammar is a piano I play by ear. All I know about grammar is its power. —Joan Didion

**NOTE:** Phrases beginning with the prepositions *as well as, in addition to, accompanied by, together with,* and *along with* do not make a singular subject plural.

▶ The governor as well as his press secretary ~~were~~ shot.
  *was*

> To emphasize that two people were shot, the writer could use *and* instead: *The governor and his press secretary were shot.*

## 21c Treat most subjects joined with *and* as plural.

A subject with two or more parts is said to be compound. If the parts are connected by *and,* the subject is nearly always plural.

*Leon and Jan* often *jog* together.

▶ Jill's natural ability and her desire to help others ~~has~~ led to a
  *have*

  career in the ministry.

> *Ability and desire* is a plural subject, so its verb should be *have.*

**EXCEPTIONS:** When the parts of the subject form a single unit or when they refer to the same person or thing, treat the subject as singular.

> Strawberries and cream was a last-minute addition to the menu.

> Sue's friend and adviser was surprised by her decision.

When a compound subject is preceded by *each* or *every,* treat it as singular.

---

**WRITERS ON WRITING**

I write what I would like to read.  —Kathleen Norris

When I say writing, O believe me, it is rewriting that I have chiefly in mind.  —Robert Louis Stevenson

Each tree, shrub, and vine needs to be sprayed.

Every car, truck, and van is required to pass inspection.

This exception does not apply when a compound subject is followed by *each: Alan and Marcia each have different ideas.*

**21d** With subjects joined with *or* or *nor* (or with *either . . . or* or *neither . . . nor*), make the verb agree with the part of the subject nearer to the verb.

A driver's *license* or credit *card is* required.

A driver's *license* or two credit *cards are* required.

▶ If an infant or a child ~~are~~ *is* having difficulty breathing, seek medical attention immediately.

▶ Neither the lab assistant nor the students ~~was~~ *were* able to download the information.

The verb must be matched with the part of the subject closer to it: *child is* in the first sentence, *students were* in the second.

**NOTE:** If one part of the subject is singular and the other is plural, put the plural one last to avoid awkwardness.

**21e** Treat most indefinite pronouns as singular.

Indefinite pronouns are pronouns that do not refer to specific persons or things. The following commonly used indefinite pronouns are singular.

---

**WRITERS ON WRITING**

Everything that is written merely to please the author is worthless. —Pascal

Any writer overwhelmingly honest about pleasing himself [or herself] is almost sure to please others. —Marianne Moore

I am dead against art's being self-expression. I see an inherent failure in any story which fails to detach itself from the author.
—Elizabeth Bowen

| anybody | each | everyone | nobody | somebody |
|---|---|---|---|---|
| anyone | either | everything | no one | someone |
| anything | everybody | neither | nothing | something |

Many of these words appear to have plural meanings, and they are often treated as such in casual speech. In formal written English, however, they are nearly always treated as singular.

*Everyone* on the team *supports* the coach.

▶ Each of the furrows ~~have~~ has been seeded.

▶ Everybody who signed up for the snowboarding trip ~~were~~ was taking lessons.

The subjects of these sentences are *Each* and *Everybody*. These indefinite pronouns are third-person singular, so the verbs must be *has* and *was*.

A few indefinite pronouns (*all, any, none, some*) may be singular or plural depending on the noun or pronoun they refer to.

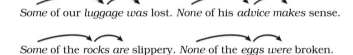

*Some* of our *luggage was* lost. *None* of his *advice makes* sense.

*Some* of the *rocks are* slippery. *None* of the *eggs were* broken.

**NOTE:** When the meaning of *none* is emphatically "not one," *none* may be treated as singular: *None* [meaning "Not one"] *of the eggs was broken.* However, some experts advise using *not one* instead: *Not one of the eggs was broken.*

---

**WRITERS ON WRITING**

The desire to write grows with writing.              —Erasmus

I can't understand how anyone can write without rewriting everything over and over again.              —Leo Tolstoy

| ON THE WEB | **dianahacker.com/bedhandbook** |
|---|---|
| | ▶ Language Debates |
| | ▶ *none* |

**21f** Treat collective nouns as singular unless the meaning is clearly plural.

Collective nouns such as *jury, committee, audience, crowd, class, troop, family,* and *couple* name a class or a group. In American English, collective nouns are nearly always treated as singular: They emphasize the group as a unit. Occasionally, when there is some reason to draw attention to the individual members of the group, a collective noun may be treated as plural. (Also see 22b.)

**SINGULAR**    The *class respects* the teacher.

**PLURAL**    The *class are* debating among themselves.

To underscore the notion of individuality in the second sentence, many writers would add a clearly plural noun such as *members.*

**PLURAL**    The class *members are* debating among themselves.

▶ The board of trustees ~~meet~~ meets in Denver twice a year.

The board as a whole meets; there is no reason to draw attention to its individual members.

▶ A young couple ~~was~~ were arguing about politics while holding hands.

The meaning is clearly plural. Only individuals can argue and hold hands.

**NOTE:** The phrase *the number* is treated as singular, *a number* as plural.

**SINGULAR**    *The number* of school-age children *is* declining.

**PLURAL**    *A number* of children *are* attending the wedding.

**NOTE:** In general, when units of measurement are used with a singular noun, treat them as singular; when they are used with a plural noun, treat them as plural.

**SINGULAR**    *Three-fourths* of the pie *has* been eaten.

**PLURAL**    *One-fourth* of the drivers *were* drunk.

**21g** Make the verb agree with its subject even when the subject follows the verb.

Verbs ordinarily follow subjects. When this normal order is reversed, it is easy to become confused. Sentences beginning with *there is* or *there are* (or *there was* or *there were*) are inverted; the subject follows the verb.

There *are* surprisingly few *children* in our neighborhood.

▶ There ~~was~~ *were* a social worker and a crew of twenty volunteers at the scene of the accident.

The subject, *worker and crew,* is plural, so the verb must be *were.*

Occasionally you may decide to invert a sentence for variety or effect. When you do so, check to make sure that your subject and verb agree.

▶ At the back of the room ~~is~~ *are* a small aquarium and an enormous

terrarium.

> The subject, *aquarium and terrarium*, is plural, so the verb must be *are*. If the correct sentence seems awkward, begin with the subject: *A small aquarium and an enormous terrarium are at the back of the room.*

**21h** Make the verb agree with its subject, not with a subject complement.

One basic sentence pattern in English consists of a subject, a linking verb, and a subject complement: *Jack is a securities lawyer.* Because the subject complement names or describes the subject (*Jack*), it is sometimes mistaken for the subject. (See 63b on subject complements.)

> These *exercises are* a way to test your ability to perform under pressure.

▶ A tent and a sleeping bag ~~is~~ *are* the required equipment for all

campers.

> *Tent and bag* is the subject, not *equipment.*

▶ A major force in today's economy ~~are~~ *is* women—as earners,

consumers, and investors.

> *Force* is the subject, not *women.* If the corrected version seems awkward, make *women* the subject: *Women are a major force in today's economy—as earners, consumers, and investors.*

**21i** *Who, which,* and *that* take verbs that agree with their antecedents.

Like most pronouns, the relative pronouns *who, which,* and *that* have antecedents, nouns or pronouns to which they refer. Relative pronouns used as subjects of subordinate clauses take verbs that agree with their antecedents.

Take a *suit that travels* well.

Constructions such as *one of the students who* [or *one of the things that*] cause problems for writers. Do not assume that the antecedent must be *one.* Instead, consider the logic of the sentence.

▶ Our ability to use language is one of the things that sets us

apart from animals.

The antecedent of *that* is *things,* not *one.* Several things set us apart from animals.

When the word *only* comes before *one,* you are safe in assuming that *one* is the antecedent of the relative pronoun.

▶ Veronica was the only one of the first-year Spanish students

        was
who ~~were~~ fluent enough to apply for the exchange program.

The antecedent of *who* is *one,* not *students.* Only one student was fluent enough.

| ON THE WEB | **dianahacker.com/bedhandbook** ▶ Language Debates ▶ *one of those who* (or *that*) |
|---|---|

**21j** Words such as *athletics, economics, mathematics, physics, statistics, measles, mumps,* and *news* are usually singular, despite their plural form.

▶     Statistics ~~are~~ *is* among the most difficult courses in our

    program.

**EXCEPTION:** When they describe separate items rather than a collective body of knowledge, words such as *athletics, mathematics, physics,* and *statistics* are plural: *The statistics on steroid use are alarming.*

**21k** Titles of works, company names, words mentioned as words, and gerund phrases are singular.

▶     *Lost Cities* ~~describe~~ *describes* the discoveries of many ancient

    civilizations.

▶     Delmonico Brothers ~~specialize~~ *specializes* in organic produce and

    additive-free meats.

▶     *Controlled substances* ~~are~~ *is* a euphemism for illegal drugs.

A gerund phrase consists of an *-ing* verb form followed by any objects, complements, or modifiers (see 64c). Treat gerund phrases as singular.

▶     Encountering busy signals ~~are~~ *is* troublesome to our clients, so

    we have hired two new switchboard operators.

**EXERCISE 21–1** Underline the subject (or compound subject) and then select the verb that agrees with it. (If you have difficulty identifying the subject, consult 63a.) Answers to lettered sentences appear in the back of the book. Example:

Everyone in the telecom focus group (has/have) experienced

problems with cell phones.

a. Your friendship over the years and your support (has/have) meant a great deal to us.
b. Shelters for teenage runaways (offers/offer) a wide variety of services.
c. The main source of income for Trinidad (is/are) oil and pitch.
d. The chances of your being promoted (is/are) excellent.
e. There (was/were) a Yu-Gi-Oh! card and a quirky haiku stuck to the refrigerator.

1. Neither the professor nor his assistants (was/were) able to solve the mystery of the eerie glow in the laboratory.
2. Many hours at the driving range (has/have) led us to design golf balls with GPS locators in them.
3. Discovered in the soil of our city garden (was/were) a button dating from the Civil War and three marbles dating from the turn of the century.
4. Every year, during the midsummer festival, the smoke of village bonfires (fills/fill) the sky.
5. The story performers (was/were) surrounded by children and adults eager to see magical tales.

**EXERCISE 21–2** Edit the following sentences to eliminate problems with subject-verb agreement. If a sentence is correct, write "correct" after it. Answers to lettered sentences appear in the back of the book. Example:

*were*
Jack's first days in the infantry ~~was~~ grueling.
^

**EXERCISE 21–1 Answers:**

a. Subject: friendship and support; verb: have; b. Subject: Shelters; verb: offer; c. Subject: source; verb: is; d. Subject: chances; verb: are; e. Subject: card and haiku; verb: were

1. Subject: professor nor assistants; verb: were; 2. Subject: hours; verb: have; 3. Subject: button and marbles; verb: were; 4. Subject: smoke; verb: fills; 5. Subject: performers; verb: were

**EXERCISE 21–2 Answers:**

a. One of the main reasons for elephant poaching is the profits received from selling the ivory tusks.
b. Correct
c. A number of students in the seminar were aware of the importance of joining the discussion.

a. One of the main reasons for elephant poaching are the profits received from selling the ivory tusks.
b. Not until my interview with Dr. Hwang were other possibilities opened to me.
c. A number of students in the seminar was aware of the importance of joining the discussion.
d. Batik cloth from Bali, blue and white ceramics from Delft, and a bocce ball from Turin has made Angelie's room the talk of the dorm.
e. The board of directors, ignoring the wishes of the neighborhood, has voted to allow further development.

1. Measles is a contagious childhood disease.
2. Adorning a shelf in the lab is a Vietnamese figurine, a set of Korean clay gods, and an American plastic village.
3. The presence of certain bacteria in our bodies is one of the factors that determines our overall health.
4. Sheila is the only one of the many applicants who has the ability to step into this job.
5. Neither the explorer nor his companions was ever seen again.

| ON THE WEB | **dianahacker.com/bedhandbook** ▶ Electronic grammar exercises ▶ E-ex 21–1 to 21–3 |
|---|---|

# 22

## Make pronouns and antecedents agree.

A pronoun is a word that substitutes for a noun. (See 62b.) Many pronouns have antecedents, nouns or pronouns to which they refer. A pronoun and its antecedent agree when they are both singular or both plural.

**EXERCISE 21–2 (continued)**
d. Batik cloth from Bali, blue and white ceramics from Delft, and a bocce ball from Turin have made Angelie's room the talk of the dorm.
e. Correct

1. Correct
2. Adorning a shelf in the lab are a Vietnamese figurine, a set of Korean clay gods, and an American plastic village.
3. The presence of certain bacteria in our bodies is one of the factors that determine our overall health.
4. Correct
5. Neither the explorer nor his companions were ever seen again.

**SINGULAR**   *Dr. Ava Berto* finished *her* rounds.

**PLURAL**   The hospital *interns* finished *their* rounds.

 **ESL**
The pronouns *he, his, she, her, it,* and *its* must agree in gender (masculine, feminine, or neuter) with their antecedents, not with the words they modify.

*Steve* visited *his* [not *her*] sister in Seattle.

✓ **GRAMMAR CHECKERS** do not flag problems with pronoun-antecedent agreement. It takes a human eye to see that a singular noun, such as *logger,* does not agree with a plural pronoun, such as *their,* in a sentence like this: *The logger in the Northwest relies on the old forest growth for their living.*

When grammar checkers do flag agreement problems, they often suggest (correctly) substituting the singular phrase *his or her* for the plural pronoun *their.* For other revision strategies that avoid the wordy *his or her* construction, see the chart on page 274.

## 22a Do not use plural pronouns to refer to singular antecedents.

Writers are frequently tempted to use plural pronouns to refer to two kinds of singular antecedents: indefinite pronouns and generic nouns.

**SCHOLARS ON PRONOUN-ANTECEDENT AGREEMENT**

Nilsen, Alleen Pace. "Why Keep Searching When It's Already *Their*? Reconsidering *Everybody's* Pronoun Problem." *English Journal* 90.4 (2001): 68–73. Nilsen describes the problems caused by the use of dual pronouns to avoid sexist language and analyzes the real-world use of *they* as a singular, nonsexist pronoun. She categorizes examples of such errors according to speakers' or writers' reasons for their choices: including and persuading, avoiding accusations, moving from general to specific and vice versa, and choosing efficiency. Nilsen concludes with a list of reasons why it might be counterproductive to battle the gradual change from *he/she* to *they.*

### Indefinite pronouns

Indefinite pronouns refer to nonspecific persons or things. Even though some of the following indefinite pronouns may seem to have plural meanings, treat them as singular in formal English.

| anybody | each | everyone | nobody | somebody |
|---|---|---|---|---|
| anyone | either | everything | no one | someone |
| anything | everybody | neither | nothing | something |

In class *everyone* performs at *his or her* [not *their*] own fitness level.

When a plural pronoun refers mistakenly to a singular indefinite pronoun, you can usually choose one of three options for revision:

1. Replace the plural pronoun with *he or she* (or *his or her*).
2. Make the antecedent plural.
3. Rewrite the sentence so that no problem of agreement exists.

▶ When someone has been drinking, ~~they are~~ *he or she is* likely to speed.

▶ When ~~someone has~~ *drivers have* been drinking, they are likely to speed.

▶ ~~When someone~~ *A driver who* has been drinking/ ~~they are~~ *is* likely to speed.

Because the *he or she* construction is wordy, often the second or third revision strategy is more effective. Be aware that the traditional use of *he* (or *his*) to refer to persons of either sex is now widely considered sexist. (See 17f.)

**SCHOLARS ON PRONOUN-ANTECEDENT AGREEMENT**

Sklar, Elizabeth S. "The Tribunal of Use: Agreement in Indefinite Constructions." *College Composition and Communication* 39 (1988): 410–22. Sklar argues that the rule prohibiting constructions such as "*everyone . . . their*" is "pragmatically cumbersome, linguistically unreliable, and ideologically provocative."

Bryony, Shannon. "Pronouns: Male, Female, and Undesignated." *ETC: A Review of General Semantics* 45 (1988): 334–36. Bryony reviews complaints about the "awkwardness" of alternatives to the generic *he*. She argues that since the trend in writing is toward a direct and informal style, either the second-person pronoun or a plural pronoun may be an appropriate choice.

### Choosing a revision strategy that avoids sexist language

Because many readers object to sexist language, avoid the use of *he, him,* and *his* to refer to both men and women. Also try to be sparing in your use of the wordy expressions *he or she* and *his or her.* Where possible, seek out more graceful alternatives.

***Use an occasional*** *he or she (or his or her).*

▶ In our office, everyone works at ~~their~~ own pace.
                                        *his or her*

***Make the antecedent plural.***

▶ ~~An employee~~ on extended leave may continue their life
   *Employees*
insurance.

***Recast the sentence.***

▶ The amount of annual leave a federal worker may

accrue depends on ~~their~~ length of service.

▶ ~~If a~~ child ~~is~~ born to parents who are both bipolar,/ ~~they~~
   *A*                                                    *has*
~~have~~ a high chance of being bipolar.

▶ A year later someone finally admitted ~~that they were~~
                                          *to being*

involved in the kidnapping.

▶ I was taught that no one could escape the fires of
                        *who wanted to reach heaven*

purgatory. ~~if they wanted to reach heaven.~~

---

**SCHOLARS ON PRONOUN-ANTECEDENT AGREEMENT**

Kolin, Martha. "Everyone's Right to Their Own Language." *College Composition and Communication* 37 (1986): 100–02. Kolin discusses the *"everyone . . . their"* debate and asserts that such constructions should not be marked as usage problems.

*Generic nouns*

A generic noun represents a typical member of a group, such as a typical student, or any member of a group, such as any lawyer. Although generic nouns may seem to have plural meanings, they are singular.

Every *runner* must train rigorously if *he or she wants* [not *they want*] to excel.

When a plural pronoun refers mistakenly to a generic noun, you will usually have the same three revision options as mentioned on page 273 for indefinite pronouns.

▶ A medical student must study hard if ~~they want~~ *he or she wants* to succeed.

▶ ~~A medical student~~ *Medical students* must study hard if they want to succeed.

▶ A medical student must study hard ~~if they want~~ to succeed.

**ON THE WEB**   **dianahacker.com/bedhandbook**
▶ Language Debates
▶ Pronoun-antecedent agreement

**22b** Treat collective nouns as singular unless the meaning is clearly plural.

Collective nouns such as *jury, committee, audience, crowd, class, troop, family, team,* and *couple* name a class or a group. Ordinarily the group functions as a unit, so the noun should be treated as singular; if the members of the group function as individuals, however, the noun should be treated as plural. (See also 21f.)

AS A UNIT       The *committee* granted *its* permission to build.

AS INDIVIDUALS  The *committee* put *their* signatures on the document.

> ► The jury has reached ~~their~~ *its* decision.

There is no reason to draw attention to the individual members of the jury, so *jury* should be treated as singular. Notice also that the writer treated the noun as singular when choosing the verb *has*, so for consistency the pronoun must be *its*.

> ► The audience shouted "Bravo" and stamped ~~its~~ *their* feet.

It is difficult to see how the audience as a unit can stamp *its* feet. The meaning here is clearly plural, requiring *their*.

**22c** Treat most compound antecedents connected by *and* as plural.

*Jill and John* moved to Luray, where *they* built a cabin.

**22d** With compound antecedents connected by *or* or *nor* (or by *either . . . or* or *neither . . . nor*), make the pronoun agree with the nearer antecedent.

Either *Bruce* or *Tom* should receive first prize for *his* poem.

**EXERCISE 22–1  Possible revisions:**

a. Every presidential candidate must appeal to a wide variety of ethnic and social groups to win the election.
b. David lent his motorcycle to someone who allowed a friend to use it.
c. The aerobics teacher motioned for all the students to move their arms in wide, slow circles.
d. Correct
e. Applicants should be bilingual if they want to qualify for this position.

1. Drivers who refuse to take a blood or breath test will have their licenses suspended for six months.

Neither the *mouse* nor the *rats* could find *their* way through the maze.

**NOTE:** If one of the antecedents is singular and the other plural, as in the second example, put the plural one last to avoid awkwardness.

**EXCEPTION:** If one antecedent is male and the other female, do not follow the traditional rule. The sentence *Either Bruce or Elizabeth should receive first prize for her short story* makes no sense. The best solution is to recast the sentence: *The prize for best short story should go to Bruce or Elizabeth.*

**EXERCISE 22–1**   Edit the following sentences to eliminate problems with pronoun-antecedent agreement. Most of the sentences can be revised in more than one way, so experiment before choosing a solution. If a sentence is correct, write "correct" after it. Revisions of lettered sentences appear in the back of the book. Example:

> *Recruiters*
> ~~The recruiter~~ may tell the truth, but there is much that they
> ^
> choose not to tell.

a. Every presidential candidate must appeal to a wide variety of ethnic and social groups if they want to win the election.
b. David lent his motorcycle to someone who allowed their friend to use it.
c. The aerobics teacher motioned for everyone to move their arms in wide, slow circles.
d. The parade committee was unanimous in its decision to allow all groups and organizations to join the festivities.
e. The applicant should be bilingual if they want to qualify for this position.

**EXERCISE 22–1 (continued)**

2. Why should people learn a second language? One reason is to sharpen their minds.
3. Trying to anticipate problems and avert disaster, the Department of Education issued new guidelines for school security.
4. Seven qualified Hispanic agents applied, all hoping for a career move that would let them use their language and cultural training on more than just translations.
5. Anyone who notices any suspicious activity should report it to the police.

1. If a driver refuses to take a blood or breath test, he or she will have their licenses suspended for six months.
2. Why should anyone learn a second language? One reason is to sharpen their minds.
3. The Department of Education issued new guidelines for school security. They were trying to anticipate problems and avert disaster.
4. Seven qualified Hispanic agents applied, each hoping for a career move that would let them use their language and cultural training on more than just translations.
5. If anyone notices any suspicious activity, they should report it to the police.

**EXERCISE 22–2** Edit the following paragraph to eliminate problems with pronoun-antecedent agreement or sexist language.

A common practice in businesses is to put each employee in their own cubicle. A typical cubicle resembles an office, but their walls don't reach the ceiling. Many office managers feel that a cubicle floor plan has its advantages. Cubicles make a large area feel spacious. In addition, they can be moved around so that each new employee can be accommodated in his own work area. Of course, the cubicle model also has problems. The typical employee is not as happy with a cubicle as they would be with a traditional office. Also, productivity can suffer. Neither a manager nor a frontline worker can ordinarily do their best work in a cubicle because of noise and lack of privacy. Each worker can hear his neighbors tapping on computer keyboards, making telephone calls, and muttering under their breath.

**ON THE WEB** **dianahacker.com/bedhandbook**
▶ Electronic grammar exercises
  ▶ E-ex 22–1 to 22–3

**EXERCISE 22–2 Possible revisions:**

A common practice in businesses is to put each employee in a cubicle. A typical cubicle resembles an office, but its walls don't reach the ceiling. Many office managers feel that a cubicle floor plan has its advantages. Cubicles make a large area feel spacious. In addition, they can be moved around so that new employees can be accommodated in their own work areas. Of course, the cubicle model also has problems. Typical employees are not as happy with a cubicle as they would be with a traditional office. Also, productivity can suffer. Neither a manager nor a frontline worker can ordinarily do his or her best work in a cubicle because of noise and lack of privacy. Workers can hear their neighbors tapping on computer keyboards, making telephone calls, and muttering under their breath.

# 23

## Make pronoun references clear.

Pronouns substitute for nouns; they are a kind of shorthand. In a sentence like *After Andrew intercepted the ball, he kicked it as hard as he could,* the pronouns *he* and *it* substitute for the nouns *Andrew* and *ball.* The word a pronoun refers to is called its *antecedent.*

> **GRAMMAR CHECKERS** do not flag problems with faulty pronoun reference. Although a computer program can identify pronouns, it has no way of knowing which words, if any, they refer to. For example, grammar checkers miss the fact that the pronoun *it* has an ambiguous reference in the following sentence: *The thief stole the woman's purse and her car and then destroyed it.* Did the thief destroy the purse or the car? It takes human judgment to realize that readers might be confused.

### 23a Avoid ambiguous or remote pronoun reference.

Ambiguous pronoun reference occurs when a pronoun could refer to two possible antecedents.

▶ *The pitcher broke when Gloria set it*
~~When Gloria set the pitcher~~ on the glass-topped table~~/~~. ~~it~~
^
~~broke.~~

▶ Tom told James, *"You have* ~~that he had~~ won the lottery.*"*
^                                      ^

What broke—the table or the pitcher? Who won the lottery—Tom or James? The revisions eliminate the ambiguity.

**SCHOLARS ON PRONOUN REFERENCE**

Mathews, Alison, and Martin S. Chodorow. "Pronoun Resolution in Two-Clause Sentences: Effects of Ambiguity, Antecedent Location, and Depth of Imbedding." *Journal of Memory and Language* 27 (1988): 245–60. This empirical study focuses on students' comprehension when reading a two-clause sentence. The authors discover that students resolve any ambiguity if the antecedent is located early in the first clause.

Moskovit, Leonard. "When Is Broad Reference Clear?" *College Composition and Communication* 34 (1983): 454–69. Focusing on the pronoun *this,* Moskovit uses a linguistic approach to examine why some broad references are clear and others are not.

Remote pronoun reference occurs when a pronoun is too far away from its antecedent for easy reading.

▶ After the court ordered my ex-husband to pay child support, he refused. Approximately eight months later, we were back in court. This time the judge ordered him to make payments directly to the Support and Collections Unit, which would in turn pay me. For the first six months I received regular payments, but then they stopped. Again ~~he~~ *my ex-husband* was summoned to appear in court; he did not respond.

The pronoun *he* was too distant from its antecedent, *ex-husband,* which appeared several sentences earlier.

## 23b Generally, avoid broad reference of *this, that, which,* and *it.*

For clarity, the pronouns *this, that, which,* and *it* should ordinarily refer to specific antecedents rather than to whole ideas or sentences. When a pronoun's reference is needlessly broad, either replace the pronoun with a noun or supply an antecedent to which the pronoun clearly refers.

▶ More and more often, especially in large cities, we are finding ourselves victims of serious crimes. We learn to accept ~~this~~ *our fate* with minor gripes and groans.

For clarity the writer substituted a noun (*fate*) for the pronoun *this,* which referred broadly to the idea expressed in the preceding sentence.

**WRITERS ON WRITING**

The chief difference between good writing and better writing may be measured by the number of imperceptible hesitations the reader experiences as he [or she] goes along.     —James J. Kilpatrick

Writing is just work—there's no secret. If you dictate or use a pen or type or write with your toes—it is still just work.
                                        —Sinclair Lewis

▶ Romeo and Juliet were both too young to have acquired
                 *a fact*
  much wisdom, which accounts for their rash actions.
          ^

The writer added an antecedent (*fact*) that the pronoun *which* clearly refers to.

**EXCEPTION:** Many writers view broad reference as acceptable when the pronoun refers clearly to the sense of an entire clause.

> If you pick up a starving dog and make him prosperous, he will not bite you. *This* is the principal difference between a dog and a man.      —Mark Twain

**23c** Do not use a pronoun to refer to an implied antecedent.

A pronoun should refer to a specific antecedent, not to a word that is implied but not present in the sentence.

                                    *the braids*
▶ After braiding Ann's hair, Sue decorated ~~them~~ with ribbons.
                                       ^

The pronoun *them* referred to Ann's braids (implied by the term *braiding*), but the word *braids* did not appear in the sentence.

Modifiers, such as possessives, cannot serve as antecedents. A modifier may strongly imply the noun that the pronoun might logically refer to, but it is not itself that noun.

                            *Mary Gordon*
▶ In ~~Mary Gordon's~~ *The Shadow Man,* ~~she~~ writes about her
                                  ^

father's mysterious and startling past.

The pronoun *she* cannot refer logically to the possessive modifier *Mary Gordon's.* The revision substitutes the noun *Mary Gordon* for the pronoun *she,* thereby eliminating the problem.

**WRITERS ON WRITING**

It's not wise to violate the rules until you know how to observe them.      —T. S. Eliot

| ON THE WEB | dianahacker.com/bedhandbook |
| --- | --- |
| | ▶ Language Debates |
| | ▶ Possessives as antecedents |

**23d** Avoid the indefinite use of *they, it,* and *you.*

Do not use the pronoun *they* to refer indefinitely to persons who have not been specifically mentioned. *They* should always refer to a specific antecedent.

>         *Congress*
> ▶ In 2001, ~~they~~ shut down all government agencies for more
>       ^
>
> than a month until the budget crisis was finally resolved.

The word *it* should not be used indefinitely in constructions such as *It is said on television . . .* or *In the article it says that. . . .*

>   *The*
> ▶ ~~In the~~ encyclopedia ~~it~~ states that male moths can smell
>  ^
>
> female moths from several miles away.

The pronoun *you* is appropriate when the writer is addressing the reader directly: *Once you have kneaded the dough, let it rise in a warm place for at least twenty-five minutes.* Except in informal contexts, however, the indefinite *you* (meaning "anyone in general") is inappropriate. (See pp. 58–59.)

>                 *a guest*
> ▶ Ms. Pickersgill's *Guide to Etiquette* stipulates that ~~you~~ should
>                     ^
>
> not arrive at a party too early or leave too late.

The writer could have replaced *you* with *one,* but in American English the pronoun *one* can seem stilted.

**WRITERS ON WRITING**

As against having beautiful workshops, studies, etc., one writes best in a cellar on a rainy day.      —Van Wyck Brooks

The best time for planning a book is while doing the dishes.
     —Agatha Christie

. . . a thermos of tea, a quiet room, in the early morning hours.
     —Carson McCullers

| ON THE WEB | dianahacker.com/bedhandbook<br>▶ Language Debates<br>   ▶ *you* |
|---|---|

**23e** To refer to persons, use *who, whom,* or *whose,* not *which* or *that.*

In most contexts, use *who, whom,* or *whose* to refer to persons, *which* or *that* to refer to animals or things. *Which* is reserved only for animals or things, so it is impolite to use it to refer to persons.

>                                                     *whom*
> ▶ When he heard about my seven children, four of ~~which~~
>
>    live at home, Ron smiled and said, "I love children."

Although *that* is sometimes used to refer to persons, many readers will find such references dehumanizing. It is more polite to use a form of *who*—a word reserved only for people.

>                                             *who*
> ▶ Fans wondered how an out-of-shape old man ~~that~~ walked
>
>    with a limp could play football.

**NOTE:** Occasionally *whose* may be used to refer to animals and things to avoid the awkward *of which* construction.

>                    *whose*
> ▶ A local school, ~~the~~ name ~~of which~~ will be in tomorrow's
>
>    paper, has received the Governor's Gold Medal for outstand-
>
>    ing community service.

**ON THE WEB**

**dianahacker.com/bedhandbook**
▶ Language Debates
   ▶ *who* versus *which* or *that*

**EXERCISE 23–1**   Edit the following sentences to correct errors in pronoun reference. In some cases you will need to decide on an antecedent that the pronoun might logically refer to. Revisions of lettered sentences appear in the back of the book. Example:

> Following the breakup of AT&T, many other companies began
> to offer long-distance phone service. ~~This~~ *The competition* has led to lower
> long-distance rates.

a. They say that an engineering student should have hands-on experience with dismantling and reassembling machines.
b. She had decorated her living room with posters from chamber music festivals. This led her date to believe that she was interested in classical music. Actually she preferred rock.
c. In Ethiopia, you don't need much property to be considered well-off.
d. Marianne told Jenny that she was worried about her mother's illness.
e. Though Lewis cried for several minutes after scraping his knee, eventually it subsided.

1. Our German conversation group is made up of six people, three of which I had never met before.
2. Many people believe that the polygraph test is highly reliable if you employ a licensed examiner.
3. Parent involvement is high at Mission San Jose High School. They participate in many committees and activities that affect all aspects of school life.

---

**EXERCISE 23–1**   Possible revisions:

a. Some professors say that an engineering student should have hands-on experience with dismantling and reassembling machines.
b. Because she had decorated her living room with posters from chamber music festivals, her date thought she was interested in classical music. Actually she preferred rock.
c. In Ethiopia, a person doesn't need much property to be considered well-off.
d. Marianne told Jenny, "I am worried about your mother's illness." [or "... about my mother's illness."]
e. Though Lewis cried for several minutes after scraping his knee, eventually the pain subsided.

4. Because of Paul Robeson's outspoken attitude toward fascism, he was labeled a Communist.
5. In the report it points out that lifting the ban on Compound 1080 would prove detrimental, possibly even fatal, to the bald eagle.

**ON THE WEB**

**dianahacker.com/bedhandbook**
▶ Electronic grammar exercises
  ▶ E-ex 23–1 to 23–3

# 24

## Distinguish between pronouns such as *I* and *me*.

The personal pronouns in the following chart change what is known as *case form* according to their grammatical function in a sentence. Pronouns functioning as subjects (or subject complements) appear in the *subjective* case; those functioning as objects appear in the *objective* case; and those showing ownership appear in the *possessive* case.

|  | SUBJECTIVE CASE | OBJECTIVE CASE | POSSESSIVE CASE |
|---|---|---|---|
| SINGULAR | I | me | my |
|  | you | you | your |
|  | he/she/it | him/her/it | his/her/its |
| PLURAL | we | us | our |
|  | you | you | your |
|  | they | them | their |

**EXERCISE 23–1 (continued)**

1. Our German conversation group is made up of six people, three of whom I had never met before.
2. Many people believe that the polygraph test is highly reliable if conducted by a licensed examiner.
3. Parent involvement is high at Mission San Jose High School. Parents participate in many committees and activities that affect all aspects of school life.
4. Because of his outspoken attitude toward fascism, Paul Robeson was labeled a Communist.
5. The report points out that lifting the ban on Compound 1080 would prove detrimental, possibly even fatal, to the bald eagle.

Pronouns in the subjective and objective case are frequently confused. Most of the rules in this section specify when to use one or the other of these cases (*I* or *me, he* or *him,* and so on). Section 24g explains a special use of pronouns and nouns in the possessive case.

> **GRAMMAR CHECKERS** sometimes flag incorrect pronouns and suggest using the correct form: *I* or *me, he* or *him, she* or *her, we* or *us, they* or *them*. A grammar checker correctly flagged *we* in the following sentence and advised using *us* instead: *I say it is about time for we parents to revolt.* Grammar checkers miss more incorrect pronouns than they catch, however, and their suggestions for revision are sometimes off the mark. A grammar checker caught the error in the following sentence: *I am a little jealous that my dog likes my neighbor more than I.* But instead of suggesting changing the final *I* to *me* (. . . *more than me*), it suggested adding *do* (. . . *more than I do*), which does not fit the meaning of the sentence.

**24a** Use the subjective case (*I, you, he, she, it, we, they*) for subjects and subject complements.

When personal pronouns are used as subjects, ordinarily your ear will tell you the correct pronoun. Problems sometimes arise, however, with compound word groups containing a pronoun, so it is not always safe to trust your ear.

► Joel ran away from home because his stepfather and ~~him~~ *he* had quarreled.

> *His stepfather and he* is the subject of the verb *had quarreled.* If we strip away the words *his stepfather and,* the correct pronoun becomes clear: *he had quarreled* (not *him had quarreled*).

**WRITERS ON WRITING**

If you want to be a writer, you must do two things above all others: read a lot and write a lot. There's no way around these two things that I'm aware of, no shortcut.   —Stephen King

If you're talking about writing, the first and most important thing—and this will sound silly but I mean it with all my heart—is you must write every day.   —Stephen J. Cannell

When a pronoun is used as a subject complement (a word following a linking verb), your ear may mislead you, since the incorrect form is frequently heard in casual speech. (See "subject complement," 63b.)

▶ During the Lindbergh trial, Bruno Hauptmann repeatedly

    *he.*
  denied that the kidnapper was ~~him.~~
                                  ^

  If *kidnapper was he* seems too stilted, rewrite the sentence: *During the Lindbergh trial, Bruno Hauptmann repeatedly denied that he was the kidnapper.*

**24b** Use the objective case (*me, you, him, her, it, us, them*) for all objects.

When a personal pronoun is used as a direct object, an indirect object, or the object of a preposition, ordinarily your ear will lead you to the correct pronoun. When an object is compound, however, you may occasionally become confused.

▶ Janice was indignant when she realized that the salesclerk

    *her.*
  was insulting her mother and ~~she.~~
                                ^

  *Her mother and her* is the direct object of the verb *was insulting*. Strip away the words *her mother and* to hear the correct pronoun: *was insulting her* (not *was insulting she*).

                                              *me*
▶ The most traumatic experience for her father and ~~I~~ occurred
                                                    ^

  long after her operation.

  *Her father and me* is the object of the preposition *for*. Strip away the words *her father and* to test for the correct pronoun: *for me* (not *for I*).

---

**WRITERS ON WRITING**

To be a writer is to sit down at one's desk in the chill portion of every day, and to write; not waiting for the little jet of the blue flame of genius to start from the breastbone—just plain going at it, in pain and delight. To be a writer is to throw away a great deal, not to be satisfied, to type again, and then again, and once more, and over and over.
                                                    —John Hersey

When in doubt about the correct pronoun, some writers try to avoid making the choice by using a reflexive pronoun such as *myself.* Such evasions are nonstandard, even though they are used by some educated persons.

> ► The Indian cab driver gave my husband and ~~myself~~ some
> *me*
>
> good tips on traveling in New Delhi.

> ► The independent film company hired my sister and ~~myself~~
> *me*
>
> as marketing consultants.

> *My husband and me* is the indirect object of the verb *gave. My sister and me* is the direct object of the verb *hired.* For correct uses of *myself,* see the Glossary of Usage.

| ON THE WEB | dianahacker.com/bedhandbook |
|---|---|
| | ► Language Debates |
| | ► *myself* |

**24c** Put an appositive and the word to which it refers in the same case.

Appositives are noun phrases that rename nouns or pronouns. A pronoun used as an appositive has the same function (usually subject or object) as the word(s) it renames.

> ► The chief strategists, Dr. Bell and ~~me,~~ could not agree on a
> *I,*
>
> plan.

> The appositive *Dr. Bell and I* renames the subject, *strategists.* Test: *I could not agree* (not *me could not agree*).

**WRITERS ON WRITING**

What the devil to do with the sentence "Who the devil does he think he's fooling?" You can't write "Whom the devil—"

—Paul Goodman

▶ The reporter interviewed only two witnesses, the bicyclist

*me.*
and ~~I.~~
   ^

The appositive *the bicyclist and me* renames the direct object, *witnesses.* Test: *interviewed me* (not *interviewed I*).

**24d** Following *than* or *as,* choose the pronoun that expresses your meaning.

When a comparison begins with *than* or *as,* your choice of a pronoun will depend on your intended meaning. Consider, for example, the difference in meaning between these sentences.

> My husband likes football more than I.

> My husband likes football more than me.

Finish each sentence mentally and its meaning becomes clear: *My husband likes football more than I [do]. My husband likes football more than [he likes] me.*

▶ Even though he is sometimes ridiculed by the other boys,

*they.*
Nathan is much better off than ~~them.~~
   ^

*They* is the subject of the verb *are,* which is understood: *Nathan is much better off than they [are].* If the correct English seems too formal, you can always add the verb.

▶ We respected no other candidate for the city council as

*her.*
much as ~~she.~~
   ^

This sentence means that we respected no other candidate as much as *we respected her. Her* is the direct object of the understood verb *respected.*

**WRITERS ON WRITING**

As far as I'm concerned, "whom" is a word that was invented to make everyone sound like a butler. —Calvin Trillin

## Checking for problems with pronoun case

*Look for the most common trouble spots; where possible, apply a test for the correct pronoun.*

### COMPOUND WORD GROUPS (24a, 24b)

Test: Mentally strip away the rest of the compound word group.

> While diving for pearls, [Ikiko and] *she* found a treasure chest full of gold bars.

> Geoffrey went with [my family and] *me* to King's Dominion.

### PRONOUN AFTER *IS, ARE, WAS,* OR *WERE* (24a)

In formal English, remember to use the subjective-case pronouns *I, he, she, we,* and *they* after the linking verbs *is, are, was,* and *were.*

> The panel was shocked to learn that the undercover agent was *she.*

### APPOSITIVES (24c)

Test: Mentally strip away the word group that the appositive renames. (You may need to apply one of the other tests as well.)

> [Two actors], Chris and *I,* were selected to do the last scene of *King Lear.*

> The company could afford to send only [one of two researchers], Dr. Davis or *me,* to Paris.

**PRONOUN AFTER *THAN* OR *AS* (24d)**

Test: Mentally complete the sentence.

> The supervisor claimed that she was much more experienced than *I* [was].

> Gloria admitted that she liked Greg's twin better than [she liked] *him*.

**WE OR US BEFORE A NOUN (24e)**

Test: Mentally delete the noun.

> *We* [women] really have come a long way.

> Sadly, discrimination against *us* [women] occurs in most cultures.

**PRONOUN BEFORE OR AFTER AN INFINITIVE (24f)**

Remember that both subjects and objects of infinitives take the objective case.

> Everyone expected Alan and *me* to defeat Tracy and *him* in the doubles tournament.

**PRONOUN OR NOUN BEFORE A GERUND (24g)**

Remember to use the possessive case when a pronoun modifies a gerund.

> There is only a small chance of *his* bleeding excessively because of this procedure.

**24e** For *we* or *us* before a noun, choose the pronoun that would be appropriate if the noun were omitted.

▶ ~~Us~~ <sup>We</sup> tenants would rather fight than move.

▶ Management is short-changing ~~we~~ <sup>us</sup> tenants.

> No one would say *Us would rather fight than move* or *Management is short-changing we.*

**24f** Use the objective case for subjects and objects of infinitives.

An infinitive is the word *to* followed by the base form of a verb. (See 64c.) Subjects of infinitives are an exception to the rule that subjects must be in the subjective case. Whenever an infinitive has a subject, it must be in the objective case. Objects of infinitives also are in the objective case.

▶ Ms. Wilson asked John and ~~I~~ <sup>me</sup> to drive the senator and ~~she~~ <sup>her</sup> to the airport.

> *John and me* is the subject of the infinitive *to drive; senator and her* is the direct object of the infinitive.

**24g** Use the possessive case to modify a gerund.

A pronoun that modifies a gerund or a gerund phrase should appear in the possessive case (*my, our, your, his, her, its, their*). A gerund is a verb form ending in *-ing* that functions as a noun. Gerunds frequently appear in phrases, in which case the whole gerund phrase functions as a noun. (See 64c.)

▶ The chances of ~~you~~ *your* being hit by lightning are about two

million to one.

*Your* modifies the gerund phrase *being hit by lightning.*

Nouns as well as pronouns may modify gerunds. To form the possessive case of a noun, use an apostrophe and an *-s* (*victim's*) or just an apostrophe (*victims'*). (See 36a.)

▶ The old order in France paid a high price for the ~~aristocracy~~ *aristocracy's*

exploiting the lower classes.

The possessive noun *aristocracy's* modifies the gerund phrase *exploiting the lower classes.*

Gerund phrases should not be confused with participial phrases, which function as adjectives, not as nouns: *We saw Brenda driving a yellow convertible.* Here *driving a yellow convertible* is a participial phrase modifying the noun *Brenda.* (See 64c.)

Sometimes the choice between the objective or the possessive case conveys a subtle difference in meaning:

We watched *them* dancing.

We watched *their* dancing.

In the first sentence the emphasis is on the people; *dancing* is a participle modifying the pronoun *them.* In the second sentence the emphasis is on the dancing; *dancing* is a gerund, and *their* is a possessive pronoun modifying the gerund.

**NOTE:** Do not use the possessive if it creates an awkward effect. Try to reword the sentence instead.

| AWKWARD | The president agreed to the applications' being reviewed by a faculty committee. |
|---|---|
| REVISED | The president agreed that the applications could be reviewed by a faculty committee. |
| REVISED | The president agreed that a faculty committee could review the applications. |

**ON THE WEB**

**dianahacker.com/bedhandbook**
▶ Language Debates
  ▶ Possessive before a gerund

**EXERCISE 24–1** Edit the following sentences to eliminate errors in case. If a sentence is correct, write "correct" after it. Answers to lettered sentences appear in the back of the book. Example:

> Grandfather cuts down trees for neighbors much younger
> than ~~him.~~ *he.*
>       ^

a. Rick applied for the job even though he heard that other candidates were more experienced than he.
b. The volleyball team could not believe that the coach was she.
c. She appreciated him telling the truth in such a difficult situation.
d. The director has asked you and I to draft a proposal for a new recycling plan.
e. Five close friends and myself rented a station wagon, packed it with food, and drove to Mardi Gras on a three-day weekend.

1. The squawk of the brass horns nearly overwhelmed us oboe and bassoon players.
2. Ushio, the last rock climber up the wall, tossed Teri and she the remaining pitons and carabiners.
3. The programmer realized that her and the interface designers were creating an entirely new Web application.

**EXERCISE 24–1  Answers:**

a. Correct [But the writer could change the end of the sentence: . . . *than he is.*]
b. Correct [But the writer could change the end of the sentence: . . . *that she was the coach.*]
c. She appreciated his telling the truth in such a difficult situation.
d. The director has asked you and me to draft a proposal for a new recycling plan.
e. Five close friends and I rented a station wagon, packed it with food, and drove to Mardi Gras on a three-day weekend.

4. My desire to understand classical music was aided by me working as an usher at Symphony Hall.
5. The shower of sinking bricks caused he and his diving partner to race away from the collapsing seawall.

**EXERCISE 24–2**  Choose the correct pronoun in each set of parentheses.

We may blame television for the number of products based on characters in children's TV shows—from Big Bird to SpongeBob—but in fact merchandising that capitalizes on a character's popularity started long before television. Raggedy Ann began as a child's rag doll, and a few years later books about (she / her) and her brother, Raggedy Andy, were published. A cartoonist named Johnny Gruelle painted a cloth face on a family doll and applied for a patent in 1915. Later Gruelle began writing and illustrating stories about Raggedy Ann, and in 1918 (he / him) and a publisher teamed up to publish the books and sell the dolls. He was not the only one to try to sell products linked to children's stories. Beatrix Potter published the first of many Peter Rabbit picture books in 1902, and no one was better than (she / her) at making a living from spin-offs. After Peter Rabbit and Benjamin Bunny became popular, Potter began putting pictures of (they / them) and their little animal friends on merchandise. Potter had fans all over the world, and she understood (them / their) wanting to see Peter Rabbit not only in books but also on teapots and plates and lamps and other furnishings for the nursery. Potter and Gruelle, like countless others before and since, knew that entertaining children could be a profitable business.

**ON THE WEB**  **dianahacker.com/bedhandbook**
▶ Electronic grammar exercises
▶ E-ex 24–1 and 24–2

**EXERCISE 24–1 (continued)**

1. Correct
2. Ushio, the last rock climber up the wall, tossed Teri and her the remaining pitons and carabiners.
3. The programmer realized that she and the interface designers were creating an entirely new Web application.
4. My desire to understand classical music was aided by my working as an usher at Symphony Hall.
5. The shower of sinking bricks caused him and his diving partner to race away from the collapsing seawall.

**EXERCISE 24–2  Answers:**

her, he, she, them, their

# 25

---

## Distinguish between *who* and *whom*.

---

The choice between *who* and *whom* (or *whoever* and *whomever*) occurs primarily in subordinate clauses and in questions. *Who* and *whoever*, subjective-case pronouns, are used for subjects and subject complements. *Whom* and *whomever*, objective-case pronouns, are used for objects. (See 25a and 25b.)

An exception to this general rule occurs when the pronoun functions as the subject of an infinitive (see 25c). See also 24f.

 **GRAMMAR CHECKERS** catch misuses of *who* and *whom* (*whoever* and *whomever*) only about half the time. A grammar checker flagged the incorrect use of *whomever* in the sentence *Daniel always volunteers this information to whomever will listen*, recognizing that *whoever* is required as the subject of the verb *will listen*. But it did not flag the incorrect use of *who* in this sentence: *My cousin Sylvie, who I am teaching to fly a kite, watches us every time we compete.*

**25a** In subordinate clauses, use *who* and *whoever* for subjects or subject complements, *whom* and *whomever* for all objects.

When *who* and *whom* (or *whoever* and *whomever*) introduce subordinate clauses, their case is determined by their function *within the clause they introduce.* To choose the correct pronoun, you must isolate the subordinate clause and then decide how the pronoun functions within it. (See "subordinate clauses," 64b.)

In the following two examples, the pronouns *who* and *whoever* function as the subjects of the clauses they introduce.

▶ First prize goes to the runner ~~whom~~ *who* collects the most points.

> The subordinate clause is *who collects the most points.* The verb of the clause is *collects,* and its subject is *who.*

▶ He tells the story of his narrow escape to ~~whomever~~ *whoever* will listen.

> The writer selected the pronoun *whomever,* thinking that it was the object of the preposition *to.* However, the object of the preposition is the entire subordinate clause *whoever will listen.* The verb of the clause is *will listen,* and the subject of the verb is *whoever.*

*Who* occasionally functions as a subject complement in a subordinate clause. Subject complements occur with linking verbs (usually *be, am, is, are, was, were, being,* and *been*). (See 63b.)

▶ From your social security number, anyone can find out ~~whom~~ *who* you are.

> The subordinate clause is *who you are.* Its subject is *you,* and its subject complement is *who.*

When functioning as an object in a subordinate clause, *whom* (or *whomever*) appears out of order, before both the subject and the verb. To choose the correct pronoun, you must mentally restructure the clause.

▶ You will work with our senior traders, ~~who~~ *whom* you will meet later.

> The subordinate clause is *whom you will meet later.* The subject of the clause is *you* and the verb is *will meet. Whom* is the direct object of the verb. The correct choice becomes clear if you mentally restructure the clause: *you will meet whom.*

When functioning as the object of a preposition in a subordinate clause, *whom* is often separated from its preposition.

▶ The tutor ~~who~~ *whom* I was assigned to was very supportive.

> *Whom* is the object of the preposition *to.* In this sentence, the writer might choose to drop *whom: The tutor I was assigned to was very supportive.*

**NOTE:** Inserted expressions such as *they know, I think,* and *she says* should be ignored in determining whether to use *who* or *whom.*

▶ All of the show-offs, bullies, and tough guys in school want to take on a big guy ~~whom~~ *who* they know will not hurt them.

> *Who* is the subject of *will hurt,* not the object of *know.*

**25b** In questions, use *who* and *whoever* for subjects, *whom* and *whomever* for all objects.

When *who* and *whom* (or *whoever* and *whomever*) are used to open questions, their case is determined by their function within the question. In the example at the bottom of the next page, *who* functions as the subject of the question.

## Checking for problems with *who* and *whom*

*Look for common trouble spots; where possible, apply a test for correct usage.*

### IN A SUBORDINATE CLAUSE

Isolate the subordinate clause. Then read its subject, verb, and any objects, restructuring the clause if necessary. Some writers find it helpful to substitute *he* for *who* and *him* for *whom.*

> Samuels hoped to become the business partner of (who-ever / whomever) found the treasure.
>
> **Test:** . . . *whoever* found the treasure. [. . . *he* found the treasure.]
>
> Ada always seemed to be bestowing a favor on (whoever / whomever) she worked for.
>
> **Test:** . . . she worked for *whomever*. [. . . she worked for *him.*]

### IN A QUESTION

Read the subject, verb, and any objects, rearranging the sentence structure if necessary.

> (Who / Whom) conferred with Roosevelt and Stalin at Yalta in 1945?
>
> **Test:** *Who* conferred . . . ?
>
> (Who / Whom) did the committee nominate?
>
> **Test:** The committee did nominate *whom?*

---

▶ *Who*
~~Whom~~ was responsible for creating that computer virus?
   ^

*Who* is the subject of the verb *was.*

When *whom* functions as the object of a verb or the object of a preposition in a question, it appears out of normal order. To choose the correct pronoun, you must mentally restructure the question.

> ► ~~Who~~ *Whom* did the Democratic Party nominate in 1992?

> *Whom* is the direct object of the verb *did nominate*. This becomes clear if you restructure the question: *The Democratic Party did nominate whom in 1992?*

> ► ~~Who~~ *Whom* did you enter into the contract with?

> *Whom* is the object of the preposition *with,* as is clear if you recast the question: *You did enter into the contract with whom?*

## 25c  Use *whom* for subjects or objects of infinitives.

An infinitive is the word *to* followed by the base form of a verb. (See 64c.) Subjects of infinitives are an exception to the rule that subjects must be in the subjective case. Whenever an infinitive has a subject, it must be in the objective case. Objects of infinitives also are in the objective case.

> ► On the subject of health care, I don't know ~~who~~ *whom* to believe.

**NOTE:** In spoken English, *who* is frequently used when the correct *whom* sounds too stuffy. Even educated speakers are likely to say *Who* [not *Whom*] *did Joe replace?* Although some readers will accept such constructions in informal written English, it is safer to use *whom* in formal English: *Whom did Joe replace?*

**EXERCISE 25–1   Answers:**

a.  The roundtable featured scholars whom I had never heard of. [*or* . . . scholars I had never heard of.]
b.  Correct
c.  Correct
d.  Daniel always gives a holiday donation to whoever needs it.
e.  So many singers came to the audition that Natalia had trouble deciding whom to select for the choir.

**ON THE WEB**

**dianahacker.com/bedhandbook**
▶ Language Debates
▶ *who* versus *whom*

**EXERCISE 25–1**   Edit the following sentences to eliminate errors in the use of *who* and *whom* (or *whoever* and *whomever*). If a sentence is correct, write "correct" after it. Answers to lettered sentences appear in the back of the book. Example:

> *whom*
> What is the address of the artist ~~who~~ Antonio hired?
>                                    ^

a.   The roundtable featured scholars who I had never heard of.
b.   Arriving late for rehearsal, we had no idea who was supposed to dance with whom.
c.   Whom did you support in the last presidential election?
d.   Daniel always gives a holiday donation to whomever needs it.
e.   So many singers came to the audition that Natalia had trouble deciding who to select for the choir.

1.   My cousin Sylvie, who I am teaching to fly a kite, watches us every time we compete.
2.   Who decided to research the history of Hungarians in New Brunswick?
3.   According to the Greek myth, the Sphinx devoured those who could not answer her riddles.
4.   The people who ordered their medications from Canada were retirees whom don't have health insurance.
5.   Who did the committee select?

**ON THE WEB**

**dianahacker.com/bedhandbook**
▶ Electronic grammar exercises
▶ E-ex 25–1 and 25–2

**EXERCISE 25–1 (continued)**

1.   My cousin Sylvie, whom I am teaching to fly a kite, watches us every time we compete.
2.   Correct
3.   Correct
4.   The people who ordered their medications from Canada were retirees who don't have health insurance.
5.   Whom did the committee select?

# 26

## Choose adjectives and adverbs with care.

Adjectives ordinarily modify nouns or pronouns; occasionally they function as subject complements following linking verbs. Adverbs modify verbs, adjectives, or other adverbs. (See 62d and 62e.)

Many adverbs are formed by adding *-ly* to adjectives (*normal, normally; smooth, smoothly*). But don't assume that all words ending in *-ly* are adverbs or that all adverbs end in *-ly*. Some adjectives end in *-ly* (*lovely, friendly*) and some adverbs don't (*always, here, there*). When in doubt, consult a dictionary.

In English, adjectives are not pluralized to agree with the words they modify: *The red* [not *reds*] *roses were a wonderful surprise.*

**GRAMMAR CHECKERS** can flag a number of problems with adjectives and adverbs: some misuses of *bad* or *badly* and *good* or *well;* some double comparisons, such as *more meaner;* some absolute comparisons, such as *most unique;* and some double negatives, such as *can't hardly.* However, the programs miss more problems than they find. Programs ignored errors like these: *could have been handled more professional* and *hadn't been bathed regular.*

**26a** Use adverbs, not adjectives, to modify verbs, adjectives, and adverbs.

When adverbs modify verbs (or verbals), they nearly always answer the question When? Where? How? Why? Under what conditions? How often? or To what degree? When adverbs

---

**WRITERS ON WRITING**

One of the problems we have as writers is we don't take ourselves seriously while writing; being serious is setting aside a time and saying if it comes, good; if it doesn't come, good, I'll just sit here.
— Maya Angelou

I just sit at my typewriter and curse a bit.  — P. G. Wodehouse modify adjectives or other adverbs, they usually qualify or intensify the meaning of the word they modify. (See 62e.)

Adjectives are often used incorrectly in place of adverbs in casual or nonstandard speech.

► The arrangement worked out ~~perfect~~ *perfectly* for everyone.

► The manager must see that the office runs ~~smooth~~ *smoothly* and *efficiently.* ~~efficient.~~

The adverb *perfectly* modifies the verb *worked out;* the adverbs *smoothly* and *efficiently* modify the verb *runs.*

► In the early 1970s, chances for survival of the bald eagle looked ~~real~~ *really* slim.

Only adverbs can be used to modify adjectives or other adverbs. *Really* intensifies the meaning of the adjective *slim.*

**NOTE:** The incorrect use of the adjective *good* in place of the adverb *well* to modify a verb is especially common in casual and nonstandard speech. Use *well,* not *good,* to modify a verb in your writing.

► We were glad that Sanya had done ~~good~~ *well* on the CPA exam.

The adverb *well* should be used to modify the verb *had done.*

The word *well* is an adjective, however, when it means "healthy," "satisfactory," or "fortunate."

I feel very well today.

All is well.

It is just as well.

---

> **ESL**  Placement of adjectives and adverbs can be a tricky matter
> for multilingual speakers. See 31d.

## 26b Use adjectives, not adverbs, as complements.

Adjectives ordinarily precede nouns, but they can also function as subject complements or as object complements.

### Subject complements

A subject complement follows a linking verb and completes
the meaning of the subject. (See 63b.) When an adjective
functions as a subject complement, it describes the subject.

*Justice* is *blind.*

Problems can arise with verbs such as *smell, taste, look,* and
*feel,* which sometimes, but not always, function as linking
verbs. If the word following one of these verbs describes
the subject, use an adjective; if it modifies the verb, use an
adverb.

> **ADJECTIVE**    The detective looked *cautious.*
>
> **ADVERB**    The detective looked *cautiously* for fingerprints.

The adjective *cautious* describes the detective; the adverb
*cautiously* modifies the verb *looked.*

Linking verbs suggest states of being, not actions. Notice, for example, the different meanings of *looked* in the
preceding examples. To look cautious suggests the state of
being cautious; to look cautiously is to perform an action in
a cautious way.

► The lilacs in our backyard smell especially ~~sweetly~~ this year.
<br>*(sweet)*

► Lori looked ~~well~~ in her new go-go boots.
<br>*(good)*

The verbs *smell* and *looked* suggest states of being, not actions. Therefore, they should be followed by adjectives, not adverbs. (Contrast with action verbs: *We smelled the flowers. Lori looked for her go-go boots.*)

When the verb *feel* refers to the state of a person's health or emotions, it is a linking verb and should be followed by an adjective.

► We felt ~~badly~~ upon hearing of your grandmother's death.
<br>*(bad)*

Another adjective, such as *saddened*, could be used in place of *bad*.

---

**ON THE WEB**

**dianahacker.com/bedhandbook**
► Language Debates
   ► *bad* versus *badly*

---

### Object complements

An object complement follows a direct object and completes its meaning. (See 63b.) When an adjective functions as an object complement, it describes the direct object.

   Sorrow makes *us wise.*

Object complements occur with verbs such as *call, consider, create, find, keep,* and *make.* When a modifier follows the direct object of one of these verbs, it can function as an adjective describing the direct object or as an adverb modifying the verb.

**ADJECTIVE**   The referee called the plays *perfect.*

**ADVERB**   The referee called the plays *perfectly.*

The first sentence means that the referee considered the plays to be perfect; the second means that the referee did an excellent job of calling the plays.

▶ God created all men and women ~~equally.~~ *equal.*

The adjective *equal* is an object complement describing the direct object *men and women.*

## 26c Use comparatives and superlatives with care.

Most adjectives and adverbs have three forms: the positive, the comparative, and the superlative.

| POSITIVE | COMPARATIVE | SUPERLATIVE |
|---|---|---|
| soft | softer | softest |
| fast | faster | fastest |
| careful | more careful | most careful |
| bad | worse | worst |
| good | better | best |

### Comparative versus superlative

Use the comparative to compare two things, the superlative to compare three or more.

▶ Which of these two low-carb drinks is ~~best?~~ *better?*

▶ Though Shaw and Jackson are impressive, Hobbs is the
 *most*
 ~~more~~ qualified of the three candidates running for mayor.
 ^

## Form of comparatives and superlatives

To form comparatives and superlatives of most one- and two-syllable adjectives, use the endings *-er* and *-est: smooth, smoother, smoothest; easy, easier, easiest.* With longer adjectives, use *more* and *most* (or *less* and *least* for downward comparisons): *exciting, more exciting, most exciting; helpful, less helpful, least helpful.*

Some one-syllable adverbs take the endings *-er* and *-est* (*fast, faster, fastest*), but longer adverbs and all of those ending in *-ly* form the comparative and superlative with *more* and *most* (or *less* and *least*).

The comparative and superlative forms of the following adjectives and adverbs are irregular: *good, better, best; well, better, best; bad, worse, worst; badly, worse, worst.*

 *most talented*
▶ The Kirov is the ~~talentedest~~ ballet company we have seen.
 ^

 *worse*
▶ Lloyd's luck couldn't have been ~~worser~~ than David's.
 ^

## Double comparatives or superlatives

Do not use double comparatives or superlatives. When you have added *-er* or *-est* to an adjective or adverb, do not also use *more* or *most* (or *less* or *least*).

▶ Of all her family, Julia is the ~~most~~ happiest about the move.

 *likely*
▶ All the polls indicated that Gore was more ~~likelier~~ to win
 ^
 than Bush.

## Absolute concepts

Avoid expressions such as *more straight, less perfect, very round,* and *most unique.* Either something is unique or it isn't. It is illogical to suggest that absolute concepts come in degrees.

▶ That is the most ~~unique~~ wedding gown I have ever seen.
  *unusual*

▶ The painting would have been even more ~~priceless~~ had it
  *valuable*

  been signed.

---

**ON THE WEB**

**dianahacker.com/bedhandbook**
▶ Language Debates
  ▶ Absolute concepts such as *unique*

---

## 26d Avoid double negatives.

Standard English allows two negatives only if a positive meaning is intended: *The orchestra was not unhappy with its performance.* Double negatives used to emphasize negation are nonstandard.

Negative modifiers such as *never, no,* and *not* should not be paired with other negative modifiers or with negative words such as *neither, none, no one, nobody,* and *nothing.*

▶ Management is not doing ~~nothing~~ to see that the trash is
  *anything*

  picked up.

The double negative *not . . . nothing* is nonstandard.

---

EXERCISE 26–1   Possible revisions:
a.  Did you do well on last week's chemistry exam?
b.  With the budget deadline approaching, our office has hardly had time to handle routine correspondence.
c.  Correct
d.  The customer complained that he hadn't been treated nicely.
e.  Of all my relatives, Uncle Roberto is the cleverest.

The modifiers *hardly, barely,* and *scarcely* are considered negatives in standard English, so they should not be used with negatives such as *not, no one,* or *never.*

▶ Maxine is so weak she ~~can't~~ *can* hardly climb stairs.

**EXERCISE 26–1** Edit the following sentences to eliminate errors in the use of adjectives and adverbs. If a sentence is correct, write "correct" after it. Answers to lettered sentences appear in the back of the book. Example:

We weren't surprised by how ~~good~~ *well* the sidecar racing team flowed through the tricky course.

   a. Did you do good on last week's chemistry exam?
   b. With the budget deadline approaching, our office hasn't hardly had time to handle routine correspondence.
   c. Some flowers smell surprisingly bad.
   d. The customer complained that he hadn't been treated nice.
   e. Of all my relatives, Uncle Roberto is the most cleverest.

   1. When you answer the phone, speak clear and courteous.
   2. Who was more upset about the loss? Was it the coach or the quarterback or the owner of the team?
   3. To a novice skateboarder, even the basic ollie seems real challenging.
   4. After checking how bad I had been hurt, my sister dialed 911.
   5. If the college's Web page had been updated more regular, students would have learned about the new course offerings.

| ON THE WEB | **dianahacker.com/bedhandbook**<br>▶ Electronic grammar exercises<br>   ▶ E-ex 26–1 and 26–2 |
| --- | --- |

**EXERCISE 26–1 (continued)**

   1. When you answer the phone, speak clearly and courteously.
   2. Who was most upset about the loss? Was it the coach or the quarterback or the owner of the team?
   3. To a novice skateboarder, even the basic ollie seems really challenging.
   4. After checking how badly I had been hurt, my sister dialed 911.
   5. If the college's Web page had been updated more regularly, students would have learned about the new course offerings.

# 27

## Choose standard English verb forms.

In nonstandard English, spoken by those who share a regional or cultural heritage, verb forms sometimes differ from those of standard English. In writing, use standard English verb forms unless you are quoting nonstandard speech or using nonstandard forms for literary effect. (See 17d.)

Except for the verb *be*, all verbs in English have five forms. The following list shows the five forms and provides a sample sentence in which each might appear.

| | |
|---|---|
| **BASE FORM** | Usually I (*walk, ride*). |
| **PAST TENSE** | Yesterday I (*walked, rode*). |
| **PAST PARTICIPLE** | I have (*walked, ridden*) many times before. |
| **PRESENT PARTICIPLE** | I am (*walking, riding*) right now. |
| **-*S* FORM** | He/she/it (*walks, rides*) regularly. |

Both the past-tense and past-participle forms of regular verbs end in *-ed* (*walked, walked*). Irregular verbs form the past tense and past participle in other ways (*rode, ridden*).

The verb *be* has eight forms instead of the usual five: *be, am, is, are, was, were, being, been.*

 **GRAMMAR CHECKERS** sometimes flag misused irregular verbs in sentences, such as *I had drove the car to school* and *Lucia seen the movie already.* But you cannot rely on grammar checkers to identify problems with irregular verbs—they miss about twice as many errors as they find.

**SCHOLARS ON STANDARD ENGLISH VERB FORMS**

Epes, Mary. "Tracing Errors to the Sources: A Study of the Encoding Processes of Adult Basic Writers." *Journal of Basic Writing* 41 (1985): 4–33. In a study of basic writers, Epes discovered that phonological and grammatical features of nonstandard English significantly affected students' ability to "encode" a dictated text. Epes concludes that speakers of nonstandard English need "direct instruction in the grammar of standard written English," with special focus on whole-word verb forms, hypercorrections, and omitted suffixes.

## 27a Use the correct forms of irregular verbs.

For all regular verbs, the past-tense and past-participle forms are the same (ending in -*ed* or -*d*), so there is no danger of confusion. This is not true, however, for irregular verbs, such as the following.

| BASE FORM | PAST TENSE | PAST PARTICIPLE |
|---|---|---|
| go | went | gone |
| fight | fought | fought |
| fly | flew | flown |

The past-tense form, which never has a helping verb, expresses action that occurred entirely in the past. The past participle is used with a helping verb—either with *has, have,* or *had* to form one of the perfect tenses (see 28a) or with *be, am, is, are, was, were, being,* or *been* to form the passive voice (see 8a).

**PAST TENSE**  Last July, we *went* to Paris.

**PAST PARTICIPLE**  We have *gone* to Paris twice.

When you aren't sure which verb form to choose (*went* or *gone, began* or *begun,* and so on), consult the list of common irregular verbs that starts on the next page. Choose the past-tense form if the verb in your sentence doesn't have a helping verb; choose the past-participle form if it does.

In nonstandard English speech, the past-tense and past-participle forms may differ from those of standard English, as in the following sentences.

▶ Yesterday we ~~seen~~ *saw* an unidentified flying object.

The past-tense form *saw* is required because there is no helping verb.

### SCHOLARS ON STANDARD ENGLISH VERB FORMS

Wolfram, Walt, and Ralph W. Fasold. *The Study of Social Dialects in American English.* Saddle River: Prentice, 1974. Linguists Wolfram and Fasold report sociolinguistic studies on the phonological and grammatical features of American dialects. Their treatment of the verb forms of vernacular black English is especially thorough. The final chapter of the book considers the educational implications of linguistic variations.

See also SCHOLARS ON NONSTANDARD ENGLISH (17d).

> *stolen*
> ► The truck was apparently ~~stole~~ while the driver ate lunch.
>                               ^

> *fallen*
> ► By the end of the day, the stock market had ~~fell~~ two hundred
>                                               ^
> points.

Because of the helping verbs, the past-participle forms are required: *was stolen, had fallen.*

When in doubt about the standard English forms of irregular verbs, consult the following list or look up the base form of the verb in the dictionary, which also lists any irregular forms. (If no additional forms are listed in the dictionary, the verb is regular, not irregular.)

*Common irregular verbs*

| BASE FORM | PAST TENSE | PAST PARTICIPLE |
|---|---|---|
| arise | arose | arisen |
| awake | awoke, awaked | awaked, awoke |
| be | was, were | been |
| beat | beat | beaten, beat |
| become | became | become |
| begin | began | begun |
| bend | bent | bent |
| bite | bit | bitten, bit |
| blow | blew | blown |
| break | broke | broken |
| bring | brought | brought |
| build | built | built |
| burst | burst | burst |
| buy | bought | bought |
| catch | caught | caught |
| choose | chose | chosen |
| cling | clung | clung |
| come | came | come |
| cost | cost | cost |

| BASE FORM | PAST TENSE | PAST PARTICIPLE |
|---|---|---|
| deal | dealt | dealt |
| dig | dug | dug |
| dive | dived, dove | dived |
| do | did | done |
| drag | dragged | dragged |
| draw | drew | drawn |
| dream | dreamed, dreamt | dreamed, dreamt |
| drink | drank | drunk |
| drive | drove | driven |
| eat | ate | eaten |
| fall | fell | fallen |
| fight | fought | fought |
| find | found | found |
| fly | flew | flown |
| forget | forgot | forgotten, forgot |
| freeze | froze | frozen |
| get | got | gotten, got |
| give | gave | given |
| go | went | gone |
| grow | grew | grown |
| hang (suspend) | hung | hung |
| hang (execute) | hanged | hanged |
| have | had | had |
| hear | heard | heard |
| hide | hid | hidden |
| hurt | hurt | hurt |
| keep | kept | kept |
| know | knew | known |
| lay (put) | laid | laid |
| lead | led | led |
| lend | lent | lent |
| let (allow) | let | let |
| lie (recline) | lay | lain |
| lose | lost | lost |
| make | made | made |
| prove | proved | proved, proven |
| read | read | read |
| ride | rode | ridden |
| ring | rang | rung |

*(continued)*

| BASE FORM | PAST TENSE | PAST PARTICIPLE |
|---|---|---|
| rise (get up) | rose | risen |
| run | ran | run |
| say | said | said |
| see | saw | seen |
| send | sent | sent |
| set (place) | set | set |
| shake | shook | shaken |
| shoot | shot | shot |
| shrink | shrank | shrunk |
| sing | sang | sung |
| sink | sank | sunk |
| sit (be seated) | sat | sat |
| slay | slew | slain |
| sleep | slept | slept |
| speak | spoke | spoken |
| spin | spun | spun |
| spring | sprang | sprung |
| stand | stood | stood |
| steal | stole | stolen |
| sting | stung | stung |
| strike | struck | struck, stricken |
| swear | swore | sworn |
| swim | swam | swum |
| swing | swung | swung |
| take | took | taken |
| teach | taught | taught |
| throw | threw | thrown |
| wake | woke, waked | waked, woken |
| wear | wore | worn |
| wring | wrung | wrung |
| write | wrote | written |

**27b** Distinguish among the forms of *lie* and *lay.*

Writers and speakers frequently confuse the various forms of *lie* (meaning "to recline or rest on a surface") and *lay* (meaning "to put or place something"). *Lie* is an intransitive verb; it does not take a direct object: *The tax forms lie on the table.* The verb *lay* is transitive; it takes a direct object: *Please lay the tax forms on the table.* (See 63b.)

In addition to confusing the meaning of *lie* and *lay,* writers and speakers are often unfamiliar with the standard English forms of these verbs.

| BASE FORM | PAST TENSE | PAST PARTICIPLE | PRESENT PARTICIPLE |
|---|---|---|---|
| lie | lay | lain | lying |
| lay | laid | laid | laying |

▶ Sue was so exhausted that she ~~laid~~ *lay* down for a nap.

The past-tense form of *lie* ("to recline") is *lay.*

▶ The patient had ~~laid~~ *lain* in an uncomfortable position all night.

The past-participle form of *lie* ("to recline") is *lain.* If the correct English seems too stilted, recast the sentence: *The patient had been lying in an uncomfortable position all night.*

▶ The prosecutor ~~lay~~ *laid* the pistol on a table close to the jurors.

The past-tense form of *lay* ("to place") is *laid.*

▶ Letters dating from the Civil War were ~~laying~~ *lying* in the corner of the chest.

The present participle of *lie* ("to rest on a surface") is *lying.*

---

| ON THE WEB | **dianahacker.com/bedhandbook**<br>▶ Language Debates<br>  ▶ *lie* versus *lay* |
|---|---|

**EXERCISE 27–1** Edit the following sentences to eliminate problems with irregular verbs. If a sentence is correct, write "correct" after it. Answers to lettered sentences appear in the back of the book. Example:

> saw
> Was it you I ~~seen~~ last night at the concert?
> ^

a. When I get the urge to exercise, I lay down until it passes.
b. Grandmother had drove our new SUV to the sunrise church service on Savage Mountain, so we were left with the station wagon.
c. A pile of dirty rags was laying at the bottom of the stairs.
d. How did the computer know that the gamer had went from the room with the blue ogre to the hall where the gold was heaped?
e. Abraham Lincoln took good care of his legal clients; the contracts he drew for the Illinois Central Railroad could never be broke.

1. The burglar must have gone immediately upstairs, grabbed what looked good, and took off.
2. Have you ever dreamed that you were falling from a cliff or flying through the air?
3. Tomás reached for the pen, signed the title page of his novel, and then laid the book on the table for the first customer in line.
4. In her junior year, Cindy run the 440-yard dash in 51.1 seconds.
5. Larry claimed that he had drank a bad soda, but Esther suspected the truth.

| ON THE WEB | **dianahacker.com/bedhandbook**
▶ Electronic grammar exercises
▶ E-ex 27–1 |
|---|---|

**EXERCISE 27–1 Answers:**

a. When I get the urge to exercise, I lie down until it passes.
b. Grandmother had driven our new SUV to the sunrise church service on Savage Mountain, so we were left with the station wagon.
c. A pile of dirty rags was lying at the bottom of the stairs.
d. How did the computer know that the gamer had gone from the room with the blue ogre to the hall where the gold was heaped?
e. Abraham Lincoln took good care of his legal clients; the contracts he drew for the Illinois Central Railroad could never be broken.

**27c** Use -*s* (or -*es*) endings on present-tense verbs that have third-person singular subjects.

All singular nouns (*child, tree*) and the pronouns *he, she,* and *it* are third-person singular; indefinite pronouns such as *everyone* and *neither* are also third-person singular. When the subject of a sentence is third-person singular, its verb takes an -*s* or -*es* ending in the present tense. (See also 21.)

|  | SINGULAR | | PLURAL | |
|---|---|---|---|---|
| **FIRST PERSON** | I | know | we | know |
| **SECOND PERSON** | you | know | you | know |
| **THIRD PERSON** | he/she/it | knows | they | know |
|  | child | knows | parents | know |
|  | everyone | knows | | |

In nonstandard speech, the -*s* ending required by standard English is sometimes omitted.

> ▶ My cousin ~~drive~~ *drives* to Cape Cod every weekend in the summer.

> ▶ Sulfur dioxide ~~turn~~ *turns* leaves yellow, ~~dissolve~~ *dissolves* marble, and ~~eat~~ *eats* away iron and steel.

The subjects *cousin* and *sulfur dioxide* are third-person singular, so the verbs must end in -*s*.

**TIP:** Do not add the -*s* ending to the verb if the subject is not third-person singular.

The writers of the following sentences, knowing they sometimes dropped -*s* endings from verbs, overcorrected by adding the endings where they don't belong.

**EXERCISE 27-1 (continued)**

1. The burglar must have gone immediately upstairs, grabbed what looked good, and taken off.
2. Correct
3. Correct
4. In her junior year, Cindy ran the 440-yard dash in 51.1 seconds.
5. Larry claimed that he had drunk a bad soda, but Esther suspected the truth.

▶ I prepare̸ program specifications and logic diagrams.

The writer mistakenly concluded that the -s ending belongs on present-tense verbs used with *all* singular subjects, not just *third-person* singular subjects. The pronoun *I* is first-person singular, so its verb does not require the -s.

▶ The dirt floors require̸ continual sweeping.

The writer mistakenly thought that the -s ending on the verb indicated plurality. The -s goes on present-tense verbs used with third-person *singular* subjects.

### Has *versus* have

In the present tense, use *has* with third-person singular subjects; all other subjects require *have.*

|  | **SINGULAR** |  | **PLURAL** |  |
|---|---|---|---|---|
| **FIRST PERSON** | I | have | we | have |
| **SECOND PERSON** | you | have | you | have |
| **THIRD PERSON** | he/she/it | has | they | have |

In some dialects, *have* is used with all subjects. But standard English requires *has* for third-person singular subjects.

▶ This respected musician almost always ~~have~~ has a message to convey in his work.

▶ As for the retirement income program, it ~~have~~ has finally been established.

The subjects *musician* and *it* are third-person singular, so the verb should be *has* in each case.

### SCHOLARS ON VERB TENSE

Shaughnessy, Mina P. *Errors and Expectations: A Guide for the Teacher of Basic Writing.* New York: Oxford UP, 1979. In the chapter "Common Errors," Shaughnessy discusses the difficulties of teaching the English tense system and suggests that two kinds of learning are involved in mastering the system: "One kind requires that the student have a grasp of the formal system for producing tense changes; the other that he [or she] develop an 'ear' for tense combinations in a range of situations."

**TIP:** Do not use *has* if the subject is not third-person singular. The writers of the following sentences were aware that they often wrote *have* when standard English requires *has*. Here they are using what appears to them to be the "more correct" form, but in an inappropriate context.

▶ My business law classes ~~has~~ *have* helped me to understand more about contracts.

▶ I ~~has~~ *have* much to be thankful for.

The subjects of these sentences—*classes* and *I*—are third-person plural and first-person singular, so standard English requires *have*. *Has* is used with third-person singular subjects only.

### Does *versus* do *and* doesn't *versus* don't

In the present tense, use *does* and *doesn't* with third-person singular subjects; all other subjects require *do* and *don't*.

|  | SINGULAR |  | PLURAL |  |
|---|---|---|---|---|
| **FIRST PERSON** | I | do/don't | we | do/don't |
| **SECOND PERSON** | you | do/don't | you | do/don't |
| **THIRD PERSON** | he/she/it | does/doesn't | they | do/don't |

The use of *don't* instead of the standard English *doesn't* is a feature of many dialects in the United States. Use of *do* for *does* is rarer.

▶ Grandfather really ~~don't~~ *doesn't* have a place to call home.

▶ ~~Do~~ *Does* she know the correct procedure for setting up the experiment?

---

### WRITERS ON WRITING

Wit ought to be a glorious treat, like caviar; never spread it about like marmalade. —Noel Coward

The language of the street is always strong. —Ralph Waldo Emerson

I heard an old Negro street singer last week, Reverend Pearly Brown, singing, "God don't never change!" This is a precise thing he is singing. He does not mean "God does not ever change!" He means "God don't never change." —Imamu Amiri Baraka

*vb*

*Grandfather* and *she* are third-person singular, so the verbs should be *doesn't* and *does*.

**Am, is, *and* are; was *and* were**

The verb *be* has three forms in the present tense (*am, is, are*) and two in the past tense (*was, were*). Use *am* and *was* with first-person singular subjects; use *is* and *was* with third-person singular subjects. With all other subjects, use *are* and *were*.

|  | SINGULAR |  | PLURAL |  |
|---|---|---|---|---|
| **FIRST PERSON** | I | am/was | we | are/were |
| **SECOND PERSON** | you | are/were | you | are/were |
| **THIRD PERSON** | he/she/it | is/was | they | are/were |

▶ Judy wanted to borrow Tim's notes, but she ~~were~~ too shy to

   *was*

   ask for them.

The subject *she* is third-person singular, so the verb should be *was*.

   *were*

▶ Did you think you ~~was~~ going to drown?

The subject *you* is second-person singular, so the verb should be *were*.

---

**GRAMMAR CHECKERS** are fairly good at catching missing -*s* endings on verbs and some misused -*s* forms of the verb, consistently flagging errors such as *The training session take place later today* and *The careful camper learn to feel the signs of a coming storm.* (See the grammar checker advice on p. 261 for more information about subject-verb agreement.)

**27d** Do not omit *-ed* endings on verbs.

Speakers who do not fully pronounce *-ed* endings sometimes omit them unintentionally in writing. Failure to pronounce *-ed* endings is common in many dialects and in informal speech even in standard English. In the following frequently used words and phrases, for example, the *-ed* ending is not always fully pronounced.

| | | | |
|---|---|---|---|
| advised | developed | prejudiced | supposed to |
| asked | fixed | pronounced | used to |
| concerned | frightened | stereotyped | |

When a verb is regular, both the past tense and the past participle are formed by adding *-ed* to the base form of the verb.

*Past tense*

Use an *-ed* or *-d* ending to express the past tense of regular verbs. The past tense is used when the action occurred entirely in the past.

▶ Over the weekend, Ed ~~fix~~ **fixed** his brother's skateboard and tuned up his mother's 1977 Cougar.

▶ Last summer, my counselor ~~advise~~ **advised** me to ask my chemistry instructor for help.

*Past participles*

Past participles are used in three ways: (1) following *have, has,* or *had* to form one of the perfect tenses; (2) following *be, am, is, are, was, were, being,* or *been* to form the passive voice; and (3) as adjectives modifying nouns or pronouns. The perfect tenses are listed on pages 326–27, and the passive voice is discussed in 8a. For a discussion of participles functioning as adjectives, see 64c.

▶ Robin has ~~ask~~ *asked* me to go to California with her.

*Has asked* is present perfect tense (*have* or *has* followed by a past participle).

▶ Though it is not a new phenomenon, domestic violence is ~~publicize~~ *publicized* more frequently than before.

*Is publicized* is a verb in the passive voice (a form of *be* followed by a past participle).

▶ All aerobics classes end in a cool-down period to stretch ~~tighten~~ *tightened* muscles.

The past participle *tightened* functions as an adjective modifying the noun *muscles*.

 **GRAMMAR CHECKERS** flag missing *-ed* endings on verbs more often than not. Unfortunately, they often suggest an *-ing* ending (*passing*) rather than the missing *-ed* ending (*passed*), as in the following sentence: *The law was pass last week.*

## 27e Do not omit needed verbs.

Although standard English allows some linking verbs and helping verbs to be contracted, at least in informal contexts, it does not allow them to be omitted.

Linking verbs, used to link subjects to subject complements, are frequently a form of *be: be, am, is, are, was, were, being, been.* (See 63b.) Some of these forms may be contracted (*I'm, she's, we're, you're, they're*), but they should not be omitted altogether.

▶ When we *are* quiet in the evening, we can hear crickets in the  
    ^

  woods.

▶ Alvin *is* a man who can defend himself.  
    ^

Helping verbs, used with main verbs, include forms of *be, do,* and *have* or the words *can, will, shall, could, would, should, may, might,* and *must.* (See 62c.) Some helping verbs may be contracted (*he's leaving, we'll celebrate, they've been told*), but they should not be omitted altogether.

▶ We *have* been in Chicago since last Thursday.  
    ^

▶ Do you know someone who *would* be good for the job?  
                 ^

**ESL** Speakers of English as a second language sometimes have problems with omitted verbs and correct use of helping verbs. See 29e and 29a.

**GRAMMAR CHECKERS** flag omitted verbs about half the time—but they often miss needed helping verbs. For example, a grammar checker caught the missing verb in this sentence: *We seen the* Shrek *sequel three times already.* However, this sentence went unflagged: *The plot built around a family reunion.*

**EXERCISE 27–2** Edit the following sentences to eliminate problems with *-s* and *-ed* verb forms and with omitted verbs. If a sentence is correct, write "correct" after it. Answers to lettered sentences appear in the back of the book. Example:

> *covers*
> The Pell Grant sometimes ~~cover~~ the student's full
>                          ^
> tuition.

a. The glass sculptures of the Swan Boats was prominent in the brightly lit lobby.
b. Visitors to the glass museum were not suppose to touch the exhibits.
c. Our church has all the latest technology, even a close-circuit television.
d. Christos didn't know about Marlo's promotion because he never listens. He always talking.
e. Most psychologists agree that no one performs well under stress.

1. Have there ever been a time in your life when you were too depressed to get out of bed?
2. My days in this department have taught me to do what I'm told without asking questions.
3. We have change our plan and are waiting out the storm before leaving.
4. Winter training for search-and-rescue divers consist of building up a tolerance to icy water temperatures.
5. How would you feel if a love one had been a victim of a crime like this?

<table><tr><td>ON THE WEB</td><td>**dianahacker.com/bedhandbook**<br>▶ Electronic grammar exercises<br>  ▶ E-ex 27–2</td></tr></table>

**EXERCISE 27–2 Answers:**

a. The glass sculptures of the Swan Boats were prominent in the brightly lit lobby.
b. Visitors to the glass museum were not supposed to touch the exhibits.
c. Our church has all the latest technology, even a closed-circuit television.
d. Christos didn't know about Marlo's promotion because he never listens. He is always talking.
e. Correct

# 28

## Use verbs in the appropriate tense and mood.

**28a** Choose the appropriate verb tense.

Tenses indicate the time of an action in relation to the time of the speaking or writing about that action.

The most common problem with tenses — shifting confusingly from one tense to another — is discussed in 13. Other problems with tenses are detailed in this section, after the following survey of tenses.

 **GRAMMAR CHECKERS** do not flag most problems with tense discussed in this section: special uses of the present tense, use of past versus past perfect, and sequence of tenses.

*Survey of tenses*

English has three simple tenses (past, present, and future) and three perfect tenses (present perfect, past perfect, and future perfect). In addition, each of these six tenses has a progressive form.

**SIMPLE TENSES** The simple present tense is used primarily to describe habitual actions (*Jane walks to work*) or to refer to actions occurring at the time of speaking (*I see a cardinal in our maple tree*). It is also used to state facts or general truths and to describe fictional events in a literary work (see p. 328). The present tense may even be used to express future actions that are to occur at some specified time (*The semester begins tomorrow*).

**EXERCISE 27–2 (continued)**

1. Has there ever been a time in your life when you were too depressed to get out of bed?
2. Correct
3. We have changed our plan and are waiting out the storm before leaving.
4. Winter training for search-and-rescue divers consists of building up a tolerance to icy water temperatures.
5. How would you feel if a loved one had been a victim of a crime like this?

The simple past tense is used for actions completed entirely in the past (*Yesterday Jane walked to work*).

The simple future tense is used for actions that will occur in the future (*Tomorrow Jane will walk to work*) or for actions that are predictable, given certain causes (*Meat will spoil if not properly refrigerated*).

In the following list, the simple tenses are given for the regular verb *walk,* the irregular verb *ride,* and the highly irregular verb *be.*

**SIMPLE PRESENT**

| SINGULAR | | PLURAL | |
|---|---|---|---|
| I | walk, ride, am | we | walk, ride, are |
| you | walk, ride, are | you | walk, ride, are |
| he/she/it | walks, rides, is | they | walk, ride, are |

**SIMPLE PAST**

| SINGULAR | | PLURAL | |
|---|---|---|---|
| I | walked, rode, was | we | walked, rode, were |
| you | walked, rode, were | you | walked, rode, were |
| he/she/it | walked, rode, was | they | walked, rode, were |

**SIMPLE FUTURE**

I, you, he/she/it, we, they    will walk, ride, be

**PERFECT TENSES**    More complex time relations are indicated by the perfect tenses (which consist of a form of *have* plus the past participle). The present perfect tense is used for an action that began in the past and is still going on in the present (*Jane has walked to work for years*) or an action that began in the past and is finished by the time of speaking or writing (*Jane has discovered a new restaurant on Elm Street*).

The past perfect tense is used for an action already completed by the time of another past action (*Jane hailed a cab after she had walked several blocks in the rain*) or for an action already completed at some specific past time (*By 8:30, Jane had walked two miles*). (See also pp. 329–30.)

The future perfect tense is used for an action that will be completed before or by a certain future time (*Jane will have left Troy by the time Jo arrives*).

**PRESENT PERFECT**
I, you, we, they — have walked, ridden, been
he/she/it — has walked, ridden, been

**PAST PERFECT**
I, you, he/she/it, we, they — had walked, ridden, been

**FUTURE PERFECT**
I, you, he/she/it, we, they — will have walked, ridden, been

**PROGRESSIVE FORMS** The simple and perfect tenses already discussed have progressive forms that describe actions in progress. The present progressive form is used for actions currently in progress (*Jane is writing a letter*) or for future actions that are to occur at some specified time (*Jane is leaving for Chicago on Monday*).

The past progressive is used for past actions in progress (*Jane was writing a letter last night*).

The future progressive is used for future actions in progress (*Jane will be traveling next week*).

**PRESENT PROGRESSIVE**
I — am walking, riding, being
he/she/it — is walking, riding, being
you, we, they — are walking, riding, being

**PAST PROGRESSIVE**
I, he/she/it — was walking, riding, being
you, we, they — were walking, riding, being

**FUTURE PROGRESSIVE**
I, you, he/she/it, we, they — will be walking, riding, being

Like the simple tenses, the perfect tenses have progressive forms. The perfect progressive forms express the length of time an action is, was, or will be in progress: *Jane has been walking to work for five years* (present perfect progressive). *Jane had been walking to work until she was mugged* (past perfect progressive). *Jane will have been walking to work for five years by the end of this month* (future perfect progressive).

**PRESENT PERFECT PROGRESSIVE**

| I, you, we, they | have been walking, riding, being |
| he/she/it | has been walking, riding, being |

**PAST PERFECT PROGRESSIVE**

I, you, he/she/it, we, they   had been walking, riding, being

**FUTURE PERFECT PROGRESSIVE**

I, you, he/she/it, we, they   will have been walking, riding, being

 The progressive forms are not normally used with mental activity verbs such as *believe*. See page 339.

### Special uses of the present tense

Use the present tense when writing about events in a literary work, when expressing general truths, and when quoting, summarizing, or paraphrasing an author's views.

When writing about a work of literature, you may be tempted to use the past tense. The convention, however, is to describe fictional events in the present tense. (See also 13b.)

► In Masuji Ibuse's *Black Rain,* a child r̶e̶a̶c̶h̶e̶d̶ for a pome-
   granate in his mother's garden, and a moment later he
   ̶w̶a̶s̶ dead, killed by the blast of the atomic bomb.

*reaches*

*is*

Scientific principles or general truths should appear in the present tense, unless such principles have been disproved.

▶ Galileo taught that the earth ~~revolved~~ around the sun.
   ^revolves

> Since Galileo's teaching has not been discredited, the verb should be in the present tense. The following sentence, however, is acceptable: *Ptolemy taught that the sun revolved around the earth.*

When you are quoting, summarizing, or paraphrasing the author of a nonliterary work, use present-tense verbs such as *writes, reports, asserts,* and so on. (See p. 603 for a longer list.) This convention is usually followed even when the author is dead (unless a date specifies the time of writing).

▶ Baron Bowan of Colwood ~~wrote~~ that "a metaphysician is one
   ^writes

who goes into a dark cellar at midnight without a light,

looking for a black cat that is not there."

**EXCEPTION:** When you are documenting a paper with the APA (American Psychological Association) style of in-text citations, use past-tense verbs such as *reported* or *demonstrated* or present perfect verbs such as *has reported* or *has demonstrated.* (See p. 708.)

> E. Wilson (1996) reported that positive reinforcement alone was a less effective teaching technique than a mixture of positive reinforcement and constructive criticism.

### The past perfect tense

The past perfect tense consists of a past participle preceded by *had* (*had worked, had gone, had had*). (See pp. 326–27.) This tense is used for an action already completed by the time of another past action or for an action already completed at some specific past time.

Everyone *had spoken* by the time the ballots were cast.

Everyone *had spoken* by 10:00 a.m.

Writers sometimes use the simple past tense when they should use the past perfect.

▶ We built our cabin high on a pine knoll, forty feet above
an abandoned quarry that ~~was~~ *had been* flooded in 1920 to create
a lake.

The building of the cabin and the flooding of the quarry both occurred in the past, but the flooding was completed before the time of building.

▶ By the time dinner was served, the guest of honor *had* left.

The past perfect tense is needed because the action of leaving was completed at a specific past time (*by the time dinner was served*).

Some writers tend to overuse the past perfect tense. Do not use the past perfect if two past actions occurred at the same time.

▶ When we arrived in Paris, Pauline ~~had~~ met us at the train

station.

### Sequence of tenses with infinitives and participles

An infinitive is the base form of a verb preceded by *to.* (See 64c.) Use the present infinitive to show action at the same time as or later than the action of the verb in the sentence.

> ▶ The club had hoped to ~~have raised~~ a thousand dollars by
>   *raise*
>   ^
>
> April 1.

The action expressed in the infinitive (*to raise*) occurred later than the action of the sentence's verb (*had hoped*).

Use the perfect form of an infinitive (*to have* followed by the past participle) for an action occurring earlier than that of the verb in the sentence.

> ▶ Dan would like to ~~join~~ the navy, but he did not pass the
>   *have joined*
>   ^
>
> physical.

The liking occurs in the present; the joining would have occurred in the past.

Like the tense of an infinitive, the tense of a participle is also governed by the tense of the sentence's verb. Use the present participle (ending in *-ing*) for an action occurring at the same time as that of the sentence's verb.

> Hiking the Appalachian Trail in early spring, we spotted many wildflowers.

Use the past participle (such as *given* or *helped*) or the present perfect participle (*having* plus the past participle) for an action occurring before that of the verb.

> *Discovered* off the coast of Florida, the *Atocha* yielded many treasures.
>
> *Having worked* her way through college, Melanie graduated debt-free.

**28b** Use the subjunctive mood in the few contexts that require it.

There are three moods in English: the *indicative*, used for facts, opinions, and questions; the *imperative*, used for orders or advice; and the *subjunctive*, used in certain contexts to express wishes, requests, or conditions contrary to fact. Of these moods, only the subjunctive causes problems for writers.

### Forms of the subjunctive

In the subjunctive mood, present-tense verbs do not change form to indicate the number and person of the subject (see 21). Instead, the subjunctive uses the base form of the verb (*be, drive, employ*) with all subjects.

> It is important that you *be* [not *are*] prepared for the interview.
>
> We asked that she *drive* [not *drives*] more slowly.

Also, in the subjunctive mood, there is only one past-tense form of *be: were* (never *was*).

> If I *were* [not *was*] you, I'd proceed more cautiously.

### Uses of the subjunctive

The subjunctive mood appears only in a few contexts: in contrary-to-fact clauses beginning with *if* or expressing a wish; in *that* clauses following verbs such as *ask, insist, recommend, request,* and *suggest;* and in certain set expressions.

**IN CONTRARY-TO-FACT CLAUSES BEGINNING WITH *IF*** When a subordinate clause beginning with *if* expresses a condition contrary to fact, use the subjunctive mood.

> *were*
> ▶ If I ~~was~~ a member of Congress, I would vote for that bill.
> ^

**WRITERS ON WRITING**

Damn the subjunctive. It brings all our writers to shame.

—Mark Twain

>              *were*
> We could be less cautious if Jake ~~was~~ more trustworthy.

The verbs in these sentences express conditions that do not exist: The writer is not a member of Congress, and Jake is not trustworthy.

Do not use the subjunctive mood in *if* clauses expressing conditions that exist or may exist.

> If Dana *wins* the contest, she will leave for Barcelona in June.

**IN CONTRARY-TO-FACT CLAUSES EXPRESSING A WISH**    In formal English, the subjunctive is used in clauses expressing a wish or desire; in informal speech, however, the indicative is more common.

> **FORMAL**    I wish that Dr. Vaughn *were* my professor.
>
> **INFORMAL**    I wish that Dr. Vaughn *was* my professor.

**IN *THAT* CLAUSES FOLLOWING VERBS SUCH AS *ASK, INSIST, REQUEST*, AND *SUGGEST***    Because requests have not yet become reality, they are expressed in the subjunctive mood.

>                                     *be*
> Professor Moore insists that her students ~~are~~ on time.

>                         *file*
> We recommend that Lambert ~~files~~ form 1050 soon.

**IN CERTAIN SET EXPRESSIONS**    The subjunctive mood, once more widely used, remains in certain set expressions: *Be that as it may, as it were, far be it from me,* and so on.

    **GRAMMAR CHECKERS** only sometimes flag problems with the subjunctive mood. What they catch is very spotty, so you must be alert to the correct uses of the subjunctive in your own writing.

**EXERCISE 28–1**   **Possible revisions:**

a. Correct

b. Watson and Crick discovered the mechanism that controls inheritance in all life: the workings of the DNA molecule.

c. When Hitler decided to kill the Jews in 1941, did he know that Himmler and his SS had had mass murder in mind since 1938?

d. Correct

e. Correct

1. Don Quixote, in Cervantes's novel, is an idealist ill suited for life in the real world.

**EXERCISE 28–1**　Edit the following sentences to eliminate errors in verb tense or mood. If a sentence is correct, write "correct" after it. Answers to lettered sentences appear in the back of the book. Example:

> *had been*
> After the path ~~was~~ plowed, we were able to walk through the park.
>                    ^

a. The palace of Knossos in Crete is believed to have been destroyed by fire around 1375 BCE.

b. Watson and Crick discovered the mechanism that controlled inheritance in all life: the workings of the DNA molecule.

c. When Hitler decided to kill the Jews in 1941, did he know that Himmler and his SS had mass murder in mind since 1938?

d. Tonight's concert begins at 9:30. If it were earlier, I'd consider going.

e. As soon as my aunt applied for the position of pastor, the post was filled by an inexperienced seminary graduate who had been so hastily snatched that his mortarboard was still in midair.

1. Don Quixote, in Cervantes's novel, was an idealist ill suited for life in the real world.

2. Visiting the technology museum inspired the high school seniors and had reminded them that science could be fun.

3. I would like to have been on the *Mayflower* but not to have lived through the first winter.

4. When the director yelled "Action!" I forgot my lines, even though I practiced my part every waking hour for three days.

5. If midday naps were a regular practice in American workplaces, employees would be far more productive.

---

| ON THE WEB | **dianahacker.com/bedhandbook** |
|---|---|
| | ▶ Electronic grammar exercises |
| | ▶ E-ex 28–1 |

---

**EXERCISE 28–1 (continued)**

2. Visiting the technology museum inspired the high school seniors and reminded them that science could be fun.

3. Correct

4. When the director yelled "Action!" I forgot my lines, even though I had practiced my part every waking hour for three days.

5. Correct

# Part VI

## ESL Trouble Spots

29 Be alert to special problems with verbs.

30 Use the articles *a, an,* and *the* appropriately.

31 Be aware of other potential trouble spots.

# 29

## Be alert to special problems with verbs.

Both native and nonnative speakers of English encounter the following problems with verbs, which are treated elsewhere in this handbook:

> problems with active and passive voice (8)
>
> problems with subject-verb agreement (21)
>
> misuse of verb forms (27)
>
> problems with tense and mood (28)

This section focuses on features of the English verb system that cause special problems for multilingual speakers.

### 29a Match helping verbs and main verbs appropriately.

Only certain combinations of helping verbs and main verbs are allowed in English. The correct combinations are discussed in this section, after the following review of helping verbs and main verbs.

#### Review of helping verbs and main verbs

Helping verbs always appear before main verbs. (See 62c.)

    HV  MV                             HV     MV
We *will leave* for the picnic at noon. *Do* you *want* a ride?

---

**SCHOLARS ON ESL WRITING**

Leki, Ilona, and Tony Silva, eds. *Journal of Second Language Writing Online* <http://www.jslw.org>. This refereed quarterly journal includes the most current scholarship on the characteristics, attitudes, and composing processes of second-language (L2) writers; features of L2 writers' texts and readers' responses to those texts; the assessment and evaluation of L2 writing; and analyses of the social, cultural, political, and situational contexts for L2 writing. In addition, each issue includes an annotated bibliography of recent L2 books and articles.

Some helping verbs—*have, do,* and *be*—change form to indicate tense; others, known as modals, do not.

**FORMS OF *HAVE, DO,* AND *BE***
have, has, had
do, does, did
be, am, is, are, was, were, being, been

**MODALS**
can, could, may, might, must, shall, should, will, would (*also* ought to)

Every main verb has five forms (except *be,* which has eight forms). The following list shows these forms for the regular verb *help* and the irregular verb *give.* (See 27a for a list of common irregular verbs.)

| | |
|---|---|
| **BASE FORM** | help, give |
| **PAST TENSE** | helped, gave |
| **PAST PARTICIPLE** | helped, given |
| **PRESENT PARTICIPLE** | helping, giving |
| **-*S* FORM** | helps, gives |

## *Modal + base form*

After the modals *can, could, may, might, must, shall, should, will,* and *would,* use the base form of the verb.

▶  My cousin will sends us photographs from her wedding.

        *speak*
▶  We could ~~spoke~~ Spanish when we were young.
        ^

**CAUTION:** Do not use *to* in front of a main verb that follows a modal. (*Ought to* is an exception.)

**SCHOLARS ON ESL WRITING**
Cooper, Charles R., and Lee Odell, eds. *Evaluating Writing: The Role of Teachers' Knowledge about Text, Learning, and Culture.* Urbana: NCTE, 1999. Two chapters in this useful collection focus on the writing of ESL students: Guadalupe Valdes and Patricia Anloff Sanders's "Latino ESL Students and the Development of Writing Abilities" and Guanjun Cai's "Texts in Contexts: Understanding Chinese Students' English Compositions." Both chapters synthesize previous research and offer teachers fresh perspectives for teaching ESL students and evaluating their writing.

▶ Gina can ~~to~~ drive us home if we miss the bus.

## Do, does, *or* did + *base form*

After helping verbs that are a form of *do*, use the base form of the verb.

The helping verbs *do, does,* and *did* are used in three ways: (1) to express a negative meaning with the adverb *not* or *never,* (2) to ask a question, and (3) to emphasize a main verb used in a positive sense.

▶ Mariko does not want~~s~~ any more dessert.

▶ Did Janice ~~bought~~ *buy* the gift for Katherine?

▶ We do ~~hoping~~ *hope* that you will come to the retirement party.

## Have, has, *or* had + *past participle (perfect tenses)*

After the helping verb *have, has,* or *had,* use the past participle to form one of the perfect tenses. (See 28a.) Past participles usually end in *-ed, -d, -en, -n,* or *-t.* (See 27a.)

▶ On cold nights many churches in the city have ~~offer~~ *offered* shelter to the homeless.

▶ An-Mei has not ~~speaking~~ *spoken* Chinese since she was a young child.

The helping verb *have* is sometimes preceded by a modal helping verb such as *will: By nightfall, we will have driven five hundred miles.* (See also "perfect tenses," 28a.)

### SCHOLARS ON ESL WRITING

Robinson, William S. "ESL and Dialect Features in the Writing of Asian American Students." *Teaching English in the Two-Year College* 22 (1995): 303–09. Robinson focuses on the features of language that cause the most difficulty for Asian American students, arguing that errors are often the result of hypercorrection and other typical problems with dialect differences. He identifies six of the most common problems and offers instructional strategies for teachers to consider.

### Form of *be* + present participle (progressive forms)

After the helping verb *be, am, is, are, was, were,* or *been,* use the present participle to express a continuing action. (See "progressive forms," 28a.)

▶ Carlos is ~~build~~ building his house on a cliff overlooking the Pacific Ocean.

▶ Uncle Roy was ~~driven~~ driving a brand-new Hummer.

The helping verb *be* must be preceded by a modal (*can, could, may, might, must, shall, should, will,* or *would*): *Edith will be going to Germany soon.* The helping verb *been* must be preceded by *have, has,* or *had: Andy has been studying English for five years.* (See also progressive forms, 28a.)

**CAUTION:** Certain verbs are not normally used in the progressive sense in English. In general, these verbs express a state of being or mental activity, not a dynamic action. Common examples are *appear, believe, belong, contain, have, hear, know, like, need, see, seem, taste, think, understand,* and *want.*

▶ I ~~am wanting~~ want to see August Wilson's *Gem of the Ocean.*

Some of these verbs, however, have special uses in which progressive forms are normal: *We are thinking about going to the Bahamas.* You will need to make a note of exceptions as you encounter them.

### Form of *be* + past participle (passive voice)

When a sentence is written in the passive voice, the subject receives the action instead of doing it: *Melissa was given a special award.* (See 8a.)

**SCHOLARS ON TEACHING ESL STUDENTS**

Reynolds, Nedra, Bruce Herzberg, and Patricia Bizzell. "Teaching English as a Second Language." *The Bedford Bibliography for Teachers of Writing.* 6th ed. Boston: Bedford, 2003. <http://bedfordstmartins.com/bb/curr9.html>. Bizzell and Herzberg list twenty-five sources—including several essay collections—that address the wide range of teachers' concerns. Their annotations are extensive and helpful.

To form the passive voice, use *be, am, is, are, was, were, being,* or *been* followed by a past participle (usually ending in *-ed, -d, -en, -n,* or *-t*).

▶ Dreaming in Cuban was ~~write~~ by Cristina García.
   <br>*written*

▶ The scientists were ~~honor~~ for their work with dolphins.
   <br>*honored*

When the helping verb is *be, being,* or *been,* it must be preceded by another helping verb. *Be* must be preceded by a modal such as *will: Senator Dixon will be defeated. Being* must be preceded by *am, is, are, was,* or *were: The child was being teased. Been* must be preceded by *have, has,* or *had: I have been invited to a party.*

**CAUTION:** Although they may seem to have passive meanings, verbs such as *occur, happen, sleep, die,* and *fall* may not be used to form the passive voice because they are intransitive. Only transitive verbs, those that take direct objects, may be used to form the passive voice. (See transitive and intransitive verbs, 63b.)

▶ The earthquake ~~was~~ occurred last Wednesday night.

**EXERCISE 29–1** Revise any sentences in which helping and main verbs do not match. You may need to look at the list in 27a to determine the correct form of some irregular verbs. Answers to lettered sentences appear in the back of the book. Example:

Moira should find̸ an apartment closer to campus.

a. The new manager should making her first announcement in the next hour.

**EXERCISE 29–1 Answers:**

a. The new manager should be making her first announcement in the next hour.
b. There is nothing in the world that TV has not touched on.
c. Did the landlord tell you that he's going to raise the rent?
d. With luck, visitors can find a beautiful view of the old temple in the rain and mist.
e. The benefits of diet and exercise have been given much attention by health care providers.

1. The swimming pool was filled early this year, on May 1.
2. A serious accident happened at the corner of Main Street and First Avenue last night.

b. There is nothing in the world that TV has not touch on.
c. Did the landlord told you that he's going to raise the rent?
d. With luck, visitors can to find a beautiful view of the old temple in the rain and mist.
e. The benefits of diet and exercise have been giving much attention by health care providers.

1. The swimming pool was fill early this year, on May 1.
2. A serious accident was happened at the corner of Main Street and First Avenue last night.
3. My family has going to Sam's restaurant ever since we moved to this neighborhood.
4. I have ate Thai food only once before.
5. How often does Sandy takes her daughter to the doctor?

**ON THE WEB**

**dianahacker.com/bedhandbook**
▶ Electronic grammar exercises
  ▶ E-ex 29–1

**GRAMMAR CHECKERS** can catch some mismatches of helping and main verbs. They can tell you, for example, that the base form of the verb should be used after certain helping verbs, such as *did* and *could,* in incorrect sentences like these: *Did you understood my question? Could Alan comes with us?*

Grammar checkers also catch some, but not all, problems with main verbs following forms of *have* or *be.* For example, a grammar checker flagged the following sentence, correctly explaining that the past participle *spent* must follow the helping verb *have: We have spend six nights in Rome.* However, the program failed to flag problems in many sentences, such as the following: *The provisions of the contract were broke by both parties.*

**EXERCISE 29–1 (continued)**

3. My family has been going to Sam's restaurant ever since we moved to this neighborhood.
4. I have eaten Thai food only once before.
5. How often does Sandy take her daughter to the doctor?

**SCHOLARS ON TEACHING ESL STUDENTS**

Celce-Murcia, Marianne, Diane Larsen-Freeman, and Stephen Thewlis. *The Grammar Book: An ESL/EFL Teacher's Course.* 2nd ed. Boston: Heinle, 1999. This book, written for ESL and EFL teachers, is a thorough description of English grammar. The authors provide practical teaching suggestions.

**29b** In conditional sentences, choose verbs with care.

Conditional sentences state that one set of circumstances depends on whether another set of circumstances exists. Choosing verbs in such sentences can be tricky, partly because two clauses are involved: usually an *if* or a *when* or an *unless* clause and an independent clause.

Three kinds of conditional sentences are discussed in this section: factual, predictive, and speculative.

### Factual

Factual conditional sentences express factual relationships. If these relationships are scientific truths, the present tense is used in both clauses.

> If water *cools* to 32°, it *freezes.*

If they are present or past relationships that are habitually true, the same tense is used in both clauses.

> When Sue *bicycles* along the canal, her dog *runs* ahead of her.

> Whenever the coach *asked* for help, I *volunteered.*

### Predictive

Predictive conditional sentences are used for predictions about the future or for future plans or possibilities. In such a sentence, an *if* or *unless* clause contains a present-tense verb; the verb in the independent clause usually consists of the modal *will, can, may, should,* or *might* followed by the base form of the verb.

> If you *practice* regularly, your tennis game *will improve.*

> We *will lose* our remaining wetlands unless we *act* now.

---

**SCHOLARS ON TEACHING ESL STUDENTS**

Cook, Lenora, and Helen C. Lodge, eds. *Voices in English Classrooms: Honoring Diversity and Change.* Classroom Practices in Teaching English 28. Urbana: NCTE, 1996. Nineteen essays describe assignments designed for diverse student populations. The essays are grouped into three categories: language, composition, and literature.

## Speculative

Speculative conditional sentences are used for three purposes: (1) to speculate about unlikely possibilities in the present or future, (2) to speculate about events that did not happen in the past, and (3) to speculate about conditions that are contrary to fact. Each of these purposes requires its own combination of verbs.

**UNLIKELY POSSIBILITIES** Somewhat confusingly, English uses the past tense in an *if* clause to speculate about a possible but unlikely condition in the present or future. The verb in the independent clause consists of *would, could,* or *might* plus the base form of the verb.

> If I *had* the time, I *would travel* to Senegal.
>
> If Stan *studied* harder, he *could master* calculus.

In the *if* clause, the past-tense form *were* is used with subjects that would normally take *was: Even if I were* [not *was*] *invited, I wouldn't go to the picnic.* (See also 28b.)

**EVENTS THAT DID NOT HAPPEN** English uses the past perfect tense in an *if* clause to speculate about an event that did not happen in the past or to speculate about a state of being that was unreal in the past. (See past perfect tense, 28a.) The verb in the independent clause consists of *would have, could have,* or *might have* plus the past participle.

> If I *had saved* enough money, I *would have traveled* to Senegal last year.
>
> If Aunt Grace *had been* at the show last night, she *would have enjoyed* your performance.

**CONDITIONS CONTRARY TO FACT** To speculate about conditions that are currently unreal or contrary to fact, English usually uses the past-tense verb *were* (never *was*) in an *if* clause. (See 28b.) The verb in the independent clause consists of *would, could,* or *might* plus the base form of the verb.

> If Yiayia *were* alive today, she *would be* very proud of you.
>
> I *would make* children's issues a priority if I *were* president.

> **GRAMMAR CHECKERS** do not flag problems with conditional sentences. The programs miss even obvious errors, such as this one: *Whenever I washed my car, it rains.*

**EXERCISE 29–2**  Edit the following conditional sentences for problems with verbs. In some cases, more than one revision is possible. Suggested revisions of lettered sentences appear in the back of the book. Example:

> had
> If I ~~have~~ time, I would study both French and Russian next
>        ^
> semester.

a. The electrician might have discovered the broken circuit if she went through the modules one at a time.
b. If Verena wins a scholarship, she would go to graduate school.
c. Whenever there is a fire in our neighborhood, everybody came out to watch.
d. Sarah will take the paralegal job unless she would get a better offer.
e. If I live in Budapest with my cousin Szusza, she would teach me Hungarian cooking.

1. If the science fiction festival starts Monday, we wouldn't need to plan entertainment for our visitors.
2. If everyone has voted in the last election, the results would have been very different.

**EXERCISE 29–2  Possible revisions:**
a. The electrician might have discovered the broken circuit if she had gone through the modules one at a time.
b. If Verena wins a scholarship, she will go to graduate school.
c. Whenever there is a fire in our neighborhood, everybody comes out to watch.
d. Sarah will take the paralegal job unless she gets a better offer.
e. If I lived in Budapest with my cousin Szusza, she would teach me Hungarian cooking.

1. If the science fiction festival started Monday, we wouldn't need to plan entertainment for our visitors.
2. If everyone had voted in the last election, the results would have been very different.

3. The tenants will not pay the rent unless the landlord fixed the furnace.
4. When dark gray clouds appeared on a hot summer afternoon, a thunderstorm often follows.
5. Our daughter would have drowned if Officer Blake didn't risk his life to save her.

---

**ON THE WEB**

**dianahacker.com/bedhandbook**
▶ Electronic grammar exercises
  ▶ E-ex 29–2

---

**29c** Become familiar with verbs that may be followed by gerunds or infinitives.

A gerund is a verb form that ends in -*ing* and is used as a noun: *sleeping, dreaming.* (See 64c.) An infinitive is the base form of the verb preceded by the word *to: to sleep, to dream.* The word *to* is not a preposition in this use but an infinitive marker. (See 64c.)

A few verbs may be followed by either a gerund or an infinitive; still others may be followed by an infinitive (either directly or with a noun or pronoun intervening) but not by a gerund.

*Verb + gerund or infinitive*

These commonly used verbs may be followed by a gerund or an infinitive, with little or no difference in meaning:

| | | | |
|---|---|---|---|
| begin | continue | like | start |
| can't stand | hate | love | |

I love *skiing.*    I love *to ski.*

---

**EXERCISE 29–2 (continued)**

3. The tenants will not pay the rent unless the landlord fixes the furnace.
4. When dark gray clouds appear on a hot summer afternoon, a thunderstorm often follows.
5. Our daughter would have drowned if Officer Blake hadn't risked his life to save her.

With a few verbs, however, the choice of a gerund or an infinitive changes the meaning dramatically:

> forget    remember    stop    try

> She stopped *speaking* to Lucia. [She no longer spoke to Lucia.]

> She stopped *to speak* to Lucia. [She paused so that she could speak to Lucia.]

### Verb + gerund

These verbs may be followed by a gerund but not by an infinitive:

| | | | |
|---|---|---|---|
| admit | enjoy | postpone | resist |
| appreciate | escape | practice | risk |
| avoid | finish | put off | suggest |
| deny | imagine | quit | tolerate |
| discuss | miss | recall | |

> Have you finished *decorating* [not *to decorate*] the tree?

> Bill enjoys *playing* [not *to play*] the piano.

### Verb + infinitive

These verbs may be followed by an infinitive but not by a gerund:

| | | | | |
|---|---|---|---|---|
| agree | decide | manage | pretend | want |
| ask | expect | mean | promise | wish |
| beg | have | offer | refuse | |
| claim | hope | plan | wait | |

> We plan *to visit* [not *visiting*] the Yucatán next week.

> Jill has offered *to water* [not *watering*] the plants.

---

**SCHOLARS ON TEACHING ESL STUDENTS**

Zamel, Vivian. "Strangers in Academia: The Experiences of Faculty and ESL Students across the Curriculum." *College Composition and Communication* 46 (1995): 506–21. Reporting on a survey of ESL students and faculty across the disciplines, Zamel contrasts two groups of faculty: those who value ESL students' knowledge and abilities, in spite of their struggles with language, and those who equate language difficulties with lack of intellect. She argues that when we build on students' strengths we are not compromising our standards.

### Verb + noun or pronoun + infinitive

With certain verbs in the active voice, a noun or pronoun must come between the verb and the infinitive that follows it. The noun or pronoun usually names a person who is affected by the action.

| | | | | |
|---|---|---|---|---|
| advise | command | instruct | remind | urge |
| allow | convince | order | require | warn |
| cause | encourage | persuade | tell | |

The dean encouraged *Juanita to apply* for the athletic scholarship.

The class asked *Luis to tell* the story of his escape.

A few verbs may be followed either by an infinitive directly or by an infinitive preceded by a noun or pronoun.

| | |
|---|---|
| ask | need |
| expect | want |
| have | would like |

We asked *to speak* to the congregation.

We asked *Rabbi Abrams to speak* to the congregation.

### Verb + noun or pronoun + unmarked infinitive

An unmarked infinitive is an infinitive without *to*. A few verbs (known as "causative verbs") may be followed by a noun or pronoun and an unmarked (but not a marked) infinitive.

| | | |
|---|---|---|
| have ("cause") | let ("allow") | make ("force") |

I've always believed that absence makes *the heart grow* [not *to grow*] fonder.

Please let *me pay* [not *to pay*] for the tickets.

---

**SCHOLARS ON TEACHING ESL STUDENTS**

Fox, Helen. *Listening to the World: Cultural Issues in Academic Writing.* Urbana: NCTE, 1994. Fox argues that the communication style promoted in US academic settings—favoring argument, analysis, and critical thinking—is "shared by only a tiny fraction of the world's peoples." She urges us to be respectful of other communication styles.

**GRAMMAR CHECKERS** can flag some, but not all, problems with gerunds and infinitives following verbs. For example, a program flagged many sentences with misused infinitives, such as this one: *Chris enjoys to play tennis.* But it was less successful at flagging sentences with misused gerunds, skipping past incorrect sentences like this one: *We want traveling to Hawaii next spring.*

**EXERCISE 29–3**    Form sentences by adding gerund or infinitive constructions to the following sentence openings. In some cases, more than one kind of construction may be possible. Possible answers to lettered items appear in the back of the book. Example:

> Please remind your sister to call me.
>                    ^

a.  I enjoy
b.  The tutor told Samantha
c.  The team hopes
d.  Ricardo and his brothers miss
e.  The babysitter let

1.  Pollen makes
2.  The club president asked
3.  Next summer we plan
4.  My supervisor intends
5.  Please stop

**ON THE WEB**    **dianahacker.com/bedhandbook**
▶ Electronic grammar exercises
  ▶ E-ex 29–3

---

**EXERCISE 29–3    Possible answers:**

a.  I enjoy riding my motorcycle.
b.  The tutor told Samantha to come to the writing center.
c.  The team hopes to work hard and win the championship.
d.  Ricardo and his brothers miss surfing during the winter.
e.  The babysitter let Roger stay up until midnight.

1.  Pollen makes me sneeze.
2.  The club president asked us to work three hours at the rummage sale. *Or* The club president asked to speak to us about the next fundraiser.
3.  Next summer we plan to visit six countries in Europe.
4.  My supervisor intends to argue for larger bonuses for our group.

## 29d Become familiar with commonly used two-word verbs.

Many verbs in English consist of a verb followed by a preposition or adverb known as a *particle*. (See 62c.) A two-word verb (also known as a *phrasal verb*) often expresses an idiomatic meaning that cannot be understood literally. Consider the verbs in the following sentences, for example.

> We *ran across* Professor Magnotto on the way to the bookstore.
>
> Calvin *dropped in* on his adviser this morning.
>
> Regina told me to *look* her *up* when I got to Seattle.

As you may know, *ran across* means "encountered," *dropped in* means "paid an unexpected visit," and *look up* means "get in touch with." When you were first learning English, however, these two-word verbs must have suggested strange meanings.

Some two-word verbs are intransitive; they do not take direct objects. (See 63b.)

> This morning I *got up* at dawn.

Transitive two-word verbs (those that take direct objects) have particles that are either separable or inseparable. Separable particles may be separated from the verb by the direct object.

> Lucy *called* the wedding *off.*

When the direct object is a noun, a separable particle may also follow the verb immediately.

> Lucy *called off* the wedding.

---

**EXERCISE 29–3 (continued)**

5. **Please stop running in the halls.** *Or* **Please stop to buy milk on your way home from school.**

When the direct object is a pronoun, however, the particle must be separated from the verb.

> Why was there no wedding? Lucy *called* it *off* [not *called off* it].

Inseparable particles must follow the verb immediately. A direct object cannot come between the verb and the particle.

> The police will *look into* the matter [not *look* the matter *into*].

## 29e Do not omit needed verbs.

Some languages allow the omission of the verb when the meaning is clear without it; English does not.

▶ Jim ^is^ exceptionally intelligent.

▶ Many streets in San Francisco ^are^ very steep.

# 30

## Use the articles *a, an,* and *the* appropriately.

Except for occasional difficulty in choosing between *a* and *an,* native speakers of English encounter few problems with articles. To speakers whose native language is not English, however, articles can prove troublesome, for the rules governing their use are surprisingly complex. This section summarizes those rules.

The definite article *the* and the indefinite articles *a* and *an* signal that a noun is about to appear. The noun may fol-

---

**SCHOLARS ON TUTORING ESL STUDENTS**

Bruce, Shanti, and Ben Rafoth, eds. *ESL Writers: A Guide for Writing Tutors.* Portsmouth: Boynton, 2004. This is the first book to focus on the theory and practice of tutoring ESL writers. The articles in Parts 1 and 3 provide a theoretical context for the issues addressed in Part 2 on the tutoring session itself. The twelve articles in Part 2 offer practical suggestions for conducting tutoring sessions with ESL writers, including how to avoid appropriating the writer's text, how and when to pay attention to global and local concerns, how to deal with plagiarism, and how to address needs that go beyond writing, such as interpreting syllabi, assigned readings, and teachers' assignments.

low the article immediately or modifiers may intervene (see 62a and 62d).

> *the candidate, the* exceptionally well qualified *candidate*
>
> *a sunset, a* spectacular *sunset*
>
> *an apple, an* appetizing *apple*

Articles are not the only words used to mark nouns. Other noun markers (sometimes called *determiners*) include possessive nouns (*Helen's*), numbers, and the following pronouns: *my, your, his, her, its, our, their, whose, this, that, these, those, all, any, each, either, every, few, many, more, most, much, neither, several, some.*

Usually an article is not used with another noun marker. Common exceptions include expressions such as *a few, the most,* and *all the.*

 **GRAMMAR CHECKERS** rarely flag missing or misused articles. They cannot distinguish when *a* or *an* is appropriate and when *the* is correct, nor can they tell when an article is missing.

### 30a Use *a* (or *an*) with singular count nouns whose specific identity is not known to the reader.

Count nouns refer to persons, places, or things that can be counted: *one girl, two girls; one city, three cities; one apple, four apples.* Noncount nouns refer to entities or abstractions that cannot be counted: *water, steel, air, furniture, patience, knowledge.* It is important to remember that noncount nouns vary from language to language. To see what nouns English categorizes as noncount nouns, refer to the list on page 354.

**SCHOLARS ON TUTORING ESL STUDENTS**

Rafoth, Ben. "Tutoring ESL Papers Online." *ESL Writers: A Guide for Writing Tutors.* Ed. Shanti Bruce and Ben Rafoth. Portsmouth: Boynton, 2004. 94–104. Rafoth describes the lessons he and his tutors learned about the kinds of online responses that are most useful to both ESL and native-speaking writers. He concludes with the following advice to online tutors: Rather than making lots of comments on a paper, focus on a few changes that need to be made; separate comments on rhetorical matters involving key points from comments on items that do not interfere with comprehension; state advice plainly and directly rather than couching it with qualifiers about what readers might think; offer a clear and consistent message and reinforce it throughout the paper.

If a singular count noun names something not known to the reader—perhaps because it is being mentioned for the first time, perhaps because its specific identity is unknown even to the writer—the noun should be preceded by *a* or *an* unless it has been preceded by another noun marker. *A* (or *an*) usually means "one among many" but can also mean "any one."

> ► Mary Beth arrived in limousine.
>                     ^a

> ► We are looking for apartment close to the lake.
>                          ^an

**NOTE:** *A* is used before a consonant sound: *a banana, a tree, a picture, a hand, a happy child. An* is used before a vowel sound: *an eggplant, an occasion, an uncle, an hour, an honorable person.* Notice that words beginning with *h* can have either a consonant sound (*hand, happy*) or a vowel sound (*hour, honorable*). (See also *a, an* in the Glossary of Usage.)

## 30b Do not use *a* (or *an*) with noncount nouns.

*A* (or *an*) is not used to mark noncount nouns, such as *sugar, gold, honesty,* or *jewelry.* A list of commonly used noncount nouns is given in the chart on page 354.

> ► Claudia asked her mother for ~~an~~ advice.

If you want to express an approximate amount, you can often use one of the following quantifiers with a noncount noun.

| QUANTIFIER | NONCOUNT NOUN |
|---|---|
| a great deal of | candy, courage |
| a little | salt, rain |

### SCHOLARS ON TUTORING ESL STUDENTS

Severino, Carol. "Avoiding Appropriation." *ESL Writers: A Guide for Writing Tutors.* Ed. Shanti Bruce and Ben Rafoth. Portsmouth: Boynton, 2004. 48–59. Drawing on her experience learning to write in Italian, Severino explains the loss of voice and ownership ESL writers often feel when their writing has been reformulated by teachers or tutors. Severino offers ten specific recommendations for honoring the writer's voice, with an emphasis on addressing the student's expressed needs in a session and on meta-tutoring, that is, explaining how and why one is using particular tutoring techniques.

| QUANTIFIER | NONCOUNT NOUN |
|---|---|
| any | sugar, homework |
| enough | bread, wood, money |
| less | meat, violence |
| little (*or* a little) | knowledge, time |
| more | coffee, information |
| much (*or* a lot of) | snow, pollution |
| plenty of | paper, lumber |
| some | tea, news, work |

To express a more specific amount, you can often precede a noncount noun with a unit word that is typically associated with it. Here are some common combinations.

| *A OR AN* + UNIT + *OF* | NONCOUNT NOUNS |
|---|---|
| a bottle of | water, vinegar |
| a carton of | ice cream, milk, yogurt |
| an ear of | corn |
| a head of | cabbage, lettuce |
| a loaf of | bread |
| a piece of | meat, furniture, advice |
| a pound of | butter, sugar |
| a quart of | milk, ice cream |
| a slice of | bread, bacon |

**CAUTION:** Noncount nouns do not have plural forms, and they should not be used with numbers or words suggesting plurality (such as *several, many, a few, a couple of, a number of*).

▶ We need some informations/ about rain forests.

▶ Do you have ~~many~~ money with you?
　　　　　　 ^much^

▶ We bought new furnitures/ for our living room.

**SCHOLARS ON TUTORING ESL STUDENTS**

Harris, Muriel, and Tony Silva. "Tutoring ESL Students: Issues and Options." *College Composition and Communication* 44 (1995): 525–37. Harris and Silva help writing center tutors learn to work with ESL students. They show tutors how to prioritize errors, analyze patterns in writing, understand composing differences, categorize sentence-level problems, resist excessive correction, and teach proofreading.

## Commonly used noncount nouns

### Food and drink

bacon, beef, bread, broccoli, butter, cabbage, candy, cauliflower, celery, cereal, cheese, chocolate, coffee, corn, cream, fish, flour, fruit, ice cream, meat, milk, oil, pasta, rice, salt, spinach, sugar, tea, water, wine

### Nonfood substances

air, cement, coal, dirt, gasoline, gold, paper, petroleum, plastic, rain, silver, snow, soap, steel, wood, wool

### Abstract nouns

advice, anger, beauty, confidence, courage, fun, happiness, health, honesty, information, intelligence, knowledge, love, poverty, satisfaction, truth, wealth

### Other

biology (and other areas of study), clothing, equipment, furniture, homework, jewelry, luggage, lumber, machinery, mail, money, news, poetry, pollution, research, scenery, traffic, transportation, violence, weather, work

**NOTE:** A few noncount nouns may also be used as count nouns, especially in informal English: *Bill loves chocolate; Bill offered me a chocolate. I'll have coffee; I'll have a coffee.*

---

**30c** Use *the* with most nouns whose specific identity is known to the reader.

The definite article *the* is used with most nouns whose identity is known to the reader. (For exceptions, see 30d.) Usually the identity will be clear to the reader for one of the following reasons:

---

**SCHOLARS ON TEACHING ESL STUDENTS**

Leki, Ilona. "Classroom Expectations and Behaviors." *Understanding ESL Writers*. Portsmouth: Boynton, 1992. 47–57. Leki points out that ESL students may be "surprised at some of the customs and behaviors they encounter in U.S. classrooms" and examines numerous causes for this surprise. Instructors who are aware of ESL students' expectations can help them adjust more easily to American teaching and learning styles.

- The noun has been previously mentioned.
- A phrase or a clause following the noun restricts its identity.
- A superlative such as *best* or *most intelligent* makes the noun's identity specific.
- The noun describes a unique person, place, or thing.
- The context or situation makes the noun's identity clear.

▶ A truck loaded with manure cut in front of our van.
  *the*
When ^truck skidded a few seconds later, we almost hit it.

The noun *truck* is preceded by *A* when it is first mentioned. When the noun is mentioned again, it is preceded by *the* since readers now know the specific truck being discussed.

              *the*
▶ Bob warned me that ^platter on the top shelf of the cupboard

was cracked.

The phrase *on the top shelf of the cupboard* identifies the specific platter.

                  *the*
▶ Our petite daughter dated ^tallest boy in her class.

The superlative *tallest* restricts the identity of the noun *boy*.

                          *the*
▶ During an eclipse, one should not look directly at ^sun.

There is only one sun in our solar system, so its identity is clear.

            *the*
▶ Please don't slam ^door when you leave.

Both the speaker and the listener know which door is meant.

## SCHOLARS ON TEACHING ESL STUDENTS

Dean, Terry. "Multicultural Classrooms, Monocultural Teachers." *College Composition and Communication* 40 (1989): 23–37. Dean offers a number of teaching strategies for multicultural classes, including the use of culturally oriented topics, peer response groups, and class newsletters. Dean believes that "in helping students make cultural transitions, we learn from them how to make transitions ourselves."

**30d** Do not use *the* with plural or noncount nouns meaning "all" or "in general"; do not use *the* with most singular proper nouns.

When a plural or a noncount noun means "all" or "in general," it is not marked with *the.*

▶ ~~The~~ Fountains are an expensive element of landscape design.

▶ In some parts of the world, ~~the~~ rice is preferred to all other

  grains.

As you probably know, proper nouns—which name specific people, places, or things—are capitalized. Although there are many exceptions, *the* is not used with most singular proper nouns, such as *Judge Hennessey, Spring Street,* or *Lake Huron.* However, *the* is used with plural proper nouns, such as *the United Nations, the Bahamas,* and *the Finger Lakes.*

Geographical names create problems because there are so many exceptions to the rules. When in doubt, consult the chart on the next page or ask a native speaker.

**EXERCISE 30–1**   Articles have been omitted from the following story, adapted from *Zen Flesh, Zen Bones,* compiled by Paul Reps. Insert the articles *a, an,* and *the* where English requires them and be prepared to explain the reasons for your choices.

Moon Cannot Be Stolen

Ryokan, who was Zen master, lived simple life in little hut at foot of mountain. One evening thief visited hut only to discover there was nothing in it to steal.

Ryokan returned and caught him. "You may have come long way to visit me," he told prowler, "and you should not re-

**EXERCISE 30–1   Answers:**

The Moon Cannot Be Stolen

Ryokan, who was a Zen master, lived a simple life in a little hut at the foot of a mountain. One evening a thief visited the hut only to discover there was nothing in it to steal.

Ryokan returned and caught him. "You may have come a long way to visit me," he told the prowler, "and you should not return empty-handed. Please take my clothes as a gift." The thief was bewildered. He took Ryokan's clothes and slunk away. Ryokan sat naked, watching the moon. "Poor fellow," he mused. "I wish I could give him this beautiful moon."

turn empty-handed. Please take my clothes as gift." Thief was bewildered. He took Ryokan's clothes and slunk away. Ryokan sat naked, watching moon. "Poor fellow," he mused. "I wish I could give him this beautiful moon."

**ON THE WEB**

**dianahacker.com/bedhandbook**
▸ Electronic grammar exercises
  ▸ E-ex 30–1

## Geographical names

### When to omit the

| | |
|---|---|
| streets, squares, parks | Ivy Street, Union Square, Denali National Park |
| cities, states, counties | Miami, Idaho, Bee County |
| most countries | Italy, Nigeria, China |
| continents | South America, Africa |
| bays, single lakes | Tampa Bay, Lake Geneva |
| single mountains, islands | Mount Everest, Crete |

### When to use the

| | |
|---|---|
| united countries | the United States, the Republic of China |
| large regions, deserts | the East Coast, the Sahara |
| peninsulas | the Iberian Peninsula |
| oceans, seas, gulfs | the Pacific, the Dead Sea, the Persian Gulf |
| canals and rivers | the Panama Canal, the Amazon |
| mountain ranges | the Rocky Mountains, the Alps |
| groups of islands | the Solomon Islands |

# 31

---

## Be aware of other potential trouble spots.

---

**31a** Do not omit subjects or the expletive *there* or *it*.

English requires a subject for all sentences except imperatives, in which the subject *you* is understood (*Give to the poor*). (See 63a.) If your native language allows the omission of an explicit subject in other sentences or clauses, be especially alert to this requirement in English.

▶ *I have*
~~Have~~ a large collection of baseball cards, including Mickey
 ^
Mantle's rookie card.

▶ *she*
Aunt Geraldine is very energetic; seems young for her age.
 ^

When the subject has been moved from its normal position before the verb, English sometimes requires an expletive (*there* or *it*) at the beginning of the sentence or clause. (See 63c.) *There* is used at the beginning of a sentence or clause to draw the reader's (or listener's) attention to the location or existence of something.

▶ *There is*
~~Is~~ an apple on the counter.
 ^

▶ *there*
As you know, are many religious sects in India.
 ^

Notice that the verb agrees with the subject that follows it: *apple is, sects are.* (See 21g.)

In one of its uses, the word *it* functions as an expletive, to call attention to a subject following the verb.

---

### SCHOLARS ON TEACHING ESL STUDENTS

Schlumberger, Ann, and Diane Clymer. "Tailoring Composition Classes to ESL Students' Needs." *Teaching English in the Two-Year College* 16 (1989): 121–28. Arguing that learning a language and learning to write are analogous, Schlumberger and Clymer advocate using a process methodology with ESL writers rather than product-oriented approaches. They explain clearly why and how their four general recommendations for teaching ESL writers will contribute to a more effective pedagogy. Their bibliography helps teachers explore these recommendations further.

> ~~Is~~ *It is* healthy to eat fruit and grains.
> ^

> ~~Is~~ *It is* clear that we must change our approach.
> ^

The subjects of these sentences are *to eat fruit and grains* (an infinitive phrase) and *that we must change our approach* (a noun clause). (See 64c and 64b.)

As you probably know, the word *it* is also used as the subject of sentences describing the weather or temperature, stating the time, indicating distance, or suggesting an environmental fact.

> It is raining in the valley, and it is snowing in the mountains.

> In July, it is very hot in Arizona.

> It is 9:15 a.m.

> It is three hundred miles to Chicago.

> It gets noisy in our dorm on weekends.

> **GRAMMAR CHECKERS** flag some sentences with a missing expletive (*there* or *it*), but they often misdiagnose the problem, suggesting that if a sentence opens with a word such as *Is* or *Are,* it may need a question mark at the end. Consider this sentence, which a grammar checker flagged: *Are two grocery stores on Elm Street.* Clearly, the sentence doesn't need a question mark. What it needs is an expletive: *There are two grocery stores on Elm Street.*

## 31b Do not repeat the subject of a sentence.

English does not allow a subject to be repeated in its own clause.

**SCHOLARS ON TEACHING ESL STUDENTS**

Anzaldúa, Gloria. "How to Tame a Wild Tongue." *Borderlands/La Frontera.* San Francisco: Aunt Lute, 1987. 53–64. In richly textured prose, Anzaldúa tells of the complexities of growing up as a Chicana in southwest Texas—the "borderland" between the United States and Mexico. She describes the several linguistic cultures in which she participates and discusses language differences from several perspectives, reminding us of the necessity to respect all cultures and of the difficulties associated with being "a synergy" of several cultures.

▶ The doctor ~~she~~ advised me to cut down on salt

and sweets.

The pronoun *she* repeats the subject, *doctor.*

The subject of a sentence should not be repeated even if a word group intervenes between the subject and the verb.

▶ The car that had been stolen ~~it~~ was found.

The pronoun *it* repeats the subject, *car.*

## 31c Do not repeat an object or an adverb in an adjective clause.

In some languages, an object or an adverb is repeated later in the adjective clause in which it appears; in English, such repetitions are not allowed. Adjective clauses begin with relative pronouns (*who, whom, whose, which, that*) or relative adverbs (*when, where*), and these words always serve a grammatical function within the clauses they introduce. (See 64b.) Another word in the clause cannot also serve that same grammatical function.

When a relative pronoun functions as the object of a verb or the object of a preposition, do not add another word with the same function later in the clause.

▶ The puppy ran after the car that we were riding in. ~~it.~~

The relative pronoun *that* is the object of the preposition *in,* so the object *it* is not allowed.

Even when the relative pronoun has been omitted, do not add another word with its same function.

**SCHOLARS ON ESL PROBLEMS WITH ARTICLES**

Master, Peter. "Teaching the English Articles as a Binary System." *TESOL Quarterly* 24 (1990): 461–78. Master argues that English articles can be taught as a "binary division between classification (*a*) and identification (*the*). All the other elements of article usage can be understood within this framework, allowing a one form/one function correspondence for *a* and *the.*"

▶ The puppy ran after the car we were riding in. ~~it.~~
  ^

The relative pronoun *that* is understood even though it is not present in the sentence.

Like a relative pronoun, a relative adverb should not be echoed later in its clause.

▶ The place where I work ~~there~~ is one hour from my apartment in the city.

The adverb *there* should not echo the relative adverb *where*.

---

**GRAMMAR CHECKERS** usually fail to flag sentences with repeated subjects or objects, such as this one: *The bulbs that she planted they will bloom next spring.*

---

**EXERCISE 31–1** In the following sentences, add needed subjects or expletives and delete any repeated subjects, objects, or adverbs. Answers to lettered sentences appear in the back of the book. Example:

The new geology professor is the one whom we saw ~~him~~ on

TV this morning.

a. Are some cartons of ice cream in the freezer.
b. I don't use the subway because am afraid.
c. The prime minister she is the most popular leader in my country.
d. We tried to get in touch with the same manager whom we spoke to him earlier.
e. Recently have been a number of earthquakes in Turkey.

---

**EXERCISE 31–1   Answers:**

a. There are some cartons of ice cream in the freezer.
b. I don't use the subway because I am afraid.
c. The prime minister is the most popular leader in my country.
d. We tried to get in touch with the same manager whom we spoke to earlier.
e. Recently there have been a number of earthquakes in Turkey.

1. We visited an island where several ancient ruins are being excavated.
2. In this city it is difficult to find a high-paying job.
3. Beginning knitters are often surprised that their fingers are sore at first.

1. We visited an island where several ancient ruins are being excavated there.
2. In this city is difficult to find a high-paying job.
3. Beginning knitters they are often surprised that their fingers are sore at first.
4. Is a banyan tree in our backyard.
5. The CD that teaches Italian for opera lovers it was stolen from my backpack.

| ON THE WEB | **dianahacker.com/bedhandbook**<br>▶ Electronic grammar exercises<br>▶ E-ex 31–1 |
|---|---|

## 31d  Place adjectives and adverbs with care.

Adjectives modify nouns or pronouns; adverbs modify verbs, adjectives, or other adverbs (see 62d and 62e). Both native and nonnative speakers encounter problems in the use of adjectives and adverbs (see 26). For nonnative speakers, the placement of adjectives and adverbs can also be troublesome.

### Placement of adjectives

No doubt you have already learned that in English adjectives usually precede the nouns they modify and that they may also appear following linking verbs. (See 26b and 63b.)

Janine wore a *new* necklace. Janine's necklace was *new*.

When adjectives pile up in front of a noun, however, you may sometimes have difficulty arranging them. English is

---

**EXERCISE 31–1 (continued)**

4. There is a banyan tree in our backyard.
5. The CD that teaches Italian for opera lovers was stolen from my backpack.

quite particular about the order of cumulative adjectives, those not separated by commas. (See 32d.)

> Janine was wearing a *beautiful antique silver* necklace [not *silver antique beautiful* necklace].

The chart on page 365 shows the order in which cumulative adjectives ordinarily appear in front of the noun they modify. This list is just a general guide; don't be surprised when you encounter exceptions.

**NOTE:** Long strings of cumulative adjectives tend to be awkward. As a rule, use no more than two or three of them between the article (or other noun marker) and the noun modified. Here are several examples:

| | |
|---|---|
| a beautiful old pine table | Susan's large round painting |
| two enormous French urns | some small blue medicine |
| an exotic purple jungle flower | bottles |

### Placement of adverbs

Adverbs modifying verbs appear in various positions: at the beginning or end of the sentence, before or after the verb, or between a helping verb and its main verb.

> *Slowly,* we drove along the rain-slick road.
>
> Mia handled the teapot *very carefully.*
>
> Martin *always* wins our tennis matches.
>
> Christina is *rarely* late for our lunch dates.
>
> My daughter has *often* spoken of you.

An adverb may not, however, be placed between a verb and its direct object.

**SCHOLARS ON ESL STUDENTS AND PEER GROUPS**

Nelson, Gayle L., and John M. Murphy. "Peer Response Groups: Do L2 Writers Use Peer Comments in Revising Their Drafts?" *TESOL Quarterly* 27 (1993): 135–41. According to several studies, peer response groups have been successful in L1 writing classes, but "findings of L1 studies do not necessarily apply to L2 students." L2 writers may not trust responses from a peer who is struggling as they are trying to learn English; and in some cases, cultural differences may lead writers to devalue the comments of peers and view the teacher as the sole authority in the class. Nelson and Murphy's study suggests that students are more likely to use peer comments when writing groups promote cooperation and negotiation.

*carefully.*
▶ Mother wrapped ~~carefully~~ the gift/
                                      ^

The adverb *carefully* may be placed at the beginning or at the end of this sentence or before the verb. It cannot appear after the verb because the verb is followed by a direct object, *the gift.*

> **GRAMMAR CHECKERS** do not flag problems with the placement of adjectives and adverbs. They can, however, flag a few other problems with adjectives and adverbs. See the grammar checker advice on page 302.

**EXERCISE 31–2**   Using the chart on the next page, arrange the following modifiers and nouns in their proper order. Answers to lettered items appear in the back of the book. Example:

> *two new French racing bicycles*
> **new, French, two, bicycles, racing**

a.  woman, young, an, Vietnamese, attractive
b.  dedicated, a, priest, Catholic
c.  old, her, sweater, blue, wool
d.  delicious, Joe's, Scandinavian, bread
e.  many, cages, bird, antique, beautiful

1.  oval, nine, brass, lamps, miniature
2.  several, yellow, tulips, tiny
3.  the, tree, gingko, yellow, ancient, Mongolian
4.  courtyard, a, square, small, brick
5.  charming, restaurants, Italian, several

**ON THE WEB**   **dianahacker.com/bedhandbook**
   ▶ Electronic grammar exercises
      ▶ E-ex 31–2

**EXERCISE 31–2   Answers:**

a.  an attractive young Vietnamese woman
b.  a dedicated Catholic priest
c.  her old blue wool sweater
d.  Joe's delicious Scandinavian bread
e.  many beautiful antique bird cages

1.  nine miniature oval brass lamps
2.  several tiny yellow tulips
3.  the ancient yellow Mongolian gingko tree
4.  a small square brick courtyard
5.  several charming Italian restaurants

## Usual order of cumulative adjectives

**ARTICLE OR OTHER NOUN MARKER**

a, an, the, her, Joe's, two, many, some

**EVALUATIVE WORD**

attractive, dedicated, delicious, ugly, disgusting

**SIZE**

large, enormous, small, little

**LENGTH OR SHAPE**

long, short, round, square

**AGE**

new, old, young, antique

**COLOR**

yellow, blue, crimson

**NATIONALITY**

French, Scandinavian, Vietnamese

**RELIGION**

Catholic, Protestant, Jewish, Muslim

**MATERIAL**

silver, walnut, wool, marble

**NOUN/ADJECTIVE**

tree (as in *tree* house), kitchen (as in *kitchen* table)

**THE NOUN MODIFIED**

house, sweater, bicycle, bread, woman, priest

---

**SCHOLARS ON RESPONDING TO ESL WRITING**

Cai, Guanjun. "Texts in Contexts: Understanding Students' English Compositions." *Evaluating Writing: The Role of Teachers' Knowledge about Text, Learning, and Culture.* Ed. Charles R. Cooper and Lee Odell. Urbana: NCTE, 1999. 279–97. Cai writes that expectations of what constitutes an academic essay depend on rhetorical conventions—conventions that are connected to ideological and cultural values. Cai argues that instructors can better respond to ESL writing if they are familiar with typical rhetorical strategies of other cultures. Using a case study of a Chinese student writer, he demonstrates ways to analyze ESL compositions and to help students revise their academic writing with an understanding of audience.

**31e** Distinguish between present participles and past participles used as adjectives.

Both present and past participles may be used as adjectives. The present participle always ends in *-ing*. Past participles usually end in *-ed, -d, -en, -n,* or *-t.* (See 27a.)

| | |
|---|---|
| **PRESENT PARTICIPLES** | confusing, speaking |
| **PAST PARTICIPLES** | confused, spoken |

Participles used as adjectives can precede the nouns they modify; they can also follow linking verbs, in which case they describe the subject of the sentence. (See 63b.)

It was a *depressing* movie. Jim was a *depressed* young man.

The essay was *confusing.* The student was *confused.*

A present participle should describe a person or thing causing or stimulating an experience; a past participle should describe a person or thing undergoing an experience.

The lecturer was *boring* [not *bored*].

The audience was *bored* [not *boring*].

In the first example, the lecturer is causing boredom, not experiencing it. In the second example, the audience is experiencing boredom, not causing it.

Participles describing mental states are often troublesome for nonnative speakers.

| | |
|---|---|
| annoying / annoyed | exhausting / exhausted |
| boring / bored | fascinating / fascinated |
| confusing / confused | frightening / frightened |
| depressing / depressed | satisfying / satisfied |
| exciting / excited | surprising / surprised |

**EXERCISE 31–3   Answers:**

a. Listening to everyone's complaints all day was irritating.
b. The long flight to Singapore was exhausting.
c. Correct
d. After a great deal of research, the scientist made a fascinating discovery.
e. That blackout was one of the most frightening experiences I've ever had.

1. Correct
2. The directions to the new board game seem extremely complicated.
3. Correct

**GRAMMAR CHECKERS** do not flag problems with present and past participles used as adjectives. Not surprisingly, the programs have no way of knowing the meaning a writer intends. For example, both of the following sentences could be correct, depending on the writer's meaning: *My roommate was annoying. My roommate was annoyed.*

**EXERCISE 31–3**  Edit the following sentences for proper use of present and past participles. If a sentence is correct, write "correct" after it. Answers to lettered sentences appear in the back of the book. Example:

> Danielle and Monica were very ~~exciting~~ *excited* to be going to a
>
> Broadway show for the first time.

a.  Listening to everyone's complaints all day was irritated.
b.  The long flight to Singapore was exhausted.
c.  His skill at chess is amazing.
d.  After a great deal of research, the scientist made a fascinated discovery.
e.  That blackout was one of the most frightened experiences I've ever had.

1.  I couldn't concentrate on my homework because I was distracted.
2.  The directions to the new board game seem extremely complicating.
3.  How interested are you in visiting Civil War battlefields?
4.  The aerial view of the devastated villages was depressing.
5.  Even after the lecturer went over the main points again, the students were still confusing.

**ON THE WEB**  **dianahacker.com/bedhandbook**
▶ Electronic grammar exercises
▶ E-ex 31–3

**EXERCISE 31–3 (continued)**
4.  Correct
5.  Even after the lecturer went over the main points again, the students were still confused.

**31f** Become familiar with common prepositions that show time and place.

The most frequently used prepositions in English are *at, by, for, from, in, of, on, to,* and *with.* Each of these prepositions has a variety of uses that must be learned gradually, in context.

Prepositions that indicate time and place can be difficult to master because the differences among them are subtle and idiomatic. The chart on the next page is limited to four troublesome prepositions that show time and place: *at, on, in,* and *by.*

Not every use is listed in the chart, so don't be surprised to encounter exceptions and idiomatic uses that you must learn one at a time. For example, in English we ride *in* a car but *on* a bus, train, or subway. And when we fly *on* (not *in*) a plane, we are not sitting on top of the plane.

 **GRAMMAR CHECKERS** do not recognize incorrect prepositions showing time and place. They miss errors that would be obvious to native speakers, such as the following: *Only the adults in the family were allowed to sit on the dining room table.*

**EXERCISE 31–4** In the following sentences, replace prepositions that are not used correctly. If a sentence is correct, write "correct" after it. Answers to lettered sentences appear in the back of the book. Example:

> The play begins ~~on~~ *at* 7:20 p.m.

a. Whenever we eat at the Centerville Diner, we sit at a small table on the corner of the room.
b. At the beginning of the dotcom wave, students created new businesses in record numbers.

**SCHOLARS ON RESPONDING TO ESL WRITING**

Leki, Ilona. "Coaching from the Margins: Issues in Written Response." *Second Language Writing: Research Insights for the Classroom.* Ed. Barbara Kroll. Cambridge: Cambridge UP, 1990. 57–68. Though there is little evidence that thorough annotation of papers helps students improve their writing, a survey of ESL students showed that "these students wanted to have every error marked." Leki offers suggestions for responding to ESL papers, including dialogues with writers (written or oral) about works in progress or about comments they have received on their work.

**WRITERS ON WRITING**

Who does not know another language, does not know his own.
— Goethe

## *At, on, in,* and *by* to show time and place

### *Showing time*

**AT**    *at* a specific time: *at* 7:20, *at* dawn

**ON**    *on* a specific day or date: *on* June 4

**IN**    *in* a part of a 24-hour period: *in* the afternoon, *in* the daytime [but *at* night]

       *in* a year or month: *in* 1999, *in* July

       *in* a period of time: finished *in* three hours

**BY**    *by* a specific time or date: *by* 4:15, *by* Christmas

### *Showing place*

**AT**    *at* a meeting place or location: *at* home, *at* the club

       *at* the edge of something: sitting *at* the desk

       *at* the corner of something: turning *at* the intersection

       *at* a target: throwing the snowball *at* Lucy

**ON**    *on* a surface: placed *on* the table, hanging *on* the wall

       *on* an electronic medium: *on* television, *on* the Internet

**IN**    *in* an enclosed space: *in* the garage, *in* the envelope

       *in* a geographic location: *in* San Diego, *in* Texas

       *in* a print medium: *in* a book, *in* a magazine

**BY**    *by* a landmark: *by* the fence, *by* the flagpole

**EXERCISE 31–4 Answers:**

a. Whenever we eat at the Centerville Diner, we sit at a small table in the corner of the room.
b. Correct
c. On Thursday, Nancy will attend her first Pilates class at the community center.
d. Correct
e. We decided to go to a restaurant because there was no fresh food in the refrigerator.

1. I don't feel safe walking in my neighborhood at night.
2. If the train is on time, it will arrive at six o'clock in the morning.

c. In Thursday, Nancy will attend her first Pilates class at the community center.
d. Alex began looking for her lost mitten in another location.
e. We decided to go to a restaurant because there was no fresh food on the refrigerator.

1. I don't feel safe walking on my neighborhood in night.
2. If the train is on time, it will arrive on six o'clock at the morning.
3. In the corner of the room there is a large bookcase with a pair of small Russian dolls standing at the top shelf.
4. She licked the stamp, stuck it in the envelope, put the envelope on her pocket, and walked to the nearest mailbox.
5. The mailbox was in the intersection of Laidlaw Avenue and Williams Street.

| ON THE WEB | **dianahacker.com/bedhandbook** |
|---|---|
| | ▶ Electronic grammar exercises |
| | ▶ E-ex 31–4 |

**EXERCISE 31–4 (continued)**

3. In the corner of the room there is a large bookcase with a pair of small Russian dolls standing on the top shelf.
4. She licked the stamp, stuck it on the envelope, put the envelope in her pocket, and walked to the nearest mailbox.
5. The mailbox was at the intersection of Laidlaw Avenue and Williams Street.

# Part VII

# Punctuation

**ON THE WEB**

**dianahacker.com/bedhandbook/instructor**
▶ Exercise masters
▶ Quiz masters
▶ Transparency masters

371

# 32

---

## The comma

---

The comma was invented to help readers. Without it, sentence parts can collide into one another unexpectedly, causing misreadings.

> **CONFUSING**　If you cook Elmer will do the dishes.
>
> **CONFUSING**　While we were eating a rattlesnake approached our campsite.

Add commas in the logical places (after *cook* and *eating*), and suddenly all is clear. No longer is Elmer being cooked, the rattlesnake being eaten.

Various rules have evolved to prevent such misreadings and to speed readers along through complex grammatical structures. Those rules are detailed in this section. (Section 33 explains when not to use commas.)

**32a**　Use a comma before a coordinating conjunction joining independent clauses.

When a coordinating conjunction connects two or more independent clauses—word groups that could stand alone as separate sentences—a comma must precede it. There are seven coordinating conjunctions in English: *and, but, or, nor, for, so,* and *yet.*

A comma tells readers that one independent clause has come to a close and that another is about to begin.

▶　Nearly everyone has heard of love at first sight‸ but I fell in love at first dance.

**SCHOLARS ON PUNCTUATION**

Dawkins, John. "Teaching Punctuation as a Rhetorical Tool." *College Composition and Communication* 46 (1995): 533–48. Dawkins argues that the rules approach to punctuation used in handbooks is wrongheaded because good writers often break the rules for rhetorical reasons. Believing that handbook rules are both oversimplified and too complicated, Dawkins proposes a new system based on rhetoric. He classifies punctuation marks according to the degree of separation they signal and claims that good writers choose a maximum or minimum separation to raise or lower the emphasis. Dawkins uses a patterns approach to show students which choices are allowed in sentences with one or multiple independent clauses.

**GRAMMAR CHECKERS** rarely flag missing or misused commas. They sometimes recognize that a comma belongs before a *which* clause but not before a *that* clause (see 32e). For all other uses of the comma—after introductory word groups, between items in a series, between coordinate adjectives, around appositives, and so on—they are unreliable. When a grammar checker does note a missing comma, its suggested revision is often incorrect and sometimes even amusing. One program, for example, suggested a comma after the word *delivery* in the following sentence: *While I was driving a huge delivery truck ran through a red light.*

**EXCEPTION:** If the two independent clauses are short and there is no danger of misreading, the comma may be omitted.

The plane took off and we were on our way.

**TIP:** As a rule, do *not* use a comma to separate coordinate word groups that are not independent clauses. (See 33a.)

▶ A good money manager controls expenses/ and invests

surplus dollars to meet future needs.

The word group following *and* is not an independent clause; it is the second half of a compound predicate.

## 32b Use a comma after an introductory clause or phrase.

The most common introductory word groups are clauses and phrases functioning as adverbs. Such word groups usually tell when, where, how, why, or under what conditions the main action of the sentence occurred. (See 64a–64c.)

**SCHOLARS ON PUNCTUATION**

Hassett, Michael. "Toward a Broader Understanding of the Rhetoric of Punctuation." *College Composition and Communication* 47 (1996): 419–21. Although he agrees with Dawkins that punctuation is a rhetorical tool, Hassett criticizes Dawkins's 1995 article on four grounds. First, because Dawkins used literary essayists in his study, his conclusions may not apply to other genres, such as technical writing. Second, professional essayists can break the rules in ways that job applicants and college students cannot. Third, writers and readers may interpret the emphasis of marks of punctuation in different ways. And finally, weak student writers may be tempted to mimic literary writers by using punctuation not for their own purposes but to make their writing "*look* like the work of those valued writers."

A comma tells readers that the introductory clause or phrase has come to a close and that the main part of the sentence is about to begin.

▶ When Irwin was ready to iron, his cat tripped on the cord.

Without the comma, readers may have Irwin ironing his cat. The comma signals that *his cat* is the subject of a new clause, not part of the introductory one.

▶ Near a small stream at the bottom of the canyon, the park rangers discovered an abandoned mine.

The comma tells readers that the introductory prepositional phrase has come to a close.

**EXCEPTION:** The comma may be omitted after a short adverb clause or phrase if there is no danger of misreading.

In no time we were at 2,800 feet.

Sentences also frequently begin with participial phrases describing the noun or pronoun immediately following them. The comma tells readers that they are about to learn the identity of the person or thing described; therefore, the comma is usually required even when the phrase is short. (See 64c.)

▶ Thinking his motorcade drive through Dallas was routine, President Kennedy smiled and waved at the crowds.

▶ Buried under layers of younger rocks, the earth's oldest rocks contain no fossils.

**SCHOLARS ON PUNCTUATION**

Vasallo, Phillip. "'How's the Weather': Ice-Breaking and Fog-Lifting in Your Written Messages." *ETC: A Review of General Semantics* 50 (1993–94): 484–91. In his analysis of several problems that affect readability, Vasallo observes that the misuse of punctuation causes as much confusion as improper word choice. He cautions writers to be especially sensitive to their use of commas and semicolons.

**NOTE:** Other introductory word groups include transitional expressions and absolute phrases (see 32f).

**EXERCISE 32–1** Add or delete commas where necessary in the following sentences. If a sentence is correct, write "correct" after it. Answers to lettered sentences appear in the back of the book. Example:

> Because we had been saving molding for a few weeks, we had
>
> enough wood to frame all thirty paintings.

a. Alisa brought the injured bird home, and fashioned a splint out of Popsicle sticks for its wing.
b. Considered a classic of early animation *The Adventures of Prince Achmed* used hand-cut silhouettes against colored backgrounds.
c. If you complete the enclosed evaluation form, and return it within two weeks, you will receive a free breakfast during your next stay.
d. After retiring from the New York City Ballet in 1965, legendary dancer Maria Tallchief went on to found the Chicago City Ballet.
e. Roger had always wanted a handmade violin but he couldn't afford one.

1. While I was driving a huge delivery truck ran through a red light.
2. He pushed the car beyond the tollgate, and poured a bucket of water on the smoking hood.
3. Lit by bright halogen lamps hundreds of origami cranes sparkled like diamonds in sunlight.
4. As the first chord sounded, Aileen knew that her spirits were about to rise.
5. Many musicians of Bach's time played several instruments but few mastered them as early or played with as much expression as Bach.

**EXERCISE 32–1 Answers:**

a. Alisa brought the injured bird home and fashioned a splint out of Popsicle sticks for its wing.
b. Considered a classic of early animation, *The Adventures of Prince Achmed* used hand-cut silhouettes against colored backgrounds.
c. If you complete the enclosed evaluation form and return it within two weeks, you will receive a free breakfast during your next stay.
d. Correct
e. Roger had always wanted a handmade violin, but he couldn't afford one.

1. While I was driving, a huge delivery truck ran through a red light.

## 32c Use a comma between all items in a series.

When three or more items are presented in a series, those items should be separated from one another with commas. Items in a series may be single words, phrases, or clauses.

▶ Bubbles of air, leaves, ferns, bits of wood‸ and insects are

often found trapped in amber.

Although some writers view the comma between the last two items as optional, most experts advise using the comma because its omission can result in ambiguity or misreading.

▶ Uncle David willed me all of his property, houses‸ and

warehouses.

Did Uncle David will his property *and* houses *and* warehouses—or simply his property, consisting of houses and warehouses? If the former meaning is intended, a comma is necessary to prevent ambiguity.

▶ The activities include a search for lost treasure, dubious

financial dealings, much discussion of ancient heresies‸ and

midnight orgies.

Without the comma, the activities seem to include discussing orgies, not participating in them. The comma makes it clear that *midnight orgies* is a separate item in the series.

**ON THE WEB**  dianahacker.com/bedhandbook
▶ Language Debates
  ▶ Commas with items in a series

**EXERCISE 32–1 (continued)**

2. He pushed the car beyond the tollgate and poured a bucket of water on the smoking hood.
3. Lit by bright halogen lamps, hundreds of origami cranes sparkled like diamonds in sunlight.
4. Correct
5. Many musicians of Bach's time played several instruments, but few mastered them as early or played with as much expression as Bach.

**32d** Use a comma between coordinate adjectives not joined with *and.* Do not use a comma between cumulative adjectives.

When two or more adjectives each modify a noun separately, they are coordinate.

> Roberto is a *warm, gentle, affectionate* father.

Adjectives are coordinate if they can be joined with *and* (warm *and* gentle *and* affectionate).
Adjectives that do not modify the noun separately are cumulative.

> *Three large gray* shapes moved slowly toward us.

Beginning with the adjective closest to the noun *shapes,* these modifiers lean on one another, piggyback style, with each modifying a larger word group. *Gray* modifies *shapes,* *large* modifies *gray shapes,* and *three* modifies *large gray shapes.* Cumulative adjectives cannot be joined with *and* (three *and* large *and* gray shapes).

**COORDINATE ADJECTIVES**

▶ Patients with severe, irreversible brain damage should not be put on life support systems.

> Adjectives are coordinate if they can be connected with *and:* *severe and irreversible.*

**CUMULATIVE ADJECTIVES**

▶ Ira ordered a rich/ chocolate/ layer cake.

> Ira didn't order a cake that was rich and chocolate and layer: He ordered a *layer cake* that was *chocolate,* a *chocolate layer cake* that was *rich.*

**SCHOLARS ON PUNCTUATION**
Bruthiaux, Paul. "Knowing When to Stop: Investigating the Nature of Punctuation." *Language and Communication* 13 (1993): 27–43. Bruthiaux traces the history of punctuation and suggests that we recognize punctuation's dual roles: to record prosodic contours and to mark syntactic structure.

**EXERCISE 32–2**   Add or delete commas where necessary in the following sentences. If a sentence is correct, write "correct" after it. Answers to lettered sentences appear in the back of the book. Example:

> We gathered our essentials, took off for the great outdoors,
>
> and ignored the fact that it was Friday the 13th.

a. The cold impersonal atmosphere of the university was unbearable.
b. An ambulance threaded its way through police cars, fire trucks and irate citizens.
c. The *1812 Overture* is a stirring, magnificent piece of music.
d. After two broken arms, three cracked ribs and one concussion, Ken quit the varsity football team.
e. My cat's pupils had constricted to small black shining dots.

1. We prefer our staff to be orderly, prompt and efficient.
2. For breakfast the children ordered cornflakes, English muffins with peanut butter and cherry Cokes.
3. It was a small, unimportant part, but I was happy to have it.
4. Cyril was clad in a luminous orange rain suit and a brilliant white helmet.
5. Animation master Hironobu Sakaguchi makes computer-generated scenes look realistic, vivid and seductive.

**32e**  Use commas to set off nonrestrictive elements. Do not use commas to set off restrictive elements.

Word groups describing nouns or pronouns (adjective clauses, adjective phrases, and appositives) are restrictive or nonrestrictive. A *restrictive* element defines or limits the meaning of the word it modifies and is therefore essential to the meaning of the sentence. Because it contains essential information, a restrictive element is not set off with commas.

---

**EXERCISE 32–2   Answers:**

a. The cold, impersonal atmosphere of the university was unbearable.
b. An ambulance threaded its way through police cars, fire trucks, and irate citizens.
c. Correct
d. After two broken arms, three cracked ribs, and one concussion, Ken quit the varsity football team.
e. Correct

1. We prefer our staff to be orderly, prompt, and efficient.
2. For breakfast the children ordered cornflakes, English muffins with peanut butter, and cherry Cokes.

RESTRICTIVE      For camp the children need clothes *that are washable.*

If you remove a restrictive element from a sentence, the meaning changes significantly, becoming more general than you intended. The writer of the example sentence does not mean that the children need clothes in general. The intended meaning is more limited: the children need *washable clothes.*

A *nonrestrictive* element describes a noun or pronoun whose meaning has already been clearly defined or limited. Because it contains nonessential or parenthetical information, a nonrestrictive element is set off with commas.

NONRESTRICTIVE      For camp the children need sturdy shoes, *which are expensive.*

If you remove a nonrestrictive element from a sentence, the meaning does not change dramatically. Some meaning is lost, to be sure, but the defining characteristics of the person or thing described remain the same as before. The children need *sturdy shoes,* and these happen to be expensive.

**NOTE:** Often it is difficult to tell whether a word group is restrictive or nonrestrictive without seeing it in context and considering the writer's meaning. Both of the following sentences are grammatically correct, but their meaning is slightly different.

The dessert made with fresh raspberries was delicious.

The dessert, made with fresh raspberries, was delicious.

In the example without commas, the phrase *made with fresh raspberries* tells readers which of two or more desserts the writer is referring to. In the example with commas, the phrase merely adds information about the particular dessert.

**EXERCISE 32–2 (continued)**

3. Correct
4. Correct
5. Animation master Hironobu Sakaguchi makes computer-generated scenes look realistic, vivid, and seductive.

### *Adjective clauses*

Adjective clauses are patterned like sentences, containing subjects and verbs, but they function within sentences as modifiers of nouns or pronouns. They always follow the word they modify, usually immediately. Adjective clauses begin with a relative pronoun (*who, whom, whose, which, that*) or with a relative adverb (*where, when*).

Nonrestrictive adjective clauses are set off with commas; restrictive adjective clauses are not.

**NONRESTRICTIVE CLAUSE**

▶ Ed's house, which is located on thirteen acres, was completely

furnished with bats in the rafters and mice in the kitchen.

The adjective clause *which is located on thirteen acres* does not restrict the meaning of *Ed's house*, so the information is nonessential.

**RESTRICTIVE CLAUSE**

▶ Ramona's cat/ that just had kittens/ became defensive

around the other cats in the house.

Because the adjective clause *that just had kittens* identifies the particular cat, the information is essential.

**NOTE:** Use *that* only with restrictive clauses. Many writers prefer to use *which* only with nonrestrictive clauses, but usage varies.

---

| ON THE WEB | **dianahacker.com/bedhandbook**<br>▶ Language Debates<br> ▶ *that* versus *which* |
|---|---|

---

### SCHOLARS ON PUNCTUATION

Chafe, Wallace. "What Good Is Punctuation?" *Quarterly of the National Writing Project and the Center for the Study of Writing* 10.1 (1988): 8–11. *ERIC.* CD-ROM. SilverPlatter. 1995. Chafe argues that punctuation functions to signal both grammar and prosody. He advocates teaching punctuation in the context of the "sound of written language" as well as teaching "the rules."

### Phrases functioning as adjectives

Prepositional or verbal phrases functioning as adjectives may be restrictive or nonrestrictive. Nonrestrictive phrases are set off with commas; restrictive phrases are not.

#### NONRESTRICTIVE PHRASE

▶ The helicopter, with its million-candlepower spotlight illuminating the area, circled above.

The *with* phrase is nonessential because its purpose is not to specify which of two or more helicopters is being discussed.

#### RESTRICTIVE PHRASE

▶ One corner of the attic was filled with newspapers/ dating from the turn of the century.

*Dating from the turn of the century* restricts the meaning of *newspapers*, so the comma should be omitted.

### Appositives

An appositive is a noun or noun phrase that renames a nearby noun. Nonrestrictive appositives are set off with commas; restrictive appositives are not.

#### NONRESTRICTIVE APPOSITIVE

▶ Darwin's most important book, *On the Origin of Species,* was the result of many years of research.

*Most important* restricts the meaning to one book, so the appositive *On the Origin of Species* is nonrestrictive and should be set off with commas.

---

**SCHOLARS ON PUNCTUATION**

Meyer, Charles F. *A Linguistic Study of American Punctuation.* New York: Lang, 1987. Meyer introduces a hierarchy for punctuation marks based on syntax, semantics, and prosody. The period, question mark, and exclamation point are level one, setting off sentences. The colon, parentheses, and the dash are level two, setting off sentences, clauses, and phrases. The semicolon is level three, setting off clauses or clauses and phrases in a series. The comma is level four, setting off clauses and phrases.

**RESTRICTIVE APPOSITIVE**

▶ The song/ "Vertigo/" was blasted out of huge amplifiers at

the concert.

Once they've read *song*, readers still don't know precisely which song the writer means. The appositive following *song* restricts its meaning.

**EXERCISE 32–3** Add or delete commas where necessary in the following sentences. If a sentence is correct, write "correct" after it. Answers to lettered sentences appear in the back of the book. Example:

My youngest sister, who plays left wing on the soccer

team, now lives at The Sands, a beach house near

Los Angeles.

a. Choreographer Alvin Ailey's best-known work *Revelations* is more than just a crowd pleaser.
b. Twyla Tharp's contemporary ballet *Push Comes to Shove* was made famous by Russian dancer Baryshnikov. [Tharp has written more than one contemporary ballet.]
c. The glass sculptor sifting through hot red sand explained her technique to the other glassmakers.
d. A member of an organization, that provides housing for AIDS patients, was also appointed to the commission.
e. Brian Eno who began his career as a rock musician turned to meditative compositions in the late seventies.

1. I had the pleasure of talking to a woman who had just returned from India where she had lived for ten years.
2. Patrick's oldest sister Fiona graduated from MIT with a degree in aerospace engineering.
3. The artist painting a portrait of Aung San Suu Kyi, the Burmese civil rights leader, was once a political prisoner himself.

**EXERCISE 32–3 Answers:**

a. Choreographer Alvin Ailey's best-known work, *Revelations*, is more than just a crowd pleaser.
b. Correct
c. Correct
d. A member of an organization that provides housing for AIDS patients was also appointed to the commission.
e. Brian Eno, who began his career as a rock musician, turned to meditative compositions in the late seventies.

1. I had the pleasure of talking to a woman who had just returned from India, where she had lived for ten years.
2. Patrick's oldest sister, Fiona, graduated from MIT with a degree in aerospace engineering.

4. *The Polar Express,* the 1986 Caldecott Medal winner, is my nephew's favorite book.
5. The flame crawled up a few blades of grass to reach a low-hanging palmetto branch which quickly ignited.

**32f** **Use commas to set off transitional and parenthetical expressions, absolute phrases, and elements expressing contrast.**

*Transitional expressions*

Transitional expressions serve as bridges between sentences or parts of sentences. They include conjunctive adverbs such as *however, therefore,* and *moreover* and transitional phrases such as *for example, as a matter of fact,* and *in other words.* (For more complete lists, see 34b.)

When a transitional expression appears between independent clauses in a compound sentence, it is preceded by a semicolon and is usually followed by a comma. (See 34b.)

▶ Minh did not understand our language; moreover, he was

unfamiliar with our customs.

When a transitional expression appears at the beginning of a sentence or in the middle of an independent clause, it is usually set off with commas.

▶ As a matter of fact, American football was established by

fans who wanted to play a more organized game of rugby.

▶ Natural foods are not always salt free; celery, for example,

contains more sodium than most people would imagine.

**EXERCISE 32–3 (continued)**
3. Correct
4. Correct
5. The flame crawled up a few blades of grass to reach a low-hanging palmetto branch, which quickly ignited.

**EXCEPTION:** If a transitional expression blends smoothly with the rest of the sentence, calling for little or no pause in reading, it does not need to be set off with a comma. Expressions such as *also, at least, certainly, consequently, indeed, of course, moreover, no doubt, perhaps, then,* and *therefore* do not always call for a pause.

> Alice's bicycle is broken; *therefore* you will need to borrow Sue's.

**NOTE:** The conjunctive adverb *however* always calls for a pause, but it should not be confused with *however* meaning "no matter how," which does not: *However hard Bill tried, he could not match his previous record.*

### Parenthetical expressions

Expressions that are distinctly parenthetical should be set off with commas. Providing supplemental information, they interrupt the flow of a sentence or appear at the end as afterthoughts.

▶ Evolution‸ as far as we know‸ doesn't work this way.

▶ The bass weighed about twelve pounds‸ give or take a few ounces.

### Absolute phrases

An absolute phrase, which modifies the whole sentence, usually consists of a noun followed by a participle or participial phrase. (See 64e.) Absolute phrases may appear at the beginning or at the end of a sentence. Wherever they appear, they should be set off with commas.

---

**WRITERS ON WRITING**

Punctuation marks are the road signs placed along the highway of our communications—to control speeds, provide directions, and prevent head-on collisions. A period has the unblinking finality of a red light; the comma is a flashing yellow light that asks us only to slow down; and the semicolon is a stop sign that tells us to ease gradually to a halt, before gradually starting up again.

—Pico Iyer

▶ The sun appearing for the first time in a week, we were at last able to begin the archaeological dig.

▶ Elvis Presley made music industry history in the 1950s, his records having sold more than ten million copies.

**CAUTION:** Do not insert a comma between the noun and the participle in an absolute construction.

▶ The next contestant/ being five years old, the emcee adjusted the height of the microphone.

### Contrasted elements

Sharp contrasts beginning with words such as *not, never,* and *unlike* are set off with commas.

▶ The Epicurean philosophers sought mental, not bodily, pleasures.

▶ Unlike Robert, Celia loved dance contests.

**32g** Use commas to set off nouns of direct address, the words *yes* and *no,* interrogative tags, and mild interjections.

▶ Forgive us, Dr. Atkins, for having rolls with dinner tonight.

**WRITERS ON WRITING**

Commas in *The New Yorker* fall with the precision of knives in a circus act, outlining the victim.            —E. B. White

▶ Yes, the loan will probably be approved.

▶ The film was faithful to the book, wasn't it?

▶ Well, cases like these are difficult to decide.

## 32h Use commas with expressions such as *he said* to set off direct quotations. (See also 37f.)

▶ Naturalist Arthur Cleveland Bent remarked, "In part the peregrine declined unnoticed because it is not adorable."

▶ "Convictions are more dangerous foes of truth than lies," wrote philosopher Friedrich Nietzsche.

## 32i Use commas with dates, addresses, titles, and numbers.

*Dates*

In dates, the year is set off from the rest of the sentence with a pair of commas.

▶ On December 12, 1890, orders were sent out for the arrest of Sitting Bull.

**EXCEPTIONS:** Commas are not needed if the date is inverted or if only the month and year are given.

The recycling plan went into effect on 15 April 2001.

January 2004 was an extremely cold month.

---

**SCHOLARS ON PUNCTUATION**

Meyer, Charles F. "Teaching Punctuation to Advanced Writers." *Journal of Advanced Composition* 6 (1985–86): 117–29. Meyer discusses how the deliberate violation of punctuation norms affects meaning. He recommends that writers not violate punctuation norms if the violation confuses the reader, creates a stylistically awkward construction, or goes against the tone of a formal piece of writing. Meyer lists numerous examples of how norms can be violated to create an effect, including the use of semicolons instead of commas to punctuate coordinated clauses.

### Addresses

The elements of an address or a place name are separated by commas. A zip code, however, is not preceded by a comma.

▶ John Lennon was born in Liverpool, England, in 1940.

▶ Please send the package to Greg Tarvin at 708 Spring Street, Washington, IL 61571.

### Titles

If a title follows a name, separate it from the rest of the sentence with a pair of commas.

▶ Sandra Belinsky, MD, has been appointed to the board of trustees.

### Numbers

In numbers more than four digits long, use commas to separate the numbers into groups of three, starting from the right. In numbers four digits long, a comma is optional.

> 3,500 [*or* 3500]
> 100,000
> 5,000,000

**EXCEPTIONS:** Do not use commas in street numbers, zip codes, telephone numbers, or years.

---

**SCHOLARS ON PUNCTUATION**

Shaughnessy, Mina P. *Errors and Expectations: A Guide for the Teacher of Basic Writing*. New York: Oxford UP, 1979. 14–43. Shaughnessy points out that basic writers use "only the three most common marks: the period, the comma, and the capital" and that because of inexperience they are "restricted" by "uncertain use of these marks." As usual, Shaughnessy's examples and explanations are practical and insightful.

## 32j Use a comma to prevent confusion.

In certain contexts, a comma is necessary to prevent confusion. If the writer has omitted a word or phrase, for example, a comma may be needed to signal the omission.

▶ To err is human; to forgive‸ divine.

If two words in a row echo each other, a comma may be needed for ease of reading.

▶ All of the catastrophes that we had feared might happen‸

happened.

Sometimes a comma is needed to prevent readers from grouping words in ways that do not match the writer's intention.

▶ Patients who can‸ walk up and down the halls several times

a day.

**EXERCISE 32–4: Major uses of the comma**   This exercise covers the major uses of the comma listed in the chart on the next page. Add or delete commas where necessary. If a sentence is correct, write "correct" after it. Answers to lettered sentences appear in the back of the book. Example:

Even though Pavel had studied Nigella Lawson's recipes for a

week‸ he underestimated how long it would take to juice

two hundred lemons.

**EXERCISE 32–4   Answers:**

a. Cricket, which originated in England, is also popular in Australia, South Africa, and India.
b. At the sound of the starting pistol, the horses surged forward toward the first obstacle, a sharp incline three feet high.
c. After seeing an exhibition of Western art, Gerhard Richter escaped from East Berlin and smuggled out many of his notebooks.
d. Corrie's new wet suit has an intricate blue pattern.
e. Correct

1. Correct
2. Founded in 1868, Hampton University was one of the first colleges for African Americans.

## Major uses of the comma

**BEFORE A COORDINATING CONJUNCTION
JOINING INDEPENDENT CLAUSES (32a)**

> No grand idea was ever born in a conference, but a lot of foolish ideas have died there. —F. Scott Fitzgerald

**AFTER AN INTRODUCTORY CLAUSE OR PHRASE (32b)**

> If thought corrupts language, language can also corrupt thought. —George Orwell

**BETWEEN ALL ITEMS IN A SERIES (32c)**

> All the things I really like to do are either immoral, illegal, or fattening. —Alexander Woollcott

**BETWEEN COORDINATE ADJECTIVES (32d)**

> There is a mighty big difference between good, sound reasons and reasons that sound good. —Burton Hillis

**TO SET OFF NONRESTRICTIVE ELEMENTS (32e)**

> Silence, which will save me from shame, will also deprive me of fame. —Igor Stravinsky

---

a. Cricket, which originated in England is also popular in Australia, South Africa and India.
b. At the sound of the starting pistol the horses surged forward toward the first obstacle, a sharp incline three feet high.
c. After seeing an exhibition of Western art Gerhard Richter escaped from East Berlin, and smuggled out many of his notebooks.
d. Corrie's new wet suit has an intricate, blue pattern.
e. The cookies will keep for two weeks in sturdy airtight plastic containers.

---

**EXERCISE 32–4 (continued)**

3. Aunt Emilia was an impossible, demanding guest.
4. Correct
5. At the bottom of the ship's rusty hold sat several well-preserved trunks, reminders of a bygone era of sea travel.

1. Research on Andean condors has shown that high levels of the chemical pesticide chlorinated hydrocarbon can cause the thinning of eggshells.
2. Founded in 1868 Hampton University was one of the first colleges for African Americans.
3. Aunt Emilia was an impossible demanding guest.
4. The French Mirage, a high-tech fighter, is an astonishing machine to fly.
5. At the bottom of the ship's rusty hold sat several, well-preserved trunks, reminders of a bygone era of sea travel.


**EXERCISE 32–5: All uses of the comma**   Add or delete commas where necessary in the following sentences. If a sentence is correct, write "correct" after it. Answers to lettered sentences appear in the back of the book. Example:

> "Yes, dear, you can have dessert," my mother said.
>      ∧

a. On January 15, 2004 our office moved to 29 Commonwealth Avenue, Mechanicsville VA 23111.
b. The coach having bawled us out thoroughly, we left the locker room with his harsh words ringing in our ears.
c. Ms. Carlson you are a valued customer whose satisfaction is very important to us.
d. Mr. Mundy was born on July 22, 1939 in Arkansas, where his family had lived for four generations.
e. Her board poised at the edge of the half-pipe, Nina waited her turn to drop in.

1. President Lincoln's original intention was to save the Union, not to destroy slavery.
2. For centuries people believed that Greek culture had developed in isolation from the world. Today however scholars are acknowledging the contributions made by Egypt and the Middle East.
3. Putting together a successful fundraiser, Patricia discovered, requires creativity and good timing.

---

**EXERCISE 32–5   Answers:**

a. On January 15, 2004, our office moved to 29 Commonwealth Avenue, Mechanicsville, VA 23111.
b. Correct
c. Ms. Carlson, you are a valued customer whose satisfaction is very important to us.
d. Mr. Mundy was born on July 22, 1939, in Arkansas, where his family had lived for four generations.
e. Correct

1. Correct
2. For centuries people believed that Greek culture had developed in isolation from the world. Today, however, scholars are

4. Fortunately science is creating many alternatives to research performed on animals.
5. While the machine was printing the oversize paper jammed.

# 33

## Unnecessary commas

Many common misuses of the comma result from an incomplete understanding of the major comma rules presented in 32. In particular, writers frequently form misconceptions about rules 32a–32e, either extending the rules inappropriately or misinterpreting them. Such misconceptions can lead to the errors described in 33a–33e; rules 33f–33h list other common misuses of the comma.

**33a** Do not use a comma between compound elements that are not independent clauses.

Though a comma should be used before a coordinating conjunction joining independent clauses (see 32a), this rule should not be extended to other compound word groups.

▶ Marie Curie discovered radium/ and later applied her work

on radioactivity to medicine.

---

**EXERCISE 32–5 (continued)**
   acknowledging the contributions made by Egypt and the Middle East. [A comma after *centuries* is optional.]
3. Correct
4. Fortunately, science is creating many alternatives to research performed on animals.
5. While the machine was printing, the oversize paper jammed.

▶ Jake still doesn't realize that his illness is serious̷ and

that he will have to alter his diet to improve his chances of

survival.

> In the first example, *and* links two verbs in a compound predicate: *discovered* and *applied*. In the second example, *and* links two subordinate clauses, each beginning with *that.*

**33b** Do not use a comma after a phrase that begins an inverted sentence.

Though a comma belongs after most introductory phrases (see 32b), it does not belong after phrases that begin an inverted sentence. In an inverted sentence, the subject follows the verb, and a phrase that ordinarily would follow the verb is moved to the beginning (see 63c).

▶ At the bottom of the hill̷ sat the stubborn mule.

**33c** Do not use a comma before the first or after the last item in a series.

Though commas are required between items in a series (32c), do not place them either before or after the whole series.

▶ Other causes of asthmatic attacks are̷ stress, change in

temperature, and cold air.

▶ Ironically, this job that appears so glamorous, carefree, and

easy̷ carries a high degree of responsibility.

---

**WRITERS ON WRITING**

This morning I took out a comma and this afternoon I put it back
again.                                                    — Oscar Wilde

**33d** Do not use a comma between cumulative adjectives, between an adjective and a noun, or between an adverb and an adjective.

Commas are required between coordinate adjectives (those that can be joined with *and*), but they do not belong between cumulative adjectives (those that cannot be joined with *and*). (For a full discussion, see 32d.)

▶ In the corner of the closet we found an old⁄ maroon hatbox

from Sears.

A comma should never be used between an adjective and the noun that follows it.

▶ It was a senseless, dangerous⁄ mission.

Nor should a comma be used between an adverb and an adjective that follows it.

▶ The Hurst Home is unsuitable as a mental facility for

severely⁄ disturbed youths.

**33e** Do not use commas to set off restrictive or mildly parenthetical elements.

Restrictive elements are modifiers or appositives that restrict the meaning of the nouns they follow. Because they are essential to the meaning of the sentence, they are not set off with commas. (For a full discussion of both restrictive and nonrestrictive elements, see 32e.)

**WRITERS ON WRITING**

Punctuation, whether we call it a science that contains touches of art or an art reared on underpinnings of science, is a graphic device for showing how sentences are constructed.

—Wilson Follett

Many writers profess great exactness of punctuation, who never yet made a point. —George Dennison Prentice

▶ Drivers/ who think they own the road/ make cycling a

dangerous sport.

> The modifier *who think they own the road* restricts the meaning of *Drivers* and is therefore essential to the meaning of the sentence. Putting commas around the *who* clause falsely suggests that all drivers think they own the road.

▶ Margaret Mead's book/ *Coming of Age in Samoa*/ stirred

up considerable controversy when it was published

in 1928.

> Since Mead wrote more than one book, the appositive contains information essential to the meaning of the sentence.

Although commas should be used with distinctly parenthetical expressions (see 32f), do not use them to set off elements that are only mildly parenthetical.

▶ Charisse believes that the Internet is/ essentially/ a bastion

of advertising.

**33f** Do not use a comma to set off a concluding adverb clause that is essential to the meaning of the sentence.

When adverb clauses introduce a sentence, they are nearly always followed by a comma (see 32b). When they conclude a sentence, however, they are not set off by commas if their content is essential to the meaning of the earlier part of the sentence. Adverb clauses beginning with *after, as soon as, because, before, if, since, unless, until,* and *when* are usually essential.

**WRITERS ON WRITING**

The most important fact about a comma is that there are places where it must not be used.     —Bergen Evans and Cornelia Evans

The drive toward a lean punctuation is such that even if we still wrote the complex, periodic sentences of Johnson or of Macaulay, we should punctuate them much less heavily.     —Wilson Follett

I like to use as few commas as possible so that sentences will go down in one swallow without touching the sides.

—Pamela Frankau

▶ Don't visit Paris at the height of the tourist season/ unless

  you have booked hotel reservations.

  Without the *unless* clause, the meaning of the sentence might
  at first seem broader than the writer intended.

  When a concluding adverb clause is nonessential, it should
  be preceded by a comma. Clauses beginning with *although,
  even though, though,* and *whereas* are usually nonessential.

▶ The lecture seemed to last only a short time, although the

  clock said it had gone on for more than an hour.

## 33g Do not use a comma to separate a verb from its subject or object.

A sentence should flow from subject to verb to object without
unnecessary pauses. Commas may appear between these major
sentence elements only when a specific rule calls for them.

▶ Zoos large enough to give the animals freedom to roam/ are

  becoming more popular.

  The comma should not separate the subject, *Zoos,* from the
  verb, *are becoming.*

▶ Francesca explained to him/ that she was busy and would

  see him later.

  The comma should not separate the verb, *explained,* from its
  object, the subordinate clause *that she was busy and would
  see him later.*

**WRITERS ON WRITING**

The commas are the most useful and usable of all the stops. It is
highly important to put them in place as you go along. If you try to
come back after doing a paragraph and stick them in the various
spots that tempt you you will discover that they tend to swarm like
minnows into all sorts of crevices whose existence you hadn't realized and before you know it the whole long sentence becomes
immobilized and lashed up squirming in commas. Better to use
them sparingly, and with affection, precisely when the need for
each one arises, nicely, by itself.                    —Lewis Thomas

**33h** Avoid other common misuses of the comma.

Do not use a comma in the following situations.

### AFTER A COORDINATING CONJUNCTION (*AND, BUT, OR, NOR, FOR, SO, YET*)

▶ Occasionally soap operas are performed live, but̸ more often they are taped.

### AFTER *SUCH AS* OR *LIKE*

▶ Many shade-loving plants, such as̸ begonias, impatiens, and coleus, can add color to a shady garden.

### BEFORE *THAN*

▶ Touring Crete was more thrilling for us̸ than visiting the Greek islands frequented by rich Europeans.

### AFTER *ALTHOUGH*

▶ Although̸ the air was balmy, the water was too cold for swimming.

### BEFORE A PARENTHESIS

▶ At Nextel Sylvia began at the bottom̸ (with only three and a half walls and a swivel chair), but within five years she had been promoted to supervisor.

---

**EXERCISE 33–1  Answers:**

a. Correct
b. Tricia's first artwork was a big blue clay dolphin.
c. Some modern musicians (trumpeter John Hassell is an example) blend several cultural traditions into a unique sound.
d. Myra liked hot, spicy foods such as chili, jambalaya, and buffalo wings.
e. On the display screen was a soothing pattern of light and shadow.

1. Correct
2. Jolie's parents encouraged independent thinking but required respect for others' opinions.

**TO SET OFF AN INDIRECT (REPORTED) QUOTATION**

▶ Samuel Goldwyn once said/ that a verbal contract isn't worth the paper it's written on.

**WITH A QUESTION MARK OR AN EXCLAMATION POINT**

▶ "Why don't you try it?/" she coaxed. "You can't do any worse than the rest of us."

**EXERCISE 33–1**  Delete commas where necessary in the following sentences. If a sentence is correct, write "correct" after it. Answers to lettered sentences appear in the back of the book. Example:

> In his Silk Road Project, Yo-Yo Ma has incorporated work by musicians such as/ Kayhan Kahlor and Richard Danielpour.

a. After the morning rains cease, the swimmers emerge from their cottages.
b. Tricia's first artwork was a big, blue, clay dolphin.
c. Some modern musicians, (trumpeter John Hassell is an example) blend several cultural traditions into a unique sound.
d. Myra liked hot, spicy foods such as, chili, jambalaya, and buffalo wings.
e. On the display screen, was a soothing pattern of light and shadow.

1. Mesquite, the hardest of the softwoods, grows primarily in the Southwest.
2. Jolie's parents encouraged independent thinking, but required respect for others' opinions.
3. Miranda told her boss, that she had discovered a new plastic as strong as metal.

**EXERCISE 33–1 (continued)**
3. Miranda told her boss that she had discovered a new plastic as strong as metal.
4. The streets that three hours later would be bumper to bumper with commuters were quiet and empty except for a few prowling cats.
5. Some first-year architecture students expect to design intricate structures immediately.

4. The streets that three hours later would be bumper to bumper with commuters, were quiet and empty except for a few prowling cats.

5. Some first-year architecture students, expect to design intricate structures immediately.

---

**ON THE WEB**    **dianahacker.com/bedhandbook**
▶ Electronic grammar exercises
  ▶ E-ex 33–1

---

# 34

---

## The semicolon

---

The semicolon is used to connect major sentence elements of equal grammatical rank.

---

 **GRAMMAR CHECKERS** flag some, but not all, misused semicolons (34d). In addition, they can alert you to some run-on sentences (34a). However, they miss more run-on sentences than they identify, and they sometimes flag correct sentences as possible run-ons.

---

**34a** Use a semicolon between closely related independent clauses not joined with a coordinating conjunction.

When related independent clauses appear in one sentence, they are ordinarily linked with a comma and a coordinating conjunction (*and, but, or, nor, for, so, yet*). The coordinating

---

**WRITERS ON WRITING**

It is almost always a greater pleasure to come across a semicolon than a period. The period tells you that that is that; if you didn't get all the meaning you wanted or expected, anyway you got all the writer intended to parcel out and now you have to move along. But with a semicolon there you get a pleasant little feeling of expectancy; there is more to come; read on; it will get clearer.
                                                                    —Lewis Thomas

Semicolons . . . signal, rather than shout, a relationship. . . . A semicolon is a compliment from the writer to the reader. It says: "I don't have to draw you a picture; a hint will do."        —George Will

conjunction signals the relation between the clauses. If the clauses are closely related and the relation is clear without a conjunction, they may be linked with a semicolon instead.

> Injustice is relatively easy to bear; what stings is justice.
> —H. L. Mencken

> When I was a boy, I was told that anybody could become president; I'm beginning to believe it.  —Clarence Darrow

A semicolon must be used whenever a coordinating conjunction has been omitted between independent clauses. To use merely a comma creates a kind of run-on sentence known as a *comma splice.* (See 20.)

▶ In 1800, a traveler needed six weeks to get from New York City to Chicago; in 1860, the trip by railroad took only two days.

**TIP:** Do not overuse the semicolon as a means of revising run-on sentences. For other revision strategies, see 20a, 20c, and 20d.

**34b** Use a semicolon between independent clauses linked with a transitional expression.

Transitional expressions include conjunctive adverbs and transitional phrases.

**CONJUNCTIVE ADVERBS**

| | | | |
|---|---|---|---|
| accordingly | anyway | certainly | conversely |
| also | besides | consequently | finally |

**SCHOLARS ON THE SEMICOLON**

Bruthiaux, Paul. "The Rise and Fall of the Semicolon: English Punctuation Theory and English Teaching Practice." *Applied Linguistics* 16 (1995): 1–14. Exploring semicolon use from the mid-sixteenth century, compared with the use of colons and dashes, Bruthiaux concludes that the semicolon may have become a marginal part of our punctuation system.

**CONJUNCTIVE ADVERBS (continued)**

| | | | |
|---|---|---|---|
| furthermore | likewise | now | then |
| hence | meanwhile | otherwise | therefore |
| however | moreover | similarly | thus |
| incidentally | nevertheless | specifically | |
| indeed | next | still | |
| instead | nonetheless | subsequently | |

**TRANSITIONAL PHRASES**

| | | |
|---|---|---|
| after all | even so | in fact |
| as a matter of fact | for example | in other words |
| as a result | for instance | in the first place |
| at any rate | in addition | on the contrary |
| at the same time | in conclusion | on the other hand |

When a transitional expression appears between independent clauses, it is preceded by a semicolon and usually followed by a comma.

▶ Many corals grow very gradually; in fact, the creation of a

coral reef can take centuries.

When a transitional expression appears in the middle or at the end of the second independent clause, the semicolon goes *between the clauses.*

▶ Most singers gain fame through hard work and dedication;

Evita, however, found other means.

Transitional expressions should not be confused with the coordinating conjunctions *and, but, or, nor, for, so,* and *yet,* which are preceded by a comma when they link independent clauses. (See 32a.)

**SCHOLARS ON THE SEMICOLON**

Shaughnessy, Mina P. *Errors and Expectations: A Guide for the Teacher of Basic Writing.* New York: Oxford UP, 1979. 14–33. Shaughnessy notes that the "semicolon usually becomes epidemic" when writers first learn its use, "especially if the teacher mistakenly promotes it as a way out of comma splices rather than as one device for stressing a close or parallel thought relationship between sentences."

**34c** Use a semicolon between items in a series containing internal punctuation.

▶ Classic science fiction sagas are *Star Trek,* with Mr. Spock⁄**;**

Battlestar Galactica, with Cylon Raiders⁄**;** and *Star Wars,*

with Han Solo, Luke Skywalker, and Darth Vader.

Without the semicolons, the reader would have to sort out the major groupings, distinguishing between important and less important pauses according to the logic of the sentence. By inserting semicolons at the major breaks, the writer does this work for the reader.

**34d** Avoid common misuses of the semicolon.

Do not use a semicolon in the following situations.

**BETWEEN A SUBORDINATE CLAUSE AND THE REST OF THE SENTENCE**

▶ Unless you brush your teeth within ten or fifteen minutes

after eating⁄**,** brushing does almost no good.

**BETWEEN AN APPOSITIVE AND THE WORD IT REFERS TO**

▶ The scientists were fascinated by the species *Argyroneta*

*aquatica*⁄**,** a spider that lives underwater.

**TO INTRODUCE A LIST**

▶ Some of my favorite film stars have home pages on the Web⁄**:**

Uma Thurman, Billy Bob Thornton, and Halle Berry.

**BETWEEN INDEPENDENT CLAUSES JOINED BY *AND, BUT, OR, NOR, FOR, SO,* OR *YET***

▶ Five of the applicants had worked with spreadsheets/, but only one was familiar with database management.

**EXCEPTIONS:** If at least one of the independent clauses contains internal punctuation, you may use a semicolon even though the clauses are joined with a coordinating conjunction.

> As a vehicle [the model T] was hard-working, commonplace, and heroic; and it often seemed to transmit those qualities to the person who rode in it. —E. B. White

Although a comma would also be correct in this sentence, the semicolon is more effective, for it indicates the relative weights of the pauses.

Occasionally, a semicolon may be used to emphasize a sharp contrast or a firm distinction between clauses joined with a coordinating conjunction.

> We hate some persons because we do not know them; and we will not know them because we hate them. —Charles Caleb Colton

**EXERCISE 34–1** Add commas or semicolons where needed in the following well-known quotations. If a sentence is correct, write "correct" after it. Answers to lettered sentences appear in the back of the book. Example:

> If an animal does something, we call it instinct; if we do the same thing, we call it intelligence. —Will Cuppy

**EXERCISE 34–1 Answers:**

a. Do not ask me to be kind; just ask me to act as though I were.
b. When men talk about defense, they always claim to be protecting women and children, but they never ask the women and children what they think.
c. When I get a little money, I buy books; if any is left, I buy food and clothes.
d. Correct
e. Wit has truth in it; wisecracking is simply calisthenics with words.

1. Standing in the middle of the road is very dangerous; you get knocked down by the traffic from both sides.
2. Correct

a. Do not ask me to be kind just ask me to act as though I were.
— Jules Renard

b. When men talk about defense they always claim to be protecting women and children but they never ask the women and children what they think. — Pat Schroeder

c. When I get a little money I buy books if any is left I buy food and clothes. — Desiderius Erasmus

d. America is a country that doesn't know where it is going but is determined to set a speed record getting there.
— Lawrence J. Peter

e. Wit has truth in it wisecracking is simply calisthenics with words. — Dorothy Parker

1. Standing in the middle of the road is very dangerous you get knocked down by the traffic from both sides.
— Margaret Thatcher

2. I do not believe in an afterlife, although I am bringing a change of underwear. — Woody Allen

3. Once the children were in the house the air became more vivid and more heated every object in the house grew more alive.
— Mary Gordon

4. We don't know what we want but we are ready to bite someone to get it. — Will Rogers

5. I've been rich and I've been poor rich is better.
— Sophie Tucker

**EXERCISE 34–2** Edit the following sentences to correct errors in the use of the comma and the semicolon. If a sentence is correct, write "correct" after it. Answers to lettered sentences appear in the back of the book. Example:

> Love is blind; envy has its eyes wide open.
>         ^

a. Strong black coffee will not sober you up, the truth is that time is the only way to get alcohol out of your system.

b. It is not surprising that our society is increasingly violent, after all, television desensitizes us to brutality at a very early age.

---

**EXERCISE 34–1 (continued)**

3. Once the children were in the house, the air became more vivid and more heated; every object in the house grew more alive.

4. We don't know what we want, but we are ready to bite someone to get it.

5. I've been rich and I've been poor; rich is better.

**EXERCISE 34–2 Answers:**

a. Strong black coffee will not sober you up; the truth is that time is the only way to get alcohol out of your system.

b. It is not surprising that our society is increasingly violent; after all, television desensitizes us to brutality at a very early age.

c. There is often a fine line between right and wrong; good and bad; truth and deception.

d. At Weight Watchers, we believe that being fat is not hereditary; it is a choice.

e. Severe, unremitting pain is a ravaging force; especially when the patient tries to hide it from others.

1. Another delicious dish is the chef's special; a roasted duck rubbed with spices and stuffed with wild rice.

2. Martin Luther King Jr. had not intended to be a preacher, initially, he had planned to become a lawyer.

3. We all assumed that the thief had been Jean's boyfriend; even though we had seen him only from the back.

4. The Victorians avoided the subject of sex but were obsessed with death, our contemporaries are obsessed with sex but avoid thinking about death.

5. Some educators believe that African American history should be taught in separate courses, others prefer to see it integrated into survey courses.

---

**ON THE WEB**

**dianahacker.com/bedhandbook**
▶ Electronic grammar exercises
  ▶ E-ex 34–1 and 34–2

---

# 35

## The colon

The colon is used primarily to call attention to the words that follow it. In addition, the colon has some conventional uses.

---

**EXERCISE 34–2 (continued)**

c. There is often a fine line between right and wrong, good and bad, truth and deception.

d. Correct

e. Severe, unremitting pain is a ravaging force, especially when the patient tries to hide it from others.

1. Another delicious dish is the chef's special, a roasted duck rubbed with spices and stuffed with wild rice.

2. Martin Luther King Jr. had not intended to be a preacher; initially, he had planned to become a lawyer.

3. We all assumed that the thief had been Jean's boyfriend, even though we had seen him only from the back.

**GRAMMAR CHECKERS** are fairly good at flagging colons that incorrectly follow a verb (*The office work includes: typing, filing, and answering the phone*). They also point out semicolons used where colons are needed, although they don't suggest revisions.

**35a** Use a colon after an independent clause to direct attention to a list, an appositive, or a quotation.

**A LIST**
The daily routine should include at least the following: twenty knee bends, fifty sit-ups, fifteen leg lifts, and five minutes of running in place.

**AN APPOSITIVE**
My roommate is guilty of two of the seven deadly sins: gluttony and sloth.

**A QUOTATION**
Consider the words of John F. Kennedy: "Ask not what your country can do for you; ask what you can do for your country."

For other ways of introducing quotations, see "Introducing quoted material" on pages 418–19.

**35b** Use a colon between independent clauses if the second summarizes or explains the first.

Faith is like love: It cannot be forced.

**NOTE:** When an independent clause follows a colon, it may begin with a capital or a lowercase letter (see 45f).

**EXERCISE 34–2 (continued)**
4. The Victorians avoided the subject of sex but were obsessed with death; our contemporaries are obsessed with sex but avoid thinking about death.
5. Some educators believe that African American history should be taught in separate courses; others prefer to see it integrated into survey courses.

**35c** Use a colon after the salutation in a formal letter, to indicate hours and minutes, to show proportions, between a title and subtitle, and between city and publisher in bibliographic entries.

> Dear Sir or Madam:
>
> 5:30 p.m.
>
> The ratio of women to men was 2:1.
>
> *The Glory of Hera: Greek Mythology and the Greek Family*
>
> Boston: Bedford, 2005

**NOTE:** In biblical references, a colon is ordinarily used between chapter and verse (Luke 2:14). The Modern Language Association recommends a period instead (Luke 2.14).

**35d** Avoid common misuses of the colon.

A colon must be preceded by a full independent clause. Therefore, avoid using it in the following situations.

#### BETWEEN A VERB AND ITS OBJECT OR COMPLEMENT

▶ Some important vitamins found in vegetables are:/ vitamin A, thiamine, niacin, and vitamin C.

#### BETWEEN A PREPOSITION AND ITS OBJECT

▶ The heart's two pumps each consist of:/ an upper chamber, or atrium, and a lower chamber, or ventricle.

#### AFTER *SUCH AS, INCLUDING,* OR *FOR EXAMPLE*

▶ The trees on our campus include many fine Japanese specimens such as:/ black pines, ginkgos, and weeping cherries.

---

**EXERCISE 35–1  Answers:**

a. Correct [Either *It* or *it* is correct.]
b. If we have come to fight, we are far too few; if we have come to die, we are far too many.
c. The travel package includes a round-trip ticket to Athens, a cruise through the Cyclades, and all hotel accommodations.
d. The media portray my generation as lazy, although polls show that we work as hard as the twentysomethings before us.
e. Fran Lebowitz has this advice for parents: "Never allow your child to call you by your first name. He hasn't known you long enough."

**EXERCISE 35–1**  Edit the following sentences to correct errors in the use of the comma, the semicolon, or the colon. If a sentence is correct, write "correct" after it. Answers to lettered sentences appear in the back of the book. Example:

> Lifting the cover gently, Luca found the source of the odd
>
> sound/: a marble in the gears.

a. We always looked forward to Thanksgiving in Vermont: It was our only chance to see our Grady cousins.
b. If we have come to fight, we are far too few, if we have come to die, we are far too many.
c. The travel package includes: a round-trip ticket to Athens, a cruise through the Cyclades, and all hotel accommodations.
d. The media portray my generation as lazy; although polls show that we work as hard as the twentysomethings before us.
e. Fran Lebowitz has this advice for parents, "Never allow your child to call you by your first name. He hasn't known you long enough."

1. Harry Potter prevails against pain and evil for one reason, his heart is pure.
2. While traveling through France, Rose visited: the Loire Valley, Chartres, the Louvre, and the McDonald's stand at the foot of the Eiffel Tower.
3. There are three types of leave; annual leave, used for vacations, sick leave, used for medical appointments and illness, and personal leave, used for a variety of personal reasons.
4. Carl Sandburg once asked these three questions, "Who paid for my freedom? What was the price? And am I somehow beholden?"
5. Amelie had four goals: to be encouraging, to be effective, to be efficient, and to be elegant.

**ON THE WEB**

**dianahacker.com/bedhandbook**
▶ Electronic grammar exercises
  ▶ E-ex 35–1

**EXERCISE 35–1 (continued)**

1. Harry Potter prevails against pain and evil for one reason: His [*or* his] heart is pure.
2. While traveling through France, Rose visited the Loire Valley, Chartres, the Louvre, and the McDonald's stand at the foot of the Eiffel Tower.
3. There are three types of leave: annual leave, used for vacations; sick leave, used for medical appointments and illness; and personal leave, used for a variety of personal reasons.
4. Carl Sandburg once asked these three questions: "Who paid for my freedom? What was the price? And am I somehow beholden?"
5. Correct

# 36

## The apostrophe

 **GRAMMAR CHECKERS** flag only some missing or misused apostrophes. They catch missing apostrophes in contractions, such as *don't.* They also flag problems with possessives (*sled dogs feet, a babys eyes*), although they miss as many problems as they identify. Only you can decide when to add an apostrophe and whether to put it before or after the *-s* in possessives.

### 36a Use an apostrophe to indicate that a noun is possessive.

Possessive nouns usually indicate ownership, as in *Tim's hat* or *the lawyer's desk.* Frequently, however, ownership is only loosely implied: *the tree's roots, a day's work.* If you are not sure whether a noun is possessive, try turning it into an *of* phrase: *the roots of the tree, the work of a day.*

#### When to add -'s

1. If the noun does not end in *-s,* add *-'s.*

   Roy managed to climb out on the driver's side.

   Thank you for refunding the children's money.

2. If the noun is singular and ends in *-s,* add *-'s.*

   Lois's sister spent last year in India.

   Sophocles's plays are among my favorites.

---

**WRITERS ON WRITING**

Lately, I've been trying to be a lot more calm about apostrophes. I still mark a fair number of them in the margin and try to help students to learn how to write "it's" for "it is" and how to recognize simple problems like the "dogs bone" and "Hashimotos brain." But I'm slowly learning how difficult such ideas are for some students in a world where apostrophes are not so important, where life goes on with or without punctuation.     —Irvin Hashimoto

**NOTE:** To avoid potentially awkward pronunciation, some writers use only the apostrophe with a singular noun ending in *-s: Sophocles'.*

| | |
|---|---|
| **ON THE WEB** | **dianahacker.com/bedhandbook**<br>▶ Language Debates<br>  ▶ -'s for singular nouns ending in -s |

### When to add only an apostrophe

If the noun is plural and ends in *-s,* add only an apostrophe.

> Both diplomats' briefcases were searched by guards.

### Joint possession

To show joint possession, use *-'s* or (*-s'*) with the last noun only; to show individual possession, make all nouns possessive.

> Have you seen Joyce and Greg's new camper?

> John's and Marie's expectations of marriage couldn't have been more different.

Joyce and Greg jointly own one camper. John and Marie individually have different expectations.

### Compound nouns

If a noun is compound, use *-'s* (or *-s'*) with the last element.

> My father-in-law's sculpture won first place.

**36b** Use an apostrophe and *-s* to indicate that an indefinite pronoun is possessive.

Indefinite pronouns refer to no specific person or thing: *everyone, someone, no one, something.* (See 62b.)

> Someone's raincoat has been left behind.

**36c** Use an apostrophe to mark omissions in contractions and numbers.

In contractions the apostrophe takes the place of missing letters.

> It's a shame that Frank can't go on the tour.

*It's* stands for *it is, can't* for *cannot.*
The apostrophe is also used to mark the omission of the first two digits of a year (*the class of '95*) or years (*the '60s generation*).

**36d** Do not use an apostrophe to form the plural of numbers, letters, abbreviations, and words mentioned as words.

An apostrophe typically is not used to pluralize numbers, letters, abbreviations, and words mentioned as words. Note the few exceptions and be consistent throughout your paper.

**PLURAL NUMBERS**   Omit the apostrophe in the plural of all numbers, including decades.

> Oksana skated nearly perfect figure 8s.
>
> The 1920s are known as the Jazz Age.

**PLURAL LETTERS**   Italicize the letter and use roman (regular) font style for the *-s* ending. Do not italicize academic grades.

Two large *J*s were painted on the door.

He received two Ds for the first time in his life.

**EXCEPTIONS:** To avoid misreading, use an apostrophe to form the plural of lowercase letters and the capital letters *A* and *I*: *p*'s, *A*'s.

Beginning readers often confuse *b*'s and *d*'s.

**MLA NOTE:** The Modern Language Association recommends using an apostrophe for the plural of both capital and lowercase letters: *J*'s, *p*'s.

**PLURAL ABBREVIATIONS**   Do not use an apostrophe to pluralize an abbreviation.

We collected only four IOUs out of forty.

Marco earned two PhDs before his thirtieth birthday.

**PLURAL OF WORDS MENTIONED AS WORDS**   Generally, omit the apostrophe to form the plural of words mentioned as words. If the word is italicized, the *-s* ending appears in roman type.

We've heard enough *maybe*s.

Words mentioned as words may also appear in quotation marks. When you choose this option, use the apostrophe.

We've heard enough "maybe's."

**36e** Avoid common misuses of the apostrophe.

Do not use an apostrophe in the following situations.

**WITH NOUNS THAT ARE NOT POSSESSIVE**

▶ Some ~~outpatient's~~ *outpatients* have special parking permits.

**IN THE POSSESSIVE PRONOUNS *ITS, WHOSE, HIS, HERS, OURS, YOURS,* AND *THEIRS***

▶ Each area has ~~it's~~ *its* own conference room.

*It's* means "it is." The possessive pronoun *its* contains no apostrophe despite the fact that it is possessive.

▶ This course was taught by a professional florist ~~who's~~ *whose* technique was Japanese.

*Who's* means "who is." The possessive pronoun is *whose*.

**EXERCISE 36–1** Edit the following sentences to correct errors in the use of the apostrophe. If a sentence is correct, write "correct" after it. Answers to lettered sentences appear in the back of the book. Example:

> We rented an art studio above a barbecue restaurant, Poor ~~Richards~~ *Richard's* Ribs.

a. This diet will improve almost anyone's health.
b. The innovative shoe fastener was inspired by the designers young son.
c. Each days menu features a different European country's dish.
d. Sue worked overtime to increase her families earnings.
e. Ms. Jacobs is unwilling to listen to students complaints about computer failures and damaged disks.

**EXERCISE 36–1   Answers:**

a. Correct
b. The innovative shoe fastener was inspired by the designer's young son.
c. Each day's menu features a different European country's dish.
d. Sue worked overtime to increase her family's earnings.
e. Ms. Jacobs is unwilling to listen to students' complaints about computer failures and damaged disks.

1. Correct
2. Three teenage sons can devour about as much food as four full-grown field hands. The only difference is that they don't do half as much work.

1. Siddhartha sat by the river and listened to its many voices.
2. Three teenage son's can devour about as much food as four full-grown field hands. The only difference is that they dont do half as much work.
3. We handle contracts with NASA and many other government agency's.
4. Patience and humor are key tools in a travelers survival kit.
5. My sister-in-law's quilts are being shown at the Fendrick Gallery.

| ON THE WEB | **dianahacker.com/bedhandbook**<br>▶ Electronic grammar exercises<br>  ▶ E-ex 36–1 |
| --- | --- |

# 37

## Quotation marks

 **GRAMMAR CHECKERS** are no help with quotation marks. They do not recognize direct and indirect quotations, they fail to identify quotation marks used incorrectly inside periods and commas, and they do not point out a missing quotation mark in a pair.

**37a** Use quotation marks to enclose direct quotations.

Direct quotations of a person's words, whether spoken or written, must be in quotation marks.

> "A foolish consistency is the hobgoblin of little minds," wrote Ralph Waldo Emerson.

**EXERCISE 36–1 (continued)**
3. We handle contracts with NASA and many other government agencies.
4. Patience and humor are key tools in a traveler's survival kit.
5. Correct

**NOTE:** Do not use quotation marks around indirect quotations. An indirect quotation reports someone's ideas without using that person's exact words.

> Ralph Waldo Emerson believed that consistency for its own sake is the mark of a small mind.

In dialogue, begin a new paragraph to mark a change in speaker.

> "Mom, his name is Willie, not William. A thousand times I've told you, it's *Willie*."
>
> "Willie is a derivative of William, Lester. Surely his birth certificate doesn't have Willie on it, and I like calling people by their proper names."
>
> "Yes, it does, ma'am. My mother named me Willie K. Mason."
>
> —Gloria Naylor

If a single speaker utters more than one paragraph, introduce each paragraph with quotation marks, but do not use closing quotation marks until the end of the speech.

## 37b Set off long quotations of prose or poetry by indenting.

The guidelines in this section are those of the Modern Language Association (MLA). The American Psychological Association (APA) and *The Chicago Manual of Style* have slightly different guidelines (see pp. 706–07 and 764–65).

When a quotation of prose runs to more than four typed lines in your paper, set it off by indenting one inch (or ten spaces) from the left margin. Quotation marks are not required because the indented format tells readers that the quotation is taken word-for-word from a source. Long quotations are ordinarily introduced by a sentence ending with a colon.

**WRITERS ON WRITING**

I quote others in order to better express my own self.

—Montaigne

After making an exhaustive study of the historical record, James Horan evaluates Billy the Kid like this:

> The portrait that emerges of [the Kid] from the thousands of pages of affidavits, reports, trial transcripts, his letters, and his testimony is neither the mythical Robin Hood nor the stereotyped adenoidal moron and pathological killer. Rather Billy appears as a disturbed, lonely young man, honest, loyal to his friends, dedicated to his beliefs, and betrayed by our institutions and the corrupt, ambitious, and compromising politicians in his time. (158)

The number in parentheses is a citation handled according to MLA style. (See 57a.)

**NOTE:** When you quote two or more paragraphs from the source, indent the first line of each paragraph an additional one-half inch (or five spaces).

When you quote more than three lines of a poem, set the quoted lines off from the text by indenting one inch (or ten spaces) from the left margin. Use no quotation marks unless they appear in the poem itself. (To quote two or three lines of poetry, see 39e.)

Although many anthologizers "modernize" her punctuation, Emily Dickinson relied heavily on dashes, using them, perhaps, as a musical device. Here, for example, is the original version of the opening stanza from "The Snake":

> A narrow Fellow in the Grass
> Occasionally rides--
> You may have met Him--did you not
> His notice sudden is--

**37c** Use single quotation marks to enclose a quotation within a quotation.

> According to Paul Eliott, Eskimo hunters "chant an ancient magic song to the seal they are after: 'Beast of the sea! Come and place yourself before me in the early morning!'"

**37d** Use quotation marks around the titles of short works: newspaper and magazine articles, poems, short stories, songs, episodes of television and radio programs, and chapters or subdivisions of books.

> Katherine Mansfield's "The Garden Party" provoked a lively discussion in our short-story class last night.

**NOTE:** Titles of books, plays, Web sites, television and radio programs, films, magazines, and newspapers are put in italics or underlined. (See 42a.)

**37e** Quotation marks may be used to set off words used as words.

Although words used as words are ordinarily italicized (see 42d), quotation marks are also acceptable. Just be sure to follow consistent practice throughout a paper.

> The words "accept" and "except" are frequently confused.
>
> The words *accept* and *except* are frequently confused.

**37f** Use punctuation with quotation marks according to convention.

This section describes the conventions used by American publishers in placing various marks of punctuation inside or outside quotation marks. It also explains how to punctuate when introducing quoted material.

### Periods and commas

Place periods and commas inside quotation marks.

> "This is a stick-up," said the well-dressed young couple. "We want all your money."

This rule applies to single quotation marks as well as double quotation marks. (See 37c.) It also applies to all uses of quotation marks: for quoted material, for titles of works, and for words used as words.

**EXCEPTION:** In the Modern Language Association's style of parenthetical in-text citations (see 57a), the period follows the citation in parentheses.

> James M. McPherson comments, approvingly, that the Whigs "were not averse to extending the blessings of American liberty, even to Mexicans and Indians" (48).

### Colons and semicolons

Put colons and semicolons outside quotation marks.

> Harold wrote, "I regret that I am unable to attend the fundraiser for AIDS research"; his letter, however, came with a substantial contribution.

### Question marks and exclamation points

Put question marks and exclamation points inside quotation marks unless they apply to the whole sentence.

> Contrary to tradition, bedtime at my house is marked by "Mommy, can I tell you a story now?"

Have you heard the old proverb "Do not climb the hill until you reach it"?

In the first sentence, the question mark applies only to the quoted question. In the second sentence, the question mark applies to the whole sentence.

**NOTE:** In MLA style for a quotation that ends with a question mark or an exclamation point, the parenthetical citation and a period should follow the entire quotation: *Rosie Thomas asks, "Is nothing in life ever straight and clear, the way children see it?" (77).*

## Introducing quoted material

After a word group introducing a quotation, choose a colon, a comma, or no punctuation at all, whichever is appropriate in context.

**FORMAL INTRODUCTION**  If a quotation has been formally introduced, a colon is appropriate. A formal introduction is a full independent clause, not just an expression such as *he said* or *she remarked.*

Morrow views personal ads in the classifieds as an art form: "The personal ad is like a haiku of self-celebration, a brief solo played on one's own horn."

**EXPRESSION SUCH AS *HE SAID***  If a quotation is introduced with an expression such as *he said* or *she remarked*—or if it is followed by such an expression—a comma is needed.

Stephan Leacock once said, "I am a great believer in luck, and I find the harder I work the more I have of it."

"You can be a little ungrammatical if you come from the right part of the country," writes Robert Frost.

**BLENDED QUOTATION**  When a quotation is blended into the writer's own sentence, either a comma or no punctuation is appropriate, depending on the way in which the quotation fits into the sentence structure.

> The future champion could, as he put it, "float like a butterfly and sting like a bee."

> Charles Hudson notes that the prisoners escaped "by squeezing through a tiny window eighteen feet above the floor of their cell."

**BEGINNING OF SENTENCE**  If a quotation appears at the beginning of a sentence, set it off with a comma unless the quotation ends with a question mark or an exclamation point.

> "We shot them like dogs," boasted Davy Crockett, who was among Jackson's troops.

> "What is it?" I asked, bracing myself.

**INTERRUPTED QUOTATION**  If a quoted sentence is interrupted by explanatory words, use commas to set off the explanatory words.

> "A great many people think they are thinking," observed William James, "when they are merely rearranging their prejudices."

If two successive quoted sentences from the same source are interrupted by explanatory words, use a comma before the explanatory words and a period after them.

> "I was a flop as a daily reporter," admitted E. B. White. "Every piece had to be a masterpiece—and before you knew it, Tuesday was Wednesday."

## 37g Avoid common misuses of quotation marks.

Do not use quotation marks to draw attention to familiar slang, to disown trite expressions, or to justify an attempt at humor.

▶ Between Thanksgiving and Super Bowl Sunday, many American wives become ̸football widows.̸

Do not use quotation marks around indirect quotations. (See also 37a.)

▶ After leaving the scene of the domestic quarrel, the officer said that ̸he was due for a coffee break.̸

Do not use quotation marks around the title of your own essay.

| ON THE WEB | **dianahacker.com/bedhandbook** <br> ▶ Electronic grammar exercises <br> ▶ E-ex 37–1 |
|---|---|

**EXERCISE 37–1** Add or delete quotation marks as needed and make any other necessary changes in punctuation in the following sentences. If a sentence is correct, write "correct" after it. Answers to lettered sentences appear in the back of the book. Example:

Gandhi once said, "An eye for an eye only ends up making the whole world blind."

**EXERCISE 37–1 Answers:**

a. As for the advertisement "Sailors have more fun," if you consider chipping paint and swabbing decks fun, then you will have plenty of it.
b. Correct
c. After winning the lottery, Juanita said that she would give half the money to charity.
d. After the movie Vicki said, "The reviewer called this flick 'trash of the first order.' I guess you can't believe everything you read."
e. Correct

a. As for the advertisement "Sailors have more fun", if you consider chipping paint and swabbing decks fun, then you will have plenty of it.
b. Even after forty minutes of discussion, our class could not agree on an interpretation of Robert Frost's poem "The Road Not Taken."
c. After winning the lottery, Juanita said that "she would give half the money to charity."
d. After the movie Vicki said, "The reviewer called this flick "trash of the first order." I guess you can't believe everything you read."
e. "Cleaning your house while your kids are still growing," quipped Phyllis Diller, "is like shoveling the walk before it stops snowing."

1. "That's the most beautiful seashell I've ever seen!", shouted Alexa.
2. "Get your head in the game, and the rest will come" advised the coach just before the whistle.
3. Gloria Steinem once twisted an old proverb like this, "A woman without a man is like a fish without a bicycle."
4. "Even when freshly washed and relieved of all obvious confections," says Fran Lebowitz, "children tend to be sticky."
5. Have you heard the Cowboy Junkies' rendition of Hank Williams's "I'm So Lonesome I Could Cry?"

# 38

## End punctuation

 **GRAMMAR CHECKERS** occasionally flag sentences beginning with words like *Why* or *Are* and suggest that a question mark may be needed. On the whole, however, grammar checkers are of little help with end punctuation. Most notably, they neglect to tell you when your sentence is missing end punctuation.

**EXERCISE 37–1 (continued)**

1. "That's the most beautiful seashell I've ever seen!" shouted Alexa.
2. "Get your head in the game, and the rest will come," advised the coach just before the whistle.
3. Gloria Steinem once twisted an old proverb like this: "A woman without a man is like a fish without a bicycle."
4. Correct
5. Have you heard the Cowboy Junkies' rendition of Hank Williams's "I'm So Lonesome I Could Cry"?

## 38a The period

Use a period to end all sentences except direct questions or genuine exclamations. Also use periods in abbreviations according to convention.

### *To end sentences*

Everyone knows that a period should be used to end most sentences. The only problems that arise concern the choice between a period and a question mark or between a period and an exclamation point.

If a sentence reports a question instead of asking it directly, it should end with a period, not a question mark.

▶ Joelle asked whether the picnic would be canceled?.
                                                    ^

If a sentence is not a genuine exclamation, it should end with a period, not an exclamation point.

▶ After years of working her way through school, Geeta finally

graduated with high honors!.
                          ^

### *In abbreviations*

A period is conventionally used in abbreviations of titles and Latin words or phrases, including the time designations for morning and afternoon.

| | | |
|---|---|---|
| Mr. | i.e. | a.m. (or AM) |
| Ms. | e.g. | p.m. (or PM) |
| Dr. | etc. | |

**NOTE:** If a sentence ends with a period marking an abbreviation, do not add a second period.

**WRITERS ON WRITING**

There's not much to be said about the period except that most writers don't reach it soon enough.       —William Zinsser

Exclamation points are the most irritating of all. Look! they say, look at what I just said! How amazing is my thought! It is like being forced to watch someone else's small child jumping up and down crazily in the center of the living room shouting to attract attention. If a sentence really has something of importance to say, something quite remarkable, it doesn't need a mark to point it out. And if it is really, after all, a banal sentence needing more zing, the exclamation point simply emphasizes its banality!

—Lewis Thomas

A period is not used with US Postal Service abbreviations for states: MD, TX, CA.

Current usage is to omit the period in abbreviations of organization names, academic degrees, and designations for eras.

| | | | | |
|---|---|---|---|---|
| NATO | UNESCO | UCLA | BS | BC |
| IRS | AFL-CIO | NIH | PhD | AD |
| USA | NAACP | SEC | RN | BCE |

## 38b The question mark

Obviously a direct question should be followed by a question mark.

What is the horsepower of a 777 engine?

If a polite request is written in the form of a question, it may be followed by a period.

Would you please send me your catalog of lilies.

**TIP:** Do not use a question mark after an indirect question, one that is reported rather than asked directly. Use a period instead.

▶ He asked me who was teaching the mythology course

this year?.
       ^

**NOTE:** Questions in a series may be followed by question marks even when they are not complete sentences.

We wondered where Calamity had hidden this time. Under the sink? Behind the furnace? On top of the bookcase?

**WRITERS ON WRITING**

Exclamation marks, also called "notes of admiration," should be sparingly used. Queen Victoria used so many of them in her letters that a sentence by her that ends with a mere full-stop seems hardly worth reading. —Robert Graves and Alan Hodge

Cut out all these exclamation points. An exclamation point is like laughing at your own joke. —F. Scott Fitzgerald

## 38c The exclamation point

Use an exclamation point after a word group or sentence to express exceptional feeling or to provide special emphasis.

> When Gloria entered the room, I switched on the lights and we all yelled, "Surprise!"

**TIP:** Do not overuse the exclamation point.

▶ In the fisherman's memory the fish lives on, increasing in

length and weight with each passing year, until at last it is

big enough to shade a fishing boat~~!~~.

This sentence doesn't need to be pumped up with an exclamation point. It is emphatic enough without it.

▶ Whenever I see Venus lunging forward to put away an

overhead smash, it might as well be me~~!~~. She does it just

the way I would!

The first exclamation point should be deleted so that the second one will have more force.

**EXERCISE 38–1**   Add appropriate end punctuation in the following paragraph.

> Although I am generally rational, I am superstitious I never walk under ladders or put shoes on the table If I spill the salt, I go into frenzied calisthenics picking up the grains and tossing them over my left shoulder As a result of these

---

**EXERCISE 38–1**

Although I am generally rational, I am superstitious. I never walk under ladders or put shoes on the table. If I spill the salt, I go into frenzied calisthenics picking up the grains and tossing them over my left shoulder. As a result of these curious activities, I've always wondered whether knowing the roots of superstitions would quell my irrational responses. Superstition has it, for example, that one should never place a hat on the bed. This superstition arises from a time when head lice were common and placing a guest's hat on the bed stood a good chance of spreading lice through the host's bed. Doesn't this make good sense? And doesn't it stand to reason that if I know that my guests don't have

curious activities, I've always wondered whether knowing the roots of superstitions would quell my irrational responses Superstition has it, for example, that one should never place a hat on the bed This superstition arises from a time when head lice were common and placing a guest's hat on the bed stood a good chance of spreading lice through the host's bed Doesn't this make good sense And doesn't it stand to reason that if I know that my guests don't have lice I shouldn't care where their hats go Of course it does It is fair to ask, then, whether I have changed my ways and place hats on beds Are you kidding I wouldn't put a hat on a bed if my life depended on it

# 39

## Other punctuation marks: the dash, parentheses, brackets, the ellipsis mark, the slash

 **GRAMMAR CHECKERS** rarely flag problems with the punctuation marks in this section: the dash, parentheses, brackets, the ellipsis mark, and the slash.

## 39a The dash

When typing, use two hyphens to form a dash (--). Do not put spaces before or after the dash. (If your word processing program has what is known as an "em-dash," you may use it instead, with no space before or after it.) Dashes are used for the following purposes.

**EXERCISE 38–1 (continued)**

lice I shouldn't care where their hats go? Of course it does. It is fair to ask, then, whether I have changed my ways and place hats on beds. Are you kidding? I wouldn't put a hat on a bed if my life depended on it!

*To set off parenthetical material that deserves emphasis*

> Everything that went wrong—from the peeping Tom at her window last night to my head-on collision today—we blamed on our move.

*To set off appositives that contain commas*

An appositive is a noun or noun phrase that renames a nearby noun. Ordinarily most appositives are set off with commas (32e), but when the appositive itself contains commas, a pair of dashes helps readers see the relative importance of all the pauses.

> In my hometown the basic needs of people—food, clothing, and shelter—are less costly than in a big city like Los Angeles.

*To prepare for a list, a restatement, an amplification, or a dramatic shift in tone or thought*

> Along the wall are the bulk liquids—sesame seed oil, honey, safflower oil, and that half-liquid "peanuts only" peanut butter.

> Consider the amount of sugar in the average person's diet— 104 pounds per year, 90 percent more than that consumed by our ancestors.

> Everywhere we looked there were little kids—a box of Cracker Jacks in one hand and mommy or daddy's sleeve in the other.

> Kiere took a few steps back, came running full speed, kicked a mighty kick—and missed the ball.

> Laws now restrict the activities of one of the most cunning predators—the telemarketer.

**WRITERS ON WRITING**

The most frequent use of the dash is in pairs, to interrupt and set off a thought, long or short, which does not form an integral part of the sentence. In this capacity it serves somewhat the same purpose as the parentheses, though writers who like distinctions tend to think of the latter as slipping in a thought under the breath, perhaps for explanation, whereas the paired dashes throw in a fresh, not easily assimilable thought. —Wilson Follett

In the first two examples, the writer could also use a colon. (See 35a.) The colon is more formal than the dash and not quite as dramatic.

**TIP:** Unless there is a specific reason for using the dash, avoid it. Unnecessary dashes create a choppy effect.

▶ Insisting that students use computers as instructional

    tools⁻⁄for information retrieval⁻⁄makes good sense. Herding

    them⁻⁄sheeplike⁻⁄into computer technology does not.

## 39b Parentheses

Use parentheses to enclose supplemental material, minor digressions, and afterthoughts.

> After taking her vital signs (temperature, pulse, and blood pressure), the nurse made Becky as comfortable as possible.

> The weights James was first able to move (not lift, mind you) were measured in ounces.

Use parentheses to enclose letters or numbers labeling items in a series.

> Regulations stipulated that only the following equipment could be used on the survival mission: (1) a knife, (2) thirty feet of parachute line, (3) a book of matches, (4) two ponchos, (5) an *E* tool, and (6) a signal flare.

**TIP:** Do not overuse parentheses. Rough drafts are likely to contain more afterthoughts than necessary. As writers head into a sentence, they often think of additional details, occasionally working them in as best they can with parentheses.

---

### WRITERS ON WRITING

Its overuse is [the dash's] greatest danger, and the writer who can't resist dashes may be suspected of uncoordinated thinking.
        —Bergen Evans and Cornelia Evans

One has to dismount from an idea, and get into the saddle again, at every parenthesis.         —Oliver Wendell Holmes Sr.

[Lionell Trilling] returned [my] paper with a wounding reprimand: "Never, never begin an essay with a parenthesis in the first sentence." Ever since then, I've made a point of starting out with a parenthesis in the first sentence.         —Cynthia Ozick

Usually such sentences should be revised so that the additional details no longer seem to be afterthoughts.

*from thirteen to eighteen million*
► Researchers have said that ~~thirteen million (estimates run as~~
^
~~high as eighteen million)~~ Americans have diabetes.

## 39c Brackets

Use brackets to enclose any words or phrases that you have inserted into an otherwise word-for-word quotation.

> *Audubon* reports that "if there are not enough young to balance deaths, the end of the species [California condor] is inevitable."

The sentence quoted from the *Audubon* article did not contain the words *California condor* (since the context made clear what species was meant), so the writer needed to add the name in brackets.

The Latin word "sic" in brackets indicates that an error in a quoted sentence appears in the original source.

> According to the review, Nelly Furtado's performance was brilliant, "exceding [sic] the expectations of even her most loyal fans."

Do not overuse "sic," however, since calling attention to others' mistakes can appear snobbish. The preceding quotation, for example, might have been paraphrased instead: *According to the review, even Nelly Furtado's most loyal fans were surprised by the brilliance of her performance.*

### WRITERS ON WRITING

My attitude toward punctuation is that it ought to be as conventional as *possible.* The game of golf would lose a great deal if croquet mallets and billiard cues were allowed on the putting green. You ought to be able to show that you can do it a good deal better than anyone else with the regular tools before you have a license to bring in your own improvements.                 —Ernest Hemingway

## 39d The ellipsis mark

The ellipsis mark consists of three spaced periods. Use an ellipsis mark to indicate that you have deleted words from an otherwise word-for-word quotation.

> Reuben reports that "when the amount of cholesterol circulating in the blood rises over . . . 300 milligrams per 100, the chances of a heart attack increase dramatically."

If you delete a full sentence or more in the middle of a quoted passage, use a period before the three ellipsis dots.

> "Most of our efforts," writes Dave Erikson, "are directed toward saving the bald eagle's wintering habitat along the Mississippi River. . . . It's important that the wintering birds have a place to roost, where they can get out of the cold wind."

**TIP:** Ordinarily, do not use the ellipsis mark at the beginning or at the end of a quotation. Readers will understand that the quoted material is taken from a longer passage. If you have cut some words from the end of the final sentence quoted, however, MLA requires an ellipsis mark, as in the second example on page 599.

In quoted poetry, use a full line of ellipsis dots to indicate that you have dropped a line or more from the poem.

> Had we but world enough, and time,
> This coyness, lady, were no crime.
> . . . . . . . . . . . . . . . . . . . . . . . . . . . . . .
> But at my back I always hear
> Time's winged chariot hurrying near;
> —Andrew Marvell

The ellipsis mark may also be used to indicate a hesitation or an interruption in speech or to suggest unfinished thoughts.

> "The apartment building next door . . . it's going up in flames!" yelled Marcia.

> Before falling into a coma, the victim whispered, "It was a man with a tattoo on his . . . ."

## 39e The slash

Use the slash to separate two or three lines of poetry that have been run into your text. Add a space both before and after the slash.

> In the opening lines of "Jordan," George Herbert pokes gentle fun at popular poems of his time: "Who says that fictions only and false hair / Become a verse? Is there in truth no beauty?"

More than three lines of poetry should be handled as an indented quotation. (See 37b.)

The slash may occasionally be used to separate paired terms such as *pass/fail* and *producer/director.* Do not use a space before or after the slash.

> Roger, the producer/director, announced a casting change.

Be sparing, however, in this use of the slash. In particular, avoid the use of *and/or, he/she,* and *his/her.* Instead of using *he/she* and *his/her* to solve sexist language problems, you can usually find more graceful alternatives. (Also see 17f and 22a.)

▶ ~~Each camper was~~ All campers were on ~~his or her~~ their own during free swim.

---

**EXERCISE 39–1**    Edit the following sentences to correct errors in punctuation, focusing especially on appropriate use of the dash, parentheses, brackets, ellipsis mark, and slash. If a sentence is correct, write "correct" after it. Answers to lettered sentences appear in the back of the book. Example:

> Social insects/— bees, for example/— are able to
>
> communicate quite complicated messages to one
>
> another.

a.  A client has left his/her cell phone in our conference room.
b.  The films we made of Kilauea—on our trip to Hawaii Volcanoes National Park—illustrate a typical spatter cone eruption.
c.  Samantha selected the pass/fail option for Chemistry 101.
d.  Masahiro poked through his backpack—laptop, digital camera, guidebook—to make sure he was ready for a day's study at the Ryoanji Temple garden.
e.  Of three engineering fields, chemical, mechanical, and materials, Keegan chose materials engineering for its application to toy manufacturing.

1.  The old Valentine verse we used to chant says it all: "Sugar is sweet, /And so are you."
2.  In studies in which mothers gazed down at their infants in their cribs but remained facially unresponsive, for example, not smiling, laughing, or showing any change of expression, the infants responded with intense weariness and eventual withdrawal.
3.  There are three points of etiquette in poker: 1. always allow someone to cut the cards, 2. don't forget to ante up, and 3. never stack your chips.
4.  In *Lifeboat,* Alfred Hitchcock appears [some say without his knowledge] in a newspaper advertisement for weight loss.
5.  The writer Chitra Divakaruni explained her work with other Indian American immigrants: "Many women who came to Maitri [a women's support group in San Francisco] needed to know

**EXERCISE 39–1 (continued)**

not smiling, laughing, or showing any change of expression), the infants responded with intense weariness and eventual withdrawal. [or . . . unresponsive—for example, not smiling, laughing, or showing any change of expression—the infants responded. . . .]
3.  There are three points of etiquette in poker: (1) always allow someone to cut the cards, (2) don't forget to ante up, and (3) never stack your chips.
4.  In *Lifeboat,* Alfred Hitchcock appears (some say without his knowledge) in a newspaper advertisement for weight loss.
5.  Correct

simple things like opening a bank account or getting citizen-ship. . . . Many women in Maitri spoke English, but their English was functional rather than emotional. They needed someone who understands their problems and speaks their language."

**ON THE WEB**

**dianahacker.com/bedhandbook**
▶ Electronic grammar exercises
   ▶ E-ex 39–1

# Part VIII

# Mechanics

**ON THE WEB**

**dianahacker.com/bedhandbook/instructor**
- Exercise masters
- Quiz masters
- Transparency masters

433

# 40

## Abbreviations

 **GRAMMAR CHECKERS** can flag a few inappropriate abbreviations, such as *Xmas* and *e.g.*, but do not assume that a program will catch all problems with abbreviations.

**40a** Use standard abbreviations for titles immediately before and after proper names.

| TITLES BEFORE PROPER NAMES | TITLES AFTER PROPER NAMES |
|---|---|
| Mr. Rafael Zabala | William Albert Sr. |
| Ms. Nancy Linehan | Thomas Hines Jr. |
| Mrs. Edward Horn | Anita Lor, PhD |
| Dr. Margaret Simmons | Robert Simkowski, MD |
| the Rev. John Stone | Margaret Chin, LLD |
| Prof. James Russo | Polly Stein, DDS |

Do not abbreviate a title if it is not used with a proper name.

>          *professor*
> ► My history ~~prof.~~ is an expert on race relations in South Africa.
>        ^

Avoid redundant titles such as *Dr. Amy Day, MD.* Choose one title or the other: *Dr. Amy Day* or *Amy Day, MD.*

**40b** Use abbreviations only when you are sure your readers will understand them.

Familiar abbreviations, written without periods, are acceptable.

**WRITERS ON WRITING**

There is no royal path to good writing; and such paths as exist do not lead through neat critical gardens, various as they are, but through the jungles of self, the world, and of craft.

        — Jessamyn West

Having imagination, it takes you an hour to write a paragraph that, if you were unimaginative, would take you only a minute. Or you might not write the paragraph at all.      —Franklin P. Adams

You don't write because you want to say something; you write because you've got something to say.      —F. Scott Fitzgerald

| | | | |
|---|---|---|---|
| CIA | FBI | MD | NAACP |
| NBA | NEA | PhD | CD-ROM |
| YMCA | CBS | USA | ESL |

Talk show host Conan O'Brien is a Harvard graduate with a BA in history.

The YMCA has opened a new gym close to my office.

**NOTE:** When using an unfamiliar abbreviation (such as NASW for National Association of Social Workers) throughout a paper, write the full name followed by the abbreviation in parentheses at the first mention of the name. Then use the abbreviation throughout the rest of the paper.

## 40c  Use BC, AD, a.m., p.m., No., and $ only with specific dates, times, numbers, and amounts.

The abbreviation BC ("before Christ") follows a date, and AD (*"anno Domini"*) precedes a date. Acceptable alternatives are BCE ("before the common era") and CE ("common era"), both of which follow a date.

| | | |
|---|---|---|
| 40 BC (or 40 BCE) | 4:00 a.m. (or AM) | No. 12 (or no. 12) |
| AD 44 (or 44 CE) | 6:00 p.m. (or PM) | $150 |

Avoid using a.m., p.m., No., or $ when not accompanied by a specific figure.

▶ We set off for the lake early in the ~~a.m.~~ *morning.*

## 40d  Be sparing in your use of Latin abbreviations.

Latin abbreviations are acceptable in footnotes and bibliographies and in informal writing for comments in parentheses.

---

**WRITERS ON WRITING**

The first rule for a good style is to have something to say; in fact, this in itself is almost enough.　　　　　—Schopenhauer

In many ways writing is the act of saying *I*, of imposing oneself upon other people, of saying *listen to me, see it my way, change your mind.*　　　　　—Joan Didion

cf. (Latin *confer*, "compare")
e.g. (Latin *exempli gratia*, "for example")
et al. (Latin *et alia*, "and others")
etc. (Latin *et cetera*, "and so forth")
i.e. (Latin *id est*, "that is")
N.B. (Latin *nota bene*, "note well")

Harold Simms et al., *The Race for Space*

Alfred Hitchcock directed many classic thrillers (e.g., *Psycho, Rear Window,* and *Vertigo*).

In formal writing, use the appropriate English phrases.

▶ Many obsolete laws remain on the books, e̶.̶g̶.̶, *for example,* a law in

Vermont forbidding an unmarried man and woman to sit

closer than six inches apart on a park bench.

## 40e Avoid inappropriate abbreviations.

In formal writing, abbreviations for the following are not commonly accepted: personal names, units of measurement, days of the week, holidays, months, courses of study, divisions of written works, states, and countries (except in complete addresses and except Washington, DC). Do not abbreviate *Company* and *Incorporated* unless their abbreviated forms are part of an official name.

**PERSONAL NAME**   Charles (not Chas.)

**UNITS OF MEASUREMENT**   pound (not lb.)

**DAYS OF THE WEEK**   Monday (not Mon.)

**HOLIDAYS**   Christmas (not Xmas)

**MONTHS**   January, February, March (not Jan., Feb., Mar.)

**EXERCISE 40–1   Answers:**

a. Correct
b. Some combat soldiers are trained by government diplomats to be sensitive to issues of culture, history, and religion.
c. Correct
d. How many pounds have you lost since you began running four miles a day?
e. Denzil spent all night studying for his psychology exam.

1. My favorite professor, Dr. Barker, is on sabbatical this semester.
2. Correct
3. Correct

**COURSES OF STUDY**    political science (not poli. sci.)

**DIVISIONS OF WRITTEN WORKS**    chapter, page (not ch., p.)

**STATES AND COUNTRIES**    Massachusetts (not MA or Mass.)

**PARTS OF A BUSINESS NAME**    Adams Lighting Company (not Adams Lighting Co.); Kim and Brothers (not Kim and Bros.)

▶ Eliza promised to buy me one ~~lb.~~ *pound* of Godiva chocolate for my birthday, which was last ~~Fri.~~ *Friday.*

**EXERCISE 40–1**    Edit the following sentences to correct errors in abbreviations. If a sentence is correct, write "correct" after it. Answers to lettered sentences appear in the back of the book. Example:

> This year ~~Xmas~~ *Christmas* will fall on a ~~Tues.~~ *Tuesday.*

a. Since its inception, the BBC has maintained a consistently high standard of radio and television broadcasting.
b. Some combat soldiers are trained by govt. diplomats to be sensitive to issues of culture, history, and religion.
c. "Mahatma" Gandhi has inspired many modern leaders, including Martin Luther King Jr.
d. How many lb. have you lost since you began running four miles a day?
e. Denzil spent all night studying for his psych. exam.

1. My favorite prof., Dr. Barker, is on sabbatical this semester.
2. When we visited NYU in early September, we were charmed by the lull of summer crickets in Washington Square Park.
3. Some historians think that the New Testament was completed by AD 100.
4. My mother's birthday was on Fri. the 13th this year.
5. Many first-time users of Flash panic before the complex menus— i.e., some develop a blank stare and the tingling of a migraine.

**EXERCISE 40–1 (continued)**

4. My mother's birthday was on Friday the 13th this year.
5. Many first-time users of Flash panic before the complex menus—that is, some develop a blank stare and the tingling of a migraine.

**WRITERS ON WRITING**

Don't fake enthusiasms. Say what you think, not what you think you ought to think.                    —Darcy O'Brien

If you can speak what you will never hear, if you can write what you will never read, you have done rare things.
                    —Henry David Thoreau

| ON THE WEB | **dianahacker.com/bedhandbook**<br>▶ Electronic grammar exercises<br>   ▶ E-ex 40–1 |

# 41

## Numbers

 **GRAMMAR CHECKERS** can tell you to spell out certain numbers, such as *thirty-three* and numbers that begin a sentence, but they won't help you understand when it is acceptable to use figures.

**41a** Spell out numbers of one or two words or those that begin a sentence. Use figures for numbers that require more than two words to spell out.

▶ It's been ~~8~~ *eight* years since I visited Peru.

▶ I counted ~~one hundred seventy-six~~ *176* DVDs on the shelf.

If a sentence begins with a number, spell out the number or rewrite the sentence.

▶ *One hundred fifty* ~~150~~ children in our program need expensive dental treatment.

Rewriting the sentence will also correct the error and may be less awkward if the number is long: *In our program, 150 children need expensive dental treatment.*

---

**WRITERS ON WRITING**

A writer's job is sticking his [or her] neck out.     —Sloan Wilson

**EXCEPTIONS:** In technical and some business writing, figures are preferred even when spellings would be brief, but usage varies. When in doubt, consult the style guide of the organization for which you are writing.

When several numbers appear in the same passage, many writers choose consistency rather than strict adherence to the rule.

When one number immediately follows another, spell out one and use figures for the other: *three 100-meter events, 25 four-poster beds.*

**41b** Generally, figures are acceptable for dates, addresses, percentages, fractions, decimals, scores, statistics and other numerical results, exact amounts of money, divisions of books and plays, pages, identification numbers, and the time.

**DATES**    July 4, 1776, 56 BC, AD 30

**ADDRESSES**    77 Latches Lane, 519 West 42nd Street

**PERCENTAGES**    55 percent (or 55%)

**FRACTIONS, DECIMALS**    ½, 0.047

**SCORES**    7 to 3, 21–18

**STATISTICS**    average age 37, average weight 180

**SURVEYS**    4 out of 5

**EXACT AMOUNTS OF MONEY**    $105.37, $106,000

**DIVISIONS OF BOOKS**    volume 3, chapter 4, page 189

**DIVISIONS OF PLAYS**    act 3, scene 3 (or act III, scene iii)

**IDENTIFICATION NUMBERS**    serial number 10988675

**TIME OF DAY**    4:00 p.m., 1:30 a.m.

▶ Several doctors put up ~~two hundred fifty-five thousand dollars~~ *$255,000* for the construction of a golf course.

**NOTE:** When not using *a.m.* or *p.m.*, write out the time in words (*two o'clock in the afternoon, twelve noon, seven in the morning*).

**EXERCISE 41–1**  Edit the following sentences to correct errors in the use of numbers. If a sentence is correct, write "correct" after it. Answers to lettered sentences appear in the back of the book. Example:

$3.06
By the end of the evening, Ashanti had only ~~three dollars and six cents~~ left.
                                          ^

a.  The carpenters located 3 maple timbers, 21 sheets of cherry, and 10 oblongs of polished ebony for the theater set.
b.  The program's cost is well over one billion dollars.
c.  The score was tied at 5–5 when the momentum shifted and carried the Standards to a decisive 12–5 win.
d.  8 students in the class had been labeled "learning disabled."
e.  The Vietnam Veterans Memorial in Washington, DC, had fifty-eight thousand one hundred thirty-two names inscribed on it when it was dedicated in 1982.

1.  One of my favorite scenes in Shakespeare is the property division scene in act 1 of *King Lear.*
2.  The botany lecture will begin at precisely 3:30 p.m.
3.  50 percent of the gamers who play *The Sims* are female.
4.  In two thousand and four, Fox TV's *American Idol* earned more advertising dollars than any other reality show.
5.  On a normal day, I spend at least 4 to 5 hours surfing the Internet.

**ON THE WEB**  **dianahacker.com/bedhandbook**
▶  Electronic grammar exercises
  ▶  E-ex 41–1

**EXERCISE 41–1  Answers:**
a.  The carpenters located three maple timbers, twenty-one sheets of cherry, and ten oblongs of polished ebony for the theater set.
b.  Correct
c.  Correct
d.  Eight students in the class had been labeled "learning disabled."
e.  The Vietnam Veterans Memorial in Washington, DC, had 58,132 names inscribed on it when it was dedicated in 1982.

1.  Correct
2.  Correct
3.  Fifty percent of the gamers who play *The Sims* are female.

# 42

## Italics (underlining)

*Italics*, a slanting font style used in printed material, can be produced by word processing programs. In handwritten or typed papers, <u>underlining</u> is used instead. Some instructors prefer underlining even though their students can produce italics.

**NOTE:** Some e-mail systems do not allow for italics or underlining. Many people indicate words that should be italicized by preceding and ending them with underscore marks or asterisks. Punctuation should follow the coding.

> I am planning to write my senior thesis on _Memoirs of a
> Geisha_.

In less formal e-mail messages, normally italicized words aren't marked at all.

> I finally finished reading Memoirs of a Geisha--what
> a story!

**TIP:** In World Wide Web documents, underlining indicates a hot link. When creating a Web document, use italics, not underlining, for the conventions described in this section.

 **GRAMMAR CHECKERS** do not flag problems with italics or underlining.

---

**EXERCISE 41–1 (continued)**

4. In 2004, Fox TV's *American Idol* earned more advertising dollars than any other reality show.
5. On a normal day, I spend at least four to five hours surfing the Internet.

**42a** Underline or italicize the titles of works according to convention.

Titles of the following works, including electronic works, should be underlined or italicized.

**TITLES OF BOOKS** *The Color Purple, Middlesex, Encarta*

**MAGAZINES** *Time, Scientific American, Salon.com*

**NEWSPAPERS** the *Baltimore Sun*, the *New York Times on the Web*

**PAMPHLETS** *Common Sense, Facts about Marijuana*

**LONG POEMS** *The Waste Land, Paradise Lost*

**PLAYS** *King Lear, Rent*

**FILMS** *Casablanca, American Beauty*

**TELEVISION PROGRAMS** *Survivor, 60 Minutes*

**RADIO PROGRAMS** *All Things Considered*

**MUSICAL COMPOSITIONS** *Porgy and Bess*

**CHOREOGRAPHIC WORKS** *Brief Fling*

**WORKS OF VISUAL ART** Rodin's *The Thinker*

**COMIC STRIPS** *Dilbert*

**ELECTRONIC DATABASES** *InfoTrac*

**WEB SITES** *ZDNet, Google*

**ELECTRONIC GAMES** *Free Cell, Zuma*

The titles of other works, such as short stories, essays, episodes of radio and television programs, songs, and short poems, are enclosed in quotation marks. (See 37d.)

**NOTE:** Do not use underlining or italics when referring to the Bible, titles of books in the Bible (Genesis, not *Genesis*), or titles of legal documents (the Constitution, not the *Consti-*

**WRITERS ON WRITING**

Literature is strewn with the wreckage of men who have minded beyond reason the opinions of others. —Virginia Woolf

The ancients wrote at a time when the great art of writing badly had not yet been invented. In those days to write at all meant to write well. —G. C. Lichtenberg

The reason why so few good books are written is that so few people who can write know anything. —Walter Bagehot

Writing doesn't get easier with experience. The more you know, the harder it is to write. —Tim O'Brien

When I stepped from hard manual work to writing, I just stepped from one kind of hard work to another. —Sean O'Casey

*tution*). Do not underline the titles of computer software (WordPerfect, Photoshop). Do not underline the title of your own paper.

**42b** Underline or italicize the names of spacecraft, aircraft, ships, and trains.

> *Challenger, Spirit of St. Louis, Queen Mary 2, Silver Streak*

▶ The success of the Soviets' <u>Sputnik</u> galvanized the US

space program.

**42c** Underline or italicize foreign words used in an English sentence.

▶ Caroline's <u>joie de vivre</u> should be a model for all of us.

**EXCEPTION:** Do not underline or italicize foreign words that have become a standard part of the English language — "laissez-faire," "fait accompli," "modus operandi," and "per diem," for example.

**42d** Underline or italicize words mentioned as words, letters mentioned as letters, and numbers mentioned as numbers.

▶ Tim assured us that the howling probably came from

his bloodhound, Hill Billy, but his <u>probably</u> stuck in

our minds.

---

**WRITERS ON WRITING**

Writing a book is like driving a car at night. You only see as far as your headlights go, but you can make the whole trip that way.
—E. L. Doctorow

To hold a pen is to be at war.                    —Voltaire

Writing is easy; all you do is sit staring at a blank sheet of paper until the drops of blood form on your forehead.     —Gene Fowler

Wearing down seven number two pencils is a good day's work.
—Ernest Hemingway

► Sarah called her father by his given name, Johnny, but she

was unable to pronounce the J.

► A big 3 was painted on the door.

**NOTE:** Quotation marks may be used instead of underlining or italics to set off words mentioned as words. (See 37e.)

## 42e Avoid excessive underlining or italics for emphasis.

Underlining or italicizing to emphasize words or ideas is distracting and should be used sparingly.

► In-line skating is a popular sport that has become almost

an addiction.

**EXERCISE 42–1**   Edit the following sentences to correct errors in the use of italics. If a sentence is correct, write "correct" after it. Answers to lettered sentences appear in the back of the book. Example:

We had a lively discussion about Gini Alhadeff's memoir

The Sun at Midday.

a. Howard Hughes commissioned the Spruce Goose, a beautifully built but thoroughly impractical wooden aircraft.
b. The old man *screamed* his anger, *shouting* to all of us, "I will not leave my money to you worthless layabouts!"
c. I learned the Latin term ad infinitum from an old nursery rhyme about fleas: "Great fleas have little fleas upon their back to bite 'em, / Little fleas have lesser fleas and so on ad infinitum."

**EXERCISE 42–1   Answers:**

a. Howard Hughes commissioned the *Spruce Goose*, a beautifully built but thoroughly impractical wooden aircraft.
b. The old man screamed his anger, shouting to all of us, "I will not leave my money to you worthless layabouts!"
c. I learned the Latin term *ad infinitum* from an old nursery rhyme about fleas: "Great fleas have little fleas upon their back to bite 'em, / Little fleas have lesser fleas and so on *ad infinitum.*"
d. Correct
e. Neve Campbell's lifelong interest in ballet inspired her involvement in the film *The Company,* which portrays a season with the Joffrey Ballet.

d. Cinema audiences once gasped at hearing the word *damn* in *Gone with the Wind.*

e. Neve Campbell's lifelong interest in ballet inspired her involvement in the film "The Company," which portrays a season with the Joffrey Ballet.

1. Yasmina spent a year painting white flowers in imitation of Georgia O'Keeffe's Calla Lilies.

2. On the monastery walls are murals depicting scenes from the book of Kings and the book of Proverbs.

3. My per diem allowance was two hundred dollars.

4. Cecily watched in amazement as the tattoo artist made angles and swooping loops into the Gothic letter G.

5. The blend of poetic lyrics and progressive instruments on Seal's "Human Being " makes it one of my favorite CDs.

| ON THE WEB | **dianahacker.com/bedhandbook** |
|---|---|
| | ▶ Electronic grammar exercises |
| | ▶ E-ex 42–1 |

# 43

## Spelling

You learned to spell from repeated experience with words in both reading and writing, but especially writing. Words have a look, a sound, and even a feel to them as the hand moves across the page. As you proofread, you can probably tell if a word doesn't look quite right. In such cases, the solution is obvious: Look up the word in the dictionary.

**EXERCISE 42–1 (continued)**

1. Yasmina spent a year painting white flowers in imitation of Georgia O'Keeffe's *Calla Lilies.*

2. Correct

3. Correct

4. Cecily watched in amazement as the tattoo artist made angles and swooping loops into the Gothic letter *G.*

5. The blend of poetic lyrics and progressive instruments on Seal's *Human Being* makes it one of my favorite CDs.

> ☑ **SPELL CHECKERS** are useful alternatives to a dictionary, but only to a point. A spell checker will not tell you how to spell words not listed in its dictionary; nor will it help you catch words commonly confused, such as *accept* and *except*, or some typographical errors, such as *own* for *won*. You will still need to proofread, and for some words you may need to turn to the dictionary.

## 43a Become familiar with your dictionary.

A good dictionary, whether print or online—such as *The American Heritage Dictionary of the English Language, The Random House College Dictionary, Merriam-Webster's Collegiate Dictionary,* or *Webster's New World Dictionary of the American Language*—is an indispensable writer's aid.

A sample print dictionary entry, taken from *The American Heritage Dictionary,* appears on the following page. Labels show where various kinds of information about a word can be found in that dictionary.

A sample online dictionary entry, taken from *Merriam-Webster Online,* appears on page 448.

### Spelling, word division, pronunciation

The main entry (*re•gard* in the sample entries) shows the correct spelling of the word. When there are two correct spellings of a word (as in *collectible, collectable,* for example), both are given, with the preferred spelling usually appearing first.

The main entry also shows how the word is divided into syllables. The dot between *re* and *gard* separates the word's two syllables and indicates where the word should be divided if it can't fit at the end of a line of type (see 44f). When a word is compound, the main entry shows how to write it: as one word (*crossroad*), as a hyphenated word (*cross-stitch*), or as two words (*cross section*).

---

**WRITERS ON WRITING**

I knew I couldn't spell but I knew I could write.

—Stephen J. Cannell

The word's pronunciation is given just after the main entry. The accents indicate which syllables are stressed; the other marks are explained in the dictionary's pronunciation key. In print dictionaries this key usually appears at the

**PRINT DICTIONARY ENTRY**

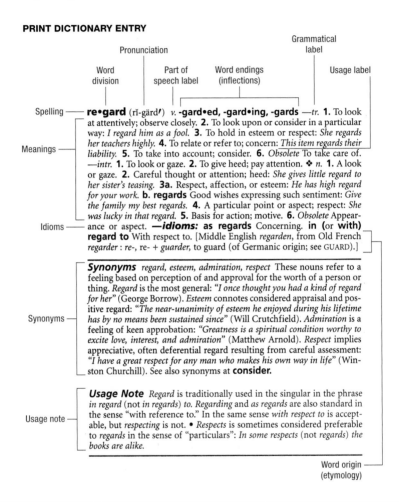

**SCHOLARS ON SPELLING**

"Vygotsky and the Bad Speller's Nightmare." *English Journal* 80.8 (1991): 65–70. The anonymous author of this article is a high school English teacher who never could, and still cannot, spell. He describes his experiences writing doctoral comprehensive exams in English education, arguing that spelling problems are not an "error in thinking." Instead, following Vygotsky, the author suggests that bad spellers are merely "displaying a faulty translation of perfectly sensible inner speech." The writer proposes that students with spelling problems need more effective editing strategies, familiarity with spelling aids, and opportunities for multiple revisions.

bottom of every page or every other page. Many online entries include an audio link to a person's voice pronouncing the word. And most online dictionaries have an audio pronunciation guide.

**ONLINE DICTIONARY ENTRY**

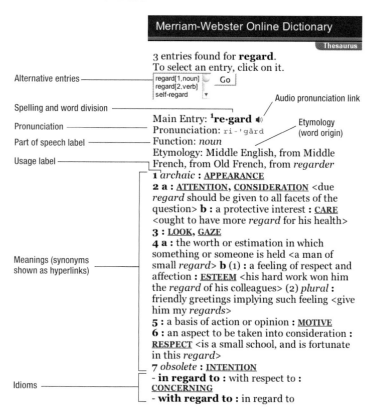

Merriam-Webster Online Dictionary

Thesaurus

3 entries found for **regard**.
To select an entry, click on it.

Alternative entries — regard[1,noun]   Go
regard[2,verb]
self-regard

Audio pronunciation link

Spelling and word division —

Pronunciation —
Part of speech label —
Usage label —

Main Entry: ¹**re·gard** ◄))
Pronunciation: ri-'gärd
Function: *noun*
Etymology: Middle English, from Middle French, from Old French, from *regarder*

Etymology (word origin)

**1** *archaic* : APPEARANCE
**2 a** : ATTENTION, CONSIDERATION <due *regard* should be given to all facets of the question> **b** : a protective interest : CARE <ought to have more *regard* for his health>
**3** : LOOK, GAZE
**4 a** : the worth or estimation in which something or someone is held <a man of small *regard*> **b** (1) : a feeling of respect and affection : ESTEEM <his hard work won him the *regard* of his colleagues> (2) *plural* : friendly greetings implying such feeling <give him my *regards*>
**5** : a basis of action or opinion : MOTIVE
**6** : an aspect to be taken into consideration : RESPECT <is a small school, and is fortunate in this *regard*>
**7** *obsolete* : INTENTION

- **in regard to** : with respect to : CONCERNING
- **with regard to** : in regard to

Meanings (synonyms shown as hyperlinks) —

Idioms —

**SCHOLARS ON SPELLING**

White, Linda F. "Spelling Instruction in the Writing Center." *Writing Center Journal* 12.1 (1991): 34–47. White describes a four-lesson sequence to help students improve their spelling. Beginning with a lesson that has students explore their feelings about being labeled bad spellers, the sequence moves to a lesson on self-assessment in which students identify error patterns and tailor proofreading strategies. Following these lessons, students learn how to use tools such as dictionaries and spell checkers. The sequence ends with a lesson on the rules of spelling. White suggests that students can learn to spell, but not by memorizing or by having instructors or tutors mark every spelling error.

## Word endings and grammatical labels

When a word takes endings to indicate grammatical functions (called *inflections*), the endings are listed in boldface, as with *-garded, -garding,* and *-gards* in the sample print entry.

Labels for the parts of speech and for other grammatical terms are sometimes abbreviated, as they are in the print entry. The most commonly used abbreviations are these:

| | | | |
|---|---|---|---|
| n. | noun | adj. | adjective |
| pl. | plural | adv. | adverb |
| sing. | singular | pron. | pronoun |
| v. | verb | prep. | preposition |
| tr. | transitive verb | conj. | conjunction |
| intr. | intransitive verb | interj. | interjection |

## Meanings, word origin, synonyms, and antonyms

Each meaning for the word is given a number. Occasionally a word's use is illustrated in a quoted sentence.

Sometimes a word can be used as more than one part of speech (*regard*, for instance, can be used as either a verb or a noun). In such a case, all the meanings for one part of speech are given before all the meanings for another, as in the sample entries. The entries also give idiomatic uses of the word.

The origin of the word, called its *etymology*, appears in brackets after all the meanings in the print version; in the online version, it appears before the meanings.

Synonyms, words similar in meaning to the main entry, are frequently listed. In the sample print entry, the dictionary draws distinctions in meaning among the various synonyms. In the online entry, synonyms appear as hyperlinks. Antonyms, which do not appear in the sample entries, are words having a meaning opposite from that of the main entry.

### SCHOLARS ON SPELLING

Martin, Charles L., and Dorothy E. Ranson. "Spelling Skills of Business Students: An Empirical Investigation." *Journal of Business Communication* 27 (1990): 377–400. Recognizing the importance of spelling skills in business settings, Martin and Ranson seek answers to three questions: How widespread are spelling problems? How concerned are business educators and professionals about spelling skills? How can educators identify and help problem spellers? The authors point to numerous studies that document the increased concern with written communication skills of business students, but they point out that most studies do not address the importance of spelling. Martin and Ranson propose that spelling problems are serious, affecting readability and conveying negative impressions.

*Usage*

Usage labels indicate when, where, or under what conditions a particular meaning for a word is appropriately used. Common labels are *informal* (or *colloquial*), *slang*, *nonstandard*, *dialect*, *obsolete*, *archaic*, *poetic*, and *British*. In the print entry, two meanings of *regard* are labeled *obsolete* because they are no longer in use. The online entry has meanings labeled both *archaic* and *obsolete*.

Dictionaries sometimes include usage notes as well. In the print sample entry, the dictionary offers advice on several uses of *regard* not specifically covered by the meanings. Such advice is based on the opinions of many experts and on actual usage in current magazines, newspapers, and books.

**ON THE WEB** dianahacker.com/bedhandbook
▶ Links Library
▶ Grammar, style, and punctuation

**43b** Discriminate between words that sound alike but have different meanings.

Words that sound alike or nearly alike but have different meanings and spellings are called *homophones*. The following sets of words are so commonly confused that a good proofreader will double-check their every use.

affect (verb: to exert an influence)
effect (verb: to accomplish; noun: result)

its (possessive pronoun: of or belonging to it)
it's (contraction for *it is*)

**SCHOLARS ON SPELLING**

Meyer, Emily, and Louise Z. Smith. *The Practical Tutor.* New York: Oxford UP, 1987. 286–96. In their chapter on tutoring spelling, Meyer and Smith outline several causes for spelling problems. They suggest that instructors help students recognize patterns of error and introduce them to "a few basic principles of phonics and syllabication that underlie spelling rules." The authors offer several examples of exchanges between students and tutors, providing teachers with specific models for talking with students.

loose (adjective: free, not securely attached)
lose (verb: to fail to keep, to be deprived of)

principal (adjective: most important; noun: head of a school)
principle (noun: a general or fundamental truth)

their (possessive pronoun: belonging to them)
they're (contraction for *they are*)
there (adverb: that place or position)

who's (contraction for *who is*)
whose (possessive form of *who*)

your (possessive form of *you*)
you're (contraction of *you are*)

To check for correct use of these and other commonly confused words, consult the Glossary of Usage, which begins on page 841.

## 43c Become familiar with the major spelling rules.

### i *before* e *except after* c

Use *i* before *e* except after *c* or when sounded like *ay*, as in *neighbor* and *weigh*.

| | |
|---|---|
| **I BEFORE *E*** | relieve, believe, sieve, niece, fierce, frieze |
| ***E* BEFORE *I*** | receive, deceive, sleigh, freight, eight |
| **EXCEPTIONS** | seize, either, weird, height, foreign, leisure |

### Suffixes

**FINAL SILENT -*E*** Generally, drop a final silent -*e* when adding a suffix that begins with a vowel. Keep the final -*e* if the suffix begins with a consonant.

---

**SCHOLARS ON SPELLING**

Dobie, Ann R. "Orthographical Theory and Practice, or How to Teach Spelling." *Journal of Basic Writing* 5 (Fall 1986): 41–48. Dobie surveys research on the teaching of spelling, suggests methods to help poor spellers, and proposes frequent short periods of practice.

| | |
|---|---|
| combine, combination | achieve, achievement |
| desire, desiring | care, careful |
| prude, prudish | entire, entirety |
| remove, removable | gentle, gentleness |

Words such as *changeable, judgment, argument,* and *truly* are exceptions.

**FINAL -Y**    When adding -s or -d to words ending in -y, ordinarily change -y to -ie when the -y is preceded by a consonant but not when it is preceded by a vowel.

| | |
|---|---|
| comedy, comedies | monkey, monkeys |
| dry, dried | play, played |

With proper names ending in -y, however, do not change the -y to -ie even if it is preceded by a consonant: *the Dougherty family, the Doughertys.*

**FINAL CONSONANTS**    If a final consonant is preceded by a single vowel *and* the consonant ends a one-syllable word or a stressed syllable, double the consonant when adding a suffix beginning with a vowel.

| | |
|---|---|
| bet, betting | occur, occurrence |
| commit, committed | |

## Plurals

**-S OR -ES**    Add -s to form the plural of most nouns; add -es to singular nouns ending in -s, -sh, -ch, and -x.

| | |
|---|---|
| table, tables | church, churches |
| paper, papers | dish, dishes |

**SCHOLARS ON SPELLING**

Shaughnessy, Mina P. *Errors and Expectations: A Guide for the Teacher of Basic Writing.* New York: Oxford UP, 1979. 160–86. Shaughnessy reminds us that "the ability to spell grows slowly out of a number of different kinds of encounters with words—with sounds of words (phonological encounters), the looks of words on paper (visual encounters), the feel of words as the hand moves to form them in writing (kinesthetic encounters), and the meanings of words as they take their places in the contexts of sentences (semantic encounters)."

**ESL** Spelling varies slightly among English-speaking countries. This can prove particularly confusing for ESL students, who may have learned British or Canadian English. Following is a list of some common words spelled differently in American and British English. Consult a dictionary for others.

| AMERICAN | BRITISH |
|---|---|
| canceled, traveled | cancelled, travelled |
| color, humor | colour, humour |
| judgment | judgement |
| check | cheque |
| realize, apologize | realise, apologise |
| defense | defence |
| anemia, anesthetic | anaemia, anaesthetic |
| theater, center | theatre, centre |
| fetus | foetus |
| mold, smolder | mould, smoulder |
| civilization | civilisation |
| connection, inflection | connexion, inflexion |
| licorice | liquorice |

Ordinarily add -*s* to nouns ending in -*o* when the -*o* is preceded by a vowel. Add -*es* when it is preceded by a consonant.

radio, radios          hero, heroes

video, videos          tomato, tomatoes

**OTHER PLURALS** To form the plural of a hyphenated compound word, add -*s* to the chief word even if it does not appear at the end.

mother-in-law, mothers-in-law

English words derived from other languages such as Latin or French sometimes form the plural as they would in their original language.

medium, media          chateau, chateaux
criterion, criteria

## 43d Be alert to commonly misspelled words.

| | | | |
|---|---|---|---|
| absence | bureau | emphasize | intelligence |
| academic | business | entirely | irrelevant |
| accidentally | calendar | environment | irresistible |
| accommodate | candidate | especially | knowledge |
| achievement | cemetery | exaggerated | library |
| acknowledge | changeable | exercise | license |
| acquaintance | column | exhaust | lightning |
| acquire | commitment | existence | loneliness |
| address | committed | extraordinary | maintenance |
| all right | committee | extremely | maneuver |
| amateur | competitive | familiar | marriage |
| analyze | completely | fascinate | mathematics |
| answer | conceivable | February | mischievous |
| apparently | conscience | foreign | necessary |
| appearance | conscientious | forty | noticeable |
| arctic | conscious | fourth | occasion |
| argument | criticism | friend | occurred |
| arithmetic | criticize | government | occurrence |
| arrangement | decision | grammar | pamphlet |
| ascend | definitely | guard | parallel |
| athlete | descendant | harass | particularly |
| athletics | desperate | height | pastime |
| attendance | dictionary | humorous | permanent |
| basically | different | incidentally | permissible |
| beautiful | disastrous | incredible | perseverance |
| beginning | eighth | independence | phenomenon |
| believe | eligible | indispensable | physically |
| benefited | embarrass | inevitable | playwright |

| | | | |
|---|---|---|---|
| practically | quiet | separate | tragedy |
| precede | quite | sergeant | transferred |
| preference | quizzes | siege | tries |
| preferred | receive | similar | truly |
| prejudice | recognize | sincerely | unnecessarily |
| presence | referred | sophomore | usually |
| prevalent | restaurant | strictly | vacuum |
| privilege | rhythm | subtly | vengeance |
| proceed | roommate | succeed | villain |
| professor | sandwich | surprise | weird |
| pronunciation | schedule | thorough | whether |
| publicly | seize | tomorrow | writing |

**EXERCISE 43–1**   The following memo has been run through a spell checker. Proofread it carefully, editing the spelling and typographical errors that remain.

November 1, 2004

To:          Patricia Wise
cc:          Richard Chang
From:        Constance Mayhew
Subject:     Express Tours annual report

Thank you for agreeing to draft the annual report for Express Tours. Before you begin you're work, let me outline the initial steps.

First, its essential for you to include brief profiles of top management. Early next week, I'll provide profiles for all manages accept Samuel Heath, who's biographical information is being revised. You should edit these profiles carefully, than format them according to the enclosed instructions. We may ask you to include other employee's profiles at some point.

Second, you should arrange to get complete financial information for fiscal year 2004 from our comptroller, Richard Chang. (Helen Boyes, to, can provide the necessary figures.) When you get this information, precede according tot he plans we

---

**EXERCISE 43–1   Answer:**

November 1, 2004

To:          Patricia Wise
cc:          Richard Chang
From:        Constance Mayhew
Subject:     Express Tours annual report

Thank you for agreeing to draft the annual report for Express Tours. Before you begin your work, let me outline the initial steps.

First, it's essential for you to include brief profiles of top management. Early next week, I'll provide profiles for all managers except

discuss in yesterday's meeting. By the way, you will notice from the figures that the sale of our Charterhouse division did not significantly effect net profits.

Third, you should submit first draft of the report by December 15. I assume that you won a laser printer, but if you don't, you can submit a disk and we'll print out a draft here. Of coarse, you should proofread you writing.

I am quiet pleased that you can take on this project. If I or anyone else at Express Tours can answers questions, don't hesitate to call.

# 44

## The hyphen

 **GRAMMAR CHECKERS** can flag some, but not all, missing or misused hyphens. For example, the programs can often tell you that a hyphen is needed in compound numbers, such as *sixty-four.* They can also tell you how to spell certain compound words, such as *breakup* (not *break-up*).

**44a** Consult the dictionary to determine how to treat a compound word.

The dictionary will tell you whether to treat a compound word as a hyphenated compound (*water-repellent*), one word (*waterproof*), or two words (*water table*). If the compound word is not in the dictionary, treat it as two words.

▶  The prosecutor chose not to cross ˰-examine any witnesses.

---

**EXERCISE 43–1 (continued)**

Samuel Heath, whose biographical information is being revised. You should edit these profiles carefully, then format them according to the enclosed instructions. We may ask you to include other employees' profiles at some point.

Second, you should arrange to get complete financial information for fiscal year 2004 from our comptroller, Richard Chang. (Helen Boyes, too, can provide the necessary figures.) When you get this information, proceed according to the plans we discussed in yesterday's meeting. By the way, you will notice from the figures that the sale of our Charterhouse division did not significantly affect net profits.

▶ Imogene kept her sketches in a small note⌒book.

▶ Alice walked through the looking/glass into a backward world.

**44b** Use a hyphen to connect two or more words functioning together as an adjective before a noun.

▶ Mrs. Douglas gave Toshiko a seashell and some newspaper‑⌃wrapped fish to take home to her mother.

▶ Richa Gupta is not yet a well‑known candidate.

   *Newspaper-wrapped* and *well-known* are adjectives used before the nouns *fish* and *candidate*.

   Generally, do not use a hyphen when such compounds follow the noun.

▶ After our television campaign, Richa Gupta will be well/ known.

   Do not use a hyphen to connect *-ly* adverbs to the words they modify.

▶ A slowly/moving truck tied up traffic.

**NOTE:** In a series, hyphens are suspended.

   Do you prefer first-, second-, or third-class tickets?

---

**EXERCISE 43–1 (continued)**

Third, you should submit a [*or* the] first draft of the report by December 15. I assume that you own a laser printer, but if you don't, you can submit a disk and we'll print out a draft here. Of course, you should proofread your writing.

I am quite pleased that you can take on this project. If I or anyone else at Express Tours can answer questions, don't hesitate to call.

**44c** Hyphenate the written form of fractions and of compound numbers from twenty-one to ninety-nine.

▶ One-fourth of my income goes to pay my child care expenses.

**44d** Use a hyphen with the prefixes *all-, ex-* (meaning "former"), and *self-* and with the suffix *-elect.*

▶ The charity is funneling more money into self-help projects.

▶ Anne King is our club's president-elect.

**44e** Use a hyphen in certain words to avoid ambiguity or to separate awkward double or triple letters.

Without the hyphen there would be no way to distinguish between words such as *re-creation* and *recreation.*

Bicycling in the city is my favorite form of recreation.

The film was praised for its astonishing re-creation of nineteenth-century London.

Hyphens are sometimes used to separate awkward double or triple letters in compound words (*anti-intellectual, cross-stitch*). Always check a dictionary for the standard form of the word.

**44f** If a word must be divided at the end of a line, divide it correctly.

1. Divide words between syllables.

**WRITERS ON WRITING**

The pleasure *is* the rewriting: The first sentence can't be written until the final sentence is written. This is a koan-like statement, and I don't mean to sound needlessly obscure or mysterious, but it's simply true. The completion of any work automatically necessitates its revisioning.                — Joyce Carol Oates

▶ When I returned from my semester overseas, I didn't ~~reco-~~ *recog-*
*nize*
~~gnize~~ one face on the magazine covers.

2. Never divide one-syllable words.

▶ He didn't have the courage or the ~~stren-~~
*strength*
~~gth~~ to open the door.

3. Never divide a word so that a single letter stands alone at the end of a line or fewer than three letters begin a line.

▶ She'll bring her brother with her when she comes ~~a-~~
*again.*
~~gain.~~

▶ As audience to the play *The Mousetrap,* Hamlet is a ~~watch-~~
*watcher*
~~er~~ watching watchers.

4. When dividing a compound word at the end of a line, either make the break between the words that form the compound or put the whole word on the next line.

▶ My niece Marielena is determined to become a long-~~dis-~~
*distance*
~~tance~~ runner when she grows up.

5. To divide long e-mail and Internet addresses, do not use a hyphen. Break an e-mail address after the @ symbol or before a period. Break a URL after a colon, a slash, or a double slash or before a period or other punctuation mark.

**WRITERS ON WRITING**

Avoid theatrical flourishes—the phrases that sound so damned good that they stand up and beg to be recognized as "good writing," and therefore must be struck from the text.

—Donald Spoto

A good style must, first of all, be clear. It must not be mean or above the dignity of the subject. It must be appropriate.

—Aristotle

I revel in the prospect of being able to torture a phrase once more.

—S. J. Perelman

Be obscure clearly.

—E. B. White

I repeatedly e-mailed Janine at janine.r.rose@dunbaracademy
.org before I gave up and called her cell phone.

To find a zip code quickly, I always use the United States
Postal Service Web site at http://zip4.usps.com/zip4/
welcome.jsp.

**NOTE:** For breaks in URLs in MLA and APA documentation
styles, see 58a and 60e.

**EXERCISE 44–1**   Edit the following sentences to correct errors
in hyphenation. If a sentence is correct, write "correct" after it.
Answers to lettered sentences appear in the back of the book. Example:

> **Zola's first readers were scandalized by his slice-of-life**
> **novels.**

a. Gold is the seventy-ninth element in the periodic table.
b. The swiftly-moving tugboat pulled alongside the barge and
   directed it away from the oil spill in the harbor.
c. The Moche were a pre-Columbian people who established a
   sophisticated culture in ancient Peru.
d. Your dog is well-known in our neighborhood.
e. Road-blocks were set up along all the major highways leading
   out of the city.

1. We knew we were driving too fast when our tires skidded on the
   rain slick surface.
2. The Black Death reduced the population of some medieval
   villages by two thirds.
3. Sewing forty-eight sequined tutus for the ballet recital nearly
   made Karyn cross-eyed.
4. Olivia had hoped to find a pay as you go plan to finance the
   construction of her observatory.
5. Gail Sheehy writes that at age twenty five many people assume
   that the choices they make are irrevocable.

**EXERCISE 44–1   Answers:**

a. Correct
b. The swiftly moving tugboat pulled alongside the barge and directed it away from the oil spill in the harbor.
c. Correct
d. Your dog is well known in our neighborhood.
e. Roadblocks were set up along all the major highways leading
   out of the city.

1. We knew we were driving too fast when our tires skidded on
   the rain-slick surface.
2. The Black Death reduced the population of some medieval villages by two-thirds.

| ON THE WEB | **dianahacker.com/bedhandbook** ▶ Electronic grammar exercises ▶ E-ex 44–1 |
|---|---|

# 45

## Capital letters

In addition to the rules in this section, a good dictionary can tell you when to use capital letters.

> **GRAMMAR CHECKERS** remind you that sentences should begin with capital letters and that some words, such as *Cherokee*, are proper nouns. Many words, however, should be capitalized only in certain contexts, and you must determine when to do so.

**45a** Capitalize proper nouns and words derived from them; do not capitalize common nouns.

Proper nouns are the names of specific persons, places, and things. All other nouns are common nouns. The following types of words are usually capitalized: names for the deity, religions, religious followers, sacred books; words of family relationship used as names; particular places; nationalities and their languages, races, tribes; educational institutions, departments, degrees, particular courses; government departments, organizations, political parties; historical movements, periods, events, documents; specific electronic sources; and trade names.

---

**EXERCISE 44–1 (continued)**

3. Correct
4. Olivia had hoped to find a pay-as-you-go plan to finance the construction of her observatory.
5. Gail Sheehy writes that at age twenty-five many people assume that the choices they make are irrevocable.

| PROPER NOUNS | COMMON NOUNS |
|---|---|
| God (used as a name) | a god |
| Book of Common Prayer | a book |
| Uncle Pedro | my uncle |
| Father (used as a name) | my father |
| Lake Superior | a picturesque lake |
| the Capital Center | a center for advanced studies |
| the South | a southern state |
| Wrigley Field | a baseball stadium |
| University of Wisconsin | a good university |
| Geology 101 | geology |
| Environmental Protection Agency | a federal agency |
| Phi Kappa Psi | a fraternity |
| a Democrat | an independent |
| the Enlightenment | the eighteenth century |
| the Declaration of Independence | a treaty |
| the World Wide Web, the Web | a home page |
| the Internet, the Net | a computer network |
| Advil | a painkiller |

Months, holidays, and days of the week are treated as proper nouns; the seasons and numbers of the days of the month are not.

> Our academic year begins on a Tuesday in early September, right after Labor Day.

> My mother's birthday is in early summer, on the second of June.

**EXCEPTION:** Capitalize Fourth of July (or July Fourth) when referring to the holiday.

Names of school subjects are capitalized only if they are names of languages. Names of particular courses are capitalized.

### SCHOLARS ON CAPITALIZATION

Shaughnessy, Mina P. *Errors and Expectations: A Guide for the Teacher of Basic Writing.* New York: Oxford UP, 1979. 36–38. According to Shaughnessy, basic writers do not have many problems with capitalizing first words of sentences or proper nouns; however, they often have problems with using capitals in other places. She attributes this difficulty in part to handwriting habits or to attempts to increase emphasis and suggests that writers are not aware that it is a problem.

This semester Austin is taking math, geography, geology, French, and English.

Professor Obembe offers Modern American Fiction 501 to graduate students.

**CAUTION:** Do not capitalize common nouns to make them seem important: *Our company is currently hiring computer programmers* (not *Company, Computer Programmers*).

## 45b Capitalize titles of persons when used as part of a proper name but usually not when used alone.

Professor Margaret Barnes; Dr. Sinyee Sein; John Scott Williams Jr.; Anne Tilton, LLD

District Attorney Marshall was reprimanded for badgering the witness.

The district attorney was elected for a two-year term.

Usage varies when the title of an important public figure is used alone: *The president* [or *President*] *vetoed the bill.*

## 45c Capitalize the first, last, and all major words in titles and subtitles of works such as books, articles, songs, and online documents.

In both titles and subtitles, major words such as nouns, pronouns, verbs, adjectives, and adverbs should be capitalized. Minor words such as articles, prepositions, and coordinating conjunctions are not capitalized unless they are the first or last word of a title or subtitle. Capitalize the second part of a hyphenated term in a title if it is a major word but not if it is a minor word. Capitalize chapter titles and the titles of other major divisions of a work following the same guidelines used for titles of complete works.

**WRITERS ON WRITING**

One writes to find words' meanings.　　　　　　— Joy Williams

Words have basic inalienable meanings, departure from which is either conscious metaphor or inexcusable vulgarity.
　　　　　　　　　　　　　　　　　　—Evelyn Waugh

Words are weapons.　　　　　　　　　　—George Santayana

*Seizing the Enigma: The Race to Break the German U-Boat Codes*
"Fire and Ice"
"I Want to Hold Your Hand"
*The Canadian Green Page*
"Work and Play" in Santayana's *The Nature of Beauty*

To see why some of the titles in the list are italicized and some are put in quotation marks, see 42a and 37d.

**45d** Capitalize the first word of a sentence.

Obviously the first word of a sentence should be capitalized.

When lightning struck the house, the chimney collapsed.

When a sentence appears within parentheses, capitalize its first word unless the parentheses appear within another sentence.

Early detection of breast cancer significantly increases survival rates. (See table 2.)

Early detection of breast cancer significantly increases survival rates (see table 2).

**45e** Capitalize the first word of a quoted sentence but not a quoted phrase.

In *Time* magazine Robert Hughes writes, "There are only about sixty Watteau paintings on whose authenticity all experts agree."

Russell Baker has written that in our country, sports are "the opiate of the masses."

If a quoted sentence is interrupted by explanatory words, do not capitalize the first word after the interruption. (See 37f.)

**WRITERS ON WRITING**

The words! I collected them in all shapes and sizes and hung them like bangles in my mind. —Hortense Calisher

The South understands language. You should live there if you want to be a writer. —Rita Mae Brown

The secret of good writing is to say an old thing a new way or to say a new thing an old way. —Richard Harding Davis

"If you want to go out," he said, "tell me now."

When quoting poetry, copy the poet's capitalization exactly. Many poets capitalize the first word of every line of poetry; a few contemporary poets dismiss capitalization altogether.

> When I consider everything that grows
> Holds in perfection but a little moment          —Shakespeare

> it was the week          that
> i felt the city's narrow breezes rush about
> me                                           —Don L. Lee

**45f** Capitalize the first word after a colon if it begins an independent clause.

> I came to a startling conclusion: The house at the end of the street must be haunted.

**NOTE:** MLA and *Chicago* styles use a lowercase letter to begin an independent clause following a colon; APA style uses a capital letter.

Use lowercase after a colon to introduce a list or an appositive.

> The students were divided into two groups: residents and commuters.

**45g** Capitalize abbreviations for departments and agencies of government, other organizations, and corporations; capitalize the call letters of radio and television stations.

> EPA, FBI, OPEC, IBM, WCRB, KNBC-TV

**EXERCISE 45–1   Answers:**

a. Assistant Dean Shirin Ahmadi recommended offering more world language courses.
b. Correct
c. Kalindi has an ambitious semester, studying differential calculus, classical Hebrew, brochure design, and Greek literature.
d. Lydia's aunt and uncle make modular houses as beautiful as modernist works of art.
e. We amused ourselves on the long flight by discussing how spring in Kyoto stacks up against summer in London.

**EXERCISE 45–1** Edit the following sentences to correct errors in capitalization. If a sentence is correct, write "correct" after it. Answers to lettered sentences appear in the back of the book. Example:

On our trip to the West we visited the g̶rand c̶anyon and the
g̶reat s̶alt d̶esert.

a. Assistant dean Shirin Ahmadi recommended offering more world language courses.
b. We went to the Mark Taper Forum to see a production of *Angels in America.*
c. Kalindi has an ambitious semester, studying differential calculus, classical hebrew, brochure design, and greek literature.
d. Lydia's Aunt and Uncle make modular houses as beautiful as modernist works of art.
e. We amused ourselves on the long flight by discussing how Spring in Kyoto stacks up against Summer in London.

1. When the Ducati will not start, I try a few tricks with the ignition key: Jiggling it to the left, pulling it out a quarter of an inch, and gently pulling down on it.
2. When you slowly bake a clove of garlic, the most amazing thing happens: It loses its bitter tang and becomes sweet and buttery.
3. After World War II, aunt Helena left Poland to study in Italy.
4. When we drove through the south last summer, we were amazed to see kudzu growing wild along the road.
5. Following in his sister's footsteps, Leonid is pursuing a degree in Marketing Research.

**ON THE WEB**
**dianahacker.com/bedhandbook**
▶ Electronic grammar exercises
  ▶ E-ex 45–1

**EXERCISE 45–1 (continued)**

1. When the Ducati will not start, I try a few tricks with the ignition key: jiggling it to the left, pulling it out a quarter of an inch, and gently pulling down on it.
2. Correct [Either *It* or *it* is correct.]
3. After World War II, Aunt Helena left Poland to study in Italy.
4. When we drove through the South last summer, we were amazed to see kudzu growing wild along the road.
5. Following in his sister's footsteps, Leonid is pursuing a degree in marketing research.

# Part IX

## Critical
## Thinking

**ON THE WEB**

**dianahacker.com/bedhandbook/instructor**
▶ Exercise masters
▶ Quiz masters
▶ Transparency masters

Most college assignments, especially those based on reading, call for critical thinking: an open-minded, reasoned response to a political or scholarly debate. At times you will be asked to write a researched essay in which you draw conclusions about a variety of sources advancing different points of view (see 50–53). Many assignments, however, ask you to respond critically to just one or two texts (see 46) or to construct your own argument (see 47 and 48).

# 46

## Writing about texts

The word *texts* can refer to a variety of works: essays, periodical articles, government reports, books, and even visuals such as advertisements and photographs. Most assignments that ask you to respond to a text call for a summary or an analysis or both.

A summary is neutral in tone and demonstrates that you have understood the author's key ideas. Assignments calling for an analysis of a text vary widely, but they will usually ask you to look at how the text's parts contribute to its central argument or purpose, often with the aim of judging its evidence or overall effect.

When you write about a written text, obviously you need to read it first. Less obvious, perhaps, is the need to reread it and digest its full meaning. Two techniques will help you move beyond a superficial first reading: (1) annotating the text with your observations and questions and (2) outlining the text's key points. The same techniques will help you analyze visual texts.

Sections 46a–46d will help you understand how to write about written texts; section 46e offers advice about how to write about visual texts.

**WRITERS ON WRITING**
To read without reflecting is like eating without digesting.
—Kenneth Burke

## 46a Read actively: Annotate the text.

Read actively by jotting down your questions and thoughts in the text's margins or in a notebook. When you annotate a text as you read, you are doing something—engaging with the work, not just letting the words slip past you. Although you may be fond of using a highlighter to interact with a text, consider using a pencil instead: A pencil promotes active reading in ways that a highlighter cannot. With a highlighter, you just identify key sentences, usually on a first reading; on a second reading, you are often tempted to read only what's highlighted. More important, you can't write down your thoughts, questions, and reactions with a highlighter.

A pencil offers greater flexibility. You can underline key concepts or draw an asterisk or other symbol in the margins to mark them. And you can scribble your observations and questions all over the pages—not just on a first reading but on rereadings as well. Finally, if you change your mind while rereading, you can erase your early annotations and replace them with new ones.

**TIP:** If you are working on an electronic text, you can use the commenting tools in your word processor as you would use a pencil. Word processors also have highlighting tools, which are less restrictive than highlighting on paper—on the computer you can change your mind and remove highlighting, for instance. Using colors either in your comments or in your highlighting can also help you categorize your notes.

---

### TIPS FROM WRITING TUTORS

"While reading, I always underline, make notes on important quotes, and circle repeated imagery and phrases. After I decide on a topic for my paper, I go back and reread all of my notes and everything I've underlined, trying to make connections. Then I record quotes I think I might use for support in my paper. From there, I write my first outline."

—*Lauren M. Carlson, Gonzaga University*

---

### WRITERS ON WRITING

It's important for me to have someone read the work who won't let me get away with things. —Rick Moody

## Guidelines for active reading

*Familiarize yourself with the basic features and structure of a text.*

- What kind of text are you reading? An essay? An editorial? A scholarly article? An advertisement?
- What is the author's purpose? To inform? To persuade? To call to action?
- Who is the author's audience? How does the author attempt to appeal to the audience?
- What is the author's thesis? What question (or questions) does the text attempt to answer?
- What evidence does the author provide to support the thesis?

*Note details that surprise, puzzle, or intrigue you.*

- Has the author revealed a fact or made a point that runs counter to what you had assumed was true? What exactly is surprising?
- Has the author made a generalization you disagree with? Can you think of evidence that would challenge the generalization?
- Are there any contradictions or inconsistencies in the text that don't make sense to you?
- Are there any words, statements, or phrases in the text that you don't understand? If so, what reference materials do you need to consult?

*Read and reread to discover meaning.*

- What do you notice on a second, third, or fourth reading that you didn't notice earlier?
- Does the text raise questions that it does not resolve?
- If you could address the author directly, what questions would you pose? Where do you agree and disagree with the author? Why?

If you are examining a visual text, see the additional questions on pages 482 and 484–85.

**WRITERS ON WRITING**

As soon as I open [a book], I occupy the book, I stomp around in it. I underline passages, scribble in the margins, leave my mark. . . . I like to be able to hear myself responding to a book, answering it, agreeing and disagreeing in a manner I recognize as peculiarly my own.
—George Bernard Shaw

Following is an article with a student's annotations. The student, Carmen Lopez, was assigned to write a summary and an analysis of the article (see pp. 474–75 and 477–80). She began by annotating and then outlining the article.

---

## A Question of Ethics

**JANE GOODALL**

David Greybeard first showed me how fuzzy the distinction between animals and humans can be. Forty years ago I befriended David, a chimpanzee, during my first field trip to Gombe in Tanzania. One day I offered him a nut in my open palm. He looked directly into my eyes, took the nut out of my hand and dropped it. At the same moment he very gently squeezed my hand as if to say, I don't want it, but I understand your motives.

*Firsthand account gives her credibility.*

*Anecdote makes chimpanzee seem human.*

Since chimpanzees are thought to be physiologically close to humans, researchers use them as test subjects for new drugs and vaccines. In the labs, these very sociable creatures often live isolated from one another in 5-by-5-foot cages, where they grow surly and sometimes violent. Dogs, cats and rats are also kept in poor conditions and subjected to painful procedures. Many people would find it hard to sympathize with rats, but dogs and cats are part of our lives. Ten or 15 years ago, when the use of animals in medical testing was first brought to my attention, I decided to visit the labs myself. Many people working there had forced themselves to believe that animal testing is the only way forward for medical research.

*Examples appeal to our sympathy.*

*Why "forced"? Because no one could reasonably support animal testing? Is her statement based on researchers' words?*

Once we accept that animals are sentient beings, is it ethical to use them in research? From the point of view of the animals, it is quite simply wrong. From our standpoint, it seems ridiculous to equate a rat with a human being. If we clearly and honestly believe that using animals in research will, in the end, reduce massive human suffering, it would be difficult to argue that doing so is unethical. How do we find a way out of this dilemma?

*Goodall's central question.*

*Answer is not simple if we balance the needs of animals and humans.*

---

**WRITERS ON WRITING**

Louis Pasteur said, "Chance favors the prepared mind." If you're really engaged in the writing, you'll work yourself out of whatever jam you find yourself in.                    —Michael Chabon

One thing we can do is change our mind-set. We can begin by questioning the assumption that animals are (essential) to medical research. Scientists have concluded that chimpanzees are not useful for AIDS research because, even though their genetic makeup differs from ours by about 1 percent, their immune systems deal much differently with the AIDS virus. Many scientists test drugs and vaccines on animals simply because they are required to by law rather than out of scientific merit. This is a shame, because our medical technology is beginning to provide alternatives. We can perform many tests on cell and tissue cultures without recourse to systemic testing on animals. Computer simulations can also cut down on the number of animal tests we need to run. We aren't exploring these alternatives vigorously enough.

Ten or 15 years ago animal-rights activists resorted to violence against humans in their efforts to break through the public's terrible apathy and lack of imagination on this issue. This extremism is counterproductive. I believe that more and more people are becoming aware that to use animals thoughtlessly, without any anguish or making an effort to find another way, diminishes us as human beings.

*Jane Goodall, an animal behaviorist widely recognized as the world's foremost authority on chimpanzees, speaks and writes about wildlife conservation, animal testing, and environmental issues.*

---

### 46b Try sketching a brief outline of the text.

After reading, rereading, and annotating a text, attempt to outline it. A brief outline serves as an X-ray of the text, revealing the skeleton that lies beneath the words and visuals on the page. Seeing how the author has constructed a text can help you understand it.

---

**SCHOLARS ON CRITICAL THINKING**

*Critical Thinking Project.* Washington State U. 2004 <http://wsuctproject.wsu.edu/ctr.htm>. This project Web site offers detailed information and advice on how to assess students' higher-order thinking skills during college along with a rubric consisting of seven important dimensions of critical thinking as they can be identified in student writing. The project was begun when an assessment of junior writing portfolios at WSU revealed that students were demonstrating satisfactory proficiency in writing but were scoring low in critical thinking abilities.

As you sketch an outline, pay special attention to the text's thesis (central idea) and its topic sentences. The thesis of a written text usually appears in the introduction, often in the first or second paragraph. Topic sentences can be found at the beginnings of most body paragraphs, where they announce a shift to a new topic. (See 2a and 4b.)

In your outline, put the author's thesis and key points in your own words. Here, for example, is the outline that Carmen Lopez developed as she prepared to write her summary and analysis of the text printed on pages 471–72. Notice that the outline does not simply trace the author's ideas paragraph by paragraph; instead, it sums up the article's central points.

> **OUTLINE OF "A QUESTION OF ETHICS"**
>
> Thesis: It is wrong to use animals for scientific research if that research can be done without harming animals.
>
> I. Animals are "sentient"—feeling, conscious—and similar to human beings in many ways.
>    A. A chimpanzee can show empathy with and understanding of humans.
>    B. One of the reasons we use chimpanzees for research is that they're so similar to us.
>    C. We sympathize with animals because pets are such an important part of our lives.
>
> II. Since animals are conscious beings, it is unethical to harm them through unnecessary research.
>    A. The way animals are treated in labs is often stressful and painful to them.
>    B. Animal experimentation is not necessarily the only way to research new medicines.
>    C. Frequently the law requires animal testing even when it is not useful.
>    D. Technology has made other testing options available.

**SCHOLARS ON CRITICAL THINKING**

Sullivan, Patricia. "Composing Culture: A Place for the Personal." *College English* 66 (2003): 41–54. As part of a special issue focused on "the personal" in academic writing, Sullivan suggests that we become "students" of our students' personal narratives to see how their texts record particular cultural moments. She demonstrates, by analyzing several student narratives, what to look for in such a reading: what do the writers consider significant enough to write about, how do they convey their experiences, and how do they construct their identities and actions in relation to others around them?

**46c** Summarize to demonstrate your understanding.

Your goal in summarizing a text is to articulate an author's main idea and key points as simply and briefly as possible, without sacrificing accuracy. Since most summaries must be fairly short, part of your challenge will be in deciding what *not* to include. That means making judgments about what is most important.

---

**TIPS FROM WRITING TUTORS**

"It takes time, practice, and patience to become a good writer in any language. For native and nonnative speakers, doing lots of reading in English is also helpful. Reading for fun gives you a broad look at writing styles, more examples to learn from, and a stronger vocabulary."
— *Cari-Sue Wilmot, University of Houston*

---

When you sit down to write a summary, don't get tangled up in details: Think big. Find the author's central idea for the whole piece — the thesis — and then try to divide the whole into a few major and perhaps minor ideas. If you have sketched a brief outline of the text (see 46b), refer to it as you draft your summary.

Following is Carmen Lopez's summary of the article by Jane Goodall that is printed on pages 471–72.

> In her essay "A Question of Ethics," Jane Goodall argues that using animals for scientific research is unethical if testing can be accomplished without harming animals. Opening with an anecdote about a chimpanzee that was able to communicate his capacity for understanding, Goodall claims that animals deserve our compassion and protection because they are "sentient," or feeling, beings (62). She describes the poor conditions to which test animals are subjected and the effects that test procedures can have on their behavior. Goodall reasons

**SCHOLARS ON CRITICAL THINKING**

Paley, Karen Surman. *I-Writing: The Politics and Practice of Teaching First-Person Writing.* Carbondale: Southern Illinois UP, 2001. Paley criticizes the arguments that pit social constructionist against expressivist pedagogies. First-person narratives are valuable, she says, in helping students understand how their own experiences are "invested with political tension and the political, in turn, [is] imbued with pathos and with family memories." The first chapter offers a thoughtful discussion of how expressivism has been wrongly constructed as naive, self-absorbed, and apolitical; middle chapters report on her ethnographic research in two classrooms where the teachers teach their students critical approaches to their personal narratives; the final chapter suggests an ethics of assigning and responding to personal narratives.

## Guidelines for writing a summary

- In the first sentence, mention the title of the text, the name of the author, and the author's thesis, or central idea.
- Use a neutral tone; be objective.
- Write from the third-person point of view, and use the present tense: *Goodall argues* . . . [not *I thought that* or *You will see that*].
- Keep your focus on the author of the text. Don't state the author's ideas as if they were your own.
- Put all or most of your summary in your own words; if you borrow a phrase or a sentence from the author, put it in quotation marks and give the page number in parentheses.
- Limit yourself to presenting the author's key points.
- Be concise; make every word count.

that since scientists test drugs on chimpanzees and other species because they are genetically close to human beings, humans should consider alternatives to tests that cause animals pain. She suggests that researchers test cell and tissue cultures or use computer simulations as alternatives to animal testing.

**NOTE:** For advice on using summaries in researched writing, see 52c.

## 46d Analyze to demonstrate your critical thinking.

To analyze is to separate the whole for the purpose of studying the parts. Whereas a summary most often answers the question of *what* a text says, an analysis looks at *how* a text makes its point. When an assignment calls for an analysis, read the whole assignment carefully, along with any models provided, to see what your instructor expects.

### SCHOLARS ON CRITICAL THINKING

McComiskey, Bruce. *Teaching Composition as a Social Process.* Logan: Utah State UP, 2000. McComiskey provides a thoughtfully practical discussion of how cultural studies theory can be integrated into composition instruction. As an antidote to classroom practices centered on producing cultural critiques, he presents a series of assignments that lead students through a critical process, culminating in their own rewriting of the cultural texts being analyzed. One such assignment asks students to analyze the cultural and social values in college viewbooks. Students then produce their own version of a viewbook, representing the values and identities they think are important to develop in college. Students should be not only critical consumers of cultural texts, McComiskey argues, but also generators of alternative texts representing other perspectives.

## Guidelines for writing an analysis

Instructors who ask you to analyze a nonfiction text often expect you to address some of the following questions.

- What is the author's thesis or central idea? Who is the audience?
- What questions does the author address (implicitly or explicitly)? What questions are left unanswered?
- How does the author structure the text? What are the key parts and how do they relate to one another and to the thesis?
- What strategies has the author used to generate interest in the argument and to persuade readers of its merit?
- What evidence does the author use to support the thesis? How persuasive is the evidence?
- Does the author anticipate objections and counter opposing views? (See 47f.)
- Does the author fall prey to any faulty reasoning? (See 48.)

**NOTE:** For guidelines on analyzing a literary text, see 59. Questions for analyzing a visual text appear on pages 484–85.

Typically, your analysis will be in the form of an essay that makes its own argument about an author's text. Like other kinds of essays, your analysis should include an introduction that briefly summarizes the text, a thesis that states your own judgment about the author's text, and body paragraphs that support your thesis with details (see 2).

If you have written a summary of the text (46c), you may find it useful to refer to the main points of the summary as you write your analysis. When you summarize the author's key points, you will enhance your credibility as a writer by giving a fair reading of the text.

Following is Carmen Lopez's analysis of the article by Jane Goodall that appears on pages 471–72. Lopez used Modern Language Association (MLA) style to format her paper and cite the source.

### SCHOLARS ON CRITICAL THINKING

Galotti, Kathleen M. "Valuing Connected Knowing in the Classroom." *Clearing House* 71.5 (1998): 281–83. Galotti describes the traditional view of critical thinking as that which questions assumptions, searches for flaws in an argument, and takes nothing for granted — thinking that is rational, unemotional, rigorous, and even adversarial. Galotti discusses the ongoing work of scholars who distinguish critical thinking (*separate* knowing) from appreciative thinking (*connected* knowing). Connected knowing, unlike critical thinking, is collaborative and draws on personal experience, empathy, and a desire to consider the story behind another's perspective. Galotti raises the question of what this may mean in her classroom and in her teaching of critical thinking skills.

Lopez 1

Carmen Lopez

Professor Sykes

English 101

4 November 2004

"A Question of Ethics" Left Unanswered

In her essay "A Question of Ethics," Jane Goodall, a scientist who has studied chimpanzees for years, tries to resolve a
complicated ethical dilemma: Under what circumstances is it
acceptable to cause animal suffering to prevent human suffering? Her answer, however, remains somewhat unclear. Although
Goodall challenges scientists to avoid conducting unnecessary
tests on animals, she does not explain the criteria by which
scientists should determine necessity.

Goodall argues that her readers have an ethical obligation
to protect animals from suffering, but she also implies that it
might be necessary sometimes to abandon that obligation. She
points out that animals share similar traits with human beings:
they have a capacity for certain human emotions, and they
may be capable of legitimate friendship. Goodall's evidence for
this claim is an anecdote from her research. She recounts that
one chimpanzee in her study, named David Greybeard, "gently
squeezed [her] hand" when she offered him food (62).
Appealing to readers' emotions, Goodall hopes to persuade
readers that the chimp is "sociable" and "sentient," or feeling
(62). According to Goodall's logic, if researchers are careful
to avoid tests that cause human suffering, they should also
be careful to avoid tests that cause suffering for other life
forms.

*Marginal annotations:*

Opening summarizes
the article's purpose
and notes the au-
thor's credentials.

Thesis expresses
Lopez's own judg-
ment of Goodall's
article.

Lopez summarizes
Goodall's main
points.

Quotation is cited
with an MLA in-text
citation.

Lopez's summary
helps readers under-
stand her analysis
and gives her
credibility.

Marginal annotations indicate MLA-style formatting and effective writing.

## SCHOLARS ON CRITICAL THINKING

Marzano, Robert J. "What Are the General Skills of Thinking and
Reasoning and How Do You Teach Them?" *Clearing House* 71.5
(1998): 268–73. Marzano reports on a study that examines definitions of thinking and reasoning in various disciplines. He synthe-
sizes the study's findings into a list of core skills desired across
the curriculum and includes a sample task and an analysis of how
it incorporates critical thinking.

Lopez 2

Lopez begins to identify and question Goodall's assumptions.

When Goodall asserts that scientists shouldn't mindlessly test animals if alternative tests are available, she is in effect conceding that sometimes animals will have to suffer for the sake of helping human beings. Yet if it is unacceptable in some cases to cause sentient beings to suffer, why would it not always be unacceptable? When could compassionate people be comfortable with the prospect of causing David Greybeard mental and physical pain?

Goodall attempts to draw the line between ethical and unethical animal testing by stressing the idea of "essential" tests--those without which scientists could not adequately study certain human illnesses at all. In other words, Goodall seems to imply that it would be unethical for scientists not to test animals when such tests are the only tool available to alleviate human suffering.

Question serves as a transition and advances Lopez's argument.

But might there be other criteria that could determine whether animal testing is necessary? For example, the severity of a given human illness might lead scientists to identify medical conditions that justify subordinating animal welfare to human needs. For nonterminal illnesses that cause people far less pain, researchers might delay animal testing or use alternative methods because in these cases concern about animal suffering outweighs concern about manageable human suffering.

By contrast, Goodall's criterion of "essential" testing leaves open the possibility that as long as alternatives are un-available or ineffective and as long as researchers do not dif-ferentiate among degrees of human suffering, mindless animal

## SCHOLARS ON CRITICAL THINKING

Fishman, Stephen M., and Lucille Parkinson McCarthy. "Teaching for Student Change: A Deweyan Alternative to Radical Pedagogy." *College Composition and Communication* 47 (1996): 342–66. Seeking an alternative to radical, confrontational pedagogy, Fishman and McCarthy describe a course that uses a Deweyan approach stressing "cooperative inquiry."

Salvatori, Mariolina. "Conversations with Texts: Reading in the Teaching of Composition." *College English* 58 (1996): 440–54. Building on the notion of critical reading as conversing with a text, Salvatori observes that readers have the responsibility of "giving a voice, and therefore a sort of life, to the text's argument." Writers have the responsibility of "writing a text that asks (rather than

Lopez 3

testing would be acceptable. Her assumption suggests that David Greybeard could suffer, for example, because inadequate computer simulations have prevented researchers from finding a cure for the common headache or for mildly unpleasant pollen allergies. To make a more persuasive case, Goodall should define essential and nonessential human needs.

Goodall could use another standard to determine whether animal tests are essential. Researchers might consider how society values the species of animal used in tests. Goodall has chosen in her David Greybeard example an animal whose physiological similarity to human beings encourages people to grant personhood to it. But other animals have much lower capacity for understanding and empathy than do chimps, dolphins, dogs, or cats. Rats, for example, are not typically conferred with human qualities because their emotional capacity is assumed to be far more limited than humans'. If rats are more distant from human beings than chimpanzees are, and if they justify less stringent protection, then might a test be "essential" if it could be performed on a rat, but "nonessential" if it could be performed only on a chimpanzee? Researchers could conduct more ethically responsible animal testing if they used some species and exempted others from testing based on a reasoned determination of their similarity to or difference from human beings in mental capacity.

Although Goodall perhaps intended to call for improving animal laboratory conditions, her essay has also raised some questions about this important ethical issue. The stakes of animal testing are too high and the issue too complex to

*Clear topic sentence announces a shift to a new topic.*

*Lopez raises questions.*

*Lopez treats the author fairly.*

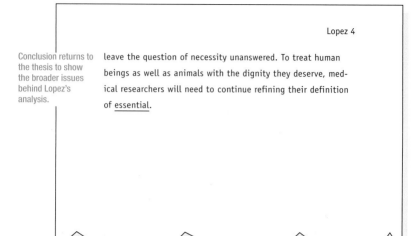

Lopez 4

Conclusion returns to the thesis to show the broader issues behind Lopez's analysis.

leave the question of necessity unanswered. To treat human beings as well as animals with the dignity they deserve, medical researchers will need to continue refining their definition of <u>essential</u>.

In MLA style, the list of works cited begins on a new page.

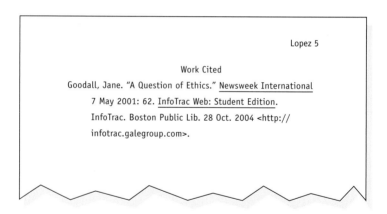

Lopez 5

Work Cited

Goodall, Jane. "A Question of Ethics." <u>Newsweek International</u>
      7 May 2001: 62. <u>InfoTrac Web: Student Edition</u>.
      InfoTrac. Boston Public Lib. 28 Oct. 2004 <http://
      infotrac.galegroup.com>.

**46e** Apply critical thinking strategies to visual texts.

Like a nonfiction work, an image has a purpose and communicates with an audience. Think, for example, of how an advertisement tries to sell toothpaste or of how a photograph shows the struggles of poverty. Writing about visual texts is comparable to writing about written texts. An image, however, doesn't state an explicit thesis. Instead, you must infer the meaning beneath the image's surface and interpret its central idea from its elements of design.

In writing about an article or a book, you usually analyze the text's argument; the goal of writing about a visual text is to argue for a valid interpretation of the image's meaning or to evaluate its message.

*Annotating visual texts*

Rather than take an image at face value, explore its purpose and effect by annotating it. Look at the visual text closely and write down any initial thoughts and questions it raises for you. Then circle or draw arrows to elements that you find interesting, surprising, or puzzling. Try to determine what elements of the visual text are most important to its meaning.

Most of the guidelines for active reading on page 470 are useful for assessing a visual text. In addition, the following questions will help you understand your responses to an image's meaning.

**ADDITIONAL RESOURCE ON VISUAL RHETORIC**

Handa, Carolyn, ed. *Visual Rhetoric in a Digital World: A Critical Sourcebook.* Boston: Bedford, 2004. This collection brings together current and intellectually interesting scholarship in this emerging field. Part 1, "Toward a Pedagogy of the Visual," includes essays that discuss how teachers can balance the verbal and the visual in their composition classrooms. Parts 2 and 3, "The Rhetoric of the Image" and "The Rhetoric of Design," focus on the persuasive power of illustrations and typography in written texts. The essays in Parts 4 and 5, "Visual Rhetoric and Argument" and "Visual Rhetoric and Culture," address the logic of visual arguments and the pervasiveness of the visual in shaping cultural perceptions.

See also SCHOLARS ON VISUAL RHETORIC (5d).

- What first strikes you about the image?
- What elements do you notice immediately?
- Who or what is the main subject of the image?
- What colors and textures dominate?
- What is in the background? In the foreground?
- What role, if any, do words play in the visual text?
- What questions does the image raise for you?

On the following page is an advertisement with a student's annotations. After annotating the advertisement and outlining its key features, the student, Albert Lee, wrote a summary and an analysis (see pp. 484 and 486–89).

### Outlining a visual text's key features

Although you can't trace an explicit line of reasoning for an image, try to define the visual text's purpose and sketch a list of its key elements.

Here, for example, are the key features that student Albert Lee identified for the advertisement printed on the following page.

**KEY FEATURES OF THE MCDONALD'S ADVERTISEMENT**
Purpose: To persuade readers that McDonald's is concerned about its customers' health.

Key features:

- A close-up of a fresh, green lettuce leaf makes up the entire background.
- Near the center there's a comment card with a handwritten question from a "real" McDonald's customer: "What makes your lettuce so crisp?"
- A photograph of a smiling woman in her twenties is clipped to the card.
- Beneath the comment card is the company's response, which emphasizes the farm-fresh quality and purity of its vegetables and urges customers to ask other candid questions.
- At the bottom of the ad is the McDonald's slogan "I'm lovin' it."

**WRITERS ON WRITING**
There are things that would take me fifteen pages to write in words, whereas the right animation, the right visual, can communicate the idea in fifteen seconds. —Brian Greene

## FULL-PAGE McDONALD'S ADVERTISEMENT

Why lettuce? When I think of McDonald's I think of burgers and fries.

Beads of water from recent washing?

Lettuce is larger than life and fills whole ad.

So green. Crisp edges. Suggests freshness.

A real customer?

"M" sounds like a person.

Looks healthy, not like fast food.

Trying to build trust with the customer

## SCHOLARS ON CRITICAL THINKING AND THE WEB

Browne, Neill M., Kari E. Freeman, and Carrie L. Williamson. "The Importance of Critical Thinking for Student Use of the Internet." *College Student Journal* 34 (2000): 391–98. The authors offer strategies for helping students become more critical of what they find on the Web. They argue that if students are not equipped to evaluate the information and the multiple perspectives they find online, they can become passive consumers and not active, critical users of information.

Sosnoski, James. "Hyper-readers and Their Reading Engines." *Passions, Pedagogies, and Twenty-first Century Technologies.* Logan: Utah State UP, 1999. 161–77. Critical reading of electronic texts—especially those found on the Web—requires specific reading strategies. Sosnoski explores the ways that reading on-screen

*Summarizing a visual text*

To summarize a visual text, begin with essential information such as who created the visual, who the intended audience is, where the visual appeared, and when it was created. Then in a few sentences explain the visual's main point or purpose and describe the image by pointing to its key features. (See also 46c.)

Following is Albert Lee's summary of the McDonald's advertisement printed on page 483.

> An advertisement for McDonald's in the July–August 2004 issue of *Men's Health* magazine represents an attempt by the restaurant chain to remake its image. The implicit reason for the ad is that McDonald's world-famous fast food has come under increasingly harsh attack for unhealthful processing and preparation. The fresh, spring-green lettuce that dominates this ad is a signal to customers that McDonald's has changed its menu and now offers food as fresh and healthful as any found in a supermarket. By publicizing this new direction, McDonald's clearly hopes to attract health-conscious customers. Moreover, by framing this advertisement as a response to an individual customer's question, McDonald's attempts to show that the vast size of the chain does not prevent it from tending personally to its customers' concerns.

*Analyzing a visual text*

To analyze a visual text, examine it as a whole and then reflect on how the individual elements contribute to its overall effect. The guidelines for writing an analysis on page 476 can be applied to visual texts as well as written ones. In addition, the following questions will help you evaluate an image's purpose and meaning.

• What surprises, perplexes, or intrigues you about the image?

**SCHOLARS ON CRITICAL THINKING AND THE WEB (continued)**

has affected reading practices and describes a number of different ways of "hyper-reading" that have evolved. His discussion will be of interest to instructors who incorporate online texts in their teaching of critical thinking.

Sorapure, Madeleine, Pamela Inglesby, and George Yatchisin. "Web Literacy: Challenges and Opportunities for Research in a New Medium." *Computers and Composition* 15 (1998): 409–24. The authors offer ways to help students become more careful readers of Web content. They suggest adapting traditional strategies for evaluating print sources to develop guidelines for assessing the various texts (and nontextual information) that students will encounter online.

- What clues suggest the visual text's intended audience? How does the image appeal to its audience?
- If the text is an advertisement, what product is it selling? Does it attempt to sell an idea or a message as well?
- If the visual text includes words, how do the words contribute to the meaning of the image?
- How do design elements—colors, shapes, perspective, background, foreground—shape the visual text's meaning or serve its purpose?

On the following pages is Albert Lee's analysis of the McDonald's ad that appears on page 483.

Lee 1

Albert Lee

Professor McIntosh

English 101

4 November 2004

The Golden Arches Go Green: McDonald's and Real Lettuce

Dominating a McDonald's advertisement in the July-August 2004 issue of <u>Men's Health</u> magazine is a highly magnified head of lettuce, the centerpiece of a new healthful menu that McDonald's promoted during the summer. The lettuce looms over the ad's two other elements, a comment card from a smiling female customer with a question about lettuce and a friendly note in reply from McDonald's. For a restaurant chain known for its supersized meals of Double Quarter Pounders with Cheese, the close-up of a lettuce leaf might come as a surprise. A superficial interpretation of the McDonald's ad would point out that the fast-food giant is attempting to remake its image into a health-conscious restaurant. After all, the greening of the Golden Arches follows a shift in public attitudes toward diet and a sometimes environmentally unfriendly food industry.

Less obvious are the associations that the ad creates to persuade people that McDonald's is committed to a product--an entire experience--not usually offered by fast-food restaurants. If fast food has become synonymous in many consumers' minds with the impersonal and artificial conditions of modern life-- from assembly-line food to robotic exchanges at the counter or drive-through window--then the McDonald's ad seeks to replace those associations with images of authenticity and familiarity.

*Lee summarizes the content of the ad.*

*Lee suggests a simple interpretation to highlight his more compelling interpretation.*

*Lee's thesis offers his analysis of the ad's message.*

Marginal annotations indicate MLA-style formatting and effective writing.

Lee 2

The ad's underlying message emphasizes for viewers the real over the artificial, a quality in both McDonald's food and its relationship with its customers. Through vivid graphics McDonald's shows, rather than tells, viewers that its ingredients are wholesome. The head of lettuce that creates the ad's entire background is the picture of mouth-watering wholesomeness. Enlarged to many times its natural size, the lettuce reveals its sharp, spring-green edges and beads of water standing on its leaves, presumably from recent washing. The fast-food chain could have bombarded the public with nutritional statistics about its food items, as many other restaurants do, but it seems to recognize that numbers can begin to read like cold data from a science textbook. Instead, McDonald's invites us to take a closer look at its ingredients, a chance to verify for ourselves that the lettuce is as "pure" and "fresh" as it claims. The lettuce does in fact look "so crisp" that we can easily believe it would produce a "crunch" if we bit into it, just as McDonald's reports.

The ad's copy suggests that McDonald's wishes to convince viewers that its commitment to serving customers' needs is as genuine as its lettuce. The prominent repetition of the word <u>real</u> in the tagline expresses McDonald's policy of plain dealing with individual customers. The picture of a supposedly real customer, a paper clip holding her photograph, and the ragged left edge of the comment card all contribute to a sense that this exchange between customer and McDonald's is as real, as "pure," as McDonald's claims its lettuce is.

Lee describes the dominant image in the visual text.

Lee quotes words from the text.

Clear topic sentence announces a shift to a new topic.

Lee 3

Lee analyzes the ad's language.

Indeed, the heading to the comment card, "Ask M," gives McDonald's a personal identity, which intensifies the impression of the company's accessibility. "Ask M" conjures up the image of a straight-shooting, small-town newspaper advice columnist. McDonald's lettuce, "M" says, comes "from the same place you buy yours." This comparison with the neighborhood market emphasizes the local presence of the restaurant by association. The lettuce we eat at McDonald's, the ad suggests, is in fact the very same we would feel confident putting on our family's plate at home. The opening phrase of the second sentence, "Simply put," is a signal that McDonald's earnestly desires to explain its operations to its customers. As with the close-up of the lettuce, the wording suggests that the company has nothing to hide.

Lee concludes with his interpretation of the ad's overall effect.

It might be difficult to imagine that people will be persuaded to abandon their local markets for McDonald's. But then again, we cannot easily forget the ad's image of lettuce, its curling, serrated edges and finely branched veins, enlarged to a slightly unsettling size. And if this green image conjures up in our minds a golden "M"--a place where we can reconnect with real people and the bounty of the land--then maybe one of the most successful companies in history has done it again.

Lee 4

Work Cited

McDonald's Corporation. Advertisement. <u>Men's Health</u> July-
     Aug. 2004: 95.

ON
THE
WEB

**dianahacker.com/bedhandbook**
▶ Additional resources
   ▶ Analyzing a photograph

# 47

## Constructing reasonable arguments

In writing an argument, you take a stand on a debatable issue. The question being debated might be a matter of public policy:

> Should religious groups be allowed to meet on public school property?
>
> What is the least dangerous way to dispose of nuclear waste?
>
> Should a state enact laws rationing medical care?

On such questions, reasonable people may disagree.

Reasonable men and women also disagree about many scholarly issues. Psychologists debate the validity of behaviorism; historians interpret the causes of the Civil War quite

**SCHOLARS ON ARGUMENT**

Bizzell, Patricia. "The 4th of July and the 22nd of December: The Function of Cultural Archives in Persuasion, as Shown by Frederick Douglass and William Apess." *College Composition and Communication* 48 (1997): 44–60. Bizzell observes that when judging the effectiveness of student writing, teachers usually talk about what writers do, ignoring what they know. Using Douglass and Apess as examples, she shows that a broad display of knowledge can be rhetorically effective and can help build common ground to effect social change.

differently; biologists conduct genetic experiments to challenge the conclusions of other researchers. (See 49.)

When you construct a *reasonable* argument, your goal is not simply to win or to have the last word. Your aim is to reveal your current understanding of the truth about a subject or to propose the best solution available for solving a problem—without being needlessly combative. In constructing your argument, you join a conversation with other writers and readers. Your aim is to convince readers to reconsider their opinions by offering new reasons to question an old viewpoint.

**ESL** The conventions of argument vary from culture to culture. In the United States, most arguments are direct, not subtle; explicitly organized, not discursive; plainspoken, not poetic. Evidence is usually specific and factual; appeals to intuition or communal wisdom are rare. If you have difficulty writing the kinds of arguments that are valued in the United States, ask your instructor for help or visit your school's writing center.

## 47a Examine your issue's social and intellectual contexts.

Arguments appear in social and intellectual contexts. Public policy debates obviously arise in social contexts. Grounded in specific times and places, such debates are conducted among groups with competing values and interests. For example, the debate over nuclear power plants has been renewed in the United States in light of energy concerns and the September 11 attacks—with environmentalists, nuclear industry officials, and consumers all weighing in on the argument. Most public policy debates also have intellectual dimensions that address scientific or theoretical concerns. In the case of the nuclear power issue, physicists, biologists, and economists all contribute their expertise.

**SCHOLARS ON ARGUMENT**

Lynch, Dennis A., Diana George, and Marilyn M. Cooper. "Moments of Argument: Agonistic Inquiry and Confrontational Cooperation." *College Composition and Communication* 48 (1997): 61–85. Instead of viewing arguments as "for or against" stances, the authors see arguments as having "moments of conflict and agonistic positioning as well as moments of understanding and communication." They describe two courses in which they applied their methods.

Scholarly debates clearly play themselves out in intellectual contexts, but they have a social dimension too. Scholars and researchers rarely work in a vacuum: They respond to the contributions of other specialists in the field, often building on others' views and refining them, but at times challenging them.

Because many of your readers will be aware of the social and intellectual contexts in which your issue is grounded, you will be at a serious disadvantage if you are not informed. That's why it is a good idea to conduct some research before preparing your argument; consulting even a few sources can help. For example, the student whose paper appears on pages 500–04 became more knowledgeable about his issue—whether to ban recreational snowmobiles from Yellowstone National Park—after consulting a handful of brief sources.

## 47b View your audience as a panel of jurors.

Do not assume that your audience already agrees with you; instead, envision skeptical readers who, like a panel of jurors, will make up their minds after listening to all sides of the argument. If you are arguing a public policy issue, aim your paper at readers who represent a variety of opinions. In the case of the debate over nuclear power, for example, imagine a jury representative of those who have a stake in the matter: environmentalists, nuclear industry officials, and consumers.

At times, you can deliberately narrow your audience. If you are working within a word limit, for example, you might not have the space in which to address the concerns of all parties to the nuclear energy debate. Or you might be primarily interested in reaching one segment of a general audience, such as consumers. In such instances, you can still view your audience as a panel of jurors; the jury will simply be a less diverse group.

### SCHOLARS ON ARGUMENT

Fulkerson, Richard. *Teaching the Argument in Writing.* Urbana: NCTE, 1996. Drawing on classical and contemporary theories of argument, Fulkerson challenges teachers to rethink some conventional views about reasoning. He asserts that the usual English textbook treatment of inductive and deductive reasoning and the fallacies is misguided—worth little classroom time. We should focus instead on the kinds of argumentative strategies used in real life; many of these strategies, such as drawing analogies, can be legitimate in one context, fallacious in another. To Fulkerson, the goal of argument is not to win but to reach intelligent, yet tentative, conclusions after giving all points of view a fair hearing. Fulkerson's motive for writing his book is, as he puts it, "a profound commitment to the importance of argument in a free society."

In the case of scholarly debates, you will be addressing readers who share your interest in a discipline such as literature or psychology. Such readers belong to a group with an agreed-upon way of investigating and talking about issues. Though they generally agree about procedures, scholars in an academic discipline often disagree about particular issues. Once you see how they disagree about your issue, you should be able to imagine a jury that reflects the variety of opinions they hold.

## 47c In your introduction, establish credibility and state your position.

When you are constructing an argument, make sure your introduction contains a thesis sentence that states your position on the issue you have chosen to debate (see 2a). In the sentences leading up to the thesis, establish your credibility with readers by showing that you are knowledgeable and fair-minded. If possible, build common ground with readers who may not be in initial agreement with your views and show them why they need to consider your thesis.

In the following introduction, student Kevin Smith presents himself as someone worth listening to. His opening sentence shows that he is familiar with the legal issues surrounding school prayer. His next sentence reveals him to be fair-minded, as he presents the views of both sides. Even Smith's thesis builds common ground: "Prayer is too important to be trusted to our public schools." Because Smith introduces both sides of the debate, readers are likely to approach his essay with an open mind.

> Although the Supreme Court has ruled against prayer in public schools on First Amendment grounds, many people still

**SCHOLARS ON ARGUMENT**

Trail, George Y. "Teaching Argument and the Rhetoric of Orwell's 'Politics and the English Language.'" *College English* 57 (1995): 570–83. Trail recommends that instructors resist ahistorical, decontextualized approaches to teaching argument and proposes instead three principles: (1) Recognize that all arguments are situated in a historical time and place; (2) think of an argument's appeal in psychological as opposed to emotional terms; and (3) view logic as a rhetorical device.

feel that prayer should be allowed. Such people value prayer as a practice central to their faith and believe that prayer is a way for schools to reinforce moral principles. They also compellingly point out a paradox in the First Amendment itself: at what point does the separation of church and state restrict the freedom of those who wish to practice their religion? What proponents of school prayer fail to realize, however, is that the Supreme Court's decision, although it was made on legal grounds, makes sense on religious grounds as well. Prayer is too important to be trusted to our public schools.

— Kevin Smith, student

**TIP:** A good way to test a thesis while drafting and revising is to imagine a counterargument to your argument (see 47f). If you can't think of an opposing point of view, rethink your thesis or ask a classmate to respond to your argument.

---

**TIPS FROM WRITING TUTORS**

"I spent my childhood as an ESL student who struggled with writing. Now as I tutor other nonnative speakers, I find that most have a hard time with their thesis because they cannot take a definite side on an issue. Many write to explain rather than to persuade or argue a point."

— *Shabnam Tehrani, George Mason University*

---

**47d** Back up your thesis with persuasive lines of argument.

Arguments of any complexity contain lines of argument that, when taken together, might reasonably persuade readers that the thesis has merit. The following, for example, are the main lines of argument used by Aaron Lund in his paper supporting a ban on snowmobiles in Yellowstone National Park (see pp. 500–04).

**SCHOLARS ON ARGUMENT**

Lamb, Catherine E. "Beyond Argument in Feminist Composition." *College Composition and Communication* 42 (1991): 11–24. The feminist approach to argument begins with "understanding the range of power relationships available to a writer and her readers," Lamb says. "One then determines which are consistent with the emphasis on cooperation, collaboration, shared leadership, and integration of the cognitive and affective which is characteristic of feminist pedagogy." Lamb discusses how the oral discourse methods of negotiation and mediation can be adapted for composition courses.

Thesis: Recreational snowmobiles should be banned from Yellowstone National Park.

- The air pollution caused by snowmobiles is a health risk to park employees and visitors.
- The noise made by snowmobiles disturbs the peace and quiet that park visitors have a right to expect.
- The National Park Service cannot afford to spend funds and time responding to the problems created by snowmobiles in the park.
- The Park Service has a mandate to preserve the park's natural resources for the future.

If you sum up your main lines of argument, as Lund did, you will have a rough outline of your essay. The outline will consist of your central claim—the thesis—and any supporting claims that back it up. In your paper, you will provide evidence for each of these claims.

### 47e Support your claims with specific evidence.

You will need to support your central claim and any subordinate claims with evidence: facts, statistics, examples and illustrations, expert opinion, and so on. Depending on the issue you have chosen to write about, you may or may not need to do some reading to gather evidence. Some topics, such as whether your college should continue to support its

**SCHOLARS ON ARGUMENT**

Secor, Marie J. "Recent Research in Argumentation Theory." *Technical Writing Teacher* 14 (1987): 337–54. This bibliographic essay proposes incorporating the study of argumentation in the teaching of technical writing.

travel study program, can be developed through personal experience and research tools such as questionnaires and interviews. Most debatable topics, however, require that you consult some written sources.

If any of your evidence is based on reading, you must document your sources. Documentation gives credit to the authors and shows readers how to locate a source in case they want to assess its credibility or explore the issue further (see 53).

### Using facts and statistics

A fact is something that is known with certainty because it has been objectively verified: The capital of Wyoming is Cheyenne. Carbon has an atomic weight of 12. John F. Kennedy was assassinated on November 22, 1963. Statistics are collections of numerical facts: Alcohol abuse is a factor in nearly 40 percent of traffic fatalities. Almost six out of ten US households currently own a DVD player. As of 2004, about 48 percent of privately held businesses in the United States were owned by women.

Most arguments are supported at least to some extent by facts and statistics. For example, in the following passage the writer uses statistics to show that college students are carrying unreasonably high credit card debt.

> A 2001 study by Nellie Mae revealed that while the average credit card debt per college undergraduate is $2,327, more than 20% of undergraduates who have at least one credit card maintain a much higher debt level, from $3,000 to $7,000 (Barrett).

Writers often use statistics in selective ways to bolster their own views. If you suspect that a writer's handling of statistics is not quite fair, read authors with opposing views, who may give you a fuller understanding of the numbers. For example, one writer might argue that because sales of

**SCHOLARS ON ARGUMENT**

Bator, Paul. "Aristotelian and Rogerian Rhetoric." *College Composition and Communication* 31 (1980): 427–32. In this clear discussion of the differences between two approaches to argumentation, Bator offers practical advice to help students sense "when it is appropriate to confront 'opponents' and when it is more advantageous to strive for change through mutual acceptance and understanding."

recorded music have dropped 31 percent since Internet file sharing became popular, the practice of file sharing has severely affected musicians' earnings. By researching the subject further, however, you might find another source that claims that musicians seldom receive royalties from CD sales and that the bulk of their earnings come from the sale of concert tickets and merchandise.

### Using examples and illustrations

Examples and illustrations (extended examples, often in story form) rarely prove a point by themselves, but when used in combination with other forms of evidence they flesh out an argument and bring it to life. Because they often have an emotional dimension, they can reach readers in ways that statistics cannot.

In a paper arguing in favor of banning snowmobiles from Yellowstone National Park, student Aaron Lund refers to park rangers wearing respirators at work. He supplements this vivid example with specific findings from scientific investigations that link snowmobiles to air pollution.

### Citing expert opinion

Although they are no substitute for careful reasoning of your own, the views of an expert can contribute to the force of your argument. For example, in a paragraph describing the link between snowmobiles and air pollution, Aaron Lund relies on scientific expertise:

> The Bluewater Network, an environmental group, reports that the most common snowmobiles, those with two-stroke engines, "discharge up to one-third of their fuel unburned into the environment and are one of the largest unchecked sources of hydrocarbon pollution nationwide" (1).

**WRITERS ON WRITING**

"For example" is not proof.                    —Yiddish proverb

We have become so democratic in our habits of thought that we are convinced that truth is determined through a plebiscite of facts.                    —Erich Heller

Any mental activity is easy if it need not take reality into account.
                    —Marcel Proust

When you rely on expert opinion, make sure that your source is an expert in the field you are writing about. In some cases, you may need to provide credentials showing why your source is worth listening to. When including expert testimony in your paper, you can summarize or paraphrase the expert's opinion or you can quote the expert's exact words. You will of course need to document the source, as Lund did in the example just given (see 53).

## 47f Anticipate objections; counter opposing arguments.

Readers who already agree with you need no convincing, although they should welcome a well-argued case for their point of view. But indifferent or skeptical readers may resist your arguments. To be willing to give up a position that seems reasonable, a reader has to see that there is an even more reasonable one. In addition to presenting your own case, therefore, you should review the opposing arguments and attempt to counter them.

It might seem at first that drawing attention to an opposing point of view or contradictory piece of evidence would weaken your argument. But by anticipating and countering objections to your argument, you show yourself as a reasonable and well-informed writer. You also establish your purpose, demonstrate the significance of the issue you are debating, and ultimately strengthen your argument.

There is no best place in an essay to deal with opposing views. Often it is useful to summarize the opposing position early in your essay. After stating your thesis but before developing your own arguments, you might have a paragraph that takes up the most important counterargument. Or you can anticipate objections paragraph by paragraph as you develop your case. Wherever you decide to deal with opposing arguments, do your best to explain the arguments of others accurately and fairly (see 48c).

**WRITERS ON WRITING**

A writer has a facility with words. A good writer can also think.
—Cynthia Ozick

The world is divided into people who think they are right.
—Anonymous

The truth is rarely pure and never simple.     —Oscar Wilde

Seeking to know is only too often learning to doubt.
—Antoinette Deshoulières

Few people think more than two or three times a year; I have made an international reputation for myself by thinking once or twice a week.     —George Bernard Shaw

## Anticipating and countering objections

To anticipate a possible objection, consider the following questions.

- Could a reasonable person draw a different conclusion from your facts or examples?
- Might a reader question any of your assumptions?
- Could a reader offer an alternative explanation of this issue?
- Is there any evidence that might undermine your position?

The following questions may help you respond to a potential objection.

- Can you concede the point to the opposition but challenge the point's importance or usefulness?
- Can you explain why readers should consider a new perspective or question a piece of evidence?
- Should you qualify your position in light of contradictory evidence?
- Can you suggest a different interpretation of the evidence?

When you write, use phrasing to signal to readers that you're about to present an objection. Often the signal phrase can go in the lead sentence of a paragraph:

Critics of this view argue that. . . .

Some readers might point out that. . . .

There might appear to be compelling challenges to. . . .

But isn't it possible that . . . ?

**TIP:** It's always helpful to ask yourself whether a reasonable person might disagree with your argument. If a reasonable person would disagree, you have an arguable thesis. If not, you'll need to revise your thesis.

### WRITERS ON WRITING

Convictions are more dangerous foes of truth than lies.
—Friedrich Nietzsche

People are usually more firmly convinced that their opinions are precious than that they are true. —George Santayana

Opinion is a flitting thing, / But truth outlasts the Sun—/ If then we cannot own them both—/ Possess the oldest one—
—Emily Dickinson

A great many people think they are thinking when they are only rearranging their prejudices. —William James

**47g** Build common ground.

As you counter opposing arguments, try to build common ground with readers who do not initially agree with your views. If you can show that you share your readers' concerns, they will be more likely to acknowledge the validity of your argument. For example, to persuade people opposed to shooting deer, a state wildlife commission would have to show that it too cares about preserving deer and does not want them to die needlessly. Having established these values in common, the commission might be able to persuade critics that a carefully controlled hunting season is good for the deer population because it prevents starvation caused by overpopulation.

People believe that intelligence and decency support their side of an argument. To change sides, they must continue to feel intelligent and decent. Otherwise they will persist in their opposition.

## SAMPLE ARGUMENT PAPER

In the paper that begins on the following page, student Aaron Lund argues that recreational snowmobiling should be banned from Yellowstone National Park. Notice that Lund is careful to establish common ground with readers who may hold a different view. Notice too that he attempts to counter the arguments of the opposition.

In writing the paper, Lund consulted print and electronic sources. When he quotes from or uses statistics from a source, he cites the source with an MLA (Modern Language Association) in-text citation. Citations in the paper refer readers to the list of works cited at the end of the paper (see 57).

*arg*
**47g**

*Critical thinking*

Lund 1

Aaron Lund

Professor Dorn

English 102

15 November 2002

Preserving Yellowstone's Winter Wilderness

Although a few recreational snowmobilers destroy fragile ecosystems and harass animals as they ride through the wilderness, most love and respect this country's natural heritage. That's why they brave the cold to explore what is left of wild America--including Yellowstone National Park. Unfortunately, however, even respectful snowmobilers are unwittingly damaging what they love. Because snowmobiles create both air and noise pollution and because their use in the park strains the already lean budget of the park service, recreational snowmobiles should be banned from Yellowstone National Park.

In 2002, the Bush administration, under pressure from the snowmobile industry, proposed to reverse the National Park Service's 2000 plan that would have phased out recreational snowmobile use in Yellowstone. In addition to reversing the earlier plan, the new policy would increase the number of snowmobiles allowed into the park per day. This policy is a step in the wrong direction.

It may be hard to imagine that 1,100 snowmobiles a day (the proposed limit) could cause an air pollution problem in a park half the size of Connecticut, but in fact they can. The air pollution at park entrances has already become so bad in winter, according to environmental reporter Julie Cart, that fresh air has to be pumped into the kiosks where snowmobiles line

*Marginal notes:*

Lund builds common ground with readers who may disagree with him.

Thesis states the main point.

Background information puts the thesis in context.

Lund introduces his first line of argument.

**Marginal annotations indicate MLA-style formatting and effective writing.**

Lund 2

up and park rangers have been forced to wear respirators
(A12). Park visitors, including the snowmobilers themselves,
have no such protection.

Sources are docu-
mented with MLA
citations.

The Bluewater Network, an environmental group, reports
that the most common snowmobiles, those with two-stroke
engines, "discharge up to one-third of their fuel unburned into
the environment and are one of the largest unchecked sources
of hydrocarbon pollution nationwide" (1). Bluewater Network
cites numerous scientific studies linking carbon monoxide pol-
lutants to snowmobiles. One of these studies, which was conducted in the mid-1990s after many rangers complained of
dizziness and nausea, found that carbon monoxide levels at
park entrances exceeded those allowed by the National Ambient Air Quality Standard (2). Clearly, such a level of pollution
is a health risk to the park's employees and to its visitors.

Lund supports his
points with specific
evidence.

In addition to polluting the air, snowmobiles are noisy,
disturbing the peace and quiet that park visitors have a right
to expect. One study cited by Bluewater Network reports that
twelve snowmobiles traveling together could be heard as far
as two miles away (5). Even a travel writer for <u>Yellowstone
Journal</u>, a magazine financed to a great extent by advertising
from snowmobile manufacturers and rental services, advises
readers about areas in the park free from "the constant hum of
the other snowmobiles" (Johnson 7). Whether such noise ad-
versely affects the park's wildlife remains a debated question,
but the possibility exists.

Transition prepares
readers for the sec-
ond line of argument.

Some who favor keeping the park open to snowmobiles
argue that newer, four-stroke machines cause less air and noise

Lund counters an
opposing argument.

*Critical thinking*

Lund 3

pollution than older models. While this is true, the new machines still pollute more than cars, and their decibel level is
reduced only slightly ("Snowmobile" B25). Also, because the
newer snowmobiles cost at least $3,000 more than the older
ones, it is unlikely that individuals would choose to buy them
or that rental companies could afford to upgrade. At present
there are no strict guarantees that only the newer models
would be allowed into the park.

Lund presents
his third line of
argument.

Like most federal agencies, the National Park Service faces
serious budget constraints. Funds that should be used to
preserve Yellowstone National Park and its wildlife have been
diverted to deal with the snowmobile issue. A single environmental impact study of the problem cost taxpayers nearly
$250,000 in early 2002 (Greater Yellowstone Coalition), and
the park service estimates that implementing the new plan
would cost one million dollars ("Snowmobile" B25). Also, park
rangers are spending an increasing amount of their valuable
time policing snowmobilers. In 2002, park rangers issued 338
citations for illegal snowmobiling activity, twice as many as in
2001, in addition to hundreds of warnings (Greater Yellowstone
Coalition). Although most snowmobilers remain law-abiding, a
disturbing number of joyriders violate speed limits, stray from
marked trails, and pursue animals for the thrill of the chase.
Policing such activities takes away from park rangers' primary
responsibility--preserving this country's treasured natural
resources.

Opponents of a ban argue that a central mission of the
park service is to provide access to national parks--access

Lund 4

not only to the physically fit (such as snowshoers and cross-country skiers) but to ordinary people, including those who are handicapped. Admittedly, winter access is important, but ordinary people can enjoy the park by means other than snow-mobiles. Snowcoaches (buses on skis) already take visitors into the park, and one road into the park is plowed and open to cars in winter. Also, the park service's mission is not just to provide access to the parks; no less important is its mission to pre-serve the parks' pristine natural resources for future generations.

Lund counters a possible objection to his thesis.

Even with a ban on snowmobiling in the park itself, the Yellowstone area would still earn the title of Snowmobiling Capital of America. Virtually all of the streets of West Yellow-stone, the area's major town, are open to snowmobilers, and many trails run out of the town. The Big Sky Trail extends for 110 miles, and the 360-mile Continental Divide Snowmobile Trail offers sledders "groomed trails, spectacular mountain scenery, wide-open spaces, and lots of opportunities to view wildlife" (Johnson 7). Because the Yellowstone area offers so many winter trails, there is no need to allow snowmobiles in the park itself.

Lund suggests a rea-sonable alternative for snowmobilers.

A ban on snowmobiles would give park visitors a quiet, pollution-free experience, and it would allow the park service to devote more of its limited resources to one of its primary missions: the protection of natural resources. Whether on cross-country skis or from the heated comfort of a snowcoach, visitors would still be able to appreciate Yellowstone's beauty-- its geysers, its wildlife, and its snow-covered vistas--through-out the park's long winter.

Conclusion echoes the thesis without dully repeating it.

Lund 5

Works Cited

Works cited page uses MLA style.

Bluewater Network. <u>Snowmobile Position Paper</u>. Apr. 2002.

11 pp. 12 Nov. 2002 <www.bluewaternetwork.org/

reports/rep_pl_snow_snowposition.pdf>.

Cart, Julie. "Plan Backs Snowmobiles at Parks." <u>Los Angeles</u>

<u>Times</u> 8 Nov. 2002: A12. <u>National Newspaper Index</u>.

InfoTrac. Auraria Lib., Denver. 11 Nov. 2002 <http://

infotrac.galegroup.com>.

Greater Yellowstone Coalition. "Yellowstone Experiences Worst

Year Ever for Illegal Snowmobile Activity." <u>Greater</u>

<u>Yellowstone Coalition</u>. 4 Apr. 2002. 6 Nov. 2002

<http://greateryellowstone.org/

snowmobiles_violations_nr.html>.

Johnson, Shelli. "Greater Yellowstone Region Is a Snowmobil-

ing Mecca." <u>Yellowstone Journal</u> Winter 2002-03: 6-7.

"Snowmobile Plan All Wet." Editorial. <u>Denver Post</u> 9 Nov. 2002:

B25. <u>Colorado Newsstand</u>. ProQuest. Auraria Lib., Denver.

10 Nov. 2002 <http://proquest.umi.com>.

# 48

## Evaluating arguments

In your reading and in your own writing, evaluate all arguments for logic and fairness. Many arguments can stand up to critical scrutiny. Often, however, a line of argument that at first seems reasonable turns out to be fallacious, unfair, or both.

**48a** Distinguish between reasonable and fallacious argumentative tactics.

A number of unreasonable argumentative tactics are known as *logical fallacies.* Most of the fallacies—such as hasty generalizations and false analogies—are misguided or dishonest uses of legitimate argumentative strategies. The examples in this section suggest when such strategies are reasonable and when they are not.

---

**SCHOLARS ON EVALUATING ARGUMENTS**

Browne, M. Neil, and Stuart M. Keeley. *Asking the Right Questions: A Guide to Critical Thinking.* 4th ed. Englewood Cliffs: Prentice, 1994. A practical and accessible guide to analysis and evaluation, this book emphasizes "values and moral reasoning as an integral part of critical thinking." It discusses how to question organization, evidence, assumptions, reasoning, and language.

*Generalizing (inductive reasoning)*

Writers and thinkers generalize all the time. We look at a sample of data and conclude that data we have not observed will most likely conform to what we have seen before. From a spoonful of soup, we conclude just how salty the whole bowl will be. After numerous bad experiences with an airline, we decide to book future flights with one of its competitors instead.

When we draw a conclusion from an array of facts, we are engaged in inductive reasoning. Such reasoning deals in probability, not certainty. For a conclusion to be highly probable, it must be based on evidence that is sufficient, representative, and relevant. (See the chart on p. 508.)

The fallacy known as *hasty generalization* is a conclusion based on insufficient or unrepresentative evidence.

**HASTY GENERALIZATION**
Deaths from drug overdoses in Metropolis have doubled in the past three years. Therefore, more Americans than ever are dying from drug abuse.

Data from one city do not justify a conclusion about the whole United States.

A *stereotype* is a hasty generalization about a group. Here are a few examples.

**STEREOTYPES**
Women are bad bosses.

Politicians are corrupt.

Asian students are exceptionally intelligent.

Stereotyping is common because of our human tendency to perceive selectively. We tend to see what we want to see; that is, we notice evidence confirming our already formed opinions and fail to notice evidence to the contrary. For example,

**SCHOLARS ON EVALUATING ARGUMENTS**
Lazere, Donald. "Teaching the Political Conflicts: A Rhetorical Schema." *College Composition and Communication* 43 (1992): 194–213. Lazere describes a set of assignments that ask students to think critically about politics by using a rhetorical schema. The assignments focus on interpreting semantics, perceiving bias, seeing through deceptive rhetoric, and evaluating partisan sources.

if you have concluded that politicians are corrupt, your stereotype will be confirmed by news reports of legislators being indicted—even though every day the media describe conscientious officials serving the public honestly and well.

**NOTE:** Many hasty generalizations contain words like *all, ever, always,* and *never,* when qualifiers such as *most, many, usually,* and *seldom* would be more accurate.

### Drawing analogies

An analogy points out a similarity between two things that are otherwise different. Analogies can be an effective means of arguing a point. In fact, our system of case law, which relies heavily on precedents, makes extensive use of reasoning by analogy. A prosecutor may argue, for example, that Z is guilty because his actions resemble those of X and Y, who were judged guilty in previous rulings. In response, the defense may maintain that the actions of Z bear only a superficial resemblance to those of X and Y and that in legally relevant respects they are in fact quite different.

It is not always easy to draw the line between a reasonable and an unreasonable analogy. At times, however, an analogy is clearly off-base, in which case it is called a *false analogy.*

> **FALSE ANALOGY**
> If we can put humans on the moon, we should be able to find a cure for the common cold.

The writer has falsely assumed that because two things are alike in one respect, they must be alike in others. Putting human beings on the moon and finding a cure for the common cold are both scientific challenges, but the problems confronting medical researchers are quite different from those solved by space scientists.

**SCHOLARS ON LOGIC**

Kaufer, David S., and Christine M. Neuwirth. "Integrating Formal Logic and the New Rhetoric: A Four Stage Heuristic." *College English* 45 (1983): 380–89. Kaufer and Neuwirth develop a four-part heuristic, moving from summary to a polished essay, based on their belief that formal logic is important in teaching argumentation.

## Testing inductive reasoning

Though inductive reasoning leads to probable and not absolute truth, you can assess a conclusion's likely probability by asking three questions. This chart shows how to apply those questions to a sample conclusion based on a survey.

CONCLUSION    The majority of students on our campus would subscribe to wireless Internet access if it were available.

EVIDENCE    In a recent survey, 923 of 1,515 students questioned say they would subscribe to wireless Internet access.

1. Is the evidence sufficient?
   That depends. On a small campus (say, 3,000 students), the pool of students surveyed would be sufficient for market research, but on a large campus (say, 30,000), 1,515 students are only 5 percent of the population. If that 5 percent were known to be truly representative of the other 95 percent, however, even such a small sample would be sufficient (see question 2).
2. Is the evidence representative?
   The evidence is representative if those responding to the survey reflect the characteristics of the entire student population: age, sex, level of technical expertise, amount of disposable income, and so on. If most of those surveyed are majoring in technical fields, for example, the researchers would be wise to question the survey's conclusion.
3. Is the evidence relevant?
   The answer is yes. The survey question is directly linked to the conclusion. A question about the number of hours spent online, by contrast, would not be relevant, because it would not be about *subscribing to wireless Internet access.*

**SCHOLARS ON ASSESSMENT**

Huot, Brian. *(Re)Articulating Writing Assessment for Teaching and Learning.* Logan: Utah State UP, 2002. Huot defines assessment as the judgments we make about student writing, the form these judgments take, and the context in which they are made. By looking at each aspect of this definition, he hopes to neutralize the negative influence of assessment and emphasize the benefits. He calls for increased attention to the ways in which writing assessment can enhance teaching and learning, beginning with the importance of teaching students to assess their own writing and understanding the impact of our judgments on student writers. In Chapter 5, he argues for increased attention to how we read and respond to student texts, which he sees as an integral part of

## Tracing causes and effects

Demonstrating a connection between causes and effects is rarely a simple matter. For example, to explain why a chemistry course has a high failure rate, you would begin by listing possible causes: inadequate preparation of students, poor teaching, large class size, lack of qualified tutors, and so on. Next you would investigate each possible cause. To see whether inadequate preparation contributes to the high failure rate, for instance, you might compare the math and science backgrounds of successful and failing students. To see whether large class size is a contributing factor, you might run a pilot program of small classes and compare grades in the small classes with those in the larger ones. Only after investigating the possible causes would you be able to weigh the relative impact of each cause and suggest appropriate remedies.

Because cause-and-effect reasoning is so complex, it is not surprising that writers frequently oversimplify it. In particular, writers sometimes assume that because one event follows another, the first is the cause of the second. This common fallacy is known as *post hoc*, from the Latin *post hoc, ergo propter hoc*, meaning "after this, therefore because of this."

### POST HOC FALLACY

Since Governor Cho took office, unemployment of minorities in the state has decreased by 7 percent. Governor Cho should be applauded for reducing unemployment among minorities.

The writer must show that Governor Cho's policies are responsible for the decrease in unemployment; it is not enough to show that the decrease followed the governor's taking office.

### SCHOLARS ON ASSESSMENT (continued)

teaching writing. In his final chapters, Huot focuses on writing assessment as a practical, self-conscious, and reflective practice that can enrich teaching and program development.

## Weighing options

Especially when reasoning about problems and solutions, writers must weigh options. To be fair, a writer should mention the full range of options, showing why one is superior to the others or might work well in combination with others.

It is unfair to suggest that there are only two alternatives when in fact there are more. Writers who set up a false choice between their preferred option and one that is clearly unsatisfactory are guilty of the *either . . . or* fallacy.

> **EITHER . . . OR FALLACY**
> Our current war against drugs has not worked. Either we should legalize drugs or we should turn the drug war over to our armed forces and let them fight it.

Clearly there are other options, such as increased funding for drug prevention and treatment.

## Making assumptions

An assumption is a claim that is taken to be true—without the need of proof. Most arguments are based to some extent on assumptions, since writers rarely have the time and space to prove all of the conceivable claims on which the argument is based. For example, someone arguing about the best means of limiting population growth in developing countries might well assume that the goal of limiting population growth is worthwhile. For most audiences, there would be no need to articulate this assumption or to defend it.

There is a danger, however, in failing to spell out and prove a claim that is clearly controversial. Consider the following short argument, in which a key claim is missing.

**SCHOLARS ON ASSESSMENT**

Haswell, Richard, ed. *Beyond Outcomes: Assessment and Instruction within a University Writing Program*. Westport: Ablex, 2001. This collection of articles focuses on Washington State University's successful writing assessment initiative, which integrates instruction and assessment so that each informs the other in productive ways. While the authors describe local problems and solutions, the collection provides guidance for writing program administrators planning a similar assessment approach. For teachers, the value of this collection lies in its thoughtful analysis in Parts 3 and 4, "The Circle of Assessment and Instruction" and "Beyond Outcomes," respectively, both of which include articles related to faculty and student stakeholders.

**ARGUMENT WITH MISSING CLAIM**
Violent crime is increasing.
Therefore, we should vigorously enforce the death penalty.

The writer seems to be assuming that the death penalty deters violent criminals—and that most audiences will agree. Neither is a safe assumption.

When a missing claim is an assertion that few would agree with, we say that a writer is guilty of a *non sequitur* (Latin for "does not follow").

**NON SEQUITUR**
Leah loves good food; therefore, she will be an excellent chef.

Few people would agree with the missing claim—that lovers of good food always make excellent chefs.

### Deducing conclusions (deductive reasoning)

When we deduce a conclusion, we—like Sherlock Holmes — put things together. We establish that a general principle is true, that a specific case is an example of that principle, and that therefore a particular conclusion about that case is a certainty. In real life, such absolute reasoning rarely happens. Approximations of it, however, sometimes occur.

Deductive reasoning can often be structured in a three-step argument called a *syllogism*. The three steps are the major premise, the minor premise, and the conclusion.

1. Anything that increases radiation in the environment is dangerous to public health. (Major premise)
2. Nuclear reactors increase radiation in the environment. (Minor premise)
3. Therefore, nuclear reactors are dangerous to public health. (Conclusion)

---

**SCHOLARS ON ASSESSMENT**

Hamp-Lyons, Liz, and William Condon. *Assessing the Portfolio: Principles for Practice, Theory, and Research.* Cresskill: Hampton, 2000. The authors, both noted experts in writing assessment, begin with an overview of the history and practice of portfolio-based writing assessment. Chapter 2 lists nine characteristics of portfolios, connects them to theories of writing, and then examines the use of portfolios in broader WAC and ESL contexts. Perhaps most useful to teachers is Chapter 3, with its focus on practices for using portfolios in the writing classroom and for measuring entry to and exit from writing courses. The final two chapters suggest a theory of portfolio assessment and a research agenda for those interested in the field.

The major premise is a generalization. The minor premise is a specific case. The conclusion follows from applying the generalization to the specific case.

Deductive arguments break down if one of the premises is not true or if the conclusion does not logically follow from the premises. In the following short argument, the major premise is very likely untrue.

> **UNTRUE PREMISE**
> The police do not give speeding tickets to people driving less than five miles per hour over the limit. Sam is driving fifty-nine miles per hour in a fifty-five-mile-per-hour zone. Therefore, the police will not give Sam a speeding ticket.

The conclusion is true only if the premises are true. If the police sometimes give tickets for less than five-mile-per-hour violations, Sam cannot safely conclude that he will avoid a ticket.

In the following argument, both premises might be true, but the conclusion does not follow logically from them.

> **CONCLUSION DOES NOT FOLLOW**
> All members of our club ran in this year's Boston Marathon. Jay ran in this year's Boston Marathon. Therefore, Jay is a member of our club.

The fact that Jay ran the marathon is no guarantee that he is a member of the club. Presumably, many runners are nonmembers.

Assuming that both premises are true, the following argument holds up.

> **CONCLUSION FOLLOWS**
> All members of our club ran in this year's Boston Marathon. Jay is a member of our club. Therefore, Jay ran in this year's Boston Marathon.

**SCHOLARS ON ASSESSMENT**

Smith, Jane Bowman, and Kathleen Blake Yancey, eds. *Self-assessment and Development in Writing: A Collaborative Inquiry.* Cresskill: Hampton, 2000. The essays in this collection argue for self-assessment as an integral part of a writer's development. Students' reflections on their writing also provide useful data for course and program assessment, as many of the authors explain.

## 48b Distinguish between legitimate and unfair emotional appeals.

There is nothing wrong with appealing to readers' emotions. After all, many issues worth arguing about have an emotional as well as a logical dimension. Even the Greek logician Aristotle lists *pathos* (emotion) as a legitimate argumentative tactic.

In the essay printed in 46a, Jane Goodall has a good reason for tugging at readers' emotions: Her subject is animal testing. In her conclusion, Goodall appeals to readers' emotions by invoking their desire to be compassionate.

**LEGITIMATE EMOTIONAL APPEAL**
Ten or 15 years ago animal-rights activists resorted to violence against humans in their efforts to break through the public's terrible apathy and lack of imagination on this issue. This extremism is counterproductive. I believe that more and more people are becoming aware that to use animals thoughtlessly, without any anguish or making an effort to find another way, diminishes us as human beings.

As we all know, however, emotional appeals are frequently misused. Many of the arguments we see in the media, for instance, strive to win our sympathy rather than our intelligent agreement. A TV commercial suggesting that you will be thin and sexy if you drink a certain diet beverage is making a pitch to emotions. So is a political speech that recommends electing John D'Eau because he is a devoted husband and father who coordinated relief efforts in Indonesia after the 2004 tsunami.

The following passage illustrates several types of unfair emotional appeals.

**UNFAIR EMOTIONAL APPEALS**
This progressive proposal to build a ski resort in the state park has been carefully researched by Western Trust, the

---

**SCHOLARS ON ASSESSMENT**

Angelo, Thomas A., and K. Patricia Cross. *Classroom Assessment Techniques: A Handbook for College Teachers.* 2nd ed. San Francisco: Jossey, 1993. While not focused specifically on writing assessment, most of the fifty techniques described in this book use writing of one kind or another to assess learning. Part 1 defines classroom assessment and its underlying goals and assumptions and offers twelve examples of successful assessment projects in courses across the disciplines. Part 2 consists of detailed descriptions of and step-by-step procedures for the fifty techniques. These include, for example, the minute paper, analytic memos, one-sentence summaries, concept maps, directed paraphrasing,

**(continued)**

largest bank in the state; furthermore, it is favored by a majority of the local merchants. The only opposition comes from narrow-minded, do-gooder environmentalists who care more about trees than they do about people; one of their leaders was actually arrested for disturbing the peace several years ago.

Words with strong positive or negative connotations, such as *progressive* and *do-gooder*, are examples of *biased language*. Attacking the persons who hold a belief (environmentalists) rather than refuting their argument is called *ad hominem*, a Latin term meaning "to the man." Associating a prestigious name (Western Trust) with the writer's side is called *transfer*. Claiming that an idea should be accepted because a large number of people are in favor (the majority of merchants) is called the *bandwagon appeal*. Bringing in irrelevant issues (the arrest) is a *red herring*, named after a trick used in fox hunts to mislead the dogs by dragging a smelly fish across the trail.

## 48c Judge how fairly a writer handles opposing views.

The way in which a writer deals with opposing views is telling. Some writers address the arguments of the opposition fairly, conceding points when necessary and countering others, all in a civil spirit. Other writers will do almost anything to win an argument: either ignoring opposing views altogether or misrepresenting such views and attacking their proponents.

In your own writing, you build credibility by addressing opposing arguments fairly. (See also 47f.) In your reading, you can assess the credibility of your sources by looking at how they deal with views not in agreement with their own.

**SCHOLARS ON ASSESSMENT (continued)**

double-entry journals, autobiographical sketches, diagnostic learning logs, chain notes, and e-mail. The book concludes with advice on how to build on the lessons learned from assessment.

### Describing the views of others

Writers and politicians often deliberately misrepresent the views of others. One way they do this is by setting up a "straw man," a character so weak that he is easily knocked down. The *straw man* fallacy consists of an oversimplification or outright distortion of opposing views. For example, in a California debate over attempts to control the mountain lion population, pro-lion groups characterized their opponents as trophy hunters bent on shooting harmless lions and sticking them on the walls of their dens. In truth, such hunters were only one faction of those who saw a need to control the lion population.

In response to the District of Columbia's request for voting representation, some politicians have set up a straw man, as shown in the following example.

**STRAW MAN FALLACY**
Washington, DC, residents are lobbying for statehood. Giving a city such as the District of Columbia the status of a state would be unfair.

The straw man wants statehood. In fact, most District citizens are lobbying for voting representation in any form, not necessarily through statehood.

### Quoting opposing views

Writers often quote the words of writers who hold opposing views. In general, this is a good idea, for it assures some level of fairness and accuracy. At times, though, both the fairness and accuracy are an illusion.

A source may be misrepresented when it is quoted out of context. All quotations are to some extent taken out of context, but a fair writer will explain the context to readers. To select a provocative sentence from a source and to ignore the more moderate sentences surrounding it is both unfair and misleading. Sometimes a writer deliberately distorts a source through the device of ellipsis dots. Ellipsis dots tell readers that words have been omitted from the original source. When those words are crucial to an author's meaning, omitting them is obviously unfair. (See also 39d.)

**ORIGINAL SOURCE**
Johnson's *History of the American West* is riddled with inaccuracies and astonishing in its blatantly racist description of the Indian wars. —B. R., reviewer

**MISLEADING QUOTATION**
According to B. R., Johnson's *History of the American West* is "astonishing in its . . . description of the Indian wars."

**EXERCISE 48–1**    Explain what is illogical in the following brief arguments. It may be helpful to identify the logical fallacy or fallacies by name. Answers to lettered sentences appear in the back of the book.

a. My roommate, who is an engineering major, is taking a course called Structures of Tall Buildings. All engineers have to know how to design tall buildings.
b. If you're old enough to vote, you're old enough to drink. Therefore, the drinking age should be lowered to eighteen.
c. Cable stations that rely on nauseating reality shows, annoying infomercials for useless products, idiotic talk shows, and second-rate movies should have their licenses pulled.
d. Most young people can't afford to buy a house in Silicon Valley because they spend too much money on new clothes and computer games.
e. If you're not part of the solution, you're part of the problem.

1. Whenever I wash my car, it rains. I have discovered a way to end all droughts — get all the people to wash their cars.
2. Either learn how to build a Web site or you won't be able to get a decent job after college.

**EXERCISE 48–1    Answers:**

a. hasty generalization; b. false analogy; c. biased language; d. faulty cause-and-effect reasoning; e. *either...or* fallacy

1. faulty cause-and-effect reasoning; 2. *either...or* fallacy; 3. hasty generalization; 4. *ad hominem*; 5. biased language; 6. faulty cause-and-effect reasoning; 7. non sequitur; 8. false analogy; 9. hasty generalization; 10. non sequitur

3. College professors tend to be sarcastic. Three of my five professors this semester make sarcastic remarks.

4. Although Ms. Bell's book on Joe DiMaggio was well researched, I doubt that an Australian historian can contribute much to our knowledge of an American baseball player.

5. Slacker co-workers and crazy, big-mouthed clients make our spineless managers impose ridiculous workloads on us hardworking, conscientious employees.

6. If professional sports teams didn't pay athletes such high salaries, we wouldn't have so many kids breaking their legs at hockey and basketball camps.

7. Ninety percent of the students oppose a tuition increase; therefore, the board of trustees should not pass the proposed increase.

8. If more people would take a long, close look at businesses like Microsoft and Amazon, they could reorganize their family lives to run successfully.

9. A mandatory ten-cent deposit on bottles and cans will eliminate litter because everyone I know will return the containers for the money rather than throw them away.

10. Researching what voters think during an election campaign is useless when most citizens don't vote anyway.

# 49

## Writing in the disciplines

Writing is a fact of college life. No matter what you study, you will be expected to write for a variety of audiences in a variety of formats. College courses expose you to the thinking of scholars in many disciplines, such as the humanities (literature, music, art), the social sciences (psychology, anthropology, sociology), and the sciences (biology, physics, chemistry). Writing in any discipline provides the opportunity to practice the methods used by scholars in these fields and to enter into their debates.

### SCHOLARS ON WRITING IN THE DISCIPLINES

*The WAC Clearinghouse* <http://wac.colostate.edu/>. Ed. **Mike Palmquist.** This invaluable online resource brings together five journals, four book series, and a host of resources on teaching with writing across the disciplines. The journals are *Language and Learning across the Disciplines; Academic.Writing: Interdisciplinary Perspectives on Communication across the Curriculum; Across the Disciplines: Interdisciplinary Perspectives on Language, Learning, and Academic Writing; The WAC Journal;* and *RhetNet.* The book series present online books sponsored by the *WAC Clearinghouse,* including reference books on rhetoric and composition, and republished books that have made a significant impact on WAC theory and practice. In addition to these publications, readers will find a rich array of links to programs, research, and teaching exchanges.

Each field has its own questions, evidence, language, and methods. But all disciplines share certain expectations for good writing. As you write in college courses, be aware of both the commonalities and the variations in different fields.

## 49a Find commonalities across disciplines.

If you understand the features that are common to writing in all disciplines, you will have an easier time sorting out the unique aspects of writing in a particular field.

A good paper in any field needs to communicate a writer's purpose to an audience (see 1a) and to explore an engaging question about a subject (see 1b). All effective writers make an argument and support their claims with evidence (see 47). Writers in any field need to show readers the thesis they're developing (or, in the sciences, the hypothesis they're testing) and how they counter opposing explanations or objections of other writers. All disciplines require writers to document where they found their evidence and from whom they borrowed ideas (see 49e).

## 49b Recognize the questions writers in a discipline ask.

Disciplines are characterized by the kinds of questions their scholars attempt to answer. Social scientists, who analyze human behavior, might ask about the factors that cause people to act in certain ways. Humanities scholars interpret texts within their cultural contexts; they ask questions about the society at the time a text was written or about the connections between an author's life and work. Historians, who seek an understanding of the past, ask questions about the causes and effects of events and about connections between present and past events. Scientists collect data and ask questions to help them interpret the data.

**SCHOLARS ON WRITING IN THE DISCIPLINES**

Coffin, Caroline, et al. *Teaching Academic Writing: A Toolkit for Higher Education.* New York: Routledge, 2003. This book offers a wealth of approaches to teaching writing across the disciplines and to reflecting on the purposes for such writing. The first chapter explains the authors' theoretical framework and the goals of the book. The rest of the chapters focus on integrating process approaches with textual analysis, introducing students to the conventions of writing in the disciplines, assessing student writing, giving effective feedback, and teaching writing in electronic environments. Each chapter includes detailed suggestions for teaching activities and sample assignments.

One way to understand how disciplines ask different questions is to look at assignments on the same topic in various fields. Many disciplines, for example, might be interested in cults. The following are some questions that writers in different fields might ask in response to an assignment about cults.

| | |
|---|---|
| **SOCIOLOGY** | What role does gender play in cult leadership? |
| **FILM** | How does the movie *Fight Club* portray contemporary cults? |
| **HISTORY** | Why did the cult of Caesar take hold in ancient Rome? |
| **BIOLOGY** | Do individuals susceptible to cult influence share genetic characteristics? |

The questions you will ask in any discipline will form the basis of the thesis for your paper. The questions themselves don't communicate a central idea, but they may lead you to one. For a history paper, for example, you might begin with the question "Why did the cult of Caesar take hold in ancient Rome?" You might work your way around to a thesis like this:

> By raising Caesar to the status of a deity, imperial Rome attempted to unify the various peoples in its far-flung realm into one cult of worship centered on the emperor.

Whenever you write for a college course, try to determine the kinds of questions scholars in the field might ask about a topic. You can find clues in assigned readings, lecture or discussion topics, e-mail discussion groups, and the paper assignment itself. When in doubt, ask your instructor for guidance.

**SCHOLARS ON WRITING IN THE DISCIPLINES**

Russell, David R., and Arturo Yañez. " 'Big Picture People Rarely Become Historians': Genre Systems and the Contradictions of General Education." *Writing Selves/Writing Societies: Research from Activity Perspectives.* Ed. Charles Bazerman and David R. Russell. *WAC Clearinghouse.* 2003 <http://wac.colostate.edu/books/selves_societies/russell/>. As Russell and Yañez show in their study of students' motivations for writing in an introductory history course, the teacher and the students may have very different conceptions of what constitutes a disciplinary genre. From their findings the authors conclude that composition teachers need to help students learn not just the *what* or *how* of a genre but also the *why* — that is, the underlying motives that shape genres. With this deeper understanding, they will become more flexible and versatile writers across the disciplines.

## 49c Understand the kinds of evidence writers in a discipline use.

Regardless of the discipline in which you're writing, you must support any claims you make with evidence — facts, statistics, examples and illustrations, expert opinion, and so on. Familiarize yourself with the kinds of evidence most writers use to support claims in the field you are writing in. For an English paper that examines three types of parent-child relationships in *King Lear,* you would look closely at lines from Shakespeare's play. For a psychology paper on the connection between medication and suicidal impulses, you might study the results of clinical trials. For a history paper on Renaissance attitudes toward marriage, you might examine historical artifacts such as letters, diaries, and church records.

The kinds of evidence used in different disciplines commonly overlap. Students of geography, media studies, and political science, for example, all might use census data to explore different topics. The evidence that one discipline values, however, might not be sufficient to support an interpretation or a conclusion in another field. You might use personal anecdotes or interviews in an anthropology paper, for example, but such evidence would be irrelevant in a biology lab report. The chart on page 521 lists the kinds of evidence accepted in various disciplines.

## 49d Become familiar with a discipline's language conventions.

Every discipline has a specialized vocabulary. As you read the articles and books in a field, you'll notice certain words and phrases that come up repeatedly. Sociologists, for example, use terms like *independent variables, political opportunity resources,* and *dyads* to describe social phenomena;

---

**SCHOLARS ON WRITING IN THE DISCIPLINES**

Young, Art. "Writing across and against the Curriculum." *College Composition and Communication* 54 (2003): 472–85. Young argues that the succinctness of poetic language provides students with another way to enter disciplinary conversations. Poetic language, he says, "engages, recasts, and critiques disciplinary knowledge without having to conform to conventions." Academic conventions are an alien discourse to some students and are so familiar to others that they can write on autopilot. Poetic language requires both types of student writers to rethink form and content, and the resulting disequilibrium can lead to connections that otherwise might not have been available. Young suggests that poetry assignments be brief and informal writing-to-learn experiences rather than graded writing. Students should also be given a chance to share and reflect on their writing.

## Acceptable evidence in various disciplines

### Humanities: Literature, art, film, music, philosophy

- Passages of text or lines of a poem
- Details from an image or a work of art
- Passages of a musical composition
- Critical essays that analyze original works

### Humanities: History

- Firsthand sources such as photographs, letters, maps, and government documents
- Scholarly books and articles that interpret evidence

### Social sciences: Psychology, sociology, political science, anthropology

- Data from original experiments
- Results of field research such as interviews, observations, or surveys
- Reports that interpret or analyze data or that place data in context

### Sciences: Biology, chemistry, physics

- Data from original experiments
- Scholarly articles that report findings from experiments

computer scientists might refer to *algorithm design* and *loop invariants* to describe programming methods. At its best, a discipline's specialized vocabulary allows researchers to conduct academic conversations efficiently; at its worst, it can mystify or alienate readers. Use discipline-specific terms only when you are certain that you and your readers fully understand their meaning. If a simple, widely understood alternative exists, use it. Keep your focus on expressing your points as clearly as possible. (See 17a.)

**SCHOLARS ON WRITING IN THE DISCIPLINES**

Young, Richard E. "Toward a Taxonomy of 'Small' Genres and Writing Techniques for WAC." Introd. Mike Palmquist. *WAC Clearinghouse.* 2003 <http://wac.colostate.edu/young/>. Young has collected 155 examples of typical writing tasks in courses across the disciplines. Each example includes short directions for carrying out the task. Palmquist introduces the list (available in printable PDF format) and invites readers to make their own contributions.

In addition to vocabulary, many fields of study have developed specialized writing conventions. As you read articles and books in a discipline, note how writers express their ideas. In some fields, for example, writers use the first-person point of view, while in others the third person is preferred. Scientists and most social scientists, who depend on quantitative research, tend to use more impersonal language because they are attempting to present objective findings. By contrast, writers in the humanities and in some social sciences often use the personal pronoun *I* or discuss their personal experiences.

Note, too, the conventions in a field for verb tenses. Literature scholars use the present tense to discuss a text: *Hughes effectively dramatizes different views of minority assertiveness.* (See 59e.) Social scientists use the past tense to describe experiments and the present tense to discuss the findings: *In 2003, Berkowitz released the first double-blind placebo study. . . . These results paint a murky picture.* (See 60c.)

Specialists frequently adapt their language and tone to suit their purpose and audience. Influencing public policy or explaining research to the general public, for example, demands a different writing style than does sharing ideas with colleagues. Be sure to assess your own writing situation for purpose and audience (see 1a).

## 49e Use a discipline's preferred citation style.

In any discipline, you must give credit to those whose ideas or words you have borrowed. Whenever you write, it is your responsibility to avoid plagiarism by citing sources honestly and accurately (see 52).

While all disciplines emphasize careful documentation, each follows a particular system of citation that its members have agreed on. Writers in the humanities usually use the system established by the Modern Language Association

---

**SCHOLARS ON WRITING IN THE DISCIPLINES**

Kiefer, Kate, and Jamie Neufeld. "Making the Most of Response: Reconciling Coaching and Evaluating Roles for Teachers across the Curriculum." *Academic.Writing* 7 May 2002 <http://wac.colostate.edu/aw/articles/kiefer_neufeld_2002.htm>. Through detailed examples drawn from experience, the authors illustrate how teachers in any discipline can use portfolios and electronic bulletin boards as techniques to balance the often conflicting roles of writing coach and writing gatekeeper. By building room in the course for supportive advice on writing, the authors argue, teachers can shift more effectively to final evaluation.

(MLA); scholars in some social sciences, such as psychology and anthropology, follow the style guidelines of the American Psychological Association (APA); scholars in history and some humanities typically follow *The Chicago Manual of Style*. For guidance on using the MLA, APA, or *Chicago* format, see section 57, 60, or 61, respectively.

## 49f Look closely at one discipline: Psychology.

To write for a psychology class, you need to ask the kinds of questions writers typically ask in psychology, to determine what counts as evidence and what language conventions writers follow, and to familiarize yourself with the citation style used in psychology. (For a research essay on childhood obesity for a psychology class, see 60f.)

Psychologists generally investigate human behavior and perceptions. Here are a few examples of questions they might ask on the topic of childhood obesity. Any one of these questions could form the basis of a thesis for a paper.

- To what degree can obesity be explained by social or cultural influences?
- What is the relationship between childhood obesity and adult obesity?
- Does obesity affect cognitive functioning and, therefore, performance in school?

Psychologists look for evidence in case studies and the results of experiments. They do not use expert opinion as evidence. Following are some examples of the kinds of evidence they use.

- Facts and statistics (such as "Subjects taking orlistat achieved an average reduction in body-mass index of 0.55%")
- Results of original experiments

**SCHOLARS ON WRITING IN THE DISCIPLINES**

Thaiss, Christopher, and Terry Myers Zawacki. "Questioning Alternative Discourses: Reports from across the Disciplines." *ALT DIS: Alternative Discourses and the Academy.* Ed. Christopher Schroeder, Helen Fox, and Patricia Bizzell. Portsmouth: Heinemann, 2002. 80–96. The authors argue that academic discourse structures and conventions are not as resistant to alternatives as they are often assumed to be. They present their research in seven social and natural science disciplines to show how teachers, as writers, make choices about using alternative structures and how, in turn, their choices influence the writing assignments they give their students. The authors conclude that teachers cannot simply provide students with templates for writing in a discipline; rather, both teachers and students need to investigate the varied ways that writing takes shape.

- Examples and illustrations (such as "One child in the study reported that her weight prevented her from seeking out new friends")

Psychologists use straightforward and concise language and depend on special terms to explain their findings.

- Specialized vocabulary includes *methods, results, double-blind study, review of literature, social identity perspective,* and *nonverbal emotions.*
- Often researchers have specific definitions for terms that nonspecialists use differently. For example, if a psychologist asks whether obese children are "depressed," the term refers to a specific mental disorder, not to a general mood of sadness.
- When reporting conclusions, writers in psychology use the past tense (*Berkowitz found*) or the present perfect tense (*Berkowitz has found*). When discussing results, they use the present tense (*The results confirm*).

When citing sources, psychologists generally follow the citation guidelines of the American Psychological Association (APA). See 60d.

**EXERCISE 49–1**   Interview a faculty member in a field that interests you. Find out what questions writers in the field ask, what counts as evidence in the field, what its language conventions are, and what citation style it requires. Summarize your findings.

**SCHOLARS ON WRITING IN THE DISCIPLINES**

McLeod, Susan, et al. *WAC for the New Millennium: Strategies for Continuing Writing across the Curriculum Programs.* Urbana: NCTE, 2001. This collection of articles by noted WAC scholars focuses on higher education initiatives and developments that have shaped and continue to shape WAC programs, including assessment, technology, service learning, learning communities, writing centers, and writing fellows programs.

## Approaching an assignment in any discipline

The following three assignments might seem to have nothing in common; but in fact they all use key terms specific to the field, they all use the vocabulary of the field to describe the purpose of the assignment, and they all explain or suggest the kinds of evidence the writers should use.

### Environmental Science

The El Niño Southern Oscillation (ENSO) is a worldwide climatic oscillation. Evaluate the scientific issues involved in enhancing our ability to predict ENSO events and current limitations to our forecasting ability. Use scientific papers, abstracts, review articles, and course readings to support your conclusions.

1. Key terms
2. Purpose: to summarize and analyze research findings
3. Appropriate evidence: articles and visuals, especially conflicting data

### Anthropology

Compare and contrast the male rites of passage among the Sambia of New Guinea and the Maasai of southern Kenya. Consult ethnographic descriptions of Sambian and Maasai rituals in course readings.

1. Key terms
2. Purpose: to analyze similarities and differences
3. Appropriate evidence: anthropologists' field research

(*continued*)

---

**SCHOLARS ON WRITING IN THE DISCIPLINES**

Reiss, Donna, and Art Young. "WAC Wired: Electronic Communication across the Curriculum." *WAC for the New Millennium: Strategies for Continuing Writing across the Curriculum Programs.* Ed. Susan McLeod et al. Urbana: NCTE, 2001. 52–85. The authors begin by listing the electronic communication skills required in today's workplaces and describe the ways WAC is changing in a digital age. They examine the range of approaches to writing online and how these affect traditional WAC practices, such as writing to learn, multiple-draft requirements, collaborative writing, and peer response. They conclude by reflecting on the future of electronic communication across the curriculum, including the use of electronic portfolios, access and intellectual property issues, and the role of the professor in a wired classroom.

## Approaching an assignment in any discipline (*continued*)

### Business

Develop a position in response to the following question:
Do corporate takeovers (changes in corporate control)
create or destroy value? To determine how these value
changes come about, analyze case studies and
Securities and Exchange Commission documents.

1. Key terms
2. Purpose: to analyze certain evidence and to argue a position based on that analysis
3. Appropriate evidence: examples of corporate takeovers

Once you have determined the expectations of a writing assignment, you must be sure to do the following, regardless of the discipline you are writing in.

- Determine your audience and purpose (see 1a).
- Ask questions appropriate to the field (see 49b).
- Formulate a thesis (see 2a).
- Gather evidence. Conduct research if necessary (see 50).
- Identify the required citation style (see 53).

For more advice on interpreting a writing assignment, see the chart on pages 10–11.

**SCHOLARS ON WAC AND ESL**

Johns, Ann M. "ESL Students and WAC Programs: Varied Populations and Diverse Needs." *WAC for the New Millennium: Strategies for Continuing Writing across the Curriculum Programs.* Ed. Susan McLeod et al. Urbana: NCTE, 2001. 141–64. Johns reviews the literature on second-language acquisition, error, and contrastive rhetorics and suggests ways to help faculty across the curriculum in their work with ESL writers, including how to approach errors and head off plagiarism.

# Part X

# Researched Writing

**ON THE WEB**

**dianahacker.com/bedhandbook/instructor**
- Exercise masters
- Quiz masters
- Transparency masters

College research assignments ask you to pose a question worth exploring, to read widely in search of possible answers, to interpret what you read, to draw reasoned conclusions, and to support those conclusions with valid and well-documented evidence. Such assignments may at first seem overwhelming, but if you pose a question that intrigues you and approach it with genuine curiosity, you will soon learn how rewarding research can be.

The process takes time: time for researching and time for drafting, revising, and documenting the paper in the appropriate style (see 53). Before beginning a research project, set a realistic schedule of deadlines. One student constructed the following schedule for a research paper assigned on October 3 and due October 31.

| SCHEDULE | FINISHED BY |
|---|---|
| 1. Pose possible questions worth exploring. | October 5 |
| 2. Talk with a reference librarian and plan a search strategy. | 6 |
| 3. Settle on a topic. | 7 |
| 4. Locate sources. | 10 |
| 5. Read and take notes. | 12 |
| 6. Draft a tentative thesis and an outline. | 13 |
| 7. Draft the paper. | 18 |
| 8. Visit the writing center to get help with ideas for revision. | 19 |
| 9. Do further research if necessary. | 22 |
| 10. Revise the paper. | 27 |
| 11. Prepare a list of works cited. | 28 |
| 12. Proofread the final draft. | 30 |
| 13. Final draft due. | 31 |

Notice that this student has budgeted more than a week for drafting and revising the paper. It's easy to spend too much time gathering sources; make sure you allow a significant portion of your schedule for drafting and editing your work.

**SCHOLARS ON RESEARCH ASSIGNMENTS**

Davis, Robert, and Mark Shadle. " 'Building a Mystery': Alternative Research Writing and the Academic Act of Seeking." *College Composition and Communication* 51 (2000): 417–41. Davis and Shadle argue that the explosion of and access to information have made the research process more complex and that traditional approaches need to be reconsidered. They argue for four alternatives to the traditional research paper that they believe will help students think of research in terms of "uncertainty, passionate exploration, and mystery." This article offers a brief history of the traditional research paper, a description of the proposed four alternatives, and strategies for teaching them.

**SAMPLE CALENDAR FOR A RESEARCH ASSIGNMENT**

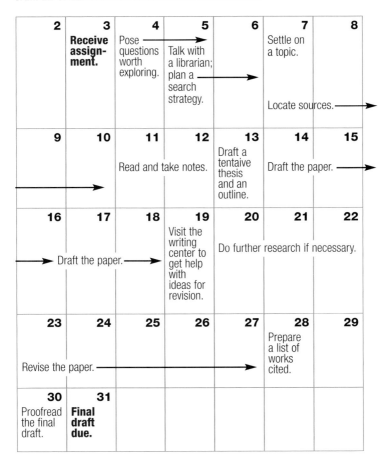

| 2 | 3 | 4 | 5 | 6 | 7 | 8 |
|---|---|---|---|---|---|---|
| | **Receive assign-ment.** | Pose questions worth exploring. | Talk with a librarian; plan a search strategy. | | Settle on a topic. | |
| | | | | | Locate sources. | |
| **9** | **10** | **11** | **12** | **13** | **14** | **15** |
| | | Read and take notes. | | Draft a tentaive thesis and an outline. | Draft the paper. | |
| **16** | **17** | **18** | **19** | **20** | **21** | **22** |
| | Draft the paper. | | Visit the writing center to get help with ideas for revision. | Do further research if necessary. | | |
| **23** | **24** | **25** | **26** | **27** | **28** | **29** |
| | Revise the paper. | | | | Prepare a list of works cited. | |
| **30** | **31** | | | | | |
| Proofread the final draft. | **Final draft due.** | | | | | |

**SCHOLARS ON RESEARCH ASSIGNMENTS**

Isaksen, Judy L., Tim Waggoner, Nancy Christensen, and Dianne Fallon. "World Wide Web Research Assignments." *Teaching English in the Two-Year College* 26 (1998): 196–98. These four straightforward assignments engage students in the "process of research," not just "the production of research findings." Using the Web as a tool and a resource for these assignments encourages students to think critically as they research, evaluate, and integrate their results in their writing.

# 50

## Conducting research

Throughout sections 50 and 51, you will encounter examples related to the three sample research papers in Part X:

- A paper on the issue of whether to limit use of cell phones while driving, written by a student in an English composition class (see pp. 659–66). The student, Angela Daly, uses the MLA (Modern Language Association) style of documentation.
- A paper on the limitations of medications to treat childhood obesity, written by a student in a psychology class (see pp. 743–55). The student, Luisa Mirano, uses the APA (American Psychological Association) style of documentation.
- A paper on the extent to which Civil War general Nathan Bedford Forrest can be held responsible for the Fort Pillow massacre, written by a student in a history class (see pp. 785–90). The student, Ned Bishop, uses *Chicago*-style documentation, a style preferred by most historians.

### 50a  Pose possible questions worth exploring.

Working within the guidelines of your assignment, pose a few questions that seem worth researching. Here, for example, are some preliminary questions jotted down by students enrolled in a variety of classes in different disciplines.

- Should the FCC broaden its definition of indecent programming to include violence?

---

**SCHOLARS ON RESEARCH ASSIGNMENTS**

Houdyshell, Mara L. "Navigating the Library: What Students (and Faculty) Need to Know." *College Teaching* 51.2 (2003): 76–78. Houdyshell, a reference librarian, offers practical tips for designing effective library research assignments.

- Which geological formations are the safest repositories for nuclear waste?
- Will a ban on stem cell research threaten important medical advancements?
- What was Marcus Garvey's contribution to the fight for racial equality?
- How can governments and zoos help preserve China's endangered panda?
- Why was amateur archaeologist Heinrich Schliemann such a controversial figure in his own time?

As you formulate possible questions, make sure that they are appropriate lines of inquiry for a research paper. Choose questions that are narrow (not too broad), challenging (not too bland), and grounded (not too speculative).

### Choosing a narrow question

If your initial question is too broad, given the length of the paper you plan to write, look for ways to restrict your focus (see also p. 6). Here, for example, is how some students narrowed their initial questions.

**TOO BROAD**

What are the hazards of fad diets?

Is the United States seriously addressing the problem of prisoner abuse?

What causes depression?

**NARROWER**

What are the hazards of low-carbohydrate diets?

To what extent has the US military addressed the problem of prisoner abuse since the Abu Ghraib discoveries?

How has the widespread use of antidepressant drugs affected teenage suicide rates?

**SCHOLARS ON RESEARCH ASSIGNMENTS**

Melzer, Daniel, and Pavel Zemliansky. "Research Writing in First-Year Composition and across Disciplines: Assignments, Attitudes, and Student Performance." *Kairos* 8.1 (2003) <http://english.ttu.edu/Kairos/8.1/index.html>. The authors report on two studies. The first explores first-year composition students' reactions to nontraditional research assignments — "ethnographic, multi-genre, hypertext, and other 'alternative' types of research projects." The second study examines the kinds of research assignments students are asked to do in other disciplines.

### Choosing a challenging question

Your research paper will be more interesting to both you and your audience if you base it on an intellectually challenging line of inquiry. Avoid bland questions that fail to provoke thought or engage readers in a debate.

**TOO BLAND**

What is obsessive-compulsive disorder?

Where is wind energy being used?

How does DNA testing work?

**CHALLENGING**

What treatments for obsessive-compulsive disorder show the most promise?

Does investing in wind energy make economic sense?

How reliable is DNA testing?

You may well need to address a bland question in the course of answering a more challenging one. For example, if you were writing about promising treatments for obsessive-compulsive disorder, you would no doubt answer the question "What is obsessive-compulsive disorder?" at some point in your paper. It would be a mistake, however, to use the bland question as the focus for the whole paper.

### Choosing a grounded question

Finally, you will want to make sure that your research question is grounded, not too speculative. Although speculative questions — such as those that address philosophical, ethical, or religious issues — are worth asking and may receive some attention in a research paper, they are inappropriate central questions. The central argument of a research paper should be grounded in facts; it should not be based entirely on beliefs.

**SCHOLARS ON RESEARCH ASSIGNMENTS**

Sutton, Brian. "Writing in the Disciplines, First-Year Composition, and the Research Paper." *Language and Learning across the Disciplines* 2.1 (1997): 46–57. Should the research assignments in first-year courses be designed to prepare students for specific writing assignments and discourse communities they will encounter in other academic disciplines? Or should they provide writers with general research skills that will transfer to a variety of settings? Building on existing scholarly work, Sutton revisits these questions, suggesting that we consider ways to incorporate both goals.

**TOO SPECULATIVE**

Is it wrong to share music files on the Internet?

Do medical scientists have the right to experiment on animals?

Are youth sports too dangerous?

**GROUNDED**

How has Internet file sharing affected the earning potential of musicians?

How have technical breakthroughs made medical experiments on animals increasingly unnecessary?

How should coaches respond to angry parents at youth sporting events?

---

**ON THE WEB**

**dianahacker.com/bedhandbook**
▶ Electronic research exercises
▶ E-ex 50–1

---

## 50b Map out a search strategy.

A search strategy is a systematic plan for tracking down sources. To create a search strategy appropriate for your research question, consult a reference librarian and take a look at your library's Web site, which will give you an overview of available resources.

### Getting started

Reference librarians are information specialists who can save you time by steering you toward relevant and reliable sources. With the help of an expert, you can make the best use of electronic databases, Web search engines, and other reference tools.

---

**SCHOLARS ON RESEARCH ASSIGNMENTS**

Shapiro, Jeremy J., and Shelley K. Hughes. "Information Literacy as a Liberal Art." *Educom Review* 31.2 (1996): 31–35. Shapiro and Hughes ask what we mean by the vague term *information literacy*. They take a broad view, suggesting that it is both a technological and a liberal art — one that requires not only the knowledge of how to use a computer to access information but also the ability to reflect critically on the information itself. The authors define seven aspects of information literacy: tool literacy, resource literacy, social structural literacy, research literacy, publishing literacy, emerging technology literacy, and critical literacy.

When you ask a reference librarian for help, be prepared to answer a number of questions:

- What is your assignment?
- In which academic discipline are you writing?
- What is your tentative research question?
- How long will the paper be?
- How much time can you spend on the project?

It's a good idea to bring a copy of the assignment with you.

In addition to speaking with a reference librarian, take some time to explore your library's Web site. You will typically find links to the library's catalog and to a variety of databases and electronic sources that you can access from any networked computer. In addition, you may find resources listed by subject, research guides, information about interlibrary loans, and links to Web sites selected by librarians for their quality. What's more, many libraries offer online reference assistance to help you locate information and refine your search strategy.

**NOTE:** If you connect to the library's Web site from off campus, you may have to set up a remote account to access subscription databases such as *InfoTrac*; ask a librarian for help.

### Including the library in your plan

Resist the temptation to do all of your work on the Internet. Even though it may seem tedious at first, becoming familiar with your library's print and electronic resources will save you time and money in the end. Libraries offer a wider range of quality materials than the Web does. The Web is not the best place to find literary criticism, historical analysis, or reports of scientific research, for example; all of these are more likely to be published in traditional ways.

**SCHOLARS ON RESEARCH ASSIGNMENTS**

Zebroski, James Thomas. "Using Ethnographic Writing to Construct Classroom Knowledge." *Thinking through Theory.* Portsmouth: Boynton, 1994. 31–43. Because his students considered the "research paper" to be "some occult art that only depraved English teachers practice (and force their students to commit)," Zebroski turned to an ethnographic research assignment instead. His article describes this assignment.

**LIBRARY HOME PAGE**

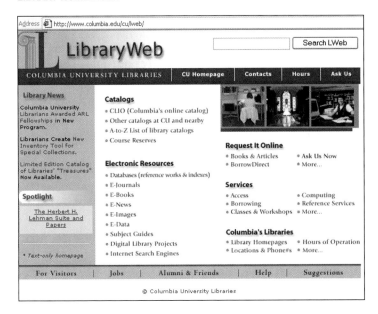

Most college assignments will require using at least some formally published sources, such as books and journal articles. Although you can locate some newspaper and magazine articles online, you may have to pay a fee or purchase a subscription to access them. Most libraries subscribe to databases that will give you unlimited access to many of these materials as well as to scholarly resources that won't turn up in a Web search. You will be able to do some of your work from any computer that can connect to the campus network. Keep in mind, however, that databases don't always include full-text articles of everything they cite. More often than not, you'll need to track down print copies in your library's stacks or request them through interlibrary loan.

**SCHOLARS ON RESEARCH ASSIGNMENTS**

Dixon, Deborah. *Writing Your Heritage: A Sequence of Thinking, Reading, and Writing Assignments.* Berkeley: Natl. Writing Project, 1993. Dixon describes an assignment sequence that introduces students to several research strategies. The assignments are a challenging alternative to the traditional "library paper."

Lazere, Donald. "Teaching the Political Conflicts: A Rhetorical Schema." *College Composition and Communication* 43 (1992): 194–213. Lazere discusses a course plan that uses a rhetorical schema to foster critical thinking for students writing about current public controversies.

*Choosing an appropriate search strategy*

No single search strategy works for every topic. For some topics, it may be appropriate to search for information in newspapers, magazines, and Web sites. For others, the best sources might be found in scholarly journals and books and specialized reference works. Still other topics might be enhanced by field research—interviews, surveys, or direct observation.

With the help of a reference librarian, each of the students mentioned on page 530 constructed a search strategy appropriate for his or her research question.

**ANGELA DALY**   Angela Daly's topic, the dangers of using cell phones while driving, was so current that books were an unlikely source (by the time a book is published, it is already dated). To find up-to-date information on her topic, Daly decided to

- search a general database for articles in magazines, newspapers, and journals
- use Web search engines, such as *Google,* to locate relevant sites, online articles, and government publications

**LUISA MIRANO**   Luisa Mirano's topic, the limitations of medications for childhood obesity, has recently become the subject of psychological studies as well as articles in the popular press (newspapers and magazines aimed at the general public). Thinking that both popular and scholarly works would be appropriate, Mirano decided to

- locate books through the library's online catalog
- check a specialized encyclopedia in psychology
- search a general database for popular articles
- search a specialized database, *PsycINFO,* for scholarly articles

**SCHOLARS ON RESEARCH ASSIGNMENTS**

Kantz, Margaret. "Helping Students Use Textual Sources Persuasively." *College English* 52 (1990): 74–91. Kantz argues that even students who come up with original ideas for argumentative research papers can have difficulty with the assignment. She points to three possible causes: (1) Students "misunderstand sources because they read them as stories." (2) Students "expect their sources to tell the truth; hence, they equate persuasive writing . . . with making things up." (3) Students "do not understand that facts are a kind of claim and are often used persuasively in so-called objective writing to create an impression."

**NED BISHOP** Ned Bishop's topic, the role played by Nathan Bedford Forrest in the Fort Pillow massacre, is an issue that has been investigated and debated by professional historians. Given the nature of his historical topic, Ned Bishop decided to

- locate books through the library's online catalog
- locate scholarly articles by searching a specialized database, *America: History and Life*
- locate 1864 newspaper articles by using a print index
- search the Web for historical primary sources that have been posted online

**50c** To locate articles, search a database or consult a print index.

Libraries subscribe to a variety of electronic databases (sometimes called *periodical databases*) that give students access to articles and other materials without charge. Many databases are limited to works published in the last ten to twenty years. To find older articles, you may need to consult a print index such as the *New York Times Index* or *Readers' Guide to Periodical Literature*.

**NOTE:** There is a difference between Web-based databases a library pays for through a subscription and those that are free to the public at large. Subscription sites provide edited material that has been scrutinized before being published. That isn't always the case with sites that are free.

*What databases offer*

Your library has access to databases that can lead you to articles in periodicals such as newspapers, magazines, and scholarly or technical journals. Some databases cover

---

**SCHOLARS ON RESEARCH ASSIGNMENTS**

Coon, Anne C. "Using Ethical Questions to Develop Autonomy in Student Researchers." *College Composition and Communication* 40 (1989): 85–89. Coon describes an assignment sequence called "breaking the law" that requires students to research an ethical issue, examine it from several perspectives, and then take a stand on it.

several subjects; others cover one subject in depth. Though each library is unique, your library might subscribe to some of the following databases and collections of databases.

**GENERAL DATABASES**

*EBSCOhost.* A portal to more than one hundred databases that include periodical articles, government documents, pamphlets, and other types of documents, many available in full text. Through *EBSCOhost,* your library may also subscribe to a wide variety of subject-specific databases.

*InfoTrac.* A collection of databases. Some of them index periodical articles, many available in full text. Through *InfoTrac,* your library may also subscribe to specialized databases in business, health, and other fields.

*LexisNexis.* A set of databases that are particularly strong in coverage of news, business, legal, and political topics. Nearly all of the material is available in full text.

*ProQuest.* A database of periodical articles, many available in full text. Through *ProQuest,* your library may also subscribe to databases in subjects such as nursing, biology, and psychology.

**SUBJECT-SPECIFIC DATABASES**

*ERIC.* An education database offering abstracts of articles published in education journals and other education-related documents.

*PubMed.* A database offering millions of abstracts of medical research studies.

*MLA Bibliography.* A database of literary criticism, with references to articles, books, and dissertations.

*PsycINFO.* A comprehensive database of psychology research, including abstracts to articles in journals and books.

Many databases include the full text of at least some articles; others list only citations or citations with short summaries called *abstracts.* In the case of full-text articles, you may have the option to print an article, save it to a disk, or e-mail it to yourself.

## Refining keyword searches in databases and search engines

Although command terms and characters vary among electronic databases and Web search engines, some of the most commonly used functions are listed here.

- Use quotation marks around words that are part of a phrase: "Broadway musicals".
- Use AND to connect words that must appear in a document: Ireland AND peace. In some search engines— *Google,* for example— *and* is assumed, so typing it is unnecessary. Other search engines require a plus sign instead: Ireland +peace.
- Use NOT in front of words that must not appear in a document: Titanic NOT movie. Some search engines require a minus sign (hyphen) instead: Titanic -movie.
- Use OR if only one of the terms must appear in a document: "mountain lion" OR cougar.
- Use an asterisk as a substitute for letters that might vary: "marine biolog*" (to find *marine biology* or *marine biologist,* for example).
- Use parentheses to group a search expression and combine it with another: (cigarettes OR tobacco OR smok*) AND lawsuits.

**NOTE:** Many search engines and databases offer an advanced search option that makes it easy to refine your search.

When full text is not available, the citation will give you enough information to track down an article. Check your library's catalog to find out if the library owns the periodical or book in which the article appears and, if so, where it is shelved. If the library does not own the item you want, you can usually request a copy through interlibrary loan; check with a librarian to find out how long the source will take to arrive.

*How to search a database*

To find articles on your topic in a database, start with a keyword search. If the first keyword you try results in no matches, don't give up; experiment with synonyms or ask a librarian for suggestions. If your keyword search results in too many matches, narrow your search. The most common way to narrow a search is to connect two search terms with AND: *childhood obesity AND treatments.* These and other strategies for narrowing or broadening a search are included in the chart on page 539.

For her paper on the dangers of using a cell phone while driving, Angela Daly conducted a keyword search in a general periodical database. She typed in *"cell phones"* and *driving* and *safety* (see screen 1 on p. 541). This search brought up thirty-five possible articles, some of which looked promising (see screen 2). Daly sent several full-text articles to her e-mail account and printed out citations to others so that she could locate them in the library.

For his history paper, Ned Bishop turned to a specialized database, *America: History and Life.* He found thirty items relevant to his topic of Nathan Bedford Forrest and the Fort Pillow massacre. Full texts of the articles were not available, but Bishop e-mailed abstracts of the articles to himself. Later he decided which articles were worth tracking down in the library.

*When to use a print index*

If you want to search for articles published before the 1980s, you may need to turn to a print index. For example, Ned Bishop consulted the *New York Times Index* to locate newspaper articles written in April 1864, just after the battle at Fort Pillow. To find older magazine articles, consult *Readers' Guide to Periodical Literature* or *Poole's Index to Periodical Literature* or ask a librarian for help.

**SCHOLARS ON RESEARCH ASSIGNMENTS**

Lutzker, Marilyn. *Research Projects for College Students: What to Write across the Curriculum.* Westport: Greenwood, 1988. Lutzker, a librarian, advocates designing research projects that are "intellectually meaningful and pedagogically useful." Her suggestions include discussing with students the various forms their finished product can take and encouraging them to "imaginatively exploit" library resources, with a special emphasis on primary sources. The book includes lists of research topics and of periodical resources.

**DATABASE SCREEN 1: KEYWORD SEARCH**

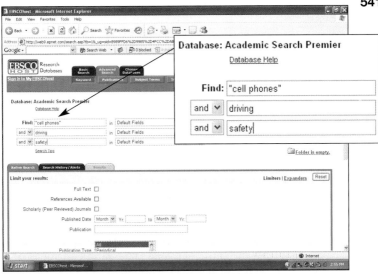

**DATABASE SCREEN 2: RESULTS OF A DATABASE SEARCH**

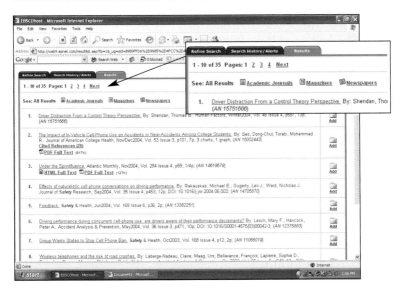

## SCHOLARS ON RESEARCH ASSIGNMENTS

Bizzell, Patricia, and Bruce Herzberg. "Research as a Social Act." *Clearing House* 60 (1987): 303–06. The authors ask us to recognize that research is "a social, collaborative act that draws on and contributes to the work of a community that cares about a given body of knowledge." They offer specific suggestions for a range of activities that will engage students as active participants in knowledge communities.

**50d** To locate books, consult the library's catalog.

The books your library owns are listed in its computer catalog, along with other resources such as videos. You can search the catalog by author, title, or topic keywords. The screens on pages 543 and 544 illustrate Luisa Mirano's search of the library catalog.

Don't be surprised if your first search calls up too few or too many results. If you have too few results, try different keywords or search for books on broader topics. If those strategies don't work, ask a librarian for suggestions. Sometimes catalogers don't use the words you would expect—for example, *motion pictures* might be used as a subject heading instead of *movies* or *films*.

If a search gives you too many results, you will need to narrow your search. Many catalogs offer an advanced search tool that will help you combine concepts and limit your results. When Luisa Mirano, whose topic was childhood obesity, entered the term *obesity* into the computer catalog, she was faced with more than fifty hits, an unmanageable number. She narrowed her search by adding two more specific terms to *obesity*: *child** (to include the terms *child, children,* and *childhood*) and *treatment.* When she still got too many results, she limited the first two terms to subject searches, which focused the search on books that had obesity in children as their primary subject. Mirano's advanced search and the seven records she retrieved are illustrated in screens 1 and 2.

Once you have narrowed your search to a list of relevant sources, you can display or print the complete record for each source, which includes its bibliographic information (author, title, publication data) and a call number. Screen 3 shows the complete record for the second title on the list generated by Mirano's search. The call number, listed beside *Availability,* is the book's address on the library shelf. When you're retrieving a book from the shelf, take the time to scan other books in the area since they are likely to be on the same topic.

**SCHOLARS ON RESEARCH ASSIGNMENTS**

Schmersahl, Carmen B. "Teaching Library Research: Process, Not Product." *Journal of Teaching Writing* 6 (1987): 231–38. Schmersahl suggests an assignment sequence that introduces students to using the library for research in a number of writing tasks. The sequence separates reading/summarizing and reference/documentation tasks from the problems of finding sources, and the assignments move students beyond the library's catalog and periodical indexes. The author argues that her approach will lead students to "adopt the spirit of inquiry that makes doing research an indispensable part of any writing project."

**LIBRARY CATALOG SCREEN 1:**
**ADVANCED SEARCH**

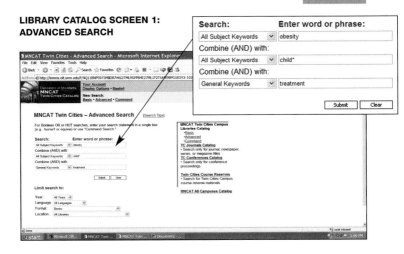

**LIBRARY CATALOG SCREEN 2: SEARCH RESULTS**

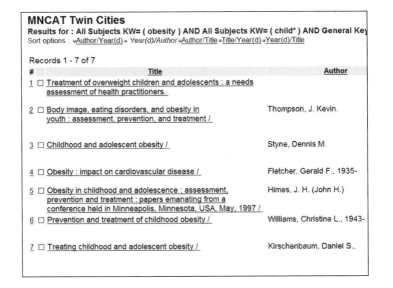

**MNCAT Twin Cities**
Results for : All Subjects KW= ( obesity ) AND All Subjects KW= ( child* ) AND General Key
Sort options : •Author/Year(d)• Year(d)/Author •Author/Title •Title/Year(d) •Year(d)/Title

Records 1 - 7 of 7

| # | Title | Author |
|---|-------|--------|
| 1 ☐ | Treatment of overweight children and adolescents : a needs assessment of health practitioners. | |
| 2 ☐ | Body image, eating disorders, and obesity in youth : assessment, prevention, and treatment / | Thompson, J. Kevin. |
| 3 ☐ | Childhood and adolescent obesity / | Styne, Dennis M. |
| 4 ☐ | Obesity : impact on cardiovascular disease / | Fletcher, Gerald F., 1935- |
| 5 ☐ | Obesity in childhood and adolescence : assessment, prevention and treatment : papers emanating from a conference held in Minneapolis, Minnesota, USA, May, 1997 / | Himes, J. H. (John H.) |
| 6 ☐ | Prevention and treatment of childhood obesity / | Williams, Christine L., 1943- |
| 7 ☐ | Treating childhood and adolescent obesity / | Kirschenbaum, Daniel S., |

## SCHOLARS ON RESEARCH ASSIGNMENTS

Strickland, James. "The Research Sequence: What to Do before the Term Paper." *College Composition and Communication* 37 (1986): 233–36. To help instructors avoid receiving research papers consisting of various sources pasted together, Strickland outlines a sequence of assignments beginning with an opinion paper, gradually incorporating research, and ending with a fully researched argument.

**LIBRARY CATALOG SCREEN 3: COMPLETE RECORD FOR A BOOK**

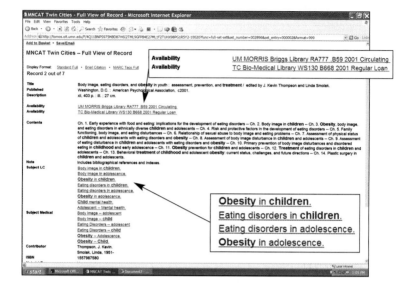

**LIBRARIAN'S TIP:** The record for a book lists related subject headings. These headings are a good way to locate other books on your subject. For example, the record above lists the terms *Obesity in children* and *Obesity in adolescence* as related subject headings. By clicking on these new terms, Mirano found a few more books on her subject.

## 50e To locate a wide variety of sources, turn to the Web.

For some—but not all—topics, the Web is an excellent resource. For example, most government agencies post information on the Web, and federal and state governments use Web sites to communicate with citizens. The sites of many

**SCHOLARS ON THE RESEARCH PROCESS**

Profozich, Richard. "Coping with the Research Paper." *Teaching English in the Two-Year College* 24 (1997): 304–07. In this brief piece, Profozich shares his methods for engaging students in inquiry and making students more comfortable with the research paper. Throughout his course, Profozich emphasizes process rather than final product, giving students ongoing opportunities to practice research. He places the research assignment early in the semester and provides social context for reading, research, discussion, and writing.

private organizations, such as the American Cancer Society and the Sierra Club, contain useful information about current issues. Even if your subject is not current, you may find the Web useful. Museums and libraries often post digital versions of primary sources, such as photographs, political speeches, and classic literary texts.

Although the Web may be a rich source of information, some of which can't be found anywhere else, it lacks quality control. Anyone can publish on the Web, so you'll need to evaluate online sources with special care (see 51d).

This section describes the following Web resources: search engines, directories, digital archives, government and news sites, and discussion forums.

---

**ON THE WEB** | **dianahacker.com/bedhandbook**
▶ Links Library
  ▶ Conducting research

---

*Search engines*

Search engines take your search terms and seek matches among millions of Web pages. Some search engines go into more depth than others, but none can search the entire Web.

For information about search engines, visit *Search Engine Showdown* at <http://www.searchengineshowdown.com>. This site classifies search engines, evaluates them, and provides updates on new search features. Following are some popular search engines:

> *Google* <http://www.google.com>
>
> *MSN Search* <http://search.msn.com>
>
> *Teoma* <http://www.teoma.com>
>
> *Yahoo!* <http://www.yahoo.com>

---

**SCHOLARS ON THE RESEARCH PROCESS**

Gibson, Craig. "Research Skills across the Curriculum: Connections with Writing-across-the-Curriculum." *Writing across the Curriculum and the Academic Library: A Guide for Librarians, Instructors, and Writing Program Directors.* Ed. Jean Sheridan. Westport: Greenwood, 1995. 55–70. Gibson traces the connections between writing and researching as processes, drawing on the work of cognitivists such as Linda Flower and constructivists such as Kenneth Bruffee. Many librarians believe that traditional library skills are no longer sufficient to help students develop information literacy. Gibson offers suggestions for how librarians and writing teachers can collaborate in helping students develop the literacies they will need.

In using a search engine, focus your search as narrowly as possible. You can sharpen your search by using many of the tips listed in the chart on page 539 or by using the search engine's advanced search form. For her paper on using cell phones while driving, Angela Daly typed *cell phones and driving* into a search engine. She got over a million matches, so she clicked on Advanced Search. On the advanced search screen she used the exact phrase *"cell phones while driving"* and restricted her search to recently updated government-sponsored sites with URLs ending in *.gov.* She further refined the search by adding the terms *accidents* and *statistics.* The resulting list of forty-one items included promising sites sponsored by the National Highway Traffic Safety Administration. Later, Daly performed a similar advanced search on URLs ending in *.org* to explore reactions among organizations to proposed legislation banning cell phone use while driving.

### Directories

Unlike search engines, which hunt for Web pages automatically, directories are put together by information specialists who choose reputable sites and arrange them by topic: education, health, politics, and so on.

Some directories are more selective and therefore more useful for scholarly research than the directories that typically accompany a search engine. For example, the directory for the *Internet Scout Project* was created for a research audience; it includes annotations that are both descriptive and evaluative. The following list includes directories especially useful for scholarly research:

> *Internet Scout Project* <http://scout.wisc.edu/Archives>
>
> *Librarian's Index to the Internet* <http://www.lii.org>
>
> *Open Directory Project* <http://www.dmoz.org>
>
> *WWW Virtual Library* <http://www.vlib.org>

**SCHOLARS ON THE RESEARCH PROCESS**

Marino, Sarah R., and Elin K. Jacob. "Questions and Answers: The Dialogue between Composition Teachers and Reference Librarians." *Reference Librarian* 37 (1992): 129–42. According to Marino and Jacob, writing teachers and reference librarians have different ideas about library research, and their contradictory views can confuse students. The authors argue that although "no one solution for this rift in communication is possible, understanding the different approaches is necessary to restore the dialogue between the two fields."

## Digital archives

Archives contain the texts of poems, books, speeches, political cartoons, and historically significant documents such as the Declaration of Independence and the Emancipation Proclamation. The materials in these sites are usually limited to official documents and older works because of copyright laws. The following online archives are impressive collections:

*American Memory* <http://memory.loc.gov>

*Archival Research Catalog* <http://www.archives.gov/research_room/arc>

*Avalon Project* <http://www.yale.edu/lawweb/avalon/avalon.htm>

*Electronic Text Center* <http://etext.lib.virginia.edu>

*Eurodocs* <http://library.byu.edu/~rdh/eurodocs>

*Internet History Sourcebooks* <http://www.fordham.edu/halsall/index.html>

*Online Books Page* <http://digital.library.upenn.edu/books>

## Government and news sites

For current topics, both government and news sites can prove useful. Many government agencies at every level provide online information. Government-maintained sites include resources such as legal texts, facts and statistics, government reports, and searchable reference databases. Here are just a few government sites:

*Census Bureau* <http://www.census.gov>

*Fedstats* <http://www.fedstats.gov>

*FirstGov* <http://www.firstgov.gov>

*GPO Access* <http://www.gpoaccess.gov>

*United Nations* <http://www.un.org>

**SCHOLARS ON THE RESEARCH PROCESS**

Zemelman, Steven, and Harvey Daniels. "Collaborative Research and Term Papers." *A Community of Writers.* Portsmouth: Boynton, 1988. 256–67. Zemelman and Daniels explore alternatives for the traditional research paper. In addition to "I-Search" strategies, they offer examples of community-based research assignments and ethnographic assignments. They advocate teaching research as a process and as a social practice; further, they suggest that students should be doing and using research in a variety of ways for a variety of purposes.

**NOTE:** You can access a state's Web site by putting the two-letter state abbreviation into a standard URL: <http://www.state.ca.us>. Substitute any state's two-letter abbreviation for the letters *ca*, which in this case stand for California.

Many popular newsletters, magazines, and television networks offer up-to-date information on the Web. These online services often allow nonsubscribers to read current stories for free. Some allow users to log on as guests and search archives without cost, but to read actual articles users typically must pay a fee. The following are some free news sites:

> *Google News* <http://news.google.com>
> *Kidon Media-Link* <http://www.kidon.com/media-link>
> *NewsLink* <http://newslink.org>

**NOTE:** Your library may subscribe to *LexisNexis* or other online databases with more full-text news sources than are available for free on the Web (see 50c).

### Discussion forums

The Web offers ways of communicating with experts and others who have an interest in your topic. You might join an online mailing list, for example, to send and receive e-mail messages relevant to your topic. Or you may wish to search a newsgroup's postings. Newsgroups resemble bulletin boards on which messages are posted and connected through "threads" as others respond. To find mailing lists and newsgroups, check a subject directory (see p. 546) to see if any are listed for the discipline you are interested in, or try one of these sites:

> *CataList* <http://www.lsoft.com/catalist.html>
> *Google Groups* <http://groups.google.com>
> *Tile.net* <http://tile.net>

**SCHOLARS ON FIELD RESEARCH**

Dellinger, Dixie G. "Alternatives to Clip and Stitch: Real Research and Writing in the Classroom." *English Journal* 78 (1989): 31–38. Dellinger demonstrates the importance of having students use various tools of inquiry — interviews, surveys, experiments — to create their own research and then write about their discoveries.

In addition to mailing lists and newsgroups, you might log on to real-time discussion forums such as chats.

**TIP:** Be aware that many of the people you contact in discussion forums will not be experts on your topic. Although you are more likely to find serious and worthwhile commentary in moderated mailing lists and scholarly discussion forums than in more freewheeling newsgroups, it is difficult to guarantee the credibility of anyone you meet online.

**50f** Consider other search tools.

In addition to articles, books, and Web sources, you may want to consult reference works such as encyclopedias and almanacs. Bibliographies (lists of works written on a topic) and citations in scholarly works can lead you to additional sources.

### Reference works

The reference section of the library holds both general and specialized encyclopedias, dictionaries, almanacs, atlases, and biographical references. Some are available in electronic format. Reference works provide information in easily digested nuggets; they often serve as a good overview of your subject and include references to the most significant works on a topic. Check with a reference librarian to see which works are most appropriate for your project.

**GENERAL REFERENCE WORKS** General reference works are good places to check facts and get basic information. Here are a few frequently used general references:

*American National Biography*
*National Geographic Atlas of the World*

The New Encyclopaedia Britannica

The Oxford English Dictionary

Statistical Abstract of the United States

World Almanac and Book of Facts

**NOTE:** Although general reference works are often a good place to find background about your topic, you should rarely use them in your final paper. Most instructors expect you to rely on more specialized sources.

**SPECIALIZED REFERENCE WORKS** Specialized reference works often go into a topic in depth, sometimes in the form of articles written by leading authorities. Many specialized works are available, including these:

Contemporary Authors

Encyclopedia of Applied Ethics

Encyclopedia of Crime and Justice

Encyclopedia of Psychology

McGraw-Hill Encyclopedia of Science and Technology

Check with a reference librarian to see what specialized references are available in your library.

| ON THE WEB | **dianahacker.com/bedhandbook** ▶ Research and Documentation Online   ▶ Finding sources |
|---|---|

### Bibliographies and scholarly citations

Bibliographies are lists of works written on a particular topic. They include enough information about each work (author's name, title, and publication data) so that you can locate the book or article.

Many bibliographies are annotated: They contain abstracts giving a brief overview of each work's contents. You can find book-length bibliographies by adding the term *bibliography* to a catalog search. For example, Ned Bishop typed the search term *"Civil War" AND bibliography* and found a book that listed and described publications about all aspects of the Civil War. It included a section on the Fort Pillow massacre.

In addition to book-length bibliographies, scholarly books and articles list the works the author has cited, usually at the end. These lists of sources are tremendously useful shortcuts: Often the author of the work has done some of your research for you. For example, most of the scholarly articles Luisa Mirano consulted contained citations to related research studies; through these citations, she quickly located additional relevant sources on her topic, treatments for childhood obesity. (For help tracking down works cited in a bibliography or a scholarly work, see the chart on p. 552.)

## 50g Consider doing field research.

For a composition class, you might want to visit your local historical society to research some aspect of your town's early history, such as the role it played in the underground railroad. For a sociology class, you might decide to study campus trends in classroom participation: Which students are most, and least, involved in class discussions, and why? At work, you might need to learn how food industry executives have responded to reports that their products are contributing to health problems. Projects like these may be enhanced by, and sometimes centered on, your own field research.

### Interviewing

Interviews can often shed new light on a topic. Look for an expert who has firsthand knowledge of the subject or seek

## Tracking down a source cited in a reference or scholarly work

| | | |
|---|---|---|
| Is the reference to a book? | YES → | Check the book title in your library's catalog. |

NO ↓

| | | |
|---|---|---|
| Is the reference to a chapter or an essay in a book? | YES → | Check the book title in your library's catalog. |

NO ↓

| | | |
|---|---|---|
| Is the reference to a periodical article? | YES → | Check the periodical title in your library's catalog or search for the article title in an electronic database. |

NO ↓

Ask a librarian for help.

If the work you need is not listed in the library catalog, ask a reference librarian about interlibrary loan service.

out someone whose personal experience provides an enlightening perspective on your topic.

When asking for an interview, be clear about who you are, what the purpose of the interview is, and how you would prefer to conduct it: via e-mail, over the phone, or in person. Plan for an interview by writing down a series of questions. Try to avoid questions with yes or no answers or those that encourage vague rambling. Instead, ask questions that elicit facts, anecdotes, and opinions that will add a meaningful dimension to your paper.

**INEFFECTIVE QUESTIONS**

How many years have you spent studying childhood obesity?

Is your work interesting?

**EFFECTIVE QUESTIONS**

What are some current interpretations of the causes of childhood obesity?

What treatments have you found to be most effective? Why do you think they work?

Accuracy is important. To ensure accuracy, you might want to ask permission to tape the interview; if you cannot tape the interview, take careful notes or conduct it by e-mail. When quoting your source in your paper, be as accurate and fair as possible.

## Surveying opinion

For some topics, you may find it useful to survey opinions through written questionnaires, telephone or e-mail polls, or questions posted on a Web forum. Many people are reluctant to fill out long questionnaires or answer long-winded telephone pollsters, so if you want a good response rate, you will need to limit your questions and frame them carefully.

When possible, ask yes/no questions or give multiple-choice options. Surveys with such queries can be filled out quickly, and they are easy to tabulate.

**SAMPLE YES/NO QUESTION**

Do you favor restricting the use of handheld cell phones while driving?

You may also want to ask a few open-ended questions to elicit more individual responses, some of which may be worth quoting in your paper.

> **SAMPLE OPEN-ENDED QUESTION**
> What, if any, experiences have you had with drivers distracted by cell phones?

## Visiting and observing

Your firsthand observations of a significant place—such as a museum, a park, or a historic site—can enhance a paper in a variety of disciplines. For example, while researching trends in contemporary American folk art, a student living in New York City went to an exhibit on folk art at the Museum of Modern Art. To gather information for a paper on nineteenth-century utopian experiments, a student in Peoria, Illinois, drove to nearby Bishop Hill, a commune founded in 1846 by Swedish refugees seeking religious freedom. A student studying in England visited Stonehenge and other ancient stone circles to make on-site observations for an essay in physical anthropology.

## Contacting organizations

Many organizations, both public and private, have information on their Web sites and may mail you literature in response to a phone call, an e-mail, or a letter. Although this literature can provide up-to-date information, use it judiciously. Groups tend to promote their own interests; you can't always count on them to present a balanced view.

*The Encyclopedia of Associations* (available both electronically and in print) lists groups by their concerns, such as environment or family planning, and provides addresses and phone numbers.

# 51

## Evaluating sources

With electronic search tools, you can often locate dozens or even hundreds of potential sources for your topic — far more than you will have time to read. Your challenge will be to zero in on a reasonable number of quality sources, those truly worth your time and attention.

Later, once you have decided on some sources worth consulting, your challenge will be to read them with an open mind and a critical eye.

## 51a  Select sources worth your time and attention.

Section 50 showed you how to refine your searches in the library's book catalog, in databases, and in search engines. This section shows you how to scan through the results looking for those sources that seem most promising. It also gives you tips on previewing possible sources — without actually reading them — to see whether they are likely to live up to your expectations and meet your needs.

### Scanning search results

As you scan through a list of search results, be alert for any clues indicating whether a source might be useful for your purposes or not worth pursuing. You will need to use somewhat different scanning strategies when looking at lists of hits from a book catalog, a database, and a Web search engine.

**SCHOLARS ON EVALUATING SOURCES**

Elder, Linda, and Richard Paul. "Critical Thinking and the Art of Close Reading, Part IV." *Journal of Developmental Education* 28.2 (2004): 36–37. In the last of a series of four columns on the topic of close reading, Elder and Paul outline skills needed for reading at different levels: paraphrasing the text, explicating the thesis, analyzing the author's logic, and evaluating or assessing that logic.

**BOOK CATALOGS** The library's book catalog will usually give a fairly short list of hits (see p. 543 for an example). A book's title and date of publication will often be your first clues as to whether the book is worth consulting. If a title looks interesting, you can click on it for further information: the book's subject matter and its length, for example. The table of contents may also be available, offering a glimpse of what's inside.

**DATABASES** Most databases, such as *ProQuest* and *Lexis-Nexis*, list at least the following information, which can help you decide if a source is relevant, current, scholarly enough, and a suitable length for your purposes.

Title and brief description (How relevant?)

Date (How current?)

Name of periodical (How scholarly?)

Length (How extensive in coverage?)

The following are just a few of the hits Ned Bishop came up with when he consulted a general database in search of articles on the Fort Pillow massacre, using the search term *Fort Pillow*.

---

☐ **Black, blue and gray: the other Civil War; African-American soldiers, sailors and spies were the unsung heroes.** *Ebony* Feb 1991 v46 n4 p96(6)
Mark     View <u>text and retrieval choices</u>

☐ **The Civil War.** (movie reviews) Lewis Cole. *The Nation* Dec 3, 1990 v251 n19 p694(5)
Mark     View <u>text and retrieval choices</u>

☐ **The hard fight was getting into the fight at all.** (black soldiers in the Civil War) Jack Fincher. *Smithsonian* Oct 1990 v21 n7 p46(13)
Mark     View <u>text and retrieval choices</u>

☑ **The Fort Pillow massacre: a statistical note.** John Cimprich, Robert C. Mainfort Jr.. *Journal of American History* Dec 1989 v76 n3 p830(8)
Mark     View <u>extended citation and retrieval choices</u>

---

**SCHOLARS ON EVALUATING SOURCES**

Grobman, Laurie. "'Found It on the Web, so Why Can't I Put It in My Paper?' Authorizing Basic Writers." *Journal of Basic Writing* 18 (1999): 76–90. Grobman suggests that Web sources—more than traditional library sources—provide students with opportunities to analyze and evaluate information with a greater sense of authority. Grobman writes that when students search the Web, they are making decisions throughout the process that they don't make when they use library sources. Also, because of the range of information available on the Web, they are developing a broader understanding of "texts" and the ways they are used.

By scanning the titles, Bishop saw that only one contained the words *Fort Pillow.* The article title and the name of the periodical, *Journal of American History,* suggested that the source was scholarly. The 1989 publication date was not a problem, since currency is not necessarily a key issue for historical topics. The article's length (eight pages) is given in parentheses at the end of the citation. While the article may seem short, the topic — a statistical note — is narrow enough to ensure adequate depth of coverage. Bishop decided the article was worth consulting, even though it required a trip to the library because it was not available online in full text.

Bishop chose not to consult the other sources. The first is a brief article in a popular magazine, the second is a movie review, and the third surveys a topic that is far too broad, "black soldiers in the Civil War."

**WEB SEARCH ENGINES**   Anyone can publish on the Web, and unreliable sites often masquerade as legitimate sources of information. As you scan through search results, look for the following clues about the probable relevance, currency, and reliability of a site — but be aware that the clues are by no means foolproof.

Title, keywords, and lead-in text (How relevant?)

A date (How current?)

An indication of the site's sponsor or purpose (How reliable?)

The URL, especially the domain name (How relevant? How reliable?)

The following are a few of the results that Luisa Mirano retrieved after typing the keywords *childhood obesity* into a search engine; she limited her search to works with those words in the title.

## SCHOLARS ON EVALUATING SOURCES

Gillette, Mary Ann, and Carol Videon. "Seeking Quality on the Internet: A Case Study of Composition Students' Works Cited." *Teaching English in the Two-Year College* 26 (1998): 189–94. A case study conducted by Gillette and Videon uncovered problems with the quality of Web sources cited in student research papers, highlighting the need for providing students with clear guidelines for locating quality sites. In the assignment analyzed, nearly half of the cited sources were student papers posted on the Web; some came from extremely brief sources or other sources lacking credibility. The authors provide a list of suggested guidelines for students using Web sources and an example of a worksheet to help students evaluate Web sources.

American **Obesity** Association - **Childhood Obesity**
**Childhood Obesity**. **Obesity** in children ... Note: The term "childhood obesity" may refer to both **children** and adolescents. In general, we ...
www.**obesity**.org/subs/**childhood**/ - 17k - Jan 8, 2005 - Cached - Similar pages

**Childhood Obesity**
KS Logo, **Childhood Obesity**. advertisement. Source. ERIC Clearinghouse on Teaching and Teacher Education. Contents. ... Back to the Top Causes of **Childhood Obesity**. ...
www.kidsource.com/kidsource/content2/**obesity**.html - 18k - Cached - Similar pages

**Childhood Obesity**, June 2002 Word on Health - National Institutes ...
**Childhood Obesity** on the Rise, an article in the June 2002 edition of The NIH Word on Health - Consumer Information Based on Research from the National ...
www.nih.gov/news/WordonHealth/ jun2002/**childhoodobesity**.htm - 22k -
Cached - Similar pages

MayoClinic.com - **Childhood obesity**: Parenting advice
... **Childhood obesity**: Parenting advice By Mayo Clinic staff. ... Here are some other tips to help your **obese child** — and yourself: Be a positive role model. ...
www.mayoclinic.com/invoke.cfm?id=FL00058 - 42k - Jan 8, 2005 - Cached - Similar pages

Mirano found the first site, which was sponsored by a research-based organization, promising enough to explore for her paper. The second and fourth sites held less promise, however, because they seemed to offer popular rather than scholarly information. In addition, the *KidSource* site was populated by distracting commercial advertisements. Mirano rejected the third source not because of its reliability — in fact, research from the National Institutes of Health was what she was looking for — but because a quick skim of its contents revealed that the information was too general for her purposes.

### Previewing sources

Once you have decided that a source looks promising, preview it quickly to see whether it lives up to its promise. If you can reject irrelevant or unreliable sources before actually reading them, you will save yourself time. Techniques for previewing a book or an article are relatively simple; strategies for investigating the likely worth of a Web site are more complicated.

**PREVIEWING A BOOK**   As you preview a book, keep in mind that even if the entire book is not worth your time, parts of it may prove useful. For example, by using the indexes of several books on Civil War history, Ned Bishop quickly located useful passages describing the Fort Pillow massacre. As you preview a book, try any or all of the following techniques:

- Glance through the table of contents, keeping your research question in mind.
- Skim the preface in search of a statement of the author's purposes.
- Use the index to look up a few words related to your topic.
- If a chapter looks useful, read its opening and closing paragraphs and skim any headings.
- Consider the author's style and approach. Does the style suggest enough intellectual depth, or is the book too specialized for your purposes? Does the author present ideas in an unbiased way?

**PREVIEWING AN ARTICLE**   As with books, the techniques for previewing an article are fairly straightforward. In researching her paper on childhood obesity, for example, Luisa Mirano spent no more than a few minutes scanning an article before deciding whether it was worth her time.

Here are a few strategies for previewing an article:

- Consider the publication in which the article is printed. Is it a scholarly journal? A popular magazine? A newspaper with a national reputation?
- For a magazine or journal article, look for an abstract or a statement of purpose at the beginning; also look for a summary at the end.

**SCHOLARS ON RESEARCH WRITING**

Bean, John C. "Encouraging Engagement and Inquiry in Research Papers." *Engaging Ideas: The Professor's Guide to Integrating Writing, Critical Thinking, and Active Learning in the Classroom.* San Francisco: Jossey, 1996. 197–214. Recognizing that many students "regard a research project as an encyclopedic 'all about' report on a topic area rather than as a thesis-governed response to a significant and interesting problem or question," Bean presents numerous practical, classroom-tested suggestions for helping students engage the research process more meaningfully. Especially useful are Bean's examples from across the curriculum.

- For a newspaper article, focus on the headline and the opening, known as the *lead.*
- Skim any headings and take a look at any visuals—charts, graphs, diagrams, or illustrations—that might indicate the article's focus and scope.

**PREVIEWING A WEB SITE**    It is a fairly quick and easy job to track down numerous potentially useful sources on the Web, but evaluating those sources can require some detective work. Web sites can be created by anyone, and their authors and purposes are not always readily apparent. In addition, there are no set standards for the design of Web sites, so you may need to do a fair amount of clicking and scrolling before locating clues about a site's reliability. In researching her paper on the dangers of using a cell phone while driving, Angela Daly spent considerable time previewing Web sites, many of which she rejected.

As you preview a Web site, check for relevance, reliability, and currency:

- Browse the home page. Do its contents and links seem relevant to your research question? What is the site trying to do: Sell a product? Promote an idea? Inform the public? Provide Web versions of print sources (such as newspaper stories or government reports)? Is the site's purpose consistent with your research?
- Look for the name of an author or a Webmaster, and if possible assess his or her credibility. Often a site's author is named at the bottom of the home page. If you have landed on an internal page of a site and no author is evident, try linking to the home page.
- Check for a sponsor name, and consider possible motives the organization might have in sponsoring the site. Is the group likely to look at only one side of an issue?
- Find out when the site was created or last updated. Is it current enough for your purposes?

**SCHOLARS ON RESEARCH WRITING**

Penrose, Ann M., and Cheryl Geisler. "Reading and Writing without Authority." *College Composition and Communication* 45 (1994): 505–20. Penrose and Geisler report on a first-year student and a doctoral candidate who were writing about the same topic. The two writers adopted different approaches to the assignment based on their different levels of authority. The doctoral candidate operated "with an awareness that text and knowledge claims are authored and negotiable," the first-year student "with a more traditional information-transfer model in which texts are definitive and unassailable." Penrose and Geisler suggest ways to help students engage research assignments with authority in spite of their apparent status as novices.

## Determining if a source is scholarly

For many college assignments, you will be asked to use scholarly sources. These are written by experts for a knowledgeable audience and usually go into more depth than books and articles written for a general audience. (Scholarly sources are sometimes called *refereed* or *peer-reviewed* because the work is evaluated by experts in the field before publication.) To determine if a source is scholarly, look for the following:

- Formal language and presentation
- Authors who are academics or scientists, not journalists
- Footnotes or a bibliography documenting the works cited in the source
- Original research and interpretation (rather than a summary of other people's work)
- Quotations from and analysis of primary sources (in humanities disciplines such as literature, history, and philosophy)
- A description of research methods or a review of related research (in the sciences and social sciences)

**NOTE:** In some databases, searches can be limited to refereed or peer-reviewed journals.

**NOTE:** If a site gives very little information about its authors or sponsors, be suspicious. Do not rely on such sites when conducting academic research.

### Distinguishing between primary and secondary sources

As you begin assessing evidence in a source, determine whether you are reading a primary or a secondary source. Primary sources are original documents such as letters, diaries, legislative bills, laboratory studies, field research reports, and eyewitness accounts. Secondary sources are

**SCHOLARS ON RESEARCH WRITING**

Brent, Doug. *Reading as Rhetorical Invention: Knowledge, Persuasion, and the Teaching of Research-Based Writing.* Urbana: NCTE, 1992. By introducing teachers to the work of theorists who see knowledge as a social construct, Brent helps us understand research-based writing as involving more than a set of surface conventions.

Macrorie, Ken. *The I-Search Paper.* Rev. ed. of *Searching Writing.* Portsmouth: Boynton, 1988. Macrorie describes in detail his now-famous approach to research writing. Teachers and students will find his assignment sequences useful and interesting. And Macrorie offers practical advice for managing all stages of the process.

commentaries on primary sources. A primary source for Ned Bishop was Nathan Bedford Forrest's official report on the battle at Fort Pillow. Bishop also consulted a number of secondary sources, some of which relied heavily on primary sources such as letters.

Although a primary source is not necessarily more reliable than a secondary source, it has the advantage of being a firsthand account. Naturally, you can better evaluate what a secondary source says if you have first read any primary sources it discusses.

## 51b Select appropriate versions of electronic sources.

An electronic source may appear as an abstract, an excerpt, or a full-text article or book. It is important to distinguish among these versions of sources and to use a complete version of a source, preferably one with page numbers, for your research.

Abstracts and excerpts are shortened versions of complete works. An abstract—a summary of a work's contents—typically appears in a database record for a periodical article (see p. 563). (It can also appear in a catalog listing for a book.) An abstract can give you clues about the usefulness of an article for your paper. But because an abstract is so brief (usually fewer than five hundred words), by itself it does not contain enough information to cite in your paper. To understand the author's argument and use it in your own paper, you must read the complete article. When you determine that the full article is worth reading, scroll through the record to find a link to the complete article. If you cannot access the complete article from the database, you may be able to obtain a copy of the periodical from the library stacks; if you are unsure whether your library keeps the periodical, ask a librarian for assistance.

**WRITERS ON WRITING**

What is research but a blind date with knowledge?
—Anonymous

The beginning of research is curiosity, its essence is discernment, and its goal truth and justice. —Isaac H. Satanov

res

**DATABASE RECORD WITH AN ABSTRACT**

---

**LINCC, Library Information Network for Community Colleges**
Expanded Academic ASAP

—— Article 1 of 2 —— ⊙

☐ *Civil War History*, June 1996 v42 n2 p116(17)
Mark

> "These devils are not fit to live on God's earth": war crimes and
> the Committee on the Conduct of the War, 1864-1865. *Bruce Tap.*

**Abstract:** The Committee on the Conduct of the War's report on the April 1864 Fort
Pillow massacre of black Union soldiers by Confederate forces influenced public
opinion against the atrocities of the Confederate troops and accelerated the
reconstruction program. Hostility against blacks and abolition in the South prompted
the Confederates to target black troops and deny them prisoner of war status.
Investigation exposed the barbaric act and the Northern prisoners' suffering in
Southern prisons. The report helped the inclusion of black troops in the prisoner
exchange program.

Article A18749078

---

An excerpt is the first few sentences or paragraphs (the
*lead*) of a newspaper or magazine article and usually appears
in a list of hits in an online search (see the top of p. 565).
From an excerpt you can sometimes determine whether the
complete article is useful for your paper. Sometimes, however, the thesis or topic sentence of the article is buried
deeper in the article than the excerpt reveals. In these cases,
the headline might be a clue to the usefulness of the complete article. You may find that you are required to pay a fee
to access the complete article. Before paying a fee, try searching your library's electronic databases for the article. Or your
library may have a subscription to the online publication or
may keep a copy of the periodical in its stacks.

**WRITERS ON WRITING**

Research is formalized curiosity. It is poking and prying with a
purpose.                                              —Zora Neale Hurston

The way to do research is to attack the facts at the point of greatest astonishment.                                    —Celia Green

A full-text work may appear online as a PDF (for *portable document format*) file or as an HTML file (sometimes called a *text file*). (See the database record at the bottom of p. 565.) A PDF file is usually an exact copy of the pages of a periodical article as they appeared in print, including the page numbers. Some corporate and government reports are presented online as PDF files, and these too are usually paginated. A full-text document that appears as an HTML or a text file is not paginated. If your source is available in both formats, use the PDF file in your paper because you will be able to cite specific page numbers.

## 51c Read with an open mind and a critical eye.

As you begin reading the sources you have chosen, keep an open mind. Do not let your personal beliefs prevent you from listening to new ideas and opposing viewpoints. Your research question—not a snap judgment about the question—should guide your reading.

When you read critically, you are not necessarily judging an author's work harshly; you are simply examining its assumptions, assessing its evidence, and weighing its conclusions.

**TIP:** When researching on the Web, it is easy to ignore views different from your own. Web pages that appeal to you will often link to other pages that support the same viewpoint. If your sources all seem to agree with you—and with one another—seek out opposing views and evaluate them with an open mind.

### Being alert for signs of bias

Both in print and online, some sources are more objective than others. If you were exploring the conspiracy theories

---

**WRITERS ON WRITING**

Scholarship is polite argument. —Philip Rieff

Ideas, as distinguished from events, are never unprecedented.
—Hannah Arendt

**SEARCH RESULT WITH AN EXCERPT**

> ▾ BOSTON GLOBE ARCHIVES
>
> Your search for ( ( fort AND pillow AND massacre ) ) returned **1** article(s) matching your terms.
> To purchase the full-text of an article, follow the link that says "Click for complete article."
>
> | **Perform a new search** |
>
> Your search results:
>
> TALES OF BLACKS IN THE CIVIL WAR, FOR ALL AGES
> *Published on March 23, 1998*
> **Author(s):**   Scott Alarik, Globe Correspondent
>
> For African Americans, the Civil War was always two wars. It was, of course, the war to save the
> union and destroy slavery, but for the nearly 180,000 black soldiers who served in the Union
> Army, it was also a war to establish their rights as citizens and human beings in the United
> States. Their role in defeating the Confederacy is grandly chronicled in two new books, the
> massively complete "Like Men of War" and the superbly readable children's book "Black, Blue
> and
> **Click for complete article** *(782 words)*

**DATABASE RECORD SHOWING HTML (TEXT) AND PDF OPTIONS**

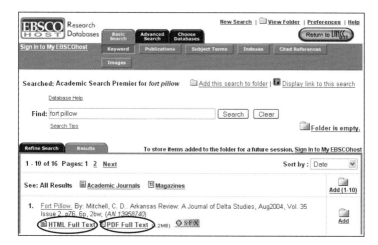

surrounding John F. Kennedy's assassination, for example, you wouldn't look to a supermarket tabloid, such as the *National Enquirer,* for answers. Even publications that are considered reputable can be editorially biased. For example, *USA Today, National Review,* and *Ms.* are all credible sources, but they are also likely to interpret events quite differently from one another. If you are uncertain about a periodical's special interests, consult *Magazines for Libraries.* To check for bias in a book, see *Book Review Digest.* A reference librarian can help you locate these resources.

Like publishers, some authors are more objective than others. If you have reason to believe that a writer is particularly biased, you will want to assess his or her arguments with special care. For a list of questions worth asking, see the chart on page 567.

### Assessing the author's argument

In nearly all subjects worth writing about, there is some element of argument, so don't be surprised to encounter experts who disagree. When you find areas of disagreement, you will want to read each source's arguments with special care, testing them with your own critical intelligence. Questions such as those in the chart on page 567 can help you weigh the strengths and weaknesses of each author's arguments.

### 51d Assess Web sources with special care.

As you may have discovered, Web sources can be deceptive. Sophisticated-looking sites can be full of dubious information, and the identities of those who created a site are often hidden, along with their motives for having created it. Even

## Evaluating all sources

**CHECKING FOR SIGNS OF BIAS**

- Does the author or publisher have political leanings or religious views that could affect objectivity?
- Is the author or publisher associated with a special-interest group, such as Greenpeace or the National Rifle Association, that might promote one side of an issue?
- Are alternative views presented and addressed? How fairly does the author treat opposing views? (See 48c.)
- Does the author's language show signs of bias? (See 48b.)

**ASSESSING AN ARGUMENT**

- What is the author's central claim or thesis?
- How does the author support this claim—with relevant and sufficient evidence or with just a few anecdotes or emotional examples?
- Are statistics consistent with those you encounter in other sources? Have they been used fairly? Does the author explain where the statistics come from? (It is possible to "lie" with statistics by using them selectively or by omitting mathematical details.)
- Are any of the author's assumptions questionable?
- Does the author consider opposing arguments and refute them persuasively? (See 48c.)
- Does the author fall prey to any logical fallacies? (See 48a.)

**TIPS FROM WRITING TUTORS**

"One of a researcher's main challenges today is ensuring that information from the Internet is accurate and credible. Asking questions—lots of them—is a researcher's best approach when finding sources online."
— *Justin Camarata, Tacoma Community College*

hate sites may be cleverly disguised to look legitimate. In contrast, sites with reliable information can stand up to careful scrutiny. For a checklist on evaluating Web sources, see page 569.

Ned Bishop came across deceptive Web sources while researching his topic, the Fort Pillow massacre. This topic is of great interest to Civil War buffs, many of them amateurs and some still fighting the war. One site looked legitimate, but when Bishop went to the home page, he was not reassured by the Confederate flags emblazoned behind the title "The War for States' Rights." Another impressive-looking site turned out to have been created by a high school junior — an intelligent young man, no doubt, but by no means an authority on the subject.

In researching her topic on the dangers of using a cell phone while driving, Angela Daly encountered sites that raised her suspicions. In particular, some sites were sponsored by the wireless communications industry, which has an obvious interest in preventing laws restricting use of its products. Even a site sponsored by the Harvard Center for Risk Analysis seemed somewhat suspect, since the wireless industry funded the center's study concluding that the risk of using a cell phone while driving is low compared with other risks.

Knowing that the creator of a site is an amateur or could be biased is not sufficient reason, however, to reject the site's information out of hand. For example, the Harvard Center for Risk Analysis offered evidence for its conclusions, and the high school junior had intelligent things to say about the Fort Pillow massacre. Nevertheless, when you know something about the creator of a site and have a sense of a site's purpose, you will be in a good position to evaluate the likely worth of its information. Consider, for example, the two sites pictured on pages 570 and 571. Not surprisingly, Angela Daly decided that the first Web site was more useful for her project than the second.

## Evaluating Web sources

**TIP:** If the sponsorship and the authorship of a site are both unclear, think twice about using the site for your research.

**AUTHORSHIP**

- Is there an author? You may need to do some clicking and scrolling to find the author's name. If you are on an internal page of a site, for example, you may need to go to the home page or click an "about this site" link to learn the name of the author.
- If there is an author, can you tell whether he or she is knowledgeable and credible? When the author's qualifications aren't listed on the site itself, look for links to the author's home page, which may provide evidence of his or her interests and expertise.

**SPONSORSHIP**

- Who, if anyone, sponsors the site? The sponsor of a site is often named and described on the home page.
- What does the URL ending tell you? The URL often specifies the type of group hosting the site: commercial (.com), educational (.edu), nonprofit (.org), governmental (.gov), military (.mil), or network (.net). URLs may also indicate a country of origin: uk (United Kingdom) or jp (Japan), for instance.

**PURPOSE AND AUDIENCE**

- Why was the site created: To argue a position? To sell a product? To inform readers?
- Who is the site's intended audience? If you do not fit the audience profile, is information on the site still relevant to your topic?

**CURRENCY**

- How current is the site? Check for the date of publication or the latest update.
- How current are the site's links? If many of the links no longer work, the site may be too dated for your purposes.

**EVALUATING A WEB SITE**

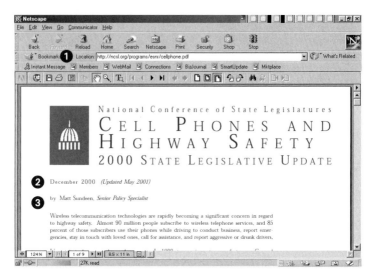

❶ The source is within a site sponsored by the National Conference of State Legislatures, an organization of state lawmakers
   and members of their staffs who track state-level policy issues
   and activity. The URL ending *.org* marks this sponsor as a nonprofit organization.

❷ Clear dates of publication and update show currency.

❸ The author is a credible expert whose credentials can be verified. Contact information is given at the end of the article.

**EVALUATING A WEB SITE**

The site is sponsored by a law firm that specializes in personal-injury law.

The relative size and placement of the toll-free number suggest the site's intended audience: injured people seeking to file a personal-injury lawsuit (probably not researchers seeking objective information about relevant legislation or even statistics).

The site mentions an article in a reputable journal, but ultimately the purpose of the site is to sell a service.

# 52

## Managing information; avoiding plagiarism

An effective researcher is a good record keeper. Whether you decide to keep records on paper or on your computer—or both—your challenge as a researcher will be to find systematic ways of managing information. More specifically, you will need methods for maintaining a working bibliography (see 52a), keeping track of source materials (see 52b), and taking notes without plagiarizing (stealing from) your sources (see 52c).

### 52a Maintain a working bibliography.

Keep a record of any sources you decide to consult. You will need this record, called a *working bibliography,* when you compile the list of works cited that will appear at the end of your paper. (The format of this list depends on the documentation style you are using. For MLA style, see 57b; for APA style, see 60d; for *Chicago* style, see 61d.) Your working bibliography will probably contain more sources than you will actually use and put in your list of works cited.

Most researchers print or save bibliographic information from the library's computer catalog, its periodical databases, and the Web. The information you need to collect is given in the chart on pages 573–74.

For Web sources, some bibliographic information may not be available, but spend time looking for it before assuming that it doesn't exist. When information isn't available on the home page, you may have to drill into the site, following links to interior pages. Look especially for the author's name, the date of publication (or latest update), and the

---

**WRITING CENTER DIRECTORS ON PLAGIARISM**

Plagiarism often results from a lack of comprehension or impatience with reading; true paraphrasing, for example, depends on true understanding of the original text. Documentation trouble may start at the most global level of writing, when a writer lacks a strong sense of purpose and decides that some other author's purpose will do. The citations may be perfect, but the writing reflects nothing more than somebody else's focus and organization.

—Deanne Gute, writing specialist, University of Northern Iowa

## Information for a working bibliography

For examples of where to locate the information in these lists, see the "Citation at a glance" charts in 57b and 60d.

**FOR A BOOK**

- All authors; any editors or translators
- Title and subtitle
- Edition (if not the first)
- Publication information: city, publisher, and date

**FOR A PERIODICAL ARTICLE**

- All authors of the article
- Title and subtitle of the article
- Title of the magazine, journal, or newspaper
- Date; volume, issue, and page numbers, if relevant

**FOR A PERIODICAL ARTICLE RETRIEVED FROM A DATABASE (IN ADDITION TO PRECEDING INFORMATION)**

- Name of the database and an item number, if available
- Name of the subscription service
- URL of the subscription service (for an online database)
- Library where you retrieved the source
- Date you retrieved the source

**NOTE:** Use particular care when printing or saving articles in PDF files. These may not include some of the elements you need to cite the electronic source properly.

**FOR A WEB SOURCE**

- All authors, editors, or translators of the source
- Editor or compiler of the Web site, if there is one
- Title and subtitle of the source and title of the longer work, if applicable
- Title of the site, if available
- Publication information for the source, if available
- Page or paragraph numbers, if any

(*continued*)

### SCHOLARS ON PLAGIARISM

Klausman, Jeffrey. "Teaching Plagiarism in the Age of the Internet." *Teaching English in the Two-Year College* 27 (1999): 209–12. Klausman writes that the use of electronic texts as sources, which may be easy to copy and incorporate in student writing, combined with students' attitudes toward text ownership on the Web, may lead to increased instances of unintentional plagiarism. Klausman describes his classroom activities that show students how to avoid plagiarism. He reinforces his discussion of plagiarism by pointing out to students how easily the reader can check electronic sources and how quickly an instructor can track down a suspected plagiarized passage.

## Information for a working bibliography (*continued*)

- Date of online publication (or latest update), if available
- Sponsor of the site
- Date you accessed the source
- The site's URL

**NOTE:** For the exact bibliographic format to use in the final paper, see 57b (MLA), 60d (APA), or 61d (*Chicago*).

name of any sponsoring organization. The following diagram illustrates what you may find on successive layers of a Web site. Do not omit publication information unless it is genuinely unavailable (see also item 28 on p. 637).

**FINDING BIBLIOGRAPHIC INFORMATION ON A WEB SITE**

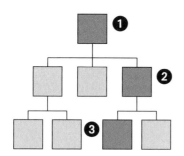

1 Home page (where you may find the sponsor and the title of the site)

2 First interior layer (where you may find the author's name and the title of the source)

3 Second interior layer (where you may find the date of publication)

## 52b Keep track of source materials.

The best way to keep track of source materials is to photocopy them or print them out. Most libraries provide photocopy machines so you can copy pages from reference books and magazines and other sources that can't be removed from the library. In addition, many databases allow you to

**SCHOLARS ON PLAGIARISM**

Rose, Shirley K. "What's Love Got to Do with It? Scholarly Citation Practices as Courtship Rituals." *Language and Learning across the Disciplines* 1.3 (1996): 34–48. Rose proposes that students' difficulties in working with sources may in part result from the typical presentation of citation in economic terms of property, ownership, and borrowing. Instead, Rose suggests, we should think of citation in terms of identification (courtship) and division (battle): Our use of citations either invites our readers to identify with us or causes readers to dismiss our work. Rose argues that the research paper offers students the opportunity to join an existing conversation, to contribute to that conversation, and to see their citation practices as a way of identifying with their readers.

print the full text of articles, and you can easily print information from the Web. Some researchers choose to save online sources on their computer so they can work with the material electronically. Many database subscription services will allow you to send yourself electronic copies of articles as e-mail attachments.

Working with photocopies, printouts, and electronic files—as opposed to relying on memory or hastily written notes—has several benefits. You save time spent in the library. You can highlight key passages, perhaps even color-coding passages to reflect topics in your outline. You can annotate the text in the margins and get a head start on note taking. Finally, you reduce the chances of unintentional plagiarism, since you will be able to compare your use of a source in your paper with the actual source, not just with your notes (see 52c).

**NOTE:** It's especially important to keep print or electronic copies of Web sources, which may change or even become inaccessible. Make sure that your copy includes the site's URL and your date of access, information needed for your list of works cited.

**TIP:** Some schools make citation management software available for free to students. These programs—which allow researchers to download references directly from databases, import saved searches, or type in citations—often promise to compile formatted bibliographies with a single mouse click. You must proofread the results carefully, however; the programs are not foolproof.

---

**TIPS FROM WRITING TUTORS**

"Students need to be reminded to collect all the information for the citation at the time they find the source. Many of the students I tutor will consult an Internet site and then have no idea how to get back to the site to find the information they need when it's time to write the works cited list."
　　　　　　　　　　　*—Amber Weiss, Northern Kentucky University*

---

**SCHOLARS ON PLAGIARISM**

Kroll, Barry M. "How College Freshmen View Plagiarism." *Written Communication* 5 (1988): 203–21. In this empirical study, Kroll reports the results of an extensive survey. Freshmen rated plagiarism as a serious offense, relating it to "three major issues: fairness to authors and other students, the responsibility of students to do independent work, and respect for ownership rights." In his analysis, Kroll points out the infrequent reference to "moral principles" such as "truthfulness, fidelity, and trust," suggesting that teachers could begin to discuss plagiarism in those terms too.

## 52c As you take notes, avoid unintentional plagiarism.

When you take notes and jot down ideas, be very careful not to borrow language from your sources. Even if you half-copy the author's sentences—either by mixing the author's phrases with your own without using quotation marks or by plugging your synonyms into the author's sentence structure—you are committing plagiarism, a serious academic offense. (See 55b, 60b, and 61b.)

There are three kinds of note taking: summarizing, paraphrasing, and quoting. Be sure to include exact page references for all three types of notes, since you will need the page numbers later if you use the information in your paper.

To prevent unintentional borrowing when you summarize or paraphrase, resist the temptation to look at the source as you take notes or to copy chunks of text from an electronic source directly into your notes. Keep the source close by so you can check for accuracy, but don't try to put ideas in your own words with the source's sentences in front of you. When you need to quote the exact words of a source, make sure you copy the words precisely and put quotation marks around them.

**TIP:** Be especially careful when working with electronic files. Some researchers have unwittingly plagiarized their sources because they lost track of which words came from sources

---

**TIPS FROM WRITING TUTORS**

"Students I tutor are often shocked when I explain plagiarism. Some think that if they invert a few phrases from a source then they no longer need to credit the source. I work with students on ways to give sources proper credit."
—*Gabriel Smith, University of Northern Iowa*

---

**SCHOLARS ON PLAGIARISM**

St. Onge, Keith R. *The Melancholy Anatomy of Plagiarism.* Lanham: UP of America, 1988. This "handbook on plagiarism" offers suggestions on how to avoid plagiarism, how to handle charges of plagiarism, when to charge others with plagiarism, and "how to select and combine optimum defenses for any innocents who may stumble into plagiarism's many traps."

and which were their own. To prevent unintentional plagiarism, put quotation marks around any text that you have inserted into your own work.

 **ESL** If you come from a culture that stresses memorization and recitation of classic texts, you may not see the need to document such sources—or even to use quotation marks to indicate that you are using the exact words of your source. In the United States, however, written texts and any original ideas they contain are viewed as the author's property. When using an author's property, writers must follow certain conventions or risk being charged with the ethical and legal offense known as *plagiarism*.

### Summarizing without plagiarizing

A summary condenses information, perhaps reducing a chapter to a short paragraph or a paragraph to a single sentence. A summary should be written in your own words; if you use phrases from the source, put them in quotation marks.

Here is a passage from an original source read by John Garcia in researching a paper on mountain lions. Following the passage is Garcia's summary of the source.

**ORIGINAL SOURCE**

In some respects, the increasing frequency of mountain lion encounters in California has as much to do with a growing *human* population as it does with rising mountain lion numbers. The scenic solitude of the western ranges is prime cougar habitat, and it is falling swiftly to the developer's spade. Meanwhile, with their ideal habitat already at its carrying capacity, mountain lions are forcing younger cats into less suitable terrain, including residential areas. Add that cougars have generally grown bolder under a lengthy ban on their being hunted, and an unsettling scenario begins to emerge.
—Ray Rychnovsky, "Clawing into Controversy," p. 40

**SCHOLARS ON PLAGIARISM**

Drum, Alice. "Responding to Plagiarism." *College Composition and Communication* 37 (1986): 241–43. Pointing out that plagiarism continues to be a problem, Drum claims that instructors traditionally respond only to the legal aspects of plagiarism, warning students without teaching them how to avoid the problem. She advocates a more balanced approach, emphasizing the pedagogical implications of plagiarism as much as the legal aspects.

**SUMMARY**

> Source: Rychnovsky, "Clawing into Controversy" (40)
>
> Encounters between mountain lions and humans are on the rise in California because increasing numbers of lions are competing for a shrinking habitat. As the lions' wild habitat shrinks, older lions force younger lions into residential areas. These lions have lost some of their fear of humans because of a ban on hunting.

### Paraphrasing without plagiarizing

Like a summary, a paraphrase is written in your own words; but whereas a summary reports significant information in fewer words than the source, a paraphrase retells the information in roughly the same number of words. If you retain occasional choice phrases from the source, use quotation marks so you will know later which phrases are not your own.

As you read the paraphrase on page 579 of the original source (see p. 577), notice that the language is significantly different from that in the original.

### Using quotation marks to avoid plagiarizing

A quotation consists of the exact words from a source. In your notes, put all quoted material in quotation marks; do not assume that you will remember later which words, phrases, and passages you have quoted and which are your own. When you quote, be sure to copy the words of your

**WRITING CENTER DIRECTORS ON INTEGRATING SOURCES**

Besides the risk of plagiarism, intentional or otherwise, student writers can lose or become confused about their own stylistic voices as they cut and paste, insert and delete snippets from other sources. The technological ease with which these changes can be made may also mask many of the most important steps in the writing process; one result of technologically "easier" writing is that students not only are less aware of their own writing steps, moves, or strategies but often have a more limited repertoire of such steps or strategies to call upon.

—Scott Hendrix, director of writing, Albion College

**PARAPHRASE**

Source: Rychnovsky, "Clawing into Controversy" (40)

Californians are encountering mountain lions more frequently because increasing numbers of humans and a rising population of lions are competing for the same territory. Humans have moved into mountainous regions once dominated by the lions, and the wild habitat that is left cannot sustain the current lion population. Therefore, the older lions are forcing younger lions into residential areas. And because of a ban on hunting, these younger lions have become bolder — less fearful of encounters with humans.

**QUOTATION**

Source: Rychnovsky, "Clawing into Controversy" (40)

Rychnovsky explains that as humans expand residential areas into mountain ranges, the cougar's natural habitat "is falling swiftly to the developer's spade."

source exactly, including punctuation and capitalization. In the example above, John Garcia quotes from the original source on page 577.

**SCHOLARS ON SUMMARIZING**

Sherrard, Carol. "Summary Writing: A Topographical Study." *Written Communication* 3 (1986): 324–43. Sherrard studied paragraph summaries written by university students and concluded that most were "mechanical." She found that students favored several strategies: "omitting text sentences, mapping existing sentences into summary sentences, and combining only those sentences that were next to each other."

# 53

## Choosing a documentation style

The various academic disciplines use their own editorial style for citing sources and for listing the works that are cited in a paper. *The Bedford Handbook* describes three commonly used styles: MLA (section 57), APA (section 60), and *Chicago* (section 61). For a list of style manuals in a variety of disciplines, see 53b.

**53a** Select a style appropriate for your discipline.

In researched writing, sources are cited for several reasons. First, it is important to acknowledge the contributions of others. If you fail to credit sources properly, you commit plagiarism, a serious academic offense. Second, choosing good sources will add credibility to your work; in a sense, you are calling on authorities to serve as expert witnesses. The more care you have taken in choosing reliable sources, the stronger your case will be. Finally—and most importantly—you are helping to build knowledge by showing readers where they can pursue your topic in greater depth.

All of the academic disciplines cite sources for these same reasons. Why, then, do they use different styles for citing those sources? The answer lies in the intellectual goals and values of scholars in different disciplines.

### MLA and APA in-text citations

The Modern Language Association (MLA) style and the American Psychological Association (APA) style both use citations in the text of a paper that refer to a list of works at the end of the paper. The systems work somewhat differently, however, because MLA style was created for scholars in English composition and literature and APA style was created for researchers in the social sciences.

### MLA IN-TEXT CITATION

Brandon Conran argues that the story is written from "a bifocal point of view" (111).

### APA IN-TEXT CITATION

As researchers Yanovski and Yanovski (2002) have explained, obesity was once considered "either a moral failing or evidence of underlying psychopathology" (p. 592).

While MLA and APA styles work in a similar way, some basic disciplinary differences show up in these key elements:

- author's name
- date of publication
- page numbers
- verb tense in signal phrases

MLA style, which gives the author's full name on first mention, reflects the respect that English scholars have for authors of written words. APA style uses last names only, not out of disrespect but to lend an air of scientific objectivity. APA style, which gives a date after the author's name, reflects the social scientist's concern with the currency of experimental results. MLA style omits the date because English scholars are less concerned with currency; what someone had to say a century ago may be as significant as the latest contribution to the field.

Although both styles include page numbers for quotations, MLA style requires page numbers for summaries and paraphrases as well, whereas APA does not. Humanities scholars place great value on written texts, and with a page number readers can easily find the exact passage that has been summarized or paraphrased. Social scientists are less concerned about page numbers because they value an article's ideas and research results more than its written text.

One final point about the differences between the two styles: MLA style uses the present tense (such as *argues*) to introduce cited material, whereas APA style uses the past or present perfect tense (such as *argued* or *have argued*). The present tense evokes the timelessness of a literary text; the past or present perfect tense emphasizes that an experiment was conducted in the past.

### Chicago-*style footnotes or endnotes*

Most historians and many scholars in the humanities use the style of footnotes or endnotes recommended by *The Chicago Manual of Style.* Historians base their work on a wide variety of primary and secondary sources, all of which must be cited. *Chicago*'s note system has the virtue of being relatively unobtrusive; even when a book or an article is thick with citations, readers will not be overwhelmed. In the text of the paper, only a raised number appears. Readers who are interested can consult the accompanying numbered note, which is given either at the foot of the page or at the end of the paper.

**TEXT**

Historian Albert Castel quotes several eyewitnesses on both the Union and the Confederate sides as saying that Forrest ordered his men to stop firing.[7]

**NOTE**

      7. Albert Castel, "The Fort Pillow Massacre: A Fresh Examination of the Evidence," *Civil War History* 4, no. 1 (1958): 44-45.

The *Chicago* system gives as much information as the MLA or APA system; the main difference is that less of that information is given in the text of the paper.

## 53b If necessary, consult a style manual.

*The Bedford Handbook* describes three commonly used systems of documentation: MLA, used in English and the humanities (see 54–59); APA, used in psychology and the social sciences (see 60); and *Chicago*, used in history and some humanities (see 61). Following is a list of style manuals used in a variety of disciplines.

**BIOLOGY (SEE <http://dianahacker.com/resdoc> FOR MORE INFORMATION.)**

Council of Biology Editors. *Scientific Style and Format: The CBE Manual for Authors, Editors, and Publishers.* 6th ed. New York: Cambridge UP, 1994.

**BUSINESS**

American Management Association. *The AMA Style Guide for Business Writing.* New York: AMACOM, 1996.

**CHEMISTRY**

Dodd, Janet S., ed. *The ACS Style Guide: A Manual for Authors and Editors.* 2nd ed. Washington: Amer. Chemical Soc., 1997.

**ENGINEERING**

Institute of Electrical and Electronics Engineers. *IEEE Standards Style Manual.* Rev. ed. New York: IEEE, 2005 <http://standards.ieee.org/guides/style/2005Style.pdf>.

**ENGLISH AND THE HUMANITIES (SEE 54–59.)**

Gibaldi, Joseph. *MLA Handbook for Writers of Research Papers*. 6th ed. New York: MLA, 2003.

**GEOLOGY**

Bates, Robert L., Rex Buchanan, and Marla Adkins-Heljeson, eds. *Geowriting: A Guide to Writing, Editing, and Printing in Earth Science*. 5th ed. Alexandria: Amer. Geological Inst., 1995.

**GOVERNMENT DOCUMENTS**

Garner, Diane L. *The Complete Guide to Citing Government Information Resources: A Manual for Social Science and Business Research*. 3rd ed. Bethesda: Congressional Information Service, 2002.

United States Government Printing Office. *Style Manual*. Washington: GPO, 2000.

**HISTORY (SEE 61.)**

*The Chicago Manual of Style*. 15th ed. Chicago: U of Chicago P, 2003.

**JOURNALISM**

Goldstein, Norm, ed. *Associated Press Stylebook and Briefing on Media Law*. Rev. ed. New York: Associated Press, 2005.

**LAW**

Harvard Law Review et al. *The Bluebook: A Uniform System of Citation*. 17th ed. Cambridge: Harvard Law Rev. Assn., 2000.

**LINGUISTICS**

Linguistic Society of America. "LSA Style Sheet." Published annually in the December issue of the *LSA Bulletin*.

**MATHEMATICS**

American Mathematical Society. *The AMS Author Handbook: General Instructions for Preparing Manuscripts*. Rev. ed. Providence: AMS, 1996.

**MEDICINE**

Iverson, Cheryl, et al. *American Medical Association Manual of Style: A Guide for Authors and Editors*. 9th ed. Baltimore: Williams, 1998.

**MUSIC**

Holoman, D. Kern, ed. *Writing about Music: A Style Sheet from the Editors of* 19th-Century Music. Berkeley: U of California P, 1988.

**PHYSICS**

American Institute of Physics. *Style Manual: Instructions to Authors and Volume Editors for the Preparation of AIP Book Manuscripts*. 5th ed. New York: AIP, 1995.

**POLITICAL SCIENCE**

American Political Science Association. *Style Manual for Political Science*. Rev. ed. Washington: APSA, 2001.

**PSYCHOLOGY AND OTHER SOCIAL SCIENCES (SEE 60.)**

American Psychological Association. *Publication Manual of the American Psychological Association*. 5th ed. Washington: APA, 2001.

**SCIENCE AND TECHNICAL WRITING**

American National Standards Institute. *American National Standard for the Preparation of Scientific Papers for Written or Oral Presentation*. New York: ANSI, 1979.

Microsoft Corporation. *Microsoft Manual of Style for Technical Publications*. 3rd ed. Redmond: Microsoft, 2004.

Rubens, Philip, ed. *Science and Technical Writing: A Manual of Style*. 2nd ed. New York: Routledge, 2001.

**SOCIAL WORK**

National Association of Social Workers. *Writing for the NASW Press: Information for Authors* <http://naswpress.org/resources/tools/01-write/guidelines_toc.htm>.

# WRITING MLA PAPERS

Most English instructors and some humanities instructors will ask you to document your sources with the Modern Language Association (MLA) system of citations described in section 57.

When writing an MLA paper that is based on sources, you face three main challenges: (1) supporting a thesis, (2) citing your sources and avoiding plagiarism, and (3) integrating quotations and other source material.

Examples in sections 54–56 are drawn from research two students conducted on the use of cell phones while driving. Angela Daly's research paper on this topic appears on pages 659–66. Daly calls for legislation restricting use of cell phones while driving. Paul Levi's paper opposing such legislation appears on the *Bedford Handbook* Web site (see p. 658 for the URL).

If you are writing an MLA paper about literature (a short story, novel, play, film, or poem), see section 59.

**NOTE:** For cross-disciplinary advice on finding and evaluating sources and on managing information, see sections 50–53.

# 54

## Supporting a thesis

Most research assignments ask you to form a thesis, or main idea, and to support that thesis with well-organized evidence.

### 54a Form a tentative thesis and sketch a rough outline.

Before you begin writing, you should decide on a tentative thesis and construct a preliminary outline. Remain flexible, however, because you may need to revise your approach later. Writing about a subject is a way of learning about it; as you write, your understanding of your subject will almost certainly deepen.

#### *Tentative thesis*

Once you have read a variety of sources and considered all sides of your issue, you are ready to form a tentative thesis: a one-sentence (or occasionally a two-sentence) statement of your central idea. (See also 2a and 54b.) The thesis expresses not just your opinion but your informed, reasoned judgment.

In a research paper, your thesis will answer the central research question that you posed earlier (see 50a). The following, for example, are the research question and tentative thesis statement that Angela Daly wrote on the dangers of using cell phones while driving.

**DALY'S RESEARCH QUESTION**

Should states regulate use of cell phones in moving vehicles?

**DALY'S TENTATIVE THESIS**

States should regulate use of cell phones on the road because many drivers are using the phones irresponsibly and causing accidents.

After you have written a rough draft and perhaps done more reading, you may decide to revise your thesis, as Daly did.

**DALY'S REVISED THESIS**

States must regulate use of cell phones on the road because drivers using phones are seriously impaired and because laws on negligent and reckless driving are not sufficient to punish offenders.

## *Rough outline*

Before committing to a detailed outline, create a rough outline using your thesis and key supporting ideas. In his rough outline, Paul Levi supports his thesis with sentences that sum up the three main sections of his paper.

**LEVI'S THESIS**    Instead of restricting use of cell phones in moving vehicles, we should educate the public about the dangers of driving while phoning and prosecute irresponsible phone users under laws on negligent and reckless driving.

Scientific studies haven't proved a link between use of cell phones and traffic accidents.

The risks of using cell phones while driving should be weighed against the benefits.

We need to educate drivers on using cell phones responsibly and enforce laws on negligent and reckless driving.

**ON THE WEB**

**dianahacker.com/bedhandbook**
► Electronic research exercises
  ► E-ex 54–1

**54b** Include your thesis in the introduction.

In a research paper, readers are accustomed to seeing the thesis statement—the paper's main point—at the end of the first or second paragraph. The advantage of putting it in the first paragraph is that readers can immediately grasp your point. The advantage of delaying the thesis until the second paragraph is that you can provide a fuller context for your point.

As you draft your introduction, you may change your preliminary thesis, either because you have refined your thinking or because new wording fits more smoothly into the context you have provided for it. For example, Paul Levi's thesis became more complex as he drafted and polished his opening paragraph. Levi's thesis appears in the last sentence of his introduction:

> As of 2000, there were about ninety million cell phone users in the United States, with 85% of them using their phones while on the road (Sundeen 1). Because of evidence that cell phones impair drivers by distracting them, some states have considered laws restricting their use in moving vehicles. Proponents of legislation correctly point out that using phones while driving can be dangerous. The extent of the danger, however, is a matter of debate, and the benefits may outweigh the risks. Unless the risks of cell phones are shown to outweigh the benefits, we should not restrict their use in moving vehicles; instead, we should educate the

public about the dangers of driving while phoning and prosecute irresponsible phone users under laws on negligent and reckless driving.

For Angela Daly's introduction and thesis, see page 659.

In addition to stating your thesis and establishing a context for it, an introduction should hook readers. For example, in your first sentence or two you might connect your topic to something recently in the news or point to emerging trends in an academic discipline. Other strategies are to pose a puzzling problem or to cite a startling statistic. Paul Levi opens his paper with compelling statistics. Angela Daly begins her paper by linking her topic to everyday experiences: "When a cell phone goes off in a classroom or at a concert, we are irritated, but at least our lives are not endangered. When we are on the road, however, irresponsible cell phone users are more than irritating: They are putting our lives at risk."

## 54c Provide organizational cues.

Even if you are working with a good outline, your paper will appear disorganized unless you provide organizational cues: topic sentences, transitions between major sections of the paper, and perhaps headings. Paul Levi uses the following headings to set off the three sections of his paper:

Assessing the risks

Weighing risks and benefits

Educating drivers and enforcing laws

Although Angela Daly does not use headings, her paper is easy to follow because she begins paragraphs with clear topic sentences and uses transitions to help readers move from one idea to the next. Some of the annotations in the margins of Daly's paper (pp. 659–66) draw attention to such organizational cues.

For more about topic sentences, transitions, and headings, see 4a, 4d, and 5b.

## 54d Draft the paper in an appropriate voice.

A chatty, breezy voice is usually not welcome in a research paper, but neither is a stuffy, pretentious style or a timid, unsure one.

**TOO CHATTY**

Who says that cell phones and driving don't mix? Tell it to the cops who learn about wild or plastered drivers from callers dialing 911 while on the road.

**BETTER**

Cell phones contribute to traffic safety because drivers place 911 calls alerting police to accidents and reckless or drunk drivers.

**TOO STUFFY**

It has been concluded that many automotive mishaps are resultant from cell phone use.

**BETTER**

Research suggests that drivers using cell phones cause many traffic accidents.

**TOO TIMID**

I may not be an expert, but it seems to me that phoning while driving could be risky.

**BETTER**

Common sense tells us that phoning while driving presents a risk.

# 55

---

## Citing sources; avoiding plagiarism

---

In a research paper, you will be drawing on the work of other writers, and you must document their contributions by citing your sources. Sources are cited for two reasons:

1. to tell readers where your information comes from—so that they can assess its reliability and, if interested, find and read the original source
2. to give credit to the writers from whom you have borrowed words and ideas

Borrowing another writer's language, sentence structures, or ideas without proper acknowledgment is a form of dishonesty known as *plagiarism.*

You must include a citation when you quote from a source, when you summarize or paraphrase, and when you borrow facts that are not common knowledge (see also 55b).

**55a**  For most English papers, use the MLA system for citing sources. (See 57 for important details.)

Most English professors and some humanities professors require the MLA (Modern Language Association) system of in-text citations. Here, briefly, is how the MLA citation system usually works:

1. The source is introduced by a signal phrase that names its author.
2. The material being cited is followed by a page number in parentheses.

3. At the end of the paper, a list of works cited (arranged alphabetically according to authors' last names) gives complete publication information about the source.

**IN-TEXT CITATION**

According to Donald Redelmeier and Robert Tibshirani, "The use of cellular telephones in motor vehicles is associated with a quadrupling of the risk of a collision during the brief period of a call" (453).

**ENTRY IN THE LIST OF WORKS CITED**

Redelmeier, Donald A., and Robert J. Tibshirani. "Association between Cellular-Telephone Calls and Motor Vehicle Collisions." New England Journal of Medicine 336 (1997): 453-58.

Handling an MLA citation is not always this simple. For a detailed discussion of possible variations, see 57.

## 55b Avoid plagiarism.

Your research paper is a collaboration between you and your sources. To be fair and ethical, you must acknowledge your debt to the writers of these sources. If you don't, you commit plagiarism, a serious academic offense.

Three different acts are considered plagiarism: (1) failing to cite quotations and borrowed ideas, (2) failing to enclose borrowed language in quotation marks, and (3) failing to put summaries and paraphrases in your own words.

### Citing quotations and borrowed ideas

You must of course document all direct quotations. You must also cite any ideas you borrow from a source: summaries and paraphrases; statistics and other specific facts; and visuals such as cartoons, graphs, and diagrams.

The only exception is common knowledge—information your readers could find in any number of general sources because it is commonly known. For example, it is well known that Toni Morrison won the Nobel Prize in literature in 1993 and that Emily Dickinson published only a handful of her many poems during her lifetime.

As a rule, when you have seen information repeatedly in your reading, you don't need to cite it. However, when information has appeared in only one or two sources or when it is controversial, you should cite the source. If a topic is new to you and you are not sure what is considered common knowledge or what is controversial, ask someone with expertise. When in doubt, cite the source.

### Enclosing borrowed language in quotation marks

To indicate that you are using a source's exact phrases or sentences, you must enclose them in quotation marks unless they have been set off from the text by indenting (see p. 600). To omit the quotation marks is to claim—falsely—that the language is your own. Such an omission is plagiarism even if you have cited the source.

**ORIGINAL SOURCE**

Future cars will provide drivers with concierge services, web-based information, online e-mail capabilities, CD-ROM access, on-screen and audio navigation technology, and a variety of other information and entertainment services.
　　　—Matt Sundeen, "Cell Phones and Highway Safety," p. 1

**PLAGIARISM**

Matt Sundeen points out that in cars of the future drivers will have concierge services, web-based information, online e-mail capabilities, CD-ROM access, on-screen and audio navigation technology, and a variety of other information and entertainment services (1).

**ACCEPTABLE: BORROWED LANGUAGE IN QUOTATION MARKS**

Matt Sundeen points out that in cars of the future drivers will have "concierge services, web-based information, online e-mail capabilities, CD-ROM access, on-screen and audio navigation technology, and a variety of other information and entertainment services" (1).

### Putting summaries and paraphrases in your own words

A summary condenses information from a source; a paraphrase repeats the information in about the same number of words. When you summarize or paraphrase, it is not enough to name the source; you must restate the source's meaning using your own language. (See also 52c.) You commit plagiarism if you half-copy the author's sentences—either by mixing the author's phrases with your own without using quotation marks or by plugging your synonyms into the author's sentence structure.

The first paraphrase of the following source (see p. 596) is plagiarized—even though the source is cited—because too much of its language is borrowed from the original. The underlined strings of words have been copied word-for-word (without quotation marks). In addition, the writer has closely echoed the sentence structure of the source, merely plugging in some synonyms (*demonstrated* for *shown, devising* for *designing,* and *car* for *automotive*).

**ORIGINAL SOURCE**

The automotive industry has not shown good judgment in designing automotive features that distract drivers. A classic example is the use of a touch-sensitive screen to replace all the controls for radios, tape/CD players, and heating/cooling. Although an interesting technology, such devices require that the driver take his eyes off the road.

—Tom Magliozzi and Ray Magliozzi,
Letter to a Massachusetts state senator, p. 3

**PLAGIARISM: UNACCEPTABLE BORROWING**

Radio show hosts Tom and Ray Magliozzi argue that <u>the automotive</u> <u>industry has not</u> demonstrated <u>good judgment in</u> devising car features <u>that distract drivers</u>. One feature is <u>a touch-sensitive</u> <u>screen</u> that replaces <u>controls for radios, tape/CD players, and</u> <u>heating/cooling</u>. Although the technology is interesting, <u>such</u> <u>devices require that</u> a driver look away from the road (3).

To avoid plagiarizing an author's language, resist the temptation to look at the source while you are summarizing or paraphrasing. Close the book, write from memory, and then open the book to check for accuracy. This technique prevents you from being captivated by the words on the page.

**TWO ACCEPTABLE PARAPHRASES**

Radio show hosts Tom and Ray Magliozzi claim that motor vehicle manufacturers do not always design features with safety in mind. For example, when designers replaced radio, CD player, and temperature control knobs with touch-sensitive panels, they were forgetting one thing: To use the panels, drivers would need to take their eyes off the road (3).

Tom and Ray Magliozzi, hosts of the <u>Car Talk</u> radio show, criticize the motor vehicle industry for contributing to driver distractions. They give the example of new touch-sensitive technology for operating the radio, CD player, and tape deck and for controlling temperature. Unlike old-fashioned knobs, this new technology requires drivers to look away from the road (3).

**ON**
**THE**
**WEB**

**dianahacker.com/bedhandbook**
▶ Electronic research exercises
  ▶ E-ex 55–1 to 55–6

# 56

## Integrating sources

Quotations, summaries, paraphrases, and facts will support your argument, but they cannot speak for you. Several strategies will help you integrate information from research sources into your paper while maintaining your own voice.

**NOTE:** If you are integrating quotations from a literary source, see 59e.

### 56a Limit your use of quotations.

Although it is tempting to insert many quotations in your paper and to use your own words only for connecting passages, do not quote excessively. It is almost impossible to integrate numerous long quotations smoothly into your own text.

Except for the following legitimate uses of quotations, use your own words to summarize and paraphrase your sources and to explain your own ideas.

**WHEN TO USE QUOTATIONS**

- When language is especially vivid or expressive
- When exact wording is needed for technical accuracy
- When it is important to let the debaters of an issue explain their positions in their own words
- When the words of an important authority lend weight to an argument
- When language of a source is the topic of your discussion (as in an analysis or interpretation)

It is not always necessary to quote full sentences from a source. To reduce your reliance on the words of others, you

can often integrate a phrase from a source into your own
sentence structure.

> Redelmeier and Tibshirani found that hands-free phones were not
> any safer in vehicles than other cell phones. They suggest that
> crashes involving cell phones may "result from a driver's limita-
> tions with regard to attention rather than dexterity" (456).

> The Harvard Center for Risk Analysis argues that "because a signif-
> icant percentage of cellular phone calls are made from vehicles
> during rush hour," accidents caused by the phones are less likely
> to be fatal than accidents caused by other risk factors (4-5).

### Using the ellipsis mark and brackets

Two useful marks of punctuation, the ellipsis mark and
brackets, allow you to keep quoted material to a minimum
and to integrate it smoothly into your text.

**THE ELLIPSIS MARK**    To condense a quoted passage, you
can use the ellipsis mark (three periods, with spaces between) to indicate that you have omitted words. What remains must be grammatically complete.

---

**TIPS FROM WRITING TUTORS**

"Some writers have a hard time quoting from a text in a manner that retains the author's original meaning. If you neglect
to consider the author's overall argument, you can end up
misrepresenting the author's views. By establishing the
proper context for a quote, you can acknowledge the ambiguities and contradictions in the author's work and use
quotes more effectively."
                                    — *Yana Zeltser, Rutgers University*

> The University of North Carolina Highway Safety Research
> Center has begun a study assessing a variety of driver distrac-
> tions. According to Allyson Vaughan, "The research . . . is
> intended to inject some empirical evidence into the debate
> over whether talking on wireless phones while driving leads to
> accidents" (1).

The writer has omitted the words *funded by the AAA Foundation for Traffic Safety,* which appeared in the source.

On the rare occasions when you want to omit one or
more full sentences, use a period before the three ellipsis
dots.

> Redelmeier and Tibshirani acknowledge that their study "indicates
> an association but not necessarily a causal relation between the
> use of cellular telephones while driving and a subsequent motor
> vehicle collision. . . . In addition, our study did not include seri-
> ous injuries . . ." (457).

Ordinarily, do not use an ellipsis mark at the beginning
or at the end of a quotation. Your readers will understand
that the quoted material is taken from a longer passage, so
such marks are not necessary. The only exception occurs
when words have been dropped at the end of the final
quoted sentence. In such cases, put three ellipsis dots before the closing quotation mark and parenthetical reference,
as in the previous example.

Do not use an ellipsis mark to distort the meaning of
your source.

**BRACKETS**  Brackets allow you to insert your own words
into quoted material. You can insert words in brackets to explain a confusing reference or to keep a sentence grammatical in your context.

According to economists Robert Hahn and Paul Tetlock, "Some studies say they [hands-free phones] would have no impact on accidents, while others suggest the reductions could be sizable" (2).

To indicate an error such as a misspelling in a quotation, insert [sic] after the error.

Smith argues that "the dangers of driving while talking have not been exagerated [sic]" (4).

### Setting off long quotations

When you quote more than four typed lines of prose or more than three lines of poetry, set off the quotation by indenting it one inch (or ten spaces) from the left margin. Use the normal right margin and do not single-space.

Long quotations should be introduced by an informative sentence, usually followed by a colon. Quotation marks are unnecessary because the indented format tells readers that the words are taken directly from the source.

Tom and Ray Magliozzi are not impressed by economists who conduct risk-benefit analyses of phone use by drivers:

Other critics [of regulation of cell phones]--some from prestigious "think tanks"--perform what appear to be erudite cost/benefit analyses. The problem here is that the benefits are always in units of convenience and productivity while the costs are in units of injuries and people's lives! (2)

Notice that at the end of an indented quotation the parenthetical citation goes outside the final mark of punctuation. (When a quotation is run into your text, the opposite is true. See the sample citation at the top of this page.)

**56b** Introduce most source material with signal phrases.

The information you gather from sources cannot speak for itself. Whenever you include a paraphrase, summary, or direct quotation of another writer in your paper, prepare your readers for it with an introduction called a *signal phrase.* Signal phrases mark the boundaries between source material and your own words; they can also tell readers why a source is trustworthy.

When you write a signal phrase, choose a verb that is appropriate for your argument. Is your source making an observation, reporting a fact, drawing a conclusion, refuting an argument, or stating a belief? See the chart on page 603 for a list of verbs commonly used in signal phrases. Note that MLA style calls for present-tense verbs (*argues*) to introduce source material unless a date specifies the time of writing (see item 6 on p. 615).

### Using signal phrases to mark boundaries

Readers need to move from your own words to the words of your source without feeling a jolt. Avoid dropping direct quotations into your text without warning. Instead, provide clear signal phrases, including at least the author's name (as in the examples on p. 602). A signal phrase indicates the boundary between your words and the source's words.

**DROPPED QUOTATION**

In 2000, the legislature of Suffolk County passed a law restricting drivers' use of handheld phones. "The bill prohibits the use of a cell phone while driving unless it is equipped with an earpiece or can act like a speakerphone, leaving the driver's hands free" (Kelley 1).

**QUOTATION WITH SIGNAL PHRASE**

In 2000, the legislature of Suffolk County passed a law restricting drivers' use of handheld phones. As Tina Kelley explains, "The bill prohibits the use of a cell phone while driving unless it is equipped with an earpiece or can act like a speakerphone, leaving the driver's hands free" (1).

Introduce most summaries and paraphrases with a signal phrase as well. Readers will then understand that everything between the signal phrase and the parenthetical citation summarizes or paraphrases the cited source.

Without the signal phrase (underlined) in the following example, readers might think that only the quotation at the end is being cited, when in fact the whole paragraph is based on the source.

<u>Alasdair Cain and Mark Burris report that</u> scientific research on traffic accidents and cell phone use has been inconclusive. Many factors play a role: for example, the type of phone (hands-free or not), the extent to which the conversation is distracting, and the demographic profile of the driver. Although research suggests that phoning in a moving vehicle affects driver performance, studies have failed to quantify the degree of driver impairment. Cain and Burris write that drivers using cell phones on the road "were anywhere from 34 percent to 300 percent more likely to have an accident" (1).

There are times when a summary or paraphrase does not require a signal phrase. Readers will understand, for example, that the citation at the end of the following passage applies to the entire paragraph, not just part of it.

## Varying signal phrases in MLA papers

To avoid monotony, try to vary both the language and the placement of your signal phrases.

**MODEL SIGNAL PHRASES**

> In the words of researchers Redelmeier and Tibshirani, ". . ."
>
> As Matt Sundeen has noted, ". . ."
>
> Patti Pena, mother of a child killed by a driver distracted by a cell phone, points out that ". . ."
>
> ". . .," writes Christine Haughney, ". . ."
>
> ". . .," claims wireless industry spokesperson Annette Jacobs.
>
> Radio hosts Tom and Ray Magliozzi offer a persuasive counterargument: ". . ."

**VERBS IN SIGNAL PHRASES**

| | | | |
|---|---|---|---|
| acknowledges | comments | endorses | reasons |
| adds | compares | grants | refutes |
| admits | confirms | illustrates | rejects |
| agrees | contends | implies | reports |
| argues | declares | insists | responds |
| asserts | denies | notes | suggests |
| believes | disputes | observes | thinks |
| claims | emphasizes | points out | writes |

The American Automobile Association is funding a study on driver distractions, including cell phone use. In the summer of 2000, researchers at the University of North Carolina Highway Safety Research Center studied 144 drivers in Chapel Hill and Philadelphia to determine which distractions--such as tuning the radio, eating, and talking on the phone--most affect the ability to drive. The drivers allowed researchers to install cameras in their cars to study their habits while driving (Vaughan 2).

### Using signal phrases to establish authority

Good research writing uses evidence from reliable sources. The first time you mention a source, briefly include the author's title, credentials, or experience—anything that would help your readers recognize the source's authority.

**SOURCE WITH NO CREDENTIALS**

Not all writers lead solitary, sedentary lives. Novelist Alice Walker, for instance, is also a vocal and committed social activist. Evelyn C. White argues that Walker's "advocacy on behalf of the dispossessed has spanned the globe" (1).

**SOURCE WITH CREDENTIALS**

Not all writers lead solitary, sedentary lives. Novelist Alice Walker, for instance, is also a vocal and committed social activist. As Walker biographer Evelyn C. White argues, Walker's "advocacy on behalf of the dispossessed has spanned the globe" (1).

When you establish your source's authority, as with the phrase *Walker biographer* in the previous example, you also signal to readers your own credibility as a responsible researcher, one who has located trustworthy sources.

### Using signal phrases with statistics and other facts

When you are citing a statistic or another specific fact, a signal phrase is often not necessary. In most cases, readers will understand whether a citation refers to one statistic or fact or to the whole paragraph.

> As of 2000, there were about ninety million cell phone users in the United States, with 85% of them using their phones while on the road (Sundeen 1).

There is nothing wrong, however, with using a signal phrase to introduce a statistic or other fact.

> Matt Sundeen reports that as of 2000, there were about ninety million cell phone users in the United States, with 85% of them using their phones while on the road (1).

## 56c  Put direct quotations in context.

Because a source cannot reveal its meaning or function by itself, you must make the connection between a source and your own ideas. A signal phrase can show readers how a quotation supports or challenges a point you are making.

> Efforts by the music industry to stop Internet file sharing have been unsuccessful and, worse, divisive. Industry analysts share this view. Salon's Scott Rosenberg, for example, writes that the only thing the music industry's "legal strategy has accomplished is to radicalize the community of online music fans and accelerate the process of technological change" (2).

Readers should not have to guess why a quotation appears in your paper. If you use another writer's words, you must explain how they contribute to your point. It's a good idea to embed a quotation — especially a long one — between sentences of your own. In addition to introducing it with a signal phrase, follow it with interpretive comments that link the quotation to your paper's argument.

**QUOTATION WITH INSUFFICIENT CONTEXT**

By comparing the time of a collision with the drivers' phone records, Redelmeier and Tibshirani assessed the dangers of driving while phoning.

> We found that using a cellular telephone was associated with a risk of having a motor vehicle collision that was about four times as high as that among the same drivers when they were not using their cellular telephones. This relative risk is similar to the hazard associated with driving with a blood alcohol level at the legal limit. (456)

**QUOTATION WITH EFFECTIVE CONTEXT**

By comparing the time of a collision with the drivers' phone records, Redelmeier and Tibshirani assessed the dangers of driving while phoning. The results are unsettling:

> We found that using a cellular telephone was associated with a risk of having a motor vehicle collision that was about four times as high as that among the same drivers when they were not using their cellular telephones. This relative risk is similar to the hazard associated with driving with a blood alcohol level at the legal limit. (456)

The news media often exaggerated the latter claim ("similar to" is not "equal to"); nonetheless, the comparison with drunk driving suggests the extent to which cell phone use while driving can impair judgment.

## Reviewing an MLA paper: Global revisions

### Focus

- Does the paper seek to answer a compelling question?
- Is the thesis stated clearly enough? Is it placed where readers will notice it?
- Does each paragraph support the thesis?

### Organization

- Can readers follow the organization? Would headings help?
- Do topic sentences signal new ideas? Do transitions help readers move from one major group of paragraphs to another?
- Are ideas presented in a logical order?

### Content

- Is the supporting material persuasive? Are the arguments strong enough to stand up to arguments of those who disagree with the thesis?
- Are the parts proportioned sensibly? Do the major ideas receive enough attention?
- Is the draft concise—free of irrelevant, unimportant, or repetitious material?

### Style

- Is the voice appropriate—not too chatty, too stuffy, or too timid?
- Are the sentences clear, emphatic, and varied?

---

**ON THE WEB**

**dianahacker.com/bedhandbook**
- ▶ Electronic research exercises
  - ▶ E-ex 56–1 to 56–4

## Reviewing an MLA paper: Use of sources

### Use of quotations

- Is quoted material enclosed within quotation marks or set off from the text? (See 55b and p. 600.)
- Is quoted language word-for-word accurate? If not, do brackets or ellipsis marks indicate the changes or omissions? (See pp. 598–600.)
- Does a clear signal phrase (usually naming the author) prepare readers for each quotation? (See 56b.)
- Does a parenthetical citation follow each quotation? (See 57a.)
- Is each quotation put in context? (See 56c.)

### Use of summaries and paraphrases

- Are summaries and paraphrases free of plagiarized wording — not copied or half-copied from the source? (See 55b.)
- Are summaries and paraphrases documented with parenthetical citations? (See 55b and 57a.)
- Do readers know where the material being cited begins? In other words, does a signal phrase mark the boundary between the writer's words and the summary or paraphrase, unless the context makes clear exactly what is being cited? (See 56b.)

### Use of statistics and other facts

- Are statistics and facts (other than common knowledge) documented with parenthetical citations? (See 56b and 57a.)
- If there is no signal phrase, will readers understand exactly which facts are being cited? (See 56b.)

# 57

## MLA documentation style

In English and in some humanities classes, you will be asked to use the MLA (Modern Language Association) system for documenting sources, which is set forth in the *MLA Handbook for Writers of Research Papers*, 6th ed. (New York: MLA, 2003). MLA recommends in-text citations that refer readers to a list of works cited.

An in-text citation names the author of the source, often in a signal phrase, and gives the page number in parentheses. At the end of the paper, a list of works cited provides publication information about the source; the list is alphabetized by authors' last names (or by titles for works without authors). There is a direct connection between the in-text citation and the alphabetical listing. In the following example, that link is highlighted in blue.

**IN-TEXT CITATION**

Matt Sundeen notes that drivers with cell phones place an estimated 98,000 emergency calls each day and that the phones "often reduce emergency response times and actually save lives" (1).

**ENTRY IN THE LIST OF WORKS CITED**

Sundeen, Matt. "Cell Phones and Highway Safety: 2000 State
    Legislative Update." <u>National Conference of State</u>
    <u>Legislatures</u>. Dec. 2000. 9 pp. 27 Feb. 2001
    <http://ncsl.org/programs/esnr/cellphone.pdf>.

For a list of works cited with this entry, see pages 664–65.

**NOTE:** If your instructor allows italics for the titles of long
works and for the names of publications, substitute italics
for underlining in all the models in this section.

---

| ON THE WEB | **dianahacker.com/bedhandbook**<br>▶ Electronic exercises<br>    ▶ E-ex 57–1 |
|---|---|

---

## 57a MLA in-text citations

MLA in-text citations are made with a combination of signal
phrases and parenthetical references. A signal phrase indicates that something taken from a source (a quotation,
summary, paraphrase, or fact) is about to be used; usually
the signal phrase includes the author's name. The parenthetical reference, which comes after the cited material, normally includes at least a page number. In the models in this
section, the elements of the in-text citation are shown in blue.

**IN-TEXT CITATION**

One driver, Peter Cohen, says that after he was rear-ended, the
guilty party emerged from his vehicle still talking on the phone
(127).

## Directory to MLA in-text citation models

Readers can look up the author's last name in the alphabetized list of works cited, where they will learn the work's title and other publication information. If readers decide to consult the source, the page number will take them straight to the passage that has been cited.

*Basic rules for print and electronic sources*

The MLA system of in-text citations, which depends heavily on authors' names and page numbers, was created in the early 1980s with print sources in mind. Because some of today's electronic sources have unclear authorship and lack page numbers, they present a special challenge. Nevertheless, the basic rules are the same for both print and electronic sources.

The models in this section (items 1–5) show how the MLA system usually works and explain what to do if your source has no author or page numbers.

■ **1. AUTHOR NAMED IN A SIGNAL PHRASE**  Ordinarily, introduce the material being cited with a signal phrase that includes the author's name. In addition to preparing readers for the source, the signal phrase allows you to keep the parenthetical citation brief.

> Christine Haughney reports that shortly after Japan made it illegal
> to use a handheld phone while driving, "accidents caused by using
> the phones dropped by 75 percent" (A8).

The signal phrase—*Christine Haughney reports that*—names the author; the parenthetical citation gives the page number where the quoted words may be found.

Notice that the period follows the parenthetical citation. When a quotation ends with a question mark or an exclamation point, leave the end punctuation inside the quotation mark and add a period after the parentheses: ". . . ?" (8). (See also the note on p. 418.)

■ **2. AUTHOR NAMED IN PARENTHESES**  If a signal phrase does not name the author, put the author's last name in parentheses along with the page number.

> Most states do not keep adequate records on the number of times
> cell phones are a factor in accidents; as of December 2000, only
> ten states were trying to keep such records (Sundeen 2).

Use no punctuation between the name and the page number.

■  **3. AUTHOR UNKNOWN**    Either use the complete title in a
signal phrase or use a short form of the title in parentheses.
Titles of books are underlined; titles of articles are put in
quotation marks.

> As of 2001, at least three hundred towns and municipalities had
> considered legislation regulating use of cell phones while driving
> ("Lawmakers" 2).

**TIP:** Before assuming that a Web source has no author, do
some detective work. Often the author's name is available
but is not easy to find. For example, it may appear at the
end of the source, in tiny print. Or it may appear on another
page of the site, such as the home page.

**NOTE:** If a source has no author and is sponsored by a corporate entity, such as an organization or a government
agency, name the corporate entity as the author (see item 9
on p. 616).

■  **4. PAGE NUMBER UNKNOWN**    You may omit the page number if a work lacks page numbers, as is the case with many
Web sources. Although printouts from Web sites usually
show page numbers, printers don't always provide the same
page breaks; for this reason, MLA recommends treating
such sources as unpaginated.

> The California Highway Patrol opposes restrictions on the use of
> phones while driving, claiming that distracted drivers can already
> be prosecuted (Jacobs).

According to Jacobs, the California Highway Patrol opposes restrictions on the use of phones while driving, claiming that distracted drivers can already be prosecuted.

When the pages of a Web source are stable (as in PDF files), however, supply a page number in your in-text citation. (For example, the Web source by Sundeen cited in the example on p. 609 has stable pages, so a page number is included in the citation.)

**NOTE:** If a Web source numbers its paragraphs or screens, give the abbreviation "par." or "pars." or the word "screen" or "screens" in the parentheses: (Smith, par. 4).

■ **5. ONE-PAGE SOURCE**   If the source is one page long, MLA allows (but does not require) you to omit the page number. Many instructors will want you to supply the page number because without it readers may not know where your citation ends or, worse, may not realize that you have provided a citation at all.

*No page number given*
Milo Ippolito reports that the driver who struck and killed a two-year-old while using her cell phone got off with a light sentence even though she left the scene of the accident and failed to call 911 for help. In this and in similar cases, traffic offenders distracted by cell phones have not been sufficiently punished under laws on reckless driving.

*Page number given*
Milo Ippolito reports that the driver who struck and killed a two-year-old while using her cell phone got off with a light sentence even though she left the scene of the accident and failed to call 911 for help (J1). In this and in similar cases, traffic offenders

distracted by cell phones have not been sufficiently punished under laws on reckless driving.

### Variations on the basic rules

This section describes the MLA guidelines for handling a variety of situations not covered by the basic rules just given. Again, these rules on in-text citations are the same for both traditional print sources and electronic sources.

■ **6. TWO OR MORE TITLES BY THE SAME AUTHOR** If your list of works cited includes two or more titles by the same author, mention the title of the work in the signal phrase or include a short version of the title in the parentheses.

> On December 6, 2000, reporter Jamie Stockwell wrote that distracted driver Jason Jones had been charged with "two counts of vehicular manslaughter . . . in the deaths of John and Carole Hall" ("Phone" B1). The next day Stockwell reported the judge's ruling: Jones "was convicted of negligent driving and fined $500, the maximum penalty allowed" ("Man" B4).

Titles of articles and other short works are placed in quotation marks, as in the example just given. Titles of books are underlined.

In the rare case when both the author's name and a short title must be given in parentheses, separate them with a comma.

> According to police reports, there were no skid marks indicating that the distracted driver who killed John and Carole Hall had even tried to stop (Stockwell, "Man" B4).

■ **7. TWO OR THREE AUTHORS** Name the authors in a signal phrase, as in the following example, or include their last names in the parenthetical reference: (Redelmeier and Tibshirani 453).

> Redelmeier and Tibshirani found that "the risk of a collision when using a cellular telephone was four times higher than the risk when a cellular telephone was not being used" (453).

When three authors are named in the parentheses, separate the names with commas: (Alton, Davies, and Rice 56).

■ **8. FOUR OR MORE AUTHORS** Name all of the authors or include only the first author's name followed by "et al." (Latin for "and others"). Make sure that your citation matches the entry in the list of works cited (see item 2 on pp. 624–25).

> The study was extended for two years, and only after results were reviewed by an independent panel did the researchers publish their findings (Blaine et al. 35).

■ **9. CORPORATE AUTHOR** When the author is a corporation, an organization, or a government agency, name the corporate author either in the signal phrase or in the parentheses.

> Researchers at the Harvard Center for Risk Analysis claim that the risks of driving while phoning are small compared with other driving risks (3-4).

In the list of works cited, the Harvard Center for Risk Analysis is treated as the author and alphabetized under *H*.

When a government agency is treated as the author, it will be alphabetized in the list of works cited under the name of the government, such as "United States" (see item 3 on p. 625). For this reason, you must name the government in your in-text citation.

The United States Department of Transportation provides nation-wide statistics on traffic fatalities.

■ **10. AUTHORS WITH THE SAME LAST NAME** If your list of works cited includes works by two or more authors with the same last name, include the author's first name in the signal phrase or first initial in the parentheses.

> Estimates of the number of accidents caused by distracted drivers vary because little evidence is being collected (D. Smith 7).

■ **11. INDIRECT SOURCE (SOURCE QUOTED IN ANOTHER SOURCE)** When a writer's or a speaker's quoted words appear in a source written by someone else, begin the parenthetical citation with the abbreviation "qtd. in."

> According to Richard Retting, "As the comforts of home and the efficiency of the office creep into the automobile, it is becoming increasingly attractive as a work space" (qtd. in Kilgannon A23).

■ **12. ENCYCLOPEDIA OR DICTIONARY** Unless an encyclopedia or a dictionary has an author, it will be alphabetized in the list of works cited under the word or entry that you consulted—not under the title of the reference work itself (see item 13 on p. 630). Either in your text or in your parenthetical reference, mention the word or the entry. No page number is required, since readers can easily look up the word or entry.

> The word crocodile has a surprisingly complex etymology ("Crocodile").

■ **13. MULTIVOLUME WORK** If your paper cites more than one volume of a multivolume work, indicate in the parentheses the volume you are referring to, followed by a colon and the page number.

> In his studies of gifted children, Terman describes a pattern of
> accelerated language acquisition (2: 279).

If your paper cites only one volume of a multivolume work, you will include the volume number in the list of works cited and will not need to include it in the parentheses.

■ **14. TWO OR MORE WORKS** To cite more than one source in the parentheses, give the citations in alphabetical order and separate them with a semicolon.

> The effects of sleep deprivation have been well documented
> (Cahill 42; Leduc 114; Vasquez 73).

Multiple citations can be distracting, however, so you should not overuse the technique. If you want to alert readers to several sources that discuss a particular topic, consider using an information note instead (see 57c).

■ **15. AN ENTIRE WORK** Use the author's name in a signal phrase or a parenthetical reference. There is of course no need to use a page number.

> Robinson succinctly describes the status of the mountain lion con-
> troversy in California.

■ **16. WORK IN AN ANTHOLOGY** Put the name of the author of the work (not the editor of the anthology) in the signal phrase or the parentheses.

In "A Jury of Her Peers," Mrs. Hale describes both a style of quilt-ing and a murder weapon when she utters the last words of the story: "We call it--knot it, Mr. Henderson" (Glaspell 210).

In the list of works cited, the work is alphabetized under Glaspell, not under the name of the editor of the anthology.

Glaspell, Susan. "A Jury of Her Peers." Literature and Its Writers: A Compact Introduction to Fiction, Poetry, and Drama. Ed. Ann Char-ters and Samuel Charters. 3rd ed. Boston: Bedford, 2004. 194-210.

■ **17. LEGAL SOURCE** For well-known historical docu-ments, such as articles of the United States Constitution, and for laws in the United States Code, provide a parenthet-ical citation in the text: (US Const., art. 1, sec. 2) or (12 USC 3412, 2000). There is no need to provide a works cited entry.

Legislative acts and court cases are included in the works cited list (see item 50 on p. 651). Your in-text citation should name the act or case either in a signal phrase or in parentheses. In the text of a paper, names of acts are not underlined, but names of cases are.

The Jones Act of 1917 granted US citizenship to Puerto Ricans.

In 1857, Chief Justice Roger B. Taney declared in the case of Dred Scott v. Sandford that blacks, whether enslaved or free, could not be citizens of the United States.

### Literary works and sacred texts

Literary works and sacred texts are usually available in a variety of editions. Your list of works cited will specify which edition you are using, and your in-text citation will usually consist of a page number from the edition you consulted (see item 18).

However, MLA suggests that when possible you should give enough information—such as book parts, play divisions, or line numbers—so that readers can locate the cited passage in any edition of the work (see items 19–21).

■  **18. LITERARY WORKS WITHOUT PARTS OR LINE NUMBERS**  Many literary works, such as most short stories and many novels and plays, do not have parts or line numbers that you can refer to. In such cases, simply cite the page number.

> At the end of Kate Chopin's "The Story of an Hour," Mrs. Mallard drops dead upon learning that her husband is alive. In the final irony of the story, doctors report that she has died of a "joy that kills" (25).

■  **19. VERSE PLAYS AND POEMS**  For verse plays, MLA recommends giving act, scene, and line numbers that can be located in any edition of the work. Use arabic numerals, and separate the numbers with periods.

> In Shakespeare's <u>King Lear</u>, Gloucester, blinded for suspected treason, learns a profound lesson from his tragic experience: "A man may see how this world goes / with no eyes" (4.2.148-49).

For a poem, cite the part (if there are a number of parts) and the line numbers, separated by a period.

> When Homer's Odysseus comes to the hall of Circe, he finds his men "mild / in her soft spell, fed on her drug of evil" (10.209-10).

For poems that are not divided into parts, use line numbers. For a first reference, use the word "lines": (lines 5-8). Thereafter use just the numbers: (12-13).

■   **20. NOVELS WITH NUMBERED DIVISIONS**   When a novel has numbered divisions, put the page number first, followed by a semicolon, and then indicate the book, part, or chapter in which the passage may be found. Use abbreviations such as "bk." and "ch."

> One of Kingsolver's narrators, teenager Rachel, pushes her vocabulary beyond its limits. For example, Rachel complains that being forced to live in the Congo with her missionary family is "a sheer tapestry of justice" because her chances of finding a boyfriend are "dull and void" (117; bk. 2, ch. 10).

■   **21. SACRED TEXTS**   When citing a sacred text such as the Bible or the Qur'an, name the edition you are using in your works cited entry (see item 14 on p. 630). In your parenthetical citation, give the book, chapter, and verse (or their equivalent), separated by periods. Common abbreviations for books of the Bible are acceptable.

> Consider the words of Solomon: "If your enemies are hungry, give them food to eat. If they are thirsty, give them water to drink" (Holy Bible, Prov. 25.21).

| ON THE WEB | **dianahacker.com/bedhandbook** ▶ Electronic research exercises    ▶ E-ex 57–2 and 57–3 |
|---|---|

## 57b MLA list of works cited

An alphabetized list of works cited, which appears at the end of your research paper, gives publication information for each of the sources you have cited in the paper. (For information about preparing the list, see pp. 656–57; for a sample list of works cited, see pp. 665–66.)

**NOTE:** Unless your instructor asks for them, omit sources not actually cited in the paper, even if you read them.

**ON THE WEB**

**dianahacker.com/bedhandbook**
▶ Research and Documentation Online
  ▶ Humanities: Documenting sources (MLA)

*General guidelines for listing authors*

Alphabetize entries in the list of works cited by authors' last names (if a work has no author, alphabetize it by its title). The author's name is important because citations in the text of the paper refer to it and readers will be looking for it at the beginning of an entry in the alphabetized list.

**NAME CITED IN TEXT**

According to Matt Sundeen, . . .

**BEGINNING OF WORKS CITED ENTRY**

Sundeen, Matt.

Items 1–5 show how to begin an entry for a work with a single author, multiple authors, a corporate author, an unknown author, and multiple works by the same author. What comes after this first element of your citation will depend on the kind of source you are citing. (See items 6–56.)

**NOTE:** For a book, an entry in the works cited list will sometimes begin with an editor (see item 9 on p. 628).

■ **1. SINGLE AUTHOR**  For a work with one author, begin with the author's last name, followed by a comma; then give the author's first name, followed by a period.

Tannen, Deborah.

■ **2. MULTIPLE AUTHORS**  For works with two or three authors, name the authors in the order in which they are listed in the source. Reverse the name of only the first author.

Walker, Janice R., and Todd Taylor.

Wilmut, Ian, Keith Campbell, and Colin Tudge.

For a work with four or more authors, either name all of the authors or name the first author, followed by "et al." (Latin for "and others").

Sloan, Frank A., Emily M. Stout, Kathryn Whetten-Goldstein, and Lan
  Liang.

Sloan, Frank A., et al.

■ **3. CORPORATE AUTHOR**  When the author of a print document or Web site is a corporation, a government agency, or some other organization, begin your entry with the name of the group.

First Union.

United States. Bureau of the Census.

American Automobile Association.

**NOTE:** Make sure that your in-text citation also treats the organization as the author (see item 9 on p. 616).

■ **4. UNKNOWN AUTHOR**  When the author of a work is unknown, begin with the work's title. Titles of articles and other short works, such as brief documents from Web sites, are put in quotation marks. Titles of books and other long works, such as entire Web sites, are underlined.

*Article or other short work*
"Media Giants."


*Book or other long work*
Atlas of the World.

Before concluding that the author of a Web source is unknown, check carefully (see the tip on p. 613). Also remember that an organization may be the author (see item 3 on p. 625).

■ **5. TWO OR MORE WORKS BY THE SAME AUTHOR**   If your list of works cited includes two or more works by the same author, use the author's name only for the first entry. For other entries, use three hyphens followed by a period. The three hyphens must stand for exactly the same name or names as in the first entry. List the titles in alphabetical order (ignoring the article *A, An,* or *The* at the beginning of a title).

García, Cristina. The Agüero Sisters. New York: Ballantine, 1998.

---. Monkey Hunting. New York: Ballantine, 2003.

### Books

Items 6–19 apply to print books. For online books, see item 29 on page 640.

■ **6. BASIC FORMAT FOR A BOOK**   For most books, arrange the information into three units, each followed by a period and one space: the author's name; the title and subtitle, underlined; and the place of publication, the publisher, and the date.

Tan, Amy. The Bonesetter's Daughter. New York: Putnam, 2001.

Take the information about the book from its title page and copyright page. Use a short form of the publisher's name; omit terms such as *Press, Inc.,* and *Co.* except when naming university presses (Harvard UP, for example). If the copyright page lists more than one date, use the most recent one.

## Citation at a glance: Book (MLA)

To cite a book in MLA style, include the following elements:

**1** Author
**2** Title and subtitle
**3** City of publication
**4** Publisher
**5** Date of publication

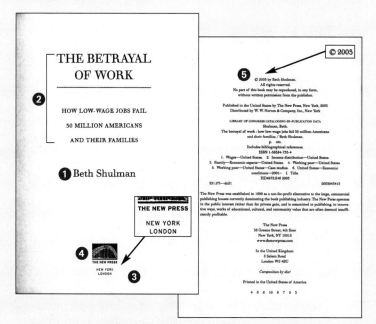

**WORKS CITED ENTRY FOR A BOOK**

```
┌─────1─────┐  ┌──────────────────2──────────────────────
Shulman, Beth. The Betrayal of Work: How Low-Wage Jobs Fail 30

────────────────────────────────┐  ┌──3──┐ ┌4┐ ┌5┐
Million Americans and Their Families. New York: New, 2003.
```

For more on citing books in MLA style, see pages 626–32.

■ **7. AUTHOR WITH AN EDITOR** Begin with the author and title, followed by the name of the editor. In this case the abbreviation "Ed." means "Edited by," so it is the same for one or multiple editors.

Plath, Sylvia. <u>The Unabridged Journals of Sylvia Plath</u>. Ed. Karen V.
    Kukil. New York: Anchor-Doubleday, 2000.

■ **8. AUTHOR WITH A TRANSLATOR** Begin with the name of the author. After the title, write "Trans." (for "Translated by") and the name of the translator.

Allende, Isabel. <u>Daughter of Fortune</u>. Trans. Margaret Sayers Peden. New
    York: Harper, 2000.

■ **9. EDITOR** An entry for a work with an editor is similar to that for a work with an author except that the name is followed by a comma and the abbreviation "ed." for "editor" (or "eds." for "editors").

Craig, Patricia, ed. <u>The Oxford Book of Travel Stories</u>. Oxford: Oxford UP,
    1996.

■ **10. WORK IN AN ANTHOLOGY** Begin with (1) the name of the author of the selection, not with the name of the editor of the anthology. Then give (2) the title of the selection; (3) the title of the anthology; (4) the name of the editor (preceded by "Ed." for "Edited by"); (5) publication information; and (6) the pages on which the selection appears.

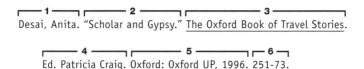

┌──1──┐ ┌────2────┐ ┌──────3──────┐
Desai, Anita. "Scholar and Gypsy." <u>The Oxford Book of Travel Stories</u>.

┌────4────┐ ┌────5────┐┌─6─┐
Ed. Patricia Craig. Oxford: Oxford UP, 1996. 251-73.

If you wish, you may cross-reference two or more works from the same anthology. Provide an entry for the anthology (see item 9 on p. 628). Then in separate entries list the author and title of each selection, followed by the last name of the editor of the anthology and the page numbers on which the selection appears.

Desai, Anita. "Scholar and Gypsy." Craig 251-73.

Malouf, David. "The Kyogle Line." Craig 390-96.

Alphabetize the entry for the anthology under the name of its editor (Craig); alphabetize the entries for the selections under the names of the authors (Desai, Malouf).

■  **11. EDITION OTHER THAN THE FIRST**  If you are citing an edition other than the first, include the number of the edition after the title (or after the names of any translators or editors that appear after the title): 2nd ed., 3rd ed., and so on.

Auletta, Ken. The Underclass. 2nd ed. Woodstock: Overlook, 2000.

■  **12. MULTIVOLUME WORK**  Include the total number of volumes before the city and publisher, using the abbreviation "vols."

Conway, Jill Ker, ed. Written by Herself. 2 vols. New York: Random, 1996.

If your paper cites only one of the volumes, give the volume number before the city and publisher and give the total number of volumes after the date.

Conway, Jill Ker, ed. Written by Herself. Vol. 2. New York: Random, 1996. 2 vols.

■ **13. ENCYCLOPEDIA OR DICTIONARY ENTRY**   When an encyclopedia or a dictionary is well known, simply list the author of the entry (if there is one), the title of the entry, the title of the reference work, the edition number (if any), and the date of the edition.

Posner, Rebecca. "Romance Languages." The New Encyclopaedia
     Britannica: Macropaedia. 15th ed. 1987.

"Sonata." The American Heritage Dictionary of the English Language.
     4th ed. 2000.

Volume and page numbers are not necessary because the entries in the source are arranged alphabetically and therefore are easy to locate.

If a reference work is not well known, provide full publication information as well.

■ **14. SACRED TEXT**   Give the title of the edition of the sacred text (taken from the title page), underlined; the editor's or translator's name (if any); and publication information.

Holy Bible. Wheaton: Tyndale, 2005.

The Qur'an: Translation. Trans. Abdullah Yusuf Ali. Elmhurst: Tahrike,
     2000.

■ **15. FOREWORD, INTRODUCTION, PREFACE, OR AFTERWORD**   Begin with the author of the foreword or other book part, followed by the name of that part. Then give the title of the book; the author of the book, preceded by the word "By"; and the editor of the book (if any). After the publication information, give the page numbers for the part of the book being cited.

Morris, Jan. Introduction. <u>Letters from the Field, 1925-1975</u>.
    By Margaret Mead. New York: Perennial-Harper, 2001.
    xix-xxiii.

If the book part being cited has a title, include it in quotation marks immediately after the author's name.

Ozick, Cynthia. "Portrait of the Essay as a Warm Body." Introduction.
    <u>The Best American Essays 1998</u>. Ed. Ozick. Boston: Houghton,
    1998. xv-xxi.

■ **16. BOOK WITH A TITLE IN ITS TITLE** If the book contains a title normally underlined, neither underline the internal title nor place it in quotation marks.

King, John N. <u>Milton and Religious Controversy: Satire and Polemic in</u>
    Paradise Lost. Cambridge: Cambridge UP, 2000.

If the title within the title is normally put in quotation marks, retain the quotation marks and underline the entire title.

Knight, Denise D., and Cynthia J. Davis. <u>Approaches to Teaching</u>
    <u>Gilman's "The Yellow Wall-Paper" and</u> Herland. New York: Mod.
    Lang. Assn., 2003.

■ **17. BOOK IN A SERIES** Before the publication information, cite the series name as it appears on the title page, followed by the series number, if any.

Malena, Anne. <u>The Dynamics of Identity in Francophone Caribbean</u>
    <u>Narrative</u>. Francophone Cultures and Lits. Ser. 24. New York: Lang,
    1998.

■ **18. REPUBLISHED BOOK** After the title of the book, cite the original publication date, followed by the current publication information. If the republished book contains new material, such as an introduction or afterword, include information about the new material after the original date.

Hughes, Langston. <u>Black Misery</u>. 1969. Afterword Robert O'Meally. New
York: Oxford UP, 2000.

■ **19. PUBLISHER'S IMPRINT** If a book was published by an imprint (a division) of a publishing company, link the name of the imprint and the name of the publisher with a hyphen, putting the imprint first.

Truan, Barry. <u>Acoustic Communication</u>. Westport: Ablex-Greenwood,
2000.

### Articles in periodicals

This section shows how to prepare works cited entries for articles in magazines, scholarly journals, and newspapers. In addition to consulting the models in this section, you will at times need to turn to other models as well:

- More than one author: see item 2
- Corporate author: see item 3
- Unknown author: see item 4
- Online article: see item 32
- Article from a subscription service: see item 31

**NOTE:** For articles appearing on consecutive pages, provide the range of pages (see items 21 and 22). When an article does not appear on consecutive pages, give the number of the first page followed by a plus sign: 32+.

■ **20. ARTICLE IN A MAGAZINE** List, in order, separated by periods, the author's name; the title of the article, in quotation marks; and the title of the magazine, underlined. Then give the date and the page numbers, separated by a colon. If the magazine is issued monthly, give just the month and year. Abbreviate the names of the months except May, June, and July.

Fay, J. Michael. "Land of the Surfing Hippos." <u>National Geographic</u> Aug.
    2004: 100+.

If the magazine is issued weekly, give the exact date.

Lord, Lewis. "There's Something about Mary Todd." <u>US News and World
    Report</u> 19 Feb. 2001: 53.

■ **21. ARTICLE IN A JOURNAL PAGINATED BY VOLUME** Many scholarly journals continue page numbers throughout the year instead of beginning each issue with page 1; at the end of the year, the issues are collected in a volume. To find an article, readers need only the volume number, the year, and the page numbers.

Ryan, Katy. "Revolutionary Suicide in Toni Morrison's Fiction." <u>African
    American Review</u> 34 (2000): 389-412.

■ **22. ARTICLE IN A JOURNAL PAGINATED BY ISSUE** If each issue of the journal begins with page 1, you need to indicate the number of the issue. After the volume number, put a period and the issue number.

Wood, Michael. "Broken Dates: Fiction and the Century." <u>Kenyon Review</u>
    22.3 (2000): 50-64.

■ **23. ARTICLE IN A DAILY NEWSPAPER** Begin with the name of the author, if known, followed by the title of the article. Next give the name of the newspaper, the date, and the page

# Citation at a glance: Article in a periodical (MLA)

To cite an article in a periodical in MLA style, include the following elements:

**1** Author
**2** Title of article
**3** Name of periodical

**4** Date of publication
**5** Page numbers

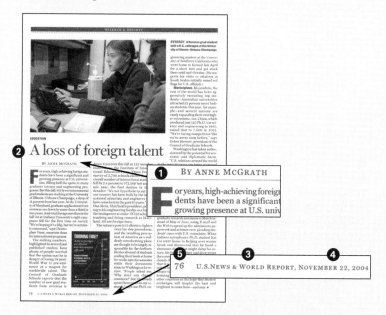

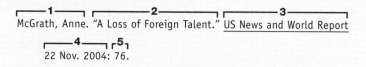

## WORKS CITED ENTRY FOR AN ARTICLE IN A PERIODICAL

```
 ┌──1──┐  ┌──────2──────┐  ┌────────3────────┐
McGrath, Anne. "A Loss of Foreign Talent." US News and World Report
       ┌──4──┐ ┌5┐
       22 Nov. 2004: 76.
```

For more on citing periodical articles in MLA style, see pages 632–36.

numbers (including the section letter). Use a plus sign (+) after the page number if the article does not appear on consecutive pages.

Brummitt, Chris. "Indonesia's Food Needs Expected to Soar." Boston
     Globe 1 Feb. 2005: A7.

If the section is marked with a number rather than a letter, handle the entry as follows:

Wilford, John Noble. "In a Golden Age of Discovery, Faraway Worlds
     Beckon." New York Times 9 Feb. 1997, late ed., sec. 1: 1+.

When an edition of the newspaper is specified on the masthead, name the edition after the date and before the page reference (eastern ed., late ed., natl. ed., and so on), as in the example just given.

If the city of publication is not obvious, include it in brackets after the name of the newspaper: *City Paper* [Washington, DC].

■ **24. EDITORIAL IN A NEWSPAPER** Cite an editorial as you would an article with an unknown author, adding the word "Editorial" after the title.

"All Wet." Editorial. Boston Globe 12 Feb. 2001: A14.

■ **25. LETTER TO THE EDITOR** Name the writer, followed by the word "Letter" and the publication information for the periodical in which the letter appears.

Shrewsbury, Toni. Letter. Atlanta Journal-Constitution 17 Feb. 2001: A13.

■ **26. BOOK OR FILM REVIEW** Name the reviewer and the title of the review, if any, followed by the words "Rev. of" and the title and author or director of the work reviewed. Add the publication information for the periodical in which the review appears.

Gleick, Elizabeth. "The Burdens of Genius." Rev. of The Last Samurai, by
Helen DeWitt. Time 4 Dec. 2000: 171.

Denby, David. "On the Battlefield." Rev. of The Hurricane, dir. Norman
Jewison. New Yorker 10 Jan. 2000: 90-92.

### Electronic sources

This section shows how to prepare works cited entries for a variety of electronic sources, including Web sites, online books, articles in online periodicals and databases, and e-mail.

**NOTE:** When a Web address in a works cited entry must be divided at the end of a line, MLA recommends that you break it after a slash. Do not insert a hyphen.

■ **27. AN ENTIRE WEB SITE** Begin with the name of the author or corporate author (if known) and the title of the site, underlined. Then give the names of any editors, the date of publication or last update, the name of any sponsoring organization, the date you accessed the source, and the URL in angle brackets. Provide as much of this information as is available.

### With author

Peterson, Susan Lynn. The Life of Martin Luther. 2002. 24 Jan. 2005
<http://www.susanlynnpeterson.com/luther/home.html>.

### With corporate (group) author

United States. Environmental Protection Agency. Drinking Water
Standards. 8 July 2004. 24 Jan. 2005 <http://www.epa.gov/
safewater/standards.html>.

*Author unknown*
Margaret Sanger Papers Project. 18 Oct. 2000. History Dept., New York
    U. 6 Dec. 2004 <http://www.nyu.edu/projects/sanger>.

*With editor*
Exploring Ancient World Cultures. Ed. Anthony F. Beavers. 1997. U of
    Evansville. 24 Jan. 2005 <http://eawc.evansville.edu/index.htm>.

**NOTE:** If the site has no title, substitute a description, such as "Home page," for the title. Do not underline the words or put them in quotation marks.

Yoon, Mina. Home page. 29 Sept. 2004. 12 Jan. 2005 <http://
    www.pa.msu.edu/~mnyoon>.

■ **28. SHORT WORK FROM A WEB SITE**   Short works are those that appear in quotation marks in MLA style: articles, poems, and other documents that are not book length. For a short work from a Web site, include as many of the following elements as apply and as are available: author's name; title of the short work, in quotation marks; title of the site, underlined; date of publication or last update; sponsor of the site (if not named as the author or given as the title of the site); date you accessed the source; and the URL in angle brackets.

Usually at least some of these elements will not apply or will be unavailable. In the following example, no sponsor or date of publication was available. (The date given is the date on which the researcher accessed the source.) For an annotated example, see pages 638–39.

*With author*
Shiva, Vandana. "Bioethics: A Third World Issue." NativeWeb. 15 Sept.
    2004 <http://www.nativeweb.org/pages/legal/shiva.html>.

## Citation at a glance: Short work from a Web site (MLA)

To cite a short work from a Web site in MLA style, include the following elements:

1. Author
2. Title of short work
3. Title of Web site
4. Date of publication or latest update
5. Sponsor of site
6. Date of access
7. URL

**ON-SCREEN VIEW OF SHORT WORK**

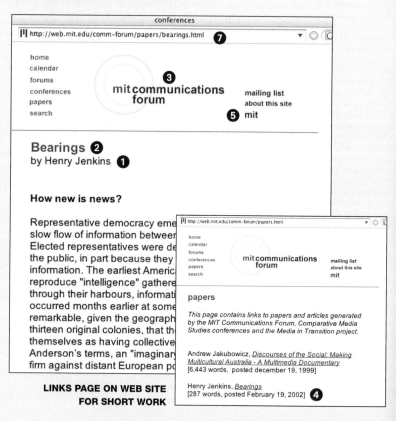

**LINKS PAGE ON WEB SITE FOR SHORT WORK**

**BROWSER PRINTOUT OF SHORT WORK**

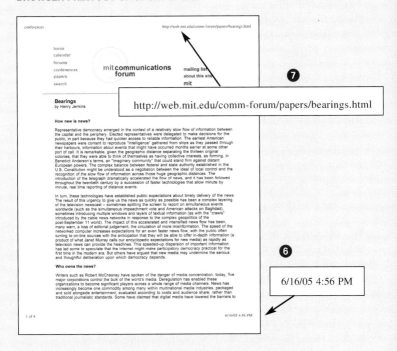

**WORKS CITED ENTRY FOR A SHORT WORK FROM A WEB SITE**

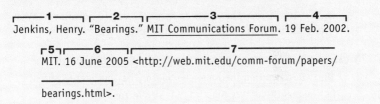

For more on citing sources from Web sites in MLA style, see pages 636–41.

*Author unknown*

"Media Giants." <u>Frontline: The Merchants of Cool</u>. 2001. PBS Online.
    7 Feb. 2005 <http://www.pbs.org/wgbh/pages/frontline/shows/
    cool/giants>.

**NOTE:** When the URL for a short work from a Web site is very long, you may give the URL for the home page and indicate the path by which readers can access the source.

"Obesity Trends among US Adults between 1985 and 2001." <u>Centers
    for Disease Control and Prevention</u>. 3 Jan. 2003. 17 Feb. 2003
    <http://www.cdc.gov>. Path: Health Topics A-Z; Obesity Trends; US
    Obesity Trends 1985 to 2001.

■  **29. ONLINE BOOK**   When a book or a book-length work such as a play or a long poem is posted on the Web as its own site, give as much publication information as is available, followed by your date of access and the URL. (See also the models for print books: items 6–19.)

Rawlins, Gregory J. E. <u>Moths to the Flame</u>. Cambridge: MIT P, 1996.
    11 Nov. 2004 <http://mitpress.mit.edu/e-books/Moths/
    contents.html>.

If the book-length work is posted on a scholarly Web site, provide information about that site.

Jacobs, Harriet Ann. <u>Incidents in the Life of a Slave Girl</u>. Boston,
    1861. <u>Documenting the American South: The Southern Experience
    in Nineteenth-Century America</u>. Ed. Ji-Hae Yoon and Natalia
    Smith. 1998. Academic Affairs Lib., U of North Carolina, Chapel
    Hill. 3 Mar. 2005 <http://docsouth.unc.edu/jacobs/
    jacobs.html>.

■ **30. PART OF AN ONLINE BOOK**   Place the part title before the book's title. If the part is a short work such as a poem or an essay, put its title in quotation marks. If the part is an introduction or other division of the book, do not use quotation marks.

Adams, Henry. "Diplomacy." The Education of Henry Adams. Boston:

Houghton, 1918. Bartleby.com: Great Books Online. 1999. 8 Jan.

2005 <http://bartleby.com/159/8.html>.

■ **31. WORK FROM A SERVICE SUCH AS *INFOTRAC***   For sources retrieved from a library's subscription database service, give as much of the following information as is available: publication information for the source (see items 20–26); the name of the database, underlined; the name of the service; the name and location of the library where you retrieved the source; your date of access; and the URL of the service.

The following models are for articles retrieved through three popular library subscription services. The *InfoTrac* source is a scholarly article in a journal paginated by volume (see item 21); the *EBSCOhost* source is an article in a bimonthly magazine (see item 20); and the *ProQuest* source is an article in a daily newspaper (see item 23).

*InfoTrac*

Johnson, Kirk. "The Mountain Lions of Michigan." Endangered Species

Update 19.2 (2002): 27+. Expanded Academic Index. InfoTrac.

U of Michigan Lib., Ann Arbor. 26 Nov. 2002 <http://

infotrac.galegroup.com>.

*EBSCOhost*

Barrera, Rebeca María. "A Case for Bilingual Education." Scholastic

Parent and Child Nov.-Dec. 2004: 72-73. Academic Search Premier.

EBSCOhost. St. Johns River Community Coll. Lib., Palatka, FL.

1 Feb. 2005 <http://search.epnet.com>.

*ProQuest*

Kolata, Gina. "Scientists Debating Future of Hormone Replacement."
    New York Times 23 Oct. 2002: A20. ProQuest. Drew U Lib.,
    Madison, NJ. 26 Nov. 2002 <http://www.proquest.com>.

**NOTE:** When you access a work through a personal subscription service such as *America Online,* give the information about the source, the name of the service, the date of access, and the keyword used to retrieve the source.

Conniff, Richard. "The House That John Built." Smithsonian
    Feb. 2001. America Online. 11 Mar. 2001. Keyword: Smithsonian
    Magazine.

■ **32. ARTICLE IN AN ONLINE PERIODICAL**   When citing online articles, follow the guidelines for printed articles (see items 20–26), giving whatever information is available in the online source. End the citation with your date of access and the URL.

**NOTE:** In some online articles, paragraphs are numbered. For such articles, include the total number of paragraphs in your citation, as in the next example.

*From an online scholarly journal*

Belau, Linda. "Trauma and the Material Signifier." Postmodern
    Culture 11.2 (2001): 37 pars. 30 Mar. 2001 <http://
    jefferson.village.virginia.edu/pmc/current.issue/11.2belau.html>.

*From an online magazine*

Morgan, Fiona. "Banning the Bullies." Salon.com 15 Mar. 2001.
    21 Sept. 2004 <http://www.salon.com/news/feature/2001/03/15/
    bullying/index.html>.

*From an online newspaper*

Rubin, Joel. "Report Faults Charter School." Los Angeles Times 22 Jan.

2005. 24 Jan. 2005 <http://pqasb.pqarchiver.com/latimes/

search.html>.

■ **33. CD-ROM**   Treat a CD-ROM as you would any other source, but name the medium before the publication information.

"Pimpernel." The American Heritage Dictionary of the English Language.

4th ed. CD-ROM. Boston: Houghton, 2000.

Wattenberg, Ruth. "Helping Students in the Middle." American Educator

19.4 (1996): 2-18. ERIC. CD-ROM. SilverPlatter. Sept. 1996.

■ **34. E-MAIL**   To cite an e-mail, begin with the writer's name and the subject line. Then write "E-mail to" followed by the name of the recipient. End with the date of the message.

Wilde, Lisa. "Review questions." E-mail to the author. 15 Mar. 2005.

■ **35. POSTING TO AN ONLINE LIST, FORUM, OR GROUP**   Communications through e-mail discussion lists (often called LISTSERVs), Web forums, and Usenet newsgroups do not take place in real time. (For real-time online communications, see item 36.) When possible, cite archived versions of postings, which are more permanent and easier to retrieve. If you cannot locate an archived version, keep a copy of the posting for your records.

Begin the entry with the author's name, followed by the title or subject line; the words "Online posting"; the date of the posting; the name of the list, forum, or newsgroup; and your date of access. Then, for a discussion list, give the URL of the list if it is available; otherwise give the e-mail address of the list moderator. For a Web forum, give the network

# Citation at a glance: Article from a database (MLA)

To cite an article from a database in MLA style, include the following elements:

1 Author
2 Title of article
3 Name of periodical, volume and issue numbers
4 Date of publication
5 Inclusive pages

6 Name of database
7 Name of subscription service
8 Library at which you retrieved the source
9 Date of access
10 URL of service

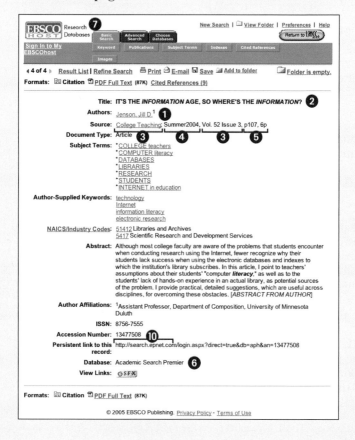

**WORKS CITED ENTRY FOR AN ARTICLE FROM A DATABASE**

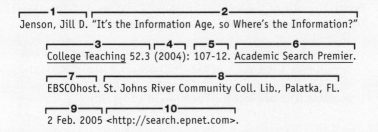

Jenson, Jill D. "It's the Information Age, so Where's the Information?" College Teaching 52.3 (2004): 107-12. Academic Search Premier. EBSCOhost. St. Johns River Community Coll. Lib., Palatka, FL. 2 Feb. 2005 <http://search.epnet.com>.

For more on citing articles from a database in MLA style, see pages 641–42.

address. For a Usenet group, use the prefix "news:" followed by the name of the newsgroup.

*Discussion list posting*

Edwards, David. "Media Lens." Online posting. 20 Dec. 2001. Media Lens
    Archives. 10 Apr. 2002 <http://groups.yahoo.com/group/
    medialens/message/25>.

*Web forum posting*

Brown, Oliver. "Welcome." Online posting. 8 Oct. 2002. Chester Coll.
    Students Web Forum. 20 Feb. 2003 <http://www.voy.com/
    113243>.

*Newsgroup posting*

Reedy, Tom. "Re: Macbeth an Existential Nightmare?" Online posting.
    9 Mar. 2002. 8 Apr. 2002 <news:humanities.lit.authors.shakespe>.

■ **36. POSTING TO A MUD OR A MOO** MUDs and MOOs are forums that allow communication in real time. Include the writer's name (if relevant), a description and date of the event, the title of the forum, the date of access, and the electronic address, beginning with the prefix "telnet://."

Carbone, Nick. Planning for the future. 1 Mar. 2001. TechRhet's Thursday
    night MOO. 1 Mar. 2001 <telnet://connections.moo.mud.org:3333>.

If possible, cite an archived version of the posting.

### Multimedia sources (including online versions)

Multimedia sources include visuals (such as works of art), audio works (such as sound recordings), audiovisuals (such as films), and live events (such as the performance of a play).

When citing multimedia sources that you retrieved online, consult the appropriate model in this section and give whatever information is available for the online source; then end the citation with your date of access and the URL. (See items 37, 40, and 44 for examples.)

■ **37. WORK OF ART** Cite the artist's name, followed by the title of the artwork, usually underlined, and the institution and city in which the artwork can be found. If you want to indicate the work's date, include it after the title. For a work of art you viewed online, end your citation with your date of access and the URL.

Constable, John. Dedham Vale. Victoria and Albert Museum, London.

van Gogh, Vincent. The Starry Night. 1889. Museum of Mod. Art,
    New York. 3 Feb. 2003 <http://moma.org/collection/depts/
    paint_sculpt/blowups/paint_sculpt_003.html>.

■ **38. CARTOON** Begin with the cartoonist's name, the title of the cartoon (if it has one) in quotation marks, the word

"Cartoon," and the publication information for the publication in which the cartoon appears.

Sutton, Ward. "Why Wait 'til November?" Cartoon. <u>Village Voice</u> 7-13
    July 2004: 6.

■ **39. ADVERTISEMENT** Name the product or company being advertised, followed by the word "Advertisement." Give publication information for the source in which the advertisement appears.

Truth by Calvin Klein. Advertisement. <u>Vogue</u> Dec. 2000: 95-98.

■ **40. MAP OR CHART** Cite a map or a chart as you would a book or a short work within a longer work. Add the word "Map" or "Chart" following the title.

<u>Serbia</u>. Map. 2 Feb. 2001. 17 Mar. 2003 <http://www.biega.com/
    serbia.html>.

Joseph, Lori, and Bob Laird. "Driving While Phoning Is Dangerous."
    Chart. <u>USA Today</u> 16 Feb. 2001: 1A.

■ **41. MUSICAL COMPOSITION** Cite the composer's name, followed by the title of the work. Underline the title of an opera, a ballet, or a composition identified by name, but do not underline or use quotation marks around a composition identified by number or form.

Ellington, Duke. <u>Conga Brava</u>.

Haydn, Franz Joseph. Symphony no. 88 in G.

■ **42. SOUND RECORDING** Begin with the name of the person you want to emphasize: the composer, conductor, or performer. For a long work, give the title, underlined, followed by names of pertinent artists (such as performers, readers, or musicians) and the orchestra and conductor (if relevant). End with the manufacturer and the date.

Bizet, Georges. <u>Carmen</u>. Perf. Jennifer Laramore, Thomas Moser, Angela

    Gheorghiu, and Samuel Ramey. Bavarian State Orch. and Chorus.

    Cond. Giuseppe Sinopoli. Warner, 1996.

For a song, put the title in quotation marks. If you include the name of the album, underline it.

Counting Crows. "Holiday in Spain." <u>Hard Candy</u>. Geffen, 2002.

■ **43. FILM OR VIDEO**   Begin with the title, underlined. For a film, cite the director and the lead actors or narrator ("Perf." or "Narr."), followed by the name of the distributor and the year of the film's release. For a videotape or DVD, add "Videocassette" or "DVD" before the name of the distributor.

<u>Finding Neverland</u>. Dir. Marc Forster. Perf. Johnny Depp, Kate Winslet,

    Julie Christie, Radha Mitchell, and Dustin Hoffman. Miramax,

    2004.

<u>High Fidelity</u>. Dir. Stephen Frears. Perf. John Cusack, Iben Hjejle,

    Jack Black, and Todd Louiso. 2000. Videocassette. Walt Disney

    Video, 2001.

■ **44. RADIO OR TELEVISION PROGRAM**   Begin with the title of the radio segment or television episode (if there is one) in quotation marks, followed by the title of the program, underlined. Next give relevant information about the program's writer ("By"), director ("Dir."), performers ("Perf."), or host ("Host"). Then name the network, the local station (if any), and the date the program was broadcast.

"Monkey Trial." <u>American Experience</u>. PBS. WGBH, Boston. 18 Mar. 2003.

"Live in 4A: Konstantin Soukhovetski." <u>Performance Today</u>. Natl. Public
    Radio. 2 May 2002. 10 May 2002 <http://www.npr.org/programs/
    pt/features/4a/soukhovetski.02.html>.

If there is a series title, include it after the title of the program, neither underlined nor in quotation marks.

<u>Mysteries of the Pyramids</u>. On the Inside. Discovery Channel. 7 Feb. 2001.

■ **45. RADIO OR TELEVISION INTERVIEW**    Begin with the name of the person who was interviewed, followed by the word "Interview." End with the information about the program as in item 44.

McGovern, George. Interview. <u>Charlie Rose</u>. PBS. WNET, New York. 1 Feb.
    2001.

■ **46. LIVE PERFORMANCE**    For a live performance of a play, a ballet, an opera, or a concert, begin with the title of the work performed. Then name the author or composer of the work (preceded by the word "By"), followed by as much information about the performance as is available: the director ("Dir."), choreographer ("Chor."), or conductor ("Cond."); the major performers ("Perf."); the theater, ballet, or opera company; the theater and its city; and the date of the performance.

<u>Art</u>. By Yasmina Reza. Dir. Matthew Warchus. Perf. Philip Franks, Leigh
    Lawson, and Simon Shephard. Whitehall Theatre, London. 3 Dec.
    2001.

<u>Cello Concerto No. 2</u>. By Eric Tanguy. Cond. Seiji Ozawa. Perf. Mstislav
    Rostropovich. Boston Symphony Orch. Symphony Hall, Boston. 5
    Apr. 2002.

■ **47. LECTURE OR PUBLIC ADDRESS**   Cite the speaker's name, followed by the title of the lecture (if any), the organization sponsoring the lecture, the location, and the date.

Cohran, Kelan. "Slavery and Astronomy." Adler Planetarium, Chicago. 21
    Feb. 2001.

■ **48. PERSONAL INTERVIEW**   To cite an interview that you conducted, begin with the name of the person interviewed. Then write "Personal interview," followed by the date of the interview.

Akufo, Dautey. Personal interview. 11 Aug. 2005.

*Other sources (including online versions)*

This section includes a variety of traditional print sources not covered elsewhere. For sources obtained on the Web, consult the appropriate model in this section and give whatever information is available for the online source; then end the citation with the date on which you accessed the source and the URL. (See the second example under item 49.)

■ **49. GOVERNMENT PUBLICATION**   Treat the government agency as the author, giving the name of the government followed by the name of the agency.

United States. Dept. of Labor. America's Dynamic Workforce. Washing-
    ton: US Dept. of Labor, 2004.

For government documents published online, give as much publication information as is available and end your citation with the date of access and the URL.

United States. Dept. of Transportation. Natl. Highway Traffic Safety
    Administration. An Investigation of the Safety Implications of

Wireless Communications in Vehicles. Nov. 1999. 20 May 2001
<http://www.nhtsa.dot.gov/people/injury/research/wireless>.

■ **50. LEGAL SOURCE**   For articles of the United States Constitution and laws in the United States Code, no works cited entry is required; instead, simply give an in-text citation (see item 17 on p. 619).

For a legislative act, begin with the name of the act. Then provide the act's Public Law number, its date of enactment, and its Statutes at Large number.

Electronic Freedom of Information Act Amendments of 1996. Pub. L.
104-418. 2 Oct. 1996. Stat. 3048.

For a court case, name the first plaintiff and first defendant. Then give the case number, the court name, and the date of the decision. In a works cited entry, the name of the case is not underlined.

Utah v. Evans. No. 01-714. Supreme Ct. of the US. 20 June 2002.

■ **51. PAMPHLET**   Cite a pamphlet as you would a book.

Commonwealth of Massachusetts. Dept. of Jury Commissioner. A Few
Facts about Jury Duty. Boston: Commonwealth of Massachusetts, 2004.

■ **52. DISSERTATION**   Begin with the author's name, followed by the dissertation title in quotation marks, the abbreviation "Diss.," the name of the institution, and the year the dissertation was accepted.

Jackson, Shelley. "Writing Whiteness: Contemporary Southern Literature
in Black and White." Diss. U of Maryland, 2000.

For dissertations that have been published in book form, underline the title. After the title and before the book's publication information, add the abbreviation "Diss.," the name of the institution, and the year the dissertation was accepted.

Damberg, Cheryl L. <u>Healthcare Reform: Distributional Consequences of an Employer Mandate for Workers in Small Firms</u>. Diss. Rand Graduate School, 1995. Santa Monica: Rand, 1996.

■ **53. ABSTRACT OF A DISSERTATION**   Cite an abstract as you would an unpublished dissertation. After the dissertation date, give the abbreviation *DA* or *DAI* (for *Dissertation Abstracts* or *Dissertation Abstracts International*), followed by the volume number, the date of publication, and the page number.

Chen, Shu-Ling. "Mothers and Daughters in Morrison, Tan, Marshall, and Kincaid." Diss. U of Washington, 2000. <u>DAI</u> 61 (2000): 2289.

■ **54. PUBLISHED PROCEEDINGS OF A CONFERENCE**   Cite published conference proceedings as you would a book, adding information about the conference after the title.

Kartiganer, Donald M., and Ann J. Abadie. <u>Faulkner at 100: Retrospect and Prospect</u>. Proc. of Faulkner and Yoknapatawpha Conf., 27 July-1 Aug. 1997, U of Mississippi. Jackson: UP of Mississippi, 2000.

■ **55. PUBLISHED INTERVIEW**   Name the person interviewed, followed by the title of the interview (if there is one). If the interview does not have a title, include the word "Interview" followed by a period after the interviewee's name. Give publication information for the work in which the interview was published.

Armstrong, Lance. "Lance in France." <u>Sports Illustrated</u> 28 June 2004: 46+.

If the name of the interviewer is relevant, include it after the name of the interviewee, as in the following example.

Prince. Interview with Bilge Ebiri. Yahoo! Internet Life 7.6 (2001):
    82-85.

■   **56. PERSONAL LETTER**   To cite a letter that you have received, begin with the writer's name and add the phrase "Letter to the author," followed by the date.

Primak, Shoshana. Letter to the author. 6 May 2005.

**ON THE WEB**   **dianahacker.com/bedhandbook**
▶ Electronic research exercises
▶ E-ex 57–4 to 57–6

## 57c MLA information notes (optional)

Researchers who use the MLA system of parenthetical documentation (see 57a) may also use information notes for one of two purposes:

1. to provide additional material that might interrupt the flow of the paper yet is important enough to include
2. to refer readers to any sources not discussed in the paper

Information notes may be either footnotes or endnotes. Footnotes appear at the foot of the page; endnotes appear on a separate page at the end of the paper, just before the list of works cited. For either style, the notes are numbered consecutively throughout the paper. The text of the paper contains a raised arabic numeral that corresponds to the number of the note.

**TEXT**

Local governments are more likely than state governments to pass legislation against using a cell phone while driving.[1]

**NOTE**

[1] For a discussion of local laws banning cell phone use, see Sundeen 8.

# 58

## MLA manuscript format; sample MLA paper

### 58a MLA manuscript format

In most English and humanities classes, you will be asked to use MLA (Modern Language Association) guidelines for formatting a paper and preparing a list of the works you have cited. The following guidelines are consistent with advice given in the *MLA Handbook for Writers of Research Papers*, 6th ed. (New York: MLA, 2003). For a sample MLA paper, see 58b.

#### Formatting the paper

MLA papers should be formatted as follows.

**MATERIALS**    For papers that you submit as hard copy, use good-quality 8½″ × 11″ white paper. Secure the pages with a paper clip. Unless your instructor suggests otherwise, do not staple or bind the pages.

**TITLE AND IDENTIFICATION**    MLA does not require a title page. On the first page of your paper, place your name, your instructor's name, the course title, and the date on separate lines against the left margin. Then center your title. (See p. 659 for a sample first page.)

If your instructor requires a title page, ask for guidelines on formatting it. A format similar to the one on page 743 may be acceptable.

**PAGINATION**    Put the page number preceded by your last name in the upper right corner of each page, one-half inch below the top edge. Use arabic numerals (1, 2, 3, and so on).

**MARGINS, LINE SPACING, AND PARAGRAPH INDENTS**    Leave margins of one inch on all sides of the page. Left-align the text.

Double-space throughout the paper. Do not add extra line spaces above or below the title of the paper or between paragraphs.

Indent the first line of each paragraph one-half inch (or five spaces) from the left margin.

**LONG QUOTATIONS**    When a quotation is longer than four typed lines of prose or three lines of verse, set it off from the text by indenting the entire quotation one inch (or ten spaces) from the left margin. Double-space the indented quotation, and don't add extra space above or below it.

Quotation marks are not needed when a quotation has been set off from the text by indenting. See pages 660–61 for an example.

**WEB ADDRESSES**    When a Web address (URL) mentioned in the text of your paper must be divided at the end of a line, do not insert a hyphen (a hyphen could appear to be part of the address). For MLA rules on dividing Web addresses in your list of works cited, see page 657.

**HEADINGS**   MLA neither encourages nor discourages the use of headings and currently provides no guidelines for their use. If you would like to insert headings in a long essay or research paper, check first with your instructor.

For a full discussion of headings, including their phrasing and placement, see 5b. A sample MLA paper with headings appears on the *Bedford Handbook* companion Web site; directions for finding the paper, written by student Paul Levi, are given in the box on page 658.

**VISUALS**   MLA classifies visuals as tables and figures (figures include graphs, charts, maps, photographs, and drawings). Label each table with an arabic numeral (Table 1, Table 2, and so on) and provide a clear caption that identifies the subject. The label and caption should appear on separate lines above the table, flush left. Below the table, give its source in a note like this one:

> Source: John M. Violanti, "Cellular Phones and Fatal Traffic
> Collisions," Accident Analysis and Prevention 30 (1998): 521.

For each figure, place a label and a caption below the figure, flush left. They need not appear on separate lines. The word "Figure" may be abbreviated to "Fig." Include source information following the caption.

Visuals should be placed in the text, as close as possible to the sentences that relate to them unless your instructor prefers them in an appendix. See page 661 for an example of a visual in the text of a paper.

### Preparing the list of works cited

Begin the list of works cited on a new page at the end of the paper. Center the title Works Cited about one inch from the top of the page. Double-space throughout. See pages 665–66 for a sample list of works cited.

**ALPHABETIZING THE LIST** Alphabetize the list by the last names of the authors (or editors); if a work has no author or editor, alphabetize by the first word of the title other than *A, An,* or *The.*

If your list includes two or more works by the same author, use the author's name only for the first entry. For subsequent entries use three hyphens followed by a period. List the titles in alphabetical order. See item 5 on page 626.

**INDENTING** Do not indent the first line of each works cited entry, but indent any additional lines one-half inch (or five spaces). This technique highlights the names of the authors, making it easy for readers to scan the alphabetized list.

**WEB ADDRESSES** Do not insert a hyphen when dividing a Web address (URL) at the end of a line. Break the line after a slash. Also insert angle brackets around the URL.

For advice about how to cite sources with long URLs, see the note on page 640.

If your word processing program automatically turns Web addresses into hot links (by underlining them and highlighting them in color), turn off this feature.

| ON THE WEB | **dianahacker.com/bedhandbook**<br>▶ Additional resources<br>    ▶ Formatting help |
| --- | --- |

## 58b Sample MLA research paper

On the following pages is a research paper on the topic of cell phones and driving, written by Angela Daly, a student in a composition class. Daly's paper is documented with

MLA-style in-text citations and list of works cited. Annotations in the margins of the paper draw your attention to Daly's use of MLA style and her effective writing.

Another student, Paul Levi, has also written a paper on the topic of cell phones and driving; his paper takes the opposite stand from that taken by Angela Daly. His paper is available on the companion Web site.

**ON THE WEB**

**dianahacker.com/bedhandbook**
▶ Model papers
   ▶ MLA papers: Daly
   ▶ MLA papers: Levi

Daly 1

Angela Daly

Professor Chavez

English 101

14 March 2001

A Call to Action:

Regulate Use of Cell Phones on the Road

When a cell phone goes off in a classroom or at a concert, we are irritated, but at least our lives are not endangered. When we are on the road, however, irresponsible cell phone users are more than irritating: They are putting our lives at risk. Many of us have witnessed drivers so distracted by dialing and chatting that they resemble drunk drivers, weaving between lanes, for example, or nearly running down pedestrians in crosswalks. A number of bills to regulate use of cell phones on the road have been introduced in state legislatures, and the time has come to push for their passage. Regulation is needed because drivers using phones are seriously impaired and because laws on negligent and reckless driving are not sufficient to punish offenders.

No one can deny that cell phones have caused traffic deaths and injuries. Cell phones were implicated in three fatal accidents in November 1999 alone. Early in November, two-year-old Morgan Pena was killed by a driver distracted by his cell phone. Morgan's mother, Patti Pena, reports that the driver "ran a stop sign at 45 mph, broadsided my vehicle and killed Morgan as she sat in her car seat." A week later, corrections officer Shannon Smith, who was guarding prisoners by the side of the road, was killed by a woman distracted by a phone call

**Title is centered.**

Opening sentences catch readers' attention.

Thesis asserts Angela Daly's main point.

Daly uses a clear topic sentence.

Signal phrase names the author of the quotation to follow.

No page number is available for this Web source.

Marginal annotations indicate MLA-style formatting and effective writing.

Daly 2

Author's name is given in parentheses; no page number is available.

Page number is given when available.

Clear topic sentences, like this one, are used throughout the paper.

Summary and long quotation are introduced with a signal phrase naming the authors.

Long quotation is set off from the text; quotation marks are omitted.

(Besthoff). On Thanksgiving weekend that same month, John and Carole Hall were killed when a Naval Academy midshipman crashed into their parked car. The driver said in court that when he looked up from the cell phone he was dialing, he was three feet from the car and had no time to stop (Stockwell B8).

Expert testimony, public opinion, and even cartoons suggest that driving while phoning is dangerous. Frances Bents, an expert on the relation between cell phones and accidents, estimates that between 450 and 1,000 crashes a year have some connection to cell phone use (Layton C9). In a survey published by Farmers Insurance Group, 87% of those polled said that cell phones affect a driver's ability, and 40% reported having close calls with drivers distracted by phones. Many cartoons have depicted the very real dangers of driving while distracted (see Fig. 1).

Scientific research confirms the dangers of using phones while on the road. In 1997 an important study appeared in the New England Journal of Medicine. The authors, Donald Redelmeier and Robert Tibshirani, studied 699 volunteers who made their cell phone bills available in order to confirm the times when they had placed calls. The participants agreed to report any nonfatal collision in which they were involved. By comparing the time of a collision with the phone records, the researchers assessed the dangers of driving while phoning. The results are unsettling:

> We found that using a cellular telephone was associated with a risk of having a motor vehicle collision that was about about four times as high as that

Daly 3

"YEP...GOT MY CELLPHONE, MY PAGER, MY INTERNET LINK, MY WIRELESS FAX, AND THANKS TO THIS NIFTY SATELLITE NAVIGATING SYSTEM, I KNOW PRECISELY WHERE I AM AT ALL TIMES!"

Fig. 1. Chan Lowe, cartoon, <u>Washington Post</u> 22 July 2000: A21.

> Illustration has figure number, label, and source information.

among the same drivers when they were not using
their cellular telephones. This relative risk is similar
to the hazard associated with driving with a blood
alcohol level at the legal limit. (456)

The news media often exaggerated the latter claim ("similar
to" is not "equal to"); nonetheless, the comparison with drunk
driving suggests the extent to which cell phone use while driving can impair judgment.

A 1998 study focused on Oklahoma, one of the few states
to keep records on fatal accidents involving cell phones. Using
police records, John M. Violanti of the Rochester Institute of
Technology investigated the relation between traffic fatalities

> Summary begins with a signal phrase naming the author and ends with page numbers in parentheses.

Daly 4

in Oklahoma and the use or presence of a cell phone. He found a ninefold increase in the risk of fatality if a phone was being used and a doubled risk simply when a phone was present in a vehicle (522-23). The latter statistic is interesting, for it suggests that those who carry phones in their cars may tend to be more negligent (or prone to distractions of all kinds) than those who do not.

Daly counters an opposing argument.

Some groups have argued that state traffic laws make legislation regulating cell phone use unnecessary. Sadly, this is not true. Laws on traffic safety vary from state to state, and drivers distracted by cell phones can get off with light punishment even when they cause fatal accidents. For example, although the midshipman mentioned earlier was charged with vehicular manslaughter for the deaths of John and Carole Hall, the judge was unable to issue a verdict of guilty. Under Maryland law, he could only find the defendant guilty of negligent driving and impose a $500 fine (Layton C1). Such a light sentence is not unusual. The driver who killed Morgan Pena in Pennsylvania received two tickets and a $50 fine--and retained his driving privileges (Pena). In Georgia, a young woman distracted by her phone ran down and killed a two-year-old; her sentence was ninety days in boot camp and five hundred hours of community service (Ippolito J1). The families of the victims are understandably distressed by laws that lead to such light sentences.

Facts are documented with in-text citations: authors' names and page numbers (if available) in parentheses.

When certain kinds of driver behavior are shown to be especially dangerous, we wisely draft special laws making them illegal and imposing specific punishments. Running red lights,

Daly 5

failing to stop for a school bus, and drunk driving are obvious examples; phoning in a moving vehicle should be no exception. Unlike more general laws covering negligent driving, specific laws leave little ambiguity for law officers and for judges and juries imposing punishments. Such laws have another important benefit: They leave no ambiguity for drivers. Currently, drivers can tease themselves into thinking they are using their car phones responsibly because the definition of "negligent driving" is vague.

> Daly uses an analogy to justify passing a special law.

As of December 2000, twenty countries were restricting use of cell phones in moving vehicles (Sundeen 8). In the United States, it is highly unlikely that legislation could be passed on the national level, since traffic safety is considered a state and local issue. To date, only a few counties and towns have passed traffic laws restricting cell phone use. For example, in Suffolk County, New York, it is illegal for drivers to use a handheld phone for anything but an emergency call while on the road (Haughney A8). The first town to restrict use of handheld phones was Brooklyn, Ohio (Layton C9). Brooklyn, the first community in the country to pass a seat belt law, has once again shown its concern for traffic safety.

> Daly explains why US laws need to be passed on the state level.

Laws passed by counties and towns have had some effect, but it makes more sense to legislate at the state level. Local laws are not likely to have the impact of state laws, and keeping track of a wide variety of local ordinances is confusing for drivers. Even a spokesperson for Verizon Wireless has said that statewide bans are preferable to a "crazy patchwork quilt of ordinances" (qtd. in Haughney A8). Unfortunately, although a

> Transition helps readers move from one paragraph to the next.

> Daly cites an indirect source: words quoted in another source.

number of bills have been introduced in state legislatures, as of early 2001 no state law seriously restricting use of the phones had passed--largely because of effective lobbying from the wireless industry.

Despite the claims of some lobbyists, tough laws regulating phone use can make our roads safer. In Japan, for example, accidents linked to cell phones fell by 75% just a month after the country prohibited using a handheld phone while driving (Haughney A8). Research suggests and common sense tells us that it is not possible to drive an automobile at high speeds, dial numbers, and carry on conversations without significant risks. When such behavior is regulated, obviously our roads will be safer.

Because of mounting public awareness of the dangers of drivers distracted by phones, state legislators must begin to take the problem seriously. "It's definitely an issue that is gaining steam around the country," says Matt Sundeen of the National Conference of State Legislatures (qtd. in Layton C9). Lon Anderson of the American Automobile Association agrees: "There is momentum building," he says, to pass laws (qtd. in Layton C9). The time has come for states to adopt legislation restricting the use of cell phones in moving vehicles.

Daly counters a claim made by some opponents.

For variety Daly places a signal phrase after a brief quotation.

The paper ends with Daly's stand on the issue.

Daly 7

Works Cited

Besthoff, Len. "Cell Phone Use Increases Risk of Accidents, but
Users Willing to Take the Risk." <u>WRAL Online</u>. 11 Nov.
1999. 12 Jan. 2001 <http://www.wral-tv.com/news/wral/
1999/1110-talking-driving>.

Farmers Insurance Group. "New Survey Shows Drivers Have Had
'Close Calls' with Cell Phone Users." <u>Farmers Insurance
Group</u>. 8 May 2000. 12 Jan. 2001 <http://
www.farmersinsurance.com/news_cellphones.html>.

Haughney, Christine. "Taking Phones out of Drivers' Hands."
<u>Washington Post</u> 5 Nov. 2000: A8.

Ippolito, Milo. "Driver's Sentence Not Justice, Mom Says."
<u>Atlanta Journal-Constitution</u> 25 Sept. 1999: J1.

Layton, Lyndsey. "Legislators Aiming to Disconnect Motorists."
<u>Washington Post</u> 10 Dec. 2000: C1+.

Lowe, Chan. Cartoon. <u>Washington Post</u> 22 July 2000: A21.

Pena, Patricia N. "Patti Pena's Letter to Car Talk." <u>Cars.com</u>.
Car Talk. 10 Jan. 2001 <http://cartalk.cars.com/About/
Morgan-Pena/letter.html>.

Redelmeier, Donald A., and Robert J. Tibshirani. "Association
between Cellular-Telephone Calls and Motor Vehicle Collisions." <u>New England Journal of Medicine</u> 336 (1997):
453-58.

Stockwell, Jamie. "Phone Use Faulted in Collision." <u>Washington
Post</u> 6 Dec. 2000: B1+.

Heading is centered.

List is alphabetized by authors' last names (or by title when a work has no author).

First line of each entry is at the left margin; extra lines are indented 1/2" (or five spaces).

Double-spacing is used throughout.

The URL is broken after a slash. No hyphen is inserted.

Sundeen, Matt. "Cell Phones and Highway Safety: 2000 State
    Legislative Update." <u>National Conference of State
    Legislatures</u>. Dec. 2000. 9 pp. 27 Feb. 2001
    <http://ncsl.org/programs/esnr/cellphone.pdf>.

Violanti, John M. "Cellular Phones and Fatal Traffic Collisions."
    <u>Accident Analysis and Prevention</u> 30 (1998): 519-24.

# 59

## Writing about literature

All good writing about literature attempts to answer a question, spoken or unspoken, about the text: "Why doesn't Hamlet kill his uncle sooner?" "How does street language function in Gwendolyn Brooks's 'We Real Cool'?" "What might the moth symbolize in Virginia Woolf's 'The Death of the Moth'?" "How does Dickens portray lawyers in *Great Expectations*?" "In what ways does James Joyce's 'The Dead' confront traditions of love and romance?"

The goal of a literature paper should be to answer such questions with a meaningful interpretation, presented forcefully and persuasively.

### 59a Get involved in the work; be an active reader.

Read the work closely and carefully. Think of the work as speaking to you: What is it telling you? Asking you? Trying to make you feel?

If the work provides an introduction and footnotes, read them attentively. They may be a source of important information. Use the dictionary to look up words unfamiliar to you or words with subtle nuances that may affect the work's meaning.

Rereading is a central part of the process. You should read short works several times, first to get an overall impression and then again to focus on meaningful details. With longer works, such as novels or plays, read the most important chapters or scenes more than once while keeping in mind the work as a whole.

As you read and reread, interact with the work by posing questions and looking for answers. The chart on pages 672–73 suggests some questions about literature that may

---

**SCHOLARS ON WRITING AND LITERATURE**

LeJeune, Susan G. "Writing for the Ignorant Reader." *Teaching English in the Two-Year College* 26.2 (1998): 163–67. In her introductory composition and literature class, LeJeune gives advice that helps students write clear, well-supported analyses without losing their voices: Write for the ignorant reader. The ignorant reader, like the student writer's classmates, has questions — the very sorts of questions that lead to an interpretation. An audience of ignorant readers won't sit still for jargon-laden academic prose; these readers expect clear, straightforward answers to their questions. In addition, ignorant readers need proof. Finally, because ignorant readers can be somewhat dense, student writers must supply them with explications and analyses.

help you become an active reader. The chart on page 470 suggests strategies for active reading.

### Annotating the work

Annotating the work is a way to focus your reading. The first time through, you may want to pencil a check mark next to passages you find especially significant. On a more careful rereading, pay particular attention to those passages and jot down your ideas and reactions in a notebook or (if you own the book) in the margins of the page.

Here is one student's annotation of a poem by Shakespeare:

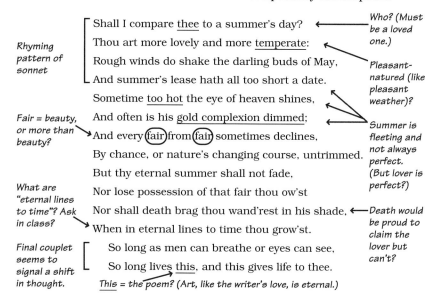

Rhyming pattern of sonnet

Shall I compare <u>thee</u> to a summer's day? ← Who? (Must be a loved one.)

Thou art more lovely and more <u>temperate</u>: ← Pleasant-natured (like pleasant weather)?

Rough winds do shake the darling buds of May,

And summer's lease hath all too short a date.

Sometime <u>too hot</u> the eye of heaven shines, ←

And often is his <u>gold complexion dimmed</u>; ← Summer is fleeting and not always perfect. (But lover is perfect?)

Fair = beauty, or more than beauty? → And every (fair) from (fair) sometimes declines,

By chance, or nature's changing course, untrimmed.

But thy eternal summer shall not fade,

What are "eternal lines to time"? Ask in class? → Nor lose possession of that fair thou ow'st

Nor shall death brag thou wand'rest in his shade, ← Death would be proud to claim the lover but can't?

When in eternal lines to time thou grow'st.

Final couplet seems to signal a shift in thought.

So long as men can breathe or eyes can see,

So long lives <u>this</u>, and this gives life to thee.

*This = the poem? (Art, like the writer's love, is eternal.)*

### Taking notes

Note taking is also an important part of rereading a work of literature. In your notes you can try out ideas and develop

**SCHOLARS ON WRITING AND LITERATURE**

Harmon, William. *A Handbook to Literature.* 10th ed. Upper Saddle River: Prentice, 2006. Including entries on literary terms, styles, and movements, this indispensable text supplements any classroom discussion of literature and offers students concise descriptions of familiar and problematic features of literature.

Lentricchia, Frank, and Thomas McLaughlin, eds. *Critical Terms for Literary Study.* 2nd ed. Chicago: U of Chicago P, 1995. For teachers and students who want more extended discussions of common terms such as *structure, narrative, figurative language,* and *author,* this text offers essays on those terms and eighteen others. The discussions rely on current concepts of critical theory and are accessible and comprehensive.

your perspective on the work. Here are some notes one student took on a short story, "Chrysanthemums," by John Steinbeck. Notice that some of these notes pose questions for further thought.

**NOTE TAKING ON A LITERARY WORK**

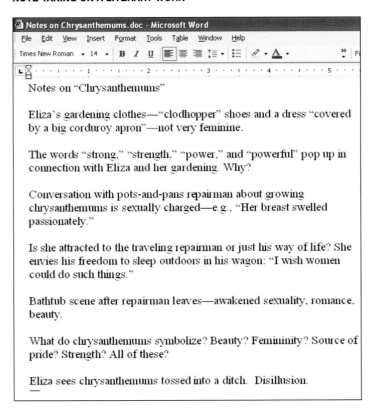

Such notes are the raw material out of which you will build an interpretation.

**SCHOLARS ON WRITING AND LITERATURE**

Steinberg, Erwin R., Michael Gamer, Erika Lindemann, Gary Tate, and Jane Peterson. "Symposium: Literature in the Composition Classroom." *College English* 57 (1995): 265–318. The authors debate whether literature has a place in the composition classroom.

Young, Art, and Toby Fulwiler, eds. *When Writing Teachers Teach Literature: Bringing Writing to Reading.* Portsmouth: Boynton, 1995. Drawing on a variety of critical approaches, this book suggests ways to help students learn to write about literature.

*Discussing the work*

As you have no doubt discovered, class discussions can lead to interesting insights about a literary work, perhaps by calling attention to details in the work that you failed to notice on a first reading. Discussions don't always need to occur face to face. Many literature instructors encourage online discussion groups, where students can explore ideas without fear of embarrassment. Here, for example, is a set of networked postings about a character in Joyce Carol Oates's short story "Where Are You Going, Where Have You Been?"

**JAKE** Do you think Arnold Friend represents the Devil? He sure seems like the incarnation of evil.

**RIMA** I was wondering about that too, Jake. He seems to have supernatural powers. He knows all about Connie and even calls up a vision of her Aunt Tillie's barbecue miles away, complete with details about a fat woman.

**BEN** There are places in the story that make me think Arnold Friend is a wolf—maybe even the wolf in "Little Red Riding Hood." Did you guys notice that he was sniffing her like he was about to gobble her up? And he has big teeth.

**DAWN** I noticed that too, Ben, and near the end of the story Arnold Friend says that Connie's house is so flimsy he could knock it down. That sounds pretty close to the fairy tale: "I'll huff and I'll puff and I'll blow your house down."

**RIMA** All I can say is that Arnold Friend is the kind of "wolf" my mother has always warned me against—a fast-talking older guy with nothing but sex on his mind. Even before he begins making threats, Connie knows she shouldn't get into a car with him. She keeps repeating, "I don't even know you." And she's worried about how old he is.

**SCHOLARS ON WRITING AND LITERATURE**

Beach, Richard. *A Teacher's Introduction to Reader-Response Theories.* Urbana: NCTE, 1993. Beach describes several reader-response theories: textual, experimental, psychological, social, and cultural. He also shows instructors how to help students develop a consistent critical stance in relation to their reading.

## 59b Form an interpretation.

After rereading, jotting notes, and perhaps discussing the work, you are ready to start forming an interpretation. At this stage, try to focus on a central issue. Look through your notes and annotations for recurring questions and insights about a single aspect of the work.

### Focusing on a central issue

In forming an interpretation, it is important to focus on a central issue. In other words, avoid trying to do everything at once. You may think, for example, that *Huckleberry Finn* is a great book because it contains brilliant descriptions of scenery, has a lot of humorous moments, but also tells a serious story of one boy's development. This is a legitimate response to the work, but your job in writing an essay will be to close in on one issue that you can develop into a sustained, in-depth interpretation. For example, you might focus on ways in which the runaway slave Jim uses humor to preserve his dignity. Or you might focus on ironic discrepancies between what Huck says and what his heart tells him. Or you could choose just one or two minor characters, such as the Duke and the Dauphin, and show how they represent flaws in the society at large.

### Asking questions that lead to an interpretation

Think of your interpretation as answering a question about the work. Some interpretations answer questions about literary techniques, such as the writer's handling of plot, setting, and character (see p. 672). Others respond to questions about social context as well: what a work reveals about the time and culture in which it was written (see pp. 672–73). Frequently you will find yourself writing about both technique

**SCHOLARS ON WRITING AND LITERATURE**

Lindemann, Erika. "Freshman Composition: No Place for Literature." *College English* 55 (1993): 311–16. Lindemann argues that literature does not belong in the composition classroom.

Tate, Gary. "A Place for Literature in Freshman Composition." *College English* 55 (1993): 317–21. Tate argues that there is value in using literature to teach writing.

## Questions to ask about literature

### Questions about technique

*Plot.* What central conflicts drive the plot? Are they internal (within a character) or external (between characters or between a character and a force)? How are conflicts resolved? Why are events revealed in a particular order?

*Setting.* Does the setting (time and place) create an atmosphere, give an insight into a character, suggest symbolic meanings, or hint at the theme of the work?

*Character.* What seems to motivate the central characters? Do any characters change significantly? If so, what—if anything—have they learned from their experiences? Do sharp contrasts between characters highlight important themes?

*Point of view.* Does the point of view—the perspective from which the story is narrated or the poem is spoken—affect our understanding of events? Does the narration reveal the character of the speaker, or does the speaker merely observe others? Is the narrator perhaps innocent, naive, or deceitful? Is the story told by multiple narrators?

*Theme.* Does the work have an overall theme (a central insight about people or a truth about life)? If so, how do details in the work illuminate this theme?

*Language.* Does language—such as formal or informal, standard or dialect, prosaic or poetic, cool or passionate—reveal the character of speakers? How do metaphors, similes, and sensory images contribute to the work? How do recurring images enrich the work and hint at its meaning? To what extent do sentence rhythms and sounds underscore the writer's meaning?

### Questions about social context

*Historical context.* What does the work reveal about the time and place in which it was written? Does the work appear to promote or undermine a philosophy that was popular in its

---

**SCHOLARS ON WRITING AND LITERATURE**

MacDonald, Susan Peck, and Charles R. Cooper. "Contributions of Academic and Dialogic Journals to Writing about Literature." *Writing, Teaching, and Learning in the Disciplines.* Ed. Anne Herrington and Charles Moran. New York: MLA, 1992. 137–55. In a research study, MacDonald and Cooper found that students who wrote academic journal responses to intellectually challenging questions earned significantly higher scores on a final exam than those who wrote "dialogic" journals without specific prompts from the instructor.

time, such as social Darwinism in the late nineteenth century or the women's movement in the mid-twentieth century?

*Class.* How does membership in a social class affect the characters' choices and their successes or failures? How does class affect the way characters view—or are viewed by—others? What do economic struggles reveal about power relationships in the society being depicted?

*Race and culture.* Are any characters portrayed as being caught between cultures: between the culture of home and work or school, or between a traditional and an emerging culture? Are any characters engaged in a conflict with society because of their race or ethnic background? To what extent does the work celebrate a specific culture and its traditions?

*Gender.* Are any characters' choices restricted because of gender? What are the power relationships between the sexes, and do these change during the course of the work? Do any characters resist the gender roles that society has assigned to them? Do other characters choose to conform to those roles?

*Archetypes.* Does a character, image, or plot fit a pattern—or archetype—that has been repeated in stories throughout history and across cultures? (For example, nearly every culture has stories about heroes, quests, redemption, and revenge.) How does an archetypal character, image, or plot line correspond to or differ from others like it?

and social context. For example, Margaret Peel, a student who wrote about Langston Hughes's poem "Ballad of the Landlord" (see pp. 689–93), addressed the following question, which touches on both language and race:

> How does the poem's language--through its four voices--
> dramatize the experience of a black man in a society dominated
> by whites?

### SCHOLARS ON WRITING AND LITERATURE

Hull, Glynda, and Mike Rose. "'This Wooden Shack Place': The Logic of an Unconventional Reading." *College Composition and Communication* 41 (1990): 287–98. Hull and Rose discuss student interpretations of literature that strike teachers as "unusual, a little off, not on the mark." The authors suggest that "our particular orientations and readings might blind us to the logic of a student's interpretation and the ways that interpretation might be sensibly influenced by the student's history."

In the introduction of your paper, you will usually announce your interpretation in a one- or two-sentence thesis. The thesis answers the central question that you posed. Here, for example, is Margaret Peel's two-sentence thesis:

> Langston Hughes's "Ballad of the Landlord" is narrated through four voices, each with its own perspective on the poem's action. These opposing voices--of a tenant, a landlord, the police, and the press--dramatize a black man's experience in a society dominated by whites.

## 59c Draft a thesis and sketch an outline.

### Drafting a thesis

A thesis, which nearly always appears in the introduction, announces an essay's main point (see also 2a). In a literature paper, your thesis will answer the central question that you have asked about the work. In drafting your thesis, aim for a strong, assertive summary of your interpretation. Here, for example, are two successful thesis statements taken from student essays, together with the central question each student had posed.

**QUESTION**

What does Stephen Crane's short story "The Open Boat" reveal about the relation between humans and nature?

**THESIS**

In Stephen Crane's gripping tale "The Open Boat," four men lost at sea discover not only that nature is indifferent to their fate but that their own particular talents make little difference as they struggle for survival.

---

**SCHOLARS ON WRITING AND LITERATURE**

Lynn, Steven. "A Passage into Critical Theory." *College English* 52 (1990): 258–71. After admitting the difficulty of incorporating theory into the classroom, Lynn uses a sample text to demonstrate various theoretical approaches to analysis: new criticism, structuralism, deconstruction, psychological criticism, and feminism.

Moran, Charles, and Elizabeth F. Penfield. *Conversations: Contemporary Critical Theory and the Teaching of Literature.* Urbana: NCTE, 1990. The essays in Part 1 address contemporary critical theory from several perspectives and include Henry Louis Gates Jr.'s "Canon Formation and the Afro-American Tradition" and Steven Mailloux on reader-response criticism. Part 2 contains essays by teachers whose understanding of critical theory informs reading lists, syllabi, and writing assignments.

**QUESTION**
In Euripides's tragedy *Electra,* how do Electra and her mother, Clytemnestra, respond to the limitations society has placed on women?

**THESIS**
The experience of powerlessness has taught Electra and her mother two very different lessons: Electra has learned the value of traditional, conservative sex roles for women, but Clytemnestra has learned just the opposite.

As in other writing, the thesis of a literature paper cannot be too factual, too broad, or too vague (see 2a). For an essay on Mark Twain's *Huckleberry Finn,* for example, the following would all make poor thesis statements.

**TOO FACTUAL**
As a runaway slave, Jim is in danger from the law.

**TOO BROAD**
In *Huckleberry Finn,* Mark Twain criticizes mid-nineteenth-century American society.

**TOO VAGUE**
*Huckleberry Finn* is Twain's most exciting work.

Here is a thesis about the novel that avoids these pitfalls.

**ACCEPTABLE THESIS**
Because Huckleberry Finn is a naive narrator, his comments on conventional religion are ironic at every turn, allowing Twain to poke fun at empty piety.

In a literature paper, your thesis should usually appear in your introductory paragraph. Often, however, you will want to present a context for the thesis and lead up to it, as in the following paragraph, which ends with the thesis (italicized).

**SCHOLARS ON WRITING AND LITERATURE**
Biddle, Arthur W., and Toby Fulwiler, eds. *Reading, Writing, and the Study of Literature.* New York: McGraw, 1989. This book provides an overview of methods that students can use to respond to literature in writing. It includes chapters on literary theory, genres, and essay exams. Each chapter includes a bibliography.

In *Electra*, Euripides depicts two women who have had too little control over their lives. Electra, ignored by her mother, Clytemnestra, has been married off to a farmer and treated more or less like a slave. Clytemnestra has fared even worse. Her husband, Agamemnon, has slashed the throat of their daughter Iphigenia as a sacrifice to the gods. *The experience of powerlessness has taught Electra and her mother two very different lessons: Electra has learned the value of traditional, conservative sex roles for women, but Clytemnestra has learned just the opposite.*

---

**ON THE WEB**  **dianahacker.com/bedhandbook**
▶ Electronic research exercises
▶ E-ex 59–1

---

### Sketching an outline

Your thesis may strongly suggest a method of organization, in which case you will have little difficulty jotting down your essay's key points. Consider, for example, the following informal outline, based on a thesis that leads naturally to a three-part organization.

> Thesis: George Bernard Shaw's *Major Barbara* depicts the ways in which three "religions" address the problem of poverty. The Established Church ignores poverty, the Salvation Army tries rather ineffectually to alleviate it, and a form of utopianism based on guns and money promises to eliminate it — but at a terrible cost.

- The Established Church (Lady Britomart)
- The Salvation Army (Major Barbara)
- Utopianism based on guns and money (Undershaft)

---

**SCHOLARS ON WRITING AND LITERATURE**

Oster, Judith. "Seeing with Different Eyes: Another View of Literature in the ESL Class." *TESOL Quarterly* 23 (1989): 85–102. Oster argues that "focusing on point of view in literature enlarges students' vision and fosters critical thinking by dramatizing the various ways a situation can be seen." She adds that "contact with literature stimulates more imaginative student writing, and with it an increase of significant detail and appropriate figurative language."

If your thesis does not by itself suggest a method of organization, turn to your notes and begin putting them into categories that relate to the thesis. For example, one student who was writing about Euripides's play *Medea* constructed the following formal outline from her notes.

Thesis:  Although Medea professes great love for her children, Euripides gives us reason to suspect her sincerity: Medea does not hesitate to use the children as weapons in her bloody battle with Jason, and from the outset she displays little real concern for their fate.

I.  From the very beginning of the play, Medea is a less than ideal mother.
   A.  Her first words about the children are hostile.
   B.  Her first actions suggest indifference.
II.  In three scenes Medea appears to be a loving mother, but in each of these scenes we have reason to doubt her sincerity.
III.  Throughout the play, as Medea plots her revenge, her overriding concern is not her children but her reputation.
   A.  Fearing ridicule, she is proud of her reputation as one who can "help her friends and hurt her enemies."
   B.  Her obsession with reputation may stem from the Greek view of reputation as a means of immortality.
IV.  After she kills her children, Medea reveals her real concern.
   A.  She shows no remorse.
   B.  She revels in Jason's agony over their death.

Whether to use a formal or an informal outline is to some extent a matter of personal preference. For most purposes, you will probably find that an informal outline is sufficient, perhaps even preferable. (See 1d.)

**SCHOLARS ON WRITING AND LITERATURE**
Herrington, Anne J. "Teaching, Writing, and Learning: A Naturalistic Study of Writing in an Undergraduate Class." *Writing in Academic Disciplines.* Ed. David Jolliffe. Norwood: Ablex, 1988. 133–66. Herrington presents three case studies that show how students learned to write about literature. The essay includes sample writing assignments and examples of student writing and teacher responses.

**59d** Support your interpretation with evidence from the work; avoid plot summary.

Your thesis and tentative outline will point you toward details in the work relevant to your interpretation. As you begin filling out the body of your paper, make good use of those details.

*Supporting your interpretation*

As a rule, the topic sentence of each paragraph in the body of your paper should focus on some aspect of your overall interpretation. The rest of the paragraph should present details and perhaps quotations from the work that back up your interpretation. In the following paragraph, which develops part of the outline sketched on page 676, the topic sentence comes first. It sums up the religious views represented by Lady Britomart, a character in George Bernard Shaw's play *Major Barbara.*

> Lady Britomart, a member of the Established Church of England, reveals her superficial attitude toward religion in a scene that takes place in her fashionable London townhouse. Religion, according to Lady Britomart, is a morbid topic of conversation. She admonishes her daughter Barbara: "Really, Barbara, you go on as if religion were a pleasant subject. Do have some sense of propriety" (1.686–87). Religion is an unpleasant subject to Lady Britomart because, unlike Barbara, she finds no joy or humor within her religion. It is not simply that she is a humorless person, for she frequently displays a sharp wit. But in Lady Britomart's upper-class world, religion has its proper place—a serious place bound by convention and cut off from the real world. When Undershaft suggests, for example, that religion can be a pleasant and profoundly important subject, Lady Britomart replies, "Well if you are determined to have it [religion], then I insist on having it in a proper and respectable way. Charles: ring for prayers" (1.690–93).

---

**SCHOLARS ON WRITING AND LITERATURE**

Gould, Christopher. "Literature in the Basic Writing Course: A Bibliographic Survey." *College English* 49 (1987): 558–74. Arguing that basic writing students are overlooked in the trend of teaching literature in composition courses, Gould encourages basic writing teachers to use literature in their courses. He provides an excellent list of relevant readers and rhetorics.

Notice that the writer has quoted dialogue from the play to lend both flavor and substance to her interpretation. Notice too that the writer is indeed *interpreting* the work: She is not merely summarizing the plot.

### Avoiding plot summary

In a literature paper, it is tempting to rely heavily on plot summary and avoid interpretation. You can resist this temptation by paying special attention to your topic sentences. The following rough-draft topic sentence, for instance, led to a plot summary rather than an interpretation.

> As they drift down the river on a raft, Huck and the runaway slave Jim have many philosophical discussions.

The student's revised topic sentence, which announces an interpretation, is much better.

> The theme of dawning moral awareness is reinforced by the many philosophical discussions between Huck and Jim, the runaway slave, as they drift down the river on a raft.

Usually a little effort is all that is needed to make the difference between a plot summary that goes nowhere and a focused, forceful interpretation. As with all forms of writing, revision is key.

**59e** Integrate quotations from the work.

Quotations from a literary work can lend vivid support to your argument, but keep most quotations fairly short. Excessive use of long quotations bores readers and interrupts the flow of your interpretation.

**WRITERS ON WRITING**

The illusion of art is to make one believe that great literature is very close to life, but exactly the opposite is true. Life is amorphous, literature is formal.  —Françoise Sagan

In good writing, words become one with things.
  —Ralph Waldo Emerson

A writer needs three things, experience, observation, and imagination, any two of which, at times any one of which, can supply the lack of the others.  —William Faulkner

The writer is more concerned to know than to judge.
  —W. Somerset Maugham

Integrating quotations smoothly into your own text can present a challenge. Because of the complexities of literature, do not be surprised to find yourself puzzling over the most graceful way to tuck in a short phrase or the clearest way to introduce a more extended passage from the work.

**NOTE:** The parenthetical citations at the ends of examples in this section follow MLA (Modern Language Association) style for documenting sources in text. They tell readers where the quoted words can be found. They indicate the lines of a poem; the act, scene, and lines of a play; or the page number of a quotation from a short story or novel. For guidelines on using citations, see pages 619–21.

### Introducing quotations

When writing about nonfiction essays and books, you have probably learned to introduce a quotation with a signal phrase naming the author: *According to Jane Doe, Jane Doe points out that, Jane Doe presents a compelling argument,* and so on.

When introducing quotations from a literary work, however, make sure that you don't confuse the author with the narrator of a story, the speaker of a poem, or a character in a play. Instead of naming the author, you can refer to the narrator or speaker—or to the work itself.

> **INAPPROPRIATE**
> Poet Andrew Marvell describes his fear of death like this: "But at my back I always hear / Time's wingèd chariot hurrying near" (21–22).

> **APPROPRIATE**
> Addressing his beloved in an attempt to win her sexual favors, the speaker of the poem argues that death gives them no time to waste: "But at my back I always hear / Time's wingèd chariot hurrying near" (21–22).

**WRITERS ON WRITING**

A writer's mind seems to be situated partly in the solar plexus and partly in the head.                                        —Ethel Wilson

It is with noble sentiments that bad literature gets written.
                                        —André Gide

It took me fifteen years to discover I had no talent for writing, but I couldn't give it up because by that time I was too famous.
                                        —Robert Benchley

Good writers have two things in common: They prefer being understood to being admired, and they do not write for the overcritical and too shrewd reader.                        —Friedrich Nietzsche

**APPROPRIATE**

The poem "To His Coy Mistress" says as much about fleeting time and death as it does about sexual passion. Its most powerful lines may well be "But at my back I always hear / Time's wingèd chariot hurrying near" (21–22).

In the last example, you could of course mention the author as well: *Marvell's poem "To His Coy Mistress" says as much. . . .* Although the author is mentioned, he is not being confused with the speaker of the poem.

If you are quoting the words of a character in a story or a play, you should name the character who is speaking and provide a context for the spoken words. In the following examples, the quoted dialogue is from Tennessee Williams's play *The Glass Menagerie* and Shirley Jackson's short story "The Lottery."

> Laura is so completely under Amanda's spell that when urged to make a wish on the moon, she asks, "What shall I wish for, Mother?" (1.5.140).

> When a neighbor suggests that the lottery should be abandoned, Old Man Warner responds, "There's *always* been a lottery" (284).

### Avoiding shifts in tense

Because it is conventional to write about literature in the present tense (see p. 328) and because literary works often use other tenses, you will need to exercise some care when weaving quotations into your own text. A first-draft attempt may result in an awkward shift, as it did for one student who was writing about Nadine Gordimer's short story "Friday's Footprint."

**TENSE SHIFT**

When Rita sees Johnny's relaxed attitude, "she blushed, like a wave of illness" (159).

To avoid the distracting shift from present to past tense, the writer decided to include the reference to Rita's blushing in her own text and reduce the length of the quotation.

**REVISED**
When Rita sees Johnny's relaxed attitude, she blushes "like a wave of illness" (159).

The writer could have changed the quotation to present tense, using brackets to indicate the change, like this: *When Rita sees Johnny's relaxed attitude, "she blushe[s], like a wave of illness" (159).* However, using brackets around just one letter of a word can seem pedantic, so the earlier revision is preferable. (For advice on using brackets around a word or more, see 39c.)

*Using quotations within quotations*

In writing about literature, you may sometimes want to use a quotation with another quotation embedded in it—when you are quoting dialogue in a novel, for example. In such cases, set off the main quotation with double quotation marks, as you usually would, and set off the embedded quotation with single quotation marks. (See also 37c.) The following example from a student paper quotes lines from Amy Tan's novel *The Hundred Secret Senses.*

Early in the novel the narrator's half-sister Kwan sees—or thinks she sees—ghosts: " 'Libby-ah,' she'll say to me. 'Guess who I see yesterday, you guess.' And I don't have to guess that she's talking about someone dead" (3).

*Formatting quotations*

Guidelines for formatting quotations from short stories (or novels), poems, and plays are slightly different.

**WRITERS ON WRITING**

A play should give you something to think about. When I see a play and understand it the first time, then I know it can't be much good. —T. S. Eliot

It is a great fault, in descriptive poetry, to describe everything. —Alexander Pope

Fiction is like a spider's web, attached ever so slightly perhaps, but still attached to life at all four corners. —Virginia Woolf

**SHORT STORIES OR NOVELS** If a quotation from a short story or a novel takes up four or fewer typed lines in your paper, put it in quotation marks and run it into the text of your essay. Include a page number in parentheses after the quotation.

> The narrator of Eudora Welty's "Why I Live at the P.O.," known to us only as "Sister," makes many catty remarks about her enemies. For example, she calls Mr. Whitaker "this photographer with the pop-eyes" (46).

If a quotation from a short story or a novel is five typed lines or longer, set it off from the text by indenting one inch (or ten spaces) from the left margin; do not use quotation marks around it. (See also 37b.) Put the page number in parentheses after the final mark of punctuation.

> Sister's tale begins with "I," and she makes every event revolve around herself, even her sister's marriage:
>> I was getting along fine with Mama, Papa-Daddy, and Uncle Rondo until my sister Stella-Rondo just separated from her husband and came back home again. Mr. Whitaker! Of course I went with Mr. Whitaker first, when he first appeared here in China Grove, taking "Pose Yourself" photos, and Stella-Rondo broke us up. (46)

**POEMS** Enclose quotations of three or fewer lines of poetry in quotation marks within your text, and indicate line breaks with a slash. (See also 39e.) Include line numbers in parentheses at the end of the quotation. (See also p. 620.)

> The opening lines of Frost's "Fire and Ice" strike a conversational tone: "Some say the world will end in fire, / Some say in ice" (1–2).

**WRITERS ON WRITING**

In certain kinds of writing, particularly in art criticism and literary criticism, it is normal to come across long passages which are almost completely lacking in meaning. —George Orwell

When you quote four or more lines of poetry, set the quotation off from the text by indenting one inch (or ten spaces) and omit the quotation marks. Put the line numbers in parentheses after the final mark of punctuation.

> The opening stanza of Louise Bogan's "Women" startles read-
> ers by presenting a negative stereotype of women:
>> Women have no wilderness in them,
>> They are provident instead,
>> Content in the tight hot cell of their hearts
>> To eat dusty bread. (1–4)

**PLAYS**    If a quotation from a play takes up four or fewer typed lines in your paper and is spoken by only one character, put quotation marks around it and run it into the text of your essay. Whenever possible, include the act number, scene number, and line numbers in parentheses at the end of the quotation. Separate the numbers with periods, and use arabic numerals unless your instructor prefers roman numerals.

> Two attendants silently watch as the sleepwalking Lady Mac-
> beth subconsciously struggles with her guilt: "Here's the smell
> of blood still. All the perfumes of Arabia will not sweeten this
> little hand" (5.1.50–51).

If a dramatic quotation by a single character is five lines or longer, set it off in the same way you would set off a long prose quotation. Include the act number, scene number, and line numbers after the final mark of punctuation.

When quoting dialogue between two or more characters in a play, no matter how many lines you use, set the quotation off from the text. Type each character's name in all capital letters at a one-inch (ten-space) indent from the left margin. Indent subsequent lines under the character's name an additional quarter inch (or three spaces).

Throughout *The Importance of Being Earnest*, Algernon criticizes romance and the institution of marriage, as in the scene when he learns of Jack's intention to marry Gwendolen:

> ALGERNON. My dear fellow, the way you flirt with Gwendolen is perfectly disgraceful. It is almost as bad as the way Gwendolen flirts with you.
> JACK. I am in love with Gwendolen. I have come up to town expressly to propose to her.
> ALGERNON. I thought you had come up for pleasure?—I call that business. (act 1)

## 59f Observe the conventions of literary papers.

When you are writing a literature paper, it is important to observe certain conventions so that your readers' attention will be focused directly on your interpretation, not on the details of your presentation.

### Referring to authors and titles

The first time you refer to authors, use their first and last names: *Virginia Woolf was one of England's most important novelists.* In subsequent references, use their last names only: *Woolf's early work was largely overlooked.* As a rule, do not use titles such as Mr. or Ms. or Dr.

Titles of short stories, essays, and most poems are put in quotation marks: "The Dead" by James Joyce, "The Death of the Moth" by Virginia Woolf, "High Windows" by Philip Larkin. (See 37d.) Titles of novels, nonfiction books, plays, and epics or other long poems are underlined (or italicized): *Heart of Darkness* by Joseph Conrad, *I Know Why the Caged Bird Sings* by Maya Angelou, *Macbeth* by William Shakespeare, *Howl* by Allen Ginsberg. (See 42a.)

### Referring to characters and events

Refer to each character by the name most often used for him or her in the work. If, for instance, a character's name is Lambert Strether and he is always referred to as "Strether," do not call him "Lambert" or "Mr. Strether." Similarly, write "Lady Macbeth," not "Mrs. Macbeth."

When describing fictional events in a work of literature, use the present tense: *Octavia demands blind obedience from James and from all of her children. When James and Ty catch two redbirds in their trap, they want to play with them; Octavia, however, has other plans for the birds.* (See also 13b and 28a.)

### Referring to parts of works

Be as accurate as possible when referring to subdivisions of a literary work. Avoid using phrases like *the part where.* Instead give specific references by using the appropriate descriptive terms: *the final stanza, the scene in which Hamlet confronts his mother, the passage that refers to Jane Austen,* and so on.

## 59g If you use secondary sources, document them appropriately and avoid plagiarism.

Many literature papers do not rely on secondary sources — works other than the literary text under discussion. (For an example of an essay without secondary sources, see pp. 689–93.)

Other literature papers use some ideas from sources such as articles or books of literary criticism, biographies of the author, the author's own essays and autobiography, and histories of the era in which the work was written. (For an example of a paper that uses secondary sources, see pp. 694–97.) Even if you use secondary sources, your main goal should always be to develop your own understanding and interpretation of the literary work.

Whenever you use secondary sources, you must document them and you must avoid plagiarism. Plagiarism is unacknowledged borrowing—whether intentional or unintentional—of a source's words or ideas. (See 55b.)

### Documenting secondary sources

Most literature papers are documented with the system recommended by the Modern Language Association (MLA). This system of documentation is discussed in detail in 57, which is easy to find because its pages have a vertical band in blue.

An MLA in-text citation usually combines a signal phrase with a page number in parentheses.

#### SAMPLE MLA IN-TEXT CITATION

Arguing that fate has little to do with the tragedy that befalls Oedipus, Bernard Knox writes that "the catastrophe of Oedipus is that he discovers his own identity; and for his discovery he is first and last responsible" (6).

The signal phrase names the author of the secondary source; the number in parentheses is the page on which the quoted words appear.

The in-text citation is used in combination with a list of works cited at the end of the paper. Anyone interested in knowing additional information about the secondary source can consult the list of works cited. Here, for example, is the works cited entry for the work referred to in the sample in-text citation.

#### SAMPLE ENTRY IN THE LIST OF WORKS CITED

Knox, Bernard. <u>Oedipus at Thebes: Sophocles' Tragic Hero and His Time</u>. New York: Norton, 1971.

As you document secondary sources with in-text citations, consult 57a; as you construct your list of works cited, consult 57b.

### Avoiding plagiarism

The rules about plagiarism are the same for literary papers as for other research writing. It is wrong to use other writers' ideas or language without giving credit to your source. If an interpretation was suggested to you by another critic's work or if an obscure point was clarified by someone else's research, it is your responsibility to cite the source. If you have borrowed any phrases or sentences from your source, you must put them in quotation marks and credit the author.

For important tips on avoiding plagiarism, see 55b.

### 59h Sample literature papers

Following are two sample essays. The first, by Margaret Peel, has no secondary sources. (Its primary source, Langston Hughes's "Ballad of the Landlord," appears on p. 693.) The second sample, excerpts from an essay by Dan Larson, uses secondary sources. The complete text of Larson's paper appears on the companion Web site.

**ON THE WEB**

**dianahacker.com/bedhandbook**
▶ Model papers
  ▶ MLA papers: Peel
  ▶ MLA papers: Larson

Peel 1

Margaret Peel
Professor Lin
English 102
20 April 2005

Opposing Voices in "Ballad of the Landlord"

Langston Hughes's "Ballad of the Landlord" is narrated
through four voices, each with its own perspective on the
poem's action. These opposing voices--of a tenant, a landlord,
the police, and the press--dramatize a black man's experience
in a society dominated by whites.

The main voice in the poem is that of the tenant, who, as
the last line tells us, is black. The tenant is characterized by
his informal, nonstandard speech. He uses slang ("Ten Bucks"),
contracted words ('member, more'n), and nonstandard grammar
("These steps is broken down"). This colloquial English suggests the tenant's separation from the world of convention,
represented by the formal voices of the police and the press,
which appear later in the poem.

Although the tenant uses nonstandard English, his argument is organized and logical. He begins with a reasonable
complaint and a gentle reminder that the complaint is already
a week old: "My roof has sprung a leak. / Don't you 'member I
told you about it / Way last week?" (lines 2-4). In the second
stanza, he appeals diplomatically to the landlord's self-
interest: "These steps is broken down. / When you come up
yourself / It's a wonder you don't fall down" (6-8). In the third
stanza, when the landlord has responded to his complaints
with a demand for rent money, the tenant becomes more

Thesis states Peel's main idea.

Details from the poem illustrate Peel's point.

The first citation to lines of the poem includes the word "lines."

Subsequent citations from the poem are cited with line numbers alone.

**Marginal annotations indicate** MLA-style formatting and effective writing.

forceful, but his voice is still reasonable: "Ten Bucks you say is due? / Well, that's Ten Bucks more'n I'll pay you / Till you fix this house up new" (10-12).

The fourth stanza marks a shift in the tone of the argument. At this point the tenant responds more emotionally, in reaction to the landlord's threats to evict him. By the fifth stanza, the tenant has unleashed his anger: "Um-huh! You talking high and mighty" (17). Hughes uses an exclamation point for the first time; the tenant is raising his voice at last. As the argument gets more heated, the tenant finally resorts to the language of violence: "You ain't gonna be able to say a word / If I land my fist on you" (19-20).

These are the last words the tenant speaks in the poem. Perhaps Hughes wants to show how black people who threaten violence are silenced. When a new voice is introduced--the landlord's--the poem shifts to a frantic tone:

> Police! Police!
>
> Come and get this man!
>
> He's trying to ruin the government
>
> And overturn the land! (21-24)

This response is clearly an overreaction to a small threat. Instead of dealing with the tenant directly, the landlord shouts for the police. His hysterical voice--marked by repetitions and punctuated with exclamation points--reveals his disproportionate fear and outrage. And his conclusions are equally excessive: This black man, he claims, is out to "ruin the government" and "overturn the land." Although the landlord's overreaction is humorous, it is sinister as well, because the

*Topic sentence focuses on an interpretation.*

*Transition prepares readers for the next topic.*

*Peel interprets the landlord's response.*

Peel 3

landlord knows that, no matter how excessive his claims are, he has the police and the law on his side.

In line 25, the regular meter and rhyme of the poem break down, perhaps showing how an arrest disrupts everyday life. The "voice" in lines 25-29 has two parts: the clanging sound of the police ("Copper's whistle! / Patrol bell!") and, in sharp contrast, the unemotional, factual tone of a police report ("Arrest. / Precinct Station. / Iron cell.").

The last voice in the poem is the voice of the press, represented in newspaper headlines: "MAN THREATENS LANDLORD / TENANT HELD NO BAIL / JUDGE GIVES NEGRO 90 DAYS IN COUNTY JAIL" (31-33). Meter and rhyme return here, as if to show that once the tenant is arrested, life can go on as usual. The language of the press, like that of the police, is cold and distant, and it gives the tenant less and less status. In line 31, he is a "man"; in line 32, he has been demoted to a "tenant"; and in line 33, he has become a "Negro," or just another statistic.

By using four opposing voices in "Ballad of the Landlord," Hughes effectively dramatizes different views of minority assertiveness. To the tenant, assertiveness is informal and natural, as his language shows; to the landlord, it is a dangerous threat, as his hysterical response suggests. The police response is, like the language that describes it, short and sharp. Finally, the press's view of events, represented by the headlines, is distant and unsympathetic.

By the end of the poem, we understand the predicament of the black man. Exploited by the landlord, politically oppressed

*Peel shows how meter and rhyme support the poem's meaning.*

*Peel sums up her interpretation.*

*Peel concludes with an analysis of the poem's political significance.*

by those who think he's out "to ruin the government," physically restrained by the police and the judicial system, and denied his individuality by the press, he is saved only by his own
sense of humor. The very title of the poem suggests his--and
Hughes's--sense of humor. The tenant is singing a <u>ballad</u> to his
oppressors, but this ballad is no love song. It portrays the oppressors, through their own voices, in an unflattering light:
the landlord as cowardly and ridiculous, the police and press as
dull and soulless. The tenant may lack political power, but he
speaks with vitality, and no one can say he lacks dignity or the
spirit to survive.

Ballad of the Landlord

Landlord, landlord,
My roof has sprung a leak.
Don't you 'member I told you about it
Way last week?

Landlord, landlord,
These steps is broken down.
When you come up yourself
It's a wonder you don't fall down.

Ten Bucks you say I owe you?
Ten Bucks you say is due?
Well, that's Ten Bucks more'n I'll pay you
Till you fix this house up new.

What? You gonna get eviction orders?
You gonna cut off my heat?
You gonna take my furniture and
Throw it in the street?

Um-huh! You talking high and mighty.
Talk on—till you get through.
You ain't gonna be able to say a word
If I land my fist on you.

*Police! Police!*
*Come and get this man!*
*He's trying to ruin the government*
*And overturn the land!*

Copper's whistle!
Patrol bell!
Arrest.

Precinct Station.
Iron cell.
Headlines in press:

MAN THREATENS LANDLORD

TENANT HELD NO BAIL

JUDGE GIVES NEGRO 90 DAYS IN COUNTY JAIL

—Langston Hughes

Larson 1

Dan Larson

Professor Duncan

English 102

18 April 2005

The Transformation of Mrs. Peters:

An Analysis of "A Jury of Her Peers"

The opening lines name the story and establish context.

In Susan Glaspell's 1917 short story "A Jury of Her Peers," two women accompany their husbands and a county attorney to an isolated house where a farmer named John Wright has

Present tense is used to describe details from the story.

been choked to death in his bed with a rope. The chief suspect, Wright's wife Minnie, is in jail awaiting trial. The sheriff's wife, Mrs. Peters, has come along to gather some personal items for Minnie, and Mrs. Hale has joined her. Early in the

Quotations from the story are cited with page numbers in parentheses.

story, Mrs. Hale sympathizes with Minnie and objects to the way the male investigators are "snoopin' round and criticizin'" her kitchen (200). In contrast, Mrs. Peters shows respect for the law, saying that the men are doing "no more than their duty" (201). By the end of the story, however, Mrs. Peters has

The opening paragraph ends with Larson's research question.

joined Mrs. Hale in a conspiracy of silence, lied to the men, and committed a crime--hiding key evidence. What causes this dramatic change?

Quotation from a secondary source: author is named in a signal phrase; page number is given in parentheses.

One critic, Leonard Mustazza, argues that Mrs. Hale recruits Mrs. Peters "as a fellow 'juror' in the case, moving the sheriff's wife away from her sympathy for her husband's position and towards identification with the accused woman" (494). While this is true, Mrs. Peters also reaches insights on her own. Her

The thesis asserts Larson's main point.

observations in the kitchen lead her to understand Minnie's grim and lonely plight as the wife of an abusive farmer, and

**Marginal annotations indicate MLA-style formatting and** effective writing.

her identification with both Minnie and Mrs. Hale is strengthened as the men conducting the investigation trivialize the
lives of women.

The first evidence that Mrs. Peters reaches understanding
on her own surfaces in the following passage:

> The sheriff's wife had looked from the stove to the
> sink--to the pail of water which had been carried in
> from outside. . . . That look of seeing into things, of
> seeing through a thing to something else, was in the
> eyes of the sheriff's wife now. (203)

Something about the stove, the sink, and the pail of water
connects with her own experience, giving Mrs. Peters a glimpse
into the life of Minnie Wright. The details resonate with
meaning.

Social historian Elaine Hedges argues that such details,
which evoke the drudgery of a farm woman's work, would not
have been lost upon Glaspell's readers in 1917. Hedges tells us
what the pail and the stove, along with another detail from
the story--a dirty towel on a roller--would have meant to
women of the time. Laundry was a dreaded all-day affair. Water
had to be pumped, hauled, and boiled; then the wash was
rubbed, rinsed, wrung through a wringer, carried outside, and
hung on a line to dry. "What the women see, beyond the pail
and the stove," writes Hedges, "are the hours of work it took
Minnie to produce that one clean towel" (56).

On her own, Mrs. Peters discovers clues about the motive
for the murder. Her curiosity leads her to pick up a sewing
basket filled with quilt pieces and then to notice something

---

A long quotation is set off by indenting; no quotation marks are needed; ellipsis dots indicate words omitted from the source.

Larson summarizes ideas from a secondary source and then quotes from that source; he names the author in a signal phrase and gives a page number in parentheses.

Topic sentence focuses on Larson's interpretation.

Larson 3

strange: a sudden row of badly sewn stitches. "What do you suppose she was so--nervous about?" asks Mrs. Peters (204). A short time later, Mrs. Peters spots another clue, an empty bird-cage. Again she observes details on her own, in this case a broken door and hinge, suggesting that the cage has been roughly handled.

In addition to noticing details, both women draw conclusions from them and speculate on their significance. When Mrs. Hale finds the dead canary beneath a quilt patch, for example, the women conclude that its neck has been wrung and understand who must have wrung it.

As the women speculate on the significance of the dead canary, each connects the bird with her own experience. Mrs. Hale knows that Minnie once sang in the church choir, an activity that Mr. Wright put a stop to, just as he put a stop to the bird's singing. Also, as a farmer's wife, Mrs. Hale understands the desolation and loneliness of life on the prairie. She sees that the bird was both a thing of beauty and a companion. "If there had been years and years of--nothing, then a bird to sing to you," says Mrs. Hale, "it would be awful--still--after the bird was still" (208). To Mrs. Peters, the stillness of the canary evokes memories of the time when she and her husband homesteaded in the northern plains. "I know what stillness is," she says, as she recalls the death of her first child, with no one around to console her (208).

Topic sentences focus on interpretation, not just plot.

Details from the story provide evidence for the interpretation.

The complete text of the paper appears on the *Bedford Handbook* Web site. See page 688 for the address.

Larson 7

Works Cited

Ben-Zvi, Linda. "'Murder, She Wrote': The Genesis of Susan
    Glaspell's Trifles." Theatre Journal 44 (1992): 141-62.
    Rpt. in Susan Glaspell: Essays on Her Theater and
    Fiction. Ed. Linda Ben-Zvi. Ann Arbor: U of Michigan P,
    1995. 19-48.

Glaspell, Susan. "A Jury of Her Peers." Literature and Its
    Writers: A Compact Introduction to Fiction, Poetry, and
    Drama. Ed. Ann Charters and Samuel Charters. 3rd ed.
    Boston: Bedford, 2004. 194-210.

Hedges, Elaine. "Small Things Reconsidered: 'A Jury of Her
    Peers.'" Women's Studies 12 (1986): 89-110. Rpt. in
    Susan Glaspell: Essays on Her Theater and Fiction. Ed.
    Linda Ben-Zvi. Ann Arbor: U of Michigan P, 1995. 49-69.

Mustazza, Leonard. "Generic Translation and Thematic Shift in
    Susan Glaspell's Trifles and 'A Jury of Her Peers.'" Studies
    in Short Fiction 26 (1989): 489-96.

The works cited page lists the primary source (Glaspell's story) and secondary sources.

# WRITING APA PAPERS
# 60

APA papers

Most writing assignments in the social sciences are either reports of original research or reviews of the literature written about a research topic. Often an original research report contains a "review of the literature" section that places the writer's project in the context of previous research.

Most social science instructors will ask you to document sources with the American Psychological Association (APA) system of in-text citations and references described in section 60d. You face three main challenges when writing a social science paper that draws on written sources: (1) supporting a thesis, (2) citing your sources and avoiding plagiarism, and (3) integrating quotations and other source material.

## 60a Supporting a thesis

A thesis, which usually appears at the end of the introduction, is a one-sentence (or occasionally a two-sentence) statement of your central idea. In a paper reviewing the literature on a topic, this thesis analyzes the often competing conclusions drawn by a variety of researchers.

### Finding a thesis

You will be reading articles and other sources that address a central research question. Your thesis will express a reasonable answer to that question, given the current state of research in the field. Here, for example, is a research question posed by Luisa Mirano, a student in a psychology class, followed by a thesis that answers the question.

**RESEARCH QUESTION**

Is medication the right treatment for the escalating problem of childhood obesity?

**POSSIBLE THESIS**

Understanding the limitations of medical treatments for children highlights the complexity of the childhood obesity problem in the United States and underscores the need for physicians, advocacy groups, and policymakers to search for other solutions.

### Organizing your evidence

The American Psychological Association encourages the use of headings to help readers follow the organization of a paper. For an original research report, the major headings often follow a standard model: Method, Results, Discussion.

The introduction is not given a heading; it consists of the material between the title of the paper and the first heading.

For a literature review, headings will vary. The student who wrote about treatments for childhood obesity used four questions to focus her research; the questions then became headings in her paper (see pp. 743–55).

**NOTE:** For APA's manuscript guidelines on placing and highlighting headings, see page 739.

**ON THE WEB**

**dianahacker.com/bedhandbook**
▶ Electronic research exercises
  ▶ E-ex 60–1

**60b** Citing sources; avoiding plagiarism

In a research paper, you will be drawing on the work of other writers, and you must document their contributions by citing your sources. Sources are cited for two reasons:

1. to tell readers where your information comes from — so that they can assess its reliability and, if interested, find and read the original source
2. to give credit to the writers from whom you have borrowed words and ideas

Borrowing another writer's language, sentence structures, or ideas without proper acknowledgment is a form of dishonesty known as *plagiarism.*

*Citing sources*

Citations are required when you quote from a source, when you summarize or paraphrase a source, and when you borrow facts from a source (except for common knowledge). The American Psychological Association recommends an author-date style of citations. Here, very briefly, is how the author-date system often works. See 60d for a detailed discussion of variations.

1. The source is introduced by a signal phrase that includes the last names of the authors followed by the date of publication in parentheses.
2. The material being cited is followed by a page number in parentheses.
3. At the end of the paper, an alphabetized list of references gives complete publication information about the source.

**IN-TEXT CITATION**

As researchers Yanovski and Yanovski (2002) have explained, obesity was once considered "either a moral failing or evidence of underlying psychopathology" (p. 592).

**ENTRY IN THE LIST OF REFERENCES**

Yanovski, S. Z., & Yanovski, J. A. (2002). Drug therapy: Obesity [Electronic version]. *The New England Journal of Medicine, 346,* 591-602.

*Avoiding plagiarism*

Your research paper is a collaboration between you and your sources. To be fair and ethical, you must acknowledge your debt to the writers of those sources. If you don't, you commit plagiarism, a serious academic offense.

Three different acts are considered plagiarism: (1) failing to cite quotations and borrowed ideas, (2) failing to enclose borrowed language in quotation marks, and (3) failing to put summaries and paraphrases in your own words.

**CITING QUOTATIONS AND BORROWED IDEAS**   You must of course document all direct quotations. You must also cite any ideas borrowed from a source: summaries and paraphrases; statistics and other specific facts; and visuals such as cartoons, graphs, and diagrams.

The only exception is common knowledge—general information that your readers may know or could easily locate in any number of reference sources. For example, the current population of the United States is common knowledge among sociologists and economists, and psychologists are familiar with Freud's theory of the unconscious.

As a rule, when you have seen certain general information repeatedly in your reading, you don't need to cite it. However, when information has appeared in only a few sources, when it is highly specific (as with statistics), or when it is controversial, you should cite the source. If a topic is new to you and you are not sure what is considered common knowledge and what is considered controversial, ask your instructor or someone else with expertise. When in doubt, cite the source.

**ENCLOSING BORROWED LANGUAGE IN QUOTATION MARKS**   To indicate that you are using a source's exact phrases or sentences, you must enclose them in quotation marks. To omit the quotation marks is to claim—falsely—that the language is your own. Such an omission is plagiarism even if you have cited the source.

**ORIGINAL SOURCE**

In an effort to seek the causes of this disturbing trend, experts have pointed to a range of important potential contributors to the rise in childhood obesity that are unrelated to media: a reduction in physical education classes and after-school athletic programs, an increase in the availability of sodas and snacks in public schools, the growth in the number of fast-food outlets across the country, the trend toward "super-sizing" food portions in restaurants, and the increasing

number of highly processed high-calorie and high-fat grocery products.                    —Henry J. Kaiser Family Foundation,
"The Role of Media in Childhood Obesity" (2004), p. 1

**PLAGIARISM**

According to the Henry J. Kaiser Family Foundation (2004), experts have pointed to a range of important potential contributors to the rise in childhood obesity that are unrelated to media (p. 1).

**BORROWED LANGUAGE IN QUOTATION MARKS**

According to the Henry J. Kaiser Family Foundation (2004), "experts have pointed to a range of important potential contributors to the rise in childhood obesity that are unrelated to media" (p. 1).

**NOTE:** When quoted sentences are set off from the text by indenting, quotation marks are not needed (see pp. 706–07).

**PUTTING SUMMARIES AND PARAPHRASES IN YOUR OWN WORDS**
Summaries and paraphrases are written in your own words. A summary condenses information; a paraphrase reports information in about the same number of words as in the source. When you summarize or paraphrase, you must restate the source's meaning using your own language. You commit plagiarism if you half-copy the author's sentences — either by mixing the author's well-chosen phrases without using quotation marks or by plugging your own synonyms into the author's sentence structure. The following paraphrases are plagiarized — even though the source is cited — because their language is too close to that of the source.

**ORIGINAL SOURCE**
In an effort to seek the causes of this disturbing trend, experts have pointed to a range of important potential contributors to the rise in childhood obesity that are unrelated to media.
                    —Henry J. Kaiser Family Foundation,
"The Role of Media in Childhood Obesity" (2004), p. 1

**UNACCEPTABLE BORROWING OF PHRASES**

According to the Henry J. Kaiser Family Foundation (2004), experts have indicated a range of significant potential contributors to the rise in childhood obesity that are not linked to media (p. 1).

**UNACCEPTABLE BORROWING OF STRUCTURE**

According to the Henry J. Kaiser Family Foundation (2004), experts have identified a variety of significant factors causing a rise in childhood obesity, factors that are not linked to media (p. 1).

To avoid plagiarizing an author's language, set the source aside, write from memory, and consult the source later to check for accuracy. This strategy prevents you from being captivated by the words on the page.

**ACCEPTABLE PARAPHRASE**

A report by the Henry J. Kaiser Family Foundation (2004) described sources other than media for the childhood obesity crisis.

**ON THE WEB**

**dianahacker.com/bedhandbook**
▶ Electronic research exercises
▶ E-ex 60–2 to 60–6

## 60c Integrating sources

Quotations, summaries, paraphrases, and facts will support your argument, but they cannot speak for you. Several strategies will help you integrate information from research sources into your paper while maintaining your own voice.

*Limiting your use of quotations*

Although it is tempting to insert many long quotations in your paper and to use your own words only for connecting passages, do not quote excessively. It is almost impossible to integrate numerous long quotations smoothly into your own text.

It is not always necessary to quote full sentences from a source. At times you may wish to borrow only a phrase or to weave part of a source's sentence into your own sentence structure.

> Carmona (2004) advised the subcommittee that the situation constitutes an "epidemic" and that the skyrocketing statistics are "astounding" (para. 3).

> As researchers continue to face a number of unknowns about obesity, it may be helpful to envision treating the disorder, as Yanovski and Yanovski (2002) suggested, "in the same manner as any other chronic disease" (p. 592).

**USING THE ELLIPSIS MARK**   To condense a quoted passage, you can use the ellipsis mark (three periods, with spaces between) to indicate that you have omitted words. What remains must be grammatically complete.

> Roman (2003) reported that "social factors are nearly as significant as individual metabolism in the formation of . . . dietary habits of adolescents" (p. 345).

The writer has omitted the words *both healthy and unhealthy.*

When you want to omit a full sentence or more, use a period before the three ellipsis dots.

> According to Sothern and Gordon (2003), "Environmental factors
> may contribute as much as 80% to the causes of childhood
> obesity. . . . Research suggests that obese children demonstrate
> decreased levels of physical activity and increased psychosocial
> problems" (p. 104).

Ordinarily, do not use an ellipsis mark at the beginning or at the end of a quotation. Readers will understand that the quoted material is taken from a longer passage. The only exception occurs when you think that the author's meaning might be misinterpreted without the ellipsis mark.

**USING BRACKETS**  Brackets allow you to insert your own words into quoted material to explain a confusing reference or to keep a sentence grammatical in your context.

> The cost of treating obesity currently totals $117 billion
> per year--a price, according to the surgeon general, "second
> only to the cost of [treating] tobacco use" (Carmona, 2004,
> para. 9).

To indicate an error in a quotation, insert [sic] right after the error. Notice that the term *sic* is italicized and appears in brackets.

**SETTING OFF LONG QUOTATIONS**  When you quote forty or more words, set off the quotation by indenting it one-half inch (or five spaces) from the left margin. Use the normal right margin and do not single-space.

Long quotations should be introduced by an informative sentence, usually followed by a colon. Quotation marks are unnecessary because the indented format tells readers that the words are taken directly from the source.

Yanovski and Yanovski (2002) have described earlier treatments of obesity that focused on behavior modification:

> With the advent of behavioral treatments for obesity in the 1960s, hope arose that modification of maladaptive eating and exercise habits would lead to sustained weight loss, and that time-limited programs would produce permanent changes in weight. Medications for the treatment of obesity were proposed as short-term adjuncts for patients, who would presumably then acquire the skills necessary to continue to lose weight, reach "ideal body weight," and maintain a reduced weight indefinitely. (p. 592)

### *Using signal phrases with most material*

The information you gather from sources cannot speak for itself. Whenever you include a paraphrase, summary, or direct quotation of another writer in your paper, prepare your readers for it with an introduction called a *signal phrase.* Signal phrases mark the boundaries between source material and your own words; they can also tell readers why a source is trustworthy.

When the signal phrase includes a verb, choose one that is appropriate in context. Is your source arguing a point, making an observation, reporting a fact, drawing a conclusion, refuting an argument, or stating a belief? By choosing an appropriate verb, you can make your source's stance clear. See the chart on page 708 for a list of verbs commonly used in signal phrases.

The American Psychological Association requires using past tense or present perfect tense in phrases that introduce quotations and other source material: *Davis noted that* or *Davis has noted that* (not *Davis notes that*). Use the present tense only for discussing the results of an experiment (*the results show*) or knowledge that has clearly been established (*researchers agree*).

It is generally acceptable in the social sciences to call authors by their last name only, even on a first mention. If your paper refers to two authors with same last name, use initials as well.

## Varying signal phrases in APA papers

To avoid monotony, try to vary both the language and the placement of your signal phrases.

**MODEL SIGNAL PHRASES**

In the words of Carmona, ". . ."

As Yanovski and Yanovski have noted, ". . ."

Hoppin and Taveras, medical researchers, pointed out that ". . ."

". . . ," claimed Critser.

". . . ," wrote Duenwald, ". . ."

Researchers McDuffie et al. have offered an odd argument for this view: ". . ."

Hilts answered these objections with the following analysis: ". . ."

**VERBS IN SIGNAL PHRASES**

| | | |
|---|---|---|
| admitted | contended | reasoned |
| agreed | declared | refuted |
| argued | denied | rejected |
| asserted | emphasized | reported |
| believed | insisted | responded |
| claimed | noted | suggested |
| compared | observed | thought |
| confirmed | pointed out | wrote |

*Using signal phrases with quotations*

Readers need to move from your own words to the words of a source without feeling a jolt. Avoid dropping direct quotations into your text without warning. Instead, provide clear signal phrases, including at least the author's name and the date of publication. A signal phrase indicates the boundary between your words and the source's words.

**DROPPED QUOTATION**

Obesity was once considered in a very different light. "For many years, obesity was approached as if it were either a moral failing or evidence of underlying psychopathology" (Yanovski & Yanovski, 2002, p. 592).

**QUOTATION WITH SIGNAL PHRASE**

As researchers Yanovski and Yanovski (2002) have explained, obesity was once considered "either a moral failing or evidence of underlying psychopathology" (p. 592).

*Using signal phrases with summaries and paraphrases*

As with quotations, you should introduce most summaries and paraphrases with a signal phrase that mentions the author and the date of publication and places the material in context. Readers will then understand where the summary or paraphrase begins.

Without the signal phrase (underlined) in the following example, readers might think that only the last sentence is being cited, when in fact the whole paragraph is based on the source.

Carmona (2004) advised a Senate subcommittee that the problem of childhood obesity is dire and that the skyrocketing statistics--

which put the child obesity rate at 15%--are cause for alarm. More than 9 million children, double the number in the early 1980s, are classified as obese. Carmona warned that obesity can cause myriad physical problems that only worsen as children grow older (para. 6).

There are times, however, when a summary or a paraphrase does not require a signal phrase naming the author. Most readers will understand, for example, that the parenthetical citation at the end of the following passage applies to the entire anecdote, not just the last sentence.

A trend is under way among parents who are seeking ways to keep their children fit as school budget crunches force cuts in physical education programs. The parents of nine-year-old Daniel Shteremberg, for example, enrolled the boy in a San Diego gym and hired a personal trainer at $60 an hour. After having attempted unsuccessfully to wean Daniel from TV and junk food with other enticements, they turned to the Pacific Athletic Club, signing him up for two one-hour sessions each week (Saltzman, 2004, p. D8).

Notice that when there is no signal phrase naming the author, the author's name and the date must be included in the parentheses. Unless the work is short, also include the page number in the parentheses.

### Integrating statistics and other facts

When you are citing a statistic or another specific fact, a signal phrase is often not necessary. In most cases, readers will understand that the citation refers to the statistic or fact (not the whole paragraph).

In purely financial terms, the drugs cost more than $3 a day on average (Duenwald, 2004, paras. 33, 36).

There is nothing wrong, however, with using a signal phrase.

Duenwald (2004) reported that the drugs cost more than $3 a day on average (paras. 33, 36).

### Putting source material in context

Readers need to understand how your source is relevant to your paper's thesis. It's a good idea, in other words, to embed your quotation—especially a long one—between sentences of your own, introducing it with a signal phrase and following it up with interpretive comments that link the source material to your paper's thesis.

**QUOTATION WITH INSUFFICIENT CONTEXT**

A report by the Henry J. Kaiser Family Foundation (2004) outlined trends that may have contributed to the childhood obesity crisis, including food advertising for children as well as

a reduction in physical education classes . . . , an increase in the availability of sodas and snacks in public schools, the growth in the number of fast-food outlets . . . , and the increasing number of highly processed high-calorie and high-fat grocery products. (p. 1)

**QUOTATION WITH EFFECTIVE CONTEXT**

A report by the Henry J. Kaiser Family Foundation (2004) outlined trends that may have contributed to the childhood obesity crisis, including food advertising for children as well as

a reduction in physical education classes . . . , an increase in the availability of sodas and snacks in public schools, the growth in the number of fast-food outlets . . . , and the increasing number of highly processed high-calorie and high-fat grocery products. (p. 1)

Addressing each of these areas requires more than a doctor armed with a prescription pad; it requires a broad mobilization not just of doctors and concerned parents but of educators, food industry executives, advertisers, and media representatives.

ON THE WEB

**dianahacker.com/bedhandbook**
▶ Electronic research exercises
  ▶ E-ex 60–7 to 60–10

## 60d APA documentation style

In most social science classes, you will be asked to use the APA system for documenting sources, which is set forth in the *Publication Manual of the American Psychological Association*, 5th ed. (Washington: APA, 2001). APA recommends in-text citations that refer readers to a list of references.

An in-text citation gives the author of the source (often in a signal phrase), the date of publication, and at times a page number in parentheses. At the end of the paper, a list of references provides publication information about the source (see pp. 720–38). The direct link between the in-text citation and the entry in the reference list is highlighted in green in the following example.

**IN-TEXT CITATION**

Yanovski and Yanovski (2002) reported that "the current state of the treatment for obesity is similar to the state of the treatment of hypertension several decades ago" (p. 600).

**ENTRY IN THE LIST OF REFERENCES**

Yanovski, S. Z., & Yanovski, J. A. (2002). Drug therapy: Obesity
[Electronic version]. *The New England Journal of Medicine,*
*346,* 591-602.

For a reference list that includes this entry, see pages
754–55.

**ON THE WEB**

**dianahacker.com/bedhandbook**
▶ Electronic research exercises
  ▶ E-ex 60–11

*APA in-text citations*

The APA's in-text citations provide at least the author's last
name and the date of publication. For direct quotations and
some paraphrases, a page number is given as well.

**NOTE:** APA style requires the use of the past tense or the present perfect tense in signal phrases introducing cited material: *Smith (2005) reported, Smith (2005) has argued.*

■ **1. BASIC FORMAT FOR A QUOTATION** Ordinarily, introduce the quotation with a signal phrase that includes the author's last name followed by the year of publication in parentheses. Put the page number (preceded by "p.") in parentheses after the quotation.

> Critser (2003) noted that despite growing numbers of overweight Americans, many health care providers still "remain either in igno-rance or outright denial about the health danger to the poor and the young" (p. 5).

If the author is not named in the signal phrase, place the author's name, the year, and the page number in parentheses after the quotation: (Critser, 2003, p. 5).

**NOTE:** APA style requires the year of publication in an in-text citation. Do not include a month, even if the source is listed by month and year.

■ **2. BASIC FORMAT FOR A SUMMARY OR A PARAPHRASE** Include the author's last name and the year either in a signal phrase introducing the material or in parentheses following it. A page number or another locator is not required for a sum-mary or a paraphrase, but include one if it would help read-ers find the passage in a long work.

> According to Carmona (2004), the cost of treating obesity is exceeded only by the cost of treating illnesses from tobacco use (para. 9).

> The cost of treating obesity is exceeded only by the cost of treat-ing illnesses from tobacco use (Carmona, 2004, para. 9).

■ **3. A WORK WITH TWO AUTHORS**   Name both authors in the signal phrase or parentheses each time you cite the work. In the parentheses, use "&" between the authors' names; in the signal phrase, use "and."

> According to Sothern and Gordon (2003), "Environmental factors may contribute as much as 80% to the causes of childhood obesity" (p. 104).

> Obese children often engage in less physical activity (Sothern & Gordon, 2003, p. 104).

■ **4. A WORK WITH THREE TO FIVE AUTHORS**   Identify all authors in the signal phrase or parentheses the first time you cite the source.

> In 2003, Berkowitz, Wadden, Tershakovec, and Cronquist concluded, "Sibutramine . . . must be carefully monitored in adolescents, as in adults, to control increases in [blood pressure] and pulse rate" (p. 1811).

In subsequent citations, use the first author's name followed by "et al." in either the signal phrase or the parentheses.

> As Berkowitz et al. (2003) advised, "Until more extensive safety and efficacy data are available, . . . weight-loss medications should be used only on an experimental basis for adolescents" (p. 1811).

■ **5. A WORK WITH SIX OR MORE AUTHORS**   Use the first author's name followed by "et al." in the signal phrase or the parentheses.

> McDuffie et al. (2002) tested 20 adolescents aged 12-16 over a three-month period and found that orlistat, combined with behavioral therapy, produced an average weight loss of 4.4 kg, or 9.7 pounds (p. 646).

▨ **6. UNKNOWN AUTHOR** If the author is unknown, mention the work's title in the signal phrase or give the first word or two of the title in the parenthetical citation. Titles of articles and chapters are put in quotation marks; titles of books and reports are italicized.

> Children struggling to control their weight must also struggle with the pressures of television advertising that, on the one hand, encourages the consumption of junk food and, on the other, celebrates thin celebrities ("Television," 2002).

**NOTE:** In the rare case when "Anonymous" is specified as the author, treat it as if it were a real name: (Anonymous, 2001). In the list of references, also use the name Anonymous as author.

▨ **7. ORGANIZATION AS AUTHOR** If the author is a government agency or other organization, name the organization in the signal phrase or in the parenthetical citation the first time you cite the source.

> Obesity puts children at risk for a number of medical complications, including type 2 diabetes, hypertension, sleep apnea, and orthopedic problems (Henry J. Kaiser Family Foundation, 2004, p. 1).

If the organization has a familiar abbreviation, you may include it in brackets the first time you cite the source and use the abbreviation alone in later citations.

**FIRST CITATION** (National Institute of Mental Health [NIMH], 2001)

**LATER CITATIONS** (NIMH, 2001)

■ **8. TWO OR MORE WORKS IN THE SAME PARENTHESES** When your parenthetical citation names two or more works, put them in the same order that they appear in the reference list, separated by semicolons.

> Researchers have indicated that studies of pharmacological treatments for childhood obesity are inconclusive (Berkowitz et al., 2003; McDuffie et al., 2003).

■ **9. AUTHORS WITH THE SAME LAST NAME** To avoid confusion, use initials with the last names if your reference list includes two or more authors with the same last name.

> Research by E. Smith (1989) revealed that . . .

■ **10. PERSONAL COMMUNICATION** Interviews, memos, letters, e-mail, and similar unpublished person-to-person communications should be cited as follows:

> One of Atkinson's colleagues, who has studied the effect of the media on children's eating habits, has contended that advertisers for snack foods will need to design ads responsibly for their younger viewers (F. Johnson, personal communication, October 20, 2004).

Do not include personal communications in your reference list.

■ **11. AN ELECTRONIC DOCUMENT** When possible, cite an electronic document as you would any other document (using the author-date style).

> Atkinson (2001) found that children who spent at least four hours a day watching TV were less likely to engage in adequate physical activity during the week.

Electronic sources may lack authors' names or dates. In addition, they may lack page numbers (required in some citations). Here are APA's guidelines for handling sources without authors' names, dates, or page numbers.

*Unknown author*

If no author is named, mention the title of the document in a signal phrase or give the first word or two of the title in parentheses (see also item 6). (If an organization serves as the author, see item 7.)

> The body's basal metabolic rate, or BMR, is a measure of its at-rest energy requirement ("Exercise," 2003).

*Unknown date*

When the date is unknown, APA recommends using the abbreviation "n.d." (for "no date").

> Attempts to establish a definitive link between television programming and children's eating habits have been problematic (Magnus, n.d.).

*No page numbers*

APA ordinarily requires page numbers for quotations, and it recommends them for summaries or paraphrases from long sources. When an electronic source lacks stable numbered pages, your citation should include — if possible — information that will help readers locate the particular passage being cited.

When an electronic document has numbered paragraphs, use the paragraph number preceded by the symbol ¶ or by the abbreviation "para.": (Hall, 2001, ¶ 5) *or* (Hall, 2001, para. 5). If neither a page nor a paragraph number is given and the document contains headings, cite the appropriate heading and indicate which paragraph under that heading you are referring to.

Hoppin and Taveras (2004) pointed out that several other medications were classified by the Drug Enforcement Administration as having the "potential for abuse" (Weight-Loss Drugs section, para. 6).

**NOTE:** Electronic files using portable document format (PDF) often have stable page numbers. For such sources, give the page number in the parenthetical citation.

■ **12. INDIRECT SOURCE** If you use a source that was cited in another source (a secondary source), name the original source in your signal phrase. List the secondary source in your reference list and include it in your parenthetical citation, preceded by the words "as cited in." In the following example, Critser is the secondary source.

Former surgeon general Dr. David Satcher described "a nation of young people seriously at risk of starting out obese and dooming themselves to the difficult task of overcoming a tough illness" (as cited in Critser, 2003, p. 4).

■ **13. TWO OR MORE WORKS BY THE SAME AUTHOR IN THE SAME YEAR** When your list of references includes more than one work by the same author in the same year, use lowercase letters ("a," "b," and so on) with the year to order the entries in the reference list. (See item 6 on p. 723.) Use those same letters with the year in the in-text citation.

Research by Durgin (2003b) has yielded new findings about the role of counseling in treating childhood obesity.

**ON THE WEB**

**dianahacker.com/bedhandbook**
▶ Electronic research exercises
  ▶ E-ex 60–12 to 60–14

*APA list of references*

In APA style, the alphabetical list of works cited, which appears at the end of the paper, is titled "References." Following are models illustrating APA style for entries in the list of references. Observe all details: capitalization, punctuation, use of italics, and so on. For advice on preparing the reference list, see pages 740–41. For a sample reference list, see pages 754–55.

**ON THE WEB**

**dianahacker.com/bedhandbook**
▶ Research and Documentation Online
   ▶ Social sciences: Documenting sources (APA)

*General guidelines for listing authors*

Alphabetize entries in the list of references by authors' last names; if a work has no author, alphabetize it by its title. The first element of each entry is important because citations in the text of the paper refer to it and readers will be looking for it in the alphabetized list. The date of publication appears immediately after the first element of the citation.

**NAME AND DATE CITED IN TEXT**

Duncan (2001) has reported that . . .

**BEGINNING OF ENTRY IN THE LIST OF REFERENCES**

Duncan, B. (2001).

Items 1–4 show how to begin an entry for a work with a single author, multiple authors, an organization as author, and an unknown author. Items 5 and 6 show how to begin an entry when your list includes two or more works by the same author or two or more works by the same author in the same year. What comes after the first element of your citation will depend on the kind of source you are citing (see items 7–31).

■ **1. SINGLE AUTHOR**    Begin the entry with the author's last name, followed by a comma and the author's initial(s). Then give the date in parentheses.

Perez, E. (2001).

■ **2. MULTIPLE AUTHORS**    List up to six authors by last names followed by initials. Use an ampersand (&) between the names of two authors or, if there are more than two authors, before the name of the last author.

DuNann, D. W., & Koger, S. M. (2004).

Sloan, F. A., Stout, E. M., Whetten-Goldstein, K., & Liang, L. (2000).

If there are more than six authors, list the first six and "et al." (meaning "and others") to indicate that there are others.

■ **3. ORGANIZATION AS AUTHOR**    When the author is an organization, begin with the name of the organization.

American Psychiatric Association. (2003).

**NOTE:** If the organization is also the publisher, see item 28.

■ **4. UNKNOWN AUTHOR**    Begin the entry with the work's title. Titles of books are italicized; titles of articles are neither italicized nor put in quotation marks. (For rules on cap-italization of titles, see p. 741.)

*Oxford essential world atlas.* (2001).

Omega-3 fatty acids. (2004, November 23).

▥ **5. TWO OR MORE WORKS BY THE SAME AUTHOR** Use the author's name for all entries. List the entries by year, the earliest first.

Schlechty, P. C. (1997).

Schlechty, P. C. (2001).

▥ **6. TWO OR MORE WORKS BY THE SAME AUTHOR IN THE SAME YEAR** List the works alphabetically by title. In the parentheses, fol-lowing the year, add "a," "b," and so on. Use these same letters when giving the year in the in-text citation. (See also p. 741.)

Durgin, P. A. (2003a). At-risk behaviors in children.

Durgin, P. A. (2003b). Treating obesity with psychotherapy.

### Articles in periodicals

This section shows how to prepare an entry for an article in a periodical such as a scholarly journal, a magazine, or a newspaper. In addition to consulting the models in this sec-tion, you may need to refer to items 1–6 (general guidelines for listing authors).

**NOTE:** For articles on consecutive pages, provide the range of pages at the end of the citation (see item 7 for an example). When an article does not appear on consecutive pages, give all page numbers: A1, A17.

# Citation at a glance: Article in a periodical (APA)

To cite an article in a periodical in APA style, include the following elements:

1 Author
2 Date of publication
3 Title of article
4 Name of periodical
5 Volume and issue numbers
6 Page numbers

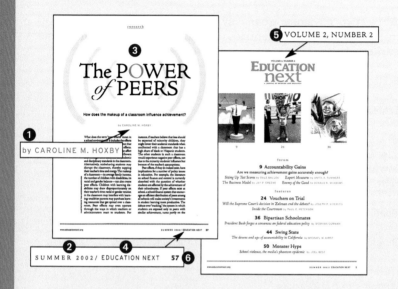

## REFERENCE LIST ENTRY FOR AN ARTICLE IN A PERIODICAL

```
┌──1──┐ ┌─2─┐   ┌────────3────────┐ ┌─────4─────┐ ┌─5─┐ ┌─6─┐
```
Hoxby, C. M. (2002). The power of peers. *Education Next, 2*(2), 57-63.

For more on citing periodicals in APA style, see pages 723–26.

▦ **7. ARTICLE IN A JOURNAL PAGINATED BY VOLUME** Many professional journals continue page numbers throughout the year instead of beginning each issue with page 1; at the end of the year, the issues are collected in a volume. After the italicized title of the journal, give the volume number (also italicized), followed by the page numbers.

Morawski, J. (2000). Social psychology a century ago. *American Psychol-*
    *ogist, 55,* 427-431.

▦ **8. ARTICLE IN A JOURNAL PAGINATED BY ISSUE** When each issue of a journal begins with page 1, include the issue number in parentheses after the volume number. Italicize the volume number but not the issue number.

Smith, S. (2003). Government and nonprofits in the modern age.
    *Society, 40*(4), 36-45.

▦ **9. ARTICLE IN A MAGAZINE** In addition to the year of publication, list the month and, for weekly magazines, the day. If there is a volume number, include it (italicized) after the title.

Raloff, J. (2001, May 12). Lead therapy won't help most kids. *Science*
    *News, 159,* 292.

▦ **10. ARTICLE IN A NEWSPAPER** Begin with the name of the author followed by the exact date of publication. (If the author is unknown, see also item 4.) Page numbers are introduced with "p." (or "pp.").

Lohr, S. (2004, December 3). Health care technology is a promise
    unfinanced. *The New York Times,* p. C5.

▦ **11. LETTER TO THE EDITOR** Letters to the editor appear in journals, magazines, and newspapers. Follow the appropriate model and insert the words "Letter to the editor" in brackets before the name of the periodical.

Carter, R. (2000, July). Shot in the dark? [Letter to the editor].
    *Scientific American, 283*(1), 8.

**12. REVIEW** Reviews of books and other media appear in a variety of periodicals. Follow the appropriate model for the periodical. For a review of a book, give the title of the review (if there is one), followed by the words "Review of the book" and the title of the book in brackets.

Gleick, E. (2000, December 14). The burdens of genius [Review of the
    book *The Last Samurai*]. *Time, 156,* 171.

For a film review, write "Review of the motion picture," and for a TV review, write "Review of the television program." Treat other media in a similar way.

*Books*

In addition to consulting the items in this section, you may need to refer to items 1–6 (general guidelines for listing authors).

**13. BASIC FORMAT FOR A BOOK** Begin with the author's name, followed by the date and the book's title. End with the place of publication and the name of the publisher. Take the information about the book from its title page and copyright page. If more than one place of publication is given, use only the first; if more than one date is given, use the most recent one.

Highmore, B. (2001). *Everyday life and cultural theory.* New York:
    Routledge.

## Citation at a glance: Book (APA)

To cite a book in APA style, include the following elements:

1 Author
2 Date of publication
3 Title and subtitle
4 City of publication
5 Publisher

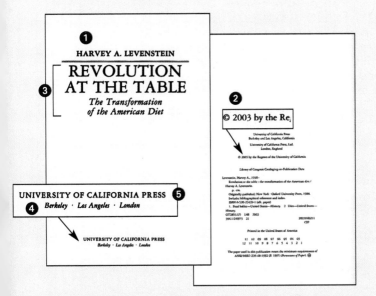

**REFERENCE LIST ENTRY FOR A BOOK**

```
┌────1────┐ ┌─2─┐ ┌──────────────3──────────────────
```
Levenstein, H. A. (2003). *Revolution at the table: The transformation of*

```
────────────┐ ┌──4──┐ ┌───────────5───────────┐
```
*the American diet.* Berkeley: University of California Press.

For more on citing books in APA style, see pages 726–29.

▓▓ **14. BOOK WITH AN EDITOR**   For a book with an editor but no author, begin with the name of the editor (or editors) followed by the abbreviation "Ed." (or "Eds.") in parentheses.

Bronfen, E., & Kavka, M. (Eds.). (2001). *Feminist consequences: Theory for a new century*. New York: Columbia University Press.

For a book with an author and an editor, begin with the author's name. Give the editor's name in parentheses after the title of the book, followed by the abbreviation "Ed." (or "Eds.").

Plath, S. (2000). *The unabridged journals* (K. V. Kukil, Ed.). New York: Anchor.

▓▓ **15. TRANSLATION**   After the title, name the translator, followed by the abbreviation "Trans.," in parentheses. Add the original date of the work's publication in parentheses at the end of the entry.

Steinberg, M. D. (2003). *Voices of revolution, 1917*. (M. Schwartz, Trans.). New Haven, CT: Yale University Press. (Original work published 2001)

▓▓ **16. EDITION OTHER THAN THE FIRST**   Include the number of the edition in parentheses after the title.

Helfer, M. E., Keme, R. S., & Drugman, R. D. (1997). *The battered child* (5th ed.). Chicago: University of Chicago Press.

▓▓ **17. ARTICLE OR CHAPTER IN AN EDITED BOOK**   Begin with the author, year of publication, and title of the article or chapter. Then write "In" and give the editor's name, followed by "Ed." in parentheses; the title of the book; and the page numbers of the article or chapter in parentheses. End with the book's publication information.

Luban, D. (2000). The ethics of wrongful obedience. In D. L. Rhode
(Ed.), *Ethics in practice: Lawyers' roles, responsibilities, and regulation* (pp. 94-120). New York: Oxford University Press.

**18. MULTIVOLUME WORK**   Give the number of volumes after the title.

Luo, J. *Encyclopedia of contemporary Chinese civilization* (Vols. 1-2).
Westport, CT: Greenwood Publishing Group.

*Electronic sources*

This section shows how to prepare reference list entries for a variety of electronic sources, including articles in online periodicals and databases, Web documents, and e-mail.

**19. ARTICLE FROM AN ONLINE PERIODICAL**   When citing online articles, follow the guidelines for printed articles (see items 7–12), giving whatever information is available in the online source. If the article also appears in a printed journal, a URL is not required; instead, include "Electronic version" in brackets after the title of the article.

Whitmeyer, J. M. (2000). Power through appointment [Electronic
version]. *Social Science Research, 29*(4), 535-555.

If there is no print version, include the date you accessed the source and the article's URL.

Ashe, D. D., & McCutcheon, L. E. (2001). Shyness, loneliness, and
attitude toward celebrities. *Current Research in Social Psychology,
6*(9). Retrieved July 3, 2001, from http://www.uiowa.edu/
~grpproc/crisp/crisp.6.9.htm

**NOTE:** When you have retrieved an article from a newspaper's searchable Web site, give the URL for the site, not for the exact source.

Cary, B. (2001, June 18). Mentors of the mind. *Los Angeles Times.*
　　Retrieved July 5, 2001, from http://www.latimes.com

■ **20. ARTICLE FROM A DATABASE**   To cite an article from a library's subscription database, include the publication information from the source (see items 7–12). End the citation with your date of access, the name of the database, and the document number (if applicable).

Holliday, R. E., & Hayes, B. K. (2001). Dissociating automatic and
　　intentional processes in children's eyewitness memory. *Journal of*
　　*Experimental Child Psychology, 75*(1), 1-5. Retrieved February 21,
　　2001, from Expanded Academic ASAP database (A59317972).

■ **21. NONPERIODICAL WEB DOCUMENT**   To cite a nonperiodical Web document, such as a report, list as many of the following elements as are available.

Author's name

Date of publication (if there is no date, use "n.d.")

Title of document (in italics)

Date you accessed the source

A URL that will take readers directly to the source

In the first model, the source has both an author and a date; in the second, the source lacks a date.

Cain, A., & Burris, M. (1999, April). *Investigation of the use of mobile*
　　*phones while driving.* Retrieved January 15, 2000, from
　　http://www.cutr.eng.usf.edu/its/mobile_phone_text.htm

Archer, Z. (n.d.). *Exploring nonverbal communication.* Retrieved July 18,
2001, from http://zzyx.ucsc.edu/~archer

If a source has no author, begin with the title and follow it
with the date in parentheses.

**NOTE:** If you retrieved the source from a university program's
Web site, name the program in your retrieval statement.

Cosmides, L., & Tooby, J. (1997). *Evolutionary psychology: A primer.*
Retrieved July 5, 2001, from the University of California, Santa
Barbara, Center for Evolutionary Psychology Web site:
http://www.psych.ucsb.edu/research/cep/primer.html

■ **22. CHAPTER OR SECTION IN A WEB DOCUMENT** Begin with
the author, the year of publication, and the title of the
chapter or section. Then write "In" and give the title of the
document, followed by any identifying information in parentheses. End with your date of access and the URL for the
chapter or section.

Heuer, R. J., Jr. (1999). Keeping an open mind. In *Psychology of
intelligence analysis* (chap. 6). Retrieved July 7, 2001, from
http://www.cia.gov/csi/books/19104/art9.html

■ **23. E-MAIL** E-mail messages and other personal communications are not included in the list of references.

■ **24. ONLINE POSTING** If an online posting is not maintained in an archive, cite it as a personal communication in
the text of your paper and do not include it in the list of references. If the posting can be retrieved from an archive, give
as much information as is available. An example appears at
the top of page 736.

# Citation at a glance: Article from a database (APA)

To cite an article from a database in APA style, include the following elements:

1 Author
2 Date of publication
3 Title of article
4 Name of periodical
5 Volume and issue numbers
6 Page numbers
7 Date of access
8 Name of database
9 Document number

**ON-SCREEN VIEW OF DATABASE RECORD**

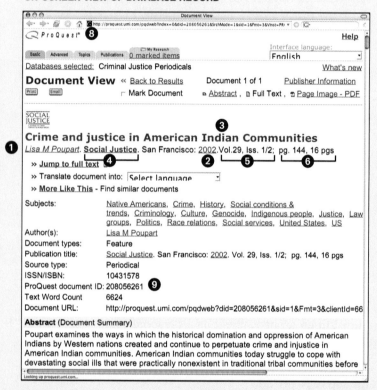

## PRINTOUT OF RECORD
## AND BEGINNING OF ARTICLE

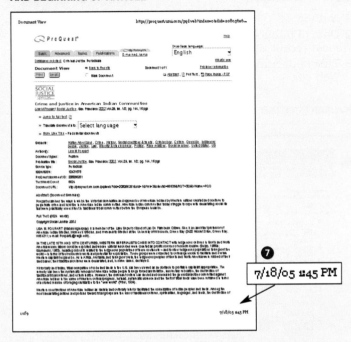

## REFERENCE LIST ENTRY FOR AN ARTICLE FROM A DATABASE

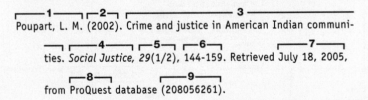

For more on citing articles from a database in APA style, see page 730.

# Citation at a glance: Document from a Web site (APA)

To cite a document from a Web site in APA style, include the following elements:

1 Author
2 Date of publication or most recent update
3 Title of document on Web site
4 Title of Web site or section of site
5 Date of access
6 URL of document

**BROWSER PRINTOUT OF WEB SITE**

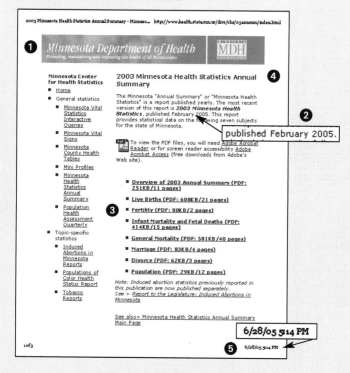

**ON-SCREEN VIEW OF DOCUMENT**

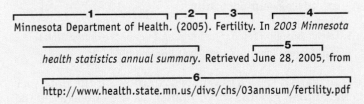

**REFERENCE LIST ENTRY FOR A DOCUMENT FROM A WEB SITE**

┌────────────1────────────┐  ┌──2──┐  ┌──3──┐      ┌──────4──────
Minnesota Department of Health. (2005). Fertility. In *2003 Minnesota*

┌──────────────────────────────┐      ┌──────5──────┐
*health statistics annual summary.* Retrieved June 28, 2005, from

┌──────────────────────────6──────────────────────────┐
http://www.health.state.mn.us/divs/chs/03annsum/fertility.pdf

For more on citing documents from Web sites in APA style, see pages 729–36.

Eaton, S. (2001, June 12). Online transactions [Msg 2]. Message posted to news://sci.psychology.psychotherapy.moderated

▦ **25. COMPUTER PROGRAM** Add the words "Computer software" in brackets after the title of the program.

Kaufmann, W. J., III, & Comins, N. F. (2003). Discovering the universe (Version 6.0) [Computer software]. New York: Freeman.

*Other sources*

▦ **26. DISSERTATION ABSTRACT**

Yoshida, Y. (2001). Essays in urban transportation (Doctoral dissertation, Boston College, 2001). *Dissertation Abstracts International, 62,* 7741A.

▦ **27. GOVERNMENT DOCUMENT**

U.S. Census Bureau. (2000). *Statistical abstract of the United States.* Washington, DC: U.S. Government Printing Office.

▦ **28. REPORT FROM A PRIVATE ORGANIZATION** If the publisher is the author, give the word "Author" as the publisher. If the report has an author, begin with the author's name, and name the publisher at the end.

American Psychiatric Association. (2000). *Practice guidelines for the treatment of patients with eating disorders* (2nd ed.). Washington, DC: Author.

▦ **29. CONFERENCE PROCEEDINGS**

Stahl, G. (Ed.). (2002). *Proceedings of CSCL '02: Computer support for collaborative learning.* Hillsdale, NJ: Erlbaum.

■ **30. MOTION PICTURE**   To cite a motion picture (film, video, or DVD), list the director and the year of the picture's release. Give the title, followed by "Motion picture" in brackets, the country where it was made, and the name of the studio. If the motion picture is difficult to find, include instead the name and address of its distributor.

Soderbergh, S. (Director). (2000). *Traffic* [Motion picture]. United
    States: Gramercy Pictures.

Spurlock, M. (Director). (2004). *Super size me* [Motion picture].
    (Available from IDP Films, 1133 Broadway, Suite 926, New York,
    NY 10010)

■ **31. TELEVISION PROGRAM**   To cite a television program, list the producer and the date it was aired. Give the title, followed by "Television broadcast" in brackets, the city, and the television network or service.

Pratt, C. (Executive Producer). (2001, December 2). *Face the nation*
    [Television broadcast]. Washington, DC: CBS News.

For a television series, use the year in which the series was produced, and follow the title with "Television series" in brackets. For an episode in a series, list the writer and director and the year. After the episode title put "Television series episode" in brackets. Follow with information about the series.

Janows, J. (Executive Producer). (2000). *Culture shock* [Television
    series]. Boston: WGBH.

Loeterman, B. (Writer), & Gale, B. (Director). (2000). Real justice
    [Television series episode]. In M. Sullivan (Executive Producer),
    *Frontline*. Boston: WGBH.

## 60e APA manuscript format

The American Psychological Association makes a number of recommendations for formatting a paper and preparing a list of references. The following guidelines are consistent with advice given in the *Publication Manual of the American Psychological Association,* 5th ed. (Washington: APA, 2001).

### Formatting the paper

APA guidelines for formatting a paper are endorsed by many instructors in the social sciences.

**MATERIALS AND TYPEFACE**  Use good-quality 8½″ × 11″ white paper. Avoid a typeface that is unusual or hard to read.

**TITLE PAGE**  The APA manual does not provide guidelines for preparing the title page of a college paper, but most instructors will want you to include one. See page 743 for an example.

**PAGE NUMBERS AND RUNNING HEAD**  The title page is numbered as page i; the abstract page, if there is one, is numbered as page ii. Use arabic numerals, beginning with 1, for the rest of the paper. In the upper right-hand corner of each page, type a short version of your title, followed by five spaces and the page number. Number all pages, including the title page.

**MARGINS, LINE SPACING, AND PARAGRAPH INDENTS**   Use margins of one inch on all sides of the page. Left-align the text.

Double-space throughout the paper, but single-space footnotes. Indent the first line of each paragraph one-half inch (or five spaces).

**LONG QUOTATIONS AND FOOTNOTES**   When a quotation is longer than forty words, set it off from the text by indenting it one-half inch (or five spaces) from the left margin. Double-space the quotation. Quotation marks are not needed when a quotation has been set off from the text. See page 752 for an example.

Place each footnote, if any, at the bottom of the page on which the text reference occurs. Double-space between the last line of text on the page and the footnote. Indent the first line of the footnote one-half inch (or five spaces). Begin the note with the superscript arabic numeral that corresponds to the number in the text. See page 745 for an example.

**ABSTRACT**   If your instructor requires one, include an abstract immediately after the title page. Center the word Abstract one inch from the top of the page; double-space the abstract as you do the body of your paper.

An abstract is a 100-to-120-word paragraph that provides readers with a quick overview of your essay. It should express your main idea and your key points; it might also briefly suggest any implications or applications of the research you discuss in the paper. See page 744 for an example.

**HEADINGS**   Although headings are not always necessary, their use is encouraged in the social sciences. For most undergraduate papers, one level of heading will usually be sufficient.

In APA style, major headings are centered. Capitalize the first word of the heading, along with all words except articles, short prepositions, and coordinating conjunctions.

**VISUALS**   The APA classifies visuals as tables and figures (figures include graphs, charts, drawings, and photographs). Keep visuals as simple as possible. Label each table with an arabic numeral (Table 1, Table 2, and so on) and provide a clear title. The label and title should appear on separate lines above the table, flush left and single-spaced. Below the table, give its source in a note. If any data in the table require an explanatory footnote, use a superscript lowercase letter in the body of the table and in a footnote following the source note. Single-space source notes and footnotes and do not indent the first line of each note. See page 748 for an example.

For each figure, place a label and a caption below the figure, flush left and single-spaced. They need not appear on separate lines.

In the text of your paper, discuss the most significant features of each visual. Place the visual as close as possible to the sentences that relate to it unless your instructor prefers it in an appendix.

*Preparing the list of references*

Begin your list of references on a new page at the end of the paper. Center the title References about one inch from the top of the page. Double-space throughout. For a sample reference list, see pages 754–55.

**INDENTING ENTRIES**   APA recommends using a hanging indent: Type the first line of an entry flush left and indent any additional lines one-half inch (or five spaces), as shown on pages 754–55.

**ALPHABETIZING THE LIST**   Alphabetize the reference list by the last names of the authors (or editors); when a work has no author or editor, alphabetize by the first word of the title other than *A, An,* or *The.*

If your list includes two or more works by the same author, arrange the entries by year, the earliest first. If your list includes two or more works by the same author in the same year, arrange them alphabetically by title. Add the letters "a," "b," and so on within the parentheses after the year. Use only the year for articles in journals: (2002a). Use the full date for articles in magazines and newspapers in the reference list: (2001a, July 7). Use only the year in the in-text citation.

**AUTHORS' NAMES**  Invert all authors' names and use initials instead of first names. With two or more authors, use an ampersand (&) before the last author's name. Separate the names with commas. Include names for the first six authors; if there are additional authors, end the list with "et al." (Latin for "and others").

**TITLES OF BOOKS AND ARTICLES**  Italicize the titles and subtitles of books; capitalize only the first word of the title and subtitle (and all proper nouns). Capitalize names of periodicals as you would capitalize them normally (see section 45).

**ABBREVIATIONS FOR PAGE NUMBERS**  Abbreviations for "page" and "pages" ("p." and "pp.") are used before page numbers of newspaper articles and articles in edited books (see item 10 on p. 725 and item 17 on p. 728) but not before page numbers of articles appearing in magazines and scholarly journals (see items 7–9 on p. 725).

**BREAKING A URL**  When a URL must be divided, break it after a slash or before a period. Do not insert a hyphen.

See pages 754–55 for an example of how to type your list of references. For information about the exact format of each entry in your list, consult the models on pages 720–37.

**60f** Sample research paper: APA style

On the following pages is a research paper written by Luisa Mirano, a student in a psychology class. Mirano's assignment was to write a review of the literature paper documented with APA-style citations and references.

| ON THE WEB | **dianahacker.com/bedhandbook**<br>▶ Model papers<br>　▶ APA papers: Mirano<br>　▶ APA papers: Haddad (annotated bibliography) |
| --- | --- |

Obesity in Children   i

Short title and page
number for student
papers. Lowercase
roman numerals are
used on title page
and abstract page,
arabic numerals on
all text pages.

Can Medication Cure Obesity in Children?
A Review of the Literature

Full title, writer's
name, and section
number of course, in-
structor's name, and
date (all centered).

Luisa Mirano
Psychology 107, Section B
Professor Kang
October 31, 2004

Marginal annotations indicate APA-style formatting and effective writing.

Abstract appears on a separate page.

Abstract

   In recent years, policymakers and medical experts have expressed alarm about the growing problem of childhood obesity
in the United States. While most agree that the issue deserves
attention, consensus dissolves around how to respond to the
problem. This literature review examines one approach to
treating childhood obesity: medication. The paper compares
the effectiveness for adolescents of the only two drugs approved by the Food and Drug Administration (FDA) for long-
term treatment of obesity, sibutramine and orlistat. This
examination of pharmacological treatments for obesity points
out the limitations of medication and suggests the need for a
comprehensive solution that combines medical, social, behavioral, and political approaches to this complex problem.

Can Medication Cure Obesity in Children?

A Review of the Literature

In March 2004, U.S. Surgeon General Richard Carmona called attention to a health problem in the United States that, until recently, has been overlooked: childhood obesity. Carmona said that the "astounding" 15% child obesity rate constitutes an "epidemic." Since the early 1980s, that rate has "doubled in children and tripled in adolescents." Now more than 9 million children are classified as obese (paras. 3, 6).[1] While the traditional response to a medical epidemic is to hunt for a vaccine or a cure-all pill, childhood obesity has proven more elusive. The lack of success of recent initiatives suggests that medication might not be the answer for the escalating problem. This literature review considers whether the use of medication is a promising approach for solving the childhood obesity problem by responding to the following questions:

1. What are the implications of childhood obesity?
2. Is medication effective at treating childhood obesity?
3. Is medication safe for children?
4. Is medication the best solution?

Understanding the limitations of medical treatments for children highlights the complexity of the childhood obesity

[1]Obesity is measured in terms of body-mass index (BMI): weight in kilograms divided by square of height in meters. An adult with a BMI 30 or higher is considered obese. In children and adolescents, obesity is defined in relation to others of the same age and gender. An adolescent with a BMI in the 95th percentile for his or her age and gender is considered obese.

Full title, centered.

The writer sets up her organization by posing four questions.

The writer states her thesis.

The writer uses a footnote to define an essential term that would be cumbersome to define within the text.

problem in the United States and underscores the need for
physicians, advocacy groups, and policymakers to search for
other solutions.

**What Are the Implications of Childhood Obesity?**

Obesity can be a devastating problem from both an individual and a societal perspective. Obesity puts children at risk
for a number of medical complications, including type 2 diabetes, hypertension, sleep apnea, and orthopedic problems
(Henry J. Kaiser Family Foundation, 2004, p. 1). Researchers
Hoppin and Taveras (2004) have noted that obesity is often
associated with psychological issues such as depression,
anxiety, and binge eating (Table 4).

Obesity also poses serious problems for a society struggling to cope with rising health care costs. The cost of treating obesity currently totals $117 billion per year--a price,
according to the surgeon general, "second only to the cost of
[treating] tobacco use" (Carmona, 2004, para. 9). And as the
number of children who suffer from obesity grows, long-term
costs will only increase.

**Is Medication Effective at Treating Childhood Obesity?**

The widening scope of the obesity problem has prompted
medical professionals to rethink old conceptions of the
disorder and its causes. As researchers Yanovski and Yanovski
(2002) have explained, obesity was once considered "either a
moral failing or evidence of underlying psychopathology"
(p. 592). But this view has shifted: Many medical professionals
now consider obesity a biomedical rather than a moral condition, influenced by both genetic and environmental factors.

---

Headings, centered, help readers follow the organization.

In a signal phrase, the word "and" links the names of two authors; the date is given in parentheses.

Because the author (Carmona) is not named in the signal phrase, his name and the date appear in parentheses, along with the paragraph number of the electronic source.

Obesity in Children    3

Yanovski and Yanovski have further noted that the development of weight-loss medications in the early 1990s showed
that "obesity should be treated in the same manner as any
other chronic disease . . . through the long-term use of
medication" (p. 592).

The search for the right long-term medication has been
complicated. Many of the drugs authorized by the Food and
Drug Administration (FDA) in the early 1990s proved to be a
disappointment. Two of the medications--fenfluramine and
dexfenfluramine--were withdrawn from the market because of
severe side effects (Yanovski & Yanovski, 2002, p. 592), and
several others were classified by the Drug Enforcement Administration as having the "potential for abuse" (Hoppin &
Taveras, 2004, Weight-Loss Drugs section, para. 6). Currently
only two medications have been approved by the FDA for long-
term treatment of obesity: sibutramine (marketed as Meridia)
and orlistat (marketed as Xenical). This section compares
studies on the effectiveness of each.

Sibutramine suppresses appetite by blocking the reuptake
of the neurotransmitters serotonin and norepinephrine in the
brain. Though the drug won FDA approval in 1998, experiments
to test its effectiveness for younger patients came considerably
later. In 2003, University of Pennsylvania researchers
Berkowitz, Wadden, Tershakovec, and Cronquist released the
first double-blind placebo study testing the effect of sibutramine on adolescents, aged 13-17, over a 12-month period.
Their findings are summarized in Table 1.

Ellipsis mark indi-
cates omitted words.

An ampersand links
the names of two au-
thors in parentheses.

The writer draws
attention to an im-
portant article.

Obesity in Children  4

The writer uses a
table to summarize
the findings pre-
sented in two
sources.

Table 1

*Effectiveness of Sibutramine and Orlistat in Adolescents*

| Medication | Subjects | Treatment[a] | Side effects | Average weight loss/gain |
|---|---|---|---|---|
| Sibutra-mine | Control | 0-6 mos.: placebo / 6-12 mos.: sibutra-mine | Mos. 6-12: increased blood pres-sure; in-creased pulse rate | After 6 mos.: loss of 3.2 kg (7 lb) / After 12 mos.: loss of 4.5 kg (9.9 lb) |
| | Medi-cated | 0-12 mos.: sibutra-mine | Increased blood pres-sure; in-creased pulse rate | After 6 mos.: loss of 7.8 kg (17.2 lb) / After 12 mos.: loss of 7.0 kg (15.4 lb) |
| Orlistat | Control | 0-12 mos.: placebo | None | Gain of 0.67 kg (1.5 lb) |
| | Medi-cated | 0-12 mos.: orlistat | Oily spot-ting; flatu-lence; abdominal discomfort | Loss of 1.3 kg (2.9 lb) |

A note gives the
source of the data.

A content note ex-
plains data common
to all subjects.

*Note.* The data on sibutramine are adapted from "Behavior Therapy and
Sibutramine for the Treatment of Adolescent Obesity" [Electronic version],
by R. I. Berkowitz, T. A. Wadden, A. M. Tershakovec, & J. L. Cronquist,
2003, *Journal of the American Medical Association, 289*, pp. 1807-1809.
The data on orlistat are adapted from *Xenical (orlistat) Capsules: Complete
Product Information*, by Roche Laboratories, December 2003, retrieved October 11, 2004, from http://www.rocheusa.com/products/xenical/pi.pdf
[a]The medication and/or placebo were combined with behavioral therapy in
all groups over all time periods.

After 6 months, the group receiving medication had lost 4.6 kg (about 10 pounds) more than the control group. But during the second half of the study, when both groups received sibutramine, the results were more ambiguous. In months 6-12, the group that continued to take sibutramine gained an average of 0.8 kg, or roughly 2 pounds; the control group, which switched from placebo to sibutramine, lost 1.3 kg, or roughly 3 pounds (p. 1808). Both groups received behavioral therapy covering diet, exercise, and mental health.

These results paint a murky picture of the effectiveness of the medication: While initial data seemed promising, the results after one year raised questions about whether medication-induced weight loss could be sustained over time. As Berkowitz et al. (2003) advised, "Until more extensive safety and efficacy data are available, . . . weight-loss medications should be used only on an experimental basis for adolescents" (p. 1811).

A study testing the effectiveness of orlistat in adolescents showed similarly ambiguous results. The FDA approved orlistat in 1999 but did not authorize it for adolescents until December 2003. Roche Laboratories (2003), maker of orlistat, released results of a one-year study testing the drug on 539 obese adolescents, aged 12-16. The drug, which promotes weight loss by blocking fat absorption in the large intestine, showed some effectiveness in adolescents: an average loss of 1.3 kg, or roughly 3 pounds, for subjects taking orlistat for one year, as opposed to an average gain of 0.67 kg, or 1.5 pounds, for the control group (pp. 8-9). See Table 1.

When this article was first cited, all four authors were named. In subsequent citations of a work with three to five authors, "et al." is used after the first author's name.

Short-term studies of orlistat have shown slightly more dramatic results. Researchers at the National Institute of Child Health and Human Development tested 20 adolescents, aged 12-16, over a three-month period and found that orlistat, combined with behavioral therapy, produced an average weight loss of 4.4 kg, or 9.7 pounds (McDuffie et al., 2002, p. 646). The study was not controlled against a placebo group; therefore, the relative effectiveness of orlistat in this case remains unclear.

For a source with six or more authors, the first author's surname followed by "et al." is used for the first and subsequent references.

Is Medication Safe for Children?

While modest weight loss has been documented for both medications, each carries risks of certain side effects. Sibutramine has been observed to increase blood pressure and pulse rate. In 2002, a consumer group claimed that the medication was related to the deaths of 19 people and filed a petition with the Department of Health and Human Services to ban the medication (Hilts, 2002). The sibutramine study by Berkowitz et al. (2003) noted elevated blood pressure as a side effect, and dosages had to be reduced or the medication discontinued in 19 of the 43 subjects in the first six months (p. 1809).

The main side effects associated with orlistat were abdominal discomfort, oily spotting, fecal incontinence, and nausea (Roche Laboratories, 2003, p. 13). More serious for long-term health is the concern that orlistat, being a fat-blocker, would affect absorption of fat-soluble vitamins, such as vitamin D. However, the study found that this side effect can be minimized or eliminated if patients take vitamin

supplements two hours before or after administration of
orlistat (p. 10). With close monitoring of patients taking the
medication, many of the risks can be reduced.

### Is Medication the Best Solution?

The data on the safety and efficacy of pharmacological
treatments of childhood obesity raise the question of whether
medication is the best solution for the problem. The treatments have clear costs for individual patients, including unpleasant side effects, little information about long-term use,
and uncertainty that they will yield significant weight loss.

In purely financial terms, the drugs cost more than $3 a
day on average (Duenwald, 2004, paras. 33, 36). In each of
the clinical trials, use of medication was accompanied by an
expensive regime of behavioral therapies, including counseling,
nutritional education, fitness advising, and monitoring. As
journalist Greg Critser (2003) noted in his book *Fat Land,* use
of weight-loss drugs is unlikely to have an effect without the
proper "support system"--one that includes doctors, facilities,
time, and money (p. 3). For some, this level of care is prohibi-
tively expensive.

A third complication is that the studies focused on adolescents aged 12-16, but obesity can begin at a much younger
age. Little data exist to establish the safety or efficacy of
medication for treating very young children.

While the scientific data on the concrete effects of these
medications in children remain somewhat unclear, medication
is not the only avenue for addressing the crisis. Both medical
experts and policymakers recognize that solutions might come

The writer develops
the paper's thesis.

not only from a laboratory but also from policy, education, and advocacy. Indeed, a handbook designed to educate doctors on obesity recommended a notably nonmedical course of action, calling for "major changes in some aspects of western culture" (Hoppin & Taveras, 2004, Conclusion section, para. 1). Cultural change may not be the typical realm of medical professionals, but the handbook urged doctors to be proactive and "focus [their] energy on public policies and interventions" (Conclusion section, para. 1).

Brackets indicate a word not in the original source.

The solutions proposed by a number of advocacy groups underscore this interest in political and cultural change. A report by the Henry J. Kaiser Family Foundation (2004) outlined trends that may have contributed to the childhood obesity crisis, including food advertising for children as well as

A quotation longer than 40 words is set off from the text without quotation marks.

> a reduction in physical education classes and after-school athletic programs, an increase in the availability of sodas and snacks in public schools, the growth in the number of fast-food outlets . . . , and the increasing number of highly processed high-calorie and high-fat grocery products. (p. 1)

The writer interprets the evidence; she doesn't just report it.

Addressing each of these areas requires more than a doctor armed with a prescription pad; it requires a broad mobilization not just of doctors and concerned parents but of educators, food industry executives, advertisers, and media representatives.

The tone of the conclusion is objective.

The barrage of possible approaches to combating childhood obesity--from scientific research to political lobbying--indicates both the severity and the complexity of the problem.

While none of the medications currently available is a miracle drug for curing the nation's 9 million obese children, research has illuminated some of the underlying factors that affect obesity and has shown the need for a comprehensive approach to the problem that includes behavioral, medical, social, and political change.

Obesity in Children    10

References

List of references be-
gins on a new page.
Heading is centered.

Berkowitz, R. I., Wadden, T. A., Tershakovec, A. M., & Cron-

quist, J. L. (2003). Behavior therapy and sibutramine for

the treatment of adolescent obesity [Electronic version].

*Journal of the American Medical Association, 289,* 1805-

1812.

List is alphabetized
by authors' last
names. All authors'
names are inverted.

Carmona, R. H. (2004, March 2). *The growing epidemic of child-*

*hood obesity.* Testimony before the Subcommittee on

Competition, Foreign Commerce, and Infrastructure of

the U.S. Senate Committee on Commerce, Science, and

Transportation. Retrieved October 10, 2004, from

http://www.hhs.gov/asl/testify/t040302.html

Critser, G. (2003). *Fat land: How Americans became the fattest*

*people in the world.* Boston: Houghton Mifflin.

The first line of an
entry is at the left
margin; subsequent
lines indent ½" (or
five spaces).

Duenwald, M. (2004, January 6). Slim pickings: Looking be-

yond ephedra. *The New York Times,* p. F1. Retrieved

October 12, 2004, from LexisNexis.

Henry J. Kaiser Family Foundation. (2004, February). *The role*

*of media in childhood obesity.* Retrieved October 10,

2004, from http://www.kff.org/entmedia/7030.cfm

Hilts, P. J. (2002, March 20). Petition asks for removal of diet

drug from market. *The New York Times,* p. A26. Retrieved

October 12, 2004, from LexisNexis.

Double-spacing is
used throughout.

Hoppin, A. G., & Taveras, E. M. (2004, June 25). Assessment

and management of childhood and adolescent obesity.

*Clinical Update.* Retrieved October 12, 2004, from

Medscape Web site: http://www.medscape.com/

viewarticle/481633

McDuffie, J. R., Calis, K. A., Uwaifo, G. I., Sebring, N. G., Fallon, E. M., Hubbard, V. S., et al. (2003). Three-month tolerability of orlistat in adolescents with obesity-related comorbid conditions [Electronic version]. *Obesity Research, 10,* 642-650.

Roche Laboratories. (2003, December). *Xenical (orlistat) capsules: Complete product information.* Retrieved October 11, 2004, from http://www.rocheusa.com/products/xenical/pi.pdf

Yanovski, S. Z., & Yanovski, J. A. (2002). Drug therapy: Obesity [Electronic version]. *The New England Journal of Medicine, 346,* 591-602.

# WRITING *CHICAGO* PAPERS
# 61

*Chicago* papers

Most assignments in history and other humanities classes are based to some extent on reading. At times you will be asked to respond to one or two readings, such as essays or historical documents. At other times you may be asked to write a research paper that draws on a wide variety of sources.

Most history instructors and some humanities instructors require you to document sources with footnotes or endnotes based on *The Chicago Manual of Style,* 15th ed. (Chicago: U of Chicago P, 2003). (See 61d.)

When you write a paper using sources, you face three main challenges in addition to documenting your sources: (1) supporting a thesis, (2) citing your sources and avoiding plagiarism, and (3) integrating quotations and other source material.

## 61a Supporting a thesis

Most assignments ask you to form a thesis, or main idea, and to support that thesis with well-organized evidence.

### Finding a thesis

A thesis is a one-sentence (or occasionally a two-sentence) statement of your central idea. Usually your thesis will appear at the end of the first paragraph (as on p. 786), but if you need to provide readers with considerable background information, you may place it in the second paragraph.

Although the thesis appears early in your paper, do not attempt to write it until fairly late in your reading and writing process. Early in the process, you can keep your mind open—yet focused—by posing questions. The thesis that you articulate later in the process will be a reasoned answer to the central question you pose. Here is a research question posed by Ned Bishop, a student in a history course, followed by a thesis that answers the question.

**RESEARCH QUESTION**

To what extent was Confederate Major General Nathan Bedford Forrest responsible for the massacre of Union troops at Fort Pillow?

**POSSIBLE THESIS**

Although we will never know whether Nathan Bedford Forrest directly ordered the massacre of Union troops at Fort Pillow, evidence suggests that he was responsible for it.

Notice that the thesis expresses a view on a debatable issue—an issue about which intelligent, well-meaning people might disagree. The writer's job is to convince such readers that this view is worth taking seriously.

**ON THE WEB**

**dianahacker.com/bedhandbook**
▶ Electronic research exercises
  ▶ E-ex 61–1

*Organizing your evidence*

The body of your paper will consist of evidence in support of your thesis. Instead of getting tangled up in a complex, formal outline, sketch an informal plan that organizes your evidence in bold strokes. Ned Bishop, the student who wrote about Fort Pillow, used a simple list of questions as the blueprint for his paper. In the paper itself, these became headings that helped readers follow Bishop's line of argument.

> What happened at Fort Pillow?
> Did Forrest order the massacre?
> Can Forrest be held responsible for the massacre?

## 61b Citing sources; avoiding plagiarism

In a research paper, you will be drawing on the work of other writers, and you must document their contributions by citing your sources. Sources are cited for two reasons:

1. to tell readers where your information comes from — so that they can assess its reliability and, if interested, find and read the original source
2. to give credit to the writers from whom you have borrowed words and ideas

Borrowing another writer's language, sentence structures, or ideas without proper acknowledgment is a form of dishonesty known as *plagiarism*.

### Citing sources

Citations are required when you quote from a source, when you summarize or paraphrase a source, and when you borrow facts that are not common knowledge. (See also the next section, "Avoiding plagiarism.")

*Chicago* citations consist of numbered notes in the text of the paper that refer readers to notes with corresponding numbers either at the foot of the page (footnotes) or at the end of the paper (endnotes).

**TEXT**

Governor John Andrew was not allowed to recruit black soldiers from out of state. "Ostensibly," writes Peter Burchard, "no recruiting was done outside Massachusetts, but it was an open secret that Andrew's agents were working far and wide."[1]

**NOTE**

1. Peter Burchard, *One Gallant Rush: Robert Gould Shaw and His Brave Black Regiment* (New York: St. Martin's, 1965), 85.

For detailed advice on using *Chicago*-style notes, see 61d. When you use footnotes or endnotes, you will usually need to provide a bibliography as well (see p. 771).

### Avoiding plagiarism

Your research paper is a collaboration between you and your sources. To be fair and ethical, you must acknowledge your debt to the writers of these sources. If you don't, you commit plagiarism, a serious academic offense.

Three different acts are considered plagiarism: (1) failing to cite quotations and borrowed ideas, (2) failing to enclose borrowed language in quotation marks, and (3) failing to put summaries and paraphrases in your own words.

**CITING QUOTATIONS AND BORROWED IDEAS**   You must of course cite the source of all direct quotations. You must also cite any ideas you borrow from a source: summaries and paraphrases; statistics and other specific facts; and visuals such as cartoons, graphs, and diagrams.

The only exception is common knowledge — general information that your readers may know or could easily locate in any number of reference sources. For example, the approximate population of the United States is common knowledge among sociologists and economists, and historians are familiar with facts such as the date of the Emancipation Proclamation. As a rule, when you have seen certain general information repeatedly in your reading, you don't need to cite it. However, when information has appeared in only a few sources, when it is highly specific (as with statistics), or when it is controversial, you should cite the source. If a topic is new to you and you are not sure what is considered common knowledge or what is a matter of controversy, ask someone with expertise. When in doubt, cite the source.

**ENCLOSING BORROWED LANGUAGE IN QUOTATION MARKS**   To indicate that you are using a source's exact phrases or sentences, you must enclose them in quotation marks. To omit the quotation marks is to claim — falsely — that the language is your own. Such an omission is plagiarism even if you have cited the source.

**ORIGINAL SOURCE**

For many Southerners it was psychologically impossible to see a black man bearing arms as anything but an incipient slave uprising complete with arson, murder, pillage, and rapine.
—Dudley Taylor Cornish, *The Sable Arm*, p. 158

**PLAGIARISM**

According to Civil War historian Dudley Taylor Cornish, for many Southerners it was psychologically impossible to see a black man bearing arms as anything but an incipient slave uprising complete with arson, murder, pillage, and rapine.[2]

**BORROWED LANGUAGE IN QUOTATION MARKS**

According to Civil War historian Dudley Taylor Cornish, "For many Southerners it was psychologically impossible to see a black man bearing arms as anything but an incipient slave uprising complete with arson, murder, pillage, and rapine."[2]

**NOTE:** When quoted sentences are set off from the text by indenting, quotation marks are not needed (see pp. 764–65).

**PUTTING SUMMARIES AND PARAPHRASES IN YOUR OWN WORDS**
Summaries and paraphrases are written in your own words. A summary condenses information; a paraphrase reports information in about the same number of words as in the source. When you summarize or paraphrase, you must restate the source's meaning using your own language. In the example on page 762, the paraphrase is plagiarized — even though the source is cited — because too much of its language is borrowed from the source without quotation marks. The underlined phrases have been copied word-for-word. In addition, the writer has closely followed the sentence structure of the original source, merely plugging in some synonyms (such as *fifty percent* for *half* and *savage hatred* for *fierce, bitter animosity*).

**ORIGINAL SOURCE**
Half of the force holding Fort Pillow were Negroes, former slaves now enrolled in the Union Army. Toward them Forrest's troops had the fierce, bitter animosity of men who had been educated to regard the colored race as inferior and who for the first time had encountered that race armed and fighting against white men. The sight enraged and perhaps terrified

many of the Confederates and aroused in them the ugly spirit
of a lynching mob.

—Albert Castel, "The Fort Pillow Massacre," pp. 46–47

**PLAGIARISM: UNACCEPTABLE BORROWING**

Albert Castel suggests that much of the brutality at Fort Pillow can
be traced to racial attitudes. Fifty percent of the troops <u>holding
Fort Pillow were Negroes, former slaves</u> who had joined the Union
Army. <u>Toward them Forrest's</u> soldiers displayed the savage hatred
<u>of men who had been</u> taught the inferiority of blacks <u>and who for
the first time had</u> confronted them <u>armed and fighting against
white men</u>. The vision angered and perhaps frightened the Confederates <u>and aroused in them the ugly spirit of a lynching mob</u>.[3]

To avoid plagiarizing an author's language, set the
source aside, write from memory, and consult the source
later to check for accuracy. This strategy prevents you from
being captivated by the words on the page.

**ACCEPTABLE PARAPHRASE**

Albert Castel suggests that much of the brutality at Fort Pillow
can be traced to racial attitudes. Half of the Union troops were
blacks, men whom the Confederates had been raised to consider
their inferiors. The shock and perhaps fear of facing armed ex-
slaves in battle for the first time may well have unleashed the fury
that led to the massacre.[3]

**ON THE WEB**

**dianahacker.com/bedhandbook**
▶ Electronic research exercises
  ▶ E-ex 61–2 to 61–6

## 61c Integrating sources

Quotations, summaries, paraphrases, and facts will support your argument, but they cannot speak for you. Several strategies will help you to integrate information from research sources into your paper while maintaining your own voice.

### *Limiting your use of quotations*

Although it is tempting to insert many long quotations in your paper and to use your own words only for connecting passages, do not quote excessively. It is almost impossible to integrate numerous long quotations smoothly into your own text.

It is not always necessary to quote full sentences from a source. At times you may wish to borrow only a phrase or to weave part of a source's sentence into your own sentence structure.

> As Hurst has pointed out, until there was "an outcry in the northern press," even the Confederates did not deny that there had been a massacre at Fort Pillow.[4]

> Union surgeon Dr. Charles Fitch testified that after being taken prisoner by Forrest he saw Southern soldiers "kill every Negro who made his appearance in Federal uniform."[5]

**USING THE ELLIPSIS MARK**   To condense a quoted passage, you can use the ellipsis mark (three periods, with spaces between) to indicate that you have omitted words. The sentence that remains must be grammatically complete.

> Union surgeon Fitch's testimony that all women and children had been evacuated from Fort Pillow before the attack conflicts with

Forrest's report: "We captured . . . about 40 negro women and children."[6]

The writer has omitted several words not relevant to the issue at hand: *164 Federals, 75 negro troops, and.*

When you want to omit a full sentence or more, use a period before the three ellipsis dots. For an example, see the long quotation on page 765.

Ordinarily, do not use the ellipsis mark at the beginning or at the end of a quotation. Readers will understand that the quoted material is taken from a longer passage.

**USING BRACKETS**  Brackets allow you to insert words of your own into quoted material to explain a confusing reference or to keep a sentence grammatical in your context.

According to Albert Castel, "It can be reasonably argued that he [Forrest] was justified in believing that the approaching steamships intended to aid the garrison [at Fort Pillow]."[7]

**NOTE:** Use [*sic*] to indicate that an error in a quoted sentence appears in the original source. (An example appears on p. 765.) However, if a source is filled with errors, as is the case with many historical documents, this use of [*sic*] can become distracting and is best avoided.

**SETTING OFF LONG QUOTATIONS**  *Chicago* style allows you some leeway in deciding whether to set off a long quotation or run it into your text. For emphasis you may want to set off a quotation of more than four or five lines of text; almost certainly you should set off quotations of ten lines or more. To set off a quotation, indent it one-half inch (or five spaces) from the left margin and use the normal right margin. Double-space the indented quotation.

Long quotations should be introduced by an informative sentence, usually followed by a colon. Quotation marks are unnecessary because the indented format tells readers that the words are taken directly from the source.

> In a letter home, Confederate officer Achilles V. Clark recounted what happened at Fort Pillow:
>
>> Words cannot describe the scene. The poor deluded negroes would run up to our men fall upon their knees and with up-lifted hands scream for mercy but they were ordered to their feet and then shot down. The whitte [*sic*] men fared but little better. . . . I with several others tried to stop the butchering and at one time had partially succeeded, but Gen. Forrest ordered them shot down like dogs, and the carnage continued.[8]

### Using signal phrases with most material

In a *Chicago*-style paper, use the present tense or present perfect tense in phrases that introduce quotations or other source materials from nonfiction sources: *Foote points out that* or *Foote has pointed out that* (not *Foote pointed out that*). If you have good reason to emphasize that the author's language or opinion was articulated in the past, however, the past tense is acceptable.

The first time you mention an author, use the full name: *Shelby Foote argues. . . .* When you refer to the author again, you may use the last name only: *Foote raises an important question.*

To avoid monotony, try to vary both the language and the placement of your signal phrases. The models in the chart on page 766 suggest a range of possibilities.

When the signal phrase includes a verb, choose one that is appropriate in the context. Is your source arguing a point, making an observation, reporting a fact, refuting an argument, or stating a belief? By choosing an appropriate verb, you can make your source's stance clear. See the following chart for a list of verbs commonly used in signal phrases.

### Using signal phrases with quotations

Readers should be able to move from your own words to the words you quote from a source without feeling a jolt. Avoid dropping quotations into the text without warning. Instead,

---

### Varying signal phrases in *Chicago* papers

To avoid monotony, try to vary both the language and the placement of your signal phrases.

**MODEL SIGNAL PHRASES**

In the words of historian James M. McPherson, ". . ."

As Dudley Taylor Cornish has argued, ". . ."

In a letter to his wife, a Confederate soldier who witnessed the massacre wrote that ". . ."

". . . ," claims Benjamin Quarles.

". . . ," writes Albert Castel, ". . ."

Shelby Foote offers an intriguing interpretation of these events: ". . ."

**VERBS IN SIGNAL PHRASES**

| | | | |
|---|---|---|---|
| admits | compares | insists | rejects |
| agrees | confirms | notes | reports |
| argues | contends | observes | responds |
| asserts | declares | points out | suggests |
| believes | denies | reasons | thinks |
| claims | emphasizes | refutes | writes |

provide clear signal phrases, usually including the author's name, to prepare readers for the source.

**DROPPED QUOTATION**

Not surprisingly, those testifying on the Union and Confederate sides recalled events at Fort Pillow quite differently. Unionists claimed that their troops had abandoned their arms and were in full retreat. "The Confederates, however, all agreed that the Union troops retreated to the river with arms in their hands."[9]

**QUOTATION WITH SIGNAL PHRASE**

Not surprisingly, those testifying on the Union and Confederate sides recalled events at Fort Pillow quite differently. Unionists claimed that their troops had abandoned their arms and were in full retreat. "The Confederates, however," writes historian Albert Castel, "all agreed that the Union troops retreated to the river with arms in their hands."[9]

### Using signal phrases with summaries and paraphrases

As with quotations, you should introduce most summaries and paraphrases with a signal phrase that mentions the author and places the material in context. Readers will then understand that everything between the signal phrase and the numbered note summarizes or paraphrases the cited source.

Without the signal phrase (underlined) in the following example, readers might think that only the last sentence is being cited, when in fact the whole paragraph is based on the source.

According to Kenneth Davis, official Confederate policy was that black soldiers were to be treated as runaway slaves; in addition, the Confederate Congress decreed that white Union officers com-manding black troops be killed. Confederate Lieutenant General Kirby Smith of Mississippi boldly announced that he would kill all captured black troops. Smith's policy never met with strong oppo-sition from the Richmond government.[10]

### *Integrating statistics and other facts*

When you are citing a statistic or another specific fact, a sig-nal phrase is often not necessary. In most cases, readers will understand that the citation refers to the statistic or fact (not the whole paragraph).

Of the 295 white troops garrisoned at Fort Pillow, 168 were taken prisoner. Black troops fared much worse, with only 58 of 262 men being taken into custody and most of the rest presumably killed or badly wounded.[11]

There is nothing wrong, however, with using a signal phrase.

Shelby Foote notes that of the 295 white troops garrisoned at Fort Pillow, 168 were taken prisoner but that black troops fared much worse, with only 58 of 262 men being taken into custody and most of the rest presumably killed or badly wounded.[11]

### *Putting source material in context*

Readers need to understand how your source is relevant to your paper's argument. It's a good idea, in other words, to embed your quotation between sentences of your own, intro-ducing it with a signal phrase and following it up with inter-pretive comments that link the source material to your paper's argument.

**QUOTATION WITH INSUFFICIENT CONTEXT**

In a biography of Nathan Bedford Forrest, Hurst suggests that the temperamental Forrest "may have ragingly ordered a massacre and even intended to carry it out--until he rode inside the fort and viewed the horrifying result" and ordered it stopped.[12]

**QUOTATION WITH EFFECTIVE CONTEXT**

In a biography of Nathan Bedford Forrest, Hurst suggests that the temperamental Forrest "may have ragingly ordered a massacre and even intended to carry it out--until he rode inside the fort and viewed the horrifying result" and ordered it stopped.[12] While this is an intriguing interpretation of events, even Hurst would probably admit that it is merely speculation.

**ON THE WEB**

**dianahacker.com/bedhandbook**
▶ Electronic research exercises
  ▶ E-ex 61–7 to 61–10

## 61d *Chicago* documentation style

Professors in history and some humanities courses often require footnotes or endnotes based on *The Chicago Manual of Style.* When you use *Chicago*-style notes, you will usually be asked to include a bibliography at the end of your paper (see p. 771).

**TEXT**

A Union soldier, Jacob Thomas, claimed to have seen Forrest order the killing, but when asked to describe the six-foot-two general, he called him "a little bit of a man."[13]

**FOOTNOTE OR ENDNOTE**

13. Brian Steel Wills, *A Battle from the Start: The Life of Nathan Bedford Forrest* (New York: HarperCollins, 1992), 187.

**BIBLIOGRAPHY ENTRY**

Wills, Brian Steel. *A Battle from the Start: The Life of Nathan Bedford Forrest.* New York: HarperCollins, 1992.

---

**ON THE WEB**

**dianahacker.com/bedhandbook**
▶ Electronic research exercises
  ▶ E-ex 61–11

---

*First and subsequent notes for a source*

The first time you cite a source, the note should include publishing information for that work as well as the page number on which the passage being cited may be found.

1. Peter Burchard, *One Gallant Rush: Robert Gould Shaw and His Brave Black Regiment* (New York: St. Martin's, 1965), 85.

For subsequent references to a source you have already cited, you may simply give the author's last name, a short form of the title, and the page or pages cited. A short form of the title of a book is italicized; a short form of the title of an article is put in quotation marks.

4. Burchard, *One Gallant Rush,* 31.

When you have two consecutive notes from the same source, you may use "Ibid." (meaning "in the same place") and the page number for the second note. Use "Ibid." alone if the page number is the same.

5. Jack Hurst, *Nathan Bedford Forrest: A Biography* (New York: Knopf, 1993), 8.

6. Ibid., 174.

## Chicago-*style bibliography*

A bibliography, which appears at the end of your paper, lists every work you have cited in your notes; in addition, it may include works that you consulted but did not cite. For advice on constructing the list, see page 784. A sample bibliography appears on page 790.

**NOTE:** If you include a bibliography, *The Chicago Manual of Style* suggests that you shorten all notes, including the first reference to a source, as described on page 770. Check with your instructor, however, to see whether using an abbreviated note for a first reference to a source is acceptable.

## Model notes and bibliography entries

The following models are consistent with guidelines set forth in *The Chicago Manual of Style,* 15th ed. For each type of source, a model note appears first, followed by a model bibliography entry. The model note shows the format you should use when citing a source for the first time. For subsequent citations of a source, use shortened notes (see p. 770).

---

**ON THE WEB**

**dianahacker.com/bedhandbook**
▶ Research and Documentation Online
  ▶ History: Documenting sources (*Chicago*)

## Books (print and online)

**■ 1. BASIC FORMAT FOR A PRINT BOOK**

1. William H. Rehnquist, *The Supreme Court: A History* (New York: Knopf, 2001), 204.

Rehnquist, William H. *The Supreme Court: A History*. New York: Knopf, 2001.

**■ 2. BASIC FORMAT FOR AN ONLINE BOOK**

2. Heinz Kramer, *A Changing Turkey: The Challenge to Europe and the United States* (Washington, DC: Brookings Press, 2000), 85, http://brookings.nap.edu/books/0815750234/html/index.html.

Kramer, Heinz. *A Changing Turkey: The Challenge to Europe and the United States*. Washington, DC: Brookings Press, 2000. http://brookings.nap.edu/books/0815750234/html/index.html.

**■ 3. TWO OR THREE AUTHORS**

3. Michael D. Coe and Mark Van Stone, *Reading the Maya Glyphs* (London: Thames and Hudson, 2002), 129-30.

Coe, Michael D., and Mark Van Stone. *Reading the Maya Glyphs*. London: Thames and Hudson, 2002.

**■ 4. FOUR OR MORE AUTHORS**

4. Lynn Hunt and others, *The Making of the West: Peoples and Cultures* (Boston: Bedford/St. Martin's, 2001), 541.

Hunt, Lynn, Thomas R. Martin, Barbara H. Rosenwein, R. Po-chia Hsia, and Bonnie G. Smith. *The Making of the West: Peoples and Cultures*. Boston: Bedford/St. Martin's, 2001.

**■ 5. UNKNOWN AUTHOR**

5. *The Men's League Handbook on Women's Suffrage* (London, 1912), 23.

*The Men's League Handbook on Women's Suffrage.* London, 1912.

### ■ 6. EDITED WORK WITHOUT AN AUTHOR

Jack Beatty, ed., *Colossus: How the Corporation Changed America* (New York: Broadway Books, 2001), 127.

Beatty, Jack, ed. *Colossus: How the Corporation Changed America.* New York: Broadway Books, 2001.

### ■ 7. EDITED WORK WITH AN AUTHOR

7. Ted Poston, *A First Draft of History,* ed. Kathleen A. Hauke (Athens: University of Georgia Press, 2000), 46.

Poston, Ted. *A First Draft of History.* Edited by Kathleen A. Hauke. Athens: University of Georgia Press, 2000.

### ■ 8. TRANSLATED WORK

8. Tonino Guerra, *Abandoned Places,* trans. Adria Bernardi (Barcelona: Guernica, 1999), 71.

Guerra, Tonino. *Abandoned Places.* Translated by Adria Bernardi. Barcelona: Guernica, 1999.

### ■ 9. EDITION OTHER THAN THE FIRST

9. Andrew F. Rolle, *California: A History,* 5th ed. (Wheeling, IL: Harlan Davidson, 1998), 243.

Rolle, Andrew F. *California: A History.* 5th ed. Wheeling, IL: Harlan Davidson, 1998.

### ■ 10. VOLUME IN A MULTIVOLUME WORK

10. James M. McPherson, *Ordeal by Fire,* vol. 2, *The Civil War* (New York: McGraw-Hill, 1993), 205.

McPherson, James M. *Ordeal by Fire.* Vol. 2, *The Civil War.* New York: McGraw-Hill, 1993.

## ■ 11. WORK IN AN ANTHOLOGY

11. Zora Neale Hurston, "From *Dust Tracks on a Road,*" in *The Norton Book of American Autobiography,* ed. Jay Parini (New York: Norton, 1999), 336.

Hurston, Zora Neale. "From *Dust Tracks on a Road.*" In *The Norton Book of American Autobiography,* edited by Jay Parini, 333-43. New York: Norton, 1999.

## ■ 12. LETTER IN A PUBLISHED COLLECTION

12. Thomas Gainsborough to Elizabeth Rasse, 1753, in *The Letters of Thomas Gainsborough,* ed. John Hayes (New Haven: Yale University Press, 2001), 5.

Gainsborough, Thomas. Letter to Elizabeth Rasse, 1753. In *The Letters of Thomas Gainsborough,* edited by John Hayes, 5. New Haven: Yale University Press, 2001.

## ■ 13. WORK IN A SERIES

13. R. Keith Schoppa, *The Columbia Guide to Modern Chinese History,* Columbia Guides to Asian History (New York: Columbia University Press, 2000), 256-58.

Schoppa, R. Keith. *The Columbia Guide to Modern Chinese History.* Columbia Guides to Asian History. New York: Columbia University Press, 2000.

## ■ 14. ENCYCLOPEDIA OR DICTIONARY

14. *Encyclopaedia Britannica,* 15th ed., s.v. "Monroe Doctrine."

**NOTE:** The abbreviation "s.v." is for the Latin *sub verbo* ("under the word").

Reference works are usually not included in the bibliography.

■   **15. SACRED TEXT**

15. Matt. 20.4-9 (Revised Standard Version).

15. Qur'an 18:1-3.

The Bible and other sacred texts are usually not included in the bibliography.

### Articles in periodicals (print and online)

■   **16. ARTICLE IN A JOURNAL**   For an article in a print journal, include the volume and issue numbers and the date; end the bibliography entry with the page range of the article.

16. Jonathan Zimmerman, "Ethnicity and the History Wars in the 1920s," *Journal of American History* 87, no. 1 (2000): 101.

Zimmerman, Jonathan. "Ethnicity and the History Wars in the 1920s." *Journal of American History* 87, no. 1 (2000): 92-111.

For an article accessed through a database service such as *EBSCOhost* or for an article published online, include a URL. If the article is paginated, give a page number in the note and a page range in the bibliography. For unpaginated articles, page references are not possible, but in your note you may include a "locator," such as a numbered paragraph or a heading from the article, as in the example for an article published online.

### Journal article from a database service

16. Eugene F. Provenzo Jr., "Time Exposure," *Educational Studies* 34, no. 2 (2003): 266, http://search.epnet.com.

Provenzo, Eugene F. Jr. "Time Exposure." *Educational Studies* 34, no. 2 (2003): 266-67. http://search.epnet.com.

*Journal article published online*

16. Linda Belau, "Trauma and the Material Signifier," *Postmodern Culture* 11, no. 2 (2001): par. 6, http://www.iath.virginia.edu/pmc/text-only/issue.101/11.2belau.txt.

Belau, Linda. "Trauma and the Material Signifier." *Postmodern Culture* 11, no. 2 (2001). http://www.iath.virginia.edu/pmc/text-only/issue.101/11.2belau.txt.

■ **17. ARTICLE IN A MAGAZINE** For a print article, provide a page number in the note and a page range in the bibliography.

17. Joy Williams, "One Acre," *Harper's,* February 2001, 62.

Williams, Joy. "One Acre." *Harper's,* February 2001, 58-65.

For an article accessed through a database service such as *FirstSearch* or for an article published online, include a URL. If the article is paginated, give a page number in the note and a page range in the bibliography. For unpaginated articles, page references are not possible.

*Magazine article from a database service*

17. David Pryce-Jones, "The Great Sorting Out: Postwar Iraq," *National Review,* May 5, 2003, 17, http://newfirstsearch.oclc.org.

Pryce-Jones, David. "The Great Sorting Out: Postwar Iraq." *National Review,* May 5, 2003, 17-18. http://newfirstsearch.oclc.org.

*Magazine article published online*

17. Fiona Morgan, "Banning the Bullies," *Salon,* March 15, 2001. http://www.salon.com/news/feature/2001/03/15/bullying/index.html.

Morgan, Fiona. "Banning the Bullies." *Salon,* March 15, 2001. http://www.salon.com/news/feature/2001/03/15/bullying/index.html.

■ **18. ARTICLE IN A NEWSPAPER** For newspaper articles—whether in print or online—page numbers are not necessary. A section letter or number, if available, is sufficient.

18. Dan Barry, "A Mill Closes, and a Hamlet Fades to Black," *New York Times,* February 16, 2001, sec. A.

Barry, Dan. "A Mill Closes, and a Hamlet Fades to Black." *New York Times,* February 16, 2001, sec. A.

For an article accessed through a database such as *ProQuest* or for an article published online, include a URL.

*Newspaper article from a database service*

18. Gina Kolata, "Scientists Debating Future of Hormone Replacement," *New York Times,* October 23, 2002, http://www.proquest.com.

Kolata, Gina. "Scientists Debating Future of Hormone Replacement." *New York Times,* October 23, 2002. http://www.proquest.com.

*Newpaper article published online*

18. Phil Willon, "Ready or Not," *Los Angeles Times,* December 2, 2001, http://www.latimes.com/news/la-foster-special.special.

Willon, Phil. "Ready or Not." *Los Angeles Times,* December 2, 2001. http://www.latimes.com/news/la-foster-special.special.

■ **19. UNSIGNED ARTICLE** When the author of a periodical article is unknown, treat the periodical itself as the author.

19. *Boston Globe,* "Renewable Energy Rules," August 11, 2003, sec. A.

*Boston Globe.* "Renewable Energy Rules." August 11, 2003, sec. A.

■ **20. BOOK REVIEW**

20. Nancy Gabin, review of *The Other Feminists: Activists in the Liberal Establishment,* by Susan M. Hartman, *Journal of Women's History* 12, no. 3 (2000): 230.

Gabin, Nancy. Review of *The Other Feminists: Activists in the Liberal
    Establishment,* by Susan M. Hartman. *Journal of Women's History*
    12, no. 3 (2000): 227-34.


## Web sites and postings

■ **21. WEB SITE** Include as much of the following information as is available: author, title of the site, sponsor of the
site, and the site's URL. When no author is named, treat the
sponsor as the author.

21. Kevin Rayburn, *The 1920s,* http://www.louisville.edu/
~kprayb01/1920s.html.

Rayburn, Kevin. *The 1920s.* http://www.louisville.edu/~kprayb01/
    1920s.html.

**NOTE:** *The Chicago Manual of Style* does not advise including
the date you accessed a Web source, but you may provide
an access date after the URL if the cited material is time-
sensitive: for example, http://www.historychannel.com/today
(accessed May 1, 2005).

■ **22. SHORT DOCUMENT FROM A WEB SITE** Include as many of
the following elements as are available: author's name, title
of the short work, title of the site, sponsor of the site, and
the URL. When no author is named, treat the site's sponsor
as the author.

22. Sheila Connor, "Historical Background," *Garden and Forest,*
Library of Congress, http://lcweb.loc.gov/preserv/prd/gardfor/
historygf.html.

Connor, Sheila. "Historical Background." *Garden and Forest.* Library of
    Congress. http://lcweb.loc.gov/preserv/prd/gardfor/historygf.html.

22. PBS Online, "Media Giants," *Frontline: The Merchants of Cool,*
http://www.pbs.org/wgbh/pages/frontline/shows/cool/giants.

PBS Online. "Media Giants." *Frontline: The Merchants of Cool.*
http://www.pbs.org/wgbh/pages/frontline/shows/cool/giants.

■ **23. ONLINE POSTING OR E-MAIL**  If an online posting has been archived, include a URL, as in the following example. E-mails that are not part of an online discussion are treated as personal communications (see item 26). Online postings and e-mails are not included in the bibliography.

23. Janice Klein, posting to State Museum Association discussion list, June 19, 2003, http://listserv.nmmnh-abq.mus.nm.us/scripts/wa.exe?A2=ind0306c&L=sma-l&F=lf&S=&P=81.

### *Other sources (print, online, multimedia)*

■ **24. GOVERNMENT DOCUMENT**

24. U.S. Department of State, *Foreign Relations of the United States: Diplomatic Papers, 1943* (Washington, DC: GPO, 1965), 562.

U.S. Department of State. *Foreign Relations of the United States: Diplomatic Papers, 1943.* Washington, DC: GPO, 1965.

■ **25. UNPUBLISHED DISSERTATION**

25. Stephanie Lynn Budin, "The Origins of Aphrodite (Greece)" (PhD diss., University of Pennsylvania, 2000), 301-2.

Budin, Stephanie Lynn. "The Origins of Aphrodite (Greece)." PhD diss., University of Pennsylvania, 2000.

■ **26. PERSONAL COMMUNICATION**

26. Sara Lehman, e-mail message to author, August 13, 2003.

Personal communications are not included in the bibliography.

■ **27. PUBLISHED OR BROADCAST INTERVIEW**

27. Ron Haviv, interview by Charlie Rose, *The Charlie Rose Show,* PBS, February 12, 2001.

Haviv, Ron. Interview by Charlie Rose. *The Charlie Rose Show,* PBS, February 12, 2001.

## 28. VIDEO OR DVD

28. *The Secret of Roan Inish,* DVD, directed by John Sayles (1993; Culver City, CA: Columbia TriStar Home Video, 2000).

*The Secret of Roan Inish.* DVD. Directed by John Sayles. 1993; Culver City, CA: Columbia TriStar Home Video, 2000.

## 29. SOUND RECORDING

29. Gustav Holst, *The Planets,* Royal Philharmonic, André Previn, Telarc compact disc 80133.

Holst, Gustav. *The Planets.* Royal Philharmonic. André Previn. Telarc compact disc 80133.

## 30. SOURCE QUOTED IN ANOTHER SOURCE

30. Adam Smith, *The Wealth of Nations* (New York: Random House, 1965), 11, quoted in Mark Skousen, *The Making of Modern Economics: The Lives and the Ideas of the Great Thinkers* (Armonk, NY: M. E. Sharpe, 2001), 15.

Smith, Adam. *The Wealth of Nations,* 11. New York: Random House, 1965. Quoted in Mark Skousen, *The Making of Modern Economics: The Lives and the Ideas of the Great Thinkers* (Armonk, NY: M. E. Sharpe, 2001), 15.

**ON THE WEB**
**dianahacker.com/bedhandbook**
▶ Electronic research exercises
▶ E-ex 61–12 to 61–16

## 61e *Chicago* manuscript format

The following guidelines for formatting a *Chicago* paper and preparing its endnotes and bibliography are based on *The Chicago Manual of Style,* 15th ed. For pages from a sample paper, see 61f.

### Formatting the paper

*Chicago* manuscript guidelines are fairly generic, since they were not created with a specific type of writing in mind.

**TITLE PAGE**   Include the full title of your paper, your name, the course title, the instructor's name, and the date. Do not number the title page but count it in the manuscript numbering; that is, the first page of the text will be numbered 2. See page 785 for a sample title page.

**PAGINATION**   Using arabic numerals, number all pages except the title page in the upper right corner. Depending on your instructor's preference, you may also use a short title or your last name before the page numbers to help identify pages in case they come loose from your manuscript.

**MARGINS AND LINE SPACING**   Leave margins of at least one inch at the top, bottom, and sides of the page. Double-space the entire manuscript, including long quotations that have been set off from the text. (For line spacing in notes and the bibliography, see pp. 783 and 784.) Left-align the text.

**LONG QUOTATIONS**   When a quotation is fairly long, set it off from the text by indenting (see also pp. 764–65). Indent the full quotation one-half inch (five spaces) from the left margin. Quotation marks are not needed when a quotation has been set off from the text.

**VISUALS**    *The Chicago Manual* classifies visuals as tables and illustrations (illustrations, or figures, include drawings, photographs, maps, and charts). Keep visuals as simple as possible. Label each table with an arabic numeral (Table 1, Table 2, and so on) and provide a clear title that identifies the subject. The label and title should appear on separate lines above the table, flush left. Below the table, give its source in a note like this one:

> *Source:* Edna Bonacich and Richard P. Appelbaum, *Behind the Label* (Berkeley: University of California Press, 2000), 145.

For each figure, place a label and a caption below the figure, flush left. The label and caption need not appear on separate lines. The word "Figure" may be abbreviated to "Fig."

In the text of your paper, discuss the most significant features of each visual. Place visuals as close as possible to the sentences that relate to them unless your instructor prefers them in an appendix.

### Preparing the endnotes

Begin the endnotes on a new page at the end of the paper. Center the title Notes about one inch from the top of the page, and number the pages consecutively with the rest of the manuscript. See pages 788–89 for an example.

**INDENTING AND NUMBERING**    Indent the first line of each note one-half inch (or five spaces) from the left margin; do not indent additional lines in the note. Begin the note with the arabic numeral that corresponds to the number in the text. Put a period after the number.

**LINE SPACING**    Single space each note and double-space between notes (unless your instructor prefers double-spacing throughout).

*Preparing the bibliography*

Typically, the notes in *Chicago*-style papers are followed by a bibliography, an alphabetically arranged list of all the works cited or consulted (see p. 790 for an example). Center the title Bibliography about one inch from the top of the page. Number bibliography pages consecutively with the rest of the paper.

**ALPHABETIZING THE LIST**   Alphabetize the bibliography by the last names of the authors (or editors); when a work has no author or editor, alphabetize it by the first word of the title other than *A, An,* or *The.*

If your list includes two or more works by the same author, use three hyphens instead of the author's name in all entries after the first. You may arrange the entries alphabetically by title or by date; be consistent throughout the bibliography.

**INDENTING AND LINE SPACING**   Begin each entry at the left margin, and indent any additional lines one-half inch (or five spaces). Single-space each entry and double-space between entries (unless your instructor prefers double-spacing throughout).

**61f** Sample pages from a research paper: *Chicago* style

Following are sample pages from a research paper by Ned Bishop, a student in a history class. (The complete paper is available on the *Bedford Handbook* Web site.) Bishop was asked to document his paper using *Chicago*-style endnotes and a bibliography. In preparing his manuscript, Bishop also followed *Chicago* guidelines.

**ON THE WEB**   dianahacker.com/bedhandbook
▶ Model papers
  ▶ *Chicago* paper

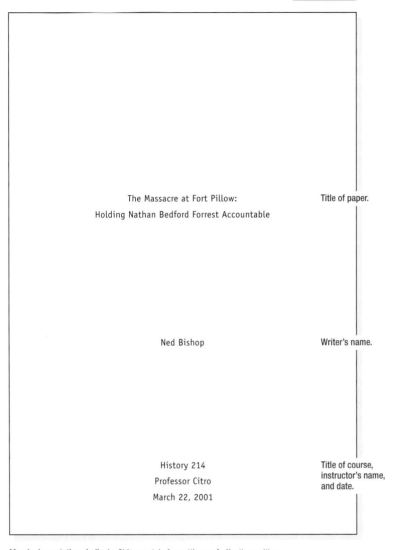

The Massacre at Fort Pillow:
Holding Nathan Bedford Forrest Accountable

Title of paper.

Ned Bishop

Writer's name.

History 214
Professor Citro
March 22, 2001

Title of course, instructor's name, and date.

Marginal annotations indicate *Chicago*-style formatting and effective writing.

Bishop 2

Although Northern newspapers of the time no doubt exaggerated some of the Confederate atrocities at Fort Pillow, most modern sources agree that a massacre of Union troops took place there on April 12, 1864. It seems clear that Union soldiers, particularly black soldiers, were killed after they had stopped fighting or had surrendered or were being held prisoner. Less clear is the role played by Major General Nathan Bedford Forrest in leading his troops. Although we will never know whether Forrest directly ordered the massacre, evidence suggests that he was responsible for it.

What happened at Fort Pillow?

Fort Pillow, Tennessee, which sat on a bluff overlooking the Mississippi River, had been held by the Union for two years. It was garrisoned by 580 men, 292 of them from the Sixth United States Colored Heavy and Light Cavalry, 285 from the white Thirteenth Tennessee Cavalry. Nathan Bedford Forrest's troops numbered about 1,500 men.[1]

The Confederates attacked Fort Pillow on April 12, 1864, and had virtually surrounded the fort by the time Forrest arrived on the battlefield. At 3:30 p.m., Forrest displayed a flag of truce and sent in a demand for unconditional surrender of the sort he had used before: "The conduct of the officers and men garrisoning Fort Pillow has been such as to entitle them to being treated as prisoners of war. . . . Should my demand be refused, I cannot be responsible for the fate of your command."[2] Union Major William Bradford, who had replaced Major Booth, killed earlier by sharpshooters, asked for an hour to consult. Forrest, worried that vessels in the river were bringing

*Thesis asserts writer's main point.*

*Headings help readers follow the organization.*

*Statistics are cited with an endnote.*

*Quotation is cited with an endnote.*

in more troops, shortened the time to twenty minutes. Bradford refused to surrender, and Forrest quickly ordered the attack.

The Confederates charged across the short distance between their lines and the fort, helping one another scale the parapet, from which they fired into the fort. Victory came quickly, with the Union forces running toward the river or surrendering. Shelby Foote describes the scene like this:

> Some kept going, right into the river, where a number drowned and the swimmers became targets for marksmen on the bluff. Others, dropping their guns in terror, ran back toward the Confederates with their hands up, and of these some were spared as prisoners, while others were shot down in the act of surrender.[3]

In his own official report, Forrest makes no mention of the massacre. He does make much of the fact that the Union flag was not taken down, saying that if his own men had not taken down the flag, "few if any, would have survived unhurt another volley."[4] However, as Jack Hurst points out and Forrest must have known, in this twenty-minute battle, "Federals running for their lives had little time to concern themselves with a flag."[5]

The federal congressional report on Fort Pillow, which charged the Confederates with appalling atrocities, drew much criticism from Southern writers, and even respected writer Shelby Foote, who does not deny a massacre occurred, says it was largely a "tissue of lies."[6] In an important article, John Cimprich and Robert C. Mainfort Jr. argue that the most trust-

*Long quotation is set off from text by indenting. Quotation marks are omitted.*

*Writer uses a primary source as well as secondary sources.*

*Quotation is introduced with a signal phrase.*

*The writer draws attention to an important article containing primary sources.*

Bishop 8

Notes

First line of each note is indented ½" (or five spaces).

1. John Cimprich and Robert C. Mainfort Jr., "Fort Pillow Revisited: New Evidence about an Old Controversy," *Civil War History* 28, no. 4 (1982): 293-94.

Note number is not raised and is followed by a period.

2. Quoted in Brian Steel Wills, *A Battle from the Start: The Life of Nathan Bedford Forrest* (New York: HarperCollins, 1992), 182.

3. Shelby Foote, *The Civil War, a Narrative: Red River to Appomattox* (New York: Vintage, 1986), 110.

Authors' names are not inverted.

4. Nathan Bedford Forrest, "Report of Maj. Gen. Nathan B. Forrest, C. S. Army, Commanding Cavalry, of the Capture of Fort Pillow," *Shotgun's Home of the American Civil War,* http://www.civilwarhome.com/forrest.htm.

5. Jack Hurst, *Nathan Bedford Forrest: A Biography* (New York: Knopf, 1993), 174.

Last name and title refer to an earlier note by the same author.

6. Foote, *Civil War,* 111.

7. Cimprich and Mainfort, "Fort Pillow," 305.

8. Ibid., 299.

9. Foote, *Civil War,* 110.

10. Wills, *Battle from the Start,* 187.

Notes are single-spaced, with double-spacing between notes. (Some instructors may prefer double-spacing throughout.)

11. Albert Castel, "The Fort Pillow Massacre: A Fresh Examination of the Evidence," *Civil War History* 4, no. 1 (1958): 44-45.

12. Cimprich and Mainfort, "Fort Pillow," 300.

13. Hurst, *Nathan Bedford Forrest,* 177.

14. Ibid.

15. Dudley Taylor Cornish, *The Sable Arm: Black Troops in the Union Army, 1861-1865* (Lawrence, KS: University Press of Kansas, 1987), 175.

16. Foote, *Civil War,* 111.

17. Cimprich and Mainfort, "Fort Pillow," 304.

18. Wills, *Battle from the Start,* 189.

19. Ibid., 215.

20. Hurst, *Nathan Bedford Forrest,* 177.

21. James M. McPherson, *Battle Cry of Freedom: The Civil War Era* (New York: Oxford University Press, 1988), 402.

22. Hurst, *Nathan Bedford Forrest,* 74.

23. Foote, *Civil War,* 106.

Bishop 10

Bibliography

Entries are alphabet-
ized by authors' last
names.

Castel, Albert. "The Fort Pillow Massacre: A Fresh Examination
of the Evidence." *Civil War History* 4, no. 1 (1958):
37-50.

Cimprich, John, and Robert C. Mainfort Jr. "Fort Pillow Revisited: New Evidence about an Old Controversy." *Civil War
History* 28, no. 4 (1982): 293-306.

First line of entry
is at left margin;
additional lines are
indented ½" (or five
spaces).

Cornish, Dudley Taylor. *The Sable Arm: Black Troops in the
Union Army, 1861-1865.* Lawrence, KS: University Press of
Kansas, 1987.

Foote, Shelby. *The Civil War, a Narrative: Red River to Appomattox.* New York: Vintage, 1986.

Forrest, Nathan Bedford. "Report of Maj. Gen. Nathan B. Forrest, C. S. Army, Commanding Cavalry, of the Capture of
Fort Pillow." *Shotgun's Home of the American Civil War.*
http://www.civilwarhome.com/forrest.htm.

Entries are single-
spaced, with double-
spacing between
entries. (Some
instructors may pre-
fer double-spacing
throughout.)

Hurst, Jack. *Nathan Bedford Forrest: A Biography.* New York:
Knopf, 1993.

McPherson, James M. *Battle Cry of Freedom: The Civil War Era.*
New York: Oxford University Press, 1988.

Wills, Brian Steel. *A Battle from the Start: The Life of Nathan
Bedford Forrest.* New York: HarperCollins, 1992.

# Part XI

# Grammar
# Basics

# 62

## Parts of speech

Traditional grammar recognizes eight parts of speech: noun, pronoun, verb, adjective, adverb, preposition, conjunction, and interjection. Many words can function as more than one part of speech. For example, depending on its use in a sentence, the word *paint* can be a noun (*The paint is wet*) or a verb (*Please paint the ceiling next*).

A quick-reference chart of the parts of speech appears on pages 807–09.

### 62a Nouns

As most schoolchildren can attest, a noun is the name of a person, place, or thing.

>     **N**       **N**             **N**
> The *cat* in *gloves* catches no *mice*.

In addition to the traditional definition of a noun, grammarians describe a noun as follows:

- the kind of word that is often marked with an article (a *spoon*, an *apple*, the *newspaper*)
- the kind of word that can usually be made plural (one *cat*, two *cats*) or possessive (the *cat's* paw)
- the kind of word that when derived from another word typically takes one of the following italicized endings: play*er*, just*ice*, happi*ness*, divis*ion*, guid*ance*, refer*ence*, pave*ment*, child*hood*, king*dom*, agen*cy*, tour*ist*, sincer*ity*, censor*ship*

---

**SCHOLARS ON GRAMMAR BASICS**

Weaver, Constance. *Teaching Grammar in Context.* Portsmouth: Boynton, 1996. Weaver's six chapters include an analysis of the meanings of "grammar," a brief overview of the history of grammar instruction, a summary of the arguments for and against teaching grammar, a discussion of error, and an exploration of the relation between learning theory and grammar instruction. Her appendix includes mini-lessons that demonstrate what she means by "teaching grammar in context."

Lindemann, Erika. *A Rhetoric for Writing Teachers.* 4th ed. New York: Oxford UP, 2001. 60–85. Lindemann examines several different approaches to grammar and provides brief overviews of structural and generative-transformational grammars.

- the kind of word that can fill one of these slots in a sentence: subject, direct object, indirect object, subject complement, object complement, object of the preposition (See 63.)

Nouns, in other words, may be identified as much by their form and function as by their meaning.

Nouns sometimes function as adjectives modifying other nouns. Because of their dual roles, nouns used in this manner may be called *noun/adjectives.*

          **N/ADJ**              **N/ADJ**
You can't make a *silk* purse out of a *sow's* ear.

Nouns are classified for a variety of purposes. When capitalization is the issue, we speak of *proper* versus *common nouns* (see 45a). If the problem is one of word choice, we may speak of *concrete* versus *abstract nouns* (see 18b). The distinction between *count nouns* and *noncount nouns* is useful primarily for nonnative speakers of English (see 30a and 30b). The term *collective noun* refers to a set of nouns that may cause problems with subject-verb or pronoun-antecedent agreement (see 21f and 22b).

**EXERCISE 62–1**    Underline the nouns (and noun/adjectives) in the following sentences. Answers to lettered sentences appear in the back of the book. Example:

    Idle <u>hands</u> are the <u>devil's</u> <u>workshop</u>.

  a.  The sun will set without your assistance.    —Hebrew proverb
  b.  Pride is at the bottom of all great mistakes.    —John Ruskin
  c.  Success breeds confidence.    —Beryl Markham
  d.  The ultimate censorship is the flick of the dial.
                          —Tom Smothers

**EXERCISE 62–1**    **Answers:**

a. sun, assistance; b. Pride, bottom, mistakes; c. Success, confidence; d. censorship, flick, dial; e. flower, concrete (noun/adjective), cloverleaf

1. Truthfulness, ruthlessness; 2. Luck, matter, preparation, opportunity; 3. Problems, opportunities, work (noun/adjective), clothes; 4. woman, money, room; 5. Language, limits, reality

e.  Our national flower is the concrete cloverleaf.
—Lewis Mumford

1.  Truthfulness so often goes with ruthlessness.   —Dodie Smith
2.  Luck is a matter of preparation meeting opportunity.
—Oprah Winfrey
3.  Problems are only opportunities in work clothes.
—Henry Kaiser
4.  A woman must have money and a room of her own.
—Virginia Woolf
5.  Language helps form the limits of our reality.   —Dale Spender

---

**ON THE WEB**

**dianahacker.com/bedhandbook**
▶ Electronic grammar exercises
  ▶ E-ex 62–1

---

## 62b Pronouns

There are thousands of nouns, and new ones come into the language every year. This is not true of pronouns, which number about one hundred and are extremely resistant to change. Most of the pronouns in English are listed in this section.

A pronoun is a word used in place of a noun. Usually the pronoun substitutes for a specific noun, known as its *antecedent.*

When the *wheel* squeaks, *it* is greased.

Although most pronouns function as substitutes for nouns, some can function as adjectives modifying nouns.

*This* bird always catches the worm.

---

**SCHOLARS ON GRAMMAR BASICS**

Parker, Frank, and Kim Sydow Campbell. "Linguistics and Writing: A Reassessment." *College Composition and Communication* 44 (1993): 295–314. Responding to arguments that linguistics has not contributed significantly to composition studies, Parker and Campbell reevaluate the relevance of linguistics to writing instruction. They point to recent approaches to linguistics that move beyond the sentence level and focus on language in its fuller discourse contexts. Such approaches, they suggest, can provide a theoretical foundation for composition pedagogy.

Because they have the form of a pronoun and the function of an adjective, such pronouns may be called *pronoun/adjectives*.

Pronouns are classified as personal, possessive, intensive and reflexive, relative, interrogative, demonstrative, indefinite, and reciprocal.

**PERSONAL PRONOUNS**   Personal pronouns refer to specific persons or things. They always function as noun equivalents.

> *Singular:* I, me, you, she, her, he, him, it
>
> *Plural:* we, us, you, they, them

**POSSESSIVE PRONOUNS**   Possessive pronouns indicate ownership.

> *Singular:* my, mine, your, yours, her, hers, his, its
>
> *Plural:* our, ours, your, yours, their, theirs

Some of these possessive pronouns function as adjectives modifying nouns: *my, your, his, her, its, our, their.*

**INTENSIVE AND REFLEXIVE PRONOUNS**   Intensive pronouns emphasize a noun or another pronoun (The senator *herself* met us at the door). Reflexive pronouns, which have the same form as intensive pronouns, name a receiver of an action identical with the doer of the action (Paula cut *herself*).

> *Singular:* myself, yourself, himself, herself, itself
>
> *Plural:* ourselves, yourselves, themselves

**RELATIVE PRONOUNS**   Relative pronouns introduce subordinate clauses functioning as adjectives (The man *who robbed us* was never caught). In addition to introducing the

---

**SCHOLARS ON GRAMMAR BASICS**

Noguchi, Rei R. *Grammar and the Teaching of Writing: Limits and Possibilities.* Urbana: NCTE, 1991. Though grammar instruction has a place in writing classes, the role of such instruction "will need to be a much more selective and efficient one than that currently played," Noguchi argues. He recommends that instructors introduce only basic categories such as subjects, verbs, and modifiers. "Ultimately," he says, "the choice and number of categories and principles will be determined by their utility in treating the most frequent and most socially consequential writing errors."

clause, the relative pronoun, in this case *who,* points back to a noun or pronoun that the clause modifies (*man*). (See 64b.)

who, whom, whose, which, that

Some textbooks also treat *whichever, whoever, whomever, what,* and *whatever* as relative pronouns. These words introduce noun clauses; they do not point back to a noun or pronoun. (See 64b.)

**INTERROGATIVE PRONOUNS**  Interrogative pronouns introduce questions (*Who* is expected to win the election?).

who, whom, whose, which, what

**DEMONSTRATIVE PRONOUNS**  Demonstrative pronouns identify or point to nouns. Frequently they function as adjectives (*This* chair is my favorite), but they may also function as noun equivalents (*This* is my favorite chair).

this, that, these, those

**INDEFINITE PRONOUNS**  Indefinite pronouns refer to nonspecific persons or things. Most are always singular (*everyone, each*); some are always plural (*both, many*); a few may be singular or plural (see 21e). Most indefinite pronouns function as noun equivalents (*Something* is burning), but some can also function as adjectives (*All* campers must check in at the lodge).

| | | | | |
|---|---|---|---|---|
| all | anything | everyone | nobody | several |
| another | both | everything | none | some |
| any | each | few | no one | somebody |
| anybody | either | many | nothing | someone |
| anyone | everybody | neither | one | something |

**SCHOLARS ON GRAMMAR BASICS**

Crowley, Sharon. "Linguistics and Composition Instruction: 1950–1980." *Written Communication* 6 (1989): 480–505. Crowley surveys the relation between composition studies and linguistics over three decades.

Harris, Muriel, and Katherine E. Rowan. "Explaining Grammatical Concepts." *Journal of Basic Writing* 8.2 (1989): 21–41. Arguing that "many tried-and-true explanations of grammar are COIK — clear only if known," Harris and Rowan describe a combination of techniques that instructors can use to teach grammatical concepts.

**RECIPROCAL PRONOUNS**   Reciprocal pronouns refer to individual parts of a plural antecedent (By turns, we helped *each other* through college).

each other, one another

**NOTE:** Pronouns cause a variety of problems for writers. See pronoun-antecedent agreement (22), pronoun reference (23), distinguishing between pronouns such as *I* and *me* (24), and distinguishing between *who* and *whom* (25).

**EXERCISE 62–2**   Underline the pronouns (and pronoun/adjectives) in the following sentences. Answers to lettered sentences appear in the back of the book. Example:

Always beware of persons <u>who</u> are praised by

<u>everyone</u>.

a.  He has every attribute of a dog except loyalty.  —Thomas Gore
b.  A fall does not hurt those who fly low.        —Chinese proverb
c.  I have written some poetry that I myself don't understand.
                                                —Carl Sandburg
d.  I am firm. You are obstinate. He is a pig-headed fool.
                                                —Katherine Whitehorn
e.  If you haven't anything nice to say about anyone, come and sit
    by me.                                —Alice Roosevelt Longworth

1.  Men are taught to apologize for their weaknesses, women for
    their strengths.                              —Lois Wyse
2.  Nothing is interesting if you are not interested.
                                                —Helen MacInness
3.  We will never have friends if we expect to find them without
    fault.                                      —Thomas Fuller
4.  The gods help those who help themselves.          —Aesop
5.  I awoke one morning and found myself famous.  —Lord Byron

**EXERCISE 62–2   Answers:**

a. He, every (pronoun/adjective); b. those, who; c. I, some (pronoun/adjective), that, I, myself; d. I, You, He; e. you, anything, anyone, me

1. their (pronoun/adjective), their (pronoun/adjective); 2. Nothing, you; 3. We, we, them; 4. those, who, themselves; 5. I, myself

**ON THE WEB**

**dianahacker.com/bedhandbook**
▶ Electronic grammar exercises
  ▶ E-ex 62–2

## 62c Verbs

The verb of a sentence usually expresses action (*jump, think*) or being (*is, become*). It is composed of a main verb possibly preceded by one or more helping verbs.

MV
The best fish *swim* near the bottom.

HV    MV
A marriage *is* not *built* in a day.

HV  HV     MV
Even God *has been defended* with nonsense.

Notice that words can intervene between the helping and the main verb (is *not* built).

### Helping verbs

There are twenty-three helping verbs in English: forms of *have, do,* and *be,* which may also function as main verbs; and nine modals, which function only as helping verbs. The forms of *have, do,* and *be* change form to indicate tense; the nine modals do not.

**FORMS OF *HAVE, DO,* AND *BE***

have, has, had

do, does, did

be, am, is, are, was, were, being, been

---

**SCHOLARS ON GRAMMAR BASICS**

Sedgwick, Ellery. "Alternatives to Teaching Formal, Analytical Grammar." *Journal of Developmental Education* 12.3 (1989): 8+. Sedgwick suggests techniques such as sentence combining, imitation exercises, and inductive grammar in place of formal grammatical instruction. He discusses a variety of ways to teach editing and proofreading skills, including peer editing, student-teacher conferences, and selective marking of errors.

**MODALS**
can, could, may, might, must, shall, should, will, would

The phrase *ought to* is often classified as a modal as well.

### Main verbs

The main verb of a sentence is always the kind of word that would change form if put into these test sentences:

| | |
|---|---|
| **BASE FORM** | Usually I (*walk, ride*). |
| **PAST TENSE** | Yesterday I (*walked, rode*). |
| **PAST PARTICIPLE** | I have (*walked, ridden*) many times before. |
| **PRESENT PARTICIPLE** | I am (*walking, riding*) right now. |
| **-S FORM** | Usually he/she/it (*walks, rides*). |

If a word doesn't change form when slipped into these test sentences, you can be certain that it is not a main verb. For example, the noun *revolution,* though it may seem to suggest an action, can never function as a main verb. Just try to make it behave like one (*Today I revolution...Yesterday I revolutioned...*) and you'll see why.

When both the past-tense and the past-participle forms of a verb end in *-ed,* the verb is regular (*walked, walked*). Otherwise, the verb is irregular (*rode, ridden*). (See 27a.)

The verb *be* is highly irregular, having eight forms instead of the usual five: the base form *be;* the present-tense forms *am, is,* and *are;* the past-tense forms *was* and *were;* the present participle *being;* and the past participle *been.*

Helping verbs combine with the various forms of main verbs to create tenses. For a survey of tenses, see 28a.

**NOTE:** Some verbs are followed by words that look like prepositions but are so closely associated with the verb

**SCHOLARS ON GRAMMAR BASICS**

Connors, Robert J. "Grammar in American College Composition: An Historical Overview." *The Territory of Language: Linguistics, Stylistics, and the Teaching of Composition.* Ed. Donald A. McQuade. Carbondale: Southern Illinois UP, 1986. 3–22. Connors surveys how grammar has affected the teaching of writing from the mid-nineteenth century and finds that a "great deal of the history of composition in America seems to be a clumsy shuffle-dance of grammar with rhetoric, with first one and then another leading."

that they are a part of its meaning. These words are known as *particles*. Common verb-particle combinations include *bring up, call off, drop off, give in, look up, run into,* and *take off.*

> A lot of parents *pack up* their troubles and *send* them *off* to camp. —Raymond Duncan

**NOTE:** Verbs cause many problems for writers. See active verbs (8), subject-verb agreement (21), standard English verb forms (27), verb tense and mood (28), and ESL problems with verbs (29).

**EXERCISE 62–3** Underline the verbs in the following sentences, including helping verbs and particles. If a verb is part of a contraction (such as *is* in *isn't* or *would* in *I'd*), underline only the letters that represent the verb. Answers to lettered sentences appear in the back of the book. Example:

A full cup <u>must</u> <u>be carried</u> steadily.

a. I can pardon everyone's mistakes except my own. —Cato
b. There are no atheists on turbulent airplanes. —Erica Jong
c. One arrow does not bring down two birds. —Turkish proverb
d. Keep your talent in the dark, and you'll never be insulted. —Elsa Maxwell
e. Throw a lucky man into the sea, and he will emerge with a fish in his mouth. —Arab proverb

1. Do not scald your tongue in other people's broth. —English proverb
2. Wrong must not win by technicalities. —Aeschylus
3. Love your neighbor, but don't pull down the hedge. —Swiss proverb
4. I'd rather have roses on my table than diamonds around my neck. —Emma Goldman
5. He is a fine friend. He stabs you in the front. —Leonard Louis Levinson

**EXERCISE 62–3 Answers:**

a. can pardon; b. are; c. does bring down; d. Keep, 'll [will] be insulted; e. Throw, will emerge

1. Do scald; 2. must win; 3. Love, do pull down; 4. 'd [would] have; 5. is, stabs

## 62d Adjectives

An adjective is a word used to modify, or describe, a noun or pronoun. An adjective usually answers one of these questions: Which one? What kind of? How many?

**ADJ**
the *lame* elephant [Which elephant?]

**ADJ  ADJ**
*valuable old* stamps [What kind of stamps?]

**ADJ**
*sixteen* candles [How many candles?]

Grammarians also define adjectives according to their form and their typical position in a sentence, as follows:

- the kind of word that usually comes before a noun in a noun phrase (a *frisky* puppy, an *amiable young* man)
- the kind of word that can follow a linking verb and describe the subject (the ship was *unsinkable;* talk is *cheap*) (See 63b.)
- the kind of word that when derived from another part of speech typically takes one of the following italicized endings: wonder*ful,* courte*ous,* luck*y,* fool*ish,* pleasur*able,* colon*ial,* help*less,* defens*ible,* urg*ent,* disgust*ing,* friend*ly,* spectacu*lar,* secret*ive*

The definite article *the* and the indefinite articles *a* and *an* are also classified as adjectives.

**WRITERS ON WRITING**

As to the adjective, when in doubt, strike it out. — Mark Twain

The adjective is the banana peel of the parts of speech.
— Clifton Fadiman

The adjective is the enemy of the noun. — Voltaire

Some possessive, demonstrative, and indefinite pronouns can function as adjectives: *their, its, this* (see 62b).

**NOTE:** Writers sometimes misuse adjectives (see 26b). Speakers of English as a second language often encounter problems with the articles *a, an,* and *the* and occasionally have trouble placing adjectives correctly (see 30 and 31d).

## 62e Adverbs

An adverb is a word used to modify, or qualify, a verb (or verbal), an adjective, or another adverb. It usually answers one of these questions: When? Where? How? Why? Under what conditions? To what degree?

> Pull *gently* at a weak rope. [Pull how?]
>
> Read the best books *first.* [Read when?]

Adverbs that modify a verb are also defined according to their form and their typical position in a sentence, as follows:

- the kind of word that can appear nearly anywhere in a sentence and is often movable (he *sometimes* jogged after work; *sometimes* he jogged after work)
- the kind of word that when derived from an adjective typically takes an *-ly* ending (nice, nice*ly;* profound, profound*ly*)

Adverbs modifying adjectives or other adverbs usually intensify or limit the intensity of the word they modify.

> **ADV** **ADV**
> Be *extremely* good, and you will be *very* lonesome.

Adverbs modifying adjectives and other adverbs are not movable. We can't say "Be good *extremely*" or "*Extremely* be good."

---

**WRITERS ON WRITING**

If the noun is good and the verb is strong, you almost never need an adjective. —J. Anthony Lukas

Don't say it "was delightful"; make us say "delightful" when we've read the description. You see, all those words (horrifying, wonderful, hideous, exquisite) are only like saying to your readers "Please will you do my job for me?" —C. S. Lewis

The negators *not* and *never* are classified as adverbs. A word such as *cannot* contains the helping verb *can* and the adverb *not*. A contraction such as *can't* contains the helping verb *can* and a contracted form of the adverb *not*.

Adverbs can modify prepositional phrases (The budget is *barely* on target), subordinate clauses (We will try to attend, *especially* if you will be there), or whole sentences (*Certainly* Joe did not intend to insult you).

**NOTE:** Writers sometimes misuse adverbs (see 26a). Speakers of English as a second language may have trouble placing adverbs correctly (see 31d).

**EXERCISE 62–4**    Underline the adjectives and circle the adverbs in the following sentences. If a word is a pronoun in form but an adjective in function, treat it as an adjective. Also treat the articles *a, an,* and *the* as adjectives. Answers to lettered sentences appear in the back of the book. Example:

> A wild goose (never) laid a tame egg.

a. General notions are generally wrong.
> —Lady Mary Wortley Montagu

b. The American public is wonderfully tolerant.
> —Anonymous

c. Wildflowers sometimes grow in an uncultivated field, but they never bloom in an uncultivated mind.
> —Anonymous

d. I'd rather be strongly wrong than weakly right.
> —Tallulah Bankhead

e. Sleep faster. We need the pillows.        —Yiddish proverb

1. Success is a public affair; failure is a private funeral.
> —Rosalind Russell

2. Their civil discussions were not interesting, and their interesting discussions were not civil.        —Lisa Alther

3. Money will buy a pretty good dog, but it will not buy the wag of its tail.        —Josh Billings

**EXERCISE 62–4    Answers:**

a. Adjectives: General, wrong; adverb: generally; b. Adjectives: The (article), American, tolerant; adverb: wonderfully; c. Adjectives: an (article), uncultivated, an (article), uncultivated; adverbs: sometimes, never; d. Adjectives: wrong, right; adverbs: rather, strongly, weakly; e. Adjective: the (article); adverb: faster

1. Adjectives: a (article), public, a (article), private; 2. Adjectives: Their (pronoun/adjective), civil, interesting, their (pronoun/adjective), interesting, civil; adverbs: not, not; 3. Adjectives: a (article), good, the (article), its (pronoun/adjective); adverbs: pretty, not; 4. Adjectives: careful, the (article), our (pronoun/adjective); adverbs: not, too; 5. Adjective: untidy

4.  We cannot be too careful in the choice of our enemies.

— Oscar Wilde

5.  Feelings are untidy.

— Esther Hautzig

> **ON THE WEB**
>
> **dianahacker.com/bedhandbook**
> ▶ Electronic grammar exercises
>   ▶ E-ex 62–5 and 62–6

## 62f Prepositions

A preposition is a word placed before a noun or pronoun to form a phrase modifying another word in the sentence. The prepositional phrase nearly always functions as an adjective or as an adverb.

P                          P

The road *to* hell is usually paved *with* good intentions.

*To hell* functions as an adjective, modifying the noun *road;* *with good intentions* functions as an adverb, modifying the verb *is paved.* (For more about prepositional phrases, see 64a.)

There are a limited number of prepositions in English. The most common ones are included in the following list.

| | | | | |
|---|---|---|---|---|
| about | before | considering | like | over |
| above | behind | despite | near | past |
| across | below | down | next | plus |
| after | beside | during | of | regarding |
| against | besides | except | off | respecting |
| along | between | for | on | round |
| among | beyond | from | onto | since |
| around | but | in | opposite | than |
| as | by | inside | out | through |
| at | concerning | into | outside | throughout |

### SCHOLARS ON GRAMMAR BASICS

Hartwell, Patrick. "Grammar, Grammars, and the Teaching of Grammar." *College English* 47 (1985): 105–27. As part of his attempt to move beyond disputes about the value of teaching formal grammar in composition courses, Hartwell carefully defines the term *grammar* and offers five meanings. These meanings range from Grammar 1, "the grammar in our heads," or the internal system of rules that native speakers of a language share, to Grammar 5, stylistic grammar, which consists of "grammatical terms used in the interest of teaching prose style."

| till | under | until | upon | without |
|------|-------|-------|------|---------|
| to | underneath | unto | with | |
| toward | unlike | up | within | |

Some prepositions are more than one word long. *Along with, as well as, in addition to,* and *next to* are common examples.

**NOTE:** Except for certain idiomatic uses (see 18d), prepositions cause few problems for native speakers of English. For multilingual speakers, however, prepositions can cause considerable difficulty (see 29d and 31f).

## 62g Conjunctions

Conjunctions join words, phrases, or clauses, and they indicate the relation between the elements joined.

**COORDINATING CONJUNCTIONS**   A coordinating conjunction is used to connect grammatically equal elements. The coordinating conjunctions are *and, but, or, nor, for, so,* and *yet.*

> Poverty is the parent of revolution *and* crime.

> Admire a little ship, *but* put your cargo in a big one.

In the first sentence, *and* connects two nouns; in the second, *but* connects two independent clauses.

**CORRELATIVE CONJUNCTIONS**   Correlative conjunctions come in pairs: *either ... or; neither ... nor; not only ... but also; whether ... or; both ... and.* Like coordinating conjunctions, they connect grammatically equal elements.

> *Either* Jack Sprat *or* his wife could eat no fat.

**SUBORDINATING CONJUNCTIONS**   A subordinating conjunction introduces a subordinate clause and indicates its

**SCHOLARS ON GRAMMAR BASICS**

Baron, Dennis. *Grammar and Good Taste: Reforming the American Language.* New Haven: Yale UP, 1982. Focusing primarily on eighteenth- and nineteenth-century America, Baron traces the history of our present-day concern for correctness in speech and writing and our continued suspicion of formal language regulation.

relation to the rest of the sentence. (See 64b.) The most common subordinating conjunctions are *after, although, as, as if, because, before, even though, how, if, in order that, once, rather than, since, so that, than, that, though, unless, until, when, where, whether, while,* and *why.*

*If* you want service, serve yourself.

**CONJUNCTIVE ADVERBS** A conjunctive adverb may be used with a semicolon to connect independent clauses; it usually serves as a transition between the clauses. The most common conjunctive adverbs are *consequently, finally, furthermore, however, moreover, nevertheless, similarly, then, therefore,* and *thus.* (See p. 809 for a longer list.)

When we want to murder a tiger, we call it sport; *however,* when the tiger wants to murder us, we call it ferocity.

**NOTE:** The ability to distinguish between conjunctive adverbs and coordinating conjunctions will help you avoid run-on sentences and make punctuation decisions (see 20, 32a, and 32b). The ability to recognize subordinating conjunctions will help you avoid sentence fragments (see 19).

## 62h Interjections

An interjection is a word used to express surprise or emotion (*Oh! Hey! Wow!*).

| | |
|---|---|
| ON THE WEB | **dianahacker.com/bedhandbook** ▶ Electronic grammar exercises      ▶ E-ex 62–7 |

**SCHOLARS ON GRAMMAR BASICS**

Quirk, Randolph, and Sidney Greenbaum. *A Concise Grammar of Contemporary English.* New York: Harcourt, 1973. This is a thorough survey of descriptive grammar.

## Parts of speech

A **NOUN** names a person, place, thing, or idea.

> N        N  N
> *Repetition* does not transform a *lie* into *truth.*

A **PRONOUN** substitutes for a noun.

>           PN PN   PN
> When the gods wish to punish *us, they* heed *our* prayers.

*Personal pronouns:* I, me, you, he, him, she, her, it, we, us, they, them

*Possessive pronouns:* my, mine, your, yours, her, hers, his, its, our, ours, their, theirs

*Intensive and reflexive pronouns:* myself, yourself, himself, herself, itself, ourselves, yourselves, themselves

*Relative pronouns:* that, which, who, whom, whose

*Interrogative pronouns:* who, whom, whose, which, what

*Demonstrative pronouns:* this, that, these, those

*Indefinite pronouns:* all, another, any, anybody, anyone, anything, both, each, either, everybody, everyone, everything, few, many, neither, nobody, none, no one, nothing, one, several, some, somebody, someone, something

*Reciprocal pronouns:* each other, one another

A **HELPING VERB** comes before a main verb.

*Modals:* can, could, may, might, must, shall, should, will, would (*also* ought to)

*Forms of* be: be, am, is, are, was, were, being, been

*Forms of* have: have, has, had

*Forms of* do: do, does, did

(*continued*)

## Parts of speech (*continued*)

(The forms of *be, have,* and *do* may also function as main verbs.)

A **MAIN VERB** asserts action, being, or state of being.

            MV                  HV      MV
Charity *begins* at home but *should* not *end* there.

A main verb will always change form when put into these positions in sentences:

| | |
|---|---|
| Usually I _____ . | (*walk, ride*) |
| Yesterday I _____ . | (*walked, rode*) |
| I have _____ many times before. | (*walked, ridden*) |
| I am _____ right now. | (*walking, riding*) |
| Usually he _____ . | (*walks, rides*) |

There are eight forms of the highly irregular verb *be: be, am, is, are, was, were, being, been.*

An **ADJECTIVE** modifies a noun or pronoun, usually answering one of these questions: Which one? What kind of? How many? The articles *a, an,* and *the* are also adjectives.

     ADJ                     ADJ
*Useless* laws weaken *necessary* ones.

An **ADVERB** modifies a verb, adjective, or adverb, usually answering one of these questions: When? Where? Why? How? Under what conditions? To what degree?

            ADV    ADV
People think *too historically.*

A **PREPOSITION** indicates the relationship between the noun or pronoun that follows it and another word in the sentence.

(*continued*)

## Parts of speech (*continued*)

　　　　　　P　　　　　　　　　　　　P
A journey *of* a thousand miles begins *with* a single step.

*Common prepositions:* about, above, across, after, against, along, among, around, as, at, before, behind, below, beside, besides, between, beyond, but, by, concerning, considering, despite, down, during, except, for, from, in, inside, into, like, near, next, of, off, on, onto, opposite, out, outside, over, past, plus, regarding, respecting, since, than, through, throughout, till, to, toward, under, underneath, unlike, until, unto, up, upon, with, within, without

A **CONJUNCTION** connects words or word groups.

*Coordinating conjunctions:* and, but, or, nor, for, so, yet

*Subordinating conjunctions:* after, although, as, as if, because, before, even though, how, if, in order that, once, rather than, since, so that, than, that, though, unless, until, when, where, whether, while, why

*Correlative conjunctions:* either . . . or, neither . . . nor, not only . . . but also, both . . . and, whether . . . or

*Conjunctive adverbs:* accordingly, also, anyway, besides, certainly, consequently, conversely, finally, furthermore, hence, however, incidentally, indeed, instead, likewise, meanwhile, moreover, nevertheless, next, nonetheless, otherwise, similarly, specifically, still, subsequently, then, therefore, thus

An **INTERJECTION** expresses surprise or emotion (*Oh! Wow! Hey! Hooray!*).

# 63

## Sentence patterns

Most English sentences flow from subject to verb to any objects or complements. The vast majority of sentences conform to one of these five patterns:

> subject / verb / subject complement
> subject / verb / direct object
> subject / verb / indirect object / direct object
> subject / verb / direct object / object complement
> subject / verb

Adverbial modifiers (single words, phrases, or clauses) may be added to any of these patterns, and they may appear nearly anywhere—at the beginning, the middle, or the end.

*Predicate* is the grammatical term given to the verb plus its objects, complements, and adverbial modifiers.

For a quick-reference chart of sentence patterns, see page 817.

### 63a  Subjects

The subject of a sentence names who or what the sentence is about. The *complete subject* is usually composed of a *simple subject,* always a noun or pronoun, plus any words or word groups modifying the simple subject.

#### The complete subject

To find the complete subject, ask Who? or What?, insert the verb, and finish the question. The answer is the complete subject.

---

**WRITERS ON WRITING**

Grammar is to a writer what anatomy is to a sculptor, or the scales to a musician. You may loathe it, it may bore you, but nothing will replace it, and once mastered it will support you like a rock.

—B. J. Chute

It is well to remember that grammar is common speech formulated.

—W. Somerset Maugham

Grammar is the analysis of language.          —Edgar Allan Poe

┌─ COMPLETE SUBJECT ─┐
The purity of a revolution usually lasts about two weeks.

Who or what lasts about two weeks? *The purity of a revolution.*

┌──────── COMPLETE SUBJECT ────────┐
Historical books that contain no lies are extremely tedious.

Who or what are extremely tedious? *Historical books that contain no lies.*

COMPLETE SUBJECT
In every country ┌the sun┐ rises in the morning.

Who or what rises in the morning? *The sun.* Notice that *In every country the sun* is not a sensible answer to the question. *In every country* is a prepositional phrase modifying the verb *rises.* Since sentences frequently open with such modifiers, it is not safe to assume that the subject must always appear first in a sentence.

### The simple subject

To find the simple subject, strip away all modifiers in the complete subject. This includes single-word modifiers such as *the* and *historical,* phrases such as *of a revolution,* and subordinate clauses such as *that contain no lies.*

┌ SS ┐
*The purity of a revolution* usually lasts about two weeks.

┌ SS ┐
*Historical books that contain no lies* are extremely tedious.

┌SS┐
In every country *the sun* rises in the morning.

A sentence may have a compound subject containing two or more simple subjects joined with a coordinating conjunction such as *and, but,* or *or.*

┌─ SS ─┐ ┌─ SS ─┐
*Much industry* and *little conscience* make us rich.

## *Understood subjects*

In imperative sentences, which give advice or issue commands, the subject is understood but not actually present in the sentence. The subject of an imperative sentence is understood to be *you*, as in the following example.

[*You*] Hitch your wagon to a star.

## *Subject after the verb*

Although the subject ordinarily comes before the verb, occasionally it does not. When a sentence begins with *There is* or *There are* (or *There was* or *There were*), the subject follows the verb. The word *There* is an expletive in such constructions, an empty word serving merely to get the sentence started.

┌─ SS ─┐
There is *no substitute* for victory.

Occasionally a writer will invert a sentence for effect.

┌ SS ┐
Happy is *the nation that has no history.*

*Happy* is an adjective, so it cannot be the subject. Turn this sentence around and its structure becomes obvious: *The nation that has no history is happy.*

In questions, the subject frequently appears in an unusual position, sandwiched between parts of the verb.

┌SS┐
Do *married men* make the best husbands?

Turn the question into a statement, and the words will appear in their usual order: *Married men do make the best husbands.* (*Do make* is the verb.)

For more about unusual sentence patterns, see 63c.

**NOTE:** The ability to recognize the subject of a sentence will help you edit for a variety of problems such as sentence fragments (19), subject-verb agreement (21), and choice of pronouns such as *I* and *me* (24). If English is not your native language, see also 31a and 31b.

**EXERCISE 63–1**　In the following sentences, underline the complete subject and write *SS* above the simple subject(s). If the subject is an understood *you,* insert it in parentheses. Answers to lettered sentences appear in the back of the book. Example:

　　SS　　　　　　　SS
Fools and their money are soon parted.

a. Sticks and stones may break my bones, and words can sting like anything. —Anonymous
b. In war, all delays are dangerous. —John Dryden
c. Speak softly and carry a big stick. —Theodore Roosevelt
d. There is nothing permanent except change. —Heraclitus
e. Most of the disputes in the world arise from words. —Lord Mansfield

1. The structure of every sentence is a lesson in logic. — J. S. Mill
2. Don't be humble. You're not that great. —Golda Meir
3. In the eyes of its mother, every beetle is a gazelle. —Moorish proverb
4. The burden of proof lies on the plaintiff. —Legal maxim
5. There are no signposts in the sea. —Vita Sackville-West

**EXERCISE 63–1　Answers:**

a. Complete subjects: Sticks and stones, words; simple subjects: Sticks, stones, words; b. Complete subject: all delays; simple subject: delays; c. Complete subject: (You); d. Complete subject: nothing except change; simple subject: nothing; e. Complete subject: Most of the disputes in the world; simple subject: Most

1. Complete subject: The structure of every sentence; simple subject: structure; 2. Complete subjects: (You), You; 3. Complete subject: every beetle; simple subject: beetle; 4. Complete subject: The burden of proof; simple subject: burden; 5. Complete subject: no signposts; simple subject: signposts

| ON THE WEB | **dianahacker.com/bedhandbook** ▶ Electronic grammar exercises ▶ E-ex 63–1 and 63–2 |

## 63b Verbs, objects, and complements

Section 62c explains how to find the verb of a sentence, which consists of a main verb possibly preceded by one or more helping verbs. A sentence's verb is classified as linking, transitive, or intransitive, depending on the kinds of objects or complements the verb can (or cannot) take.

### Linking verbs and subject complements

Linking verbs link the subject to a subject complement, a word or word group that completes the meaning of the subject by renaming or describing it. If the subject complement renames the subject, it is a noun or noun equivalent (sometimes called a *predicate noun*).

$$
\underbrace{\text{The handwriting on the wall}}_{\text{S}}\ \underbrace{\text{may be}}_{\text{V}}\ \underbrace{\text{a forgery.}}_{\text{SC}}
$$

If the subject complement describes the subject, it is an adjective or adjective equivalent (sometimes called a *predicate adjective*).

```
S   V   SC
Love is blind.
```

Whenever they appear as main verbs (rather than helping verbs), the forms of *be* — *be, am, is, are, was, were,*

*being, been*—usually function as linking verbs. In the preceding examples, for instance, the main verbs are *be* and *is*.

Verbs such as *appear, become, feel, grow, look, make,
seem, smell, sound,* and *taste* are sometimes linking, depending on the sense of the sentence.

```
                       S        V    ┌ SC ┐
        At the touch of love, everyone becomes a poet.
```

```
              ┌── S ──┐      V    SC
        At first sight, original art often looks ugly.
```

When you suspect that a verb such as *becomes* or *looks* is
linking, check to see if the word or words following it rename
or describe the subject. In the preceding examples, *a poet*
renames *everyone,* and *ugly* describes *art.*

### Transitive verbs and direct objects

A transitive verb takes a direct object, a word or word group
that names a receiver of the action.

```
        ┌── S ──┐   V   ┌────── DO ──────┐
        The little snake studies the ways of the big serpent.
```

In such sentences, the subject and verb alone will seem incomplete. Once we have read *The little snake studies,* for example, we want to know the rest: *The little snake studies
what?* The answer to the question What? (or Whom?) is
the complete direct object: *the ways of the big serpent.* The
simple direct object is always a noun or pronoun, in this
case *ways.* To find it, simply strip away all modifiers.

Transitive verbs usually appear in the active voice, with
the subject doing the action and a direct object receiving the
action. Active-voice sentences can be transformed into the
passive voice, with the subject receiving the action instead.
(See 63c.)

### Transitive verbs, indirect objects, and direct objects

The direct object of a transitive verb is sometimes preceded by an indirect object, a noun or pronoun telling to whom or for whom the action of the sentence is done.

$$\overset{\text{S}}{\text{You}}\ \overset{\text{V}}{\text{show}}\ \overset{\text{IO}}{\text{me}}\ \overset{\lceil\text{DO}\rceil}{\text{a hero}},\ \text{and}\ \overset{\text{S}}{\text{I}}\ \overset{\text{V}}{\text{will write}}\ \overset{\text{IO}}{\text{you}}\ \overset{\lceil\text{DO}\rceil}{\text{a tragedy}}.$$

You show me a hero, and I will write you a tragedy.

The simple indirect object is always a noun or pronoun. To test for an indirect object, insert the word *to* or *for* before the word or word group in question. If the sentence makes sense, the word or word group is an indirect object.

You show [to] me a hero, and I will write [for] you a tragedy.

An indirect object may be turned into a prepositional phrase using *to* or *for: You show a hero to me, and I will write a tragedy for you.*
Only certain transitive verbs take indirect objects. Some examples are *ask, bring, find, get, give, hand, lend, offer, pay, promise, read, send, show, teach, tell, throw,* and *write.*

### Transitive verbs, direct objects, and object complements

The direct object of a transitive verb is sometimes followed by an object complement, a word or word group that completes the direct object's meaning by renaming or describing it.

$$\overset{\text{S}}{\text{People now}}\ \overset{\text{V}}{\text{call}}\ \overset{\lceil\text{DO}\rceil}{\text{a spade}}\ \overset{\lceil\text{OC}\rceil}{\text{an agricultural implement}}.$$

People now call a spade an agricultural implement.

$$\overset{\text{S}}{\text{Love}}\ \overset{\text{V}}{\text{makes}}\ \overset{\lceil\text{DO}\rceil}{\text{all hard hearts}}\ \overset{\text{OC}}{\text{gentle}}.$$

Love makes all hard hearts gentle.

When the object complement renames the direct object, it is a noun or pronoun (such as *implement*). When it describes the direct object, it is an adjective (such as *gentle*).

## Sentence patterns

Subject / linking verb / subject complement

Advertising is legalized lying. [*Legalized lying* renames *Advertising*.]

Great intellects are skeptical. [*Skeptical* describes *Great intellects*.]

Subject / transitive verb / direct object

A stumble may prevent a fall.

Subject / transitive verb / indirect object / direct object

Fate gives us our relatives.

Subject / transitive verb / direct object / object complement

Our fears do make us traitors. [*Traitors* renames *us*.]

The pot calls the kettle black. [*Black* describes *the kettle*.]

Subject / intransitive verb

Time flies.

### Intransitive verbs

Intransitive verbs take no objects or complements. Their pattern is subject/verb.

**S    V**
Money talks.

**S         V**
Revolutions never go backward.

Nothing receives the actions of talking and going in these sentences, so the verbs are intransitive. Notice that such verbs may or may not be followed by adverbial modifiers. In the second sentence, *backward* is an adverb modifying *go*.

**NOTE:** The dictionary will tell you whether a verb is transitive or intransitive. Some verbs have both transitive and intransitive functions.

> **TRANSITIVE**    Sandra flew her Cessna over the canyon.
>
> **INTRANSITIVE**   A bald eagle flew overhead.

In the first example, *flew* has a direct object that receives the action: *her Cessna*. In the second example, the verb is followed by an adverb (*overhead*), not by a direct object.

**EXERCISE 63–2**    Label the subject complements and direct objects in the following sentences, using these labels: *SC, DO*. If a subject complement or direct object consists of more than one word, bracket and label all of it. Example:

```
                  ┌──── DO ────┐
You can fool most of the people most of the time.
```

a. Talk is cheap.                              — English proverb
b. An elephant never forgets an injury.        — American proverb
c. A runaway monk never praises his convent.   — Italian proverb
d. Religion is the opium of the people.        — Karl Marx
e. Good medicine always tastes bitter.         — Japanese proverb

1. You can say the nastiest things about yourself without offending anyone.                              — Phyllis Diller

**EXERCISE 63–2    Answers:**

a. Subject complement: cheap; b. Direct object: an injury; c. Direct object: his convent; d. Subject complement: the opium of the people; e. Subject complement: bitter

1. Direct object: the nastiest things about yourself; 2. Subject complement: the opportunities of foes; 3. Subject complement: the signature of civilization; 4. Direct object: the ideals of a nation; 5. Subject complement: too rich or too thin

2. The quarrels of friends are the opportunities of foes. —Aesop
3. Art is the signature of civilization. —Beverly Sills
4. You can tell the ideals of a nation by its advertising.
   —Norman Douglas
5. You can never be too rich or too thin.
   —Wallis Warfield Simpson

**EXERCISE 63–3**   Each of the following sentences has either an indirect object followed by a direct object or a direct object followed by an object complement. Label the objects and complements, using these labels; *IO, DO, OC.* If an object or complement consists of more than one word, bracket and label all of it. Example:

```
       ┌──── DO ────┐   OC
Every man thinks his own geese swans.
```

a. Sorrow makes us wise. —Alfred Lord Tennyson
b. Too many people make money their primary pursuit.
   —Anonymous
c. Make us happy and you make us good. —Robert Browning
d. Ask me no questions, and I will tell you no lies. —Anonymous
e. Show me a good loser, and I will show you a failure.
   —Paul Newman

1. Give the devil his due. —English proverb
2. God gives every bird its proper food, but all must fly for it.
   —Dutch proverb
3. A wide screen makes a bad film worse. —Samuel Goldwyn
4. Trees and fields tell me nothing. —Socrates
5. Necessity can make us surprisingly brave. —Latin proverb

**ON THE WEB**   **dianahacker.com/bedhandbook**
  ▶ Electronic grammar exercises
    ▶ E-ex 63–3 to 63–5

**EXERCISE 63–3   Answers:**

a. Direct object: us; object complement: wise; b. Direct object: money; object complement: their primary pursuit; c. Direct objects: us, us; object complements: happy, good; d. Indirect objects: me, you; direct objects: no questions, no lies; e. Indirect objects: me, you; direct objects: a good loser, a failure

1. Indirect object: the devil; direct object: his due; 2. Indirect object: every bird; direct object: its proper food; 3. Direct object: a bad film; object complement: worse; 4. Indirect object: me; direct object: nothing; 5. Direct object: us; object complement: surprisingly brave

## 63c Pattern variations

Although most sentences follow one of the five patterns in the chart on page 817, variations of these patterns commonly occur in questions, commands, sentences with delayed subjects, and passive transformations.

### Questions and commands

Questions are sometimes patterned in normal word order, with the subject preceding the verb.

> S ┌─ V ─┐
> Who will take the first step?

Just as frequently, however, the pattern of a question is inverted, with the subject appearing between the helping and main verbs or after the verb.

> HV  S  MV
> Will you take the first step?

> V ┌──── S ────┐
> Why is the first step so difficult?

In commands, the subject of the sentence is an understood *you.*

> S    V
> [You] Keep your eyes on the road.

### Sentences with delayed subjects

Writers sometimes choose to delay the subject of a sentence to achieve a special effect such as suspense or humor.

> V ┌──── S ────┐
> Behind the phony tinsel of Hollywood lies the real tinsel.

The subject of the sentence is also delayed in sentences opening with the expletive *There* or *It.* When used as expletives, the words *There* and *It* have no strict grammatical function; they serve merely to get the sentence started.

V ┌─── S ───┐
There are too many cooks spoiling the broth.

V      ┌─── S ───┐
It is not good to wake a sleeping lion.

The subject in the second example is an infinitive phrase. (See 64c.)

## Passive transformations

Transitive verbs, those that can take direct objects, usually appear in the active voice. In the active voice, the subject does the action and a direct object receives the action.

┌─ S ─┐     V ┌─ DO ─┐
**ACTIVE** The early bird sometimes catches the early worm.

Sentences in the active voice may be transformed into the passive voice, with the subject receiving the action instead.

┌── S ──┐ HV    MV
**PASSIVE** The early worm is sometimes caught by the early bird.

What was once the direct object (*the early worm*) has become the subject in the passive-voice transformation, and the original subject appears in a prepositional phrase beginning with *by.* The *by* phrase is frequently omitted in passive-voice constructions.

**PASSIVE** The early worm is sometimes caught.

Verbs in the passive voice can be identified by their form alone. The main verb is always a past participle, such as *caught* (see 62c), preceded by a form of *be* (*be, am, is, are, was, were, being, been*): *is caught.* Sometimes adverbs intervene (*is sometimes caught*).

**NOTE:** Writers sometimes use the passive voice when the active voice would be more appropriate (see 8a).

# 64

## Subordinate word groups

Subordinate word groups include prepositional phrases, subordinate clauses, verbal phrases, appositives, and absolutes. Not all of these word groups are subordinate in quite the same way. Some are subordinate because they are modifiers; others function as noun equivalents, not as modifiers.

### 64a Prepositional phrases

A prepositional phrase begins with a preposition such as *at, by, for, from, in, of, on, to,* or *with* (see 62f) and usually ends with a noun or noun equivalent: *on the table, for him, with great fanfare.* The noun or noun equivalent is known as the *object of the preposition.*

#### Functions of prepositional phrases

Prepositional phrases function either as adjectives modifying a noun or pronoun or as adverbs modifying a verb, an adjective, or another adverb. When functioning as an adjective, a prepositional phrase nearby always appears immediately following the noun or pronoun it modifies.

Variety is the *spice of life.*

Adjective phrases usually answer one or both of the questions Which one? and What kind of? If we ask Which spice? or What kind of spice? we get a sensible answer: *the spice of life.*

Adverbial prepositional phrases that modify the verb can appear nearly anywhere in a sentence.

Do not *judge* a tree *by its bark.*

Tyranny will *in time lead* to revolution.

*To the ant,* a few drops of rain *are* a flood.

Adverbial word groups usually answer one of these questions: When? Where? How? Why? Under what conditions? To what degree?

Do not judge a tree *how? By its bark.*

Tyranny will lead to revolution *when? In time.*

A few drops of rain are a flood *under what conditions? To the ant.*

If a prepositional phrase is movable, you can be certain that it is adverbial; adjectival prepositional phrases are wedded to the words they modify. At least some of the time, adverbial modifiers can be moved to other positions in the sentence.

*By their fruits* you shall know them.

You shall know them *by their fruits.*

### Objects of prepositions

Objects of prepositions range from a simple noun or pronoun (at *peace*, with *you*, and so on) to quite complex structures. For example, the object of the preposition might itself be modified by a prepositional phrase, with one phrase embedded in the other.

There are many *paths to the top of the mountain.*

The complete object of *to* is *the top of the mountain;* the simple object is *top*. The prepositional phrase *of the mountain* modifies the noun *top*. And the prepositional phrase *to the top of the mountain* modifies the noun *paths*.

The effect is something like Chinese eggs or Russian dolls nestled within one another. Consider the complexity of one such sentence:

> I am one individual
>    on a small planet
>       in a little solar system
>          in one
>            of the galaxies.

**NOTE:** In questions and subordinate clauses, a preposition may appear after its object.

> *What* are you afraid *of?*

> We avoided the bike trail *that* John had warned us *about.*

**EXERCISE 64–1** Underline the prepositional phrases in the following sentences. Be prepared to explain the function of each phrase. Answers to lettered sentences appear in the back of the book. Example:

---

**EXERCISE 64–1 Answers:**

a. On their side (adverb phrase modifying *had*); b. of several air traffic controllers (adjective phrase modifying *job*), with ease (adverb phrase modifying *could perform*); c. To my embarrassment (adverb phrase modifying *was born*), in bed (adverb phrase modifying *was born*), with a lady (adverb phrase modifying *was born*); d. of a culture (adjective phrase modifying *map*); e. In France (adverb phrase modifying *is*)

1. to freedom (adjective phrase modifying *road*), by death (adverb phrase modifying *has been stalked*); 2. of sheep (adjective phrase modifying *society*), of wolves (adjective phrase modifying *government*); 3. with their heads (adverb phrase modifying *feel*), with

Communism is fascism <u>**with a human face.**</u> *(Adjective phrase modifying fascism)*

a. On their side, the workers had only the Constitution. The other side had bayonets.                                    —Mother Jones
b. Any mother could perform the job of several air traffic controllers with ease.                                    —Lisa Alther
c. To my embarrassment, I was born in bed with a lady.
                                                    —Wilson Mizner
d. Language is the road map of a culture.        —Rita Mae Brown
e. In France, cooking is a serious art form and a national sport.
                                                    —Julia Child

1. We know that the road to freedom has always been stalked by death.                                           —Angela Davis
2. A society of sheep produces a government of wolves.
                                                —Bertrand de Jouvenal
3. Some people feel with their heads and think with their hearts.
                                                —G. C. Lichtenberg
4. By a small sample, we may know the whole piece.
                                                        —Cervantes
5. You and I come by road or rail, but economists travel on infrastructure.                                  —Margaret Thatcher

| ON THE WEB | **dianahacker.com/bedhandbook**<br>▶ Electronic grammar exercises<br>  ▶ E-ex 64–1 to 64–3 |
|---|---|

## **64b** Subordinate clauses

Subordinate clauses are patterned like sentences, having subjects and verbs and sometimes objects or complements. But they function within sentences as adjectives, adverbs, or nouns. They cannot stand alone as complete sentences.

**EXERCISE 64–1 (continued)**

their hearts (adverb phrase modifying *think*); 4. By a small sample (adverb phrase modifying *may know*); 5. by road or rail (adverb phrase modifying *come*), on infrastructure (adverb phrase modifying *travel*)

A subordinate clause usually begins with a subordinating conjunction or a relative pronoun.

**SUBORDINATING CONJUNCTIONS**

| after | before | rather than | though | where |
|---|---|---|---|---|
| although | even though | since | unless | whether |
| as | how | so that | until | while |
| as if | if | than | when | why |
| because | in order that | that | | |

**RELATIVE PRONOUNS**

| that | who | whom | whose | which |
|---|---|---|---|---|

The chart on page 830 classifies these words according to the kinds of clauses (adjective, adverb, or noun) they introduce.

## Adjective clauses

Like other word groups functioning as adjectives, adjective clauses modify nouns or pronouns. An adjective clause nearly always appears immediately following the noun or pronoun it modifies.

The *arrow that has left the bow* never returns.

Relatives are *persons who live too near and visit too often.*

To test whether a subordinate clause functions as an adjective, ask the adjective questions: Which one? What kind of? The answer should make sense. Which arrow? *The arrow that has left the bow.* What kind of persons? *Persons who live too near and visit too often.*

Most adjective clauses begin with a relative pronoun (*who, whom, whose, which,* or *that*), which marks them as grammatically subordinate. In addition to introducing the

**WRITERS ON WRITING**

A dependent clause is like a dependent child: incapable of standing on its own but able to cause a lot of trouble.   —William Safire

clause, the relative pronoun points back to the noun that the clause modifies.

The *fur that warms a monarch* once warmed a bear.

Relative pronouns are sometimes "understood."

The things [*that*] *we know best* are the things [*that*] *we haven't been taught.*

Occasionally an adjective clause is introduced by a relative adverb, usually *when, where,* or *why.*

Home is the *place where you slip in the tub and break your neck.*

The parts of an adjective clause are often arranged as in sentences (subject/verb/object or complement).

          **S   V   DO**
We often forgive the people who bore us.

Frequently, however, the object or complement appears first, violating the normal order of subject/verb/object.

        **DO   S   V**
We rarely forgive those whom we bore.

To determine the subject of a clause, ask Who? or What? and insert the verb. Don't be surprised if the answer is an echo, as in the first adjective clause above: Who bore us? *Who.* To find any objects or complements, read the subject and the verb and then ask Who? Whom? or What? Again, be prepared for a possible echo, as in the second adjective clause: We bore whom? *Whom.*

**NOTE:** For punctuation of adjective clauses, see 32e and 33e. If English is not your native language, see 31c for a common problem with adjective clauses.

### Adverb clauses

Adverb clauses usually modify verbs, in which case they may appear nearly anywhere in a sentence—at the beginning, at the end, or in the middle. Like other adverbial word groups, they tell when, where, why, under what conditions, or to what degree an action occurred or a situation existed.

*When the well is dry,* we *know* the worth of water.

Venice would *be* a fine city *if it were only drained.*

When do we know the worth of water? *When the well is dry.* Under what conditions would Venice be a fine city? *If it were only drained.*

Unlike adjective clauses, adverb clauses are frequently movable. In the preceding example sentences, for instance, the adverb clauses can be moved without affecting the meaning of the sentences.

We know the worth of water *when the well is dry.*

*If it were only drained,* Venice would be a fine city.

When an adverb clause modifies an adjective or an adverb, it is not movable; it must appear next to the word it modifies. In the following examples, the *because* clause modifies the adjective *angry,* and the *than* clause modifies the adverb *faster.*

Angry *because the mayor had not kept his promises,* we worked for his defeat.

Joan can run faster *than I can bicycle.*

Adverb clauses always begin with a subordinating conjunction (see the chart on p. 830 for a list). Subordinating conjunctions introduce clauses and express their relation to the rest of the sentence.

Adverb clauses are sometimes elliptical, with some of their words being understood but not appearing in the sentence.

*When [it is] painted,* the room will look larger.

### Noun clauses

Because they do not function as modifiers, noun clauses are not subordinate in the same sense as are adjective and adverb clauses. They are called subordinate only because they cannot stand alone: They must function within a sentence, always as nouns.

A noun clause functions just like a single-word noun, usually as a subject, subject complement, direct object, or object of a preposition.

— S —<br>Whoever gossips to you will gossip of you.

— DO —<br>We never forget that we buried the hatchet.

A noun clause begins with a word that marks it as subordinate (see the list on p. 830). The subordinating word may or may not play a significant role in the clause. In the preceding example sentences, *Whoever* is the subject of its clause, but *that* does not perform a function in its clause.

As with adjective clauses, the parts of a noun clause may appear out of their normal order (subject/verb/object).

DO  S   V<br>Talent is what you possess.

The parts of a noun clause may also appear in their normal order.

S   V   DO<br>Genius is what possesses you.

## Words that introduce subordinate clauses

### Words introducing adverb clauses

*Subordinating conjunctions:* after, although, as, as if, because, before, even though, if, in order that, rather than, since, so that, than, that, though, unless, until, when, where, whether, while

### Words introducing adjective clauses

*Relative pronouns:* that, which, who, whom, whose

*Relative adverbs:* when, where, why

### Words introducing noun clauses

*Relative pronouns:* that, which, who, whom, whose

*Other pronouns:* whoever, whomever, what, whatever, whichever

*Subordinating conjunctions:* how, if, when, whenever, where, wherever, whether, why

---

**EXERCISE 64–2** Underline the subordinate clauses in the following sentences. Be prepared to explain the function of each clause. Answers to lettered sentences appear in the back of the book. Example:

> **Dig a well before you are thirsty.** *(Adverb clause modifying Dig)*

a. It is hard to fight an enemy who has outposts in your head.
—Sally Kempton

b. A rattlesnake that doesn't bite teaches you nothing.
—Jessamyn West

c. If love is the answer, could you please rephrase the question?
—Lily Tomlin

---

**EXERCISE 64–2 Answers:**

a. who has outposts in your head (adjective clause modifying *enemy*); b. that doesn't bite (adjective clause modifying *rattlesnake*); c. If love is the answer (adverb clause modifying *could rephrase*); d. what they mean (noun clause used as direct object of *say*); e. unless I cannot resist it (adverb clause modifying *avoid*)

1. What history teaches us (noun clause used as subject of the sentence), that we have never learned anything from it (noun clause used as subject complement); 2. When the insects take over the world (adverb clause modifying *hope*), that they will remember our picnics with gratitude (noun clause used as direct object of *hope*); 3. who will tell her age (adjective clause modifying

*basic*

d. Dreams say what they mean, but they don't say it in daytime language. —Gail Godwin
e. I generally avoid temptation unless I cannot resist it.
—Mae West

1. What history teaches us is that we have never learned anything from it. —Georg Wilhelm Hegel
2. When the insects take over the world, we hope that they will remember our picnics with gratitude. —Anonymous
3. A woman who will tell her age will tell anything.
—Rita Mae Brown
4. If triangles had a god, it would have three sides.
—C. L. de Montesquieu
5. He gave her a look that you could have poured on a waffle.
—Ring Lardner

**ON THE WEB**

**dianahacker.com/bedhandbook**
▶ Electronic grammar exercises
  ▶ E-ex 64–4 to 64–6

## 64c Verbal phrases

A verbal is a verb form that does not function as the verb of a clause. Verbals include infinitives (the word *to* plus the base form of the verb), present participles (the *-ing* form of the verb), and past participles (the verb form usually ending in *-d*, *-ed*, *-n*, *-en*, or *-t*). (See 27a and 62c.)

| INFINITIVE | PRESENT PARTICIPLE | PAST PARTICIPLE |
|---|---|---|
| to dream | dreaming | dreamed |
| to choose | choosing | chosen |
| to build | building | built |
| to grow | growing | grown |

**EXERCISE 64–2 (continued)**

*woman*); 4. If triangles had a god (adverb clause modifying *would have*); 5. that you could have poured on a waffle (adjective clause modifying *look*)

Instead of functioning as the verb of a clause, a verbal or a verbal phrase functions as an adjective, a noun, or an adverb.

| | |
|---|---|
| **ADJECTIVE** | *Stolen* grapes are especially sweet. |
| **NOUN** | Continual *dripping* wears away a stone. |
| **ADVERB** | Were we born *to suffer*? |

Verbals can take objects, complements, and modifiers to form verbal phrases; the phrases usually lack subjects.

*Living well* is the best revenge.

Governments exist *to protect the rights of minorities*.

The verbal *Living* is modified by the adverb *well*; the verbal *to protect* is followed by a direct object, *the rights of minorities*.

Like single-word verbals, verbal phrases function as adjectives, nouns, or adverbs. In the sentences just given, for example, *living well* functions as a noun used as the subject of the sentence, and *to protect the rights of minorities* functions as an adverb, answering the question Why?

Verbal phrases are ordinarily classified as participles, gerunds, and infinitives. This classification is based partly on form (whether the verbal is a present participle, a past participle, or an infinitive) and partly on function (whether the whole phrase functions as an adjective, a noun, or an adverb).

**NOTE:** For advice on editing dangling verbal phrases, see 12e.

### Participial phrases

Participial phrases always function as adjectives. Their verbals are either present participles, always ending in *-ing*, or past participles, frequently ending in *-d, -ed, -n, -en,* or *-t* (see 27a).

Participial phrases frequently appear immediately following the noun or pronoun they modify.

Congress shall make no *law abridging the freedom of speech or of the press.*

*Truth kept in the dark* will never save the world.

Unlike other adjectival word groups, however, which must always follow the noun or pronoun they modify, participial phrases are often movable. They can precede the word they modify.

*Being weak, foxes* are distinguished by superior tact.

They may also appear at some distance from the word they modify.

History is *something* that never happened, *written by someone who wasn't there.*

### Gerund phrases

Gerund phrases are built around present participles (verb forms ending in *-ing*), and they always function as nouns: usually as subjects, subject complements, direct objects, or objects of a preposition.

**S**
Justifying a fault doubles it.

**SC**
The secret of education is respecting the pupil.

**DO**
Kleptomaniacs can't help helping themselves.

```
  ┌──── OBJ OF PREP ────┐
```
The hen is an egg's way of producing another egg.

## Infinitive phrases

Infinitive phrases, usually constructed around *to* plus the base form of the verb (*to call, to drink*), can function as nouns, as adjectives, or as adverbs.

When functioning as a noun, an infinitive phrase may appear in almost any noun slot in a sentence, usually as a subject, subject complement, or direct object.

```
  ┌──── S ────┐
```
To side with truth is noble.

```
  ┌──────── DO ────────┐
```
Never try to leap a chasm in two jumps.

Infinitive phrases functioning as adjectives usually appear immediately following the noun or pronoun they modify.

We do not have the *right to abandon the poor.*

The infinitive phrase modifies the noun *right*. Which right? *The right to abandon the poor.*

Adverbial infinitive phrases usually qualify the meaning of the verb, telling when, where, how, why, under what conditions, or to what degree an action occurred.

He *cut off* his nose *to spite his face.*

Why did he cut off his nose? *To spite his face.*

**NOTE:** In some constructions, the infinitive is unmarked; in other words, the *to* does not appear: *No one can make you [to] feel inferior without your consent.* (See 29c.)

---

**EXERCISE 64–3  Answers:**

a. Concealing a disease (gerund phrase used as subject), to cure it (infinitive phrase modifying *way*); b. being punctual (gerund phrase used as object of the preposition *with*), to appreciate it (infinitive phrase modifying *is*); c. to conceal him (infinitive phrase used as direct object), naming him Smith (gerund phrase used as object of the preposition *by*); d. Being weak (participial phrase modifying *children*), to beguile us with charm (infinitive phrase used as direct object); e. Wrestling with words (gerund phrase used as subject)

1. generally raised on city land (participial phrase modifying *thing*); 2. to remove a fly from your friend's forehead (infinitive

**EXERCISE 64–3**    Underline the verbal phrases in the following sentences. Be prepared to explain the function of each phrase. Answers to lettered sentences appear in the back of the book. Example:

> Do you want <u>to be a writer</u>? Then write. *(Infinitive phrase*
>
> *used as direct object of <u>Do want</u>)*

a.  Concealing a disease is no way to cure it.
                                            —Ethiopian proverb
b.  The trouble with being punctual is that nobody is there to appreciate it.                              —Franklin P. Jones
c.  Fate tried to conceal him by naming him Smith.
                                            —Oliver Wendell Holmes Jr.
d.  Being weak, children quickly learn to beguile us with charm.
                                            —Anonymous
e.  Wrestling with words gave me my moments of greatest meaning.                                        —Richard Wright

1.  The thing generally raised on city land is taxes.
                                            —C. D. Warner
2.  Do not use a hatchet to remove a fly from your friend's forehead.                                    —Chinese proverb
3.  He has the gall of a shoplifter returning an item for a refund.
                                            —W. I. E. Gates
4.  Tact is the ability to describe others as they see themselves.
                                            —Mary Pettibone Poole
5.  He could never see a belt without hitting below it.
                                            —Harriet Braiker

ON
THE
WEB

**dianahacker.com/bedhandbook**
▶ Electronic grammar exercises
   ▶ E-ex 64–7 to 64–9

**EXERCISE 64–3 (continued)**

phrase modifying *Do use*); 3. returning an item for a refund (participial phrase modifying *shoplifter*); 4. to describe others as they see themselves (infinitive phrase modifying *ability*); 5. hitting below it (gerund phrase used as object of the preposition *without*)

## 64d Appositive phrases

Though strictly speaking they are not subordinate word groups, appositive phrases function somewhat as adjectives do, to describe nouns or pronouns. Instead of modifying nouns or pronouns, however, appositive phrases rename them. In form they are nouns or noun equivalents.

Appositives are said to be "in apposition" to the nouns or pronouns they rename.

> Politicians, *acrobats at heart,* can sit on a fence and yet keep both ears to the ground.

*Acrobats at heart* is in apposition to the noun *politicians.*

## 64e Absolute phrases

An absolute phrase modifies a whole clause or sentence, not just one word, and it may appear nearly anywhere in the sentence. It consists of a noun or noun equivalent usually followed by a participial phrase.

> *His words dipped in honey,* the senator mesmerized the crowd.

> The senator mesmerized the crowd, *his words dipped in honey.*

# 65

## Sentence types

Sentences are classified in two ways: according to their structure (simple, compound, complex, and compound-complex) and according to their purpose (declarative, imperative, interrogative, and exclamatory).

## 65a Sentence structures

Depending on the number and types of clauses they contain, sentences are classified as simple, compound, complex, or compound-complex.

Clauses come in two varieties: independent and subordinate. An independent clause is a full sentence pattern that does not function within another sentence pattern: It contains a subject and its modifiers plus a verb and any objects, complements, and modifiers of that verb, and it either stands alone or could stand alone. A subordinate clause is a full sentence pattern that functions within a sentence as an adjective, an adverb, or a noun but that cannot stand alone as a complete sentence. (See 64b.)

### Simple sentences

A simple sentence is one independent clause with no subordinate clauses.

┌─────────── INDEPENDENT CLAUSE ───────────┐
Without music, life would be a mistake.

This sentence contains a subject (*life*), a verb (*would be*), a complement (*a mistake*), and an adverbial modifier (*Without music*).

A simple sentence may contain compound elements—a compound subject, verb, or object, for example—but it does not contain more than one full sentence pattern. The following sentence is simple because its two verbs (*enters* and *spreads*) share a subject (*Evil*).

```
┌──────────── INDEPENDENT CLAUSE ────────────┐
```
Evil enters like a needle and spreads like an oak.

## Compound sentences

A compound sentence is composed of two or more independent clauses with no subordinate clauses. The independent clauses are usually joined with a comma and a coordinating conjunction (*and, but, or, nor, for, so, yet*) or with a semicolon. (See 14a.)

```
┌─INDEPENDENT CLAUSE─┐     ┌── INDEPENDENT CLAUSE ──┐
```
One arrow is easily broken, but you can't break a bundle of ten.

```
┌────────── INDEPENDENT CLAUSE ──────────┐┌INDEPENDENT–
```
We are born brave, trusting, and greedy; most of us have

```
┌─ CLAUSE ──────┐
```
remained greedy.

## Complex sentences

A complex sentence is composed of one independent clause with one or more subordinate clauses. (See 64b.)

|  |  |
|--|--|
| **ADJECTIVE** | **SUBORDINATE** ┌── **CLAUSE** ──┐ <br> They that sow in tears shall reap in joy. |
| **ADVERB** | **SUBORDINATE** ┌── **CLAUSE** ──┐ <br> If you scatter thorns, don't go barefoot. |
| **NOUN** | ┌─────── **SUBORDINATE CLAUSE** ───────┐ <br> What the scientists have in their briefcases is terrifying. |

## Compound-complex sentences

A compound-complex sentence contains at least two independent clauses and at least one subordinate clause. The following sentence contains two full sentence patterns that can stand alone.

┌─────── IND CL ───────┐   ┌─────── IND CL ───────┐
Tell me what you eat, and I will tell you what you are.

And each independent clause contains a subordinate clause, making the sentence both compound and complex.

┌─────── IND CL ───────┐   ┌─────── IND CL ───────┐
    ┌─ SUB CL ─┐               ┌─ SUB CL ─┐
Tell me what you eat, and I will tell you what you are.

## 65b Sentence purposes

Writers use declarative sentences to make statements, imperative sentences to issue requests or commands, interrogative sentences to ask questions, and exclamatory sentences to make exclamations.

| | |
|---|---|
| **DECLARATIVE** | The echo always has the last word. |
| **IMPERATIVE** | Love your neighbor. |
| **INTERROGATIVE** | Are second thoughts always wisest? |
| **EXCLAMATORY** | I want to wash the flag, not burn it! |

**EXERCISE 65–1** Identify the following sentences as simple, compound, complex, or compound-complex. Be prepared to identify the subordinate clauses and classify them according to their function: adjective, adverb, or noun. (See 64b.) Answers to lettered sentences appear in the back of the book. Example:

**The frog in the well knows nothing of the ocean.** *(Simple)*

a. People who sleep like a baby usually don't have one.
— Leo Burke

**EXERCISE 65–1 Answers:**

a. Complex; who sleep like a baby (adjective clause); b. Compound; c. Simple; d. Complex; If you don't go to other people's funerals (adverb clause); e. Compound-complex; what you are afraid of (noun clause)

1. Complex; that people don't change (noun clause); 2. Complex; who cannot remember the past (adjective clause); 3. Simple; 4. Compound; 5. Complex; when it adopts a creed (adverb clause)

b. My folks didn't come over on the *Mayflower;* they were there to meet the boat. —Will Rogers

c. The impersonal hand of the government can never replace the helping hand of a neighbor. —Hubert Humphrey

d. If you don't go to other people's funerals, they won't go to yours. —Clarence Day

e. Tell us your phobias, and we will tell you what you are afraid of. —Robert Benchley

1. The tragedy of life is that people don't change. —Agatha Christie

2. Those who cannot remember the past are condemned to repeat it. —George Santayana

3. The best mind-altering drug is truth. —Lily Tomlin

4. Morality cannot be legislated, but behavior can be regulated. —Martin Luther King Jr.

5. Science commits suicide when it adopts a creed. —T. H. Huxley

---

**ON THE WEB**

**dianahacker.com/bedhandbook**
▶ Electronic grammar exercises
  ▶ E-ex 65–1

# Glossary of Usage

This glossary includes words commonly confused (such as *accept* and *except*), words commonly misused (such as *aggravate*), and words that are nonstandard (such as *hisself*). It also lists colloquialisms and jargon. Colloquialisms are expressions that may be appropriate in informal speech but are inappropriate in formal writing. Jargon is needlessly technical or pretentious language that is inappropriate in most contexts. If an item is not listed here, consult the index. For irregular verbs (such as *sing, sang, sung*), see 27a. For idiomatic use of prepositions, see 18d.

---

**ON THE WEB**

Some matters of usage included in this glossary have sparked debates. If you are interested in learning why, go to **dianahacker.com/bedhandbook** and click on

▶ **Language Debates**
  *bad* versus *badly*
  *however* at the beginning of a sentence
  *lie* versus *lay*
  *myself*
  *that* versus *which*
  Absolute concepts such as *unique*
  *who* versus *which* or *that*
  *who* versus *whom*
  *you*

**a, an**  Use *an* before a vowel sound, *a* before a consonant sound: *an apple, a peach.* Problems sometimes arise with words beginning with *h.* If the *h* is silent, the word begins with a vowel sound, so use *an: an hour, an heir, an honest senator, an honorable deed.* If the *h* is pronounced, the word begins with a consonant sound, so use *a: a hospital, a hymn, a historian, a hotel.* When an abbreviation or acronym begins with a vowel sound, use *an: an EKG, an MRI, an AIDS patient.*

**accept, except**  *Accept* is a verb meaning "to receive." *Except* is usually a preposition meaning "excluding." *I will accept all the packages except that one. Except* is also a verb meaning "to exclude." *Please except that item from the list.*

**adapt, adopt**  *Adapt* means "to adjust or become accustomed"; it is usually followed by *to. Adopt* means "to take as one's own." *Our family adopted a Vietnamese orphan, who quickly adapted to his new surroundings.*

**adverse, averse**  *Adverse* means "unfavorable." *Averse* means "opposed" or "reluctant"; it is usually followed by *to. I am averse to your proposal because it could have an adverse impact on the economy.*

**advice, advise**  *Advice* is a noun, *advise* a verb. *We advise you to follow John's advice.*

**affect, effect**  *Affect* is usually a verb meaning "to influence." *Effect* is usually a noun meaning "result." *The drug did not affect the disease, and it had adverse side effects. Effect* can also be a verb meaning "to bring about." *Only the president can effect such a change.*

**aggravate**  *Aggravate* means "to make worse or more troublesome." *Overgrazing aggravated the soil erosion.* In formal writing, avoid the colloquial use of *aggravate* meaning "to annoy or irritate." *Her babbling annoyed* (not *aggravated*) *me.*

**agree to, agree with**  *Agree to* means "to give consent." *Agree with* means "to be in accord" or "to come to an understanding." *He agrees with me about the need for change, but he won't agree to my plan.*

**ain't**  *Ain't* is nonstandard. Use *am not, are not* (*aren't*), or *is not* (*isn't*). *I am not* (not *ain't*) *going home for spring break.*

**all ready, already**  *All ready* means "completely prepared." *Already* means "previously." *Susan was all ready for the concert, but her friends had already left.*

**all right**  *All right* is written as two words. *Alright* is nonstandard.

**all together, altogether**  *All together* means "everyone gathered." *Altogether* means "entirely." *We were not altogether certain that we could bring the family all together for the reunion.*

**allude**  To *allude* to something is to make an indirect reference to it. Do not use *allude* to mean "to refer directly." *In his lecture the professor referred* (not *alluded*) *to several pre-Socratic philosophers.*

**allusion, illusion**  An *allusion* is an indirect reference. An *illusion* is a misconception or false impression. *Did you catch my allusion to Shakespeare? Mirrors give the room an illusion of depth.*

**a lot**  *A lot* is two words. Do not write *alot*. *We have had a lot of rain this spring.* See also *lots, lots of.*

**among, between**  See *between, among.*

**amongst**  In American English, *among* is preferred.

**amoral, immoral**  *Amoral* means "neither moral nor immoral"; it also means "not caring about moral judgments." *Immoral* means "morally wrong." *Until recently, most business courses were taught from an amoral perspective. Murder is immoral.*

**amount, number**  Use *amount* with quantities that cannot be counted; use *number* with those that can. *This recipe calls for a large amount of sugar. We have a large number of toads in our garden.* (See 30a and 30b.)

**an**  See *a, an.*

**and etc.**  *Et cetera* (*etc.*) means "and so forth"; therefore, *and etc.* is redundant. See also *etc.*

**and/or**  Avoid the awkward construction *and/or* except in technical or legal documents.

**angry at, angry with**  To write that one is *angry at* another person is nonstandard. Use *angry with* instead.

**ante-, anti-**  The prefix *ante-* means "earlier" or "in front of"; the prefix *anti-* means "against" or "opposed to." *William Lloyd Garrison was a leader of the antislavery movement during the antebellum period.* *Anti-* should be used with a hyphen when it is followed by a capital letter or a word beginning with *i.*

**anxious**  *Anxious* means "worried" or "apprehensive." In formal writing, avoid using *anxious* to mean "eager." *We are eager* (not *anxious*) *to see your new house.*

**anybody, anyone**   *Anybody* and *anyone* are singular. (See 21e and 22a.)

**anymore**   Reserve the adverb *anymore* for negative contexts, where it means "any longer." *Moviegoers are rarely shocked anymore by profanity.* Do not use *anymore* in positive contexts. Use *now* or *nowadays* instead. *Interest rates are so low now* (not *anymore*) *that more people can afford to buy homes.*

**anyone**   See *anybody, anyone.*

**anyone, any one**   *Anyone,* an indefinite pronoun, means "any person at all." *Any one,* the pronoun *one* preceded by the adjective *any,* refers to a particular person or thing in a group. *Anyone from Chicago may choose any one of the games on display.*

**anyplace**   *Anyplace* is informal for *anywhere.* Avoid *anyplace* in formal writing.

**anyways, anywheres**   *Anyways* and *anywheres* are nonstandard. Use *anyway* and *anywhere.*

**as**   *As* is sometimes used to mean "because." But do not use it if there is any chance of ambiguity. *We canceled the picnic because* (not *as*) *it began raining. As* here could mean "because" or "when."

**as, like**   See *like, as.*

**as to**   *As to* is jargon for *about. He inquired about* (not *as to*) *the job.*

**averse**   See *adverse, averse.*

**awful**   The adjective *awful* and the adverb *awfully* are too colloquial for formal writing.

**awhile, a while**   *Awhile* is an adverb; it can modify a verb, but it cannot be the object of a preposition such as *for.* The two-word form *a while* is a noun preceded by an article and therefore can be the object of a preposition. *Stay awhile. Stay for a while.*

**back up, backup**   *Back up* is a verb phrase. *Back up the car carefully. Be sure to back up your hard drive. Backup* is a noun meaning "a duplicate of electronically stored data." *Keep your backup in a safe place. Backup* can also be used as an adjective. *I regularly create backup disks.*

**bad, badly**   *Bad* is an adjective, *badly* an adverb. (See 26a and 26b.) *They felt bad about being early and ruining the surprise. Her arm hurt badly after she slid headfirst into second base.*

**being as, being that**  *Being as* and *being that* are nonstandard expressions. Write *because* instead. *Because* (not *Being as*) *I slept late, I had to skip breakfast.*

**beside, besides**  *Beside* is a preposition meaning "at the side of" or "next to." *Annie Oakley slept with her gun beside her bed. Besides* is a preposition meaning "except" or "in addition to." *No one besides Terrie can have that ice cream. Besides* is also an adverb meaning "in addition." *I'm not hungry; besides, I don't like ice cream.*

**between, among**  Ordinarily, use *among* with three or more entities, *between* with two. *The prize was divided among several contestants. You have a choice between carrots and beans.*

**bring, take**  Use *bring* when an object is being transported toward you, *take* when it is being moved away. *Please bring me a glass of water. Please take these flowers to Mr. Scott.*

**burst, bursted; bust, busted**  *Burst* is an irregular verb meaning "to come open or fly apart suddenly or violently." Its principal parts are *burst, burst, burst.* The past-tense form *bursted* is nonstandard. *Bust* and *busted* are slang for *burst* and, along with *bursted*, should not be used in formal writing.

**can, may**  The distinction between *can* and *may* is fading, but some writers still observe it in formal writing. *Can* is traditionally reserved for ability, *may* for permission. *Can you ski down the advanced slope without falling? May I help you?*

**capital, capitol**  *Capital* refers to a city, *capitol* to a building where lawmakers meet. *Capital* also refers to wealth or resources. *The capitol has undergone extensive renovations. The residents of the state capital protested the development plans.*

**censor, censure**  *Censor* means "to remove or suppress material considered objectionable." *Censure* means "to criticize severely." *The library's new policy of censoring controversial books has been censured by the media.*

**cite, site**  *Cite* means "to quote as an authority or example." *Site* is usually a noun meaning "a particular place." *He cited the zoning law in his argument against the proposed site of the gas station.* Locations on the Internet are usually referred to as *sites. The library's Web site improves every week.*

**climactic, climatic** *Climactic* is derived from *climax,* the point of greatest intensity in a series or progression of events. *Climatic* is derived from *climate* and refers to meteorological conditions. *The climactic period in the dinosaurs' reign was reached just before severe climatic conditions brought on an ice age.*

**coarse, course** *Coarse* means "crude" or "rough in texture." *The coarse weave of the wall hanging gave it a three-dimensional quality. Course* usually refers to a path, a playing field, or a unit of study; the expression *of course* means "certainly." *I plan to take a course in car repair this summer. Of course, you are welcome to join me.*

**compare to, compare with** *Compare to* means "to represent as similar." *She compared him to a wild stallion. Compare with* means "to examine similarities and differences." *The study compared the language ability of apes with that of dolphins.*

**complement, compliment** *Complement* is a verb meaning "to go with or complete" or a noun meaning "something that completes." *Compliment* as a verb means "to flatter"; as a noun it means "flattering remark." *Her skill at rushing the net complements his skill at volleying. Mother's flower arrangements receive many compliments.*

**conscience, conscious** *Conscience* is a noun meaning "moral principles." *Conscious* is an adjective meaning "aware or alert." *Let your conscience be your guide. Were you conscious of his love for you?*

**continual, continuous** *Continual* means "repeated regularly and frequently." *She grew weary of the continual telephone calls. Continuous* means "extended or prolonged without interruption." *The broken siren made a continuous wail.*

**could care less** *Could care less* is a nonstandard expression. Write *couldn't care less* instead. *He couldn't* (not *could*) *care less about his psychology final.*

**could of** *Could of* is nonstandard for *could have. We could have* (not *could of*) *had steak for dinner if we had been hungry.*

**council, counsel** A *council* is a deliberative body, and a *councilor* is a member of such a body. *Counsel* usually means "advice" and can also mean "lawyer"; *counselor* is one who gives advice or guidance. *The councilors met to draft the council's position paper. The pastor offered wise counsel to the troubled teenager.*

**criteria** *Criteria* is the plural of *criterion*, which means "a standard or rule or test on which a judgment or decision can be based." *The only criterion for the scholarship is ability.*

**data** *Data* is a plural noun technically meaning "facts or propositions." But *data* is increasingly being accepted as a singular noun. *The new data suggest* (or *suggests*) *that our theory is correct.* (The singular *datum* is rarely used.)

**different from, different than** Ordinarily, write *different from. Your sense of style is different from Jim's.* However, *different than* is acceptable to avoid an awkward construction. *Please let me know if your plans are different than* (to avoid *from what*) *they were six weeks ago.*

**differ from, differ with** *Differ from* means "to be unlike"; *differ with* means "to disagree." *She differed with me about the wording of the agreement. My approach to the problem differed from hers.*

**disinterested, uninterested** *Disinterested* means "impartial, objective"; *uninterested* means "not interested." *We sought the advice of a disinterested counselor to help us solve our problem. He was uninterested in anyone's opinion but his own.*

**don't** *Don't* is the contraction for *do not. I don't want any. Don't* should not be used as the contraction for *does not*, which is *doesn't. He doesn't* (not *don't*) *want any.* (See 27c.)

**due to** *Due to* is an adjective phrase and should not be used as a preposition meaning "because of." *The trip was canceled because of* (not *due to*) *lack of interest. Due to* is acceptable as a subject complement and usually follows a form of the verb *be. His success was due to hard work.*

**each** *Each* is singular. (See 21e and 22a.)

**effect** See *affect, effect.*

**e.g.** In formal writing, replace the Latin abbreviation *e.g.* with its English equivalent: *for example* or *for instance.*

**either** *Either* is singular. (See 21e and 22a.) (For *either . . . or* constructions, see 21d and 22d.)

**elicit, illicit** *Elicit* is a verb meaning "to bring out" or "to evoke." *Illicit* is an adjective meaning "unlawful." *The reporter was unable to elicit any information from the police about illicit drug traffic.*

**emigrate from, immigrate to** *Emigrate* means "to leave one country or region to settle in another." *In 1900, my grandfather emigrated from Russia to escape the religious pogroms. Immigrate* means "to enter another country and reside there." *Many Mexicans immigrate to the United States to find work.*

**eminent, imminent** *Eminent* means "outstanding" or "distinguished." *We met an eminent professor of Greek history. Imminent* means "about to happen." *The announcement is imminent.*

**enthused** Many people object to the use of *enthused* as an adjective. Use *enthusiastic* instead. *The children were enthusiastic* (not *enthused*) *about going to the circus.*

**etc.** Avoid ending a list with *etc.* It is more emphatic to end with an example, and in most contexts readers will understand that the list is not exhaustive. When you don't wish to end with an example, *and so on* is more graceful than *etc.* See also *and etc.*

**eventually, ultimately** Often used interchangeably, *eventually* is the better choice to mean "at an unspecified time in the future" and *ultimately* is better to mean "the furthest possible extent or greatest extreme." *He knew that eventually he would complete his degree. The existentialist considered suicide the ultimately rational act.*

**everybody, everyone** *Everybody* and *everyone* are singular. (See 21e and 22a.)

**everyone, every one** *Everyone* is an indefinite pronoun. *Every one,* the pronoun *one* preceded by the adjective *every,* means "each individual or thing in a particular group." *Every one* is usually followed by *of. Everyone wanted to go. Every one of the missing books was found.*

**except** See *accept, except.*

**expect** Avoid the colloquial use of *expect* meaning "to believe, think, or suppose." *I think* (not *expect*) *it will rain tonight.*

**explicit, implicit** *Explicit* means "expressed directly" or "clearly defined"; *implicit* means "implied, unstated." *I gave him explicit instructions not to go swimming. My mother's silence indicated her implicit approval.*

**farther, further** *Farther* usually describes distances. *Further* usually suggests quantity or degree. *Chicago is farther from Miami than I thought. You extended the curfew further than you should have.*

**fewer, less**  *Fewer* refers to items that can be counted; *less* refers to general amounts. *Fewer people are living in the city. Please put less sugar in my tea.*

**finalize**  *Finalize* is jargon meaning "to make final or complete." Use ordinary English instead. *The architect prepared final drawings* (not *finalized the drawings*).

**firstly**  *Firstly* sounds pretentious, and it leads to the ungainly series *firstly, secondly, thirdly, fourthly,* and so on. Write *first, second, third* instead.

**further**  See *farther, further.*

**get**  *Get* has many colloquial uses. In writing, avoid using *get* to mean the following: "to evoke an emotional response" (*That music always gets to me*); "to annoy" (*After a while his sulking got to me*); "to take revenge on" (*I got back at him by leaving the room*); "to become" (*He got sick*); "to start or begin" (*Let's get going*). Avoid using *have got to* in place of *must*. *I must* (not *have got to*) *finish this paper tonight.*

**good, well**  *Good* is an adjective, *well* an adverb. (See 26.) *He hasn't felt good about his game since he sprained his wrist last season. She performed well on the uneven parallel bars.*

**graduate**  Both of the following uses of *graduate* are standard: *My sister was graduated from UCLA last year. My sister graduated from UCLA last year.* It is nonstandard, however, to drop the word *from: My sister graduated UCLA last year.* Though this usage is common in informal English, many readers object to it.

**grow**  Phrases such as *to grow the economy* or *to grow a business* are jargon. Usually the verb *grow* is intransitive (it does not take a direct object). *Our business has grown very quickly.* When *grow* is used in a transitive sense, with a direct object, it means "to cultivate" or "to allow to grow." *We plan to grow tomatoes this year. John is growing a beard.*

**hanged, hung**  *Hanged* is the past-tense and past-participle form of the verb *hang* meaning "to execute." *The prisoner was hanged at dawn.* *Hung* is the past-tense and past-participle form of the verb *hang* meaning "to fasten or suspend." *The stockings were hung by the chimney with care.*

**hardly**  Avoid expressions such as *can't hardly* and *not hardly,* which are considered double negatives. *I can* (not *can't*) *hardly describe my elation at getting the job.* (See 26d.)

**has got, have got**   *Got* is unnecessary and awkward in such constructions. It should be dropped. *We have* (not *have got*) *three days to prepare for the opening.*

**he**   At one time *he* was commonly used to mean "he or she." Today such usage is inappropriate. (See 17f and 22a.)

**he/she, his/her**   In formal writing, use *he or she* or *his or her*. For alternatives to these wordy constructions, see 17f and 22a.

**hisself**   *Hisself* is nonstandard. Use *himself*.

**hopefully**   *Hopefully* means "in a hopeful manner." *We looked hopefully to the future.* Some usage experts object to the use of *hopefully* as a sentence adverb, apparently on grounds of clarity. To be safe, avoid using *hopefully* in sentences such as the following: *Hopefully, your son will recover soon.* At least some educated readers will want you to indicate who is doing the hoping: *I hope that your son will recover soon.*

**however**   In the past, some writers objected to *however* at the beginning of a sentence, but current experts advise you to place the word according to your meaning and desired emphasis. Any of the following sentences is correct, depending on the intended contrast. *Pam decided, however, to attend Harvard. However, Pam decided to attend Harvard.* (She had been considering other schools.) *Pam, however, decided to attend Harvard.* (Unlike someone else, Pam opted for Harvard.)

**hung**   See *hanged, hung.*

**i.e.**   In formal writing, replace the Latin abbreviation *i.e.* with its English equivalent: *that is.*

**if, whether**   Use *if* to express a condition and *whether* to express alternatives. *If you go on a trip, whether it be to Nebraska or New Jersey, remember to bring traveler's checks.*

**illusion**   See *allusion, illusion.*

**immigrate, emigrate**   See *emigrate from, immigrate to.*

**imminent**   See *eminent, imminent.*

**immoral**   See *amoral, immoral.*

**implement**   *Implement* is a pretentious way of saying "do," "carry out," or "accomplish." Use ordinary language instead. *We carried out* (not *implemented*) *the director's orders with some reluctance.*

imply, infer *Imply* means "to suggest or state indirectly"; *infer* means "to draw a conclusion." *John implied that he knew all about computers, but the interviewer inferred that John was inexperienced.*

in, into *In* indicates location or condition; *into* indicates movement or a change in condition. *They found the lost letters in a box after moving into the house.*

in regards to *In regards to* confuses two different phrases: *in regard to* and *as regards.* Use one or the other. *In regard to* (or *As regards*) *the contract, ignore the first clause.*

irregardless *Irregardless* is nonstandard. Use *regardless.*

is when, is where These mixed constructions are often incorrectly used in definitions. *A run-off election is a second election held to break a tie* (not *is when a second election breaks a tie*). (See 11c.)

it is *It is* is nonstandard when used to mean "there is." *There is* (not *It is*) *a fly in my soup.*

its, it's *Its* is a possessive pronoun; *it's* is a contraction for *it is.* (See 36c and 36e.) *The dog licked its wound whenever its owner walked into the room. It's a perfect day to walk the twenty-mile trail.*

kind(s) *Kind* is singular and should be treated as such. Don't write *These kind of chairs are rare.* Write instead *This kind of chair is rare. Kinds* is plural and should be used only when you mean more than one kind. *These kinds of chairs are rare.*

kind of, sort of Avoid using *kind of* or *sort of* to mean "somewhat." *The movie was somewhat* (not *kind of*) *boring.* Do not put *a* after either phrase. *That kind of* (not *kind of a*) *salesclerk annoys me.*

lay, lie See *lie, lay.*

lead, led *Lead* is a metallic element; it is a noun. *Led* is the past tense of the verb *lead. He led me to the treasure.*

learn, teach *Learn* means "to gain knowledge"; *teach* means "to impart knowledge." *I must teach* (not *learn*) *my sister to read.*

leave, let *Leave* means "to exit." *Let* means "to permit." *Let* (not *Leave*) *me help you with the dishes.*

less See *fewer, less.*

let, leave See *leave, let.*

**liable** *Liable* means "obligated" or "responsible." Do not use it to mean "likely." *You're likely* (not *liable*) *to trip if you don't tie your shoelaces.*

**lie, lay** *Lie* is an intransitive verb meaning "to recline or rest on a surface." Its principal parts are *lie, lay, lain. Lay* is a transitive verb meaning "to put or place." Its principal parts are *lay, laid, laid.* (See 27b.)

**like, as** *Like* is a preposition, not a subordinating conjunction. It can be followed only by a noun or a noun phrase. *As* is a subordinating conjunction that introduces a subordinate clause. In casual speech you may say *She looks like she hasn't slept* or *You don't know her like I do.* But in formal writing, use *as. She looks as if she hasn't slept. You don't know her as I do.* (See prepositions and subordinating conjunctions, 62f and 62g.)

**loose, lose** *Loose* is an adjective meaning "not securely fastened." *Lose* is a verb meaning "to misplace" or "to not win." *Did you lose your only loose pair of work pants?*

**lots, lots of** *Lots* and *lots of* are colloquial substitutes for *many, much,* or *a lot.* Avoid using them in formal writing.

**mankind** Avoid *mankind* whenever possible. It offends many readers because it excludes women. Use *humanity, humans, the human race,* or *humankind* instead.

**may** See *can, may.*

**maybe, may be** *Maybe* is an adverb meaning "possibly." *May be* is a verb phrase. *Maybe the sun will shine tomorrow. Tomorrow may be a brighter day.*

**may of, might of** *May of* and *might of* are nonstandard for *may have* and *might have. We may have* (not *may of*) *had too many cookies.*

**media, medium** *Media* is the plural of *medium. Of all the media that cover the Olympics, television is the medium that best captures the spectacle of the events.*

**most** *Most* is colloquial when used to mean "almost" and should be avoided. *Almost* (not *Most*) *everyone went to the parade.*

**must of** See *may of.*

**myself** *Myself* is a reflexive or intensive pronoun. Reflexive: *I cut myself.* Intensive: *I will drive you myself.* Do not use *myself* in place of *I* or *me*. *He gave the flowers to Melinda and me* (not *myself*). (See also 24.)

**neither** *Neither* is singular. (See 21e and 22a.) For *neither . . . nor* constructions, see 21d and 22d.

**none** *None* may be singular or plural. (See 21e.)

**nowheres** *Nowheres* is nonstandard for *nowhere*.

**number** See *amount, number.*

**of** Use the verb *have*, not the preposition *of*, after the verbs *could, should, would, may, might,* and *must. They must have* (not *of*) *left early.*

**off of** *Off* is sufficient. Omit *of. The ball rolled off* (not *off of*) *the table.*

**OK, O.K., okay** All three spellings are acceptable, but in formal speech and writing avoid these colloquial expressions for consent or approval.

**parameters** *Parameter* is a mathematical term that has become jargon for "fixed limit," "boundary," or "guideline." Use ordinary English instead. *The task force was asked to work within certain guidelines* (not *parameters*).

**passed, past** *Passed* is the past tense of the verb *pass. Mother passed me another slice of cake. Past* usually means "belonging to a former time" or "beyond a time or place." *Our past president spoke until past midnight. The hotel is just past the next intersection.*

**percent, per cent, percentage** *Percent* (also spelled *per cent*) is always used with a specific number. *Percentage* is used with a descriptive term such as *large* or *small*, not with a specific number. *The candidate won 80 percent of the primary vote. Only a small percentage of registered voters turned out for the election.*

**phenomena** *Phenomena* is the plural of *phenomenon*, which means "an observable occurrence or fact." *Strange phenomena occur at all hours of the night in that house, but last night's phenomenon was the strangest of all.*

**plus** *Plus* should not be used to join independent clauses. *This raincoat is dirty; moreover* (not *plus*), *it has a hole in it.*

**precede, proceed** *Precede* means "to come before." *Proceed* means "to go forward." *As we proceeded up the mountain path, we noticed* *fresh tracks in the mud, evidence that a group of hikers had preceded us.*

**principal, principle** *Principal* is a noun meaning "the head of a school or organization" or "a sum of money." It is also an adjective meaning "most important." *Principle* is a noun meaning "a basic truth or law." *The principal expelled her for three principal reasons. We believe in the principle of equal justice for all.*

**proceed, precede** See *precede, proceed*.

**quote, quotation** *Quote* is a verb; *quotation* is a noun. Avoid using *quote* as a shortened form of *quotation*. *Her quotations* (not *quotes*) *from Shakespeare intrigued us.*

**raise, rise** *Raise* is a transitive verb meaning "to move or cause to move upward." It takes a direct object. *I raised the shades. Rise* is an intransitive verb meaning "to go up." It does not take a direct object. *Heat rises.*

**real, really** *Real* is an adjective; *really* is an adverb. *Real* is sometimes used informally as an adverb, but avoid this use in formal writing. *She was really* (not *real*) *angry.* (See 26a.)

**reason is because** Use *that* instead of *because*. *The reason I'm late is that* (not *because*) *my car broke down.* (See 11c.)

**reason why** The expression *reason why* is redundant. *The reason* (not *The reason why*) *Jones lost the election is clear.*

**relation, relationship** *Relation* describes a connection between things. *Relationship* describes a connection between people. *There is a relation between poverty and infant mortality. Our business relationship has cooled over the years.*

**respectfully, respectively** *Respectfully* means "showing or marked by respect." *Respectively* means "each in the order given." *He respectfully submitted his opinion to the judge. John, Tom, and Larry were a butcher, a baker, and a lawyer, respectively.*

**sensual, sensuous** *Sensual* means "gratifying the physical senses," especially those associated with sexual pleasure. *Sensuous* means "pleasing to the senses," especially those involved in the experience of art, music, and nature. *The sensuous music and balmy air led the dancers to more sensual movements.*

**set, sit** *Set* is a transitive verb meaning "to put" or "to place." Its principal parts are *set, set, set. Sit* is an intransitive verb meaning "to be seated." Its principal parts are *sit, sat, sat. She set the dough in a warm corner of the kitchen. The cat sat in the warmest part of the room.*

**shall, will** *Shall* was once used as the helping verb with *I* or *we: I shall, we shall, you will, he/she/it will, they will.* Today, however, *will* is generally accepted even when the subject is *I* or *we.* The word *shall* occurs primarily in polite questions (*Shall I find you a pillow?*) and in legalistic sentences suggesting duty or obligation (*The applicant shall file form 1080 by December 31*).

**should of** *Should of* is nonstandard for *should have. They should have* (not *should of*) *been home an hour ago.*

**since** Do not use *since* to mean "because" if there is any chance of ambiguity. *Since we won the game, we have been celebrating with a pitcher of root beer. Since* here could mean "because" or "from the time that."

**sit** See *set, sit.*

**site, cite** See *cite, site.*

**somebody, someone** *Somebody* and *someone* are singular. (See 21e and 22a.)

**something** *Something* is singular. (See 21e.)

**sometime, some time, sometimes** *Sometime* is an adverb meaning "at an indefinite or unstated time." *Some time* is the adjective *some* modifying the noun *time* and is spelled as two words to mean "a period of time." *Sometimes* is an adverb meaning "at times, now and then." *I'll see you sometime soon. I haven't lived there for some time. Sometimes I run into him at the library.*

**suppose to** Write *supposed to.*

**sure and** *Sure and* is nonstandard for *sure to. We were all taught to be sure to* (not *and*) *look both ways before crossing a street.*

**take** See *bring, take.*

**than, then** *Than* is a conjunction used in comparisons; *then* is an adverb denoting time. *That pizza is more than I can eat. Tom laughed, and then we recognized him.*

**that** See *who, which, that.*

**that, which** Many writers reserve *that* for restrictive clauses, *which* for nonrestrictive clauses. (See 32e.)

**theirselves** *Theirselves* is nonstandard for *themselves*. *The two people were able to push the Volkswagen out of the way themselves* (not *theirselves*).

**them** The use of *them* in place of *those* is nonstandard. *Please send those* (not *them*) *flowers to the patient in room 220.*

**there, their, they're** *There* is an adverb specifying place; it is also an expletive. Adverb: *Sylvia is lying there unconscious.* Expletive: *There are two plums left. Their* is a possessive pronoun. *Fred and Jane finally washed their car. They're* is a contraction of *they are. They're later than usual today.*

**they** The use of *they* to indicate possession is nonstandard. Use *their* instead. *Cindy and Sam decided to sell their* (not *they*) *1975 Corvette.*

**this kind** See *kind(s).*

**to, too, two** *To* is a preposition; *too* is an adverb; *two* is a number. *Too many of your shots slice to the left, but the last two were right on the mark.*

**toward, towards** *Toward* and *towards* are generally interchangeable, although *toward* is preferred in American English.

**try and** *Try and* is nonstandard for *try to. The teacher asked us all to try to* (not *and*) *write an original haiku.*

**ultimately, eventually** See *eventually, ultimately.*

**unique** Avoid expressions such as *most unique, more straight, less perfect, very round.* Something either is unique or it isn't. It is illogical to suggest degrees of uniqueness. (See 26c.)

**usage** The noun *usage* should not be substituted for *use* when the meaning intended is "employment of." *The use* (not *usage*) *of computers dramatically increased the company's profits.*

**use to** Write *used to.*

**utilize** *Utilize* means "to make use of." It often sounds pretentious; in most cases, *use* is sufficient. *I used* (not *utilized*) *the best workers to get the job done fast.*

**wait for, wait on** *Wait for* means "to be in readiness for" or "await." *Wait on* means "to serve." *We're waiting for* (not *waiting on*) *Ruth to take us to the game.*

**ways** *Ways* is colloquial when used to mean "distance." *The city is a long way* (not *ways*) *from here.*

**weather, whether**  The noun *weather* refers to the state of the atmosphere. *Whether* is a conjunction used for a choice between alternatives. *We wondered whether the weather would clear up in time for our picnic.*

**well, good**  See *good, well.*

**where**  Do not use *where* in place of *that. I heard that* (not *where*) *the crime rate is increasing.*

**which**  See *that, which* and *who, which, that.*

**while**  Avoid using *while* to mean "although" or "whereas" if there is any chance of ambiguity. *Although* (not *While*) *Gloria lost money in the slot machine, Tom won it at roulette.* Here *While* could mean either "although" or "at the same time that."

**who, which, that**  Do not use *which* to refer to persons. Use *who* instead. *That,* though generally used to refer to things, may be used to refer to a group or class of people. *The player who* (not *that* or *which*) *made the basket at the buzzer was named MVP. The team that scores the most points in this game will win the tournament.* (See 23e.)

**who, whom**  *Who* is used for subjects and subject complements; *whom* is used for objects. (See 25.)

**who's, whose**  *Who's* is a contraction of *who is; whose* is a possessive pronoun. *Who's ready for more popcorn? Whose coat is this?* (See 36c and 36e.)

**will**  See *shall, will.*

**would of**  *Would of* is nonstandard for *would have. She would have* (not *would of*) *had a chance to play if she had arrived on time.*

**you**  In formal writing, avoid *you* in an indefinite sense meaning "anyone." (See 23d.) *Any spectator* (not *You*) *could tell by the way John caught the ball that his throw would be too late.*

**your, you're**  *Your* is a possessive pronoun; *you're* is a contraction of *you are. Is that your new motorcycle? You're on the list of finalists.* (See 36c and 36e.)

# Answers to Tutorials and Lettered Exercises

## Answers to Tutorial 1, page xxxi

1. A verb has to agree with its subject. (21)
2. Each pronoun should agree with its antecedent. (22)
3. Avoid sentence fragments. (19)
4. It's important to use apostrophes correctly. (36)
5. Check for *-ed* verb endings that have been dropped. (27d)
6. Discriminate carefully between adjectives and adverbs. (26)
7. If your sentence begins with a long introductory word group, use a comma to separate the word group from the rest of the sentence. (32b)
8. Don't write a run-on sentence; you must connect independent clauses with a comma and a coordinating conjunction or with a semicolon. (20)
9. For clarity, a writer must be careful not to shift his or her [*not* their] point of view. *Or* For clarity, writers should be careful not to shift their point of view. (13a)
10. Watch out for dangling modifiers. (12e)

## Answers to Tutorial 2, page xxxii

1. The index entry "*each*" mentions that the word is singular, so you might not need to look further to realize that the verb should be *has*, not *have*. The first page reference takes you to section 21, which explains in more detail why *has* is correct. The index entry "*has* vs. *have*" also leads you to section 21.
2. The index entry "*lying* vs. *laying*" takes you to section 27b, where you will learn that *lying* (meaning "reclining or resting on a surface") is correct.
3. Look up "*only*" and you will be directed to section 12a, which explains that limiting modifiers such as *only* should be placed before the words they modify. The sentence should read *We looked at only two houses before buying the house of our dreams.*
4. Looking up "*you*, inappropriate use of" leads you to section 23d and the Glossary of Usage, which explain that *you* should not be used to mean "anyone in general." You can revise the sentence by using *a person* or *one* instead of *you*, or you can restructure the sentence completely: *In Saudi Arabia, accepting a gift is considered ill mannered.*
5. The index entries "*I* vs. *me*" and "*me* vs. *I*" take you to section 24, which explains why *me* is correct.

## Answers to Tutorial 3, page xxxii

1. Section 32c states that, although usage varies, most experts advise using a comma between all items in a series — to prevent possible misreadings or ambiguities. To find this section, Ray Farley would probably use the menu system.
2. Maria Sanchez and Mike Lee would consult section 30, on articles. This section is easy to locate in the menu system.
3. Section 24 explains why *Jane and me* is correct. To find section 24, John Pell could use the menu system if he knew to look under "Problems with pronouns." Otherwise, he could look up "*I* vs. *me*" in the index. Pell could also look up "*myself*" in the index or he could consult the Glossary of Usage, where a cross-reference would direct him to section 24.
4. Selena Young's employees could turn to sections 21 and 27c for help. Young could use the menu system to find these sections if she knew to look under "Subject-verb agreement" or "Standard English verb forms." If she wasn't sure about the grammatical terminology, she could look up "*-s,* as verb ending" or "Verbs, *-s* form of" in the index.
5. Section 26b explains why "I felt bad about her death" is correct. To find section 26b, Joe Thompson could use the menu system if he knew that *bad* versus *badly* is a choice between an adjective and an adverb. Otherwise he could look up "*bad, badly*" in the index or the Glossary of Usage.

## Answers to Tutorial 4, page xxxiii

1. Changing attitudes toward alcohol have *affected* the beer industry.
2. It is *human* nature to think wisely and act foolishly.
3. Correct
4. Our goal this year is to *increase* our profits by 9 percent.
5. Most sleds are pulled by no *fewer* than two dogs and no more than ten.

## Answers to Tutorial 5, page xxxiv

Alim, H. Samy. "360 Degreez of Black Art Comin at You: Sista Sonia Sanchez and the Dimensions of a Black Arts Continuum." BMa: The Sonia Sanchez Literary Review 6.1 (2000): 15-33.

Chang, Jeff. Can't Stop, Won't Stop: A History of the Hip-Hop Generation. New York: St. Martin's, 2005.

Davis, Kimberly. "The Roots Redefine Hip-Hop's Past." Ebony June 2003: 162-64. Expanded Academic ASAP. InfoTrac. Ray Cosgrove Lib., Truman Coll., Chicago. 13 Apr. 2005 <http://infotrac.galegroup.com>.

Randall, Kay. "Studying a Hip-Hop Nation." University of Texas at Austin. 11 Apr. 2005. 13 Apr. 2005 <http://www.utexas.edu/features/archives/2003/hiphop.html>.

Sugarhill Gang. "Rapper's Delight." The Sugarhill Gang. LP. Sugarhill, 1979.

## EXERCISE 8–1, page 150

Possible revisions:

a. The Prussians defeated the Saxons in 1745.
b. Ahmed, the producer, manages the entire operation.
c. The video game programmers awkwardly paddled the sea kayaks.
d. Emphatic and active; no change
e. Protesters were shouting on the courthouse steps.

## EXERCISE 9–1, page 156

Possible revisions:

a. Police dogs are used for finding lost children, tracking criminals, and detecting bombs and illegal drugs.
b. Hannah told her rock climbing partner that she bought a new harness and that she wanted to climb Otter Cliffs.
c. It is more difficult to sustain an exercise program than to start one.
d. During basic training, I was told not only what to do but also what to think.
e. Jan wanted to drive to the wine country or at least to Sausalito.

## EXERCISE 10–1, page 162

Possible revisions:

a. A good source of vitamin C is a grapefruit or an orange.
b. The women entering VMI can expect haircuts as short as those of the male cadets.
c. The driver went to investigate, only to find that one of the new tires had blown.
d. The graphic designers are interested in and knowledgeable about producing posters for the balloon race.
e. Reefs are home to more species than any other ecosystem in the sea.

## EXERCISE 11–1, page 167

Possible revisions:

a. Using surgical gloves is a precaution now taken by dentists to prevent contact with patients' blood and saliva.
b. A career in medicine, which my brother is pursuing, requires at least ten years of challenging work.
c. The pharaohs had bad teeth because tiny particles of sand found their way into Egyptian bread.
d. Recurring bouts of flu caused the team to forfeit a record number of games.
e. This box contains the key to your future.

## EXERCISE 12–1, page 173

Possible revisions:

a. Our English professor asked us to reread the sonnet very carefully, looking for subtleties we had missed on a first reading.

b. The monarch arrived at the gate in a gold carriage pulled by four white horses.
c. Rhonda and Sam talked almost all night about her surgery.
d. A coolhunter is a person who can find the next wave of fashion in the unnoticed corners of modern society.
e. Not all geese fly beyond Narragansett for the winter.

## EXERCISE 12–2, page 177

Possible revisions:

a. When I was ten, my parents took me on my first balloon ride.
b. To replace the gear mechanism, you can use the attached form to order the part by mail.
c. As I nestled in the cockpit, the pounding of the engine was muffled only slightly by my helmet.
d. After studying polymer chemistry, Phuong found computer games less complex.
e. When I was a young man, my mother enrolled me in tap dance classes, hoping I would become the next Savion Glover.

## EXERCISE 13–3, page 184

Possible revisions:

a. Courtroom lawyers have more than a touch of theater in their blood.
b. The interviewer asked if we had brought our proof of birth and citizenship and our passports.
c. Reconnaissance scouts often have to make fast decisions and use sophisticated equipment to keep their teams from detection.
d. After the animators finish their scenes, the production designer arranges the clips according to the storyboard and makes synchronization notes for the sound editor and the composer.
e. Madame Defarge is a sinister figure in Dickens's *A Tale of Two Cities*. On a symbolic level, she represents fate; like the Greek Fates, she knits the fabric of individual destiny.

## EXERCISE 14–1, page 191

Possible revisions:

a. The X-Men comic books and Japanese woodcuts of kabuki dancers, all part of Marlena's research project on popular culture, covered the tabletop and the chairs.
b. Our waitress, costumed in a kimono, had painted her face white and arranged her hair in an upswept lacquered beehive.
c. Students can apply for a spot in the foundation's leadership program, which teaches thinking and communication skills.
d. Shore houses were flooded up to the first floor, beaches were washed away, and Brant's Lighthouse was swallowed by the sea.
e. Laura Thackray, an engineer at Volvo Car Corporation, designed a pregnant crash-test dummy to address women's safety needs.

## EXERCISE 14–2, page 193

Possible revisions:

a. These particles, known as "stealth liposomes," can hide in the body for a long time without detection.
b. Irena, a competitive gymnast majoring in biochemistry, intends to apply her athletic experience and her science degree to a career in sports medicine.
c. Because students, textile workers, and labor unions have loudly protested sweatshop abuses, apparel makers have been forced to examine their labor practices.
d. Developed in a European university, IRC (Internet Relay Chat) was created as a way for a group of graduate students to talk about projects from their dorm rooms.
e. The cafeteria's new menu, which has an international flavor, includes everything from enchiladas and pizza to pad thai and sauerbraten.

## EXERCISE 14–3, page 195

Possible revisions:

a. Working as an aide for the relief agency, Gina distributed food and medical supplies.
b. Janbir, who spent every Saturday learning tabla drumming, noticed with each hour of practice that his memory for complex patterns was growing stronger.
c. When the rotor hit, it gouged a hole about an eighth of an inch deep in my helmet.
d. My grandfather, who was born eighty years ago in Puerto Rico, raised his daughters the old-fashioned way.
e. By reversing the depressive effect of the drug, the Narcan saved the patient's life.

## EXERCISE 16–1, page 211

Possible revisions:

a. Martin Luther King Jr. set a high standard for future leaders.
b. Aanika has loved cooking since she could first peek over a kitchen tabletop.
c. Bloom's race for the governorship is futile.
d. A successful graphic designer must have technical knowledge and an eye for color and balance.
e. You will deliver mail to all employees.

## EXERCISE 17–1, page 216

Possible revisions:

a. In my youth, my family was poor.
b. This conference will help me serve my clients better.
c. Have you ever been accused of beating a dead horse?
d. Government studies show a need for after-school programs.

e. Passengers should try to complete the customs declaration form before leaving the plane.

## EXERCISE 17–3, page 224

Possible revisions:

a. Dr. Geralyn Farmer is the chief surgeon at University Hospital. Dr. Paul Green is her assistant.
b. All applicants want to know how much they will make.
c. Elementary school teachers should understand the concept of nurturing if they intend to be successful.
d. Students of high-tech architecture pick a favorite when they study such inspirational architects as Renzo Piano and Zaha Hadid.
e. If we do not stop polluting our environment, we will perish.

## EXERCISE 18–3, page 230

Possible revisions:

a. We regret this delay; thank you for your patience.
b. Ada's plan is to acquire education and experience to prepare herself for a position as property manager.
c. Tiger Woods, the ultimate competitor, has earned millions of dollars just in endorsements.
d. Many people take for granted that public libraries have up-to-date networked computer systems.
e. The effect of Gao Xinjian's novels on Chinese exiles is hard to gauge.

## EXERCISE 18–4, page 232

Possible revisions:

a. Queen Anne was so angry with Sarah Churchill that she refused to see her again.
b. Correct
c. The parade moved off the street and onto the beach.
d. The frightened refugees intend to make the dangerous trek across the mountains.
e. What type of wedding are you planning?

## EXERCISE 18–5, page 236

Possible revisions:

a. John stormed into the room like a hurricane.
b. Some people insist that they'll always be available to help, even when they haven't been before.
c. The Cubs easily beat the Mets, who were in trouble early in the game today at Wrigley Field.
d. We ironed out the wrinkles in our relationship.
e. My mother accused me of evading her questions when in fact I was just saying the first thing that came to mind.

## EXERCISE 19–1, page 246

Possible revisions:

a. Listening to the CD her sister had sent, Mia was overcome with a mix of emotions: happiness, homesickness, nostalgia.
b. Cortés and his soldiers were astonished when they looked down from the mountains and saw Tenochtitlán, the magnificent capital of the Aztecs.
c. Although my spoken Spanish is not very good, I can read the language with ease.
d. There are several reasons for not eating meat. One reason is that dangerous chemicals are used throughout the various stages of meat production.
e. To learn how to sculpt beauty from everyday life is my intention in studying art and archaeology.

## EXERCISE 20–1, page 255

Possible revisions:

a. The city had one public swimming pool that stayed packed with children all summer long.
b. The building is being renovated, so at times we have no heat, water, or electricity.
c. The view was not what the travel agent had described. Where were the rolling hills and the shimmering rivers?
d. All those gnarled equations looked like toxic insects; maybe I was going to have to rethink my major.
e. The city government had good reason to fear a major earthquake: Most [*or* most] of the business district was built on landfill.

## EXERCISE 20–2, page 256

Possible revisions:

a. Wind power for the home is a supplementary source of energy that can be combined with electricity, gas, or solar energy.
b. Correct
c. In the Middle Ages, when the streets of London were dangerous places, it was safer to travel by boat along the Thames.
d. "He's not drunk," I said. "He's in a state of diabetic shock."
e. Are you able to endure boredom, isolation, and potential violence? Then the army may well be the adventure for you.

## EXERCISE 21–1, page 270

a. Subject: friendship and support; verb: have; b. Subject: Shelters; verb: offer; c. Subject: source; verb: is; d. Subject: chances; verb: are; e. Subject: card and haiku; verb: were

## EXERCISE 21–2, page 270

a. One of the main reasons for elephant poaching is the profits received from selling the ivory tusks.

b. Correct
c. A number of students in the seminar were aware of the importance of joining the discussion.
d. Batik cloth from Bali, blue and white ceramics from Delft, and a bocce ball from Turin have made Angelie's room the talk of the dorm.
e. Correct

## EXERCISE 22–1, page 277

Possible revisions:

a. Every presidential candidate must appeal to a wide variety of ethnic and social groups to win the election.
b. David lent his motorcycle to someone who allowed a friend to use it.
c. The aerobics teacher motioned for all the students to move their arms in wide, slow circles.
d. Correct
e. Applicants should be bilingual if they want to qualify for this position.

## EXERCISE 23–1, page 284

Possible revisions:

a. Some professors say that an engineering student should have hands-on experience with dismantling and reassembling machines.
b. Because she had decorated her living room with posters from chamber music festivals, her date thought she was interested in classical music. Actually she preferred rock.
c. In Ethiopia, a person doesn't need much property to be considered well-off.
d. Marianne told Jenny, "I am worried about your mother's illness." [or ". . . about my mother's illness."]
e. Though Lewis cried for several minutes after scraping his knee, eventually the pain subsided.

## EXERCISE 24–1, page 294

a. Correct [But the writer could change the end of the sentence: . . . *than he is.*]
b. Correct [But the writer could change the end of the sentence: . . . *that she was the coach.*]
c. She appreciated his telling the truth in such a difficult situation.
d. The director has asked you and me to draft a proposal for a new recycling plan.
e. Five close friends and I rented a station wagon, packed it with food, and drove to Mardi Gras on a three-day weekend.

## EXERCISE 25–1, page 301

a. The roundtable featured scholars whom I had never heard of. [or . . . scholars I had never heard of.]
b. Correct
c. Correct
d. Daniel always gives a holiday donation to whoever needs it.
e. So many singers came to the audition that Natalia had trouble deciding whom to select for the choir.

## EXERCISE 26–1, page 309

Possible revisions:

a. Did you do well on last week's chemistry exam?
b. With the budget deadline approaching, our office has hardly had time to handle routine correspondence.
c. Correct
d. The customer complained that he hadn't been treated nicely.
e. Of all my relatives, Uncle Roberto is the cleverest.

## EXERCISE 27–1, page 316

a. When I get the urge to exercise, I lie down until it passes.
b. Grandmother had driven our new SUV to the sunrise church service on Savage Mountain, so we were left with the station wagon.
c. A pile of dirty rags was lying at the bottom of the stairs.
d. How did the computer know that the gamer had gone from the room with the blue ogre to the hall where the gold was heaped?
e. Abraham Lincoln took good care of his legal clients; the contracts he drew for the Illinois Central Railroad could never be broken.

## EXERCISE 27–2, page 324

a. The glass sculptures of the Swan Boats were prominent in the brightly lit lobby.
b. Visitors to the glass museum were not supposed to touch the exhibits.
c. Our church has all the latest technology, even a closed-circuit television.
d. Christos didn't know about Marlo's promotion because he never listens. He is always talking.
e. Correct

## EXERCISE 28–1, page 334

Possible revisions:

a. Correct
b. Watson and Crick discovered the mechanism that controls inheritance in all life: the workings of the DNA molecule.
c. When Hitler decided to kill the Jews in 1941, did he know that Himmler and his SS had had mass murder in mind since 1938?
d. Correct
e. Correct

## EXERCISE 29–1, page 340

a. The new manager should be making her first announcement in the next hour.
b. There is nothing in the world that TV has not touched on.
c. Did the landlord tell you that he's going to raise the rent?
d. With luck, visitors can find a beautiful view of the old temple in the rain and mist.
e. The benefits of diet and exercise have been given much attention by health care providers.

## EXERCISE 29–2, page 344

Possible revisions:

a. The electrician might have discovered the broken circuit if she had gone through the modules one at a time.
b. If Verena wins a scholarship, she will go to graduate school.
c. Whenever there is a fire in our neighborhood, everybody comes out to watch.
d. Sarah will take the paralegal job unless she gets a better offer.
e. If I lived in Budapest with my cousin Szusza, she would teach me Hungarian cooking.

## EXERCISE 29–3, page 348

Possible answers:

a. I enjoy riding my motorcycle.
b. The tutor told Samantha to come to the writing center.
c. The team hopes to work hard and win the championship.
d. Ricardo and his brothers miss surfing during the winter.
e. The babysitter let Roger stay up until midnight.

## EXERCISE 31–1, page 361

a. There are some cartons of ice cream in the freezer.
b. I don't use the subway because I am afraid.
c. The prime minister is the most popular leader in my country.
d. We tried to get in touch with the same manager whom we spoke to earlier.
e. Recently there have been a number of earthquakes in Turkey.

## EXERCISE 31–2, page 364

a. an attractive young Vietnamese woman
b. a dedicated Catholic priest
c. her old blue wool sweater
d. Joe's delicious Scandinavian bread
e. many beautiful antique bird cages

## EXERCISE 31–3, page 367

a. Listening to everyone's complaints all day was irritating.
b. The long flight to Singapore was exhausting.
c. Correct
d. After a great deal of research, the scientist made a fascinating discovery.
e. That blackout was one of the most frightening experiences I've ever had.

## EXERCISE 31–4, page 368

a. Whenever we eat at the Centerville Diner, we sit at a small table in the corner of the room.
b. Correct
c. On Thursday, Nancy will attend her first Pilates class at the community center.
d. Correct

e. We decided to go to a restaurant because there was no fresh food in the refrigerator.

## EXERCISE 32–1, page 375

a. Alisa brought the injured bird home and fashioned a splint out of Popsicle sticks for its wing.
b. Considered a classic of early animation, *The Adventures of Prince Achmed* used hand-cut silhouettes against colored backgrounds.
c. If you complete the enclosed evaluation form and return it within two weeks, you will receive a free breakfast during your next stay.
d. Correct
e. Roger had always wanted a handmade violin, but he couldn't afford one.

## EXERCISE 32–2, page 378

a. The cold, impersonal atmosphere of the university was unbearable.
b. An ambulance threaded its way through police cars, fire trucks, and irate citizens.
c. Correct
d. After two broken arms, three cracked ribs, and one concussion, Ken quit the varsity football team.
e. Correct

## EXERCISE 32–3, page 382

a. Choreographer Alvin Ailey's best-known work, *Revelations*, is more than just a crowd pleaser.
b. Correct
c. Correct
d. A member of an organization that provides housing for AIDS patients was also appointed to the commission.
e. Brian Eno, who began his career as a rock musician, turned to meditative compositions in the late seventies.

## EXERCISE 32–4, page 388

a. Cricket, which originated in England, is also popular in Australia, South Africa, and India.
b. At the sound of the starting pistol, the horses surged forward toward the first obstacle, a sharp incline three feet high.
c. After seeing an exhibition of Western art, Gerhard Richter escaped from East Berlin and smuggled out many of his notebooks.
d. Corrie's new wet suit has an intricate blue pattern.
e. Correct

## EXERCISE 32–5, page 390

a. On January 15, 2004, our office moved to 29 Commonwealth Avenue, Mechanicsville, VA 23111.
b. Correct
c. Ms. Carlson, you are a valued customer whose satisfaction is very important to us.

d. Mr. Mundy was born on July 22, 1939, in Arkansas, where his family had lived for four generations.
e. Correct

## EXERCISE 33–1, page 397

a. Correct
b. Tricia's first artwork was a big blue clay dolphin.
c. Some modern musicians (trumpeter John Hassell is an example) blend several cultural traditions into a unique sound.
d. Myra liked hot, spicy foods such as chili, jambalaya, and buffalo wings.
e. On the display screen was a soothing pattern of light and shadow.

## EXERCISE 34–1, page 402

a. Do not ask me to be kind; just ask me to act as though I were.
b. When men talk about defense, they always claim to be protecting women and children, but they never ask the women and children what they think.
c. When I get a little money, I buy books; if any is left, I buy food and clothes.
d. Correct
e. Wit has truth in it; wisecracking is simply calisthenics with words.

## EXERCISE 34–2, page 403

a. Strong black coffee will not sober you up; the truth is that time is the only way to get alcohol out of your system.
b. It is not surprising that our society is increasingly violent; after all, television desensitizes us to brutality at a very early age.
c. There is often a fine line between right and wrong, good and bad, truth and deception.
d. Correct
e. Severe, unremitting pain is a ravaging force, especially when the patient tries to hide it from others.

## EXERCISE 35–1, page 407

a. Correct [Either *It* or *it* is correct.]
b. If we have come to fight, we are far too few; if we have come to die, we are far too many.
c. The travel package includes a round-trip ticket to Athens, a cruise through the Cyclades, and all hotel accommodations.
d. The media portray my generation as lazy, although polls show that we work as hard as the twentysomethings before us.
e. Fran Lebowitz has this advice for parents: "Never allow your child to call you by your first name. He hasn't known you long enough."

## EXERCISE 36–1, page 412

a. Correct
b. The innovative shoe fastener was inspired by the designer's young son.
c. Each day's menu features a different European country's dish.
d. Sue worked overtime to increase her family's earnings.

e. Ms. Jacobs is unwilling to listen to students' complaints about computer failures and damaged disks.

## EXERCISE 37–1, page 420

a. As for the advertisement "Sailors have more fun," if you consider chipping paint and swabbing decks fun, then you will have plenty of it.
b. Correct
c. After winning the lottery, Juanita said that she would give half the money to charity.
d. After the movie Vicki said, "The reviewer called this flick 'trash of the first order.' I guess you can't believe everything you read."
e. Correct

## EXERCISE 39–1, page 431

a. A client has left his or her cell phone in our conference room.
b. The films we made of Kilauea on our trip to Hawaii Volcanoes National Park illustrate a typical spatter cone eruption.
c. Correct
d. Correct
e. Of three engineering fields — chemical, mechanical, and materials — Keegan chose materials engineering for its application to toy manufacturing.

## EXERCISE 40–1, page 437

a. Correct
b. Some combat soldiers are trained by government diplomats to be sensitive to issues of culture, history, and religion.
c. Correct
d. How many pounds have you lost since you began running four miles a day?
e. Denzil spent all night studying for his psychology exam.

## EXERCISE 41–1, page 440

a. The carpenters located three maple timbers, twenty-one sheets of cherry, and ten oblongs of polished ebony for the theater set.
b. Correct
c. Correct
d. Eight students in the class had been labeled "learning disabled."
e. The Vietnam Veterans Memorial in Washington, DC, had 58,132 names inscribed on it when it was dedicated in 1982.

## EXERCISE 42–1, page 444

a. Howard Hughes commissioned the *Spruce Goose,* a beautifully built but thoroughly impractical wooden aircraft.
b. The old man screamed his anger, shouting to all of us, "I will not leave my money to you worthless layabouts!"
c. I learned the Latin term *ad infinitum* from an old nursery rhyme about fleas: "Great fleas have little fleas upon their back to bite 'em, / Little fleas have lesser fleas and so on *ad infinitum.*"

    d. Correct
    e. Neve Campbell's lifelong interest in ballet inspired her involvement in the film *The Company*, which portrays a season with the Joffrey Ballet.

## EXERCISE 44–1, page 460

    a. Correct
    b. The swiftly moving tugboat pulled alongside the barge and directed it away from the oil spill in the harbor.
    c. Correct
    d. Your dog is well known in our neighborhood.
    e. Roadblocks were set up along all the major highways leading out of the city.

## EXERCISE 45–1, page 466

    a. Assistant Dean Shirin Ahmadi recommended offering more world language courses.
    b. Correct
    c. Kalindi has an ambitious semester, studying differential calculus, classical Hebrew, brochure design, and Greek literature.
    d. Lydia's aunt and uncle make modular houses as beautiful as modernist works of art.
    e. We amused ourselves on the long flight by discussing how spring in Kyoto stacks up against summer in London.

## EXERCISE 48–1, page 516

a. hasty generalization; b. false analogy; c. biased language; d. faulty cause-and-effect reasoning; e. *either . . . or* fallacy

## EXERCISE 62–1, page 793

a. sun, assistance; b. Pride, bottom, mistakes; c. Success, confidence; d. censorship, flick, dial; e. flower, concrete (noun/adjective), cloverleaf

## EXERCISE 62–2, page 797

a. He, every (pronoun/adjective); b. those, who; c. I, some (pronoun/adjective), that, I, myself; d. I, You, He; e. you, anything, anyone, me

## EXERCISE 62–3, page 800

a. can pardon; b. are; c. does bring down; d. Keep, 'll [will] be insulted; e. Throw, will emerge

## EXERCISE 62–4, page 803

a. Adjectives: General, wrong; adverb: generally; b. Adjectives: The (article), American, tolerant; adverb: wonderfully; c. Adjectives: an (article), uncultivated, an (article), uncultivated; adverbs: sometimes, never; d. Adjectives: wrong, right; adverbs: rather, strongly, weakly; e. Adjective: the (article); adverb: faster

## EXERCISE 63–1, page 813

a. Complete subjects: Sticks and stones, words; simple subjects: Sticks, stones, words; b. Complete subject: all delays; simple subject: delays; c. Complete subject: (You); d. Complete subject: nothing except change; simple subject: nothing; e. Complete subject: Most of the disputes in the world; simple subject: Most

## EXERCISE 63–2, page 818

a. Subject complement: cheap; b. Direct object: an injury; c. Direct object: his convent; d. Subject complement: the opium of the people; e. Subject complement: bitter

## EXERCISE 63–3, page 819

a. Direct object: us; object complement: wise; b. Direct object: money; object complement: their primary pursuit; c. Direct objects: us, us; object complements: happy, good; d. Indirect objects: me, you; direct objects: no questions, no lies; e. Indirect objects: me, you; direct objects: a good loser, a failure

## EXERCISE 64–1, page 824

a. On their side (adverb phrase modifying *had*); b. of several air traffic controllers (adjective phrase modifying *job*), with ease (adverb phrase modifying *could perform*); c. To my embarrassment (adverb phrase modifying *was born*), in bed (adverb phrase modifying *was born*), with a lady (adverb phrase modifying *was born*); d. of a culture (adjective phrase modifying *map*); e. In France (adverb phrase modifying *is*)

## EXERCISE 64–2, page 830

a. who has outposts in your head (adjective clause modifying *enemy*); b. that doesn't bite (adjective clause modifying *rattlesnake*); c. If love is the answer (adverb clause modifying *could rephrase*); d. what they mean (noun clause used as direct object of *say*); e. unless I cannot resist it (adverb clause modifying *avoid*)

## EXERCISE 64–3, page 835

a. Concealing a disease (gerund phrase used as subject), to cure it (infinitive phrase modifying *way*); b. being punctual (gerund phrase used as object of the preposition *with*), to appreciate it (infinitive phrase modifying *is*); c. to conceal him (infinitive phrase used as direct object), naming him Smith (gerund phrase used as object of the preposition *by*); d. Being weak (participial phrase modifying *children*), to beguile us with charm (infinitive phrase used as direct object); e. Wrestling with words (gerund phrase used as subject)

## EXERCISE 65–1, page 839

a. Complex; who sleep like a baby (adjective clause); b. Compound; c. Simple; d. Complex; If you don't go to other people's funerals (adverb clause); e. Compound-complex; what you are afraid of (noun clause)

(*continued from p. iv*)
Alaska Rural Systemic Initiative, front page from *Sharing Our Pathways* (September/October 2004). Reprinted with the permission of the Alaska Rural Systemic Initiative.
American Heritage Dictionary, definition for "regard" from *The American Heritage Dictionary of the English Language, Fourth Edition.* Copyright © 2000 by Houghton Mifflin Company. Reprinted with permission.
Screen shot of database search results Blackwell Synergy Web site, www.blackwell-synergy.com. Reprinted with the permission of Blackwell Publishers, Ltd.
Eugene Boe, excerpt from "Pioneers to Eternity" from *The Immigrant Experience,* edited by Thomas C. Wheeler. Copyright © 1971 by Doubleday, a division of Random House, Inc. Reprinted with the permission of Doubleday, a division of Random House, Inc.
Louise Bogan, "Women" (excerpt) from *The Blue Estuaries: Poems 1923–1968.* Copyright © 1968 by Louise Bogan, renewed 1996 by Ruth Limmer. Reprinted with the permission of Farrar, Straus & Giroux, LLC.
Columbia University Library. Library Web pages. Copyright © Columbia University Libraries. www.columbia.edu. Reprinted by permission.
Dorchester Historical Society, "This Place Is My Home Oral History Project" (brochure) and "Participants Needed for *This Place Is My Home* Dorchester Oral History Project" (flyer). Copyright © 2004 by the Dorchester Historical Society. Reprinted with permission.
Excerpt from *The Dorling Kindersley Encyclopedia of Fishing.* Copyright © 1994 by Dorling Kindersley, Ltd. Reprinted with permission.
EBSCO Information Services, various screen shots. Reprinted with the permission of EBSCO Information Services.
Robert Frost, excerpt from "Fire and Ice" from *The Poetry of Robert Frost,* edited by Edward Connery Lathem. Copyright 1923, © 1969 by Henry Holt and Company. Copyright 1951 by Robert Frost. Reprinted with the permission of Henry Holt and Company, LLC.
Global Routes screen shot. Copyright © 2004 by Global Routes. Reprinted with permission.
Jane Goodall, "A Question of Ethics" from *Newsweek International* (May 7, 2001). Copyright © 2001 by Newsweek, Inc. Reprinted with permission.
Google screen shot. Reprinted with the permission of Google, Inc.
Stephen Jay Gould, excerpt from "Were Dinosaurs Dumb?" from *The Panda's Thumb.* Copyright © 1982 by Stephen Jay Gould. Reprinted with the permission of W. W. Norton & Company, Inc.
Caroline M. Hoxby. "The Power of Peers." Front page of article and the TOC. From *Education Next,* Summer 2002. www.educationnext.org. Copyright © 2002. Reprinted by permission of the Hoover Institute, Stanford University.
Langston Hughes, from "Ballad of the Landlord" from *Collected Poems of Langston Hughes,* edited by Arnold Rampersad and David Roessel. Copyright © 1994 by the Estate of Langston Hughes. Reprinted with the permission of Alfred A. Knopf, a division of Random House, Inc. and Harold Ober Associates, Incorporated.
Henry Jenkins. Excerpted data from "Bearings." Copyright © 2002. Posted online within the *MIT Communications Forum.* Reprinted with permission.
Jill D. Jenson, excerpt from "It's the Information Age, So Where's the Information?" from *College Teaching* (Summer 2004). Copyright © 2004. Reprinted with the permission of the Helen Dwight Reed Educational Foundation. Published by Heldref Publications, 1319 18th Street NW, Washington, DC 20036.
Harvey A. Levenstein. Reprint of the title and copyright pages from *Revolution at the Table: The Transformation of the American Diet* by Harvey A. Levenstein. Copyright © 2003 by the Regents of the University of California Press. Reprinted with permission.
Chan Lowe, "Yep, got my cell" cartoon. Copyright © Tribune Media Services. All rights reserved. Reprinted with permission.
McDonald's Corporation, "What makes your lettuce so crisp?" advertisement. Copyright © 2004 by McDonald's Corporation. Reprinted with permission.
Anne McGrath, "A loss of foreign talent" from *U.S. News & World Report* (November 27, 2004). Copyright © 2004 by U.S. News & World Report, LP. Reprinted with permission.

Merriam-Webster Online, screen shot of thesaurus entry for "regard" from www.Merriam-Webster.com. Copyright © 2005 by Merriam-Webster Incorporated. Reprinted by permission.

"The Minnesota Annual Summary" or "Minnesota Health Statistics" report. Copyright © 2005 by the Minnesota Department of Health. www.health.state.mn.us.

Screen shot of National Conference of State Legislatures Web site, including excerpt from Matt Sundeen, "Cell Phones and Highway Safety: 2000 State Legislative Update," http://www.ncsl.org/print/transportation/cellphone.pdf. Reprinted with the permission of the National Conference of State Legislatures.

Photo of eggs in a frying pan from Partnership for a Drug-Free America advertisement (1987). Reprinted with the permission of the Partnership for a Drug-Free America.

Screen shot of Perenich, Carroll, Perenich, Avril, Caulfield & Noyes, P.A., Voice of the Injured web site, including excerpt from "Cell Phones in Cars: More Accidents on Highways?" http://www.voiceoftheinjured.com/a-aa-cell-phones-accidents-injuries.html. Reprinted with the permission of Perenich, Carroll, Perenich, Avril, Caulfield & Noyes, P.A.

L. M. Poupart. Page from "Crime and Justice in American Indian Communities." Copyright © 2002 ProQuest Information and Learning. Reprinted with permission.

Anne Rudloe and Jack Rudloe, excerpt from "Electric Warfare: The Fish That Kill with Thunderbolts" from *Smithsonian* (July 1993). Reprinted with the permission of the authors.

Ray Rychnovsky, from "Clawing into Controversy" from *Outdoor Life* (January 1995): 40. Reprinted with the permission of the author.

Beth Shulman. Reprint of title and copyright pages from *Betrayal of Work* by Beth Shulman. Copyright © 2003 by Beth Shulman. Reprinted by permission of The New Press.

Courtesy of the Tasmanian Museum and Art Gallery.

University of Minnesota Libraries, screen shots. Reprinted with permission.

# Index

Lodge, Helen C.  *See* Cook and Lodge.
Logan, Shirley Wilson  2
Lorinskas, Sharon.  *See* Cogie, Strain, and Lorinskas.
Lukas, J. Anthony  802
Lutz, William  213
Lutzker, Marilyn  540
Lynch, Dennis A., Diana George, and Marilyn M. Cooper  490
Lynn, Steven  674
MacDonald, Susan Peck, and Charles R. Cooper  672
Macrorie, Ken  561
Malamud, Bernard  34
Marino, Sarah R., and Elin K. Jacob  546
Markel, Mike  105
Marsella, Joy, and Thomas L. Hilgers  20
Martin, Charles L., and Dorothy E. Ranson  449
Marzano, Robert J.  477
Master, Peter  360
Mathews, Alison, and Martin S. Chodorow  279

Spear, Karen   56
Spoto, Donald   459
Starkey, David   27
Steinbeck, John   95
Steinberg, Erwin R., Michael Gamer, Erika Lindemann, Gary Tate, and Jane
    Peterson   669
Stendahl   166
Sterne, Laurence   303
Stevenson, Robert Louis   262, 681
St. Onge, Keith R.   576
Strain, Kim.   *See* Cogie, Strain, and Lorinskas.
Straub, Richard   93
Strauss, Tracy.   *See* Blau, Hall, and Strauss.
Strickland, James   543
Strunk, William, Jr., and E. B. White   207
Sullivan, Patricia   473
Sutton, Brian   532
Sweeney, Marilyn Ruth   89

Young, Art, and Toby Fulwiler  669
Young, Richard, and Yameung Liu  26
Young, Richard E.  521
Zak, Frances, and Christopher C. Weaver  91
Zamel, Vivian  346
Zawacki, Terry Myers.  *See* Thaiss and Zawacki.
Zebroski, James Thomas  534
Zemelman, Steven, and Harvey Daniels  547
Zemliansky, Pavel.  *See* Melzer and Zemliansky.
Zimmerelli, Lisa.  *See* Ryan and Zimmerelli.
Zinsser, William  41, 94, 206, 422

# ESL Menu

# A List of Charts

# Revision Symbols

*Boldface numbers refer to sections of the handbook.*

| | | | |
|---|---|---|---|
| *abbr* | faulty abbreviation **40** | *om* | omitted word **10, 30, 31a** |
| *ad* | misuse of adverb or adjective **26** | *p* | error in punctuation |
| *add* | add needed word **10** | ˆ | comma **32** |
| *agr* | faulty agreement **21, 22** | *no ,* | no comma **33** |
| *appr* | inappropriate language **17** | ; | semicolon **34** |
| *art* | article (*a, an, the*) **30** | : | colon **35** |
| *awk* | awkward | ˯ | apostrophe **36** |
| *cap* | capital letter **45** | " " | quotation marks **37** |
| *case* | error in case **24, 25** | . ? | period, question mark, |
| *cliché* | cliché **18e** | ! | exclamation point **38** |
| *coh* | coherence **4d** | — ( ) | dash, parentheses, |
| *coord* | faulty coordination **14a** | [ ] ... | brackets, ellipsis mark, |
| *cs* | comma splice **20** | / | slash **39** |
| *dev* | inadequate development **4b** | ¶ | new paragraph **4e** |
| *dm* | dangling modifier **12e** | *pass* | ineffective passive **8** |
| *-ed* | error in *-ed* ending **27d** | *pn agr* | pronoun agreement **22** |
| *emph* | emphasis **14** | *proof* | proofreading problem **3b** |
| *ESL* | English as a second language **29–31** | *ref* | error in pronoun reference **23** |
| *exact* | inexact language **18** | *run-on* | run-on sentence **20** |
| *frag* | sentence fragment **19** | *-s* | error in *-s* ending **27c, 21** |
| *fs* | fused sentence **20** | *sexist* | sexist language **17f, 22a** |
| *gl/us* | see Glossary of Usage | *shift* | distracting shift **13** |
| *hyph* | error in use of hyphen **44** | *sl* | slang **17d** |
| *idiom* | idioms **18d** | *sp* | misspelled word **43** |
| *inc* | incomplete construction **10** | *sub* | faulty subordination **14a** |
| *irreg* | error in irregular verb **27a** | *sv agr* | subject-verb agreement **21, 27c** |
| *ital* | italics (underlining) **42** | *t* | error in verb tense **28a** |
| *jarg* | jargon **17a** | *trans* | transition needed **4d** |
| *lc* | lowercase letter **45** | *usage* | see Glossary of Usage |
| *mix* | mixed construction **11** | *v* | voice **8a** |
| *mm* | misplaced modifier **12a–d** | *var* | lack of variety in sentence structure **14, 15** |
| *mood* | error in mood **28b** | *vb* | verb problem **27, 28** |
| *nonst* | nonstandard usage **17d, 27** | *w* | wordy **16** |
| *num* | error in use of numbers **41** | *//* | faulty parallelism **9** |
| | | ^ | insert |
| | | x | obvious error |
| | | # | insert space |
| | | ⌣ | close up space |

# A List of Grammatical Terms

*Boldface numbers refer to sections of the handbook.*

absolute phrase **64e**
active voice **8a, 63c**
adjective **62d**
adjective clause **64b**
adverb **62e**
adverb clause **64b**
agreement **21, 22**
antecedent **22, 23, 62b**
appositive phrase **64d**
article **30**
case **24, 25**
clause **64b, 65a**
comparative **26c**
complement **63b**
complete subject **63a**
complex sentence **65a**
compound-complex sentence **65a**
compound sentence **65a**
compound subject **63a**
conjunction **62g**
conjunctive adverb **62g**
coordinating conjunction **62g**
correlative conjunction **62g**
demonstrative pronoun **62b**
dependent clause (*See* subordinate clause.)
determiner **30**
direct object **63b**
expletive **63a, 63c**
future tense **28a**
gerund **64c**
gerund phrase **64c**
helping verb **62c**
indefinite pronoun **62b**

independent clause **65a**
indirect object **63b**
infinitive **64c**
infinitive phrase **64c**
intensive pronoun **62b**
interjection **62h**
interrogative pronoun **62b**
intransitive verb **63b**
inverted sentence pattern **63a**
irregular verb **27a**
linking verb **63b**
main clause (*See* independent clause.)
main verb **62c**
modal **29a, 62c**
mood **28b**
noun **62a**
noun/adjective **62a**
noun clause **64b**
object complement **63b**
object of the preposition **64a**
particle **29d**
participial phrase **64c**
participle, present and past **27a, 62c**
parts of speech **62**
passive voice **8a, 63c**
past tense **28a**
perfect tense **28a**
personal pronoun **62b**
possessive pronoun **62b**
predicate **63**
predicate adjective (*See* subject complement.)

predicate noun (*See* subject complement.)
preposition **62f**
prepositional phrase **62f, 64a**
present tense **28a**
progressive forms **28a**
pronoun **62b**
pronoun/adjective **62b**
reciprocal pronoun **62b**
reflexive pronoun **62b**
regular verb **27a, 62c**
relative adverb **64b**
relative pronoun **62b, 64b**
-s form of verbs **21, 27c**
sentence patterns **63**
sentence types **65**
simple sentence **65a**
simple subject **63a**
subject **63a**
subject complement **63b**
subordinate clause **64b**
subordinating conjunction **62g, 64b**
subordinate word group **64**
superlative **26c**
tense **28a**
transitive verb **63b**
understood subject **63b**
verb **27, 28, 62c, 63b**
verbal phrase **64c**

# Detailed Menu